Political and Social Philosophy

Traditional and Contemporary Readings

J. Charles King
James A. McGilvray

Department of Philosophy
Pomona College

McGraw-Hill Book Company

New York   St. Louis   San Francisco   Düsseldorf   Johannesburg
Kuala Lumpur   London   Mexico   Montreal   New Delhi
Panama   Rio de Janeiro   Singapore   Sydney   Toronto

POLITICAL AND SOCIAL PHILOSOPHY

1 2 3 4 5 6 7 8 9 0 D O D O 7 9 8 7 6 5 4 3 2

Library of Congress Cataloging in Publication Data

King, Jessie Charles, 1940-   comp.
    Political and social philosophy.

        Bibliography: p.
        1. Political science—Addresses, essays, lectures.
2. Political ethics—Addresses, essays, lectures.
I. McGilvray, James A., joint comp. II. Title.
JA71.K54   320'.08   72-3993
ISBN 0-07-034630-5

This book was set in Century by Creative Book Services, division of McGregor &
Werner, Incorporated. The editor was Samuel B. Bossard; the designer was
Creative Book Services; and the production supervisor was Sally Ellyson. The
printer and binder was R. R. Donnelley & Sons Company.

Contents

Political and Social Philosophy

PART II: CONTEMPORARY POLITICAL THOUGHT   277

SECTION I: THEORETICAL CONCERNS   277

Preface

This textbook of readings in political philosophy grew out of what the editors believed to be a need for a book which would include both historical and contemporary material. It is thus divided into two main parts. The first part contains selections from the major historical figures who wrote on issues in political philosophy; the list of individuals included in it is broadly representative of traditional political philosophy. The second part contains contemporary material and is divided into two sections. The first section contains writings which are primarily theoretical in intent, and the works of professional philosophers and other academic figures predominate. The second section contains writings, more popular in nature, which were intended to direct political action or which concern topics that have been the subject of popular debate. In this section the writings of political leaders, revolutionaries, and popular social critics predominate.

There are other needs which we believe ought to be met by a new textbook in political philosophy. Such a textbook must speak to important issues. *Important*, of course, calls for decisions. There are some issues which will probably always be important to the political philosopher, such as justice, the question of natural law, and the problem of the justification of political and social change; but there are other issues which have an immediate importance, such as civil disobedience, punishment, and war. We attempted in our editing to reflect various positions on all these issues (and some others) in a way which will, we hope, prove interesting to the readers of this book. By choosing material, in both the historical and contemporary parts, which speaks to a list of important problems, we hoped to produce a textbook which would enable one to see contemporary issues in historical perspective. There are few issues with which we have to deal today that have not appeared in similar form in the past; and this is particularly true of problems in political philosophy.

We explain those questions that have guided us in selecting material for the book in our *Introduction*, which provides a general introduction to the problems of political philosophy and explains the view of the subject that guided us in editing. We have not, however, organized the materials in either part of the book according to our conception of the problems to which they speak. In this, as in other matters, we have tried to follow a policy of editorial restraint so as to allow each person who uses the book to organize the material as he believes best. The sample *Syllabi* at the back of the book illustrate some of the many ways in which the material may be organized by topic to reflect differing approaches to political and social philosophy. In line with our policy of editorial restraint, we have kept our introductory comments to each selection to a minimum in order to allow each instructor to introduce and interpret the selections as he thinks best.

In order to aid all readers, but particularly as an aid to students undertaking independent papers we have provided a full index of terms and names; this allows students to trace issues throughout the selections and locate relevant material, which may not have been assigned reading. Further, the sample *Syllabi* may be used by students to facilitate the relating of various authors not assigned in their course to material they are pursuing for individual papers and interests. As a final aid for students beginning research in political philosophy, we have provided a short *Selected General Bibliography* to introduce them to the secondary literature and collections of articles. Since several very good and extensive bibliographies are already easily available, we have made ours selective and included references to some of the more extensive ones. It seemed better to us to use space to include more material from original sources than to use it repeating bibliographies already easily available to students and teachers.

We have used translations and editions which are, in our judgment, the best available. Where we have omitted parts of texts this fact is indicated, and where we have omitted footnotes, except in trivial cases, the reader is informed at the beginning of the selection.

Any task of editing always involves compromise, particularly if one attempts to cover a large historical period and concentrate on a rather small number of issues—and of course even more compromises are involved where there are two editors! But we believe that we have produced a balanced text within the editorial principles outlined above. We only regret—as all editors do—that we could not have included a great deal more.

We would like to thank the many authors and publishers who granted us permission to use their material. Each is credited at the beginning of the selection for which he granted permission.

Further we want to express our appreciation to several persons who provided help in various ways. Our colleague Morton Beckner first suggested our undertaking the project, and our colleagues W. T. Jones and Frederick Sontag provided encouragement as well as valuable advice. Our work was considerably improved by the suggestions of the publisher's reviewers. Robert L. Borton provided invaluable help in the final assembling of the manuscript and Ariel Strombotne provided helpful secretarial assistance.

Finally, and most importantly, we are grateful to our wives, Harriet and Joan who, as is the fate of wives of academics, shared in proofreading, typing, criticism of ungainly prose, indexing, and occasionally, in discouragement.

J. Charles King
James A. McGilvray

Introduction

In recent years controversies over public issues have led to an outpouring of popular political philosophy. The Vietnam war and the protests against it, the increasingly militant revolt of American minority groups, and the ever-growing evidence of sickening deprivation in the midst of American abundance have led to questioning of basic political institutions. We find citizens—from students and professors to "hard-hat" construction workers—earnestly explaining and defending their political philosophies. When a young man tries to decide whether he is really obligated to answer the draft call to serve in a war he despises, or when one tries to decide how much the government should do to ensure the material well-being of all citizens, questions of basic political principles—and thus, questions of political philosophy—obviously arise.

But it is not necessary to look to great disputes or unusual circumstances to discover the kinds of issues which political and social philosophers discuss. One need only imagine such everyday figures as a newspaper editorial writer or a neighborhood political pundit being subjected to the inquiries of a reasonably pertinacious questioner.

Perhaps the editorial writer has just insisted that the public interest demands the construction of a new freeway through the city. The questioner asks why the public interest demands this. He replies that the traffic jams coming into the business area are cutting down sales, lowering employment, and creating a general nuisance. The questioner says that of course he knows this, but that a group whose homes will be taken by the freeway opposes it. What about their interest. In this case, says the editorial writer, they must yield to the public interest. But the questioner says the writer must not be understanding because it certainly seems that the opposition group is part of the public, too. Yes, the writer knows that, but in this case the opposition group is merely urging its private interest. Now the questioner feels that he must have some explanation. Evidently the writer does not consider the public interest to be merely all the interests of members of the public taken together, so the questioner must ask the editorial writer what he means by the phrase 'public interest', and further, how he decides that something is in the public interest. The questioner is now asking about basic principles of political life and is asking questions of political or social philosophy (we shall, in the future, use 'political philosophy' only, but we understand the expression 'social philosophy' to be an alternative name for the same field).

Suppose a neighborhood political pundit is maintaining that all long-haired draft resisters should be given long prison terms. The questioner asks him why. He replies that (among other things) each man has a duty to serve his country when called upon. The questioner asks what happens if a man is genuinely convinced that his country is wrong in its present cause. Should the man serve even then? The pundit replies that he should because the individual cannot set himself up as a judge over the policy of the government which represents the whole society. The questioner asks if the right to pass judgments on public policy is not part of the right of free speech. The pundit replies that criticizing in some ways is part of the right of free speech, but that freedom of speech does not mean that you can say just anything. Advising against military service is one of those things which is so dangerous that it isn't covered by freedom of speech. But now the questioner must have some clarification. If freedom of speech is not the right to say what one will, then he must be told what the limits are on freedom of speech and how these can be justified. Further, if speech can be so dangerous, why then does our pundit hold that there should be freedom of speech at all.

Problems of political philosophy have arisen again, and one can easily see how other such problems arise. One might have been asking why an educator believes that justice demands a good education for all, which could have led to the question of what he thinks the principles of justice to be. Or one might have been questioning a civil rights worker on his recent activities and have been led to ask what he takes civil disobedience to be and how he justifies its use. In all these cases, when one passes just beyond the usual political debates, and asks about the basic political or social principles assumed by the participants, one has asked questions of political philosophy. Most philosophers would easily grant that the questions in these examples are questions of political philosophy.

Not only would most philosophers agree that such questions are questions of political philosophy, they would also be able to agree that many particular books attempt to answer some or all of these questions and are therefore (at least in part) books of politcal philosophy. Although they might differ radically on an assessment of their worth, few philosophers would deny that Plato's *Republic*, Aristotle's *Politics*, St. Thomas' *Treatise on Law*, Hobbes' *Leviathan*, Locke's *Second Treatise on Civil Government*, Rousseau's *Social Contract*, Hegel's *Philosophy of Right*, Marx's *Economic and Philosophical Manuscripts*, or Mill's *On Liberty* are works of political philosophy.

If one asks them, however, for an explicit definition of the terms 'political philosophy' or 'political philosopher', he can entertain no hopes of even general agreement. It seems better, therefore, to take a clue from some of the foregoing agreements and introduce this subject by discussing the central questions it tries to answer. Of course, even this approach cannot satisfy everyone since the order chosen to introduce these questions will always seem wrong from someone's point of view. We shall present what we take to be the outstanding questions of political philosophy in what seems to us a reasonably organized manner. This will serve the dual purpose of introducing some readers to the field while indicating to those in no need of introduction the interests which have guided us in making selections for this book.

I. POLITICAL OBLIGATION

Everyone has at one time or another found laws of some governmental unit distasteful, has felt the urge to disobey, and wondered why he should not. (Most have also *acted* on this urge at times, if only in what we call 'trivial cases'.) The answers so often given by parents and politicians—"because a policeman will arrest you if you do," or "because you'll be put in jail if you do"—hardly answer the serious question of political obligation: "Am I obligated to obey the laws of the government and, if so, why?"

While a desire to avoid police and jail may provide an excellent prudential reason for abiding by the existing law, it does not show that the government has the *right* to demand obedience, only that it has the power to do so. Political philosophy attempts to answer this question of the right of government to make and enforce laws and the citizen's duty to obey. One can see immediately that any number of subsidiary questions will arise in considering this question seriously—questions ranging from the meaning of the term 'authority' to the defensibility of principles of duty. Differing theories will find it necessary to raise differing subsidiary questions in order to answer this primary question of politcal obligation.

Further, one should notice that questions of two different kinds arise when this task is undertaken. These are, in the first place, analytic questions, i.e., questions about the meanings of certain crucial terms. One must try, for example, to clarify what it means to say that someone has a political obligation. While philosophers would disagree on how this analytical process may best be accomplished, few would deny its importance in answering the kinds of questions under consideration. But, in the second place, even if the analytic questions are answered there still remains the problem of formulating and defending the principles associated with these questions. Even if one has defined the saying that "a person has a right," one still must determine the principles which say what rights he has. Even if one has clarified the meaning of the term 'justice', one still must say according to what principles institutions are to be judged 'just'. This judgment is usually called the normative task of political philosophy. In some cases the conceptual clarification may dictate the associated principles, but in most cases it leaves a wide range of possible principles open, and one must formulate and defend some of these. Some writers hold that these two tasks, the analytic and the normative, mark off two very different branches of political philosophy and some have even rejected one or the other as not worth doing. But it seems clear to us that these two tasks are simply steps in attacking the questions which constitute political philosophy and give it its interest and importance. Both analytic and normative problems arise in connection with all the primary questions of political philosophy we shall state and the two tasks seem to us simply different parts of the overall problem of answering these questions.

Some philosophers, primarily those known as anarchists (represented in our readings by Peter Kropotkin), are inclined to answer the question of whether there is a political obligation with a simple "no." They argue in various ways that government has no legitimate claim over the people and that the common good calls for the abolition of all government or of all but the most rudimentary, local government with little power. On the other hand, few if any philosophers have maintained that one is obligated to obey any government under all circumstances. Most thinkers have held that, while one is obligated to obey some or even most laws of most governments, laws and/or governments must meet some standards in order to have a legitimate claim on the citizen's obedience Saint Thomas holds, for example, that only a just law as judged by divine law can really claim the place of law at all. Locke argues that the duty to obey law is based on an implicit contract to take part in the state, but that if the state breaks its part of the bargain then one is no longer bound by the contract. Marxists might argue that one is not bound by governments which are simply the reflection of the power and interests of exploiting classes, but that one is bound to obey governments established by the proletariat to end exploitation and further the classless society. Since Utilitarians, such as Mill and Bentham, base all obligation on producing happiness for all concerned, they hold that the obligation to obey particular laws and governments must be judged according to the effects on general happiness of obeying or disobeying.

As all of these differing answers make clear (many others could be listed), most philosophers have held that one is obligated to obey some laws of some governments. Deciding which laws and governments calls for an evaluation of social and political institutions in various ways. The two main parts of this task provide the next two primary questions of political philosophy.

II. EVALUATION OF SOCIAL AND POLITICAL INSTITUTIONS

Political philosophers have tried to give an account of concepts and principles used to evaluate social and political institutions not only because most of them want to use such evaluations in answering basic questions about political obligation, but also because many of them have wanted to condemn or praise particular institutions of their own time. Additionally, many of them had social schemes of their own to advance, and many of them wanted to attack the social recommendations of others. While various philosophers emphasize differing concepts and their associated principles, one finds such concepts as justice, equality, liberty, efficiency, human rights, alienation, general welfare, and common good regularly recurring in evaluations of social and political institutions. Each of these topics is, of course, vast in its own right. In each case there are problems of conceptual clarification as well as problems of stating and defending associated principles. In carrying out these tasks one must also try to clarify the relationships between the various concepts.

In order to illustrate the variety of approaches to these issues we shall consider the case of justice. Almost all political philosophers agree that justice is one of the more important, if not the most important, standards which social and political arrangements should meet. In a philosophic treatment of justice one faces the problem of clarifying the concept (or showing that it doesn't need clarifying), together with the problem of stating and defending the principles associated with the concept. For example, if someone maintained that an institution is just if it rewards people according to their merit, then he would also need to formulate and defend principles which show how merit is properly rewarded in order to give a full account of justice.

One distinction concerning philosophical theories of justice goes back at least to Aristotle, who points out that some people—Plato was doubtlessly his example and shall be ours as well—take justice not as a particular virtue of institutions, but as the summation of all virtues of institutions, so that for them a just society is more or less a perfect society. In the *Republic*, Plato holds that justice in the state consists of each part performing its proper function well and outlines what such a society would be like. In this view a just society is one which passes, at least to a fairly high degree, all legitimate tests.

Many other philosophers treat justice as did Aristotle, simply as one virtue of institutions. In this view an institution might be just, but might fail some other test. It might not, for example, be benevolent or it might be inefficient. Such views must eventually, of course, say how these competing evaluations are to be ranked—i.e., decide which takes precedence over the other.

Among philosophers who take the view that justice is only one virtue among many there is considerable disagreement on its nature. Too many have written on justice for us to give a comprehensive listing of the theories which have been advanced, but the following summary includes the more important views. Some philosophers have maintained that justice is a formal virtue only. Justice, they might say, involves treating similar cases similarly, but it gives no criteria for deciding which similarities are relevant. Charles Perelman, Alf Ross, and Hans

Kelsen have maintained variants of this position and have further maintained that since there is no way to establish a criterion for picking the relevant similarities, justice is a procedural virtue only. Justice enjoins the regular application of the law, but cannot pass on the law itself. The matter of procedural regularity is clearly one important aspect of justice. Most people do think that public officials should treat similar cases similarly in applying the existing law, but most people would probably want to maintain that the laws themselves may be unjust. H. L. A. Hart has argued that justice itself does not settle the relevant similarities, but that other aspects of one's moral outlook may do and that, accordingly, assuming a particular moral outlook, justice may be brought to bear on the law itself.

Other philosophers have held that a correct account of justice itself does go beyond mere procedural regularity and involves substantive restrictions on the content of laws and institutions. Aristotle advocates what might be called an aristocratic view of justice. He maintains that justice consists of a proportional equality: that goods are justly divided between persons when each person's share is in proportion to his merit as compared to that of the others. In Aristotle's case merit is to be determined by virtues both moral and intellectual, but, of course, this view could (and has) been advocated with different indices of merit.

A utilitarian view of justice is advocated by Hume, among others. Hume's thesis is that utility or promotion of the good of all is the foundation of justice, i.e., that rules such as those governing property are called just because they promote the common good. It is, of course, true that utilitarians must make clear in what way we judge the good of all. Bentham maintains this is to be done by measuring the amount of pleasure and pain caused for all who are affected. Then, on his account, institutions are just to the degree that they increase the total pleasure summed over all those affected.

Some philosophers have advocated a contractarian view of justice. This is found, for example, in varying forms in Locke and Rousseau, and John Rawls has presented a contemporary version of this theory. According to Rawls, institutions are just if they are in accord with principles for judging institutions which would be chosen by rational and self-interested persons in a carefully defined original position of equal liberty. He argues that two principles would be chosen in these conditions, one providing for each person the greatest liberty compatible with a like liberty for all, the other providing that inequalities supported by the institutional structure must be everyone's advantage and that the offices and positions to which such inequalities attach must be open to all.

Still other philosophers take a more explicitly equalitarian view of justice. W. K. Frankena and Gregory Vlastos have both recently maintained such views. For example, Vlastos holds that justice demands that equality of rights and rewards must be maintained except in those cases where the same ground that leads our demand for equality of right, i.e., the equal intrinsic worth of all persons, indicates that equality should be abridged—as for example in a case where old wrongs can be compensated for only by giving preferential treatment to certain people.

Marxist thinkers provide yet another view of justice. One is tempted simply to add Marx to the above list as holding the view of justice expressed in his famous maxim "from each according to his ability; to each according to his need." But, in fact, Marx's position also involves essentially a critique of the foregoing sort of view. Marx would insist that the foregoing views were expressions of the class interests of dominating groups in a society based on class exploitation. Only in a society purged of class exploitation could a genuine view of justice emerge. This means (a Marxist might say) that his view is not to be regarded as merely another competing alternative with the above, for it is not on the same footing with these others which are mere glosses on the interests of the exploiting classes.

It is, of course, obvious that much of what has been said here about justice is far too sketchy to be of any use to anyone new to political philosophy who wishes to gain a genuine understanding of the doctrines involved. Such a summary of views of justice should, however, help to show the novice the great complexity involved in the questions of political philosophy. On merely a single topic under one of our primary questions there are many views easily available, each one raising important difficulties of its own. This should serve as fair warning that the questions we indicate in a sentence or two are not in any way simple and are not easily considered.

Even if one has, however, worked out a reasonably full account of the concepts and principles used in evaluating social and political institutions he has not yet answered the problems left from the question of political obligation nor has he said how these various evaluations should be developed into a pattern for what society should be. This is our next problem.

III. IDEALS OF SOCIETY

If one were in a position to give a reasonable account of when institutions are just, he would still be faced with the task of saying how the various evaluations of institutions are to be ranked in importance in an overall assessment of a society, and further he would still need to give an account of institutions which would meet the demands of his evaluations. This overall problem of stating and defending a basic institutional structure which meets the requirements of justice, and whatever additional virtues one requires of institutions, we call the problem of ideals of society.

It is important to notice that in this task one finds of necessity a union of political philosophy and social science or at least of the kinds of concern typical

of these disciplines. After all, important as theories of justice and other evaluations of institutions may be, they will be of small use in outlining an ideal of
society without careful attention to what one can learn from political scientists,
sociologists, and psychologists about the way people and institutions actually do
function. On our present problem, social science and philosophy must work
together. The need for such cooperation has not always been realized and has led
philosophers to approach these problems armed only with the most meager
knowledge of the actual workings of institutions. Lack of recognition of this
need has led social scientists to approach the same problems with naïve or
uncritical ideas on the kinds of evaluation involved.

Perhaps the most obvious attempts to construct ideals of society are found in
the tradition of constructing utopias. Plato is, no doubt, the most philosophical-
ly illustrious contributor to this tradition. In the *Republic* Plato presents in some
detail the institutions of government, economy, education, family, etc., which
he believes would make up a perfect city-state. In fact, construction of a utopia
may provide a philosopher such as Plato not only with a model of what society
should be, but also with a basis for developing his philosophical theories
concerning the concepts used in evaluating institutions. Thus, in Plato's case the
form of an ideal society comes before his theory of justice, which he based on
his ideal plan of government. On the other hand, one might, of course, settle on
a theory of justice first and then try to construct an ideal of society on the basis
of that theory.

Many writers attempt to describe and defend, at least for some specific place and
time, broad structures of governmental, economic, and social institutions. This
approach is taken by those who write of communism, socialism, fascism,
constitutional democracy, absolute monarchy, capitalism, totalitarianism, and
the like. The fact that these labels are not all of a kind, i.e., that commitment to
constitutional democracy may be combined, for example, with commitment to
socialism, shows that differing levels of generality have been taken by those
following this pattern. In some instances several of the usual labels must be
combined to get an overall ideal of society.

Many problems and questions arise in a systematic development of ideals of
society. There is the problem of describing the kinds of institutions involved in
one's conception and the way in which these work together. Then there is the
problem of showing that the scheme one has recommended does meet the
criteria of justice and other evaluations of institutions. Each kind of system has
its own special problems which arise in the course of this task—for example, the
question of the status of majority rule in constitutional democracy and how it is
to be justified, or the status of private property in capitalism and how it is to be
justified.

Yet another kind of problem usually included in this kind of approach is the
attempt to show that the overall system one proposes has various advantages

over the primary competing systems—at least for certain times and places. Without further detail it should be clear that questions of tremendous complexity arise in this kind of task and that the difficulty for people in these times is compounded by the fact that this task does not respect our usual neat disciplinary boundaries. In any case, the major interest and importance of both the evaluation of institutions and the elaboration of ideals of society is surely the guidance of action in regard to actual institutions, and this leads to our next main problem.

IV. THE NATURE AND JUSTIFICATION OF SOCIAL CHANGE

If the developement of an ideal of society had convinced one that one's own society contained radical faults, then one would surely wish to see it changed. If one's own society seemed to measure up well against one's ideal, then one would surely want to maintain it against ill-conceived changes. In either case the question of the nature and justification of social change becomes important.

In the history of political philosophy one finds widely varying doctrines concerning the nature of changes in social and political institutions. Some thinkers maintain that institutions must grow slowly as the parts of an organism grow. In light of this fact, they argue that attempts at 'social engineering' or planned radical changes in society can lead only to disruption of the natural development and thus do more harm than good. Other thinkers argue that one can hope for decent social and political conditions only by rational planning and altering of faulty institutions. This alteration and planning may vary, of course, from piecemeal legal reforms to radical revolution. Still other thinkers claim to have found the key to developing processes in history so that they are able to discover the way in which history is moving and thus to work for those changes which must come with that development. Marx, for example, finds the key to the development of societies in the competition of classes and their inevitable dialectical clashes.

In any case, the question of the nature of social change is clearly one which must be faced by any political philosopher. It is, of course, hard to support adequately a position on such a broad question, but one may at least hope that political philosophy will raise the question and make explicit the views of the nature of social change which have remained implicit and unargued in too many cases.

Whatever one's position on the nature of social change, there is a group of concepts and associated principles related to methods of change which must be clarified, defended, and fit into any complete political philosophy, if only by rejection. For one surely wants to know from a political philosopher how one justifies, or else shows the illegitimacy of, reforms, civil disobedience, conscientious refusal, resistance, insurrection, and revolution. One may ask, for example, when an action is one of civil disobedience and when such action is justified, if ever. How is it related to majority rule, and does it have a proper place in a constitutional democracy? These are difficult questions. It is not even easy, for example, to say exactly what constitutes an act of civil disobedience. Not every case of ignoring a stop sign or robbing a bank is civil disobedience, yet civil disobedience does involve breaking the law. How does it differ from other law breaking? To take another example under this topic, the concept of revolution raises considerable difficulties. It is not clear just when resistance to a government becomes an attempt at revolution. So many differing occurrences have been called revolutions in the modern period that one probably has to distinguish various kinds of revolution. For example, if one group of generals throws out another but continues to rule under the same constitution and basic institutions, we have a different form of social change than that in which a movement overthrows the whole of an old order and attempts to start over, as in Russia or Cuba. Further, because of the violence and suffering usually associated with revolutions, the question of their justification is of particular importance. After all, a few more years of injustice when reform is at least possible may be preferable to the agony of civil war. Yet most philosophers would grant that, under some conditions, attempted revolution can be justified. Further, this question is clearly related very closely to the question of political obligation with which we began our discussion. This brings out very well the close connection between the questions of political philosophy and perhaps shows why it is that differing theories would start at different points of our scheme and arrange the questions in different order.

We certainly have not mentioned all the questions of political philosophy, but we would claim that we have provided examples of the leading questions and have provided a framework into which other questions can easily fit. It is true, however, that in particular periods some questions will be of special interest to students of political philosophy. Some of these of special contemporary interest have been treated already—civil disobedience, justice of economic institutions, the debate between socialism and capitalism. However, in selecting the readings we have been guided by a feeling that three further problems are special contemporary interest, and we should point out this fact now. These three problems can be fitted into our scheme of primary questions but they seem to us to deserve special note.

First is the problem of human rights and civil liberties. This is probably best conceived as a particular topic under the general heading of justice, but its great contemporary importance argues for special mention. Under this heading one faces such traditional philosophical questions as "What is a right?", "Are there any natural rights?", and "What is the moral basis for civil liberties in a constitutional democracy?"

But one also faces such pressingly practical problems as "Are there any legitimate limits to freedom of speech?" and "How far should the government go in trying to prevent private citizens from suffering from racial discrimination?"

Also of great contemporary interest are various problems centering around the topic of war. One group of these problems focuses on the applicability of moral judgments to relations between states. Some have maintained that moral judgments simply do not apply to relations between states. Others hold that they do, and most people certainly seem to talk and act as though they believe that they do. This raises questions about legitimate relations between states, the duties of great powers, imperialism in its various guises, etc. But it also raises the question of war itself and whether it is ever justifiable and, if so, when.

The second group of problems centering around war concerns the relations of individual citizens to war. One must ask what the duties and rights of citizens are during time of war. Is military conscription ever justified, and if it is what is the proper place of conscientious objection in response to it? Further, what are the rights and duties of citizens who believe their own nation to be involved in an unjust war? The recent experience of the United States should show that it would be well if more citizens had thought seriously on these questions before such problems suddenly came to the forefront of national policy with all the attendant bitterness and stress.

Finally, we find the question of legal punishment to be of great contemporary interest. Here again one finds traditional philosophical questions concerning what counts as genuine punishment and how such an institution can be justified. One finds three main groups in the field: those who say suffering is simply the just desert of one who commits a crime, those who say that punishment can only be justified by the resulting reform of criminals and deterrence of potential criminals, and those who say that the whole notion of punishment should be dropped in favor of treating those 'sick' enough to commit crimes. These traditional disputes take on a new urgency when large groups of citizens are crying for harsher punishments to maintain law and order, while almost every report on prisons indicates that their net effect is to make the crime problem worse.

These three questions of special contemporary interest taken together with the four primary questions of political philosophy as discussed earlier should provide an introduction to political philosophy as well as providing an indication of the kinds of problems with which we have been concerned in selecting these readings.

It will perhaps facilitate understanding if we conclude this introduction with a few comments about political philosophy in general and about its relation to other fields. First, it should be noted that we have not covered one large area which is sometimes included under the heading of social and political philosophy. There are many philosophic problems concerning the social sciences, their concepts, and methods. Thus, some writers include in social philosophy problems of clarification of concepts such as social causation or social role, and questions such as whether theories in social science are basically logical and explanatory, like theories in the natural sciences. While we would prefer to call this area 'philosophy of social science', we do not care to enter into a terminological dispute over the matter and merely wish to point out that we have not included such problems in this volume.

As we have already said, we believe that information from the social sciences is essential for dealing with many questions of political philosophy. We do not feel that a clear and definite line can be fixed between questions of political philosophy and questions of political science (especially political theory) and sociology. It is clear, however, that the questions of political philosophy, as we have explained them, are most closely related to moral philosophy or ethics. In fact, one might say that political philosophy in our conception is primarily an application and extension of moral philosophy. Thus, as we have explained it, political philosophy, like moral philosophy, is primarily concerned with principles for guiding and evaluating conduct. Social science presumably is concerned to describe and explain the causes and results of conduct. Many, indeed most, social scientists have in recent years tended to adopt the positivistic rigid distinction between facts and values. They have emphasized that their concerns are with factual questions of description and explanation, not with supposedly emotion-based value judgments. The issue of whether principles of the kind required to answer the questions of political philosophy are in the end based on emotion and therefore radically different from facts is, of course, one of the questions to be answered in the process of political philosophy. It is not necessary to prejudge this question in order to see that in any case the results of the social scientist will be very important for political philosophy (although much information needed by political philosophy has not yet been provided by social scientists). On the other hand, it seems clear that the most 'factual' social scientist cannot in the end avoid the implications of his results for questions of political philosophy, even if its principles are at bottom expressions of emotional reaction. Thus, even though we distinguish political philosophy from philosophy of social science and from social science itself we are not thereby committed to this distinction as a clear and rigid one, and we do insist that these disciplines stand in very close and complex interrelationships.

In a famous introduction to a group of essays published in 1956, Peter Laslett, a well-known British philosopher, wrote that in the English-speaking countries political philosophy was, at least at that time, dead. He was no doubt correct in that little interest in traditional topics of political philosophy was then being shown by philosophers in the English-speaking countries. The present growing interest in political philosophy seems to show, however, that the subject was merely in hibernation. The kinds of social conflict which have arisen in the 1960s, particularly in the United States, have inevitably led to renewed concern with political philosophy. Indeed, we would insist that one need only consider for a moment the questions we have outlined to see that as long as men live together in organized groups questions such as these must arise in the minds of thinking people. Further, we would insist that the importance of these questions is obvious. We are not so naïve as to believe that the mere study of political philosophy can establish justice in the world or that political philosophy can be a substitute for social action movements or political parties. But neither are we so naïve as some "practical" people who think that social action movements and political parties can move toward better societies without a great deal of serious and searching thought concerning their goals and ideals. Such thought is the task of political philosophy whether it be undertaken by professional philosophers, political leaders, or concerned citizens.

Part I
Traditional Political Thought

Plato

Plato (428/427 B.C.–348/347 B.C.) was not the first political philosopher, but he was certainly one of the most important. His views directly and indirectly influenced most of the Western political and social philosophers who followed him. His philosophical works cover a wide area of concerns and they show, even in their diversity, a highly systematic approach to philosophical questions. This is not to say, however, that his system did not undergo changes, nor that it is an easy matter to discover in his work a single, final opinion on various philosophical questions. The selections from his work on political philosophy which follow reflect both the systematic and diverse sides of Plato's work; each is from a different period in Plato's life. The first, from the *Crito*, presents views which may be more those of Plato's friend and teacher, Socrates, than of Plato himself. The second, a selection from what is usually thought to be Plato's standard work on political theory, the *Republic*, deals with the nature of justice. The last is drawn from a work in Plato's later period, the *Statesman*.

It might prove helpful in reading Plato to remember that his later work at least reflects some of the stresses of Athenian political life, and also the abortive attempt on his part to set up a government at Syracuse. Plato, a well-born patrician and Athenian citizen, was always close to the political issues of his time.

Crito

... *Socrates*: Look at it in this way. Suppose that while we were preparing to run away from here—or however one should describe it—the laws and constitution of Athens were to come and confront us and ask this question, Now, Socrates, what are you proposing to do? Can you deny that by this act which you are contemplating you intend, so far as you have the power, to destroy us, the laws, and the whole state as well? Do you imagine that a city can continue to exist and not be turned upside down, if the legal judgments which are pronounced in it have no force but are nullified and destroyed by private persons?

How shall we answer this question, Crito, and others of the same kind? There is much that could be said, especially by a professional advocate, to protest

By permission. From *The Last Days of Socrates*. Translated by Hugh Tredennick, Penguin Classics, 1954.

against the invalidation of this law which enacts that judgments once pronounced shall be binding. Shall we say, Yes, I do intend to destroy the laws, because the state wronged me by passing a faulty judgment at my trial? Is this to be our answer, or what?

Crito: What you have just said, by all means, Socrates.

Socrates: Then what supposing the laws say, Was there provision for this in the agreement between you and us, Socrates? Or did you undertake to abide by whatever judgments the state pronounced?

If we expressed surprise at such language, they would probably say, Never mind our language, Socrates, but answer our questions; after all, you are accustomed to the method of question and answer. Come now, what charge do you bring against us and the state, that you are trying to destroy us? Did we not give you life in the first place? Was it not through us that your father married your mother and begot you? Tell us, have you any complaint against those of us laws that deal with marriage?

No, none, I should say.

Well, have you any against the laws which deal with children's upbringing and education, such as you had yourself? Are you not grateful to those of us laws which were instituted for this end, for requiring your father to give you a cultural and physical education?

Yes, I should say.

Very good. Then since you have been born and brought up and educated, can you deny, in the first place, that you were our child and servant, both you and your ancestors? And if this is so, do you imagine that what is right for us is equally right for you, and that whatever we try to do to you, you are justified in retaliating? You did not have equality of rights with your father, or your employer—supposing that you had had one—to enable you to retaliate. You were not allowed to answer back when you were scolded or to hit back when you were beaten, or to do a great many other things of the same kind. Do you expect to have such license against your country and its laws that if we try to put you to death in the belief that it is right to do so, you on your part will try your hardest to destroy your country and us its laws in return? And will you, the true devotee of goodness, claim that you are justified in doing so? Are you so wise as to have forgotten that compared with your mother and father and all the rest of your ancestors your country is something far more precious, more venerable, more sacred, and held in greater honor both among gods and among all reasonable men? Do you not realize that you are even more bound to respect and placate the anger of your country than your father's anger? That if you cannot persuade your country you must do whatever it orders, and patiently submit to any punishment that it imposes, whether it be flogging or imprisonment? And if it leads you out to war, to be wounded or killed, you must comply, and it is right that you should do so. You must not give way or retreat or abandon your position. Both in war and in the law courts and everywhere else you must do whatever your city and your country command, or else persuade them in accordance with universal justice, but violence is a sin even against your parents, and it is a far greater sin against your country.

What shall we say to this, Crito—that what the laws say is true, or not?

Crito: Yes, I think so.

Socrates: Consider, then, Socrates, the laws would probably continue, whether it is also true for us to say that what you are now trying to do to us is not right. Although we have brought you into the world and reared you and educated you, and given you and all your fellow citizens a share in all the good things at our disposal, nevertheless by the very fact of granting our permission we openly proclaim this principle, that any Athenian, on attaining to manhood and seeing for himself the political organization of the state and us its laws, is permitted, if he is not satisfied with us, to take his property and go away wherever he likes. If any of you chooses to go to one of our colonies, supposing that he should not be satisfied with us and the state, or to emigrate to any other country, not one of us laws hinders or prevents him from going away wherever he likes, without any loss of property. On the other hand, if any one of you stands his ground when he can see how we administer justice and the rest of our public organization, we hold that by so doing he has in fact undertaken to do anything that we tell him. And we maintain that anyone who disobeys is guilty of doing wrong on three separate counts: first because we are his parents, and secondly because we are his guardians, and thirdly because, after promising obedience, he is neither obeying us nor persuading us to change our decision if we are at fault in any way. And although all our orders are in the form of proposals, not of savage commands, and we give him the choice of either persuading us or doing what we say, he is actually doing neither. These are the charges, Socrates, to which we say that you will be liable if you do what you are contemplating, and you will not be the least culpable of your fellow countrymen, but one of the most guilty.

If I asked why, they would no doubt pounce upon me with perfect justice and point out that there are very few people in Athens who have entered into this agreement with them as explicitly as I have. They would say, Socrates, we have substantial evidence that you are satisfied with us and with the state. You would not have been so exceptionally reluctant to cross the borders of your country if you had not been exceptionally attached to it. You have never left the city to attend a festival or for any other purpose, except on some military expedition. You have never traveled abroad as other people do, and you have never felt the impulse to acquaint yourself with another country or constitution. You have been content with us and with our city. You have definitely chosen us, and undertaken to observe us in all your activities as a citizen, and as the crowning proof that you are satisfied with our city, you have begotten children in it. Furthermore, even at the time of your trial you could have proposed the penalty of banishment, if you had chosen to do so—that is, you could have done then with the sanction of the state what you are now trying to do without it. But whereas at that time you made a noble show of indifference if you had to die, and in fact preferred death, as you said, to banishment, now you show no respect for your earlier professions, and no regard for us, the laws, whom you are trying to destroy. You are behaving like the lowest type of menial, trying to run away in spite of the contracts and undertakings by which you agreed to live as a member of our state. Now first answer this question. Are we or are we not speaking the truth when we say that you have undertaken, in deed if not in word, to live your life as a citizen in obedience to us?

What are we to say to that, Crito? Are we not bound to admit it?

Crito: We cannot help it, Socrates.

Socrates: It is a fact, then, they would say, that you are breaking covenants and undertakings made with us, although you made them under no compulsion or misunderstanding, and were not compelled to decide in a limited time. You had seventy years in which you could have left the country, if you were not satisfied with us or felt that the agreements were unfair. You did not choose Sparta or Crete—your favorite models of good government—or any other Greek or foreign state. You could not have absented yourself from the city less if you had been lame or blind or decrepit in some other way. It is quite obvious that you stand by yourself above all other Athenians in your affection for this city and for us its laws. Who would care for a city without laws? And now, after all this, are you not going to stand by your agreement? Yes, you are, Socrates, if you will take our advice, and then you will at least escape being laughed at for leaving the city.

We invite you to consider what good you will do to yourself or your friends if you commit this breach of faith and stain your conscience. It is fairly obvious that the risk of being banished and either losing their citizenship or having their property confiscated will extend to your friends as well. As for yourself, if you go to one of the neighboring states, such as Thebes or Megara, which are both well governed, you will enter them as an enemy to their constitution, and all good patriots will eye you with suspicion as a destroyer of law and order. Incidentally you will confirm the opinion of the jurors who tried you that they gave a correct verdict; a destroyer of laws might very well be supposed to have a destructive influence upon young and foolish human beings. Do you intend, then, to avoid well-governed states and the higher forms of human society? And if you do, will life be worth living? Or will you approach these people and have the impudence to converse with them? What arguments will you use, Socrates? The same which you used here, that goodness and integrity, institutions and laws, are the most precious possessions of mankind? Do you not think that Socrates and everything about him will appear in a disreputable light? You certainly ought to think so.

But perhaps you will retire from this part of the world and go to Crito's friends in Thessaly? That is the home of indiscipline and laxity, and no doubt they would enjoy hearing the amusing story of how you managed to run away from prison by arraying yourself in some costume or putting on a shepherd's smock or some other conventional runaway's disguise, and altering your personal appearance. And will no one comment on the fact that an old man of your age, probably with only a short time left to live, should dare to cling so greedily to life, at the price of violating the most stringent laws? Perhaps not, if you avoid irritating anyone. Otherwise, Socrates, you will hear a good many humiliating comments. So you will live as the toady and slave of all the populace, literally 'roistering in Thessaly,' as though you had left this country for Thessaly to attend a banquet there. And where will your discussions about goodness and uprightness be then, we should like to know? But of course you want to live for your children's sake, so that you may be able to bring them up and educate them. Indeed! By first taking them off to Thessaly and making foreigners of them, so that they may have that additional enjoyment? Or if that is not your intention, supposing that they are brought up here with you still alive, will they be better cared for and educated without you, because of course your friends will look after them? Will they look after your children if you go away to Thessaly, and not if you go away to the next world? Surely if those who profess to be your friends are worth anything, you must believe that they would care for them.

No, Socrates, be advised by us your guardians, and do not think more of your children or of your life or of anything else than you think of what is right, so that when you enter the next world you may have all this to plead in your defense before the authorities there. It seems clear that if you do this thing, neither you nor any of your friends will be the better for it or be more upright or have a cleaner conscience here in this world, nor will it be better for you when you reach the next. As it is, you will leave this place, when you do, as the victim of a wrong done not by us, the laws, but by your fellow men. But if you leave in that dishonorable way, returning wrong for wrong and evil for evil, breaking your agreements and covenants with us, and injuring those whom you least ought to injure—yourself, your friends, your country, and us—then you will have to face our anger in your lifetime, and in that place beyond when the laws of the other world know that you have tried, so far as you could, to destroy even us their brothers, they will not receive you with a kindly welcome. Do not take Crito's advice, but follow ours.

That, my dear friend Crito, I do assure you, is what I seem to hear them saying, just as a mystic seems to hear the strains of music, and the sound of their arguments rings so loudly in my head that I cannot hear the other side. I warn you that, as my opinion stands at present, it will be useless to urge a different view. However, if you think that you will do any good by it, say what you like.

Crito: No, Socrates, I have nothing to say.

Socrates: Then give it up, Crito, and let us follow this course, since God points out the way.

Republic

THE VIRTUES IN THE STATE

So now at last, son of Ariston, said I, your commonwealth is established. The next thing is to bring to bear upon it all the light you can get from any quarter, with the help of your brother and Polemarchus and all the rest, in the hope that we may see where justice is to be found in it and where injustice, how they differ, and which of the two will bring happiness to its possessor, no matter whether gods and men see that he has it or not.

From *Plato's Republic*. Translated by F. M. Cornford, 1941. By permission of the Clarendon Press, Oxford.

This passage begins in Book IV of *The Republic*. Socrates while attempting to discover the nature of justice has described an ideal city-state composed of educated and naturally superior rulers, a class of soldiers and civil servants, and the ordinary class of merchants, craftsmen, etc. He will now attempt to use this imaginary state to discover what justice is. [Eds.]

Nonsense, said Glaucon, you promised to conduct the search yourself, because it would be a sin not to uphold justice by every means in your power.

That is true; I must do as you say, but you must all help.

We will.

I suspect, then, we may find what we are looking for in this way. I take it that our state, having been founded and built upon the right lines, is good in the complete sense of the word.

It must be.

Obviously, then, it is wise, brave, temperate, and just.

Obviously.

Then if we find some of these qualities in it, the remainder will be the one we have not found. It is as if we were looking somewhere for one of any four things: if we detected that one immediately, we should be satisfied; whereas if we recognized the other three first, that would be enough to indicate the thing we wanted; it could only be the remaining one. So here we have four qualities. Had we not better follow that method in looking for the one we want?

Surely.

To begin then: the first quality to come into view in our state seems to be its wisdom; and there appears to be something odd about this quality.

What is there odd about it?

I think the state we have described really has wisdom; for it will be prudent in counsel, won't it?

Yes.

And prudence in counsel is clearly a form of knowledge; good counsel cannot be due to ignorance and stupidity.

Clearly.

But there are many and various kinds of knowledge in our commonwealth. There is the knowledge possessed by the carpenters or the smiths, and the knowledge how to raise crops. Are we to call the state wise and prudent on the strength of these forms of skill?

No; they would only make it good at furniture-making or working in copper or agriculture.

Well then, is there any form of knowledge, possessed by some among the citizens of our new-founded commonwealth, which will enable it to take thought, not for some particular interest, but for the best possible conduct of the state as a whole in its internal and external relations?

Yes, there is.

What is it, and where does it reside?

It is precisely that art of guardianship which resides in those Rulers whom we just now called Guardians in the full sense.

And what would you call the state on the strength of that knowledge?

Prudent and truly wise.

And do you think there will be more or fewer of these genuine Guardians in our state than there will be smiths?

Far fewer.

Fewer, in fact, than any of those other groups who are called after the kind of skill they possess?

Much fewer.

So if a state is constituted on natural principles, the wisdom it possesses as a whole will be due to the knowledge residing in the smallest part, the one which takes the lead and governs the rest. Such knowledge is the only kind that deserves the name of wisdom, and it appears to be ordained by nature that the class privileged to possess it should be the smallest of all.

Quite true.

Here then we have more or less made out one of our four qualities and its seat in the structure of the commonwealth.

To my satisfaction, at any rate.

Next there is courage. It is not hard to discern that quality or the part of the community in which it resides so as to entitle the whole to be called brave.

Why do you say so?

Because anyone who speaks of a state as either brave or cowardly can only be thinking of that part of it which takes the field and fights in its defence; the reason being, I imagine, that the character of the state is not determined by the bravery or cowardice of the other parts.

No.

Courage, then, is another quality which a community owes to a certain part of itself. And its being brave will mean that, in this part, it possesses the power of preserving, in all circumstances, a conviction about the sort of things that it is right to be afraid of—the conviction implanted by the education which the lawgiver has established. Is not that what you mean by courage?

I do not quite understand. Will you say it again?

I am saying that courage means preserving something.

Yes, but what?

The conviction, inculcated by lawfully established education, about the sort of things which may rightly be feared. When I added 'in all circumstances,' I meant preserving it always and never abandoning it, whether under the influence of pain or of pleasure, of desire or of fear. If you like, I will give an illustration.

Please do.

You know how dyers who want wool to take a purple dye, first select the white wool from among all the other colours, next treat it very carefully to make it take the dye in its full brilliance, and only then dip it in the vat. Dyed in that way, wool gets a fast colour, which no washing, even with soap, will rob of its brilliance; whereas if they choose wool of any colour but white, or if they neglect to prepare it, you know what happens.

Yes, it looks washed-out and ridiculous.

That illustrates the result we were doing our best to achieve when we were choosing our fighting men and training their minds and bodies. Our only purpose was to contrive influences whereby they might take the colour of our institutions like a dye, so that, in virtue of having both the right temperament and the right education, their convictions about what ought to be feared and on all other subjects might be indelibly fixed, never to be washed out by pleasure and pain, desire and fear, solvents more terribly effective than all the soap and fuller's earth in the world. Such a power of constantly preserving, in accordance with our institutions, the right conviction about the things which ought, or ought not, to be feared, is what I call courage. That is my position, unless you have some objection to make.

None at all, he replied; if the belief were such as might be found in a slave or an animal—correct, but not produced by education—you would hardly describe it as in accordance with our institutions, and you would give it some other name than courage.

Quite true.

Then I accept your account of courage.

You will do well to accept it, at any rate as applying to the courage of the ordinary citizen; if you like we will go into it more fully some other time. At present we are in search of justice, rather than of courage; and for that purpose we have said enough.

I quite agree.

Two qualities, I went on, still remain to be made out in our state, temperance and the object of our whole inquiry, justice. Can we discover justice without troubling ourselves further about temperance?

I do not know, and I would rather not have justice come to light first, if that means that we should not go on to consider temperance. So if you want to please me, take temperance first.

Of course I have every wish to please you.

Do go on then.

I will. At first sight, temperance seems more like some sort of concord or harmony than the other qualities did.

How so?

Temperance surely means a kind of orderliness, a control of certain pleasures and appetiies. People use the expression, 'master of oneself,' whatever that means, and various other phrases that point the same way.

Quite true.

Is not 'master of oneself' an absurd expression? A man who was master of himself would presumably be also subject to himself, and the subject would be master; for all these terms apply to the same person.

No doubt.

I think, however, the phrase means that within the man himself, in his soul, there is a better part and a worse; and that he is his own master when the part which is better by nature has the worse under its control. It is certainly a term of praise; whereas it is considered a disgrace, when, through bad breeding or bad company, the better part is overwhelmed by the worse, like a small force outnumbered by a multitude. A man in that condition is called a slave to himself and intemperate.

Probably that is what is meant.

Then now look at our newly founded state and you will find one of these two conditions realized there. You will agree that it deserves to be called master of itself, if temperance and self-mastery exist where the better part rules the worse.

Yes, I can see that is true.

It is also true that the great mass of multifarious appetites and pleasures and pains will be found to occur chiefly in children and women and slaves, and, among free men so called, in the inferior multitude; whereas the simple and moderate desires which, with the aid of reason and right belief, are guided by reflection, you will find only in a few, and those with the best inborn dispositions and the best educated.

Yes, certainly.

Do you see that this state of things will exist in your commonwealth, where the desires of the inferior multitude will be controlled by the desires and wisdom of the superior few? Hence, if any society can be called master of itself and in control of pleasures and desires, it will be ours.

Quite so.

On all these grounds, then, we may describe it as temperate. Furthermore, in our state, if anywhere, the governors and the governed will share the same conviction on the question who ought to rule Don't you think so?

I am quite sure of it.

Then, if that is their state of mind, in which of the two classes of citizens will temperance reside—in the governors or in the governed?

In both, I suppose.

So we were not wrong in divining a resemblance between temperance and some kind of harmony. Temperance is not like courage and wisdom, which made the state wise and brave by residing each in one particular part. Temperance works in a different way; it extends throughout the whole gamut of the state, producing a consonance of all its elements from the weakest to the strongest as measured by any standard you like to take—wisdom, bodily strength, numbers, or wealth. So we are entirely justified in identifying with temperance this unanimity or harmonious agreement between the naturally superior and inferior elements on the question which of the two should govern, whether in the state or in the individual.

I fully agree.

Good, said I. We have discovered in our commonwealth three out of our four qualities, to the best of our present judgment. What is the remaining one, required to make up its full complement of goodness? For clearly this will be justice.

Clearly.

Now is the moment, then, Glaucon, for us to keep the closest watch, like huntsmen standing round a covert, to make sure that justice does not slip through and vanish undetected. It must certainly be somewhere hereabouts; so keep your eyes open for a view of the quarry, and if you see it first, give me the alert.

I wish I could, he answered; but you will do better to give me a lead and not count on me for more than eyes to see what you show me.

Pray for luck, then, and follow me.

I will, if you will lead on.

The thicket looks rather impenetrable, said I; too dark for it to be easy to start up the game. However, we must push on.

Of course we must.

Here I gave the view halloo. Glaucon, I exclaimed, I believe we are on the track and the quarry is not going to escape us altogether.

That is good news.

Really, I said, we have been extremely stupid. All this time the thing has been under our very noses from the start, and we never saw it. We have been as absurd as a person who hunts for something he has all the time got in his hand. Instead of looking at the thing, we have been staring into the distance. No doubt that is why it escaped us.

What do you mean?

I believe we have been talking about the thing all this while without ever understanding that we were giving some sort of account of it.

Do come to the point. I am all ears.

Listen, then, and judge whether I am right. You remember how, when we first began to establish our commonwealth and several times since, we have laid down, as a universal principle, that everyone ought to perform the one function in the community for which his nature best suited him. Well I believe that that principle, or some form of it, is justice.

We certainly laid that down.

Yes, and surely we have often heard people say that justice means minding one's own business and not meddling with other men's concerns; and we have often said so ourselves.

We have.

Well, my friend, it may be that this minding of one's own business, when it takes a certain form, is actually the same thing as justice. Do you know what makes me think so?

No, tell me.

I think that this quality which makes it possible for the three we have already considered, wisdom, courage, and temperance, to take their place in the commonwealth, and so long as it remains present secures their continuance, must be the remaining one. And we said that, when three of the four were found, the one left over would be justice.

It must be so.

Well now, if we had to decide which of these qualities will contribute most to the excellence of our commonwealth, it would be hard to say whether it was the unanimity of rulers and subjects, or the soldier's fidelity to the established conviction about what is, or is not, to be feared, or the watchful intelligence of the Rulers; or whether its excellence were not above all due to the observance by everyone, child or woman, slave or freeman or artisan, ruler or ruled, of this principle that each one should do his own proper work without interfering with others.

It would be hard to decide, no doubt.

It seems, then, that this principle can at any rate claim to rival wisdom, temperance, and courage as conducing to the excellence of a state. And would you not say that the only possible competitor of these qualities must be justice?

Yes, undoubtedly.

Here is another thing which points to the same conclusion. The judging of law-suits is a duty that you will lay upon your Rulers, isn't it?

Of course.

And the chief aim of their decisions will be that neither party shall have what belongs to another or be deprived of what is his own.

Yes.

Because that is just?

Yes.

So here again justice admittedly means that a man should possess and concern himself with what properly belongs to him.

True.

Again, do you agree with me that no great harm would be done to the community by a general interchange of most forms of work, the carpenter and the cobbler exchanging their positions and their tools and taking on each other's jobs, or even the same man undertaking both?

Yes, there would not be much harm in that.

But I think you will also agree that another kind of interchange would be disastrous. Suppose, for instance, someone whom nature designed to be an artisan or tradesman should be emboldened by some advantage, such as wealth or command of votes or bodily strength, to try to enter the order of fighting men; or some member of that order should aspire, beyond his merits, to a seat in the council-chamber of the Guardians. Such interference and exchange of social positions and tools, or the attempt to combine all these forms of work in the same person, would be fatal to the commonwealth.

Most certainly.

Where there are three orders, then, any plurality of functions or shifting from one order to another is not merely utterly harmful to the community, but one might fairly call it the extreme of wrongdoing. And you will agree that to do the greatest of wrongs to one's own community is injustice.

Surely.

This, then, is injustice. And, conversely, let us repeat that when each order— tradesman, Auxiliary, Gardian—keeps to its own proper business in the common-wealth and does its own work, that is justice and what makes a just society.

I entirely agree.

THE THREE PARTS OF THE SOUL

We must not be too positive yet, said I. If we find that this same quality when it exists in the individual can equally be identified with justice, then we can at once give our assent; there will be no more to be said; otherwise, we shall have to look further. For the moment, we had better finish the inquiry which we began with the idea that it would be easier to make out the nature of justice in the individual if we first tried to study it in something on a larger scale. That larger thing we took to be a state, and so we set about constructing the best one we could, being sure of finding justice in a state that was good. The discovery we made there must now be applied to the individual. If it is confirmed, all will be well; but if we find that justice in the individual is something different, we must go back to the state and test our new result. Perhaps if we brought the two cases into contact like flint and steel, we might strike out between them the spark of justice, and in its light confirm the conception in our own minds.

A good method. Let us follow it.

Now, I continued, if two things, one large, the other small, are called by the same name, they will be alike in that respect to which the common name applies. Accordingly, in so far as the quality of justice is concerned, there will be no difference between a just man and a just society.

No.

Well, but we decided that a society was just when each of the three types of human character it contained performed its own function; and again, it was temperate and brave and wise by virtue of certain other affections and states of mind of those same types.

True.

Accordingly, my friend, if we are to be justified in attributing those same virtues to the individual, we shall expect to find that the individual soul contains the same three elements and that they are affected in the same way as are the corresponding types in society.

That follows.

Here, then, we have stumbled upon another little problem: Does the soul contain these three elements or not?

Not such a very little one, I think. It may be a true saying, Socrates, that what is worth while is seldom easy.

Apparently; and let me tell you, Glaucon, it is my belief that we shall never reach the exact truth in this matter by following our present methods of discussion; the road leading to that goal is longer and more laborious. However, perhaps we can find an answer that will be up to the standard we have so far maintained in our speculations.

Is not that enough? I should be satisfied for the moment.

Well, it will more than satisfy me, I replied.

Don't be disheartened, then, but go on.

Surely, I began, we must admit that the same elements and characters that appear in the state must exist in every one of us; where else could they have come from? It would be absurd to imagine that among peoples with a reputation for a high-spirited character, like the Thracians and Scythians and northerners generally, the states have not derived that character from their individual members; or that it is otherwise with the love of knowledge, which would be ascribed chiefly to our own part of the world, or with the love of money, which one would specially connect with Phoenicia and Egypt.

Certainly.

So far, then, we have a fact which is easily recognized. But here the difficulty begins. Are we using the same part of ourselves in all these three experiences, or a different part in each? Do we gain knowledge with one part, feel anger with another, and with yet a third desire the pleasures of food, sex, and so on? Or is the whole soul at work in every impulse and in all these forms of behavior? The difficulty is to answer that question satisfactorily.

I quite agree.

Let us approach the problem whether these elements are distinct or identical in this way. It is clear that the same thing cannot act in two opposite ways or be in two opposite states at the same time, with respect to the same part of itself, and in relation to the same object. So if we find such contradictory actions or states among the elements concerned, we shall know that more than one must have been involved.

Very well.

Consider this proposition of mine, then. Can the same thing, at the same time and with respect to the same part of itself, be at rest and in motion?

Certainly not.

We had better state this principle in still more precise terms, to guard against misunderstanding later on. Suppose a man is standing still, but moving his head and arms. We should not allow anyone to say that the same man was both at rest and in motion at the same time, but only that part of him was at rest, part in motion. Isn't that so?

Yes.

An ingenious objector might refine still further and argue that a peg-top, spinning with its peg fixed at the same spot, or indeed any body that revolves in the same place, is both at rest and in motion as a whole. But we should not agree, because the parts in respect of which such a body is moving and at rest are not the same. It contains an axis and a circumference; and in respect of the axis it is at rest inasmuch as the axis is not inclined in any direction, while in respect of the circumference it revolves; and if, while it is spinning, the axis does lean out of the perpendicular in all directions, then it is in no way at rest.

That is true.

No objection of that sort, then, will disconcert us or make us believe that the same thing can ever act or be acted upon in two opposite ways, or be two opposite things, at the same time, in respect of the same part of itself, and in relation to the same object.

I can answer for myself at any rate.

Well, anyhow, as we do not want to spend time in reviewing all such objections to make sure that they are unsound, let us proceed on this assumption, with the understanding that, if we ever come to think otherwise, all the consequences based upon it will fall to the ground.

Yes, that is a good plan.

Now, would you class such things as assent and dissent, striving after something and refusing it, attraction and repulsion, as pairs of opposite actions or states of mind—no matter which?

Yes, they are opposites.

And would you not class all appetites such as hunger and thirst, and again willing and wishing, with the affirmative members of those pairs I have just mentioned? For instance, you would say that the soul of a man who desires something is striving after it, or trying to draw to itself the thing it wishes to possess, or again, in so far as it is willing to have its want satisfied, it is giving its assent to its own longing, as if to an inward question.

Yes.

And, on the other hand, disinclination, unwillingness, and dislike, we should class on the negative side with acts of rejection or repulsion.

Of course.

That being so, shall we say that appetites form one class, the most conspicuous being those we call thirst and hunger?

Yes.

Thirst being desire for drink, hunger for food?

Yes.

Now, is thirst, just in so far as it is thirst, a desire in the soul for anything more than simply drink? Is it, for instance, thirst for hot drink or for cold, for much drink or for little, or in a word for drink of any particular kind? Is it not rather true that you will have a desire for cold drink only if you are feeling hot as well as thirsty, and for hot drink only if you are feeling cold; and if you want much drink or little, that will be because your thirst is a great thirst or a little one? But, just in itself, thirst or hunger is a desire for nothing more than its natural object, drink or food, pure and simple.

Yes, he agreed, each desire, just in itself, is simply for its own natural object. When the object is of such and such a particular kind, the desire will be correspondingly qualified.

We must be careful here, or we might be troubled by the objection that no one desires mere food and drink, but always wholesome food and drink. We shall be told that what we desire is always something that is good; so if thirst is a desire, its object must be, like that of any other desire, something—drink or whatever it may be—that will be good for one.

Yes, there might seem to be something in that objection.

But surely, wherever you have two correlative terms, if one is qualified, the other must always be qualified too; whereas if one is unqualified, so is the other.

I don't understand.

Well, 'greater' is a relative term; and the greater is greater than the less; if it is much greater, then the less is much less; if it is greater at some moment, past or future, then the less is less at that same moment. The same principle applies to all such correlatives, like 'more' and 'fewer,' 'double' and 'half'; and again to terms like 'heavier' and 'lighter,' 'quicker' and 'slower,' and to things like hot and cold.

Yes.

Or take the various branches of knowledge: is it not the same there? The object of knowledge pure and simple is the knowable—if that is the right word—without any qualification; whereas a particular kind of knowledge has an object of a particular kind. For example, as soon as men learnt how to build houses, their craft was distinguished from others under the name of architecture, because it had a unique character, which was itself due to the character of its object; and all other branches of craft and knowledge were distinguished in the same way.

True.

This, then, if you understand me now, is what I meant by saying that, where there are two correlatives, the one is qualified if, and only if, the other is so. I am not saying that the one must have the same quality as the other—that the science of health and disease is itself healthy and diseased, or the knowledge of good and evil is itself good and evil—but only that, as soon as you have a knowledge that is restricted to a particular kind of object, namely health and disease, the knowledge itself becomes a particular kind of knowledge. Hence we no longer call it merely knowledge, which would have for its object whatever can be known, but we add the qualification and call it medical science.

I understand now and I agree.

Now, to go back to thirst: is not that one of these relative terms? It is essentially thirst for something.

Yes, for drink.

And if the drink desired is of a certain kind, the thirst will be correspondingly qualified. But thirst which is just simply thirst is not for drink of any particular sort—much or little, good or bad—but for drink pure and simple.

Quite so.

We conclude, then, that the soul of a thirsty man, just in so far as he is thirsty, has no other wish than to drink. That is the object of its craving, and towards that it is impelled.

That is clear.

Now if there is ever something which at the same time pulls it the opposite way, that something must be an element in the soul other than the one which is thirsting and driving it like a beast to drink; in accordance with our principle that the same thing cannot behave in two opposite ways at the same time and towards the same object with the same part of itself. It is like an archer drawing the bow: it is not accurate to say that his hands are at the same time both pushing and pulling it. One hand does the pushing, the other the pulling.

Exactly.

Now, is it sometimes true that people are thirsty and yet unwilling to drink?

Yes, often.

What, then, can one say of them, if not that their soul contains something which urges them to drink and something which holds them back, and that this latter is a distinct thing and overpowers the other?

I agree.

And is it not true that the intervention of this inhibiting principle in such cases always has its origin in reflection; whereas the impulses driving and dragging the soul are engendered by external influences and abnormal conditions?

Evidently.

We shall have good reason, then, to assert that they are two distinct principles. We may call that part of the soul whereby it reflects, rational; and the other, with which it feels hunger and thirst and is distracted by sexual passion and all the other desires, we will call irrational appetite, associated with pleasure in the replenishment of certain wants.

Yes, there is good ground for that view.

Let us take it, then, that we have now distinguished two elements in the soul. What of that passionate element which makes us feel angry and indignant? Is that a third, or identical in nature with one of those two?

It might perhaps be identified with appetite.

I am more inclined to put my faith in a story I once heard about Leontius, son of Aglaion. On his way up from the Piraeus outside the north wall, he noticed the bodies of some criminals lying on the ground, with the executioner standing by them. He wanted to go and look at them, but at the same time he was disgusted and tried to turn away. He struggled for some time and covered his eyes, but at last the desire was too much for him. Opening his eyes wide, he ran up to the bodies and cried, 'There you are, curse you; feast yourselves on this lovely sight!'

Yes, I have heard that story too.

The point of it surely is that anger is sometimes in conflict with appetite, as if they were two distinct principles. Do we not often find a man whose desires would force him to go against his reason, reviling himself and indignant with this part of his nature which is trying to put constraint on him? It is like a struggle between two factions, in which indignation takes the side of reason. But I believe you have never observed, in your self or anyone else, indignation make common cause with appetite in behaviour which reason decides to be wrong.

No, I am sure I have not.

Again, take a man who feels he is in the wrong. The more generous his nature, the less can he be indignant at any suffering, such as hunger and cold, inflicted by the man he has injured. He recognizes such treatment as just, and, as I say, his spirit refuses to be roused against it.

That is true.

But now contrast one who thinks it is he that is being wronged. His spirit boils with resentment and sides with the right as he conceives it. Persevering all the more for the hunger and cold and other pains he suffers, it triumphs and will not give in until its gallant struggle has ended in success or death; or until the restraining voice of reason, like a shepherd calling off his dog, makes it relent.

An apt comparison, he said; and in fact it fits the relation of our Auxiliaries to the Rulers: they were to be like watchdogs obeying the shepherds of the commonwealth.

Yes, you understand very well what I have in mind. But do you see how we have changed our view? A moment ago we were supposing this spirited element to be something of the nature of appetite; but now it appears that, when the soul is divided into factions, it is far more ready to be up in arms on the side of reason.

Quite true.

Is it, then, distinct from the rational element or only a particular form of it, so that the soul will contain no more than two elements, reason and appetite? Or is the soul like the state, which had three orders to hold it together, traders, Auxiliaries, and counsellors? Does the spirited element make a third, the natural auxiliary of reason, when not corrupted by bad upbringing?

It must be a third.

Yes, I said, provided it can be shown to be distinct from reason, as we saw it was from appetite.

That is easily proved. You can see that much in children: they are full of passionate feelings from their very birth; but some, I should say, never become rational, and most of them only late in life.

A very sound observation, said I, the truth of which may also be seen in animals. And besides, there is the witness of Homer in that line I quoted before: 'He smote his breast and spoke, chiding his heart.' The poet is plainly thinking of the two elements as distinct, when he makes the one which has chosen the better course after reflection rebuke the other for its unreasoning passion.

I entirely agree.

THE VIRTUES IN THE INDIVIDUAL AND THE
DEFINITION OF JUSTICE

And so, after a stormy passage, we have reached the land. We are fairly agreed that the same three elements exist alike in the state and in the individual soul.

That is so.

Does it not follow at once that state and individual will be wise or brave by virtue of the same element in each and in the same way? Both will possess in the same manner any quality that makes for excellence.

That must be true.

Then it applies to justice: we shall conclude that a man is just in the same way that a state was just. And we have surely not forgotten that justice in the state meant that each of the three orders in it was doing its own proper work. So we may henceforth bear in mind that each one of us likewise will be a just person fulfilling his proper function, only if the several parts of our nature fulfill theirs.

Certainly.

And it will be the business of reason to rule with wisdom and forethought on behalf of the entire soul; while the spirited element ought to act as its subordinate and ally. The two will be brought into accord, as we said earlier, by that combination of mental and bodily training which will tune up one string of the instrument and relax the other, nourishing the reasoning part on the study of noble literature and allaying the other's wildness by harmony and rhythm. When both have been thus nurtured and trained to know their own true functions, they must be set in command over the appetites, which form the greater part of each man's soul and are by nature insatiably covetous. They must keep watch lest this part, by battening on the pleasures that are called bodily, should grow so great and powerful that it will no longer keep to its own work, but will try to enslave the others and usurp a dominion to which it has no right, thus turning the whole of life upside down. At the same time, those two together will be the best of guardians for the entire soul and for the body against all enemies from without: the one will take counsel, while the other will do battle, following its ruler's commands and by its own bravery giving effect to the ruler's designs.

Yes, that is all true.

And so we call an individual brave in virtue of this spirited part of his nature, when, in spite of pain or pleasure, it holds fast to the injunctions of reason about what he ought or ought not to be afraid of.

True.

And wise in virtue of that small part which rules and issues these injunctions, possessing as it does the knowledge of what is good for each of the three elements and for all of them in common.

Certainly.

And, again, temperate by reason of the unanimity and concord of all three, when there is no internal conflict between the ruling element and its two subjects, but all are agreed that reason should be ruler.

Yes, that is an exact account of temperance, whether in the state or in the individual.

Finally, a man will be just by observing the principle we have so often stated.

Necessarily.

Now is there any indistinctness in our vision of justice, that might make it seem somehow different from what we found it to be in the state?

I don't think so.

Because, if we have any lingering doubt, we might make sure by comparing it with some commonplace notions. Suppose, for instance, that a sum of money were entrusted to our state or to an individual of corresponding character and training, would anyone imagine that such a person would be specially likely to embezzle it?

No.

And would he not be incapable of sacrilege and theft, or of treachery to friend or country; never false to an oath or any other compact; the last to be guilty of adultery or of neglecting parents or the due service of the gods?

Yes.

And the reason for all this is that each part of his nature is exercising its proper function, of ruling or of being ruled.

Yes, exactly.

Are you satisfied, then, that justice is the power which produces states or individuals of whom that is true, or must we look further?

There is no need; I am quite satisfied.

And so our dream has come true—I mean the inkling we had that, by some happy chance, we had lighted upon a rudimentary form of justice from the very moment when we set about founding our commonwealth. Our principle that the born shoemaker or carpenter had better stick to his trade turns out to have been an adumbration of justice; and that is why it has helped us. But in reality justice, though evidently analogous to this principle, is not a matter of external behavior, but of the inward self and of attending to all that is, in the fullest sense, a man's proper concern. The just man does not allow the several elements in his soul to usurp one another's functions; he is indeed one who sets his house in order, by self-mastery and discipline coming to be at peace with himself, and bringing into tune those three parts, like the terms in the proportion of a musical scale, the highest and lowest notes and the mean between them, with all the intermediate intervals. Only when he has linked these parts together in well-tempered harmony and has made himself one man instead of many, will he be ready to go about whatever he may have to do, whether it be making money and satisfying bodily wants, or business transactions, or the affairs of state. In all these fields when he speaks of just and honourable conduct, he will mean the behaviour that helps to produce and to preserve this habit of mind; and by wisdom he will mean the knowledge which presides over such conduct. Any action which tends to break down this habit will be for him unjust; and the notions governing it he will call ignorance and folly.

That is perfectly true, Socrates.

Good, said I. I believe we should not be thought altogether mistaken, if we claimed to have discovered the just man and the just state, and wherein their justice consists.

Indeed we should not.

Shall we make that claim, then?

Yes, we will.

So be it, said I. Next, I suppose, we have to consider injustice.

Evidently.

This must surely be a sort of civil strife among the three elements whereby they usurp and encroach upon one another's functions and some one part of the soul rises up in rebellion against the whole, claiming a supremacy to which it has no right because its nature fits it only to be the servant of the ruling principle. Such turmoil and aberration we shall, I think, identify with injustice, intemperance, cowardice, ignorance, and in a word with all wickedness.

Exactly.

And now that we know the nature of justice and injustice, we can be equally clear about what is meant by acting justly and again by unjust action and wrongdoing.

How do you mean?

Plainly, they are exactly analogous to those wholesome and unwholesome activities which respectively produce a healthy or unhealthy condition in the body; in the same way just and unjust conduct produce a just or unjust character. Justice is produced in the soul, like health in the body, by establishing the elements concerned in their natural relations of control and subordination, whereas injustice is like disease and means that this natural order is inverted.

Quite so.

It appears, then, that virtue is as it were the health and comeliness and well-being of the soul, as wickedness is disease, deformity, and weakness.

True.

And also that virtue and wickedness are brought about by one's way of life, honourable or disgraceful.

That follows.

So now it only remains to consider which is the more profitable course: to do right and live honourably and be just, whether or not anyone knows what manner of man you are, or to do wrong and be unjust, provided that you can escape the chastisement which might make you a better man.

But really, Socrates, it seems to me ridiculous to ask that question now that the nature of justice and injustice has been brought to light. People think that all the luxury and wealth and power in the world cannot make life worth living when the bodily consitution is going to rack and ruin; and are we to believe that, when the very principle whereby we live is deranged and corrupted, life will be worth living so long as a man can do as he will, and wills to do anything rather than to free himself from vice and wrongdoing and to win justice and virtue?

Yes, I replied, it is a ridiculous question.

Statesman

TRUE STATESMANSHIP IS AN ART ABOVE ALL LAWS

Stranger: We decided, did we not, that the art of rule is one of the sciences?

Young Socrates: Yes.

Str.: Furthermore we agreed that it is a particular kind of science. Out of the whole class of sciences we selected the judging class and more particularly the directive class.

Y.S.: We did.

Str.: We divided the directive into direction of lifeless things and direction of living beings, and by this process of subdivision we arrived by regular stages where we are now, never losing sight of the fact that Statesmanship is a form of knowledge but unable as yet to say precisely what form of knowledge it is.

Y.S.: You are quite right.

Str.: Do we realize, then, that the real criterion in judging constitutions must not be whether few or many rule, whether rule is by violence or consent, or whether the rulers are poor or rich? If we are going to abide by our previous conclusions, the criterion must be the presence or absence of an art directing the ruling.

From *Plato's Statesman,* translated by J. B. Skemp, 1952. By permission of Routledge and Kegan Paul, London, and The Yale University Press, New Haven. Some translator's footnotes omitted.

Y.S.: Yes, for we simply must abide by those conclusions.

Str.: Then we are forced to look at the issue in this light. In which, if any, of these constitutions do we find the art of ruling being practised in the actual government of men? What art is more difficult to learn? But what art is more important to us? We must see it for what it is so as to be able to decide which are the other public figures we must remove from the true King's company, those personages who claim to be statesmen, who win over the mass of men to believe them to be statesmen, but are in actual fact nothing of the kind.

Y.S.: We must indeed, for this was the task set for our discussion.

Str.: Do you think that any considerable number of men in a particular city will be capable of acquiring the art of Statesmanship?

Y.S.: That is quite out of the question.

Str.: In a city with a population of a thousand, could a hundred, say, acquire it satisfactorily—or could fifty, perhaps?

Y.S.: Statesmanship would be the easiest of the arts if so many could acquire it. We know quite well that there would never be fifty first-class draughts players among a thousand inhabitants—that is, not if they were judged by proper inter-Hellenic standards. How much less can you expect to find fifty kings! For according to our former argument it is only the man possessed of the art of kingship who must be called a king, though he is just as much a king when he is not in power as when he is.

Str.: You have very rightly recalled that point. I think it follows that if the art of government is to be found in this world at all in its pure form, it will be found in the possession of one or two, or, at most, of a select few.

Y.S.: Yes.

Str.: On this principle it is the men who possess the art of ruling and these only, whom we are to regard as rulers, whatever constitutional form their rule may take. It makes no difference whether their subjects be willing or unwilling; they may rule with or without a code of laws, they may be poor or wealthy. It is the same with doctors. We do not assess the medical qualification of a doctor by the degree of willingness on our part to submit to his knife or cautery or other painful treatment. Doctors are still doctors whether they work according to fixed prescriptions or without them and whether they be poor or wealthy. So long as they control our health on a scientific basis, they may purge and reduce us or they may build us up, but they still remain doctors. The one essential condition is that they act for the good of our bodies to make them better instead of worse, and treat men's ailments in every case as healers acting to preserve life. We must insist that in this disinterested scientific ability we see the distinguishing mark of true authority in medicine—and of true authority every-where else as well.

Y.S.: Quite so.

Str.: Then the constitution *par excellence*, the only constitution worthy of the name, must be the one in which the rulers are not men making a show of political cleverness but men really possessed of scientific understanding of the art of government. Then we must not take into consideration on any sound principle of judgment whether their rule be by laws or without them over willing or unwilling subjects or whether they themselves be rich men or poor men.

Y.S.: No.

Str.: They may purge the city for its better health by putting some of the citizens to death or banishing others. They may lessen the citizen body by sending off colonies like bees swarming off from a hive, or they may bring people in from other cities and naturalize them so as to increase the number of citizens. So long as they work on a reasoned scientific principle following essential justice and act to preserve and improve the life of the state so far as may be, we must call them real statesmen according to our standards of judgment and say that the state they rule alone enjoys good government and has a real constitution. We must go on to say that all the other state-fabrics called constitutions are not genuine, but counterfeit: they imitate the true constitution. Those which we call law-abiding copy it fairly closely, but the rest are more or less shocking caricatures of it.

Y.S.: All the rest, Sir, I believe to have been spoken in due measure—but the saying about ruling without laws is a hard saying for us to hear.

Str.: You are a little too quick for me, Socrates! I was just going to cross-examine you to see if you really accepted all I have said or felt some objection. I realize, however, from what you say that the point we are anxious to discuss in detail is this question whether a good governor can govern without laws.

Y.S.: Yes, it is.

Str.: In one sense it is evident that the art of Kingship does include the art of lawmaking. But the political ideal is not full authority for laws but rather full authority for a man who understands the art of Kingship and has kingly ability. Do you understand why?

Y.S.: No, please tell me why.

Str.: Law can never issue an injunction binding on all which really embodies what is best for each: it cannot prescribe with perfect accuracy what is good and right for each member of the community at any one time. The differences of human personality, the variety of men's activities and the inevitable unsettlement attending all human experience make it impossible for any art whatsoever to issue unqualified rules holding good on all questions at all times. I suppose that so far we are agreed.

Y.S.: Most emphatically.

Str.: But we find practically always that the law tends to issue just this invariable kind of rule. It is like a self-willed, ignorant man who lets no one do anything but what he has ordered and forbids all subsequent questioning of his orders even if the situation has shown some marked improvement on the one for which he originally legislated.[1]

Y.S.: Yes, that is just how the law treats us all.

Str.: It is impossible then, for something invariable and unqualified to deal satisfactorily with what is never uniform and constant.

Y.S.: I am afraid it is impossible.

Str.: But why then must there be a system of laws, seeing that law is not the ideal form of control? We must find out why a legal system is necessary.

Y.S.: We must.

---

[1] The situation here is conceived as a parallel to the case of the patient who improves unexpectedly and does not need as rigorous medicine as that prescribed (*295c infra*). Perhaps a comparable legal situation would arise if a town which was required under an Act of 1846 to provide public wash houses built a housing scheme where houses had excellent washing facilities and cleared its slums and then, on proposing to erect new public swimming baths, was bound by the 1846 Act to provide needless wash houses as well.

Str.: You have courses of training here in Athens, have you not, just as they have in other cities—courses in which pupils are trained in a group to fit themselves for athletic contests in running or in other sports?

Y.S.: Of course. We have quite a number of them.

Str.: Let us call to mind the commands which professional trainers give to the athletes under their regimen in these courses.

Y.S.: In what particular?

Str.: The view such trainers take is that they cannot do their work in detail and issue special commands adapted to the condition of each member of the group. When they lay down rules for physical welfare they find it necessary to give bulk instructions having regard to the general benefit of the average pupil.

Y.S.: Quite so.

Str.: That is why we find them giving the same exercises to whole groups of pupils, starting or stopping all of them at the same time in their running, wrestling or whatever it may be.

Y.S.: Yes.

Str.: Similarly we must expect that the legislator who has to give orders to whole communities of human creatures in matters of right and of mutual contractual obligation, will never be able in the laws he prescribes for the whole group to give every individual his due with absolute accuracy.

Y.S.: Very probably not.

Str.: But we shall find him making the law for the generality of his subjects under average circumstances. Thus he will legislate for all individual citizens, but it will be by what may be called a 'bulk' method rather than an individual treatment; and this method of 'bulk' prescription will be followed by him whether he makes a written code of law or refrains from issuing such a code, preferring to legislate by using unwritten ancestral customs.

Y.S.: Yes, and quite rightly so.

Str.: Of course he is right, Socrates. How could any lawgiver be capable of prescribing every act of a particular individual and sit at his side, so to speak, all through his life and telling him just what to do? And if among the few who have really attained this true statesmanship there arose one who was free to give this detailed guidance to an individual, he would hardly put obstacles in his own way by deliberately framing legal codes of the kind we are criticizing.

Y.S.: That certainly follows, Sir, from what has been said.

Str.: I would rather say, Socrates, that it follows from what is going to be said.

Y.S.: And what is that?

Str.: Let us put this case to ourselves. A doctor or trainer plans to travel abroad and expects to be away from his charges for quite a long time. The doctor might well think that his patients would forget any verbal instructions he gave and the trainer might think likewise. In these circumstances each might want to leave written reminders of his orders—do you not think so yourself, Socrates?

Y.S.: Exactly so, Sir.

Str.: Well now, suppose our doctor did not stay abroad as long as he had expected and so came back the sooner to his patients. Would he hesitate to substitute different prescriptions for the original ones if his patients' condition happened to be better than anticipated because of a climatic improvement or some other unusual and unexpected development of that kind? Would the doctor feel it his duty to maintain stubbornly that there must be no transgression of the strict letter of those original prescriptions of his? Would he refuse to issue new prescriptions of conditions, or condemn a patient who was venturing to act contrary to the prescriptions he had written out for him? Would the doctor declare all such action must be wrong because those former prescriptions were the true canons of medicine and of health and therefore that all contravention of them must lead to disease and be contrary to medical science? Surely any such claims, in circumstances where a science is involved and a real art is at work, would only make the man who made the claim and his precious prescriptions supremely ridiculous.

Y.S.: Yes, it would indeed.

Str.: Imagine then the case of a scientific legislator. Suppose that by a written code or by support given to unwritten customs he has laid down what is just and honourable and what is not, and what benefits society and what hurts it. Suppose him to do this service for the several communities of the human flock who live in their cities as their appointed pasture shepherded by the codes their legislators have provided. If this man, who drew up his code by the art of statesmanship, wishes to amend it, or if another scientific legislator of this kind appears on the scene, will these be forbidden to enact new laws differing from the earlier ones? Surely such a prohibition would appear as ridiculous in the case of the legislator as it was in the case of the doctor, would it not?

Y.S.: Of course.

Str.: But are you familiar with the argument one usually hears advanced when an issue like this is raised?

Y.S.: No, I cannot remember it at the moment, at any rate.

Str.: It is quite a plausible argument: I grant that. They contend that if a man discovers better laws than those already enacted he is entitled to get them brought into effect, but only if in every instance he has first persuaded his own city to accept them.

Y.S.: But what of this? Surely this is a sound contention?

Str.: It may be: but answer this question. Suppose a man fails to persuade his city and forces his better laws upon it, what name are we to apply to force so used? But no, do not answer me that question yet, for there are others to be answered first.

Y.S.: What can they be?

Str.: Consider once more the case of the patient under the doctor's treatment. Suppose that the doctor fails to persuade the patient but has a mastery of medical knowledge; and suppose that he forces a particular course of treatment which goes against written prescription but is actually more salutary on a child patient, may be, or on a man or a woman. What are we to call force of this kind? Whatever we decide to call it, we shall not call it 'the sin against true medicine' or 'a breach of the laws of health'. Surely the very last thing a patient who is so constrained is entitled to say is that the doctor's act in applying the constraint was contrary to good medicine and an aggravation of his disease.

Y.S.: You are quite right.

Str.: By what name then, do we call the sin against the art of statesmanship? Would it not be called Dishonour, Vice, Injustice?

Y.S.: Assuredly.

Str.: What then, shall we say of citizens of a state who have been forced to do things which are contrary to written laws and ancestral customs but are nevertheless juster, more effective and more noble than the directions of these traditional authorities? How shall we regard censure by these citizens of the force which has applied in these circumstances? Unless they wish to appear ridiculous in the extreme there is one thing they must refrain from saying. They must not assert in any such instance that in being subjected to compulsion they have suffered disgrace, injustice or evil at the hands of those who compelled them.

Y.S.: That is quite true.

Str.: Can it be the case that acts imposed under compulsion are right if the compeller is rich but wrong if he is poor? Surely what matters is that with or without persuasion, rich or poor, according to a code or against it, the ruler does what is really beneficial. These are the real issues and all is well if he passes this test, the only genuine test of good government in a community and the only principle by which the understanding and upright ruler will administer the affairs of those whom he rules. The ship's captain fixes his attention on the real welfare at any given time of his ship and his crew. He lays down no written enactments but supplies a law in action by practical application of his knowledge of seamanship to the needs of the voyage. It is in this way that he preserves the lives of all in his ship. Would not a true constitution be just like this and work in the same way if the rulers really understood what government is and employed their art as a stronger power for good than any written laws? By rulers with this sound attitude of mind no wrong can possibly be done so long as they keep firmly to the one great principle, that they must always administer impartial justice to their subjects under the guidance of intelligence and the art of government. Then they will not only preserve the lives of their subjects but reform their characters too, so far as human nature permits of this.

Y.S.: There can be no objection to your last remarks at any rate.

Str.: No, nor can there be to my earlier ones either.

Y.S.: To which are you referring?

Str.: You remember that we said that in no community whatsoever could it happen that a large number of people received this gift of political wisdom and the power to govern by pure intelligence which would accompany it. Only in the hands of the select few or of the enlightened individual can we look for that right exercise of political power which is itself the one true constitution. For we must call all other constitutions mere imitations of this. Some are more perfect copies of it, others are grosser and less adequate imitations.

Y.S.: What do you really mean by this? For I must admit that I did not really understand what you said before about these 'imitations'.

Str.: But I must make you understand. It would be a serious failing to start a discussion of this issue and then simply drop it without exposing the error which is rampant today in all that is said about it.

Y.S.: And what is this error?

Str.: That is what we must now seek out, though it involves a search over unfamiliar ground and the error is hard to discover. We may say, then, that there is only one constitution in the true sense—the one we have described. For the rest of them owe their very preservation to their following a code of laws enacted for this true state and to a strict adherence to a rule which we admit to be desirable though it falls short of the ideal.

Y.S.: What rule is this?

Str.: The rule that none of the citizens may venture to do any act contrary to the laws, and that if any of them ventures to do such act, the penalty is to be death or the utmost rigour of punishment. This is the justest and most desirable course as a second-best when the ideal we have just described has been set aside. We must now go on to say how this state of affairs we have just called second-best is achieved in practice, must we not?

Y.S.: Yes, we must.

Str.: Let us go back once again to the parallel cases with which we have constantly to compare the ruler who really is a statesman.

Y.S.: Who are they?

Str.: Our good friend the ship's captain and the doctor 'worth a dozen other men'. Let us picture to ourselves a situation in which they might find themselves and see how it all works out in their case.

Y.S.: What situation?

Str.: Suppose we all suddenly decided that we are the victims of the worst possible outrages at their hands. Every doctor, you see, can preserve the life of any he will among us, and can hurt any he will by knife or cautery or by demanding fees which are nothing but imposed taxes—for only the tiniest proportion of them is spent on medicaments for the patient and all the rest goes to keep the doctor and his household. Their final enormity is to accept bribes from the patient's relations or from his enemies and put him to death. Ships' captains are guilty of a different set of crimes, but they are just as heinous. They will enter into a conspiracy to put out to sea with you and then leave you stranded, or else they will scuttle the ship and throw the passengers overboard— and these are not all their misdeeds. Suppose we formed this view of doctors and captains and then held a Council at which the following decree was passed:

I Neither medicine nor seamanship may be trusted in future with absolute control in its particular sphere, either over slaves or over free citizens.

II We therefore resolve to gather together an Assembly of all (or *of the wealthy among*) the people.

III It shall be lawful for men of no calling or men of any other calling to advise this Assembly on seamanship and medicine; that is to say:

(*a*) on the drugs and surgical instruments appropriate to the treatment of the sick;

(*b*) on ships and their tackle, on the handling of vessels and on perils of the sea, including

(*i*) risks arising from wind and tide;

(*ii*) risks arising from encountering pirates,

(*iii*) risks arising from manoeuvre of warships against enemy warships in the event of a naval engagement.

So much for the decree on these matters. The executive is to embody this decree of the Assembly of the People (based, you remember, on the advice of a few doctors and sailors maybe, but certainly on the advice of many unqualified people too) in laws which they are to inscribe on tablets of wood and of stone, and in the case of some of the rules so resolved upon, they must see that they find their place among the unwritten ancestral customs. Thereafter for ever medicine and navigation may only be practiced according to these laws and customs.

Y.S.: A pretty state of affairs this!

Str.: But we have not done yet. Suppose that they resolve further to appoint magistrates chosen by lot annually from the citizen body (whether from the wealthy only or from all citizens). Some of these magistrates, once they are appointed, are to take command of ships and navigate them; others are to cure the sick according to the written code.

Y.S.: This is getting worse!

Str.: But we have not done—see what follows. When the year of office of each of these magistrates expires, a court must be established and jury chosen by lot, perhaps from among wealthier citizens whose names are on a list of previously selected jurors, perhaps from the people as a whole. The magistrates are to be summoned before this court and it is to subject them to audit. It is open to anyone to lay an accusation against them that during their year of office they failed to sail the ships according to the written laws or the ancient custom of our forebears. Similar charges may be brought concerning the healers of the sick. If the verdict goes against any of them, the court must assess the penalty or the fine the convicted parties must pay.

Y.S.: Well then, the man who took office voluntarily in such a society would deserve any punishment and any fine that might be imposed.

Str.: Then there can be further misdemeanours, and we must enact a law to provide against them. It will be a law against independent research. If a man be found guilty of enquiry into seamanship or medicine in contravention of this law—of enquiry into nautical practice, for instance, or into climatic influences and bodily temperatures, and especially if he be guilty of airing theories of his own on such things, action must be taken to suppress him. First we must deny him the title of 'Doctor' or 'Captain'. Instead we must call him a man with his head in the clouds, one of these chattering Sophists. Furthermore it will be lawful for any citizen so desiring to indict him before a court of justice (or what passes for such a court) on the charge of corrupting the younger men and influencing them to go in for seamanship and medicine in an illegal manner by setting up as doctors or captains on their own authority. If he is found guilty of influencing young or old against the laws and written enactments, he shall suffer the utmost penalties. For there can be no claim to possess wisdom greater than the wisdom of the laws. No one need be ignorant of seamanship or medicine, of sailing regulations or health regulations. The laws are there written out for our conning, the ancient customs are firmly established in our midst. Any who really desire to learn may learn.

Suppose, Socrates, that all the arts are treated like this. How do you imagine that generalship and hunting in all its forms would be effected? What would happen to painting and other representational arts, or to building and manufacture of all types of implements under such conditions; and how could farming or any cultivation whatever be carried on? Imagine the rearing of horses and other animals tied down to legal prescription, or divination and similar ministerial functions so controlled. What would legally-governed draughts be like or legal mathematics, whether simple arithmetic, plane geometry, stereometry or kinematics? What would the world be like if everything worked on this principle, organized throughout according to written laws instead of according to the relevant arts?

Y.S.: It is quite clear that the arts as we know them would be annihilated and that they could never be resurrected because of this law which puts an embargo on all research. The result would be that life which is hard enough as it is, would be quite impossible then and not to be endured.

Str.: Yes, but there is a further possible degradation to consider. Suppose we compel each of these arts to function according to a legal code and place a magistrate in charge of this code either by election or by the fall of the lot, and make him rule according to it. Suppose then that he has no regard for the code and acts only from motives of ambition and favouritism. He embarks on a course of action contrary to law but does not act on any basis of scientific knowledge. Evil as the former state was, will not this latter one be still worse?

Y.S.: It will indeed.

Str.: The laws which have been laid down represent the fruit of experience— one must admit that. Each of them has been put forward by some advocate who has been fortunate enough to hit on the right method of commending it and who has thus persuaded the public assembly to enact it. Any man who dares by his action to infringe these laws is guilty of a wrong many times greater than the wrong done by strict laws, for such transgression, if tolerated, would do even more than a rigid code to pervert all ordered activity.

Y.S.: Yes, of course it would.

Str.: Then so long as men enact laws and written codes governing any department of life, our second-best method of government is to forbid any individual or any group to perform any act in contravention of these laws.

Y.S.: True.

Str.: Then laws would seem to be written copies of scientific truth in the various departments of life they cover, copies based as far as possible on the instructions received from those who really possess the scientific truth on these matters.

Y.S.: Yes, of course.

Str.: And yet we must never lose sight of the truth we stated before. The man with the real knowledge, the true Statesman, will in many instances allow his activities to be dictated by his art and pay no regard to written prescriptions. He will do this whenever he is convinced that there are measures which are better than the instructions he previously wrote and sent to people at a time when he could not be there to control them personally.

Y.S.: Yes, that was what we said.

Str.: So an individual or a group who possess a code of laws but try to introduce some change in them because they consider it an improvement are doing the same thing according to their lights as the true Statesman.

Y.S.: Yes.

Str.: But if they acted like this with minds unenlightened by knowledge, they would indeed try to copy the true original, but would copy it very badly. If on the other hand they possessed scientific knowledge, it would no longer be a case of copying at all: it would be the real and original statesmanship we are talking about.

Y.S.: Yes—or so I should say.

Str.: Now it has been argued already and we have agreed that no large group of men is capable of acquiring any art, be it what you will.

Y.S.: That stands as our agreed conclusion.

ON THE IMITATIVE CONSTITUTIONS

Str.: Granted then, that an art of kingly rule exists, the wealthy group or the whole citizen body would never be able to acquire this scientific art of statesmanship.

Y.S.: How could they?

Str.: It seems to follow that there is an invariable rule which these imitative constitutions must obey if they mean to reproduce as far as they can that one real constitution, which is government by a real statesman using real statecraft. They must all keep strictly to the laws once they have been laid down and never transgress written enactments or established national customs.

Y.S.: Quite right.

Str.: When the wealthy seek to copy the ideal constitution we call the constitution which results 'aristocracy', but when they disregard the laws, the constitution produced is 'oligarchy'.

Y.S.: I suppose so.

Str.: But when one individual governs according to laws imitating the truly wise ruler, we call him 'King'. We make no difference in name between the individual ruler guided by political science and the individual ruler guided by a right opinion and acting according to the laws.

Y.S.: That seems to be so

Str.: And so if there really were an example of a truly wise ruler in power his name would undoubtedly be the same—'the King': it could not be anything else. So the total of the names of the constitutions now under consideration comes to five only.[1]

. . . The passage takes up the thread laid aside at 292a. At 291d *fin.* we are told that the three main types have produced two further sub-types to make the total five—monarchy, tyranny, aristocracy, oligarchy, democracy. This we have seen (*v.* note 1, p. 192) to be the formal Academy 'division', and this corroborates M. Diès' interpretation of the present passage. We have here not a reduction of five to one but an expansion of five to seven, since the name 'monarchy' or 'kingship' covers two types, and so does 'democracy'. Plato counts up the five names for us himself at 301C *fin.* But he goes on to one more lesson on the danger of relying on names rather than things (*i.e.* real kinds). More scientific analysis provides the new total—seven—at 302c. Democracy is divided into two like the other main types, and the rule of the philosophic statesman is distinguished from them all (and in particular from law-abiding monarchy), so that a final classification is reached and may be tabulated as follows:

THE SEVEN CONSTITUTIONS

A. *Imitative*

I. Rule of one man:	(*a*)	monarchy	1
	(*b*)	tyranny	2
II. Rule of a few men:	(*a*)	aristocracy	3
	(*b*)	oligarchy	4
III. Rule of many:	(*a*)	democracy	5
	(*b*)	democracy	6

B. *Genuine*

Rule of philosophic statesman	(*c*)		7

(*a*) = law-abiding constitution, (*b*) = constitution flouting law, (*c*) = constitution above all laws.

Y.S.: So it seems.

Str.: But stay, what of the case where one man rules but does not govern his actions either by laws or by ancient customs, but claims falsely what only the truly wise ruler had a right to claim, and says that the 'best' course must be taken in defiance of written codes? If in fact it is only his passion and his ignorance that lead him to attempt to copy the true Statesman in this defiance of law, must we not call him and all like him by the name of tyrant?

Y.S.: Unquestionably.

Str.: So then we have the tyrant and the king, then oligarchy and aristocracy, then democracy, all of which arise when men turn down the idea of the one true and scientific ruler. Men doubt whether any man will ever be found fit to bear such perfect rule. They despair of finding any one man willing and able to rule with moral and intellectual insight and to render every man his due with strictest fairness. They feel sure that a man with such absolute power will be bound to employ it to the hurt and injury of his personal enemies and to put them out of the way. But it remains true that if the ideal ruler we have described were to appear on earth he would be acclaimed, and he would spend his days guiding in strictest justice and perfect felicity that one and only true Commonwealth worthy of the name.

Y.S.: That is so of course.

Str.: We must take things as they are, however, and kings do not arise in cities in the natural course of things in the way the royal bee is born in a bee-hive—one individual obviously outstanding in body and mind and capable of taking charge of things at once. And therefore it seems men gather together and work out written codes, chasing as fast as they can the fading vision of the true constitution.

Y.S.: So it would seem.

Str.: Is it any wonder that under these makeshift constitutions of ours hosts of ills have arisen and more must be expected in the future? They all rest on the sandy foundation of action according to law and custom without real scientific insight. Another art that worked on such a foundation would obviously ruin all that it sought to build up. But something even more remarkable than these besetting ills is the sheer native strength a city possesses nevertheless. For all our cities, as we know, have been subject to such ills for many generations now, and yet some of them have not come to ruin but still stand firm. However, we see many instances of cities going down like sinking ships to their destruction. There have been such wrecks in the past and there surely will be others in the future, caused by the wickedness of captains and crews alike. For these are guilty men, whose sin is supreme ignorance of what matters most. They are men who know little or nothing of real political truth and yet they consider themselves to know it from end to end and suppose that they are better instructed in this art than in any other.

Y.S.: Very true.

Str.: All these imperfect constitutions are difficult to live under, but we might ask ourselves which of them is hardest to bear and which is most tolerable. Ought we perhaps to examine this matter, though it is not directly relevant to our appointed theme? After all one must remember that, speaking quite generally, the aim of all the actions of men everywhere is to secure for themselves the most tolerable life they can.

Y.S.: Then we can hardly help considering the question.

Str.: There is one of three constitutions which you must regard as being at once the hardest to live under and the easiest.

Y.S.: How do you mean?

Str.: I just want to remind you that at the beginning of this supplementary discussion we enumerated three constitutions—the rule of one, the rule of the few and the rule of the many.

Y.S.: We did.

Str.: Dividing each of three into two let us make six, having first separated the true constitution from all, calling it the seventh.

Y.S.: How shall we divide the three others?

Str.: Under the rule of one we get kingly rule and tyranny; under the rule of the few, as we said, come the auspicious form of it, aristocracy, and also oligarchy. As for the subdividing of democracy, though we gave both forms of it one name previously, we must now treat it as twofold.

Y.S.: How is this? How can it be divided?

Str.: By the same division as the other, even though the word 'democracy' proves to be doing double duty. Rule according to law is as possible under democracy as under the other constitutions.

Y.S.: Yes, it is.

Str.: This division of democracy into two kinds was not serviceable previously as we indicated at the time; for we were seeking then to define a perfect constitution. Now, however, we have excluded the perfect constitution from our reckoning and have before us those that have to serve us as constitutions in default of it. In this group we find the principle of obedience to law or contravention of law dividing each type of ruler into two types.

Y.S.: So it seems from the argument that was put forward just now.

Str.: The rule of one man, if it has been kept within the traces, so to speak, by the written rules we call laws, is the best of all the six; but when it is lawless it is hard, and the most grievous to have to endure.

Y.S.: So it would seem.

Str.: As for the rule of a few, just as the few constitute a middle term between the one and the many, so we must regard the rule of the few as of middle potency for good or ill. The rule of the many is weakest in every way; it is not capable of any real good or of any serious evil as compared with the other two. This is because in a democracy sovereignty has been divided out in small portions among a large number of rulers. If therefore all three constitutions are law-abiding, democracy is the worst of the three; but if all three flout the laws, democracy is the best of them. Thus if all constitutions are unprincipled the best thing to do is to live in a democracy. But when constitutions are lawful and ordered, democracy is the least desirable, and monarchy, the first of the six, is by far the best to live under—unless of course the seventh is possible, for that must always be exalted, like a god among mortals, above all other constitutions.

Y.S.: Things do seem to work out in this way, and so we must take your advice and act as you say.

Str.: Therefore all who take part in one of these governments—apart from the one based on real knowledge—are to be distinguished from the true Statesman. They are not statesmen; they are party leaders, leaders of bogus governments and themselves as bogus as their systems. The supreme imitators and tricksters, they are of all Sophists the arch-sophists.

Y.S.: It seems to me that the wheel has come full circle, now that the title of sophist goes to those who most deserve it, to the men who get themselves called political leaders.

Str.: So this fantastic pageant that seemed like some strange masque of centaurs or some band of satyrs stands revealed for what it is. At much pains we have succeeded at least in distinguishing them and setting them apart, as we must, from all true practice of statesmanship.

Y.S.: So we see.

Aristotle

Aristotle (384–323 B.C.) was born in Thrace and his father was a physician to the court of Macedon, but he entered Plato's Academy at Athens as a young man and remained for twenty years until Plato's death. There followed a period during which he traveled and carried on various kinds of research as well as serving for three years as tutor to the son of Phillip of Macedon, Alexander, later to be known as Alexander the Great. After more than ten years absence he returned to Athens and founded his own school, the Lyceum. He remained there lecturing and writing until forced to leave in 323 B.C. because of his association with Macedon.

Aristotle's intellectual interests spanned almost the whole scope of learning in his day. His philosophy shows the great influence of Plato, but is developed along different lines and in fact departs in most conclusions from that of his teacher. One can see this divergence well in Aristotle's ethical and political writings.

The selection from *Politics* included here contains Aristotle's thoughts on the nature of the state and the best kind of government for most states. The selection from the *Nicomachean Ethics* presents his analysis of the concept of justice.

Politics

BOOK I THE STATE

Chapter 1

Every state is a community of some kind, and every community is established with a view to some good; for mankind always act in order to obtain that which they think good. But, if all communities aim at some good, the state or political community, which is the highest of all, and which embraces all the rest, aims, and in a greater degree than any other, at the highest good.

Now there is an erroneous opinion that a statesman, king, householder, and master are the same, and that they differ, not in kind, but only in the number of their subjects. For example, the ruler over a few is called a master; over more, the manager of a household; over a still larger number, a statesman or king, as if there were no difference between a great household and a small state. The distinction which is made between the king and the statesman is as follows: When the government is personal, the ruler is a king; when, according to the principles of the political science, the citizens rule and are ruled in turn, then he is called a statesman.

But all this is a mistake; for governments differ in kind, as will be evident to any one who considers the matter according to the method which has hitherto guided us. As in other departments of science, so in politics, the compound should always be resolved into the simple elements or least parts of the whole. We must therefore look at the elements of which the state is composed, in order that we may see in what they differ from one another, and whether any scientific distinction can be drawn between the different kinds of rule.

Chapter 2

He who thus considers things in their first growth and origin, whether a state or anything else, will obtain the clearest view of them. In the first place (1) there must be a union of those who cannot exist without each other; for example, of male and female, that the race may continue; and this is a union which is formed, not of deliberate purpose, but because, in common with other animals and with plants, mankind have a natural desire to leave behind them an image of themselves. And (2) there must be a union of natural ruler and subject, that both may be preserved. For he who can foresee with his mind is by nature intended to be lord and master, and he who can work with his body is a subject, and by nature a slave; hence master and slave have the same interest. Nature, however, has distinguished between the female and the slave. For she is not niggardly, like the smith who fashions the Delphian knife for many uses; she makes each thing for a single use, and every instrument is best made when intended for one and not for many uses. But among barbarians no distinction is made between women

From B. Jowett, *The Politics of Aristotle*, Clarendon Press, Oxford, 1885. Some footnotes deleted.

and slaves, because there is no natural ruler among them: they are a community of slaves, male and female. Wherefore the poets say—

It is meet that Hellenes should rule over barbarians;[1]

as if they thought that the barbarian and the slave were by nature one.

Out of these two relationships between man and woman, master and slave, the family first arises, and Hesiod is right when he says,—

First house and wife and an ox for the plough,[2]

for the ox is the poor man's slave. The family is the association established by nature for the supply of men's every day wants, and the members of it are called by Charondas 'companions of the cupboard' [ὁμοσιπύους] and by Epimenides the Cretan, 'companions of the manger' [ὁμκύπους]. But when several families are united, and the association aims at something more than the supply of daily needs, then comes into existence the village. And the most natural form of the village appears to be that of a colony from the family, composed of the children and grandchildren, who are said to be 'suckled with the same milk.' And this is the reason why Hellenic states were originally governed by kings; because the Hellenes were under royal rule before they came together, as the barbarians still are. Every family is ruled by the eldest, and therefore in the colonies of the family the kingly form of government prevailed because they were of the same blood. As Homer says [of the Cyclopes] :—

Each one gives law to his children and to his wives.[3]

For they lived dispersedly, as was the manner in ancient times. Wherefore men say that the gods have a king, because they themselves either are or were in ancient times under the rule of a king. For they imagine, not only the forms of the Gods, but their ways of life to be like their own.

When several villages are united in a single community, perfect and large enough to be nearly or quite self-sufficing, the state comes into existence, originating in the bare needs of life, and continuing in existence for the sake of a good life. And therefore, if the earlier forms of society are natural, so is the state, for it is the end of them, and the [completed] nature is the end. For what each thing is when fully developed, we call its nature, whether we are speaking of a man, a horse, or a family. Besides, the final cause and end of a thing is the best, and to be self-sufficing is the end and the best.

Hence it is evident that the state is a creation of nature, and that man is by nature a political animal. And he who by nature and not by mere accident is without a state, is either above humanity, or below it; he is the

Tribeless, lawless, hearthless one,

whom Homer[4] denounces—the outcast who is a lover of war; he may be compared to a bird which flies alone.

Now the reason why man is more of a political animal than bees or any other gregarious animals is evident. Nature, as we often say, makes nothing in vain, and man is the only animal whom she has endowed with the gift of speech. And whereas mere sound is but an indication of pleasure or pain, and is therefore

[1] Euripides, *Iphigenia in Aulis* 1400.
[2] *Works and Days* 405.
[3] *Odyssey* ix. 114.
[4] *Iliad* ix. 63.

found in other animals (for their nature attains to the perception of pleasure and pain and the intimation of them to one another, and no further), the power of speech is intended to set forth the expedient and inexpedient, and likewise the just and the unjust. And it is a characteristic of man that he alone has any sense of good and evil, of just and unjust, and the association of living beings who have this sense makes a family and a state.

Thus the state is by nature clearly prior to the family and to the individual, since the whole is of necessity prior to the part; for example, if the whole body be destroyed, there will be no foot or hand, except in an equivocal sense, as we might speak of a stone hand; for when destroyed the hand will be no better. But things are defined by their working and power; and we ought not to say that they are the same when they are no longer the same, but only that they have the same name. The proof that the state is a creation of nature and prior to the individual is that the individual, when isolated, is not self-sufficing; and therefore he is like a part in relation to the whole. But he who is unable to live in society, or who has no need because he is sufficient for himself, must be either a beast or a god: he is no part of a state. A social instinct is implanted in all men by nature, and yet he who first founded the state was the greatest of benefactors. For man, when perfected, is the best of animals, but, when separated from law and justice, he is the worst of all; since armed injustice is the more dangerous, and he is equipped at birth with the arms of intelligence and with moral qualities which he may use for the worst ends. Wherefore, if he have not virtue, he is the most unholy and the most savage of animals, and the most full of lust and gluttony. But justice is the bond of men in states, and the administration of justice, which is the determination of what is just, is the principle of order in political society.

BOOK III CONSTITUTIONS AND AUTHORITY

Chapter 6

... A constitution is the arrangement of magistracies in a state, especially of the highest of all. The government is everywhere sovereign in the state, and the constitution is in fact the government. For example, in democracies the people are supreme, but in oligarchies, the few; and, therefore, we say that these two forms of government are different: and so in other cases.

First, let us consider what is the purpose of a state, and how many forms of government there are by which human society is regulated. We have already said, in the former part of this treatise, when drawing a distinction between household-management and the rule of a master, that man is by nature a political animal. And therefore, men, even when they do not require one another's help, desire to live together all the same, and are in fact brought together by their common interests in proportion as they severally attain to any measure of well-being. This is certainly the chief end, both of individuals and of states. And also for the sake of mere life (in which there is possibly some noble element) mankind meet together and maintain the political community, so long as the evils of existence do not greatly overbalance the good. And we all see that men cling to life even in the midst of misfortune, seeming to find in it a natural sweetness and happiness.

There is no difficulty in distinguishing the various kinds of authority; they have been often defined already in popular works. The rule of a master, although the slave by nature and the master by nature have in reality the same interests, is nevertheless exercised primarily with a view to the interest of the master, but accidentally considers the slave, since, if the slave perish, the rule of the master perishes with him. On the other hand, the government of a wife and children and of a household, which we have called household-management, is exercised in the first instance for the good of the governed or for the common good of both parties, but essentially for the good of the governed, as we see to be the case in medicine, gymnastic, and the arts in general, which are only accidentally concerned with the good of the artists themselves. (for there is no reason why the trainer may not sometimes practise gymnastics, and the pilot is always one of the crew.) The trainer or the pilot considers the good of those committed to his care. But when he is one of the persons taken care of, he accidentally participates in the advantage, for the pilot is also a sailor, and the trainer becomes one of those in training. And so in politics: when the state is framed upon the principle of equality and likeness, the citizens think that they ought to hold office by turns. In the order of nature every one would take his turn of service; and then again, somebody else would look after his interest, just as he, while in office, had looked after theirs. [That was originally the way.] But nowadays, for the sake of the advantage which is to be gained from the public revenues and from office, men want to be always in office. One might imagine that the rulers, being sickly, were only kept in health while they continued in office; in that case we may be sure that they would be hunting after places. The conclusion is evident: that governments, which have regard to the common interest, are constituted in accordance with strict principles of justice and are therefore true forms; but those which regard only the interest of the rulers are all defective and perverted forms, for they are despotic, whereas a state is a community of freemen.

BOOK IV   THE BEST CONSTITUTION

Chapter 11

We have now to enquire what is the best constitution for most states, and the best life for most men, neither assuming a standard of virtue which is above ordinary persons, nor an education which is exceptionally favoured by nature and circumstances, nor yet an ideal state which is an aspiration only, but having regard to the life in which the majority are able to share, and to the form of government which states in general can attain. As to those aristocracies, as they are called, of which we were just now speaking, they either lie beyond the possibilities of the greater number of states, or they approximate to the so-called constitutional government, and therefore need no separate discussion. And in fact the conclusion at which we arrive respecting all these forms rests upon the same grounds. For if it has been truly said in the Ethics[1] that the happy life is the life according to unimpeded virtue, and that virtue is a mean, then the life

---

[1] *Nicomachean Ethics* **vii. 13. 2.**

which is in a mean, and in a mean attainable by every one, must be the best. And the same principles of virtue and vice are characteristic of cities and of constitutions; for the constitution is in a figure the life of the city.

Now in all states there are three elements; one class is very rich, another very poor, and a third in a mean. It is admitted that moderation and the mean are best, and therefore it will clearly be best to possess the gifts of fortune in moderation; for in that condition of life men are most ready to listen to reason. But he who greatly excels in beauty, strength, birth or wealth, or on the other hand who is very poor, or very weak, or very much disgraced, finds it difficult to follow reason. Of these two the one sort grow into violent and great criminals, the others into rogues and petty rascals. And two sorts of offences correspond to them, the one committed from violence, the other from roguery. The petty rogues are disinclined to hold office, whether military or civil, and their aversion to these two duties is as great an injury to the state as their tendency to crime. Again, those who have too much of the goods of fortune, strength, wealth, friends, and the like, are neither willing nor able to submit to authority. The evil begins at home: for when they are boys, by reason of the luxury in which they are brought up, they never learn, even at school, the habit of obedience. On the other hand, the very poor, who are in the opposite extreme, are too degraded. So that the one class cannot obey, and can only rule despotically; the other knows not how to command and must be ruled like slaves. Thus arises a city, not of freemen, but of masters and slaves, the one despising, the other envying; and nothing can be more fatal to friendship and good fellowship in states than this: for good fellowship tends to friendship; when men are at enmity with one another, they would rather not even share the same path. But a city ought to be composed, as far as possible, of equals and similars; and these are generally the middle classes. Wherefore the city which is composed of middle-class citizens is necessarily best governed; they are, as we say, the natural elements of a state. And this is the class of citizens which is most secure in a state, for they do not, like the poor, covet their neighbours' goods; nor do others covet theirs, as the poor covet the goods of the rich; and as they neither plot against others, nor are themselves plotted against, they pass through life safely. Wisely then did Phocylides pray—

> Many things are best in the mean; I desire to be of a middle condition in my city.

Thus it is manifest that the best political community is formed by citizens of the middle class, and that those states are likely to be well-administered, in which the middle class is large, and larger if possible than both the other classes, or at any rate than either singly; for the addition of the middle class turns the scale, and prevents either of the extremes from being dominant. Great then is the good fortune of a state in which the citizens have a moderate and sufficient property; for where some possess much, and the others nothing, there may arise an extreme democracy, or a pure oligarchy; or a tyranny may grow out of either extreme,—either out of the most rampant democracy, or out of an oligarchy; but it is not so likely to arise out of a middle and nearly equal condition. I will explain the reason of this hereafter, when I speak of the revolutions of states. The mean condition of states is clearly best, for no other is free from faction;

and where the middle class is large, there are least likely to be factions and dissensions. For a similar reason large states are less liable to faction than small ones, because in them the middle class is large; whereas in small states it is easy to divide all the citizens into two classes who are either rich or poor, and to leave nothing in the middle. And democracies are safer and more permanent than oligarchies, because they have a middle class which is more numerous and has a greater share in the government; for when there is no middle class, and the poor greatly exceed in number, troubles arise, and the state soon comes to an end. A proof of the superiority of the middle class is that the best legislators have been of a middle condition; for example, Solon, as his own verses testify; and Lycurgus, for he was not a king; and Charondas, and almost all legislators.

These considerations will help us to understand why most governments are either democratical or oligarchical. The reason is that the middle class is seldom numerous in them, and whichever party, whether the rich or the common people, transgresses the mean and predominates, draws the government to itself, and thus arises either oligarchy or democracy. There is another reason—the poor and the rich quarrel with one another, and whichever side gets the better, instead of establishing a just or popular government, regards political supremacy as the prize of victory, and the one party sets up a democracy and the other an oligarchy. Both the parties which had the supremacy in Hellas looked only to the interest of their own form of government, and established in states, the one, democracies, and the other, oligarchies; they thought of their own advantage, of the public not at all. For these reasons the middle form of government has rarely, if ever, existed, and among a very few only. One man alone of all who ever ruled in Hellas was induced to give this middle constitution to states. But it has now become a habit among the citizens of states, not even to care about equality; all men are seeking for dominion, or, if conquered, are willing to submit.

What then is the best form of government, and what makes it the best is evident; and of other states, since we say that there are many kinds of democracy and many of oligarchy, it is not difficult to see which has the first and which the second or any other place in the order of excellence, now that we have determined which is the best. For that which is nearest to the best must of necessity be better, and that which is furthest from it worse, if we are judging absolutely and not relatively to given conditions: I say 'relatively to given conditions,' since a particular government may be preferable for some, but another form may be better for others.

Chapter 12

We have now to consider what and what kind of government is suitable to what and what kind of men. I may begin by assuming, as a general principle common to all governments, that the portion of the state which desires permanence ought to be stronger than that which desires the reverse. Now every city is composed of quality and quantity. By quality I mean freedom, wealth, education, good birth, and by quantity, superiority of numbers. Quality may exist in one of the classes which make up the state, and quantity in the other. For example, the meanly-born may be more in number than the well-born, or the poor than the rich, yet they may not so much exceed in quantity as they fall short in quality; and therefore there must be a comparison of quantity and quality. Where the number of the poor is more than proportioned to the wealth of the rich, there will naturally be a democracy, varying in form with the sort of people who composed it in each case. If, for example, the husbandmen exceed in number, the first form of democracy will then arise; if the artisans and labouring class, the last; and so with the intermediate forms. But where the rich and the notables exceed in quality more than they fall short in quantity, there oligarchy arises, similarly assuming various forms according to the kind of superiority possessed by the oligarchs.

The legislator should always include the middle class in his government; if he makes his laws oligarchical, to the middle class let him look; if he makes them democratical, he should equally by his laws try to attach this class to the state. There only can the government ever be stable where the middle class exceeds one or both of the others, and in that case there will be no fear that the rich will unite with the poor against the rulers. For neither of them will ever be willing to serve the other, and if they look for some form of government more suitable to both, they will find none better than this, for the rich and the poor will never consent to rule in turn, because they mistrust one another. The arbiter is always the one trusted, and he who is in the middle is an arbiter. The more perfect the admixture of the political elements, the more lasting will be the state. Many even of those who desire to form aristocratical governments make a mistake, not only in giving too much power to the rich, but in attempting to overreach the people. There comes a time when out of a false good there arises a true evil, since the encroachments of the rich are more destructive to the state than those of the people.

Nicomachean Ethics

BOOK V   JUSTICE

Chapter 1

With regard to justice and injustice we must consider (1) what kind of actions they are concerned with, (2) what sort of mean justice is, and (3) between what extremes the just act is intermediate. Our investigation shall follow the same course as the preceding discussions.

We see that all men mean by justice that kind of state of character which makes people disposed to do what is just and makes them act justly and wish for what is just; and similarly by injustice that state which makes them act unjustly

By permission. From W. D. Ross, *Aristotle: Ethica Nicomachea*, Clarendon Press, Oxford, 1915. Some footnotes deleted and wish for what is unjust. Let us too, then, lay this down as a general basis. For the same is not true of the sciences and the faculties as of states of character. A faculty or a science which is one and the same is held to relate to contrary objects, but a state of character which is one of two contraries does *not* produce the contrary results; e.g. as a result of health we do not do what is the opposite of healthy, but only what is healthy; for we say a man walks healthily, when he walks as a healthy man would.

Now often one contrary state is recognized from its contrary, and often states are recognized from the subjects that exhibit them; for (A) if good condition is known, bad condition also becomes known, and (B) good condition is known from the things that are in good condition, and they from it. If good condition is firmness of flesh, it is necessary both that bad condition should be flabbiness of flesh and that the wholesome should be that which causes firmness in flesh. And it follows for the most part that if one contrary is ambiguous the other also will be ambiguous; e.g. if 'just' is so, that 'unjust' will be so too.

Now 'justice' and 'injustice' seem to be ambiguous, but because their different meanings approach near to one another the ambiguity escapes notice and is not obvious as it is, comparatively, when the meanings are far apart, e.g. (for here the difference in outward form is great) as the ambiguity in the use of κλείς for the collar-bone of an animal and for that with which we lock a door. Let us take as a starting-point, then, the various meanings of 'an unjust man'. Both the lawless man and the grasping and unfair man are thought to be unjust, so that evidently both the law-abiding and the fair man will be just. The just, then, is the lawful and the fair, the unjust the unlawful and the unfair.

Since the unjust man is grasping, he must be concerned with goods—not all goods, but those with which prosperity and adversity have to do, which taken absolutely are always good, but for a particular person are not always good. Now men pray for and pursue these things; but they should not, but should pray that the things that are good absolutely may also be good for them, and should choose the things that *are* good for them. The unjust man does not always choose the greater, but also the less—in the case of things bad absolutely; but because the lesser evil is itself thought to be in a sense good, and graspingness is directed at the good, therefore he is thought to be grasping. And he is unfair; for this contains and is common to both.

Since the lawless man was seen to be unjust and the law-abiding man just, evidently all lawful acts are in a sense just acts; for the acts laid down by the legislative art are lawful, and each of these, we say, is just. Now the laws in their enactments on all subjects aim at the common advantage either of all or of the best or of those who hold power, or something of the sort; so that in one sense we call those acts just that tend to produce and preserve happiness and its components for the political society. And the law bids us do both the acts of a brave man (e.g. not to desert our post nor take to flight nor throw away our arms), and those of a temperate man (e.g. not to commit adultery nor to gratify one's lust), and those of a good-tempered man (e.g. not to strike another nor to speak evil), and similarly with regard to the other virtues and forms of wickedness, commanding some acts and forbidding others; and the rightly-framed law does this rightly, and the hastily conceived one less well.

This form of justice, then, is complete virtue, but not absolutely, but in relation to our neighbour. And therefore justice is often thought to be the greatest of virtues, and 'neither evening nor morning star'[1] is so wonderful; and proverbially 'in justice is every virtue comprehended'.[2] And it is complete virtue in its fullest sense, because it is the actual exercise of complete virtue. It is complete because he who possesses it can exercise his virtue not only in himself but towards his neighbour also; for many men can exercise virtue in their own affairs, but not in their relations to their neighbour. This is why the saying of Bias is thought to be true, that 'rule will show the man'; for a ruler is necessarily in relation to other men and a member of a society. For this same reason justice, alone of the virtues, is thought to be 'another's good',[3] because it is related to our neighbour; for it does what is advantageous to another, either a ruler or a copartner. Now the worst man is he who exercises his wickedness both towards himself and towards another; for this is a difficult task. Justice in this sense, then, is not part of virtue but virtue entire, nor is the contrary injustice a part of vice but vice entire. What the difference is between virtue and justice in this sense is plain from what we have said; they are the same but their essence is not the same; what, as a relation to one's neighbour, is justice is, as a certain kind of state without qualification, virtue.

Chapter 2

But at all events what we are investigating is the justice which is a *part* of virtue; for there is a justice of this kind, as we maintain. Similarly it is with injustice in the particular sense that we are concerned.

That there is such a thing is indicated by the fact that while the man who exhibits in action the other forms of wickedness acts wrongly indeed, but not graspingly (e.g. the man who throws away his shield through cowardice or speaks harshly through bad temper or fails to help a friend with money through meanness), when a man acts graspingly he often exhibits none of these vices—no, nor all together, but certainly wickedness of some kind (for we blame him) and injustice. There is, then, another kind of injustice which is a part of injustice in the wide sense, and a use of the word 'unjust' which answers to a part of what is unjust in the wide sense of 'contrary to the law'. Again, if one man commits adultery for the sake of gain and makes money by it, while another does so at the bidding of appetite though he loses money and is penalized for it, the latter would be held to be self-indulgent rather than grasping, but the former is unjust, but not self-indulgent; evidently, therefore, he is unjust by reason of his making gain by his act. Again, all other unjust acts are ascribed invariably to some particular kind of wickedness, e.g. adultery to self-indulgence, the desertion of a comrade in battle to cowardice, physical violence to anger; but if a man makes gain, his action is ascribed to no form of wickedness but injustice. Evidently, therefore, there is apart from injustice in the wide sense another, 'particular', injustice which shares the name and nature of the first, because its definition falls within the same genus; for the significance of both consists in a relation to one's neighbour, but the one is concerned with honour or money or safety—or that which includes all these, if we had a single name for it—and its motive is

[1] Euripides, from *Melanippe*.
[2] Theognis 147.
[3] Plato, *Republic* 343c.

the pleasure that arises from gain; while the other is concerned with all the objects with which the good man is concerned.

It is clear, then, that there is more than one kind of justice, and that there is one which is distinct from virtue entire; we must try to grasp its genus and differentia.

The unjust has been divided into the unlawful and the unfair, and the just into the lawful and the fair. To the unlawful answers the afore-mentioned sense of injustice. But since the unfair and the unlawful are not the same, but are different as a part is from its whole (for all that is unfair is unlawful, but not all that is unlawful is unfair), the unjust and injustice in the sense of the unfair are not the same as but different from the former kind, as part from whole; for injustice in this sense is a part of injustice in the wide sense, and similarly justice in the one sense of justice in the other. Therefore we must speak also about particular justice and particular injustice, and similarly about the just and the unjust. The justice, then, which answers to the whole of virtue, and the corresponding injustice, one being the exercise of virtue as a whole, and the other that of vice as a whole, towards one's neighbour, we may leave on one side. And how the meanings of 'just' and 'unjust' which answer to these are to be distinguished is evident; for practically the majority of the acts commanded by the law are those which are prescribed from the point of view of virtue taken as a whole; for the law bids us practice every virtue and forbids us to practise any vice. And the things that tend to produce virtue taken as a whole are those of the acts prescribed by the law which have been prescribed with a view to education for the common good. But with regard to the education of the individual as such, which makes him without qualification a good *man*, we must determine later whether this is the function of the political art or of another; for perhaps it is not the same to be a good man and a good citizen of any state taken at random.

Of particular justice and that which is just in the corresponding sense, (A) one kind is that which is manifested in distributions of honour or money or the other things that fall to be divided among those who have a share in the constitution (for in these it is possible for one man to have a share either unequal or equal to that of another), and (B) one is that which plays a rectifying part in transactions between man and man. Of this there are two divisions; of transactions (1) some are voluntary and (2) others involuntary—voluntary such transactions as sale, purchase, loan for consumption, pledging, loan for use, depositing, letting (they are called voluntary because the origin of these transactions is voluntary), while of the involuntary (a) some are clandestine, such as theft, adultery, poisoning, procuring, enticement of slaves, assassination, false witness, and (b) others are violent, such as assault, imprisonment, murder, robbery with violence, mutilation, abuse, insult.

Chapter 3

(A) We have shown that both the unjust man and the unjust act are unfair or unequal; now it is clear that there is also an intermediate between the two unequals involved in either case. And this is the equal; for in any kind of action in which there is a more and a less there is also what is equal. If then, the unjust is unequal, the just is equal, as all men suppose it to be, even apart from argument. And since the equal is intermediate, the just will be an intermediate. Now equality implies at least two things. The just, then, must be both intermediate and equal and relative (i.e. for certain persons). And *qua* intermediate it must be between certain things (which are respectively greater and less); *qua* equal, it involves *two* things; *qua* just, it is for certain people. The just, therefore, involves at least four terms; for the persons for whom it is in fact just are two, and the things in which it is manifested, the objects distributed, are two. And the same equality will exist between the persons and between the things concerned; for as the latter—the things concerned—are related, so are the former; if they are not equal, they will not have what is equal, but this is the origin of quarrels and complaints—when either equals have and are awarded unequal shares, or unequals equal shares. Further, this is plain from the fact that awards should be 'according to merit'; for all men agree that what is just in distribution must be according to merit in some sense, though they do not all specify the same sort of merit, but democrats identify it with the status of freeman, supporters of oligarchy with wealth (or with noble birth), and supporters of aristocracy with excellence.

The just, then, is a species of the proportionate (proportion being not a property only of the kind of number which consists of abstract units, but of number in general). For proportion is equality of ratios, and involves four terms at least (that discrete proportion involves four terms is plain, but so does continuous proportion, for it uses one term as two and mentions it twice; e.g. 'as the line A is to the line B, so is the line B to the line C'; the line B, then, has been mentioned twice, so that if the line B be assumed twice, the proportional terms will be four); and the just, too, involves at least four terms, and the ratio between one pair is the same as that between the other pair; for there is a similar distinction between the persons and between the things. As the term A, then, is to B, so will C be to D, and therefore, *alternando*, as A is to C, B will be to D. Therefore also the whole is in the same ratio to the whole;[1] and this coupling the distribution effects, and, if the terms are so combined, effects justly. The conjunction, then, of the term A with C and of B with D is what is just in distribution,[2] and this species of the just is intermediate, and the unjust is what violates the proportion; for the proportional is intermediate, and the just is proportional. (Mathematicians call this kind of proportion geometrical; for it is in geometrical proportion that it follows that the whole is to the whole as either part is to the corresponding part.) This proportion is not continuous; for we cannot get a single term standing for a person and a thing.

This, then, is what the just is—the proportional; the unjust is what violates the proportion. Hence one term becomes too great, the other too small, as indeed happens in practice; for the man who acts unjustly has too much, and the man who is unjustly treated too little, of what is good. In the case of evil the reverse is true; for the lesser evil is reckoned a good in comparison with the greater evil,

---

[1] Person A + thing C to person B + thing D.

[2] The problem of distributive justice is to divide the distributable honour or reward into parts which are to one another as are the merits of the persons who are to participate. If A (first person) : B (second person) :: C (first portion) : D (second portion).
then (*alternando*) A : C :: B : D,
and therefore (*componendo*) A + C : B + D :: A : B.
In other words the position established answers to the relative merits of the parties.

since the lesser evil is rather to be chosen than the greater, and what is worthy of choice is good, and what is worthier of choice a greater good.

This, then, is one species of the just.

Chapter 4

(B) The remaining one is the rectificatory, which arises in connexion with transactions both voluntary and involuntary. This form of the just has a different specific character from the former. For the justice which distributes common possessions is always in accordance with the kind of proportion mentioned above (for in the case also in which the distribution is made from the common funds of a partnership it will be according to the same ratio which the funds put into the business by the partners bear to one another); and the injustice opposed to this kind of justice is that which violates the proportion. But the justice in transactions between man and man is a sort of equality; not according to that kind of proportion, however, but according to arithmetical proportion.[1] For it makes no difference whether a good man has defrauded a bad man or a bad man a good one, nor whether it is a good or a bad man that has committed adultery; the law looks only to the distinctive character of the injury, and treats the parties as equal, if one is in the wrong and the other is being wronged, and if one inflicted injury and the other has received it. Therefore, this kind of injustice being an inequality, the judge tries to equalize it; for in the case also in which one has received and the other has inflicted a wound, or one has slain and the other been slain, the suffering and the action have been unequally distributed; but the judge tries to equalize things by means of the penalty, taking away from the gain of the assailant. For the term 'gain' is applied generally to such cases, even if it be not a term appropriate to certain cases, e.g. to the person who inflicts a wound—and 'loss' to the sufferer; at all events when the suffering has been estimated, the one is called loss and the other gain. Therefore the equal is intermediate between the greater and the less, but the gain and the loss are respectively greater and less in contrary ways; more of the good and less of the evil are gain, and the contrary is loss; intermediate between them is, as we saw, the equal, which we say is just; therefore corrective justice will be the intermediate between loss and gain. This is why, when people dispute, they take refuge in the judge; and to go to the judge is to go to justice; for the nature of the judge is to be a sort of animate justice; and they seek the judge as an intermediate, and in some states they call judges mediators, on the assumption that if they get what is intermediate they will get what is just. The just, then, is an intermediate, since the judge is so. Now the judge restores equality; it is as though there were a line divided into unequal parts, and he took

[1] The problem of 'rectificatory justice' has nothing to do with punishment proper but is only that of rectifying a wrong that has been done, by awarding damages; i.e. rectificatory justice is that of the civil, not that of the criminal courts. The parties are treated by the court as equal (since a law court is not a court of morals), and the wrongful act is reckoned as having brought equal gain to the wrongdoer and loss to his victim; it brings A to the position $A + C$, and B to the position $B - C$. The judge's task is to find the arithmetical mean between these, and this he does by transferring C from A to B. Thus (A being treated as = B) we get the arithmetical 'proportion'

$$(A + C) - (A + C - C) = (A + C - C) - (B - C)$$
$$(A + C) - (B - C + C) = (B - C + C) - (B - C).$$

away that by which the greater segment exceeds the half, and added it to the smaller segment. And when the whole has been equally divided, then they say they have 'their own'—i.e. when they have got what is equal. The equal is intermediate between the greater and the lesser line according to arithmetical proportion. It is for this reason also that it is called just ($\delta\acute{\iota}\kappa\nu\iota\upsilon\upsilon$), because it is a division into two equal parts ($\delta\acute{\iota}\chi\nu$), just as if one were to call in ($\delta\acute{\iota}\chi\nu\iota\upsilon\upsilon$) and the judge ($\delta\iota\kappa\nu\sigma\tau\acute{\eta}\varsigma$) is one who bisects ($\delta\iota\chi\nu\sigma\tau\acute{\eta}\varsigma$). For when something is subtracted from one of two equals and added to the other, the other is in excess by these two; since if what was taken from the one has not been added to the other, the latter would have been in excess by one only. It therefore exceeds the intermediate by one, and the intermediate exceeds by one that from which something was taken. By this, then, we shall recognize both what we must subtract from that which has more, and what we must add to that which has less; we must add to the latter that by which the intermediate exceeds it, and subtract from the greatest that by which it exceeds the intermediate. . . .

Chapter 5

. . . We have now defined the unjust and the just. These having been marked off from each other, it is plain that just action is intermediate between acting unjustly and being unjustly treated; for the one is to have too much and the other to have too little. Justice is a kind of mean, but not in the same way as the other virtues, but because it relates to an intermediate amount, while injustice relates to the extremes. And justice is that in virtues, but because it relates to an intermediate amount, while injustice relates to the extremes. And justice is that in virtue of which the just man is said to be a doer, by choice, of that which is just, and one who will distribute either between himself and other or between two others not so as to give more of what is desirable to himself and less to his neighbour (and conversely with what is harmful), but so as to give what is equal in accordance with proportion; and similarly in distributing between two other persons. Injustice on the other hand is similarly related to the unjust, which is excess and defect, contrary to proportion, of the useful or hurtful. For which reason injustice is excess and defect, viz. because it is productive of excess and defect—in one's own case excess of what is in its own nature useful and defect of what is hurtful, while in the case of others it is as a whole like what it is in one's own case, but proportion may be violated in either direction. In the unjust act to have too little is to be unjustly treated; to have too much is to act unjustly.

Let this be taken as our account of the nature of justice and injustice, and similarly of the just and the unjust in general.

Chapter 6

. . . Now we have previously stated how the reciprocal is related to the just; but we must not forget that what we are looking for is not only what is just without qualification but also political justice. This is found among men who share their life with a view to self-sufficiency, men who are free and either proportionately or arithmetically equal, so that between those who do not fulfil this condition there is no political justice but justice in a special sense and by analogy. For justice exists only between men whose mutual relations are governed by law; and law exists for men between whom there is injustice; for legal justice is the discrimination of the just and the unjust. And between men between whom there is injustice there is also unjust action (though there is not injustice between all between whom there is unjust action), and this is assigning too much to oneself of things good in themselves and too little of things evil in themselves. This is why we do not allow a *man* to rule, but *rational principle*, because a man behaves thus in his own interests and becomes a tyrant. The magistrate on the other hand is the guardian of justice, and, if of justice, then of equality also. And since he is assumed to have no more than his share, if he is just (for he does not assign to himself more of what is good in itself, unless such a share is proportional to his merits—so that it is for others that he labours, and it is for this reason that men, as we stated previously, say that justice is 'another's good'), therefore a reward must be given him, and this is honour and privilege; but those for whom such things are not enough become tyrants.

The justice of a master and that of a father are not the same as the justice of citizens, though they are like it; for there can be no injustice in the unqualified sense towards things that are one's own, but a man's chattel,[1] and his child until it reaches a certain age and sets up for itself, are as it were part of himself, and no one chooses to hurt himself (for which reason there can be no injustice towards oneself). Therefore the justice or injustice of citizens is not manifested in these relations; for it was as we saw according to law, and between people naturally subject to law, and these as we saw are people who have an equal share in ruling and being ruled. Hence justice can more truly be manifested towards a wife than towards children and chattels, for the former is household justice; but even this is different from political justice.

Chapter 7

Of political justice part is natural, part legal—natural, that which everywhere has the same force and does not exist by people's thinking this or that; legal, that which is originally indifferent, but when it has been laid down is not indifferent, e.g. that a prisoner's ransom shall be a mina, or that a goat and not two sheep shall be sacrificed, and again all the laws that are passed for particular cases, e.g., that sacrifice shall be made in honour of Brasidas,[2] and the provisions of decrees. Now some think that all justice is of this sort, because that which is by nature is unchangeable and has everywhere the same force (as fire burns both here and in Persia), while they see change in the things recognized as just. This however, is not true in this unqualified way, but is true in a sense; or rather, with the gods it is perhaps not true at all, while with us there is something that is just even by nature, yet all of it is changeable; but still some is by nature, some not by nature. It is evident which sort of thing, among things capable of being otherwise, is by nature; and which is not but is legal and conventional, assuming that both are equally changeable. And in all other things the same distinction will apply; by nature the right hand is stronger, yet it is possible that all men should come to be ambidextrous. The things which are just by virtue of convention and expediency are like measures; for wine and corn measures are not everywhere equal, but larger in wholesale and smaller in retail markets.

[1] I.e. his slave.
[2] Thucydides V. II.

Similarly, the thing which are just not by nature but by human enactment are not everywhere the same, since constitutions also are not the same, though there is but one which is everywhere by nature the best.

Of things just and lawful each is related as the universal to its particulars; for the things that are done are many, but of *them* each is one, since it is universal.

There is a difference between the act of injustice and what is unjust, and between the act of justice and what is just; for a thing is unjust by nature or by enactment; and this very thing, when it has been done, is an act of injustice, but before it is done is not yet that but is unjust. So, too, with an act of justice (though the general term is rather 'just action', and 'act of justice' is applied to the correction of the act of injustice). . . .

Chapter 10

Our next subject is equity and the equitable (τὸ ἐπιεικές), and their respective relations to justice and the just. For on examination they appear to be neither absolutely the same nor generically different; and while we sometimes praise what is equitable and the equitable man (so that we apply the name by way of praise even to instances of the other virtues, instead of 'good', meaning by ἐπιεικέστερον that a thing is better, at other times, when we reason it out, it seems strange if the equitable, being something different from the just, is yet praiseworthy; for either the just or the equitable is not good, if they are different; or, if both are good, they are the same.

These, then, are pretty much the considerations that give rise to the problem about the equitable; they are all in a sense correct and not opposed to one another; for the equitable, though it is better than one kind of justice, yet is just, and it is not as being a different class of thing that it is better than the just. The same thing, then, is just and equitable, and while both are good the equitable is superior. What creates the problem is that the equitable is just, but not the legally just but a correction of legal justice. The reason is that all law is universal but about some things it is not possible to make a universal statement which shall be correct. In those cases, then, in which it is necessary to speak universally, but not possible to do so correctly, the law takes the usual case, though it is not ignorant of the possibility of error. And it is none the less correct; for the error is not in the law nor in the legislator but in the nature of the thing, since the matter of practical affairs is of this kind from the start. When the law speaks universally, then, and a case arises on it which is not covered by the universal statement, then it is right, where the legislator fails us and has erred by over-simplicity, to correct the omission—to say what the legislator himself would have said had he been present, and would have put into his law if he had known. Hence the equitable is just, and better than one kind of justice—not better than absolute justice but better than the error that arises from the absoluteness of the statement. And this is the nature of the equitable, a correction of law where it is defective owing to its universality. In fact this is the reason why all things are not determined by law, viz. that about some things it is impossible to lay down a law, so that a decree is needed. For when the thing is indefinite the rule also is indefinite, like the leaden rule used in making the Lesbian moulding; the rule adapts itself to the shape of the stone and is not rigid, and so too the decree is adapted to the facts.

It is plain, then, what the equitable is, and that it is just and is better than one kind of justice. It is evident also from this who the equitable man is; the man who chooses and does such acts, and is no stickler for his rights in a bad sense but tends to take less than his share though he has the law on his side, is equitable, and this state of character is equity, which is a sort of justice and not a different state of character.

St. Thomas Aquinas

St. Thomas Aquinas (1224–1274) was born the son of a count, near Aquino, Italy. He became a member of the Dominican order and spent his life in writing and teaching theology and philosophy. His philosophy was declared to be the official teaching of the Roman Catholic Church by Pope Leo XIII in 1879.

St. Thomas attempted to carry out a complete synthesis of Aristotelian philosophy and Christian theology. The selection printed here is from the unfinished *Summa Theologica*. In this selection St. Thomas presents his theory of Natural Law, which explains how just human law derives its authority from Divine Law. In effect he also tells us how in his view human law can be just.

Summa Theologica

TREATISE ON LAW

Question 90 Of the Essence of Law

We have now to consider the extrinsic principles of acts. Now the extrinsic principle inclining to evil is the devil, of whose temptations we have spoken in the First Part (Q. 114). But the extrinsic principle moving to good is God, Who

By permission. From St. Thomas Aquinas, *Summa Theologica*, trans. by Fathers of the English Dominican Province, Benziger Bros., New York, and Burns, Oates, and Washbourne, Ltd., London, 1947. Deletions are not noted in the text.

both instructs us by means of His Law, and assists us by His Grace: wherefore in the first place we must speak of law; in the second place, of grace.

Concerning law, we must consider—(1) Law itself in general; (2) its parts. Concerning law in general three points offer themselves for our consideration: (1) Its essence; (2) The different kinds of law; (3) The effects of law.

Under the first head there are four points of inquiry: (1) Whether law is something pertaining to reason? (2) Concerning the end of law; (3) Its cause; (4) The promulgation of law.

First Article *Whether law is something pertaining to reason?*

We proceed thus to the First Article:—

Objection 1. It would seem that law is not something pertaining to reason. For the Apostle says (Rom. vii. 23): *I see another law in my members*, etc. But nothing pertaining to reason is in the members; since the reason does not make use of a bodily organ. Therefore law is not something pertaining to reason.

On the contrary, It belongs to the law to command and to forbid. But it belongs to reason to command, as stated above (Q. 17, A. 1). Therefore law is something pertaining to reason.

I answer that, Law is a rule and measure of acts, whereby man is induced to act or is restrained from acting: for *lex* (law) is derived from *ligare* (to bind), because it binds one to act. Now the rule and measure of human acts is the reason, which is the first principle of human acts, as is evident from what has been stated above (Q. 1, A. 1 *ad* 3); since it belongs to the reason to direct to the end, which is the first principle in all matters of action, according to the Philosopher (*Phys.* ii). Now that which is the principle in any genus, is the rule and measure of that genus: for instance, unity in the genus of numbers, and the first movement in the genus of movements. Consequently it follows that law is something pertaining to reason.

Reply Obj. 1. Since law is a kind of rule and measure, it may be in something in two ways. First, as in that which measures and rules: and since this is proper to reason, it follows that, in this way, law is in the reason alone.—Secondly, as in that which is measured and ruled. In this way, law is in all those things that are inclined to something by reason of some law: so that any inclination arising from a law, may be called a law, not essentially but by participation as it were. And thus the inclination of the members to concupiscence is called *the law of the members*.

Second Article *Whether the law is always something directed to the common good?*

We proceed thus to the Second Article:—

Objection 1. It would seem that the law is not always directed to the common good as to its end. For it belongs to law to command and to forbid. But commands are directed to certain individual goods. Therefore the end of the law is not always the common good.

On the contrary, Isidore says (*Etym.* v. 21) that *laws are enacted for no private profit, but for the common benefit of the citizens.*

I answer that, As stated above (A. 1), the law belongs to that which is a principle of human acts, because it is their rule and measure. Now as reason is a principle of human acts, so in reason itself there is something which is the principle in respect of all the rest: wherefore to this principle chiefly and mainly law must needs be referred.—Now the first principle in practical matters, which are the object of the practical reason, is the last end: and the last end of human life is bliss or happiness, as stated above (Q. 2, A. 7; Q. 3, A. 1). Consequently the law must needs regard principally the relationship to happiness. Moreover, since every part is ordained to the whole, as imperfect to perfect; and since one man is a part of the perfect community, the law must needs regard properly the relationship to universal happiness. Wherefore the Philosopher, in the above definition of legal matters mentions both happiness and the body politic: for he says (*Ethic.* v. 1) that we call those legal matters *just, which are adapted to produce and preserve happiness and its parts for the body politic:* since the state is a perfect community, as he says in *Polit.* i. 1.

Now in every genus, that which belongs to it chiefly is the principle of the others, and the others belong to that genus in subordination to that thing: thus fire, which is chief among hot things, is the cause of heat in mixed bodies, and these are said to be hot in so far as they have a share of fire. Consequently, since the law is chiefly ordained to the common good, any other precept in regard to some individual work, must needs be devoid of the nature of a law, save in so far as it regards the common good. Therefore every law is ordained to the common good.

Reply Obj. 1. A command denotes an application of a law to matters regulated by the law. Now the order to the common good, at which the law aims, is applicable to particular ends. And in this way commands are given even concerning particular matters.

Third Article   *Whether the reason of any man is competent to make laws?*

We proceed thus to the Third Article:—

Objection 1. It would seem that the reason of any man is competent to make laws. For the Apostle says (Rom. ii. 14) that *when the Gentiles, who have not the law, do by nature those things that are of the law, ... they are a law to themselves.* Now he says this of all in general. Therefore anyone can make a law for himself.

On the contrary, Isidore says (*Etym.* v. 10): *A law is an ordinance of the people, whereby something is sanctioned by the Elders together with the Commonalty.*

I answer that, A law, properly speaking, regards first and foremost the order to the common good. Now to order anything to the common good, belongs either to the whole people, or to someone who is the viceregent of the whole people. And therefore the making of a law belongs either to the whole people or to a public personage who has care of the whole people: since in all other matters the directing of anything to the end concerns him to whom the end belongs.

Reply Obj. 1. As stated above (A. 1 *ad* 1), a law is in a person not only as in one that rules, but also by participation as in one that is ruled. In the latter way each one is a law to himself, in so far as he shares the direction that he receives from one who rules him. Hence the same text goes on: *Who show the work of the law written in their hearts.*

Fourth Article *Whether promulgation is essential to a law?*

We proceed thus to the Fourth Article:—

Objection 1. It would seem that promulgation is not essential to a law. For the natural law above all has the character of law. But the natural law needs no promulgation. Therefore it is not essential to a law that it be promulgated.

On the contrary, It is laid down in the *Decretals*, dist. 4, that *laws are established when they are promulgated.*

I answer that, As stated above (A. 1), a law is imposed on others by way of rule and measure. Now a rule or measure is imposed by being applied to those who are to be ruled and measured by it. Wherefore, in order that a law obtain the binding force which is proper to a law, it must needs be applied to the men who have to be ruled by it. Such application is made by its being notified to them by promulgation. wherefore promulgation is necessary for the law to obtain its force.

Thus from the four preceding articles, the definition of law may be gathered; and it is nothing else than an ordinance of reason for the common good, made by him who has care of the community, and promulgated.

Reply Obj. 1. The natural law is promulgated by the very fact that God instilled it into man's mind so as to be known by him naturally.

Question 91 Of the Various Kinds of Law

We must now consider the various kinds of law: under which head there are six points of inquiry: (1) Whether there is an eternal law? (2) Whether there is a natural law? (3) Whether there is a human law? (4) Whether there is a Divine law? (5) Whether there is one Divine law, or several? (6) Whether there is a law of sin?

First Article *Whether there is an eternal law?*

We proceed thus to the First Article:—

Objection 1. It would seem that there is no eternal law. Because every law is imposed on someone. But there was not someone from eternity on whom a law could be imposed: since God alone was from eternity. Therefore no law is eternal.

On the contrary, Augustine says (*De Lib. Arb.* i. 6): *That Law which is the Supreme Reason cannot be understood to be otherwise than unchangeable and eternal.*

I answer that, As stated above (Q. 90, A. 1 *ad* 2; AA. 3, 4), a law is nothing else but a dictate of practical reason emanating from the ruler who governs a perfect community. Now it is evident, granted that the world is ruled by Divine Providence, as was stated in the First Part (Q. 22, AA. 1, 2), that the whole community of the universe is governed by Divine Reason. Wherefore the very Idea of the government of things in God the Ruler of the universe, has the nature of a law. And since the Divine Reason's conception of things is not subject to time but is eternal, according to Prov. viii. 23, therefore it is that this kind of law must be called eternal.

Reply Obj. 1. Those things that are not in themselves, exist with God, inasmuch as they are foreknown and preordained by Him, according to Rom. iv. 17: *Who calls those things that are not, as those that are.* Accordingly the eternal concept of the Divine law bears the character of an eternal law, in so far as it is ordained by God to the government of things foreknown by him.

Second Article *Whether there is in us a natural law?*

We proceed thus to the Second Article:—

Objection 1. It would seem that there is no natural law in us. Because man is governed sufficiently by the eternal law: for Augustine says (*De Lib. Arb.* i) that *the eternal law is that by which it is right that all things should be most orderly.* But nature does not abound in superfluities as neither does she fail in necessaries. Therefore no law is natural to man.

On the contrary, A gloss on Rom. ii. 14: *When the Gentiles, who have not the law, do by nature those things that are of the law,* comments as follows: *Although they have no written law, yet they have the natural law, whereby each one knows, and is conscious of, what is good and what is evil.*

I answer that, As stated above (Q. 90, A. 1 *ad* 1), law, being a rule and measure, can be in a person in two ways: in one way, as in him that rules and measures; in another way, as in that which is ruled and measured, since a thing is ruled and measured, in so far as it partakes of the rule or measure. Wherefore, since all things subject to Divine providence are ruled and measured by the eternal law, as was stated above (A. 1); it is evident that all things partake somewhat of the eternal law, in so far as, namely, from its being imprinted on them, they derive their respective inclinations to their proper acts and ends. Now among all others, the rational creature is subject to Divine providence in the most excellent way, in so far as it partakes of a share of providence, by being provident both for itself and for others. Wherefore it has a share of the Eternal Reason, whereby it has a natural inclination to its proper act and end: and this participation of the eternal law in the rational creature is called the natural law. Hence the Psalmist after saying (Ps. iv. 6): *Offer up the sacrifice of justice,* as though someone asked what the works of justice are, adds: *Many say, Who showeth us good things?* in answer to which question he says: *The light of Thy countenance, O Lord, is signed upon us:* thus implying that the light of natural reason, whereby we discern what is good and what is evil, which is the function of the natural law, is nothing else than an imprint on us of the Divine light. It is therefore evident that the natural law is nothing else than the rational creature's participation of the eternal law.

Reply Obj. 1. This argument would hold, if the natural law were something different from the eternal law: whereas it is nothing but a participation thereof, as stated above.

Third Article *Whether there is a human law?*

We proceed thus to the Third Article:—

Objection 1. It would seem that there is not a human law. For the natural law is a participation of the eternal law, as stated above (A. 2). Now through the eternal law *all things are most orderly,* as Augustine states (*De Lib. Arb.* i. 6). Therefore the natural law suffices for the ordering of all human affairs. Consequently there is no need for a human law.

On the contrary, Augustine (*De Lib. Arb.* i. 6) distinguishes two kinds of law, the one eternal, the other temporal, which he calls human.

I answer that, As stated above (Q. 90, A. 1, *ad* 2), a law is a dictate of the practical reason. Now it is to be observed that the same procedure takes place in the practical and in the speculative reason: for each proceeds from principles to conclusions, as stated above (*ibid.*). Accordingly we conclude that just as, in the speculative reason, from naturally known indemonstrable principles, we draw the conclusions of the various sciences, the knowledge of which is not imparted to us by nature, but acquired by the efforts of reason, so too it is from the precepts of the natural law, as from general and indemonstrable principles, that the human reason needs to proceed to the more particular determination of certain matters. These particular determinations, devised by human reason, are called human laws, provided the other essential conditions of law be observed, as stated above (Q. 90, AA. 2, 3, 4). Wherefore Tully says in his *Rhetoric* (*De Invent. Rhet.* ii) that *justice has its source in nature; thence certain things came into custom by reason of their utility; afterwards these things which emanated from nature and were approved by custom, were sanctioned by fear and reverence for the law.*

Reply Obj. 1. The human reason cannot have a full participation of the dictate of the Divine Reason, but according to its own mode, and imperfectly. Consequently, as on the part of the speculative reason, by a natural participation of Divine Wisdom, there is in us the knowledge of certain general principles, but not proper knowledge of each single truth, such as that contained in the Divine Wisdom; so too, on the part of the practical reason, man has a natural participation of the eternal law, according to certain general principles, but not as regards the particular determinations of individual cases, which are, however, contained in the eternal law. Hence the need for human reason to proceed further to sanction them by law.

Fourth Article   *Whether there was any need for a divine law?*

We proceed thus to the Fourth Article:—

Objection 1. It would seem that there was no need for a Divine law. Because, as stated above (A. 2), the natural law is a participation in us of the eternal law. But the eternal law is a divine law, as stated above (A. 1). Therefore there is no need for a Divine law in addition to the natural law, and human laws derived therefrom.

On the contrary, David prayed God to set His law before him, saying (Ps. cxviii. 33): *Set before me for a law the way of Thy justifications, O Lord.*

I answer that, Besides the natural and the human law it was necessary for the directing of human conduct to have a Divine law. And this for four reasons. First, because it is by law that man is directed how to perform his proper acts in view of his last end. And indeed if man were ordained to no other end than that which is proportionate to his natural faculty, there would be no need for man to have any further direction on the part of his reason, besides the natural law and human law which is derived from it. But since man is ordained to an end of eternal happiness which is inproportionate to man's natural faculty, as stated above (Q. 5, A. 5), therefore it was necessary that, besides the natural and the human law, man should be directed to his end by a law given by God.

Secondly, because, on account of the uncertainty of human judgment, especially on contingent and particular matters, different people form different judgments on human acts; whence also different and contrary laws result. In order, therefore, that man may know without any doubt what he ought to do and what he ought to avoid, it was necessary for man to be directed in his proper acts by a law given by God, for it is certain that such a law cannot err.

Thirdly, because man can make laws in those matters of which he is competent to judge. but man is not competent to judge of interior movements, that are hidden, but only of exterior acts which appear: and yet for the perfection of virtue it is necessary for man to conduct himself aright in both kinds of acts. Consequently human law could not sufficiently curb and direct interior acts; and it was necessary for this purpose that a Divine law should supervene.

Fourthly, because, as Augustine says (*De Lib. Arb.* i. 5, 6), human law cannot punish or forbid all evil deeds: since while aiming at doing away with all evils, it would do away with many good things, and would hinder the advance of the common good, which is necessary for human intercourse. In order, therefore, that no evil might remain unforbidden and unpunished, it was necessary for the Divine law to supervene, whereby all sins are forbidden.

And these four causes are touched upon in Ps. cxviii. 8, where it is said: *The law of the Lord is unspotted, i.e.,* allowing no foulness of sin; *converting souls,* because it directs not only exterior, but also interior acts; *the testimony of the Lord is faithful,* because of the certainty of what is true and right; *giving wisdom to little ones,* by directing man to an end supernatural and divine.

Reply Obj. 1. By the natural law the eternal law is participated proportionately to the capacity of human nature. But to his supernatural end man needs to be directed in a yet higher way. Hence the additional law given by God, whereby man shares more perfectly in the eternal law.

Question 93   Of the Eternal Law

First Article   *Whether the eternal law is a sovereign type[1] existing in God?*

We proceed thus to the First Article:—

Objection 1. It would seem that the eternal law is not a sovereign type existing in God. For there is only one eternal law. But there are many types of things in the Divine mind; for Augustine says (*Qq.* lxxxiii, qu. 46) that God *made each thing according to its type.* Therefore the eternal law does not seem to be a type existing in the Divine mind.

On the contrary, Augustine says (*De Lib. Arb.* i. 6) that *the eternal law is the sovereign type, to which we must always conform.*

I answer that, Just as in every artificer there pre-exists a type of the things that are made by his art, so too in every governor there must pre-exist the type of the order of those things that are to be done by those who are subject to his government. And just as the type of the things yet to be made by an art is called the art or exemplar of the products of that art, so too the type in him who governs the acts of his subjects, bears the character of a law, provided the other conditions be present which we have mentioned above (Q. 90). Now God, by His wisdom, is the Creator of all things in relation to which He stands as the artificer to the products of his art, as stated in the First Part (Q. 14, A. 8). Moreover He governs all the acts and movements that are to be found in each single creature, as was also stated in the First Part (Q. 103, A. 5). Wherefore as the type of the Divine Wisdom, inasmuch as by It all things are created, has the character of art,

[1] *Ratio.*

exemplar or idea; so the type of Divine Wisdom, as moving all things to their due end, bears the character of law. Accordingly the eternal law is nothing else than the type of Divine Wisdom, as directing all actions and movements.

Reply Obj. 1. Augustine is speaking in that passage of the ideal types which regard the proper nature of each single thing; and consequently in them there is a certain distinction and plurality, according to their different relations to things, as stated in the First Part (Q. 15, A. 2). But law is said to direct human acts by ordaining them to the common good as stated above (Q. 90, A. 2). And things, which are in themselves different, may be considered as one, according as they are ordained to one common thing. Wherefore the eternal law is one since it is the type of this order.

Second Article *Whether the eternal law is known to all?*

We proceed thus to the Second Article:—

Objection 1. It would seem that the eternal law is not known to all. Because, as the Apostle says (1 Cor. ii. 11), *the things that are of God no man knoweth, but the Spirit of God.* But the eternal law is a type existing in the Divine mind. Therefore it is unknown to all save God alone.

On the contrary, Augustine says (*De Lib. Arb.* i. 6) that *knowledge of the eternal law is imprinted on us.*

I answer that, A thing may be known in two ways: first, in itself; secondly, in its effect, wherein some likeness of that thing is found: thus someone not seeing the sun in its substance, may know it by its rays. So then no one can know the eternal law, as it is in itself, except the blessed who see God in His Essence. But every rational creature knows it in its reflection, greater or less. For every knowledge of truth is a kind of reflection and participation of the eternal law, which is the unchangeable truth, as Augustine says (*De Vera Relig.* xxxi). Now all men know the truth to a certain extent, at least as to the common principles of the natural law: and as to the others, they partake of the knowledge of truth, some more, some less; and in this respect are more or less cognizant of the eternal law.

Reply Obj. 1. We cannot know the things that are of God, as they are in themselves but they are made known to us in their effects according to Rom. i. 20: *The invisible things of God . . . are clearly seen, being understood by the things that are made.*

Third Article *Whether every law is derived from the eternal law?*

We proceed thus to the Third Article:—

Objection 1. It would seem that not every law is derived from the eternal law. For there is a law of the "fomes," as stated above (Q. 91, A. 6), which is not derived from that Divine law which is the eternal law, since thereunto pertains the *prudence of the flesh,* of which the Apostle says (Rom. viii. 7), that *it cannot be subject to the law of God.* Therefore not every law is derived from the eternal law.

Obj. 2. Further, nothing unjust can be derived from the eternal law, because, as stated above (A. 2, *Obj.* 2), *the eternal law is that, according to which it is right that all things should be most orderly.* But some laws are unjust, according to Isa. x. 1: *Woe to them that make wicked laws.* Therefore not every law is derived from the eternal law.

On the contrary, Divine Wisdom says (Prov. viii. 15): *By Me kings reign, and lawgivers decree just things.* But the type of Divine Wisdom is the eternal law, as stated above (A. 1). Therefore all laws proceed from the eternal law.

I answer that, As stated above (Q. 90, AA. 1, 2), the law denotes a kind of plan directing acts towards an end. Now wherever there are movers ordained to one another, the power of the second mover must needs be derived from the power of the first mover; since the second mover does not move except in so far as it is moved by the first. Wherefore we observe the same in all those who govern, so that the plan of government is derived by secondary governors from the governor in chief; thus the plan of what is to be done in a state flows from the king's command to his inferior administrators: and again in things of art the plan of whatever is to be done by art flows from the chief craftsman to the under-craftsmen, who work with their hands. Since then the eternal law is the plan of government in the Chief Governor, all the plans of government in the inferior governors must be derived from the eternal law. But these plans of inferior governors are all other laws besides the eternal law. Therefore all laws, in so far as they partake of right reason, are derived from the eternal law. Hence Augustine says (*De Lib. Arb.* I. 6) that *in temporal law there is nothing just and lawful, but what man has drawn from the eternal law.*

Reply Obj. 1. The "fomes" has the nature of law in man, in so far as it is a punishment resulting from Divine justice; and in this respect it is evident that it is derived from the eternal law. But in so far as it denotes a proneness to sin, it is contrary to the Divine law, and has not the nature of law, as stated above (Q. 91, A. 6).

Reply Obj. 2. Human law has the nature of law in so far as it partakes of right reason; and it is clear that, in this respect, it is derived from the eternal law. But in so far as it deviates from reason, it is called an unjust law, and has the nature, not of law but of violence. Nevertheless even an unjust law, in so far as it retains some appearance of law, though being framed by one who is in power, is derived from the eternal law; since all power is from the Lord God, according to Rom. xiii. 1.

Question 94   Of the Natural Law

Second Article   *Whether the natural law contains several precepts, or one only?*

We proceed thus to the Second Article:—

Objection 1. It would seem that the natural law contains, not several precepts, but one only. For law is a kind of precept, as stated above (Q. 92, A. 2). If therefore there were many precepts of the natural law, it would follow that there are also many natural laws.

Obj. 2. Further, the natural law is consequent to human nature. But human nature, as a whole, is one; though, as to its parts, it is manifold. Therefore, either there is but one precept of the law of nature, on account of the unity of nature as a whole; or there are many, by reason of the number of parts of human nature. The result would be that even things relating to the inclination of the concupiscible faculty belong to the natural law.

On the contrary, The precepts of the natural law in man stand in relation to practical matters, as the first principles to matters of demonstration. But there are several first indemonstrable principles. Therefore there are also several precepts of the natural law.

I answer that, As stated above (Q. 91, A. 3), the precepts of the natural law are to the practical reason, what the first principles of demonstrations are to the speculative reason; because both are self-evident principles. Now a thing is said to be self-evident in two ways: first, in itself; secondly, in relation to us. Any proposition is said to be self-evident in itself, if its predicate is contained in the notion of the subject: although, to one who knows not the definition of the subject, it happens that such a proposition is not self-evident. For instance, this proposition, *Man is a rational being,* is, in its very nature, self-evident, since who says *man,* says *a rational being:* and yet to one who knows not what a man is, this proposition is not self-evident. Hence it is that, as Boethius says (*De Hebdom.*), certain axioms or propositions are universally self-evident to all; and such are those propositions whose terms are known to all, as *Every whole is greater than its part,* and *Things equal to one and the same are equal to one another.* But some propositions are self-evident only to the wise, who understand the meaning of the terms of such propositions: thus to one who understands that an angel is not a body, it is self-evident that an angel is not circumscriptively in a place: but this is not evident to the unlearned, for they cannot grasp it.

Now a certain order is to be found in those things that are apprehended universally. For that which, before aught else, falls under apprehension, is *being,* the notion of which is included in all things whatsoever a man apprehends. Wherefore the first indemonstrable principle is that *the same thing cannot be affirmed and denied at the same time,* which is based on the notion of *being* and *not-being:* and on this principle all others are based, as is stated in *Metaph.* iv, text. 9. Now as *being* is the first thing that falls under the apprehension simply, so *good* is the first thing that falls under the apprehension of the practical reason, which is directed to action: since every agent acts for an end under the aspect of good. Consequently the first principle in the practical reason is one founded on the notion of good, viz., that *good is that which all things seek after.* Hence this is the first precept of law, that *good is to be done and pursued, and evil is to be avoided.* All other precepts of the natural law are based upon this: so that whatever the practical reason naturally apprehends as man's good (or evil) belongs to the precepts of the natural law as something to be done or avoided.

Since, however, good has the nature of an end, and evil, the nature of a contrary, hence it is that all those things to which man has a natural inclination, are naturally apprehended by reason as being good, and consequently as objects of pursuit, and their contraries as evil, and objects of avoidance. Wherefore according to the order of natural inclinations, is the order of the precepts of the natural law. Because in man there is first of all an inclination to good in accordance with the nature which he has in common with all substances: inasmuch as every substance seeks the preservation of its own being, according to its nature: and by reason of this inclination, whatever is a means of preserving human life, and of warding off its obstacles, belongs to the natural law. Secondly, there is in man an inclination to things that pertain to him more specially, according to that nature which he has in common with other animals: and in virtue of this inclination, those things are said to belong to the natural law, *which nature has taught to all animals,*[1] such as sexual intercourse, education of offspring and so forth. Thirdly, there is in man an inclination to good, according to the nature of his reason, which nature is proper to him: thus man has a natural inclination to know the truth about God, and to live in society: and in this respect, whatever pertains to this inclination belongs to the natural law; for instance, to shun ignorance, to avoid offending those among whom one has to live, and other such things regarding the above inclination.

Reply Obj. 1. All these precepts of the law of nature have the character of one natural law, inasmuch as they flow from one first precept.

Reply Obj. 2. All the inclinations of any parts whatsoever of human nature, *e.g.*, of the concupiscible and irascible parts, in so far as they are ruled by reason, belong to the natural law, and are reduced to one first precept, as stated above: so that the precepts of the natural law are many in themselves, but are based on one common foundation.

Third Article   *Whether all acts of virtue are prescribed by the natural law?*

We proceed thus to the Third Article:—

Objection 1. It would seem that not all acts of virtue are prescribed by the natural law. Because, as stated above (Q. 90, A. 2) it is essential to a law that it be ordained to the common good. But some acts of virtue are ordained to the private good of the individual, as is evident especially in regards to acts of temperance. Therefore not all acts of virtue are the subject of natural law.

On the contrary, Damascene says (*De Fide Orthod.* iii. 4) that *virtues are natural.* Therefore virtuous acts also are a subject of the natural law.

I answer that, We may speak of virtuous acts in two ways: first, under the aspect of virtuous; secondly, as such and such acts considered in their proper species. If then we speak of acts of virtue, considered as virtuous, thus all virtuous acts belong to the natural law. For it has been stated (A. 2) that to the natural law belongs everything to which a man is inclined according to his nature. Now each thing is inclined naturally to an operation that is suitable to it according to its form: thus fire is inclined to give heat. Wherefore, since the rational soul is the proper form of man, there is in every man a natural inclination to act according to reason: and this is to act according to virtue. Consequently, considered thus, all acts of virtue are prescribed by the natural law: since each one's reason naturally dictates to him to act virtuously. But if we speak of virtuous acts, considered in themselves, i.e., in their proper species, thus not all virtuous acts are prescribed by the natural law: for many things are done virtuously, to which nature does not incline at first; but which, through the inquiry of reason, have been found by men to be conducive to well-living.

Reply Obj. 1. Temperance is about the natural concupiscences of food, drink and sexual matters, which are indeed ordained to the natural common good, just as other matters of law are ordained to the moral common good.

Fourth Article   *Whether the natural law is the same in all men?*

We proceed thus to the Fourth Article:—

Objection 1. It would seem that the natural law is not the same in all. For it is stated in the Decretals (*Dist.* i) that *the natural law is that which is contained in*

[1] *Pandect. Just.* I., tit. i.

the Law and the Gospel. but this is not common to all men; because, as it is written (Rom. x. 16), *all do not obey the gospel.* Therefore the natural law is not the same in all men.

On the contrary, Isidore says (*Etym.* v. 4): *The natural law is common to all nations.*

I answer that, As stated above (AA. 2, 3), to the natural law belongs those things to which a man is inclined naturally: and among these it is proper to man to be inclined to act according to reason. Now the process of reason is from the common to the proper, as stated in *Phys.* i. The speculative reason, however, is differently situated in this matter, from the practical reason. For, since the speculative reason is busied chiefly with necessary things, which cannot be otherwise than they are, its proper conclusions, like the universal principles, contain the truth without fail. The practical reason, on the other hand, is busied with contingent matters, about which human actions are concerned: and consequently, although there is necessity in the general principles, the more we descend to matters of detail, the more frequently we encounter defects. Accordingly then in speculative matters truth is the same in all men, both as to principles and as to conclusions: although the truth is not known to all as regards the conclusions, but only as regards the principles which are called common notions. But in matters of action, truth or practical rectitude is not the same for all, as to matters of detail, but only as to the general principles: and where there is the same rectitude in matters of detail, it is not equally known to all.

It is therefore evident that, as regards the general principles whether of speculative or of practical reason, truth or rectitude is the same for all, and is equally known by all. As to the proper conclusions of the speculative reason, the truth is the same for all, but is not equally known to all: thus it is true for all that the three angles of a triangle are together equal to two right angles, although it is not known to all. But as to the proper conclusions of the practical reason, neither is the truth or rectitude the same for all, nor, where it is the same, is it equally known by all. Thus it is right and true for all to act according to reason: and from this principle it follows as a proper conclusion, that goods entrusted to another should be restored to their owner. Now this is true for the majority of cases: but it may happen in a particular case that it would be injurious, and therefore unreasonable, to restore goods held in trust; for instance if they are claimed for the purpose of fighting against one's country. And this principle will be found to fail the more, according as we descend further into detail, *e.g.*, if one were to say that goods held in trust should be restored with such and such a guarantee, or in such and such a way; because the greater the number of conditions added, the greater the number of ways in which the principle may fail, so that it be not right to restore or not to restore.

Consequently we must say that the natural law, as to general principles, is the same for all, both as to rectitude and as to knowledge. But as to certain matters of detail, which are conclusions, as it were, of those general principles, it is the same for all in the majority of cases, both as to rectitude and as to knowledge; and yet in some few cases it may fail, both as to rectitude, by reason of certain obstacles (just as natures subject to generation and corruption fail in some few cases on account of some obstacle), and as to knowledge, since in some the reason is perverted by passion, or evil habit, or an evil disposition of nature; thus formerly, theft, although it is expressly contrary to the natural law, was not considered wrong among the Germans, as Julius Caesar relates (*De Bello Gall.* vi).

Reply Obj. 1. The meaning of the sentence quoted is not that whatever is contained in the Law and the Gospel belongs to the natural law, since they contain many things that are above nature; but that whatever belongs to the natural law is fully contained in them. Wherefore Gratian, after saying that *the natural law is what is contained in the Law and the Gospel*, adds at once, by way of example, by *which everyone is commanded to do to others as he would be done by.*

Fifth Article   *Whether the natural law can be changed?*

We proceed thus to the Fifth Article:—

Objection 1. It would seem that the natural law can be changed. Because on Ecclus. xvii. 9, *He gave them instructions, and the law of life*, the gloss says: *He wished the law of the letter to be written, in order to correct the law of nature.* But that which is corrected is changed. Therefore the natural law can be changed.

On the contrary, It is said in the Decretals (*Dist.* v): *The natural law dates from the creation of the rational creature. It does not vary according to time, but remains unchangeable.*

I answer that, A change in the natural law may be understood in two ways. First, by way of addition. In this sense nothing hinders the natural law from being changed: since many things for the benefit of human life have been added over and above the natural law, both by the Divine law and by human laws.

Secondly, a change in the natural law may be understood by way of subtraction, so that what previously was according to the natural law, ceases to be so. In this sense, the natural law is altogether unchangeable in its first principles: but in its secondary principles, which, as we have said (A. 4), are certain detailed proximate conclusions drawn from the first principles, the natural law is not changed so that what it prescribes be not right in most cases. But it may be changed in some particular cases of rare occurrence, through some special causes hindering the observance of such precepts, as stated above (A. 4).

Reply Obj. 1. The written law is said to be given for the correction of the natural law, either because it supplies what was wanting to the natural law; or because the natural law was perverted in the hearts of some men, as to certain matters, so that they esteemed those things good which are naturally evil; which perversion stood in need of correction.

Sixth Article   *Whether the law of nature can be abolished from from the heart of man?*

We proceed thus to the Sixth Article:—

Objection 1. It would seem that the natural law can be abolished from the heart of man. Because on Rom. ii. 14, *When the Gentiles who have not the law,* etc., a gloss says that *the law of righteousness, which sin had blotted out, is graven on the heart of man when he is restored by grace.* But the law of righteousness is the law of nature. Therefore the law of nature can be blotted out.

On the contrary, Augustine says (*Conf.* ii): *Thy law is written in the hearts of men, which iniquity itself effaces not.* But the law which is written in men's hearts is the natural law. Therefore the natural law cannot be blotted out.

I answer that, As stated above (AA. 4, 5), there belong to the natural law, first, certain most general precepts, that are known to all; and secondly, certain secondary and more detailed precepts, which are, as it were conclusions following closely from first principles. As to those general principles, the natural law, in the abstract, can nowise be blotted out from men's hearts. But it is blotted out in the case of a particular action, in so far as reason is hindered from applying the general principle to a particular point of practice, on account of concupiscence or some other passion, as stated above (Q. 77, A. 2)—But as to the other, *i.e.*, the secondary precepts, the natural law can be blotted out from the human heart, either by evil persuasions, just as in speculative matters errors occur in respect of necessary conclusions; or by vicious customs and corrupt habits, as among some men, theft, and even unnatural vices, as the Apostle states (Rom. i), were not esteemed sinful.

Reply Obj. 1. Sin blots out the law of nature in particular cases, not universally, except perchance in regard to the secondary precepts of the natural law, in the way stated above.

Question 95   Of Human Law

First Article   *Whether it was useful for laws to be framed by men?*

We proceed thus to the First Article:—

Objection 1. It would seem that it was not useful for laws to be framed by men. Because the purpose of every law is that man be made good thereby, as stated above (Q. 92, A. 1). But men are more to be induced to be good willingly by means of admonitions, than against their will, by means of laws. Therefore there was no need to frame laws.

On the contrary, Isidore says (*Etym.* v. 20): *Laws were made that in fear thereof human audacity might be held in check, that innocence might be safeguarded in the midst of wickedness, and that the dread of punishment might prevent the wicked from doing harm.* But these things are most necessary to mankind. Therefore it was necessary that human laws should be made.

I answer that, As stated above (Q. 63, A. 1; Q. 94, A. 3), man has a natural aptitude for virtue; but the perfection of virtue must be acquired by man by means of some kind of training. Thus we observe that man is helped by industry in his necessities, for instance, in food and clothing. Certain beginnings of these he has from nature, viz., his reason and his hands; but he has not the full complement, as other animals have, to whom nature has given sufficiency of clothing and food. Now it is difficult to see how man could suffice for himself in the matter of this training: since the perfection of virtue consists chiefly in withdrawing man from undue pleasures, to which above all man is inclined, and especially the young, who are more capable of being trained. Consequently a man needs to receive this training from another, whereby to arrive at the perfection of virtue. And as to those young people who are inclined to acts of virtue, by their good natural disposition, or by custom, or rather by the gift of God, paternal training suffices, which is by admonitions. But since some are found to be depraved, and prone to vice, and not easily amenable to words, it was necessary for such to be restrained from evil by force and fear, in order that, at least, they might desist from evil-doing, and leave others in peace, and that they themselves, by being habituated in this way, might be brought to do willingly what hitherto they did from fear, and thus become virtuous. Now this kind of training, which compels through fear of punishment, is the discipline of laws. Therefore, in order that man might have peace and virtue, it was necessary for laws to be framed: for, as the Philosopher says (*Polit.* i. 2), *as man is the most noble of animals if he be perfect in virtue, so is he the lowest of all, if he be severed from law and righteousness;* because man can use his reason to devise means of satisfying his lusts and evil passions, which other animals are unable to do.

Reply Obj. 1. Men who are well disposed are led willingly to virtue by being admonished better than by coercion: but men who are evilly disposed are not led to virtue unless they are compelled.

Second Article *Whether every human law is derived from the natural law?*

We proceed thus to the Second Article:—

Objection 1. It would seem that not every human law is derived from the natural law. For the Philosopher says (*Ethic.* v. 7) that *the legal just is that which originally was a matter of indifference.* But those things which arise from the natural law are not matters of indifference. Therefore the enactments of human laws are not all derived from the natural law.

On the contrary, Tully says (*Rhetor.* ii): *Things which emanated from nature and were approved by custom, were sanctioned by fear and reverence for the laws.*

I answer that, As Augustine says (*De Lib. Arb.* i. 5), *that which is not just seems to be no law at all:* wherefore the force of a law depends on the extent of its justice. Now in human affairs a thing is said to be just, from being right, according to the rule of reason. But the first rule of reason is the law of nature, as is clear from what has been stated above (Q. 92, A. 2 *ad* 2). Consequently every human law has just so much of the nature of law, as it is derived from the law of nature. But if in any point it deflects from the law of nature, it is no longer a law but a perversion of law.

But it must be noted that something may be derived from the natural law in two ways: first, as a conclusion from premises, secondly, by way of determination of certain generalities. The first way is like to that by which, in sciences, demonstrated conclusions are drawn from the principles: while the second mode is likened to that whereby, in the arts, general forms are particularized as to details: thus the craftsman needs to determine the general form of a house to some particular shape. Some things are therefore derived from the general principles of the natural law, by way of conclusions; *e.g.*, that *one must not kill* may be derived as a conclusion from the principle that *one should do harm to no man:* while some are derived therefrom by way of determination; *e.g.*, the law of nature has it that the evil-doer should be punished; but that he be punished in this or that way, is a determination of the law of nature.

Accordingly both modes of derivation are found in the human law. But those things which are derived in the first way, are contained in human law not as emanating therefrom exclusively, but have some force from the natural law also. But those things which are derived in the second way, have no other force than that of human law.

Reply Obj. 1. The Philosopher is speaking of those enactments which are by way of determination or specification of the precepts of the natural law.

Question 96   Of the Power of Human Law

Fourth Article   *Whether human law binds a man in conscience?*

We proceed thus to the Fourth Article:—

Objection 1. It would seem that human law does not bind a man in conscience. For an inferior power has no jurisdiction in a court of higher power. But the power of man, which frames human law, is beneath the Divine power. Therefore human law cannot impose its precept in a Divine court, such as is the court of conscience.

On the contrary, It is written (1 Pet. ii. 19): *This is thankworthy, if for conscience . . . a man endure sorrows, suffering wrongfully.*

I answer that, Laws framed by man are either just or unjust. If they be just, they have the power of binding in conscience, from the eternal law whence they are derived, according to Prov. viii. 15: *By Me kings reign, and lawgivers decree just things.* Now laws are said to be just, both from the end, when, to wit, they are ordained to the common good,—and from their author, that is to say, when the law that is made does not exceed the power of the lawgiver,—and from their form, when, to wit, burdens are laid on the subjects, according to an equality of proportion and with a view to the common good. For, since one man is a part of the community, each man in all that he is and has, belongs to the community; just as a part, in all that it is, belongs to the whole; wherefore nature inflicts a loss on the part, in order to save the whole: so that on this account, such laws as these which impose proportionate burdens, are just and binding in conscience, and are legal laws.

On the other hand laws may be unjust in two ways: first, by being contrary to human good, through being opposed to the things mentioned above:—either in respect of the end, as when an authority imposes on his subjects burdensome laws, conducive, not to the common good, but rather to his own cupidity or vainglory;—or in respect of the author, as when a man makes a law that goes beyond the power committed to him;—or in respect of the form, as when burdens are imposed unequally on the community, although with a view to the common good. The like are acts of violence rather than laws; because, as Augustine says (*De Lib. Arb.* i. 5), *a law that is not just, seems to be no law at all.* Wherefore such laws do not bind in conscience, except perhaps in order to avoid scandal or disturbance, for which cause a man should even yield his right, according to Matth. v. 40, 41: *If a man . . . take away thy coat, let go thy cloak also unto him; and whosoever will force thee one mile, go with him other two.*

Secondly, laws may be unjust through being opposed to the Divine good: such are the laws of tyrants inducing to idolatry, or to anything else contrary to the Divine law: and laws of this kind must nowise be observed, because, as stated in Acts v. 29, *we ought to obey God rather than men.*

Reply Obj. 1. As the Apostle says (Rom. xiii, 1, 2), all human power is from God . . . *therefore he that resisteth the power,* in matters that are within its scope, *resisteth the ordinance of God:* so that he becomes guilty according to his conscience.

Fifth Article   *Whether all are subject to the law?*

We proceed thus to the Fifth Article:—

Objection 1. It would seem that not all are subject to the law. For those alone are subject to a law for whom a law is made. But the Apostle says (1 Tim. i. 9): *The law is not made for the just man.* Therefore the just are not subject to the law.

Obj. 3. Further, the jurist says[1] that *the sovereign is exempt from the laws.* But he that is exempt from the law is not bound thereby. Therefore not all are subject to the law.

On the contrary, The Apostle says (Rom. xiii. 1): *Let every soul be subject to the higher powers.* But subjection to a power seems to imply subjection to the laws framed by that power. Therefore all men should be subject to human law.

I answer that, As stated above (Q. 90, AA. 1, 2; A. 3 *ad* 2), the notion of law contains two things; first, that it is a rule of human acts; secondly, that it has coercive power. Wherefore a man may be subject to law in two ways. First, as the regulated is subject to the regulator: and, in this way, whoever is subject to a power, is subject to the law framed by that power. But it may happen in two ways that one is not subject to a power. In one way, by being altogether free from its authority: hence the subjects of one city or kingdom are not bound by the laws of the sovereign of another city or kingdom, since they are not subject to his authority. In another way, by being under a yet higher law; thus the subject of a proconsul should be ruled by his command, but not in those matters in which the subject receives his orders from the emperor: for in these matters, he is not bound by the mandate of the lower authority, since he is directed by that of a higher. In this way, one who is simply subject to a law, may not be subject thereto in certain matters, in respect of which he is ruled by a higher law.

Secondly, a man is said to be subject to a law as the coerced is subject to the coercer. In this way the virtuous and righteous are not subject to the law, but only the wicked. Because coercion and violence are contrary to the will: but the will of the good is in harmony with the law, whereas the will of the wicked is discordant from it. Wherefore in this sense the good are not subject to the law, but only the wicked.

Reply Obj. 1. This argument is true of subjection by way of coercion: for, in this way, *the law is not made for the just men:* because *they are a law to themselves,* since they *shew the work of the law written in their hearts,* as the Apostle says (Rom. ii. 14, 15). Consequently the law does not enforce itself upon them as it does on the wicked.

Reply Obj. 3. The sovereign is said to be *exempt from the law,* as to its coercive power; since, properly speaking, no man is coerced by himself, and law has no coercive power save from the authority of the sovereign. Thus then is the sovereign said to be exempt from the law, because none is competent to pass sentence on him, if he acts against the law. Wherefore on Ps. L. 6: *To Thee only have I sinned,* a gloss says that *there is no man who can judge the deeds of a king.*—But as to the directive force of law, the sovereign is subject to the law by his own will, according to the statement (*Extra, De Constit.* cap. *Cum omnes*) that *whatever law a man makes for another, he should keep himself. And a wise authority says: "Obey the law that thou makest thyself."* Moreover the Lord reproaches those who *say and do not;* and who *bind heavy burdens and lay them on men's shoulders, but with a finger of their own they will not move them* (Matth. xxiii. 3, 4). Hence, in the judgment of God, the sovereign is not exempt

---

[1] *Pandect. Justin.* **i. ff., tit. 3,** *De Leg. et Senat.*

from the law, as to its directive force; but he should fulfil it of his own free-will and not of constraint.—Again the sovereign is above the law, in so far as, when it is expedient, he can change the law, and dispense in it according to time and place.

Niccolo Machiavelli

In the work of Niccolo Machiavelli (1469–1527) it is difficult to find something which represents a political philosophy in the full sense. His work is more famous for its tone of political realism and its emphasis on the importance of power in politics than it is for a theoretical discussion of issues such as justice or the justification of a particular variety of government. Because this is true, the selection which follows is designed primarily to give an idea of the tone of political realism which Machiavelli represents. It is drawn from *The Prince*, a piece of writing particularly designed as a practical handbook to the techniques by which a ruler must procure and retain his power. The first paragraph emphasizes the importance of military power in this project.

The Prince

The Duties of a Prince with Regard to the Militia

A prince should therefore have no other aim or thought, nor take up any other thing for his study, but war and its organisation and discipline, for that is the only art that is necessary to one who commands, and it is of such virtue that it not only maintains those who are born princes, but often enables men of private fortune to attain to that rank. And one sees, on the other hand, that when princes think more of luxury than of arms, they lose their state. The chief cause of the loss of states, is the contempt of this art, and the way to acquire them is to be well versed in the same.

Of the Things for Which Men, and Especially Princes, Are Praised or Blamed

It now remains to be seen what are the methods and rules for a prince as regards his subjects and friends. And as I know that many have written of this, I fear that my writing about it may be deemed presumptuous, differing as I do, especially in this matter, from the opinions of others. But my intention being to write something of use to those who understand, it appears to me more proper to go to the real truth of the matter than to its imagination; and many have imagined republics and principalities which have never been seen or known to exist in reality; for how we live is so far removed from how we ought to live, that he who abandons what is done for what ought to be done, will rather learn to bring about his own ruin than his preservation. A man who wishes to make a profession of goodness in everything must necessarily come to grief among so many who are not good. Therefore it is necessary for a prince, who wishes to maintain himself, to learn how not to be good, and to use this knowledge and not use it, according to the necessity of the case.

Leaving on one side, then, those things which concern only an imaginary prince, and speaking of those that are real, I state that all men, and especially princes, who are placed at a greater height, are reputed for certain qualities which bring them either praise or blame. Thus one is considered liberal, another *misero* or miserly (using a Tuscan term, seeing that *avaro* with us still means one who is rapaciously acquisitive and *misero* one who makes grudging use of his own); one a free giver, another rapacious; one cruel, another merciful; one a breaker of his word, another trustworthy; one effeminate and pusillanimous, another fierce and high-spirited; one humane, another haughty; one lascivious, another chaste; one frank, another astute; one hard, another easy; one serious, another frivolous; one religious, another an unbeliever, and so on. I know that every one will admit that it would be highly praiseworthy in a prince to possess all the above-named qualities that are reputed good, but as they cannot all be possessed or observed, human conditions not permitting of it, it is necessary that he should be prudent enough to avoid the scandal of those vices which would lose him the state, and guard himself if possible against those which will not lose it him, but if not able to, he can indulge them with less scruple. And yet he must not mind incurring the scandal of those vices, without which it would be difficult to save the state, for if one considers well, it will be found that some things which seem virtues would, if followed, lead to one's ruin, and some others which appear vices result in one's greater security and wellbeing.

Of Liberality and Niggardliness

Beginning now with the first qualities above named, I say that it would be well to be considered liberal; nevertheless liberality such as the world understands it will injure you, because if used virtuously and in the proper way, it will not be known, and you will incur the disgrace of the contrary vice. But one who wishes to obtain the reputation of liberality among men, must not omit every kind of sumptuous display, and to such an extent that a prince of this character will consume by such means all his resources, and will be at last compelled, if he wishes to maintain his name for liberality, to impose heavy taxes on his people, become extortionate, and do everything possible to obtain money. This will make his subjects begin to hate him, and he will be little esteemed being poor, so

By permission. From *The Prince* by Niccolo Machiavelli, translated by Luigi Ricci, revised by E. R. P. Vincent, published by Oxford University Press.

that having by this liberality injured many and benefited but few, he will feel the first little disturbance and be endangered by every peril. If he recognises this and wishes to change his system, he incurs at once the charge of niggardliness.

A prince, therefore, not being able to exercise this virtue of liberality without risk if it be known, must not, if he be prudent, object to be called miserly. In course of time he will be thought more liberal, when it is seen that by his parsimony his revenue is sufficient, that he can defend himself against those who make war on him, and undertake enterprises without burdening his people, so that he is really liberal to all those from whom he does not take, who are infinite in number, and niggardly to all to whom he does not give, who are few. In our times we have seen nothing great done except by those who have been esteemed niggardly; the others have all been ruined. Pope Julius II, although he had made use of a reputation for liberality in order to attain the papacy, did not seek to retain it afterwards, so that he might be able to wage war. The present King of France has carried on so many wars without imposing an extraordinary tax, because his extra expenses were covered by the parsimony he had so long praised. The present King of Spain, if he had been thought liberal, would not have engaged in and been successful in so many enterprises.

For these reasons a prince must care little for the reputation of being a miser, if he wishes to avoid robbing his subjects, if he wishes to be able to defend himself, to avoid becoming poor and contemptible, and not to be forced to become rapacious; this niggardliness is one of those vices which enable him to reign. If it is said that Caesar attained the empire through liberality, and that many others have reached the highest positions through being liberal or being thought so, I would reply that you are either a prince already or else on the way to become one. In the first case, this liberality is harmful; in the second, it is certainly necessary to be considered liberal. Caesar was one of those who wished to attain the mastery over Rome, but if after attaining it he had lived and had not moderated his expenses, he would have destroyed that empire. And should any one reply that there have been many princes, who have done great things with their armies, who have been thought extremely liberal, I would answer by saying that the prince may either spend his own wealth and that of his subjects or the wealth of others. In the first case he must be sparing, but for the rest he must not neglect to be very liberal. The liberality is very necessary to a prince who marches with his armies and lives by plunder, sack and ransom, and is dealing with the wealth of others, for without it he would not be followed by his soldiers. And you may be very generous indeed with what is not the property of yourself or your subjects, as were Cyrus, Caesar, and Alexander; for spending the wealth of others will not diminish your reputation, but increase it, only spending your own resources will injure you. There is nothing which destroys itself so much as liberality, for by using it you lose the power of using it, and become either poor and despicable, or, to escape poverty, rapacious and hated. And of all things that a prince must guard against, the most important are being despicable or hated, and liberality will lead you to one or the other of these conditions. It is, therefore, wiser to have the name of a miser, which produces disgrace without hatred, than to incur of necessity the name of being rapacious, which produces both disgrace and hatred.

Of Cruelty and Clemency, and Whether
It Is Better to Be Loved or Feared

Proceeding to the other qualities before named, I say that every prince must desire to be considered merciful and not cruel. He must, however, take care not to misuse this mercifulness. Cesare Borgia was considered cruel, but his cruelty had brought order to the Romagna, united it, and reduced it to peace and fealty. If this is considered well, it will be seen that he was really much more merciful than the Florentine people, who, to avoid the name of cruelty, allowed Pistoia to be destroyed. A prince, therefore, must not mind incurring the charge of cruelty for the purpose of keeping his subjects united and faithful; for, with a very few examples, he will be more merciful than those who, from excess of tenderness, allow disorders to arise, from whence spring bloodshed and rapine; for these as a rule injure the whole community, while the executions carried out by the prince injure only individuals. And of all princes, it is impossible for a new prince to escape the reputation of cruelty, new states being always full of dangers. Wherefore Virgil through the mouth of Dido says:

> Res dura, et regni novitas me talia cogunt
> Moliri, et late fines custode tueri.

Nevertheless, he must be cautious in believing and acting, and must not be afraid of his own shadow, and must proceed in a temperate manner with prudence and humanity, so that too much confidence does not render him incautious, and too much diffidence does not render him intolerant.

From this arises the question whether it is better to be loved more than feared, or feared more than loved. The reply is, that one ought to be both feared and loved, but as it is difficult for the two to go together, it is much safer to be feared than loved, if one of the two has to be wanting. For it may be said of men in general that they are ungrateful, voluble, dissemblers, anxious to avoid danger, and covetous of gain; as long as you benefit them, they are entirely yours; they offer you their blood, their goods, their life, and their children, as I have before said, when the necessity is remote; but when it approaches, they revolt. And the prince who has relied solely on their words, without making other preparations, is ruined; for the friendship which is gained by purchase and not through grandeur and nobility of spirit is bought but not secured, and at a pinch is not to be expended in your service. And men have less scruple in offending one who makes himself loved than one who makes himself feared; for love is held by a chain of obligation which, men being selfish, is broken whenever it serves their purpose; but fear is maintained by a dread of punishment which never fails.

Still, a prince should make himself feared in such a way that if he does not gain love, he at any rate avoids hatred; for fear and the absence of hatred may well go together, and will be always attained by one who abstains from interfering with the property of his citizens and subjects or with their women. And when he is obliged to take the life of any one, let him do so when there is a proper justification and manifest reason for it; but above all he must abstain from taking the property of others, for men forget more easily the death of their father than the loss of their patrimony. Then also pretexts for seizing property are never wanting, and one who begins to live by rapine will always find some reason for taking the goods of others, whereas causes for taking life are rarer and more fleeting.

But when the prince is with his army and has a large number of soldiers under his control, then it is extremely necessary that he should not mind being thought cruel; for without his reputation he could not keep an army united or disposed to any duty. Among the noteworthy actions of Hannibal is numbered this, that although he had an enormous army, composed of men of all nations and fighting in foreign countries, there never arose any dissension either among them or against the prince, either in good fortune or in bad. This could not be due to anything but his inhuman cruelty, which together with his infinite other virtues, made him always venerated and terrible in the sight of his soldiers, and without it his other virtues would not have sufficed to produce that effect. Thoughtless writers admire on the one hand his actions, and on the other blame the principal cause of them.

In What Way Princes Must Keep Faith

How laudable it is for a prince to keep good faith and live with integrity, and not with astuteness, every one knows. Still the experience of our times shows those princes to have done great things who have had little regard for good faith, and have been able by astuteness to confuse men's brains, and who have ultimately overcome those who have made loyalty their foundation.

You must know, then, that there are two methods of fighting, the one by law, the other by force: the first method is that of men, the second of beasts; but as the first method is often insufficient, one must have recourse to the second. It is therefore necessary for a prince to know well how to use both the beast and the man. This was covertly taught to rulers by ancient writers, who relate how Achilles and many others of those ancient princes were given to Chiron the centaur to be brought up and educated under his discipline. The parable of this semi-animal, semi-human teacher is meant to indicate that a prince must know how to use both natures, and that the one without the other is not durable.

A prince being thus obliged to know well how to act as a beast must imitate the fox and the lion, for the lion cannot protect himself from traps, and the fox cannot defend himself from wolves. One must therefore be a fox to recognise traps, and a lion to frighten wolves. Those that wish to be only lions do not understand this. Therefore, a prudent ruler ought not to keep faith when by so doing it would be against his interest, and when the reasons which made him bind himself no longer exist. If men were all good, this precept would not be a good one; but as they are bad, and would not observe their faith with you, so you are not bound to keep faith with them. Nor have legitimate grounds ever failed a prince who wished to show colourable excuse for the non-fulfilment of his promise. Of this one could furnish an infinite number of modern examples, and show how many times peace has been broken, and how many promises rendered worthless, by the faithlessness of princes, and those that have been best able to imitate the fox have succeeded best. But it is necessary to be able to disguise this character well, and to be a great feigner and dissembler; and men are so simple and so ready to obey present necessities, that one who deceives will always find those who allow themselves to be deceived.

I will only mention one modern instance. Alexander VI did nothing else but deceive men, he thought of nothing else, and found the occasion for it; no man was ever more able to give assurances, or affirmed things with stronger oaths, and no man observed them less; however, he always succeeded in his deceptions, as he well knew this aspect of things.

It is not, therefore, necessary for a prince to have all the above-named qualities, but it is very necessary to seem to have them. I would even be bound to say that to possess them and always to observe them is dangerous, but to appear to possess them is useful. Thus it is well to seem merciful, faithful, humane, sincere, religious, and also to be so; but you must have the mind so disposed that when it is needful to be otherwise you may be able to change to the opposite qualities. And it must be understood that a prince, and especially a new prince, cannot observe all those things which are considered good in men, being often obliged, in order to maintain the state, to act against faith, against charity, against humanity, and against religion. And, therefore, he must have a mind disposed to adapt itself according to the wind, and as the variations of fortune dictate, and, as I said before, not deviate from what is good, if possible, but be able to do evil if constrained.

A prince must take great care that nothing goes out of his mouth which is not full of the above-named five qualities, and, to see and hear him, he should seem to be all mercy, faith, integrity, humanity, and religion. And nothing is more necessary than to seem to have this last quality, for men in general judge more by the eyes than by the hands, for every one can see, but very few have to feel. Everybody sees what you appear to be, few feel what you are, and those few will not dare to oppose themselves to the many, who have the majesty of the state to defend them; and in the actions of men, and especially of princes, from which there is no appeal, the end justifies the means. Let a prince therefore aim at conquering and maintaining the state, and the means will always be judged honourable and praised by every one, for the vulgar is always taken by appearances and the issue of the event; and the world consists only of the vulgar, and the few who are not vulgar are isolated when the many have a rallying point in the prince. A certain prince of the present time, whom it is well not to name, never does anything but preach peace and good faith, but he is really a great enemy to both, and either of them, had he observed them, would have lost him state or reputation on many occasions.

Thomas Hobbes

Thomas Hobbes (1588–1679) was born at Malmesbury, England. The ninety-one years of his life covered one of the most turbulent periods of English history. The Spanish Armada was defeated in the year of his birth, and he lived through the civil war, Cromwell's protectorate, and the Stuart Restoration. He was an adherent of the royalist cause and was in exile for a time. After falling from the favor of the royalists because of his published political philosophy he returned to England and made his peace with the protectorate.

Hobbes was greatly influenced by the work of the new physical scientists such as Galileo and in his philosophy adheres to a strictly naturalistic basis. Although he wrote on many topics, he is best known now for his political thought. In the selection from *De Corpore Politico* printed below he presents and defends his views on the nature of government, its power, and its authority.

De Corpore Politico

PART I

CHAPTER 1   HUMAN NATURE AND THE STATE OF NATURE

1. In a former treatise of human nature already printed, hath been set forth the whole nature of man, consisting in the powers natural of his body and mind, and may all be comprehended in these four, *strength of body, experience, reason,* and *passion.*

2. In this, it will be expedient to consider in what estate of security this our nature hath placed us, and what probability it hath left us, of continuing and preserving ourselves against the violence of one another. And first, if we consider how little odds there is of strength or knowledge, between men of mature age, and with how great facility he that is the weaker in strength or in wit, or in both, may utterly destroy the power of the stronger; since there needeth but little force to the taking away of a man's life, we may conclude, that men considered in mere nature, ought to admit amongst themselves equality; and that he that claimeth no more, may be esteemed moderate.

3. On the other side, considering the great difference there is in men, from

From Thomas Hobbes *De Corpore Politico* based on the Molesworth edition, London 1839. Chapter headings added by the editors.

the diversity of their passions, how some are vainly glorious, and hope for precedency and superiority above their fellows, not only when they are equal in power, but also when they are inferior; we must needs acknowledge that it must necessarily follow, that those men who are moderate, and look for no more but equality of nature, shall be obnoxious to the force of others, that will attempt to subdue them. And from hence shall proceed a general diffidence in mankind, and mutual fear one of another.

4. Further, since men by natural passion are divers ways offensive one to another, every man thinking well of himself, and hating to see the same in others, they must needs provoke one another by words, and other signs of contempt and hatred, which are incident to all comparison, till at last they must determine the pre-eminence by strength and force of body.

5. Moreover, considering that many men's appetites carry them to one and the same end; which end sometimes can neither be enjoyed in common, nor divided, it followeth, that the stronger must enjoy it alone, and that it be decided by battle who is the stronger. And thus the greatest part of men, upon no assurance of odds, do nevertheless, through vanity, or comparison, or appetite, provoke the rest, that otherwise would be contented with equality.

6. And forasmuch as necessity of nature maketh men to will and desire *bonum sibi*, that which is good for themselves, and to avoid that which is hurtful; but most of all, the terrible enemy of nature, death, from whom we expect both the loss of all power, and also the greatest of bodily pains in the losing; it is not against reason, that a man doth all he can to preserve his own body and limbs both from death and pain. And that which is not against reason, men call *right*, or *just*, or *blameless liberty* of using our own natural power and ability. It is therefore a right of nature, that every man may preserve his own life and limbs, with all the power he hath.

7. And because where a man hath right to the end, and the end cannot be attained without the means, that is, without such things as are necessary to the end, it is consequent that it is not against reason, and therefore right, for a man to use all means, and do whatsoever action is necessary for the preservation of his body.

8. Also, every man by right of nature, is judge himself of the necessity of the means, and of the greatness of the danger. For if it be against reason, that I be judge of mine own danger myself, then it is reason, that another man be judge thereof. But the same reason that maketh another man judge of those things that concern me, maketh me also judge of that that concerneth him. And therefore I have reason to judge of his sentence, whether it be for my benefit, or not.

9. As a man's judgment in right of nature is to be employed for his own benefit, so also the strength, knowledge, and art, of every man is then rightly employed, when he useth it for himself; else must not a man have right to preserve himself.

10. Every man by nature hath right to all things, that is to say, to do whatsoever he listeth to whom he listeth, to possess, use, and enjoy all things he will and can. For seeing all things he willeth, must therefore be good unto him in his own judgment, because he willeth them, and may tend to his preservation some time or other, or he may judge so, and we have made him judge thereof, section 8, it followeth, that all things may rightly also be done by him. And for this cause it is rightly said, *Natura dedit omnia omnibus*, that Nature hath given

all things to all men; insomuch, that *jus* and *utile*, right and profit, is the same thing. But that right of all men to all things, is in effect no better than if no man had right to any thing. For there is little use and benefit of the right a man hath, when another as strong, or stronger than himself, hath right to the same.

11. Seeing then to the offensiveness of man's nature one to another, there is added a right of every man to every thing, whereby one man invadeth with right, and another man with right resisteth, and men live thereby in perpetual diffidence, and study how to preoccupate each other; the estate of men in this natural liberty, is the estate of war. For *war* is nothing else but that time wherein the will and contention of contending by force, is either by words or actions sufficiently declared; and the time which is not war, is *peace*.

12. The estate of hostility and war being such, as thereby nature itself is destroyed, and men kill one another, (as we know also that it is, both by the experience of savage nations that live at this day, and by the histories of our ancestors the old inhabitants of Germany, and other now civil countries, where we find the people few, and short lived, and without the ornaments and comforts of life, which by peace and society are usually invented and procured) he therefore that desireth to live in such an estate as is the estate of liberty and right of all to all, contradicteth himself. For every man by natural necessity desireth his own good, to which this estate is contrary, wherein we suppose contention between men by nature equal, and able to destroy one another.

13. Seeing this right of protecting ourselves by our own discretion and force, proceedeth from danger, and that danger from the equality between men's forces, much more reason is there, that a man prevent such equality before the danger cometh, and before the necessity of battle. A man therefore that hath another man in his power to rule or govern, to do good to, or harm, hath right, by the advantage of this his present power, to take caution at his pleasure, for his security against that other in time to come. He therefore that hath already subdued his adversary, or gotten into his power any other, that either by infancy, or weakness, is unable to resist him, by right of nature may take the best caution, that such infant, or such feeble and subdued person can give him, of being ruled and governed by him for the time to come. For seeing we intend always our own safety and preservation, we manifestly contradict that our intention, if we willingly dismiss such a one, and suffer him at once to gather strength and be our enemy. Out of which may also be collected, that irresistible might, in the state of nature, is right.

14. But since it is supposed by the equality of strength, and other natural faculties of men, that no man is of might sufficient, to assure himself for any long time, of preserving himself thereby, whilst he remaineth in the state of hostility and war; reason therefore dictateth to every man for his own good, to seek after peace, as far forth as there is hope to attain the same; and strengthen himself with all the help he can procure, for his own defence against those, from whom such peace cannot be obtained; and to do all those things which necessarily conduce thereunto.

CHAPTER 2 THE LAW OF NATURE

1. What it is we call the law of nature, is not agreed upon by those, that have hitherto written. For the most part, such writers as have occasion to affirm, that

anything is against the law of nature, do allege no more than this, that it is against the consent of all nations, or the wisest and most civil nations. But it is not agreed upon, who shall judge which nations are the wisest. Others make that against the law of nature, which is contrary to the consent of all mankind; which definition cannot be allowed, because then no man could offend against the law of nature; for the nature of every man is contained under the nature of mankind. But forasmuch as all men are carried away by the violence of their passion, and by evil customs do those things which are commonly said to be against the law of nature; it is not the consent of passions, or consent in some error gotten by custom, that makes the law of nature. Reason is no less of the nature of man than passion, and is the same in all men, because all men agree in the will to be directed and governed in the way to that which they desire to attain, namely, their own good, which is the work of reason: there can therefore be no other precepts of *natural law*, than those which declare unto us the ways of peace, where the same may be obtained, and of defence where it may not.

2. One precept of the law of nature therefore is this, *that every man divest himself of the right he hath to all things by nature.* For when divers men having right not only to all things else, but to one another's persons, if they use the same, there ariseth thereby invasion on the one part, and resistance on the other, which is *war*, and therefore contrary to the law of nature, the sum whereof consisteth in making peace.

3. When a man divesteth and putteth from himself his right, he either simply relinquisheth it, or transferreth the same to another man. To *relinquish* it, is by sufficient signs to declare, that it is his will no more to do that action, which of right he might have done before. To *transfer* right to another, is by sufficient signs to declare to that other accepting thereof, that it is his will not to resist, or hinder him, according to that right he had thereto before he transferred it. For seeing that by nature every man hath right to every thing, it is impossible for a man to transfer unto another any right that he had not before. And therefore all that a man doth in transferring of right, is no more but a declaring of the will, to suffer him, to whom he hath so transferred his right, to make benefit of the same, without molestation. As for example, when a man giveth his lands or goods to another, he taketh from himself the right to enter into, and make use of the said lands or goods, or otherwise to hinder him of the use of what he hath given.

4. In transferring of right, two things therefore are required: one on the part of him that transferreth, which is a sufficient signification of his will therein; the other, on the part of him to whom it is transferred, which is a sufficient signification of his acceptation thereof. Either of these failing, the right remaineth where it was: nor is it to be supposed, that he which giveth his right to one that accepteth it not, doth thereby simply relinquish it, and transfer it to whomsoever will receive it: inasmuch as the cause of transferring the same to one, rather than to another, is in the one, rather than in the rest.

8. When a man transferreth his right upon consideration of reciprocal benefit, this is not free gift, but mutual *donation*, and is called *contract*. And in all contracts, either both parties presently perform, and put each other into a certainty and assurance of enjoying what they contract for, as when men buy or sell, or barter; or one party performeth presently, and the other promiseth, as when one selleth upon trust; or else neither party performeth presently, but trust one another. And it is impossible there should be any kind of contract

besides these three. For either both the contractors trust, or neither; or else one trusteth, and the other not.

9. In all contracts where there is trust, the promise of him that is trusted, is called a *covenant*. And this, though it be a promise, and of the time to come, yet it doth transfer the right, when that time cometh, no less than an actual donation. For it is a manifest sign, that he which did perform, understood it was the will of him that was trusted, to perform also. Promises therefore, upon consideration of reciprocal benefit, are covenants and signs of the will, or last act of deliberation, whereby the liberty of performing, or not performing, is taken away, and consequently are obligatory. For where liberty ceaseth, there beginneth obligation.

10. Nevertheless, in contracts that consist of such mutual trust, as that nothing be by either party performed for the present, when the contract is between such as are not compellable, he that performeth first, considering the disposition of men to take advantage of every thing for their benefit, doth but betray himself thereby to the covetousness, or other passion of him with whom he contracteth. And therefore such covenants are of none effect. For there is no reason why the one should perform first, if the other be likely not to perform afterward. And whether he be likely or not, he that doubteth, shall be judge himself, as hath been said chap. I. sect. 8, as long as they remain in the estate and liberty of nature. But when there shall be such power coercive over both the parties, as shall deprive them of their private judgments in this point, then may such covenants be effectual, seeing he that performeth first shall have no reasonable cause to doubt of the performance of the other, that may be compelled thereunto.

CHAPTER 3   JUSTICE AND THE LAW OF NATURE

1. It is a common saying that nature maketh nothing in vain. And it is most certain, that as the truth of a conclusion, is no more but the truth of the premises that make it; so the force of the command, or law of nature, is no more than the force of the reasons inducing thereunto. Therefore the law of nature mentioned in the former chapter, section 2, namely, *That every man should divest himself of the right*, etc., were utterly vain, and of none effect, if this also were not a law of the same nature, *That every man is obliged to stand to, and perform, those covenants he maketh.* For what benefit is it to a man, that any thing be promised, or given unto him, if he that giveth, or promiseth, performeth not, or retaineth still the right of taking back what he hath given?

4. The names of *just, unjust, justice, injustice*, are equivocal, and signify diversly. For justice and injustice, when they be attributed to actions, signify the same thing with *no injury*, and *injury*, and denominate the action *just*, or *unjust*, but not the man so. For they denominate him *guilty*, or *not guilty*. But when justice or injustice, are attributed to men, they signify *proneness*, and affection and inclination of nature, that is to say, passions of the mind, apt to produce just and unjust actions. So that when a man is said to be just, or unjust; not the action, but the passion and aptitude, to do such actions, is considered. And therefore a just man may have committed an unjust act; and an unjust man may

have done justly, not only one, but most of his actions. For there is an *oderunt peccare* in the unjust, as well as in the just, but from different causes. For the unjust man who abstaineth from injuries for fear of punishment, declareth plainly, that the justice of his actions dependeth upon civil constitution, from whence punishments proceed, which would otherwise in the estate of nature be unjust, according to the fountain from whence they spring. This distinction therefore of *justice*, and *injustice*, ought to be remembered, that when injustice is taken for guilty, the action is unjust, but not therefore the man; and when justice is taken for *guiltlessness*, the actions are just, and yet not always the man. Likewise when justice and injustice are taken for habits of the mind, the man may be just, or unjust, and yet not all his actions so.

5. Concerning the justice of actions, the same is usually divided into two kinds, whereof men call the one *commutative*, and the other *distributive*; and are said to consist, the one in proportion *arithmetical*; the other in *geometrical*: and *commutative* justice, they place in permutation, as buying, selling, and bartering; *distributive*, in giving to every man according to their deserts. Which distinction is not well made, inasmuch as injury, which is the injustice of action, consisteth not in the inequality of the things changed, or distributed, but in the inequality that men, contrary to nature and reason, assume unto themselves above their fellows. Of which inequality, shall be spoken hereafter. And for *commutative* justice placed in buying and selling, though the thing bought be unequal to the price given for it, yet forasmuch as both the buyer and the seller are made judges of the value, and are thereby both satisfied, there can be no injury done on either side, neither party having trusted, or convenanted with the other. And for *distributive* justice, which consisteth in the distribution of our own benefits, seeing a thing is therefore said to be our own, because we may dispose of it at our own pleasure, it can be no injury to any man, though our liberality be farther extended towards another, than towards him; unless we be thereto obliged by covenant: and then the injustice consisteth in the violation of that covenant, and not in the inequality of distribution.

6. It happeneth many times that man benefitteth, or contributeth, to the power of another, without any convenant, but only upon confidence and trust of obtaining the grace and favour of that other, whereby he may procure a greater, or no less benefit, and assistance to himself. For by necessity of nature, every man doth in all his voluntary actions intend some good unto himself. In this case it is a law of nature, *That no man suffer him, that thus trusteth to his charity, or good affection towards him, to be in the worse estate for his trusting.* For if he shall so do, men will not dare to confer mutually to each other's defence, nor put themselves into each other's mercy upon any terms whatsoever, but rather abide the utmost and worst event of hostility; by which general diffidence, men will not only be enforced to war, but also afraid to come so much within the danger of one another, as to make any overture of peace. But this is to be understood of those only, that confer their benefits (as I have said) upon trust only, and not for triumph or ostentation. For as when they do it upon trust, the end they aimed at, namely to be well used, is the reward; so also when they do it for ostentation, they have the reward in themselves.

8. It is also a law of nature, *That every man do help and endeavour to accommodate each other as far as may be, without danger of their persons, and loss of their means, to maintain and defend themselves.* For seeing the causes of war and desolation proceed from those passions, by which we strive to accom-

modate ourselves, and to leave others as far as we can behind us, it followeth, that that passion by which we strive mutually to accommodate each other, must be the cause of peace. And this passion is that charity defined chapter IX. section 17.

9. And in this precept of nature, is included and comprehended also this, *That a man forgive and pardon him that hath done him wrong, upon his repentance and caution for the future.* For *pardon* is peace granted to him, that, having provoked to war, demandeth it. It is not therefore charity, but fear, when a man giveth peace to him that repenteth not, nor giveth caution for maintaining thereof in the time to come. For he that repenteth not, remaineth with the affection of an enemy; as also doth he that refuseth to give caution, and consequently, is presumed not to seek after peace, but advantage. And therefore to forgive him is not commanded in this law of nature, nor is charity, but may sometime be prudence. Otherwise, not to pardon upon repentance and caution, considering men cannot abstain from provoking one another, is never to give *peace.* And that is against the general definition of the law of nature.

10. And seeing the law of nature commandeth pardon, when there is repentance and caution for the future, it followeth, that the same law ordaineth, *That no revenge be taken upon the consideration only of the offence past, but of the benefit to come;* that is to say, that all revenge ought to tend to amendment, either of the person offending, or of others, by example of his punishment; which is sufficiently apparent, in that the law of nature commandeth pardon, where the future time is secured. The same is also apparent by this, that revenge when it considereth the offence past, is nothing else, but present triumph and glory, and directeth to no end: and what is directed to no end, is therefore unprofitable; and consequently the triumph of revenge, is vain glory: and whatsoever is vain, is against reason; and to hurt one another without reason, is contrary to that, which by supposition is every man's benefit, namely peace; and what is contrary to peace, is contrary to the law of nature.

11. And because all signs which we shew to one another of hatred and contempt, provoke in the highest degree to quarrel and battle, (inasmuch as life itself, with the condition of enduring scorn, is not esteemed worth the enjoying, much less peace) it must necessarily be implied as a law of nature, *That no man reproach, revile, deride, or any otherwise declare his hatred, contempt, or disesteem of any other.* But this law is very little practised. For what is more ordinary than reproaches of those that are rich, towards them that are not? or of those that sit in place of judicature, towards those that are accused at the bar? although to grieve them in that manner, be no part of the punishment for their crime, nor contained in their office. But use hath prevailed, that what was lawful in the lord towards the servant whom he maintaineth, is also practised as lawful in the more mighty towards the less; though they contribute nothing towards their maintenance.

CHAPTER 4 FURTHER LAWS OF NATURE

1. The question, which is the better man, is determinable only in the estate of government and policy, though it be mistaken for a question of nature, not only by ignorant men, that think one man's blood better than another's by

nature, but also by him, whose opinions are at this day, and in these parts, of greater authority than any other human writings. For he putteth so much difference between the powers of men by nature, that he doubteth not to set down, as the ground of all his politics, that some men are by nature worthy to govern, and others by nature ought to serve. Which foundation hath not only weakened the whole frame of his politics, but hath also given men colour and pretences, whereby to disturb and hinder the peace of one another. For though there were such a difference of nature, that master and servant were not by consent of men, but by inherent virtue; yet who hath that eminency of virtue above others, and who is so stupid, as not to govern himself, shall never be agreed upon amongst men, who do every one naturally think himself, as able, at the least, to govern another, as another to govern him. And when there was any contention between the finer and the coarser wits, (as there hath been often in times of sedition and civil war) for the most part, these latter carried away the victory; and as long as men arrogate to themselves more honour than they give to others, it cannot be imagined how they can possibly live in peace: and consequently we are to suppose, that for peace sake, nature hath ordained this law, *That every man acknowledge other for his equal.* And the breach of this law, is that we call *pride*

2. As it was necessary that a man should not retain his right to every thing, so also was it, that he should retain his right to some things; to his own body, for example, the right of defending, whereof he could not transfer; to the use of fire, water, free air, and place to live in, and to all things necessary for life. Nor doth the law of nature command any divesting of other rights, than of those only which cannot be retained without the loss of peace. Seeing then many rights are retained, when we enter into peace one with another, reason and the law of nature dictateth. *Whatsoever right any man requireth to retain, he allow every other man to retain the same.* For he that doth not so, alloweth not the equality mentioned in the former section. For there is no acknowledgment of worth, without attribution of the equality of benefit and respect. And this allowance of *aequalia aequalibus,* is the same thing with the allowing of *proportionalia proportionalibus.* For when a man alloweth to every man alike, the allowance he maketh, will be in the same proportion, in which are the numbers of men to whom they are made. And this is it men mean by *distributive justice,* and is properly termed *equity.* The breach of the law is that which the Greeks call Πλεονεξία, which is commonly rendered *covetousness,* but seemeth to be more precisely expressed by the word *encroaching.*

3. If there pass no other covenant, the law of nature is, *That such things as cannot be divided, be used in common, proportionably to the numbers of them that are to use the same, or without limitation, when the quantity thereof sufficeth.* For first supposing the thing to be used in common, not sufficient for them that are to use it without limitation, if a few shall make more use thereof than the rest, that equality is not observed, which is required in the second section. And this is to be understood, as all the rest of the laws of nature, without any other covenant antecedent: for a man may have given away his right of common, and so the case be altered.

4. In those things which neither can be divided, nor used in common, the rule of nature must needs be one of these, *lot,* or *alternate use:* for besides these two ways, there can no other equality be imagined; and for alternate use, he that beginneth, hath the advantage; and to reduce that advantage to equality, there is

no other way but lot, in things, therefore indivisible and incommunicable, it is the law of nature, *That the use be alternate, or the advantage given away by lot;* because there is no other way of equality. And equality is the law of nature.

6. Although men agree upon these laws of nature, and endeavour to observe the same; yet considering the passions of men, that make it difficult to understand by what actions, and circumstances of actions, those laws are broken, there must needs arise many great controversies about the interpretation thereof, by which the peace must needs be dissolved, and men return again to their former estate of hostility. For the taking away of which controversies, it is necessary that there be some common *arbitrator* and *judge*, to whose sentence both the parties in the controversies ought to stand. And therefore it is a law of nature, *That in every controversy, the parties thereto ought mutually to agree upon an arbitrator, whom they both trust; and mutually to covenant to stand to the sentence he shall give therein.* For where every men is his own *judge*, there properly is no judge at all; as where every man carveth out his own right, it hath the same effect, as if there were no right at all: and where is no judge, there is no end of controversy: and therefore the right of hostility remaineth.

9. A man that shall see these laws of nature set down and inferred with so many words, and so much ado, may think there is yet much more difficulty and subtlety required to acknowledge and do according to the said laws in every sudden occasion, when a man hath but a little time to consider. And while we consider man in most passions, as of *anger, ambition, covetousness, vain glory,* and the like, that tend to the excluding of natural equality, it is true. But without these passions, there is an easy rule to know upon a sudden, whether the action I be to do, be against the law of nature, or nor. And it is but this: *That a man imagine himself in the place of the party with whom he hath to do, and reciprocally him in his.* Which is no more but a changing, as it were, of the scales. For every man's passion weigheth heavy in his own scale, but not in the scale of his neighbour. And this rule is very well known and expressed in this old dictate, *Quod tibi fieri non vis, alteri ne feceris.*

10. These laws of nature, the sum whereof consisteth in forbidding us to be our own judges, and our own carvers, and in commanding us to accommodate one another, in case they should be observed by some, and not by others, would make the observers but a prey to them that should neglect them, leaving the good both without defence against the wicked, and also with a charge to assist them: which is against the scope of the said laws, that are made only for the protection and defence of them that keep them. Reason therefore, and the law of nature over and above all these particular laws, doth dictate this law in general, *That those particular laws be so far observed, as they subject us not to any incommodity, that in our own judgments may arise, by the neglect thereof in those towards whom we observe them;* and consequently requireth no more but the desire and constant intention to endeavour and be ready to observe them, unless there be cause to the contrary in other men's refusal to observe them towards us. The force therefore of the law of nature, is not *in foro externo,* till there be security for men to obey it, but is always *in foro interno,* wherein the action of obedience being unsafe, the will and readiness to perform, is taken for the performance.

11. Amongst the laws of nature, customs and prescriptions are not numbered. For whatsoever action is against reason, though it be reiterated never so

often, or that there be never so many precedents thereof, is still against reason, and therefore not a law of nature, but contrary to it. But consent and covenant may so alter the cases, which in the law of nature may be put, by changing the circumstances, that that which was reason before, may afterwards be against it; and yet is reason still the law. For though every man be bound to allow equality to another, yet if that other shall see cause to renounce the same, and make himself inferior, then, if from thenceforth he consider him as inferior, he breaketh not thereby that law of nature that commandeth to allow equality. In sum, *a man's own consent may abridge him of the liberty which the law of nature leaveth him, but custom not;* nor can either of them abrogate either these, or any other law of nature.

12. And forasmuch as law, to speak properly, is a command, and these dictates, as they proceed from nature, are not commands, they are not therefore called laws, in respect of nature, but in respect of the author of nature, God Almighty.

13. And seeing the laws of nature concern the conscience, not he only breaketh them that doth any action contrary, but also he whose action is conformable to them, in case he think it contrary. For though the action chance to be right, yet in his judgment he despiseth the law.

15. The sum of virtue is to be sociable with them that will be sociable, and formidable to them that will not. And the same is the sum of the law of nature: for in being sociable, the law of nature taketh place by way of peace and society; and to be formidable, is the law of nature in war, where to be feared is a protection a man hath from his own power: and as the former consisteth in actions of equity and justice, the latter consisteth in actions of honour. And equity, justice, and honour, contain all virtues whatsoever.

CHAPTER 6   PEACE AND THE BODY POLITIC

1. In chapter XII. section 16, of the *Treatise of Human Nature*, it hath been shewed, that the opinions men have of the rewards and punishments which are to follow their actions, are the causes that make and govern the will to those actions. In this estate of man therefore, wherein all men are equal, and every man allowed to be his own judge, the fears they have one of another are equal, and every man's hopes consist in his own sleight and strength: and consequently when any man by his natural passion, is provoked to break these laws of nature, there is no security in any other man of his own defence but *anticipation.* And for this cause, every man's right, howsoever he be inclined to peace, of doing whatsoever seemeth good in his own eyes, remaineth with him still, as the necessary means of his preservation. And therefore till there be security amongst men for the keeping of the law of nature one towards another, men are still in the estate of war, and nothing is unlawful to any man that tendeth to his own safety or commodity: and this safety and commodity consisteth in the mutual aid and help of one another, whereby also followeth the mutual fear of one another.

2. It is a proverbial saying, *inter arma silent leges.* There is a little therefore to be said concerning the laws that men are to observe one towards another in time of war, wherein every man's being and well-being is the rule of his actions.

Yet thus much the law of nature commandeth in war, that men satiate not the cruelty of their present passions, whereby in their own conscience they foresee no benefit to come. For that betrayeth not a necessity, but a disposition of the mind to war, which is against the law of nature. And in old time we read, that rapine was a trade of life, wherein nevertheless many of them that used it, did not only spare the lives of those they invaded, but left them also such things, as were necessary to preserve that life which they had given them; as namely their oxen and instruments for tillage, though they carried away all their other cattle and substance. And as the rapine itself was warranted in the law of nature, by the want of security otherwise to maintain themselves, so the exercise of cruelty was forbidden by the same law of nature, unless fear suggested anything to the contrary. For nothing but fear can justify the taking away of another's life. And because fear can hardly be made manifest, but by some action dishonourable, that betrayeth the conscience of one's own weakness, all men, in whom the passion of courage or magnanimity hath been predominant, have abstained from cruelty; insomuch, that though there be in war no law, the breach whereof is injury, yet there are in war those laws, the breach whereof is dishonour. In one word, therefore, the only law of actions in war, is *honour*; and the right of war, *providence*.

3. And seeing natural aid is necessary for defence, as mutual fear is necessary for peace, we are to consider how great aids are required for such defence, and for the causing of such mutual fear, as men may not easily adventure on one another. And first, it is evident, that the mutual aid of two or three men is of very little security. For the odds on the other side, of a man or two, giveth sufficient encouragement to an assault. And therefore before men have sufficient security in the help of one another, their number must be so great, that the odds of a few which the enemy may have, be no certain and sensible advantage.

4. And supposing how great a number soever of men assembled together for their mutual defence, yet shall not the effect follow, unless they all direct their actions to one and the same end; which direction to one and the same end is that which, chap. XII. sect. 7, is called *consent*. This *consent*, or concord, amongst so many men, though it may be made by the fear of a present invader, or by the hope of a present conquest, or booty, and endure as long as that action endureth, nevertheless, by the diversity of judgments and passions in so many men contending naturally for honour and advantage one above another, it is impossible, not only that their consent to aid each other against an enemy, but also that the peace should last between themselves, without some mutual and common fear to rule them.

5. But contrary hereunto may be objected, the experience we have of certain living creatures irrational, that neveretheless continually live in such good order and government for their common benefit, and are so free from sedition and war amongst themselves, that for peace, profit, and defence, nothing more can be imaginable. And the experience we have in this, is in that little creature the bee, which is therefore reckoned amongst *animalia politica*. Why therefore may not men, that foresee the benefit of concord, continually maintain the same without compulsion, as well as they? To which I answer, that amongst other living creatures, there is no question of precedence in their own species, nor strife about honour, or acknowledgment of one another's wisdom, as there is amongst men, from whence arise envy and hatred of one towards another, and from

thence sedition and war. Secondly, those living creatures aim every one at peace and food common to them all; men aim at dominion, superiority, and private wealth, which are distinct in every man, and breed contention. Thirdly, those living creatures that are without reason, have not learning enough to espy, or to think they espy, any defect in the government; and therefore are contented therewith. But in a multitude of men, there are always some that think themselves wiser than the rest, and strive to alter what they think amiss, and divers of them strive to alter divers ways, and that causeth war. Fourthly, they want speech, and are therefore unable to instigate one another to faction, which men want not. Fifthly, they have no conception of right and wrong, but only of pleasure and pain, and therefore also no censure of one another, nor of their commander, as long as they are themselves at ease; whereas men that make themselves judges of right and wrong, are then least at quiet, when they are most at ease. Lastly, natural concord, such as is amongst those creatures, is the work of God by the way of nature; but concord amongst men is artificial, and by way of covenant. And therefore no wonder, if such irrational creatures as govern themselves in multitude, do it much more firmly than mankind, that do it by arbitrary institution.

6. It remaineth therefore still, that consent, by which I understand the concurrence of many men's wills to one action, is not sufficient security for their common peace, without the erection of some common power, by the fear whereof they may be compelled both to keep the peace amongst themselves, and to join their strengths together, against a common enemy. And that this may be done, there is no way imaginable, but only union, which is defined, chapter XII. section 8, to be the involving, or including the wills of many in the will of one man, or in the will of the greatest part of any one number of men, that is to say, in the will of one man, or of one *council.* For a council is nothing else but an *assembly* of men deliberating concerning something common to them all.

7. The making of union consisteth in this, that every man by covenant oblige himself to some one and the same man, or to some one and the same council, by them all named and determined, to do those actions, which the said man or council shall command them to do, and to do no action, which he or they shall forbid, or command them not to do. And further, in case it be a council, whose commands they covenant to obey, that then also they covenant, that every man shall hold that for the command of the whole council, which is the command of the greater part of those men, whereof such council consisteth. And though the will of man being not voluntary, but the beginning of voluntary actions, is not subject to deliberation and covenant; yet when a man covenanteth to subject his will to the command of another, he obligeth himself to this, that he resign his strength and means to him, whom he covenanteth to obey. And hereby he that is to command, may by the use of all their means and strength, be able by the terror thereof, to frame the will of them all to unity and concord, amongst themselves.

8. This union so made, is that which men call nowadays, *a body politic*, or civil society; and the Greeks call it πόλις, that is to say, a city, which may be defined to be a multitude of men, united as one person, by a common power, for their common peace, defence, and benefit.

10. In all cities, or bodies politic not subordinate, but independent, that one man, or one council, to whom the particular members have given that common

power, is called their *sovereign*, and his power, the sovereign power; which consisteth in the power and the strength, that every of the members have transferred to him from themselves by covenant. And because it is impossible for any man really to transfer his own strength to another, or for that other to receive it; it is to be understood, that to transfer a man's power and strength, is no more but to lay by, or relinquish his own right of resisting him to whom he so transferreth it. And every member of the body politic, is called a *subject*, to wit, to the *sovereign*.

PART II

CHAPTER 1   FORMATION OF THE BODY POLITIC

1. That *Treatise of Human Nature*, which was formerly printed, hath been wholly spent in the consideration of the natural power, and the natural estate of man, namely, of his cognition and passions in the first eleven chapters, and how from thence proceed his actions; in the twelfth, how men know one another's minds: in the last, in what estate men's passions set them. In the first, second, third, fourth, and fifth chapters of the former Part of this Treatise is showed, what estate they are directed unto by the dictates of reason, that is to say, what be the principal articles of the law of nature. And lastly, how a multitude of persons natural, are united by covenants into one person civil, or body politic. In this part therefore shall be considered, the nature of a body politic, and the laws thereof, otherwise called civil laws. And whereas it hath been said in the last chapter, and last section of the former part, that there be two ways of erecting a body politic; one by arbitrary institution of many men assembled together, which is like a creation out of nothing by human wit; the other by compulsion, which is as it were a generation thereof out of natural force; I shall first speak of such erection of a body politic, as proceedeth from the assembly and consent of multitude.

2. Having in this place to consider, a multitude of men about to unite themselves into a body politic, for their security, both against one another, and against common enemies, and that by covenants; the knowledge of what covenants they must needs make, dependeth on the knowledge of the persons, and the knowledge of their end. First, for their persons they are many, and (as yet) not one; nor can any action done in a multitude of people met together, be attributed to the multitude, or truly called the action of the multitude, unless every man's hand, and every man's will, (not so much as one excepted) have concurred thereto. For multitude, though in their persons they run together, yet they concur not always in their designs. For even at that time when men are in tumult, though they agree a number of them to one mischief, and a number of them to another; yet, in the whole, they are amongst themselves in the state of hostility, and not of peace; like the seditious Jews besieged in Jerusalem, that could join against their enemies, and fight amongst themselves. Whensoever therefore any man saith, that a number of men hath done any act, it is to be understood, that every particular man in that number hath consented thereunto,

and not the greatest part only. Secondly, though thus assembled with intention to unite themselves, they are yet in that estate in which every man hath right to everything, and consequently, as hath been said, chapter I. section 10, in an estate of enjoying nothing. And therefore *meum* and *tuum* hath no place amongst them.

3. The first thing therefore they are to do, is expressly every man to consent to something, by which they may come near to their ends, which can be nothing else imaginable, but this, that they allow the wills of the major part of their whole number, or the wills of the major part of some certain number of men by them determined and named; or lastly, the will of some one man, to involve and be taken for the wills of every man. And this done, they are united, and a *body politic*. And if the major part of their whole number be supposed to involve the wills of all the particulars, then are they said to be a *democracy*, that is to say, a government wherein the whole number, or so many of them as please, being assembled together, are the sovereign, and every particular man a subject. If the major part of a certain number of men named or distinguished from the rest, be supposed to involve the wills of every one of the particulars, then are they said to be an *oligarchy*, or *aristocracy*, which two words signify the same thing, together with the divers passions of those that use them. For when the men that be in that office please, they are called an aristocracy, or otherwise an oligarchy, wherein those, the major part of which declare the wills of the whole multitude being assembled, are the sovereign, and every man severally a subject. Lastly, if their consent be such, that the will of one man, whom they name, shall stand for the wills of them all, then is their government or union called a *monarchy*, and that one man a sovereign, and every of the rest a subject.

4. And those several sorts of unions, governments, and subjections of man's will, may be understood to be made, either absolutely, that is to say, for all future time, or for a time limited only. But forasmuch as we speak here of a body politic, instituted for the perpetual benefit and defence of them that make it; which therefore men desire should last for ever, I will omit to speak of those that be temporary, and consider of those that be for ever.

5. The end for which one man giveth up, and relinquisheth to another, or others, the right of protecting and defending himself by his own power, is the security which he expecteth thereby, of protection and defence from those to whom he doth so relinquish it; and a man may then account himself in the estate of security, when he can foresee no violence to be done unto him, from which the doer may not be deterred by the power of that sovereign, to whom they have every one subjected themselves: and without that security, there is no reason for a man to deprive himself of his own advantages, and make himself a prey to others. And therefore when there is not such a sovereign power erected, as may afford this security, it is to be understood, that every man's right of doing whatsoever seemeth good in his own eyes, remaineth still with him; and contrariwise, where any subject hath right by his own judgment and discretion, to make use of his force, it is to be understood, that every man hath the like, and consequently, that there is no commonwealth at all established. How far therefore in the making of a commonwealth, man subjecteth his will to the power of others, must appear from the end, namely, security. For whatsoever is necessary to be by covenant transferred, for the attaining thereof, so much is transferred, or else every man is in his natural liberty to secure himself.

6. Covenants agreed upon by every man assembled for the making of a commonwealth, and put in writing without erecting of a power of coercion, are no reasonable security for any of them that so covenant, nor are to be called laws, and leave men still in the estate of nature and hostility. For seeing the wills of most men are governed only by fear, and where there is no power of coercion, there is no fear, the wills of most men will follow their passions of covetousness, lust, anger, and the like, to the breaking of those covenants, whereby the rest, also, who otherwise would keep them, are set at liberty, and have no law, but from themselves.

7. This power of coercion, as hath been said, chap. II. sect. 3, of the former part, consisteth in the transferring of every man's right of resistance against him, to whom he hath transferred the power of coercion. It followeth therefore, that no man in any commonwealth whatsoever, hath right to resist him, or them, to whom they have transferred this power coercive, or (as men use to call it) the sword of justice, supposing the not-resistance possible. For, Part I. chapter II. sec. 18, covenants bind but to the utmost of our endeavour.

8. And forasmuch as they who are amongst themselves in security, by the means of this sword of justice, that keeps them all in awe, are nevertheless in danger of enemies from without, if there be not some means found, to unite their strengths and natural forces, in the resistance of such enemies, their peace amongst themselves is but in vain. And therefore it is to be understood as a covenant of every member to contribute their several forces for the defence of the whole, whereby to make one power as sufficient, as is possible for their defence. Now seeing that every man hath already transferred the use of his strength to him, or them, that have the sword of justice, it followeth, that the power of defence, that is to say, the sword of war, be in the same hands wherein is the sword of justice; and consequently those two swords are but one, and that inseparably and essentially annexed to the sovercign power.

9. Moreover, seeing to have the right of the sword, is nothing else but to have the use thereof depending only on the judgment and discretion of him or them that have it, it followeth, that the power of indenture in all controversies, wherein the sword of justice is to be used; and in all deliberations concerning war, wherein the use of that sword is required, the right of resolving and determining what is to be done, belong to the same sovereign.

10. Further, considering it is no less, but much more necessary to prevent violence and rapine, than to punish the same when it is committed, and all violence proceedeth from controversies that arise between men concerning *meum* and *tuum*, right and wrong, good and bad, and the like, which men use every one to measure by their own judgments, it belongeth also to the judgment of the same sovereign power, to set forth and make known the common measure by which every man is to know what is his, and what another's; what is good, and what bad, and what he ought to do, and what not, and command the same to be observed. And these measures of the actions of the subjects are those, which men call *laws politic*, or civil: the making whereof, must of right belong to him that hath the power of the sword, by which men are compelled to observe them; for otherwise they should be made in vain.

12. And forasmuch, as the right to use the forces of every particular member, is transferred from themselves, to their sovereign, a man will easily fall upon this

conclusion of himself, that to sovereign power, whatsoever it doth, there belongeth impunity.

18. And as reason teacheth us, that a man, considered out of subjection to laws, and out of all covenants obligatory to others, is free to do and undo, and deliberate as long as he listeth, every member being obedient to the will of the whole man, that liberty being nothing else but his natural power, without which he is no better than an inanimate creature, not able to help himself; so also it teacheth us, that a body politic, of what kind soever, not subject to another, nor obliged by covenants, ought to be free, and in all actions to be assisted by the members, every one in their place, or at least, not resisted by them. For otherwise, the power of a body politic, the essence whereof is the not-resistance of the members, is none, nor a body politic of any benefit. And the same is confirmed by the use of all nations and commonwealths, wherein that man or council, which is virtually the whole, hath any absolute power over every particular member; or what nation or commonwealth is there, that hath not power and right to constitute a general in their wars? But the power of a general is absolute; and consequently there was absolute power in the commonwealth, from whom it was derived. For no person, natural or civil, can transfer unto another more power than himself hath.

19. In every commonwealth, where particular men are deprived of their right to protect themselves, there resideth an absolute sovereignty, as I have already showed. But in what man, or in what assembly of men the same is placed, is not so manifest, as not to need some marks, whereby it may be discerned. And first, it is an infallible mark of absolute sovereignty in a man, or in an assembly of men, if there be no right in any other person, natural or civil, to punish that man, or to dissolve that assembly. For he that cannot of right be punished, cannot of right be resisted; and he that cannot of right be resisted, hath coercive power over all the rest, and thereby can frame and govern their actions at his pleasure, which is absolute sovereignty. Contrariwise, he that in a commonwealth is punishable by any, or that assembly that is dissolvable, is not sovereign. For a greater power is always required to punish and dissolve, than theirs who are punished or dissolved; and that power cannot be called sovereign, than which there is a greater. Secondly, that man or assembly, that by their own right not derived from the present right of any other, may make laws, or abrogate them at his or their pleasure, have the sovereignty absolute. For seeing the laws they make, are supposed to be made by right, the members of the commonwealth, to whom they are made, are obliged to obey them, and consequently not resist the execution of them; which not-resistance, maketh the power absolute of him that ordaineth them. It is likewise a mark of this sovereignty, to have the right original of appointing magistrates, judges, counsellors, and ministers of state. For without that power, no act of sovereignty, or government, can be performed. Lastly, and generally, whosoever by his own authority independent, can do any act, which another of the same commonwealth may not, must needs be understood to have the sovereign power. For by nature men have equal right. This inequality therefore must proceed from the power of the commonwealth. He therefore that doth any act lawfully by his own authority, which another may not, doth it by the power of the commonwealth in himself, which is absolute sovereignty.

CHAPTER 2   CITIZEN AND SOVEREIGN

2. In the making of a democracy, there passeth no covenant between the sovereign, and any subject. For while the democracy is a making, there is no sovereign with whom to contract. For it cannot be imagined, that the multitude should contract with itself, or with any one man, or number of men, parcel of itself, to make itself sovereign; nor that a multitude, considered as one aggregate, can give itself anything which before it had not. Seeing then that sovereignty democratical is not conferred by the covenant of any multitude, which supposeth union and sovereignty already made, it resteth, that the same be conferred by the particular covenants of every several man; that is to say, every man with every man, for and in consideration of the benefit of his own peace and defence, covenanteth to stand to and obey whatsoever the major part of their whole number, or the major part of such a number of them, as shall be pleased to assemble at a certain time and place, shall determine and command. And this is that which giveth being to a democracy, wherein the sovereign assembly was called of the Greeks, by the name of *Demus*, that is, the people, from whence cometh democracy. So that, where to the supreme and independent court, every man may come that will, and give his vote, there the sovereign is called the people.

3. Out of this that hath been said, may readily be drawn, that whatsoever the people doth to any one particular member or subject of the commonwealth, the same by him ought not to be styled injury. For first, injury, by the definition, Part I. chap. III. sect. 2, is breach of covenant; but covenants, as hath been said in the precedent section, there passed none from the people to any private man; and consequently it, to wit, the people, can do him no injury. Secondly, how unjust soever the action be, that this sovereign *demus* shall do, is done by the will of every particular man subject to him, who are therefore guilty of the same. If therefore they style it injury, they but accuse themselves. And it is against reason for the same man, both to do and complain; implying this contradiction, that whereas he first ratified the people's acts in general, he now disalloweth the same of them in particular. It is therefore said truly *volenti non fit injuria*. Nevertheless nothing doth hinder, but that divers actions done by the people, may be unjust before God Almighty, as breaches of the laws of nature.

12. We have seen how particular men enter into subjection, by transferring their rights; it followeth to consider, how such subjection may be discharged. And first, if he or they that have the sovereign power, shall relinquish the same voluntarily, there is no doubt, but every man is again at liberty to obey, or not Likewise, if he or they retaining the sovereignty over the rest, do nevertheless exempt some one or more, from their subjection, every man so exempted, is discharged. For he or they to whom any man is obliged, hath the power to release him.

13. And here it is to be understood, that when he or they that have the sovereign power, give such exemption, or privilege, to a subject, as is not separable from the sovereignty, and nevertheless directly retaineth the sovereign power, not knowing the consequence of the privilege they grant, the person or persons exempted or privileged, are not thereby released. For in contradictory significations of the will (*Human Nature*, chap. XIII. sect. 9), that which is directly signified, is to be understood for the will, before that which is drawn from it by consequence.

14. Also exile perpetual, is a release of subjection, forasmuch, as being out of the protection of the sovereignty that expelled him, he hath no means of subsisting but from himself. Now every man may lawfully defend himself, that hath no other defence; else there had been no necessity that any man should enter into voluntary subjection, as they do in commonwealths.

15. Likewise a man is released of his subjection by conquest. For when it cometh to pass, that the power of a commonwealth is overthrown, and any particular man thereby lying under the sword of his enemy, yieldeth himself captive, he is thereby bound to serve him that taketh him, and consequently discharged of his obligation to the former. For no man can serve two masters.

16. Lastly, ignorance of the succession dischargeth obedience. For no man can be understood to be obliged to obey he knoweth not whom.

CHAPTER 5 COMMONWEALTH AND LIBERTY

1. Having set forth the nature of a Body Politic, and the three sorts thereof, democracy, aristocracy, and monarchy; in this chapter shall be declared, the *conveniences*, and *inconveniences*, that arise from the same, both in general, and of the said several sorts in particular. And first, seeing a body politic is erected only for the ruling and governing of particular men, the benefit and damage thereof, consisteth in the benefit or damage of being ruled. The benefit is that for which a body politic was instituted, namely, the peace and preservation of every particular man, than which it is not possible there can be a greater, as hath been touched before, Part I. chapter I. Section 12. And this benefit extendeth equally both to the *sovereign*, and to the *subjects*. For he or they that have the sovereign power, have but the defence of their persons, by the assistance of the particulars; and every particular man hath this defence by their union in the sovereign. As for other benefits, which pertain not to their safety and sufficiency, but to their well and delightful being, such as are superfluous riches, they so belong to the sovereign, as they must also be in the subject; and so to the subject, as they must also be in the sovereign. For the riches and treasure of the sovereign, is the dominion he hath over the riches of his subjects. If therefore the sovereign provide not so as that particular men may have means, both to preserve themselves, and also to preserve the public; the common or sovereign treasure can be none. And on the other side, if it were not for a common and public treasure belonging to the sovereign power, men's private riches would sooner serve to put them into confusion and war, than to secure and maintain them. Insomuch, as the profit of the sovereign and subject goeth always together. That distinction therefore of government, that there is one government for the good of him that governeth, and another for the good of them that be governed; whereof the former is *despotical*, that is lordly; the other, a government of *freemen*, is not right. No more is the opinion of them that hold it to be no city, which consisteth of a master and his servants. They might as well say, it were no city, that consisted in a father and his own issue, how numerous soever they were. For to a master that hath no children, the servants have in them all those respects, for which men love their children. For they are his strength and his honour. And his power is no greater over them, than over his children.

2. The inconvenience arising from government in general to him that governeth, consisteth partly in the continual care and trouble about the business of

other men, that are his subjects; and partly, in the danger of his person. For the head always is that part, not only where the care resideth, but also against which the stroke of an enemy most commonly is directed. To balance this incommodity, the sovereignty, together with the necessity of this care and danger, comprehendeth so much honour, riches, and means, whereby to delight the mind, as no private man's wealth can attain unto. The inconveniences of government in general to a subject are none at all, if well considered, but in appearance. There be two things that may trouble his mind, or two general grievances; the one is, loss of liberty; the other, the uncertainty of *meum* and *tuum*. For the first, it consisteth in this, that a subject may no more govern his own actions according to his own discretion and judgment, or, which is all one, conscience, as the present occasions from time to time shall dictate to him; but must be tied to do according to that will only, which once for all he had long ago laid up, and involved in the wills of the major part of an assembly, or in the will of some one man. But this is really no inconvenience. For, as it hath been showed before, it is the only means, by which we have any possibility of preserving ourselves. For if every man were allowed this liberty of following his conscience, in such difference of consciences, they would not live together in peace an hour. But it appeareth a great inconvenience to every man in particular, to be debarred of this liberty, because every one apart considereth it as in himself, and not as in the rest; by which means, liberty appeareth in the likeness of rule and government over others. For where one man is at liberty, and the rest bound, there that one hath government; which honour, he that understandeth not so much, demanding by the name simply of liberty, thinketh it a great grievance and injury to be denied it. For the second grievance concerning *meum* and *tuum*, it is also none, but in appearance only; it consisteth in this, that the sovereign power taketh from him that which he used to enjoy, knowing no other propriety, but use and custom. But without such sovereign power, the right of men is not propriety to anything, but a community, no better than to have no right at all, as hath been showed, Part I. chapter I. Section 10. Propriety therefore being derived from the sovereign power, is not to be pretended against the same, especially, when by it every subject hath his propriety against every other subject, which when sovereignty ceaseth, he hath not, because in that case they return to war amongst themselves. Those levies therefore which are made upon men's estates, by the sovereign authority, are no more but the price of that peace and defence which the sovereignty maintaineth for them. If this were not so, no money nor forces for the wars, nor any other public occasion, could justly be levied in the world. For neither king, nor democracy, nor aristocracy, nor the estates of any land, could do it, if the sovereignty could not. For in all those cases, it is levied by virtue of the sovereignty. Nay more, by the three estates here, the land of one man may be transferred to another, without crime of him from whom it was taken, and without pretence of public benefit, as hath been done; and this without injury, because done by the sovereign power. For the power whereby it is done, is no less than sovereign, and cannot be greater. Therefore this grievance for *meum* and *tuum* is not real, unless more be exacted than is necessary; but it seemeth a grievance, because to them that either know not the right of sovereignty, or to whom that right belongeth, it seemeth an injury; and injury, how little soever the damage, is always grievous, as putting us in mind of our disability to help ourselves, and into envy of the power to do us wrong.

John Locke

John Locke (1632–1704) was a physician by training. Through his associations he became involved with the political affairs of his time, including the Glorious Revolution. He also had a continuing interest in philosophy and spread the writing of his *Essay Concerning Human Understanding* over many years. His *Second Treatise on Civil Government* contains a detailed analysis of political questions, including the problem of authority and the issue of property. It has proven to be extremely influential in its effect on democratic political theory; indeed, to many people it appears to be just plain common sense.

Second Treatise on Civil Government

CHAPTER II   THE STATE OF NATURE

4. To understand political power aright, and derive it from its original, we must consider what estate all men are naturally in, and that is, a state of perfect freedom to order their actions, and dispose of their possessions and persons as they think fit, within the bounds of the law of Nature, without asking leave or depending upon the will of any other man.

A state also of equality, wherein all the power and jurisdiction is reciprocal, no one having more than another, there being nothing more evident than that creatures of the same species and rank, promiscuously born to all the same advantages of Nature, and the use of the same faculties, should also be equal one amongst another, without subordination or subjection, unless the lord and master of them all should, by any manifest declaration of his will, set one above another, and confer on him, by an evident and clear appointment, an undoubted right to dominion and sovereignty.

6. But though this be a state of liberty, yet it is not a state of license; though man in that state have an uncontrollable liberty to dispose of his person or possessions, yet he has not liberty to destroy himself, or so much as any creature in his possession, but where some nobler use than its bare preservation calls for it. The state of Nature has a law of Nature to govern it, which obliges everyone,

John Locke, 1690. Originally, "An Essay Concerning the True, Original, Extent and End of Civil Government." Some chapter headings have been changed by the editors.

and reason, which is that law, teaches all mankind who will but consult it, that being all equal and independent, no one ought to harm another in his life, health, liberty or possessions; for men being all the workmanship of one omnipotent and infinitely wise Maker; all the servants of one sovereign Master, sent into the world by His order and about His business; they are His property, whose workmanship they are made to last during His, not one another's pleasure. And, being furnished with like faculties, sharing all in one community of Nature, there cannot be supposed any such subordination among us that may authorize us to destroy one another, as if we were made for one another's uses, as the inferior ranks of creatures are for ours. Everyone as he is bound to preserve himself, and not to quit his station willfully, so by the like reason, when his own preservation comes not in competition, ought he as much as he can to preserve the rest of mankind, and not unless it be to do justice on an offender, take away or impair the life, or what tends to the preservation of the life, the liberty, health, limb, or goods of another.

7. And that all men may be restrained from invading others' rights, and from doing hurt to one another, and the law of Nature be observed, which willeth the peace and preservation of all mankind, the execution of the law of Nature is in that state put into every man's hands, whereby everyone has a right to punish the transgressors of that law to such a degree as may hinder its violation. For the law of Nature would, as all other laws that concern men in this world, be in vain if there were nobody that in the state of Nature had a power to execute that law, and thereby preserve the innocent and restrain offenders; and if anyone in the state of Nature may punish another for any evil he has done, everyone may do so. For in that state of perfect equality, where naturally there is no superiority or jurisdiction of one over another, what any may do in prosecution of that law, everyone must needs have a right to do.

8. And thus, in the state of Nature, one man comes by a power over another, but yet no absolute or arbitrary power to use a criminal, when he has got him in his hands, according to the passionate heats or boundless extravagancy of his own will, but only to retribute to him so far as calm reason and conscience dictate, what is proportionate to his transgression, which is so much as may serve for reparation and restraint. For these two are the only reasons why one man may lawfully do harm to another, which is that we call punishment. In transgressing the law of Nature, the offender declares himself to live by another rule than that of reason and common equity, which is that measure God has set to the actions of men for their mutual security, and so he becomes dangerous to mankind; the tie which is to secure them from injury and violence being slighted and broken by him, which being a trespass against the whole species, and the peace and safety of it, provided for by the law of Nature, every man upon this score, by the right he hath to preserve mankind in general, may restrain, or where it is necessary, destroy things noxious to them, and so may bring such evil on anyone who hath transgressed that law, as may make him repent the doing of it, and thereby deter him, and, by his example, others from doing the like mischief. And in this case, and upon this ground, every man hath a right to punish the offender, and be executioner of the law of Nature.

13. To this strange doctrine—viz., That in the state of Nature everyone has the executive power of the law of Nature—I doubt not but it will be objected

that it is unreasonable for men to be judges in their own cases, that self-love will make men partial to themselves and their friends; and, on the other side, ill-nature, passion, and revenge will carry them too far in punishing others, and hence nothing but confusion and disorder will follow, and that therefore God hath certainly appointed government to restrain the partiality and violence of men. I easily grant that civil government is the proper remedy for the inconveniences of the state of Nature, which must certainly be great where men may be judges in their own case, since it is easy to be imagined that he who was so unjust as to do his brother an injury will scarce be so just as to condemn himself for it. But I shall desire those who make this objection to remember that absolute monarchs are but men; and if government is to be the remedy of those evils which necessarily follow from men being judges in their own cases, and the state of Nature is therefore not to be endured, I desire to know what kind of government that is, and how much better it is than the state of Nature, where one man commanding a multitude has the liberty to be judge in his own case, and may do to all his subjects whatever he pleases without the least question or control of those who execute his pleasure? and in whatsoever he doth, whether led by reason, mistake, or passion, must be submitted to? which men in the state of Nature are not bound to do one to another. And if he that judges, judges amiss in his own or any other case, he is answerable for it to the rest of mankind.

14. It is often asked as a mighty objection, where are, or ever were, there any men in such a state of Nature? To which it may suffice as an answer at present, that since all princes and rulers of "independent" governments all through the world are in a state of Nature, it is plain the world never was, nor never will be, without numbers of men in that state. I have named all governors of "independent" communities, whether they are, or are not, in league with others; for it is not every compact that puts an end to the state of Nature between men, but only this one of agreeing together mutually to enter into one community, and make one body politic; other promises and compacts men may make one with another, and yet still be in the state of Nature. The promises and bargains for truck, etc., between the two men in Soldania, in or between a Swiss and an Indian, in the woods of America, are binding to them, though they are perfectly in a state of Nature in reference to one another for truth, and keeping of faith belongs to men as men, and not as members of society.

15. To those that say there were never any men in the state of Nature, I will not only oppose the authority of the judicious Hooker (*Eccl. Pol.* i. 10), where he says, "the laws which have been hitherto mentioned"—i.e., the laws of Nature—"do bind men absolutely, even as they are men, although they have never any settled fellowship, never any solemn agreement amongst themselves what to do or not to do; but for as much as we are not by ourselves sufficient to furnish ourselves with competent store of things needful for such a life as our Nature doth desire, a life fit for the dignity of man, therefore to supply those defects and imperfections which are in us, as living single and solely by ourselves, we are naturally induced to seek communion and fellowship with others; this was the cause of men uniting themselves at first in politic societies." But I, moreover, affirm that all men are naturally in that state, and remain so till, by their own consents, they make themselves members of some politic society, and I doubt not, in the sequel of this discourse, to make it very clear.

CHAPTER III   OF THE STATE OF WAR

16. The state of war is a state of enmity and destruction; and therefore declaring by word or action, not a passionate and hasty, but sedate, settled design upon another man's life puts him in a state of war with him against whom he has declared such an intention, and so has exposed his life to the other's power to be taken away by him, or anyone that joins with him in his defense, and espouses his quarrel; it being reasonable and just I should have a right to destroy that which threatens me with destruction; for by the fundamental law of Nature, man being to be preserved as much as possible, when all cannot be preserved, the safety of the innocent is to be preferred, and one may destroy a man who makes war upon him, or has discovered an enmity to his being, for the same reason that he may kill a wolf or a lion, because they are not under the ties of the common law of reason, have no other rule but that of force and violence, and so may be treated as a beast of prey, those dangerous and noxious creatures that will be sure to destroy him whenever he falls into their power.

17. And hence it is that he who attempts to get another man into his absolute power does thereby put himself into a state of war with him; it being to be understood as a declaration of a design upon his life. For I have reason to conclude that he who would get me into his power without my consent would use me as he pleased when he had got me there, and destroy me too when he had a fancy to it; for nobody can desire to have me in his absolute power unless it be to compel me by force to that which is against the right of my freedom—i.e., make me a slave. To be free from such force is the only security of my preservation, and reason bids me look on him as an enemy to my preservation who would take away that freedom which is the fence to it; so that he who makes an attempt to enslave me thereby puts himself into a state of war with me. He that in the state of Nature would take away the freedom that belongs to anyone in that state must necessarily be supposed to have a design to take away everything else, that freedom being the foundation of all the rest; as he that in the state of society would take away the freedom belonging to those of that society or commonwealth must be supposed to design to take away from them everything else, and so be looked on as in a state of war.

18. This makes it lawful for a man to kill a thief who has not in the least hurt him, or declared any design upon his life, any farther than by the use of force, so to get him in his power as to take away his money, or what he pleases, from him; because using force, where he has no right to get me into his power, let his pretense be what it will, I have no reason to suppose that he who would take away my liberty would not, when he had me in his power, take away everything else. And, therefore, it is lawful for me to treat him as one who has put himself into a state of war with me—i.e., kill him if I can; for to that hazard does he justly expose himself whoever introduces a state of war, and is aggressor in it.

19. And here we have the plain difference between the state of Nature and the state of war, which however some men have confounded, are as far distant as a state of peace, goodwill, mutual assistance, and preservation; and a state of enmity, malice, violence and mutual destruction are one from another. Men living together according to reason with a common superior on earth, with authority to judge between them, is properly the state of Nature. But force, or a declared design of force upon the person of another, where there is no common

superior on earth to appeal to for relief, is the state of war; and it is the want of such an appeal gives a man the right of war even against an aggressor, though he be in society and a fellow-subject. Thus, a thief whom I cannot harm, but by appeal to the law, for having stolen all that I am worth, I may kill when he sets on me to rob me but of my horse or coat, because the law, which was made for my preservation, where it cannot interpose to secure my life from present force, which if lost is capable of no reparation, permits me my own defense and the right of war, a liberty to kill the aggressor, because the aggressor allows not time to appeal to our common judge, nor the decision of the law, for remedy in a case where the mischief may be irreparable. Want of a common judge with authority puts all men in a state of Nature; force without right upon a man's person makes a state of war both where there is, and is not, a common judge.

20. But when the actual force is over, the state of war ceases between those that are in society and are equally on both sides subject to the judge; and, therefore, in such controversies, where the question is put, "Who shall be judge?" it cannot be meant who shall decide the controversy; everyone knows what Jephtha here tells us, that "the Lord the Judge" shall judge. Where there is no judge on earth the appeal lies to God in Heaven. That question then cannot mean who shall judge, whether another hath put himself in a state of war with me, and whether I may, as Jephtha did, appeal to Heaven in it? Of that I myself can only judge in my own conscience, as I will answer it at the great day to the Supreme Judge of all men.

CHAPTER IV   OF SLAVERY

21. The natural liberty of man is to be free from any superior power on earth, and not to be under the will or legislative authority of man, but to have only the law of Nature for his rule. The liberty of man in society is to be under no other legislative power but that established by consent in the commonwealth, nor under the dominion of any will, or restraint of any law, but what the legislative shall enact according to the trust put in it. Freedom, then, is not what Sir Robert Filmer tells us: "A liberty for everyone to do what he lists, to live as he pleases, and not to be tied by any laws"; but freedom of men under government is to have a standing rule to live by, common to everyone of that society, and made by the legislative power erected in it. A liberty to follow my own will in all things where that rule prescribes not, not to be subject to the inconstant, uncertain, unknown, arbitrary will of another man, as freedom of nature is to be under no other restraint but the law of Nature.

22. This freedom from absolute, arbitrary power is so necessary to, and closely joined with, a man's preservation, that he cannot part with it but by what forfeits his preservation and life together. For a man, not having the power of his own life, cannot by compact or his own consent enslave himself to anyone, nor put himself under the absolute, arbitrary power of another to take away his life when he pleases. Nobody can give more power than he has himself, and he that cannot take away his own life cannot give another power over it. Indeed, having by his fault forfeited his own life by some act that deserves death, he to whom he has forfeited it may, when he has him in his power, delay to take it, and make use of him to his own service; and he does him no injury by

it. For, whenever he finds the hardship of his slavery outweigh the value of his life, it is in his power, by resisting the will of his master, to draw on himself the death he desires.

23. This is the perfect condition of slavery, which is nothing else but the state of war continued between a lawful conqueror and a captive, for if once compact enter between them, and make an agreement for a limited power on the one side, and obedience on the other, the state of war and slavery ceases as long as the compact endures; for, as has been said, no man can by agreement pass over to another that which he hath not in himself—a power over his own life. . . .

CHAPTER V   OF PROPERTY

25. God, who hath given the world to men in common, hath also given them reason to make use of it to the best advantage of life and convenience. The earth and all that is therein is given to men for the support and comfort of their being. And though all the fruits it naturally produces, and beasts it feeds, belong to mankind in common, as they are produced by the spontaneous hand of Nature, and nobody has originally a private dominion exclusive of the rest of mankind in any of them, as they are thus in their natural state, yet being given for the use of men, there must of necessity be a means to appropriate them some way or other before they can be of any use, or at all beneficial, to any particular men. The fruit or venison which nourishes the wild Indian, who knows no enclosure, and is still a tenant in common, must be his, and so his—i.e., a part of him, that another can no longer have any right to it before it can do him any good for the support of his life.

26. Though the earth and all inferior creatures be common to all men, yet every man has a "property" in his own "person." This nobody has any right to but himself. The "labor" of his body and the "work" of his hands, we may say, are properly his. Whatsoever, then, he removes out of the state that Nature hath provided and left it in, he hath mixed his labor with it, and joined to it something that is his own, and thereby makes it his property. It being by him removed from the common state Nature placed it in, it hath by this labor something annexed to it that excludes the common right of other men. For this "labor" being the unquestionable property of the laborer, no man but he can have a right to what that is once joined to, at least where there is enough, and as good left in common for others.

27. He that is nourished by the acorns he picked up under an oak, or the apples he gathered from the trees in the wood, has certainly appropriated them to himself. Nobody can deny but the nourishment is his. I ask, then, when did they begin to be his? when he digested? or when he ate? or when he boiled? or when he brought them home? or when he picked them up? And it is plain, if the first gathering made them not his, nothing else could. That labor put a distinction between them and common. That added something to them more than Nature, the common mother of all, had done, and so they became his private right. And will anyone say he had no right to those acorns or apples he thus appropriated because he had not the consent of all mankind to make them his? Was it a robbery thus to assume to himself what belonged to all in common? If such a consent as that was necessary, man had starved, notwithstanding the

plenty God had given him. We see in commons, which remain so by compact, that it is the taking any part of what is common, and removing it out of the state Nature leaves it in, which begins the property, without which the common is of no use. And the taking of this or that part does not depend on the express consent of all the commoners. Thus, the grass my horse has bit, the turfs my servant has cut, and the ore I have digged in any place, where I have a right to them in common with others, become my property without the assignation or consent of anybody. The labor that was mine, removing them out of that common state they were in, hath fixed my property in them.

28. By making an explicit consent of every commoner necessary to anyone's appropriating to himself any part of what is given in common, children or servants could not cut the meat which their father or master had provided for them in common without assigning to everyone his peculiar part. Though the water running in the fountain be everyone's, yet who can doubt but that in the pitcher is his only who drew it out? His labor hath taken it out of the hands of Nature where it was common, and belonged equally to all her children, and hath thereby appropriated it to himself.

30. It will, perhaps, be objected to this, that if gathering the acorns or other fruits of the earth, etc., makes a right to them, then anyone may engross as much as he will. To which I answer, Not so. The same law of Nature that does by this means give us property, does also bound that property too. "God has given us all things richly." Is the voice of reason confirmed by inspiration? But how far has He given it us "to enjoy"? As much as anyone can make use of to any advantage of life before it spoils, so much he may by his labor fix a property in. Whatever is beyond this is more than his share, and belongs to others. Nothing was made by God for man to spoil or destroy. And thus considering the plenty of natural provisions there was a long time in the world, and the few spenders, and to how small a part of that provision the industry of one man could extend itself and engross it to the prejudice of others, especially keeping within the bounds set by reason of what might serve for his use, there could be then little room for quarrels or contentions about property so established.

31. But the chief matter of property being now not the fruits of the earth and the beasts that subsist on it, but the earth itself, as that which takes in and carries with it all the rest, I think it is plain that property in that too is acquired as the former. As much land as a man tills, plants, improves, cultivates, and can use the product of, so much is his property. He by his labor does, as it were, enclose it from the common. Nor will it invalidate his right to say everybody else has an equal title to it, and therefore he cannot appropriate, he cannot enclose, without the consent of all his fellow-commoners, all mankind. God, when He gave the world in common to all mankind, commanded man also to labor, and the penury of his condition required it of him. God and his reason commanded him to subdue the earth—i.e., improve it for the benefit of life and therein lay out something upon it that was his own, his labor. He that, in obedience to this command of God, subdued, tilled, and sowed any part of it, thereby annexed to it something that was his property, which another had no title to, nor could without injury take from him.

32. Nor was this appropriation of any parcel of land, by improving it, any prejudice to any other man, since there was still enough and as good left, and more than the yet unprovided could use. So that, in effect, there was never the

less left for others because of his enclosure for himself. For he that leaves as much as another can make use of does as good as take nothing at all. Nobody could think himself injured by the drinking of another man, though he took a good draught, who had a whole river of the same water left him to quench his thirst. And the case of land and water, where there is enough of both, is perfectly the same.

33. God gave the world to men in common, but since He gave it them for their benefit and the greatest conveniencies of life they were capable to draw from it, it cannot be supposed He meant it should always remain common and uncultivated. He gave it to the use of the industrious and rational (and labor was to be his title to it); not to the fancy or covetousness of the quarrelsome and contentious. He that had as good left for his improvement as was already taken up needed not complain, ought not to meddle with what was already improved by another's labor; if he did it is plain he desired the benefit of another's pains, which he had no right to, and not the ground which God had given him, in common with others, to labor on, and whereof there was as good left as that already possessed, and more than he knew what to do with, or his industry could reach to.

35. The measure of property Nature well set, by the extent of men's labor and the conveniency of life. No man's labor could subdue or appropriate all, nor could his enjoyment consume more than a small part; so that it was impossible for any man, this way, to entrench upon the right of another or acquire to himself a property to the prejudice of his neighbor, who would still have room for as good and as large a possession (after the other had taken out his) as before it was appropriated. Which measure did confine every man's possession to a very moderate proportion, and such as he might appropriate to himself without injury to anybody in the first ages of the world, when men were more in danger to be lost, by wandering from their company, in the then vast wilderness of the earth than to be straitened for want of room to plant in.

36. The same measure may be allowed still, without prejudice to anybody, full as the world seems. . . . Nay, the extent of ground is of so little value without labor that I have heard it affirmed that in Spain itself a man may be permitted to plow, sow, and reap, without being disturbed, upon land he has no other title to, but only his making use of it. But, on the contrary, the inhabitants think themselves beholden to him who, by his industry on neglected, and consequently waste land, has increased the stock of corn, which they wanted. But be this as it will, which I lay no stress on, this I dare boldly affirm, that the same rule of propriety—viz., that every man should have as much as he could make use of, would hold still in the world, without straitening anybody, since there is land enough in the world to suffice double the inhabitants, had not the invention of money, and the tacit agreement of men to put a value on it, introduced (by consent) larger possessions and a right to them. . . .

37. This is certain, that in the beginning, before the desire of having more than men needed had altered the intrinsic value of things, which depends only on their usefulness to the life of man, or had agreed that a little piece of yellow metal, which would keep without wasting or decay, should be worth a great piece of flesh or a whole heap of corn, though men had a right to appropriate by their labor, each one to himself, as much of the things of Nature as he could use, yet this could not be much, nor to the prejudice of others, where the same plenty was still left, to those who would use the same industry.

Before the appropriation of land, he who gathered as much of the wild fruit, killed, caught, or tamed as many of the beasts as he could—he that so employed his pains about any of the spontaneous products of Nature as any way to alter them from the state Nature put them in, by placing any of his labor on them, did thereby acquire a propriety in them; but if they perished in his possession without their due use—if the fruits rotted or the venison putrefied before he could spend it, he offended against the common law of Nature, and was liable to be punished: he invaded his neighbor's share, for he had no right farther than his use called for any of them, and they might serve to afford him conveniencies of life.

38. The same measures governed the possession of land, too. Whatsoever he tilled and reaped, laid up and made use of before it spoiled, that was his peculiar right; whatsoever he enclosed, and could feed and make use of, the cattle and product was also his. But if either the grass of his enclosure rotted on the ground, or the fruit of his planting perished without gathering and laying up, this part of the earth, notwithstanding his enclosure, was still to be looked on as waste, and might be the possession of any other. Thus, at the beginning, Cain might take as much ground as he could till and make it his own land, and yet leave enough to Abel's sheep to feed on: a few acres would serve for both their possessions. But as families increased and industry enlarged their stocks, their possessions enlarged with the need of them; but yet it was commonly without any fixed property in the ground they made use of till they incorporated, settled themselves together, and built cities, and then, by consent, they came in time to set out the bounds of their distinct territories and agree on limits between them and their neighbors, and by laws within themselves settled the properties of those of the same society. For we see that in that part of the world which was first inhabited, and therefore like to be best peopled, even as low down as Abraham's time, they wandered with their flocks and their herds, which was their substance, freely up and down—and this Abraham did in a country where he was a stranger; whence it is plain that, at least, a great part of the land lay in common, that the inhabitants valued it not, nor claimed property in any more than they made use of; but when there was not room enough in the same place for their herds to feed together, they, by consent, as Abraham and Lot did (Gen. xiii. 5), separated and enlarged their pasture where it best liked them. And for the same reason, Esau went from his father and his brother, and planted in Mount Seir (Gen. xxxvi. 6).

39. And thus, without supposing any private dominion and property in Adam over all the world, exclusive of all other men, which can no way be proved, nor anyone's property be made out from it, but supposing the world, given as it was to the children of men in common, we see how labor could make men distinct titles to several parcels of it for their private uses, wherein there could be no doubt of right, no room for quarrel.

40. Nor is it so strange as, perhaps, before consideration, it may appear, that the property of labor should be able to overbalance the community of land, for it is labor indeed that puts the difference of value on everything; and let anyone consider what the difference is between an acre of land planted with tobacco or sugar, sown with wheat or barley, and an acre of the same land lying in common without any husbandry upon it, and he will find that the improvement of labor makes the far greater part of the value. I think it will be but a very modest computation to say, that of the products of the earth useful to the life of man,

nine-tenths are the effects of labor. Nay, if we will rightly estimate things as they come to our use, and cast up the several expenses about them—what in them is purely owing to Nature and what to labor—we shall find that in most of them ninety-nine hundredths are wholly to be put on the account of labor.

44. From all which it is evident, that though the things of Nature are given in common, man (by being master of himself, and proprietor of his own person, and the actions or labor of it) had still in himself the great foundation of property; and that which made up the great part of what he applied to the support or comfort of his being, when invention and arts had improved the conveniences of life, was perfectly his own, and did not belong in common to others.

46. The greatest part of things really useful to the life of man, and such as the necessity of subsisting made the first commoners of the world look after—as it doth the Americans now—are generally things of short duration, such as—if they are not consumed by use—will decay and perish of themselves. Gold, silver, and diamonds are things that fancy or agreement hath put the value on, more than real use and the necessary support of life. Now of those good things which Nature hath provided in common, everyone has a right (as has been said) to as much as he could use, and had a property in all he could effect with his labor; all that his industry could extend to, to alter from the state Nature had put it in, was his. He that gathered a hundred bushels of acorns or apples had thereby a property in them; they were his goods as soon as gathered. He was only to look that he used them before they spoiled, else he took more than his share, and robbed others. And, indeed, it was a foolish thing, as well as dishonest, to hoard up more than he could make use of. If he gave away a part to anybody else, so that it perished not uselessly in his possession, these he also made use of. And if he also bartered away plums that would have rotten in a week, for nuts that would last good for his eating a whole year, he did no injury; he wasted not the common stock; destroyed no part of the portion of goods that belonged to others, so long as nothing perished uselessly in his hands. Again, if he would give his nuts for a piece of metal, pleased with its color, or exchange his sheep for shells, or wool for a sparkling pebble or a diamond, and keep those by him all his life, he invaded not the right of others; he might heap up as much of these durable things as he pleased; the exceeding of the bounds of his just property not lying in the largeness of his possession, but the perishing of anything uselessly in it.

47. And thus came in the use of money; some lasting thing that men might keep without spoiling, and that, by mutual consent, men would take in exchange for the truly useful but perishable supports of life.

48. And as different degrees of industry were apt to give men possessions in different proportions, so this invention of money gave them the opportunity to continue and enlarge them. For supposing an island, separate from all possible commerce with the rest of the world, wherein there were but a hundred families, but there were sheep, horses, and cows, with other useful animals, wholesome fruits, and land enough for corn for a hundred thousand times as many, but nothing in the island, either because of its commonness or perishableness, fit to supply the place of money. What reason could anyone have there to enlarge his possessions beyond the use of his family, and a plentiful supply to its consumption, either in what their own industry produced, or they could barter for like

perishable, useful commodities with others? Where there is not something both lasting and scarce, and so valuable to be hoarded up, there men will not be apt to enlarge their possessions of land, were it never so rich, never so free for them to take. For I ask, what would a man value ten thousand or a hundred thousand acres of excellent land, ready cultivated and well stocked, too, with cattle, in the middle of the inland parts of America, where he had no hopes of commerce with other parts of the world, to draw money to him by the sale of the product? It would not be worth the enclosing, and we should see him give up again to the wild common of Nature whatever was more than would supply the conveniences of life, to be had there for him and his family.

50. But since gold and silver, being little useful to the life of man, in proportion to food, raiment, and carriage, has its value only from the consent of men—whereof labor yet makes in great part the measure—it is plain that the consent of men have agreed to a disproportionate and unequal possession of the earth— I mean out of the bounds of society and compact; for in governments the laws regulate it; they having, by consent, found out and agreed in a way how a man may, rightfully and without injury, possess more than he himself can make use of by receiving gold and silver, which may continue long in a man's possession without decaying for the overplus, and agreeing those metals should have a value.

51. And thus, I think, it is very easy to conceive, without any difficulty, how labor could at first begin a title of property in the common things of Nature, and how the spending it upon our uses bounded it; so that there could then be no reason of quarreling about title, nor any doubt about the largeness of possession it gave. Right and conveniency went together. For as a man had a right to all he could employ his labor upon, so he had no temptation to labor for more than he could make use of. This left no room for controversy about the title, nor for encroachment on the right of others. What portion a man carved to himself was easily seen; and it was useless, as well as dishonest, to carve himself too much, or take more than he needed.

CHAPTER VI LAW AND AUTHORITY

57. The law that was to govern Adam was the same that was to govern all his posterity, the law of reason. But his offspring having another way of entrance into the world, different from him, by a natural birth, that produced them ignorant, and without the use of reason, they were not presently under that law. For nobody can be under a law that is not promulgated to him; and this law being promulgated or made known by reason only, he that is not come to the use of his reason cannot be said to be under this law; and Adam's children being not presently as soon as born under this law of reason, were not presently free. For law, in its true notion, is not so much the limitation as the direction of a free and intelligent agent to his proper interest, and prescribes no farther than is for the general good of those under that law. Could they be happier without it, the law, as a useless thing would of itself vanish; and that ill deserves the name of confinement which hedges us in only from bogs and precipices. So that however it may be mistaken, the end of law is not to abolish or restrain, but to preserve and enlarge freedom. For in all the states of created beings, capable of laws,

where there is no law there is no freedom. For liberty is to be free from restraint and violence from others, which cannot be where there is no law; and is not, as we are told, "a liberty for every man to do what he lists." For who could be free, when every other man's humor might domineer over him? But a liberty to dispose and order freely as he lists his person, actions, possessions, and his whole property within the allowance of those laws under which he is, and therein not to be subject to the arbitrary will of another, but freely follow his own.

58. The power, then, that parents have over their children arises from that duty which is incumbent on them, to take care of their offspring during the imperfect state of childhood. To inform the mind, and govern the actions of their yet ignorant nonage, till reason shall take its place and ease them of that trouble, is what the children want, and the parents are bound to. For God having given man an understanding to direct his actions, has allowed him a freedom of will and liberty of acting, as properly belonging thereunto within the bounds of that law he is under. But whilst he is in an estate wherein he has no understanding of his own to direct his will, he is not to have any will of his own to follow. He that understands for him must will for him too; he must prescribe to his will, and regulate his actions, but when he comes to the estate that made his father a free man, the son is a free man too.

59. This holds in all the laws a man is under, whether natural or civil. Is a man under the law of Nature? What made him free of that law? What gave him a free disposing of his property, according to his own will, within the compass of that law? I answer, an estate wherein he might be supposed capable to know that law, that so he might keep his actions within the bounds of it. When he has acquired that state, he is presumed to know how far that law is to be his guide, and how far he may make use of his freedom, and so comes to have it; till then, somebody else must guide him, who is presumed to know how far the law allows a liberty. If such a state of reason, such an age of discretion made him free, the same shall make his son free too. Is a man under the law of England? What made him free of that law—that is, to have the liberty to dispose of his actions and possessions, according to his own will, within the permission of that law? A capacity of knowing that law. Which is supposed, by that law, at the age of twenty-one, and in some cases sooner. If this made the father free, it shall make the son free too. Till then, we see the law allows the son to have no will, but he is to be guided by the will of his father or guardian, who is to understand for him. And if the father die and fail to substitute a deputy in this trust, if he hath not provided a tutor to govern his son during his minority, during his want of understanding, the law takes care to do it: some other must govern him and be a will to him till he has attained to a state of freedom, and his understanding be fit to take the government of his will. But after that the father and son are equally free, as much as tutor and pupil, after nonage, equally subjects of the same law together, without any dominion left in the father over the life, liberty, or estate of his son, whether they be only in the state and under the law of Nature, or under the positive laws of an established government.

60. But if through defects that may happen out of the ordinary course of Nature, anyone comes not to such a degree of reason wherein he might be supposed capable of knowing the law, and so living within the rules of it, he is never capable of being a free man, he is never let loose to the disposure of his own will; because he knows no bounds to it, has not understanding, its proper

guide, but is continued under the tuition and government of others all the time his own understanding is incapable of that charge. And so lunatics and idiots are never set free from the government of their parents. . . .

61. Thus we are born free as we are born rational; not that we have actually the exercise of either: age that brings one, brings with it the other too. And thus we see how natural freedom and subjection to parents may consist together, and are both founded on the same principle. A child is free by his father's title, by his father's understanding, which is to govern him till he hath it of his own. . . .

63. The freedom then of man, and liberty of acting according to his own will, is grounded on his having reason, which is able to instruct him in that law he is to govern himself by, and make him know how far he is left to the freedom of his own will. To turn him loose to an unrestrained liberty, before he has reason to guide him, is not the allowing him the privilege of his nature to be free, but to thrust him out amongst brutes, and abandon him to a state as wretched and as much beneath that of a man as theirs. This is that which puts the authority into the parents' hands to govern the minority of their children. God has made it their business to employ this care on their offspring, and has placed in them suitable inclinations of tenderness and concern to temper this power, to apply it as His wisdom designed it, to the children's good as long as they should need to be under it.

CHAPTER VII   OF POLITICAL OR CIVIL SOCIETY

77. God, having made man such a creature that, in His own judgment, it was not good for him to be alone, put him under strong obligations of necessity, convenience, and inclination, to drive him into society, as well as fitted him with understanding and language to continue and enjoy it. The first society was between man and wife, which gave beginning to that between parents and children, to which, in time, that between master and servant came to be added. . . .

85. Master and servant are names as old as history, but given to those of far different condition; for a free man makes himself a servant to another by selling him for a certain time the service he undertakes to do in exchange for wages he is to receive; and though this commonly puts him into the family of his master, and under the ordinary discipline thereof, yet it gives the master but a temporary power over him, and no greater than what is contained in the contract between them. But there is another sort of servant which by a peculiar name we call slaves, who being captives taken in a just war are, by the right of Nature, subjected to the absolute dominion and arbitrary power of their masters. These men having, as I say, forfeited their lives and, with it, their liberties, and lost their estates, and being in the state of slavery, not capable of any property, cannot in that state be considered as any part of civil society, the chief end whereof is the preservation of property.

87. Man being born, as has been proved, with a title to perfect freedom and an uncontrolled enjoyment of all the rights and privileges of the law of Nature, equally with any other man, or number of men in the world, has by nature a power not only to preserve his property—that is, his life, liberty, and estate, against the injuries and attempts of other men, but to judge of and punish the

breaches of that law in others, as he is persuaded the offense deserves, even with death itself, in crimes where the heinousness of the fact, in his opinion, requires it. But because no political society can be, nor subsist, without having in itself the power to preserve the property, and in order thereunto punish the offenses of all those of that society, there, and there only, is political society where every one of the members has quitted this natural power, resigned it up into the hands of the community in all cases that exclude him not from appealing for protection to the law established by it. And thus all private judgment of every particular member being excluded, the community comes to be umpire, and by understanding indifferent rules and men authorized by the community for their execution, decides all the differences that may happen between any members of that society concerning any matter of right, and punishes those offenses which any member hath committed against the society with such penalties as the law has established; whereby it is easy to discern who are, and are not, in political society together. Those who are united into one body, and have a common established law and judicature to appeal to, with authority to decide controversies between them and punish offenders, are in civil society one with another; but those who have no such common appeal, I mean on earth, are still in the state of Nature, each being where there is no other, judge for himself and executioner; which is, as I have before showed it, the perfect state of Nature.

88. And thus the commonwealth comes by a power to set down what punishment shall belong to the several transgressions they think worthy of it, committed amongst the members of that society (which is the power of making laws), as well as it has the power to punish any injury done unto any of its members by anyone that is not of it (which is the power of war and peace); and all this for the preservation of the property of all the members of that society, as far as is possible. But though every man entered into society has quitted his power to punish offenses against the law of Nature in prosecution of his own private judgment, yet with the judgment of offenses which he has given up to the legislative, in all cases where he can appeal to the magistrate, he has given up a right to the commonwealth to employ his force for the execution of the judgments of the commonwealth whenever he shall be called to it, which, indeed, are his own judgments, they being made by himself or his representative. And herein we have the original of the legislative and executive power of civil society, which is to judge by standing laws how far offenses are to be punished when committed within the commonwealth; and also by occasional judgments founded on the present circumstances of the fact, how far injuries from without are to be vindicated, and in both these be employ all the force of all the members when there shall be need.

89. Wherever, therefore, any number of men so unite into one society as to quit every one his executive power of the law of Nature, and to resign it to the public, there and there only is a political or civil society. And this is done wherever any number of men, in the state of Nature, enter into society to make one people one body politic under one supreme government: or else when anyone joins himself to, and incorporates with any government already made. For hereby he authorizes the society, or which is all one, the legislative thereof, to make laws for him as the public good of the society shall require, to the execution whereof his own assistance (as to his own decrees) is due. And this puts men out of a state of Nature into that of a commonwealth, by setting up a

judge on earth with authority to determine all the controversies and redress the injuries that may happen to any member of the commonwealth, which judge is the legislative or magistrates appointed by it. And wherever there are any number of men, however associated, that have no such decisive power to appeal to, there they are still in the state of Nature.

90. And hence it is evident that absolute monarchy, which by some men is counted for the only government in the world, is indeed inconsistent with civil society, and so can be no form of civil government at all. For the end of civil society being to avoid and remedy those inconveniencies of the state of Nature which necessarily follow from every man's being judge in his own case, by setting up a known authority to which every one of that society may appeal upon any injury received, or controversy that may arise, and which every one of the society ought to obey. Wherever any persons are who have not such an authority to appeal to, and decide any difference between them there, those persons are still in the state of Nature. And so is every absolute prince in respect of those who are under his dominion.

91. For he being supposed to have all, both legislative and executive, power in himself alone, there is no judge to be found, no appeal lies open to anyone, who may fairly and indifferently, and with authority decide, and from whence relief and redress may be expected of any injury or inconveniency that may be suffered from him, or by his order. . . . For wherever any two men are, who have no standing rule and common judge to appeal to on earth, for the determination of controversies of right betwixt them, there they are still in the state of Nature, and under all the inconveniencies of it, with only this woeful difference to the subject, or rather slave of an absolute prince.

CHAPTER VIII OF THE BEGINNING OF POLITICAL SOCIETIES

96. . . . When any number of men have, by the consent of every individual, made a community, they have thereby made that community one body, with a power to act as one body, which is only by the will and determination of the majority. For that which acts any community, being only the consent of the individuals of it, and it being one body, must move one way, it is necessary the body should move that way whither the greater force carries it, which is the consent of the majority, or else it is impossible it should act or continue one body, one community, which the consent of every individual that united into it agreed that it should; and so everyone is bound by that consent to be concluded by the majority. And therefore we see that in assemblies empowered to act by positive laws where no number is set by that positive law which empowers them, the act of the majority passes for the act of the whole, and of course determines as having, by the law of Nature and reason, the power of the whole.

97. And thus every man, by consenting with others to make one body politic under one government, puts himself under an obligation to everyone of that society to submit to the determination of the majority, and to be concluded by it; or else this original compact, whereby he with others incorporates into one society, would signify nothing, and be no compact if he be left free and under no other ties than he was in before in the state of Nature. For what appearance would there be of any compact? What new engagement if he were no farther tied

by any decrees of the society than he himself thought fit and did actually consent to? This would be still as great a liberty as he himself had before his compact, or anyone else in the state of Nature, who may submit himself and consent to any acts of it if he thinks fit.[1]

119. Every man being, as has been showed, naturally free, and nothing being able to put him into subjection to any earthly power, but only his own consent, it is to be considered what shall be understood to be a sufficient declaration of a man's consent to make him subject to the laws of any government. There is a common distinction of an express and a tacit consent, which will concern our present case. Nobody doubts but an express consent of any man, entering into any society, makes him a perfect member of that society, a subject of that government. The difficulty is, what ought to be looked upon as a tacit consent, and how far it binds—i.e., how far anyone shall be looked on to have consented, and thereby submitted to any government, where he has made no expressions of it at all. And to this I say, that every man that hath any possession or enjoyment of any part of the dominions of any government doth hereby give his tacit consent, and is as far forth obliged to obedience to the laws of that government, during such enjoyment, as anyone under it, whether this his possession be of land to him and his heirs forever, or a lodging only for a week; or whether it be barely traveling freely on the highway; and, in effect, it reaches as far as the very being of anyone within the territories of that government.

CHAPTER IX   OF THE ENDS OF POLITICAL SOCIETY AND GOVERNMENT

123. If man in the state of Nature be so free as has been said, if he be absolute lord of his own person and possessions, equal to the greatest and subject to nobody, why will he part with his freedom, this empire, and subject himself to the dominion and control of any other power? To which it is obvious to answer, that though in the state of Nature he has such a right, yet the enjoyment of it is very uncertain and constantly exposed to the invasion of others; for all being kings as much as he, every man his equal, and the greater part no strict observers of equity and justice, the enjoyment of the property he has in this state is very unsafe, very insecure. This makes him willing to quit this condition which, however free, is full of fears and continual dangers; and it is not without reason that he seeks out and is willing to join in society with others who are already united, or have a mind to unite for the mutual preservation of their lives, liberties and estates, which I call by the general name—property.

124. The great and chief end, therefore, of men uniting into commonwealths, and putting themselves under government, is the preservation of their property; to which in the state of Nature there are many things wanting.

Firstly, there wants an established, settled, known law, received and allowed by common consent to be the standard of right and wrong, and the common measure to decide all controversies between them. For though the law of Nature be plain and intelligible to all rational creatures, yet men, being biased by their

---

[1] "The public power of all society is above every soul contained in the same society, and the principal use of that power is to give laws unto all that are under it, which laws in such cases we must obey, unless there be reason showed which may necessarily enforce that the law of reason or of God doth enjoin the contrary."—Hooker, *Eccl. Pol.*, lib. i., s. 16.

interest, as well as ignorant for want of study of it, are not apt to allow of it as a law binding to them in the application of it to their particular cases.

125. Secondly, in the state of Nature there wants a known and indifferent judge, with authority to determine all differences according to the established law. For everyone in that state being both judge and executioner of the law of Nature, men being partial to themselves, passion and revenge is very apt to carry them too far, and with too much heat in their own cases, as well as negligence and unconcernedness, make them too remiss in other men's.

126. Thirdly, in the state of Nature there often wants power to back and support the sentence when right, and to give it due execution. They who by any injustice offended will seldom fail where they are able by force to make good their injustice. Such resistance many times makes the punishment dangerous, and frequently destructive to those who attempt it.

127. Thus mankind, notwithstanding all the privileges of the state of Nature, being but in an ill condition while they remain in it are quickly driven into society. Hence it comes to pass, that we seldom find any number of men live any time together in this state. The inconveniences that they are therein exposed to by the irregular and uncertain exercise of the power every man has of punishing the transgressions of others, make them take sanctuary under the established laws of government, and therein seek the preservation of their property. It is this makes them so willingly give up everyone his single power of punishing to be exercised by such alone as shall be appointed to it amongst them, and by such rules as the community, or those authorized by them to that purpose, shall agree on. And in this we have the original right and rise of both the legislative and executive power as well as of the governments and societies themselves.

131. But though men when they enter into society give up the equality, liberty, and executive power they had in the state of Nature into the hands of the society, to be so far disposed of by the legislative as the good of the society shall require, yet it being only with an intention in everyone the better to preserve himself, his liberty and property (for no rational creature can be supposed to change his condition with an intention to be worse), the power of the society or legislative constituted by them can never be supposed to extend farther than the common good, but is obliged to secure everyone's property by providing against those three defects above mentioned that made the state of Nature so unsafe and uneasy. And so, whoever has the legislative or supreme power of any commonwealth, is bound to govern by established standing laws, promulgated and known to the people, and not by extemporary decrees, by indifferent and upright judges, who are to decide controversies by those laws; and to employ the force of the community at home only in the execution of such laws, or abroad to prevent or redress foreign injuries and secure the community from inroads and invasion. And all this to be directed to no other end but the peace, safety, and public good of the people.

CHAPTER XI   OF THE EXTENT OF THE LEGISLATIVE POWER

134. The great end of men's entering into society being the enjoyment of their properties in peace and safety, and the great instrument and means of that being the laws established in that society, the first and fundamental positive law of all commonwealths is the establishing of the legislative power, as the first and

fundamental natural law which is to govern even the legislative. Itself is the preservation of the society and (as far as will consist with the public good) of every person in it. This legislative is not only the supreme power of the commonwealth, but sacred and unalterable in the hands where the community have once placed it. Nor can any edict of anybody else, in what form soever conceived, or by what power soever backed, have the force and obligation of a law which has not its sanction from that legislative which the public has chosen and appointed; for without this the law could not have that which is absolutely necessary to its being a law, the consent of the society, over whom nobody can have a power to make laws[1] but by their own consent and by authority received from them; and therefore all the obedience, which by the most solemn ties anyone can be obliged to pay, ultimately terminates in this supreme power, and is directed by those laws which it enacts. . . .

135. Though the legislative, whether placed in one or more, whether it be always in being or only by intervals, though it be the supreme power in every commonwealth, yet, first, it is not, nor can possibly be, absolutely arbitrary over the lives and fortunes of the people. For it being but the joint power of every member of the society given up to that person or assembly which is legislator, it can be no more than those persons had in a state of Nature before they entered into society, and gave it up to the community. For nobody can transfer to another more power than he has in himself, and nobody has an absolute arbitrary power over himself, or over any other, to destroy his own life, or take away the life or property of another.

136. Secondly, the legislative or supreme authority cannot assume to itself a power to rule by extemporary arbitrary decrees, but is bound to dispense justice and decide the rights of the subject by promulgated standing laws,[2] and known authorized judges. For the law of Nature being unwritten, and so nowhere to be found but in the minds of men, they who, through passion or interest, shall miscite or misapply it, cannot so easily be convinced of their mistake where there is no established judge; and so it serves not as it ought, to determine the rights and fence the properties of those that live under it, especially where everyone is judge, interpreter, and executioner of it too, and that in his own case; and he that has right on his side, having ordinarily but his own single

---

[1] "The lawful power of making laws to command whole politic societies of men, belonging so properly unto the same entire societies, that for any prince or potentate, of what kind soever upon earth, to exercise the same of himself, and not by express commission immediately and personally received from God, or else by authority derived at the first from their consent, upon whose persons they impose laws, it is no better than mere tyranny. Laws they are not, therefore, which public approbation hath not made so."— Hooker (*Eccl. Pol.*, lib. i., s. 10). "Of this point, therefore, we are to note that such men naturally have no full and perfect power to command whole politic multitudes of men, therefore utterly without our consent we could in such sort be at no man's commandment living. And to be commanded, we do consent when that society, whereof we be a part, hath at any time before consented, without revoking the same after by the like universal agreement.

"Laws therefore human, of what kind soever, are available by consent."—Hooker, *Eccl. Pol.*

[2] "Human laws are measures in respect of men whose actions they must direct, howbeit such measures they are as have also their higher rules to be measured by, which rules are two—the law of God and the law of Nature; so that laws human must be made according to the general laws of Nature, and without contradiction to any positive law of Scripture, otherwise they are ill made."—Hooker, *Eccl. Pol.*, lib. iii., s. 9.

"To constrain men to anything inconvenient doth seem unreasonable."—*Ibid.*, i., 10.

strength, hath not force enough to defend himself from injuries or punish delinquents. . . .

138. Thirdly, the supreme power cannot take from any man any part of his property without his own consent. For the preservation of property being the end of government, and that for which men enter into society, it necessarily supposes and requires that the people should have property, without which they must be supposed to lose that by entering into society which was the end for which then entered into it; too gross an absurdity for any man to own. . . .

140. It is true governments cannot be supported without great charge, and it is fit every one who enjoys his share of the protection should pay out of his estate his proportion for the maintenance of it. But still it must be with his own consent—i.e., the consent of the majority, giving it either by themselves or their representatives chosen by them; for if anyone shall claim a power to lay and levy taxes on the people by his own authority, and without such consent of the people, he thereby invades the fundamental law of property, and subverts the end of government. For what property have I in that which another may by right take when he pleases to himself?

141. Fourthly, the legislative cannot transfer the power of making laws to any other hands, for it being but a delegated power from the people, they who have it cannot pass it over to others. The people alone can appoint the form of the commonwealth, which by constituting the legislative, and appointing in whose hands that shall be. And when the people have said, "We will submit, and be governed by laws made by such men, and in such forms," nobody else can say other men shall make laws for them; nor can they be bound by any.

CHAPTER XIX   OF THE DISSOLUTION OF GOVERNMENT

212. Besides this overturning from without, governments are dissolved from within:

First, when the legislative is altered, civil society being a state of peace amongst those who are of it, from whom the state of war is excluded by the umpirage which they have provided in their legislative for the ending all differences that may arise amongst any of them; it is in their legislative that the members of a commonwealth are united and combined together into one coherent living body. This is the soul that gives form, life, and unity to the commonwealth; from hence the several members have their mutual influence, sympathy, and connection; and therefore when the legislative is broken, or dissolved, dissolution and death follows. For the essence and union of the society consisting in having one will, the legislative, when once established by the majority, has the declaring and, as it were, keeping of that will. The constitution of the legislative is the first and fundamental act of society, whereby provision is made for the continuation of their union under the direction of persons and bonds of laws, made by persons authorized thereunto, by the consent and appointment of the people, without which no one man, or number of men, amongst them can have authority of making laws that shall be binding to the rest. When any one, or more, shall take upon them to make laws whom the people have not appointed so to do, they make laws without authority, which the people are not therefore bound to obey; by which means they come again to be out of subjection, and may constitute to themselves a new legislative, as they think best, being in full liberty to resist the force of those who, without authority, would impose anything upon them. Everyone is at the disposure of his own will, when those who had, by the delegation of the society, the declaring of the public will, are excluded from it, and others usurp the place who have no such authority or delegation.

221. There is, secondly, another way whereby governments are dissolved, and that is, when the legislative, or the prince, either of them act contrary to their trust.

For the legislative acts against the trust reposed in them when they endeavor to invade the property of the subject, and to make themselves, or any part of the community, masters or arbitrary disposers of the lives, liberties, or fortunes of the people.

222. The reason why men enter into society is the preservation of their property; and the end while they choose and authorize a legislative is that there may be laws made, and rules set, as guards and fences to the properties of all the society, to limit the power and moderate the dominion of every part and member of the society. For since it can never be supposed to be the will of the society that the legislative should have a power to destroy that which everyone designs to secure by entering into society, and for which the people submitted themselves to legislators of their own making: whenever the legislators endeavor to take away and destroy the property of the people, or to reduce them to slavery under arbitrary power, they put themselves into a state of war with the people, who are thereupon absolved from any farther obedience, and are left to the common refuge which God hath provided for all men against force and violence. Whensoever, therefore, the legislative shall transgress this fundamental rule of society, and either by ambition, fear, folly, or corruption, endeavor to grasp themselves, or put into the hands of any other, an absolute power over the lives, liberties, and estates of the people, by this breach of trust they forfeit the power the people had put into their hands for quite contrary ends, and it devolves to the people, who have a right to resume their original liberty, and by the establishment of a new legislative (such as they shall think fit), provide for their own safety and security, which is the end for which they are in society. . . .

223. To this, perhaps, it will be said that the people being ignorant and always discontented, to lay the foundation of government in the unsteady opinion and uncertain humor of the people, is to expose it to certain ruin; and no government will be able long to subsist if the people may set up a new legislative whenever they take offense at the old one. To this I answer, quite the contrary. People are not so easily got out of their old forms as some are apt to suggest. They are hardly to be prevailed with to amend the acknowledged faults in the frame they have been accustomed to. And if there be any original defects, or adventitious ones introduced by time or corruption, it is not an easy thing to get them changed, even when all the world sees there is an opportunity for it. This slowness and aversion in the people to quit their old constitutions has in the many revolutions we have seen in this kingdom, in this and former ages, still kept us to, or after some interval of fruitless attempts, still brought us back again to our old legislative of king, lords and commons; and whatever provocations have made the crown be taken from some of our princes' heads, they never carried the people so far as to place it in another line.

224. But it will be said this hypothesis lays a ferment for frequent rebellion. To which I answer:

First, no more than any other hypothesis. For when the people are made miserable, and find themselves exposed to the ill usage of arbitrary power, cry up their governors as much as you will for sons of Jupiter, let them be scared and divine, descended or authorized from Heaven; give them out for whom or what you please, the same will happen. The people generally ill treated, and contrary to right, will be ready upon any occasion to ease themselves of a burden that sits heavy upon them. They will wish and seek for the opportunity, which in the change, weakness, and accidents of human affairs, seldom delays long to offer itself. He must have lived but a little while in the world, who has not seen examples of this in his time; and he must have read very little who cannot produce examples of it in all sorts of governments in the world.

225. Secondly, I answer, such revolutions happen not upon every little mismanagement in public affairs. Great mistakes in the ruling part, many wrong and inconvenient laws, and all the slips of human frailty will be borne by the people without mutiny or murmur. But if a long train of abuses, prevarications, and artifices, all tending the same way, make the design visible to the people, and they cannot but feel what they lie under, and see whither they are going, it is not to be wondered that they should then rouse themselves, and endeavor to put the rule into such hands which may secure to them the ends for which government was at first erected, and without which, ancient names and specious forms are so far from being better, that they are much worse than the state of Nature or pure anarchy; the inconveniences being all as great and as near, but the remedy farther off and more difficult.

226. Thirdly, I answer, that this power in the people of providing for their safety anew by a new legislative when their legislators have acted contrary to their trust by invading their property, is the best fence against rebellion, and the probablest means to hinder it. For rebellion being an opposition, not to persons, but authority, which is founded only in the constitutions and laws of the government: those, whoever they be, who, by force, break through, and, by force, justify their violation of them, are truly and properly rebels. For when men, by entering into society and civil government, have excluded force, and introduced laws for the preservation of property, peace, and unity amongst themselves, those who set up force again in opposition to the laws, do *rebellare* —that is, bring back again the state of war, and are properly rebels, which they who are in power, by the pretense they have to authority, the temptation of force they have in their hands, and the flattery of those about them being likeliest to do, the properest way to prevent the evil is to show them the danger and injustice of it who are under the greatest temptation to run into it.

Jean Jacques Rousseau

A social critic at times exiled, Jean Jacques Rousseau (1712–1778) was famous and controversial most of his life. His written work is not particularly clear and systematic from a philosophical point of view, but it is highly suggestive and original. The selection below is drawn from a translation of *the Social Contract* by Willmoore Kendall; the italicized words were inserted by the translator as an aid to reading the text.

The Social Contract

BOOK I

ON CONVENTION

1. Man was born free, but is everywhere in bondage. This or that man believes himself the master of his fellow men, but is nevertheless more of a slave than they. How did this change *from freedom into bondage* come about? I do not know. Under what conditions can it be rendered legitimate? This problem I believe I can solve.

Were I to consider only force, and the results that it produces, I should say: As long as a people is constrained to obey, and does obey, it is acting rightly: *but* once that people is capable of shaking off its yoke, and does shake it off, it is acting even more rightly—for the following reason: Since in recovering its freedom it exercises the self-same right as the man that took it away, either it is justified in recovering it, or whoever took it away was not justified in doing so.

In any case, social order is a right—a sacred right, which serves as the basis for all other rights; *it does not, that is to say, flow from force.* Yet it does not flow from nature *either*. It therefore rests upon agreements.

Our task here is to find out what those agreements are. But before going into that, I must demonstrate what I have just asserted.

2. The oldest of societies, and the only society that is *in any sense* natural, is the family. Yet *we must not overlook the rôle of agreements even here:* the children do not remain tied to the father beyond the period during which they have need of him in order to preserve themselves. Once that need disappears, the natural bond is dissolved: *i.e.*, the children are exempted from the obedience they have hitherto owed to the father, the father is exempted from the duties that he has hitherto owed to the children, and father and children alike resume

By permission. From Jean Jacques Rousseau, *The Social Contract.* Translated by Willmoore Kendall. Henry Regnery Co., Chicago, 1954. The book was originally published in French in 1762. The subtitles have been added by the editors.

their independence. If they continue together, they no longer do so out of natural necessity but rather out of choice, so that *thenceforth* even the family keeps itself alive only by agreement.

The freedom that they *subsequently* enjoy in common derives from the nature of man, whose first law is to look to his self-preservation, just as his first duties are those he owes to himself—man being, once he has attained the age of reason, the sole judge as to the means of preserving himself, and by that very token his own master.

The family, on this showing is, if you like, the earliest model of political societies: the ruler in the one corresponds to the father in the other, the people in the one to the children in the other; all, in both cases, have been born free and equal to one another, and alienate their freedom only as it is to their advantage to do so. The only difference is this: In the family, the father has his reward for the care he bestows upon his children in the love he bears them. In the state, the pleasure of giving orders takes the place of love, which the ruler does not have for the people. . . .

ON FORCE

3. The strongest—unless he transforms force into right and obedience into duty—is never strong enough to have his way all the time. Thence the *so-called* "right of the strongest"—and, for all the ironical overtones with which it is asserted, its defense on the level of principle.

But will anyone ever get around to explaining to us what the phrase *right of the strongest* means? Force is a physical cause, and what its effects have to do with morality I am quite unable to understand. When I yield to force I do not perform an act of will but one of necessity—or, at most, one of prudence. How can it be my duty to perform such an act?

Let us, *however*, assume for a moment the existence of this alleged right. I contend that it leads to nothing but inexplicable nonsense, and for this reason: If might makes right, then the effect must vary with the cause. When might overcomes might, then, it succeeds to the right *which that might had made.* As soon *therefore* as one can disobey safely, one can disobey legitimately; and since the strongest is always right the trick is, quite simply, to act in such fashion as to be the strongest. Now: what sort of right is this that disappears as soon as the force behind it is taken away? If I am forced to obey, I have no need to obey out of duty; and once I am not forced to obey, I am no longer obligated to do so either. Evidently, then, the word "right" adds nothing to the word "force." As used in the phrase we are considering, it is entirely without meaning.

Obey the powers that be. If this means, "Knuckle under to force," then it is a good rule, but also superfluous: I answer for it that no one will ever break it.

All power comes from God. I admit that too. The same thing is true, however, of all sickness. Are we, then, forbidden to call in a doctor?

A highwayman jumps me at the edge of a forest. I must—compelled as I am to do so—hand over my pocket-book. But am I also bound in conscience to hand it over—even if it lies within my power to retain it? The pistol he points at me is, after all is said and done, one of the powers that be.

Let us agree, then, that might does not make right, and that we are obligated to obey only such powers as are legitimate. . . .

4. No man, *as we have seen*, has any natural authority over his fellow-man, and might, *as we have seen also*, makes no right. We have nothing left save agreements, then, *to serve* as a basis for all legitimate authority among men.

Why, asks Grotius—if an individual can alienate his freedom, *i.e.* make himself the slave of a master—cannot an entire people alienate its freedom, *i.e.* make itself subject to a king? The question abounds in equivocal words, which evidently need some explaining. Let us, however, confine ourselves to one of them: alienate.

To alienate something is either to give it away or to sell it. Now: the man who makes himself somebody's slave does not give himself away; he sells himself—if only for his keep. But for what does a people sell itself? A king, far from furnishing his subjects their keep, gets every last bit of his own from them—and a king's keep, if Rabelais is to be believed, is no small matter. Are we to understand, then, that the subjects make the king a present of their persons, *i.e.*, *give themselves away*, on condition that he shall take their goods as well? *Then* I fail to see how they have anything further to lose.

The despot, someone will answer, guarantees his subjects civil peace—*and that, surely, is something further to lose*. Let us grant the point. But how, if the wars the despot's ambition brings down upon their heads, along with his insatiable greed and the goings-on of his ministers, are harder to bear than ever their domestic squabbles would have been—what does civil peace profit them then? How if civil peace is itself a scourge—what does it then profit them? You can live peacefully in, among other places, a dungeon; is that sufficient grounds for being happy in one? The Greeks, while they were shut up in the Cyclops' cave awaiting their turn to be devoured, were living peacefully.

The proposition that a man gives himself and receives nothing in return is not only absurd; it is also unthinkable. The act in question is illegitimate and without effect—if for no other reason than that the agent is not in his right mind. To say that an entire people performs this act *thus* presupposes a people made up of madmen. And madness does not make right *any more than force does.* . . .

The individual who renounces his freedom also renounces his status as a man, and *thus* the rights and even the duties of human beings. There is no quid pro quo that can be given to him who renounces all. Such a renunciation is incompatible with the nature of man, besides which he who strips all the freedom from his will strips all the morality from his actions.

In a word: an agreement calling for absolute authority on one side and unlimited obedience on the other is both idle and contradictory. Over against a man from whom one is entitled to demand everything, one is, surely, committed to nothing: this single clause, naming no quid pro quo, naming nothing to be given in exchange—does it not, in and of itself, nullify the agreement? Everything my slave possesses belongs to me; what right, then, could be possibly have over against me? Any right he has is mine, and the notion of a right of mine over against myself—*which is what this comes down to*—is devoid of meaning.

Grotius and the other writers *I have in mind* squeeze a further source for the supposed right to enslave out of war. The conqueror, if they are to be believed, has a right to kill the vanquished foe; the latter is, therefore, entitled to buy back his life with his freedom—such an agreement being all the more legitimate because to the advantage of both parties.

Clearly, however, the conqueror's alleged right to kill those whom he has conquered in no sense results from the state of war. The relationship between men in their primitive condition of independence is not sufficiently stable to constitute a state of either war or peace; and for that very reason men living in that condition are emphatically not natural enemies. War is a relationship between things not men, which is to say that a state of war cannot arise out of mere personal relations: it arises, rather, out of property relations. And, that being the case, private war, or war between man and man, can exist neither in the state of nature, where there is no fixed property, nor in society, where everything is under the authority of the laws. . . .

War, then, is not by any means a relation between man and man but one between state and state. It is a relation in which individuals are enemies only incidentally—not qua men, or even qua citizens, but qua soldiers, not qua sons of the fatherland but qua its defenders. . . .

In a word: since it is impossible for a genuine relation to be established between things different in nature, a State can only have other States, never men, as its enemies.

The foregoing principle is, moreover, in harmony with the rules men have laid down at all periods in the past, as also with the regular practice of all politically-organized peoples. *For instance:* A declaration of war is a warning not so much to other States as to their subjects; and the foreigner—whether king, private person, or people—who, in the absence of a declaration of war against the prince *of a given state,* robs, kills, or captures the latter's subjects, commits an act not of war but of brigandage. This applies even during open hostilities: while the just prince takes firm possession of all public property in the enemy country, he nevertheless respects both the persons and goods of individuals; *in so doing* he respects the rights upon which his own rights are based. The purpose of every war being the destruction of the enemy state, one has a right to kill its defenders as long as they have weapons in their hands. But once they lay their weapons down, and surrender, they cease to be enemies, or instruments of the enemy, and resume their status as men; *i.e.,* the right to kill them lapses. It has proved possible, on occasion, to destroy a state without killing a single one of its members; and war cannot be the source of a right that is unnecessary for the achievement of its purpose. These are different principles from those of Grotius. They are unsupported by quotations from poets. They derive, however, from the nature of things, and are underwritten by reason.

So much for the *so-called* right of conquest: its sole basis is the right of the strongest. War confers upon the conqueror no right to massacre the conquered population; and the conqueror's right to enslave the conquered population cannot, therefore, be supported by an appeal to his right, which he does not possess. One has a right to kill an enemy only when one is unable to enslave him; the right to kill him thus cannot be the source of the right to enslave him. To oblige an enemy to buy back his liberty at the price of his life, over which one has no right *to begin with,* is *to conclude* an iniquitous bargain. *In short:* Is it not clear that we are reasoning in a vicious circle when we base the right of life and death upon the right to enslave, and then base the right to enslave upon the right of life and death?

But even if we were to take this terrifying right to kill everybody off for granted, I contend that a man enslaved in a war—and, *by the same token*, a conquered people—has no obligation toward the conqueror save that of obeying for just so long as no alternative presents itself. The conqueror, by taking something of equivalent value with his life, did not spare him the latter: he merely slew him profitably rather than unprofitably. They remain—so far is the one from having acquired any authority over the other beyond his power to compel him—just as much in a state of war as they were before. To put it more strongly: the relation between them is an effect of the state of war, and the *continued* exercise of the right of war implies that there is no treaty of peace between them. They have, to be sure, made an agreement. But this agreement, far from terminating the state of war, presupposes its continuance.

Any way you look at it, then, the right to enslave is nonexistent: it is not merely illegitimate, but absurd and meaningless as well. The words slavery and right cannot keep house together; they mutually exclude one another. The following formula—*which the right of slavery puts into the mouth of the master*—will always be nonsensical, whether it be spoken by a man to a man or by a man to a people· "I make an agreement with you: it is entirely to your disadvantage, and entirely to my advantage; I shall keep it as long as I please, and you will keep it as long as I please."

THE SOCIAL CONTRACT

5. . . . There is a great difference between establishing order in a society and gaining mastery over a multitude. Let as many separate individuals as you please be bound, one after another, to one man: I see only a master and some slaves, not a people and its ruler—an aggregation, if you like, but not an association. There is no public good, and *thus* no body politic. Let the one man gain mastery over half the world: he is still a mere individual; his interest, distinct as it is from that of the other individuals, remains merely a private interest. Let him die and the empire he leaves behind—like an oak tree that breaks asunder and falls into a heap of ashes after being consumed by fire—at once disintegrates, and has nothing to draw it together.

A people, says Grotius, can give itself to a king. On his own showing, then, it is *already* a people before it gives itself to a king: *for* the gift is itself a civil act, calling for prior public discussion. In that case, *however*, it would seem a good idea to examine the act by which a people becomes a people before we examine the act by which it elects a king. For this act, which necessarily precedes the other, is for that reason the true basis of society.

In short: unless the king has been elected by unanimous vote, what, failing a prior agreement, is the source of the minority's obligation to submit to the choice of the majority? Whence the right of the hundred who do wish a master to speak for the ten who do not? The majority principle is itself a product of agreement, and presupposes unanimity on at least one occasion.

6. This is my premise: men have reached a point where the obstacles hindering their preservation in the state of nature are so obstructive as to defy the resources each individual, while in that state, can devote to his preservation. This being the case, that primitive condition cannot continue: humankind would perish if it did not change its way of life.

Now: unable as they are to add to their resources, men can only combine and channel those that are at hand. Thus their sole means of preserving themselves from now on is to create a pool of resources capable of surmounting the obstacles, to set those resources to work in response to one and the same purpose, and to see to it that they act in concert.

Such a pool of resources can arise only out of the coming together of several men. Since, however, each man's power and freedom are the chief instruments *he uses* for his self-preservation, *the following question presents itself*; How is he to pledge them without doing himself hurt, *i.e.*, without neglecting the duties he owes himself?

This difficult question may be restated, in terms appropriate to my inquiry, as follows. "Is a method of associating discoverable which will defend and protect, with all the collective might, the person and property of each associate, and in virtue of which each associate, though he becomes a member of the group, nevertheless obeys only himself, and remains as free as before?" This is the problem, a basic one, for which the social contract provides the solution.

The terms of this contract are dictated by the nature of the transaction, and in such fashion that modifying them in any way would render them nugatory and without effect: they are, therefore, everywhere the same, everywhere tacitly accepted and recognized, though nowhere perhaps have they been systematically formulated. Whence it follows that each individual immediately resumes his primitive rights, surprising as this may seem, when any violation of the social pact occurs; *i.e.*, he recovers his natural freedom, and thereby loses the contractual freedom for which he renounced it.

The contract's terms reduce themselves, when clearly grasped, to a single stipulation, namely: the total alienation to the whole community of each associate, together with every last one of his rights. The reasons for this are as follows: each gives himself completely, so that, in the first place, this stipulation places an equal burden upon everybody; and nobody, for that very reason, has any interest in making it burdensome for others.

The alienation is made without reservations, so that, in the second place, no more perfect union is possible, and no associate has any subsequent demand to make *upon the others.* For if the individual retained any rights whatever, this is what would happen: There being no common superior able to say the last word on any issue between him and the public, he would be his own judge on this or that point, and so would try before long to be his own judge on all points. The state of nature would thus persist; and the association would necessarily become useless, if not tyrannical.

Each gives himself to everybody, so that, in the third place, he gives himself to nobody; and since every associate acquires over every associate the same power he grants to every associate over himself, each gains an equivalent for all that he loses, together with greater power to protect what he possesses.

If, then, we exclude from the social contract everything not essential to it, we shall find that it reduces itself to the following terms: "Each of us puts into the common pool, and under the sovereign control of the general will, his person and all his power. And we, as a community, take each member unto ourselves as an indivisible part of the whole."

This act of association forthwith produces, in lieu of the individual persons of the several contracting parties, a collective moral body. The latter is made up of as many members as there are voices in the assembly, and it acquires, through the said act of association, its unity, its collective self, its life, and its will.

A public person formed by other persons uniting in the manner just described was in the past called a city; nowadays it is called a republic, or body politic. . . .

The members of a body politic call it "the state" when it is passive, "the sovereign" when it is active, and "a power" when they compare it with others of its kind. Collectively they use the title "people," and they refer to one another individually as "citizens" when speaking of their participation in the authority of the sovereign, and as "subjects" when speaking of their subordination to the laws of the state. These terms, however, are often confused, *i.e.*, mistaken for one another, and it is enough to know how to tell them apart when they are used with maximum precision.

BOOK II

SOVEREIGNTY INALIENABLE AND INDIVISIBLE

1. . . . Only the general will can direct the energies of the state in a manner appropriate to the end for which it was founded, *i.e.*, the common good.

But, someone will object, there is no good that is common to the individual members of a society. This I deny:

What made the establishment of societies necessary was, if you like, the fact that the interests of individuals clashed. But what made their establishment possible was the fact that those same interests *also* coincided. *In other words:* It is the overlap among different interests that creates the social bond, so that no society can possibly exist save as there is some point at which all the interests *concerned* are in harmony. Now: society should be governed exclusively in terms of the common interest *of its members*.

I affirm, then, that sovereignty is purely and simply the exercise of the general will, and can in no circumstances therefore be alienated. And I affirm further that the sovereign is purely and simply a collective being, and can be represented therefore only by itself—for the following reason: While power can indeed be communicated *to another*, will emphatically cannot.

Let us look into this a little further:

While the will of an individual may in fact coincide with the general will on this or that point, it certainly cannot do so on all points and over an indefinite period of time. For the will of the individual tends by its very nature toward partiality, while the general will tends by its very nature toward equality.

Still less can there be any *prior* guarantee that the two will coincide; it would indeed be a good thing if they always did so, but that—*if it happened*—would happen by accident not by design. The sovereign can certainly say, "As of this moment I will that which such and such a man wills, or at least that which he says he wills." But it cannot say, "Tomorrow also I shall will that which this man then wills." For (*a*) *to speak of* a will's putting limitations upon itself with regard to the future is absurd, and (*b*) no will can consent to anything contrary to the good of him who is doing the willing.

Where, therefore, the people makes a flat promise to obey, it thereby decrees its own dissolution, and divests itself of the character of a people. The instant there is an overlord there is no longer a sovereign, which is to say that the body politic is then and there destroyed.

This is not to say that the commands of rulers can never pass for general wills. If the sovereign is free to oppose them, and does not do so, we must accept universal silence as evidence of popular consent. . . .

2. Sovereignty is indivisible—and for the selfsame reason *by which I have shown* that it is inalienable: A *given* will is either general or it is not. It is either the will of the whole people, in which case it is an act of sovereignty and makes law, or it is the will of a fraction of the people only, in which case it is merely a particular will, or an act of magistracy, or, at the very most, a decree. (It is not absolutely necessary for a will to be unanimous in order for it to be general. What is necessary is that every voice be taken into account; *which is to say that* systematic exclusion of any person destroys generality.)[1] . . .

CAN THE GENERAL WILL ERR?

3. It follows from the above that the general will is always well-intentioned, *i.e., that it* always looks to the public good. It does not follow, however, that the people's deliberations are invariably and to the same extent what they ought to be. Men always will what is good for them, but do not always see what is good for them. The people is never corrupted, but is frequently misinformed. And only when it is misinformed does it give the appearance of willing what is bad *for it.*

It often happens that the will of everybody, because it is looking to private interest and is *thus* merely a sum of particular wills, is something quite different from the general will, which looks exclusively to the common interest. But if you shake out from those same particular wills those that are most so and those that are least so, in so far as they destroy each other, the general will is the sum of the remaining differences. . . .

Given a sufficiently well-informed people in the act of deliberating, the general will would always issue from the numerous small differences *of opinion* among them, which is to say deliberation would always take place to good purpose, if the citizens did not take counsel with one another *outside the assembly.* Where, however, blocs are formed, *i.e.,* lesser associations at the expense of the broader one, the will of each of these associations comes to be general with respect to its members and particular with respect to the state. It is then possible to say that there are no longer just as many voters as there are individuals, but rather as many as there are associations: the differences become less numerous than before, and produce a less general result than before.

When, finally, one of these associations assumes such proportions as to gain the ascendency over all the others, you no longer get a sum of small differences as a result, but rather a single difference: there is no longer a general will at all, and the point of view that prevails is merely a particular point of view.

If then, we are to have a clear declaration of the general will, we must see to it (*a*) that there are no partial societies within the state, so that (*b*) each citizen forms his own opinions. . . .

---

[1] *Trans. note:* The lines in parentheses are a footnote in the original.

4. The general will ceases to be itself when it has a particular object, which is to say that just as it cannot be represented by a particular will it cannot, qua general, express itself regarding either a man or a fact. When, for example, the people of Athens—appointing and removing officials, awarding honors here, imposing punishments there—indiscriminately performed, through its particular decrees, all the functions of government, it no longer had, properly speaking, a general will at all; *i.e.*, at such times it was no longer acting as the sovereign but as the government. This will no doubt seem to contradict current ideas *on this question*. But the reader must give me time to set forth my own.

The point to grasp in all this is that what generalizes a will is not so much the number of voices *that speak out in its favor* as the common interest that harmonizes them. For in the body politic each knuckles under, as a matter of course, to the terms he imposes upon others; *i.e.*, interest and justice coincide to a remarkable degree, and this confers upon the collective deliberations a quality of equitableness that is conspicuously absent during the discussion of any matter involving a particular interest—which is to say any matter in which there is no common interest to harmonize and bring into identity the ruling *in the mind* of the judge and that *in the mind* of the *other* party.

Wherever we turn in search of our principle, then, we invariably arrive at one and the same conclusion, namely: The social contract establishes among citizens an equality of such character that each binds himself on the same terms as all the others, and is *thus* entitled to enjoy the same rights as all the others. Given the nature of the pact, therefore, every act of sovereignty, that is to say, every authentic act of the general will, burdens or favors all the citizens equally. The sovereign knows only the nation as a whole, and never singles out any of the individuals of whom it is composed.

What then is an act of sovereignty, in the strict sense of that term? It is an agreement between the body politic and each of its members, not *therefore* between a superior and an inferior. It is a lawful agreement, because based on the social contract. It is an equitable agreement, because everybody is a party to it. It is a profitable agreement, because it can have no object other than the general welfare. And it is a binding agreement, because it is backed up by collective force and supreme authority.

Now: In so far as the subjects' subordination is confined to such agreements, they tender obedience to no one; rather—*in so far as they are obeying at all*—they are obeying their own wills, and only their own wills. To ask, therefore, how far the respective rights of the sovereign and the citizens extend is to ask: To what extent can the citizens—each to everybody and everybody to each— make commitments to themselves?

Clearly, then, the power of the sovereign, absolute and sacred and inviolable though it is, does not and cannot exceed the outer limits of the general agreements *among the citizens*. Clearly also each individual can freely dispose of such of his goods and his liberty as the said agreements have left him. Nor, this being the case, is the sovereign ever entitled to burden one subject more heavily than another—the reason being that this becomes a matter concerning an individual, and lies beyond the sovereign's competence. . . .

LAW

6. . . . What, then, all things considered, is a law?

So long as people are content to assign a purely metaphysical content to the word law they will go on arguing and will come to no sort of understanding. Nor, even when someone has defined a law of nature for us, shall we for that reason be any closer to comprehending a law of the state.

As I have already pointed out, there is emphatically no such thing as a general will with a particular object. Any particular object must necessarily be situated either within the state or outside it. If outside it, a will alien to it—*as a will within the state necessarily is*—is not in the least general with respect to it. If inside it, then it is a part of the state, and there arises between the whole and that part a relation that makes of them two separate entities, the part being one and the whole minus that part another. But the whole minus one of its parts is by no means the same thing as the whole—*which is to say that*, so long as the relation just described obtains there is no whole, but rather two unequal parts. And from this it follows that the will of one of these parts is not general with respect to the other.

When, however, the people is laying down statutes concerning the entire people it considers only itself. Any relation that then arises is one between a whole regarded from one point of view and the same whole regarded from another point of view, without that whole's being in any sense divided. Both the will that lays down the statute and the matter concerning which the statute is laid down are, in these circumstances, general. It is this *kind of act* that I call a law.

When I say that the object of a law is always general, I mean that the law never takes cognizance of a man as an individual, or of a specific action, but rather of the subjects *taken* as a body and of actions *defined* abstractly. While, therefore, the law may provide that there shall be such and such privileges, it cannot expressly bestow any of these privileges upon such and such a person. It can create such and such categories of citizens, or even stipulate the qualities required for membership in them, but it cannot appoint such and such persons to such membership. It can set up a monarchical form of government, and provide that the succession shall be hereditary, but it cannot elect a king, or designate a *particular family to be the* royal family. In a word, absolutely no function relating to an individual object lies within the province of the legislative power.

Once all that is granted, we readily see that it is no longer necessary to inquire who has the power to make laws, since laws are acts of the general will; or whether the prince is above the laws, since the prince is part of the state; or whether there is such a thing as an unjust law, since no man is ever unjust to himself; or how we can be free and *yet* subordinated to laws, since laws are merely the expression of our own wishes.

We see further than since *the idea of* law includes both generality of will and generality of object, that which such and such a man, whoever he is, commands on his own responsibility, is not a law at all: even the command of the sovereign with respect to a particular object is not a law, but rather a decree—not an act of sovereignty, but rather an act of government.

I therefore apply the term republic to any state that is ruled by laws, whatever the form of government under which this condition obtains. Only in such states does the public interest hold sway and the public thing have a real existence.

All legitimate forms of government—I shall explain later what government is—are *on this showing* republican. . . .

BOOK III

THE GOVERNMENT IS NOT THE SOVEREIGN

26. . . . Some writers have argued that the act by which the government is established is a contract between the people as one party and the governors it sets over itself as the other. They have argued also that this contract sets up between the two the terms on which the one accepts an obligation to give orders and the other an obligation to obey them. I am sure the reader will agree that this is a strange kind of contract to be entering into. Let us consider, nevertheless, whether this view of the matter can be sustained.

In the first place, it is no more possible for the authority of the sovereign to be limited than for it to be alienated: limit it, and you destroy it. For the sovereign to set a superior over itself, *therefore*, is not only an absurdity but also a contradiction in terms. In obligating itself to obey a master it—*or, to be more precise, each of its members*—recovers its full freedom.

Again: This contract between the people on the one hand and such and such persons on the other would evidently be a particular act. For it to be either a law or an act of sovereignty is, therefore, out of the question. And from this it follows that such a contract would be illegitimate.

Still again: the contracting parties would evidently stand over against one another without any law above them save the law of nature, and *thus* without anything whatever to enforce their reciprocal engagements—which is as different from civil society as anything could be.

The party that has force at his disposal would always decide for himself whether to live up to the terms *of the so-called contract*. We might equally well apply the term "contract," then, to that which happens when one man says to another: "I convey to you all my goods, on condition that you shall give them back to me in any amount that strikes your fancy."

The state has room for one contract and only one, namely, the act of association itself. That contract ipso facto prohibits all further contracts, so that a *further* public contract that would not violate the orginal one is inconceivable.

BOOK IV

VOTING

2. . . . When a law is proposed in the assembly of the people, the individual members are not, by any means, asked whether they approve or disapprove of

the proposal, but rather this: Does it or does it not conform to the general will, which is their own? This is the question on which the individual expresses his opinion when he votes, and it is from the totalling of *such* votes that a declaration of the general will emerges. If then the view contrary to my own carries the day, that merely proves that I was mistaken, and that what I took to be the general will was not. Had my private opinion prevailed, I should have accomplished a result different from that which I had willed. And if that had happened I should not have been free.

This view of the matter assumes, to be sure, that all the characteristics of the general will continue to be present in the majority. Once they cease to be present, freedom—however the vote may go—is no more. . . .

David Hume

David Hume (1711–1776) was born in Edinburgh and attended the university there. Throughout his life his chief interests lay in literary and philosophic pursuits. His *History of England* was better received in his own time than were his philosophical works. Most philosophers would now say that *A Treatise of Human Nature* is Hume's most important work, but it was notably unsuccessful when published. In later years Hume rewrote and revised the *Treatise* and insisted that the resulting "enquiries" were to be taken as his philosophical position.

In *An Enquiry Concerning the Principles of Morals* Hume attempts to discover the "origin of moral conceptions." The selection from that work printed here contains his account of justice. The second selection from Hume is an essay in which he subjects to keen critical analysis the theory of a social contract as it had been advocated by Locke and others.

An Enquiry Concerning the Principles of Morals

SECTION III   OF JUSTICE

Part I

That justice is useful to society, and consequently that *part* of its merit, at least, must arise from that consideration, it would be a superfluous undertaking to prove. That public utility is the *sole* origin of justice, and that reflections on the beneficial consequences of this virtue are the *sole* foundation of its merit; this proposition, being more curious and important, will better deserve our examination and enquiry.

Let us suppose that nature has bestowed on the human race such profuse *abundance* of all *external* conveniences that, without any uncertainty in the event, without any care or industry on our part, every individual finds himself fully provided with whatever his most voracious appetites can want, or luxurious imagination wish or desire. His natural beauty, we shall suppose, surpasses all acquired ornaments; the perpetual clemency of the seasons renders useless all clothes or covering; the raw herbage affords him the most delicious fare; the clear fountain, the richest beverage. No laborious occupation required; no tillage; no navigation. Music, poetry, and contemplation form his sole business; conversation, mirth, and friendship his sole amusement.

It seems evident that in such a happy state every other social virtue would flourish and receive tenfold increase; but the cautious, jealous virtue of justice would never once have been dreamed of. For what purpose make a partition of goods where every one has already more than enough? Why give rise to property where there cannot possibly be any injury? Why call this object *mine* when, upon the seizing of it by another, I need but stretch out my hand to possess myself to what is equally valuable? Justice in that case, being totally useless, would be an idle ceremonial, and could never possibly have place in the catalogue of virtues.

We see, even in the present necessitous condition of mankind, that, wherever any benefit is bestowed by nature in an unlimited abundance, we leave it always in common among the whole human race, and make no subdivisions of right and property. Water and air, though the most necessary of all objects, are not challenged as the property of individuals; nor can any man commit injustice by the most lavish use and enjoyment of these blessings. In fertile extensive countries, with few inhabitants, land is regarded on the same footing. And no topic is so much insisted on by those who defend the liberty of the seas as the unexhausted use of them in navigation. Were the advantages procured by navigation as inexhaustible, these reasoners had never had any adversaries to

From David Hume, *An Enquiry Concerning The Principles of Morals*, London, 1748. Some footnotes deleted.

refute; nor had any claims ever been advanced of a separate, exclusive dominion over the ocean. . . .

Again, suppose that, though the necessities of human race continue the same as at present, yet the mind is so enlarged, and so replete with friendship and generosity, that every man has the utmost tenderness for every man and feels no more concern for his own interest than for that of his fellows; it seems evident that the use of justice would in this case be suspended by such an extensive benevolence, nor would the divisions and barriers of property and obligation have ever been thought of. Why should I bind another by a deed or promise to do me any good office, when I know that he is already prompted by the strongest inclination to seek my happiness and would of himself perform the desired service, except the hurt he thereby receives be greater than the benefit accruing to me? in which case he knows that, from my innate humanity and friendship, I should be the first to oppose myself to his imprudent generosity. Why raise landmarks between my neighbor's field and mine, when my heart has made no division between our interests, but shares all his joys and sorrows with the same force and vivacity as if originally my own? Every man, upon this supposition, being a second self to another, would trust all his interests to the discretion of every man, without jealousy, without partition, without distinction. And the whole human race would form only one family, where all would lie in common and be used freely, without regard to property; but cautiously too, with as entire regard to the necessities of each individual as if our own interests were most intimately concerned.

In the present disposition of the human heart, it would, perhaps, be difficult to find complete instances of such enlarged affections; but still we may observe that the case of families approaches towards it; and the stronger the mutual benevolence is among the individuals, the nearer it approaches; till all distinction of property be, in a great measure, lost and confounded among them. Between married persons the cement of friendship is by the laws supposed so strong as to abolish all division of possessions, and has often, in reality, the force ascribed to it. And it is observable that during the ardour of new enthusiasms, when every principle is inflamed into extravagance, the community of goods has frequently been attempted; and nothing but experience of its inconveniences, from the returning or disguised selfishness of men, could make the imprudent fanatics adopt anew the ideas of justice and of separate property. So true is it that this virtue derives its existence entirely from its necessary *use* to the intercourse and social state of mankind.

To make this truth more evident, let us reverse the foregoing suppositions and, carrying everything to the opposite extreme, consider what would be the effect of these new situations. Suppose a society to fall into such want of all common necessaries that the utmost frugality and industry cannot preserve the greater number from perishing, and the whole from extreme misery; it will readily, I believe, be admitted that the strict laws of justice are suspended in such a pressing emergency, and give place to the stronger motives of necessity and self-preservation. Is it any crime, after a shipwreck, to seize whatever means or instrument of safety one can lay hold of, without regard to former limitations of property? Or if a city besieged were perishing with hunger, can we imagine that men will see any means of preservation before them, and lose their lives from a scrupulous regard to what, in other situations, would be the rules of equity and justice? The use and tendency of that virtue is to procure happiness and security by preserving order in society; but where the society is ready to perish from extreme necessity, no greater evil can be dreaded from violence and injustice; and every man may now provide for himself by all the means which prudence can dictate or humanity permit. The public, even in less urgent necessities, opens granaries without the consent of proprietors, as justly supposing that the authority of magistracy may, consistent with equity, extend so far; but were any number of men to assemble, without the tie of laws or civil jurisdiction, would an equal partition of bread in a famine, though effected by power and even violence, be regarded as criminal or injurious?

Suppose likewise that it should be a virtuous man's fate to fall into the society of ruffians, remote from the protection of laws and government; what conduct must he embrace in that melancholy situation? He sees such a desperate rapaciousness prevail, such a disregard to equity, such contempt of order, such stupid blindness to future consequences, as must immediately have the most tragical conclusion, and must terminate in destruction to the greater number, and in a total dissolution of society to the rest. He, meanwhile, can have no other expedient than to arm himself, to whomever the sword he seizes, or the buckler, may belong: to make provision of all means of defence and security; and his particular regard to justice being no longer of use to his own safety or that of others, he must consult the dictates of self-preservation alone, without concern for those who no longer merit his care and attention.

When any man, even in political society, renders himself by his crimes obnoxious to the public, he is punished by the laws in his goods and person; that is, the ordinary rules of justice are, with regard to him, suspended for a moment, and it becomes equitable to inflict on him, for the *benefit* of society, what otherwise he could not suffer without wrong or injury.

The rage and violence of public war: what is it but a suspension of justice among the warring parties, who perceive that this virtue is now no longer of any *use* or advantage to them? The laws of war, which then succeed to those of equity and justice, are rules calculated for the *advantage* and *utility* of that particular state in which men are now placed. And were a civilized nation engaged with barbarians, who observed no rules even of war, the former must also suspend their observance of them, where they no longer serve to any purpose, and must render every action or recounter as bloody and pernicious as possible to the first aggressors.

Thus the rules of equity or justice depend entirely on the particular state and condition in which men are placed, and owe their origin and existence to that utility which results to the public from their strict and regular observance. Reverse, in any considerable circumstance, the condition of men; produce extreme abundance or extreme necessity; implant in the human breast perfect moderation and humanity, or perfect rapaciousness and malice—by rendering justice totally *useless*, you thereby totally destroy its essence and suspend its obligation upon mankind.

The common situation of society is a medium amidst all these extremes. We are naturally partial to ourselves and to our friends; but are capable of learning the advantage resulting from a more equitable conduct. Few enjoyments are given us from the open and liberal hand of nature; but by art, labour, and industry, we can extract them in great abundance. Hence the ideas of property become necessary in all civil society; hence justice derives its usefulness to the public; and hence alone arises its merit and moral obligation.

These conclusions are so natural and obvious that they have not escaped even the poets, in their descriptions of the felicity attending the golden age or the reign of Saturn. The seasons in that first period of nature were so temperate, if we credit these agreeable fictions, that there was no necessity for men to provide themselves with clothes and houses as a security against the violence of heat and cold. The rivers flowed with wine and milk; the oaks yielded honey; and nature spontaneously produced her greatest delicacies. Nor were these the chief advantages of that happy age. Tempests were not alone removed from nature; but those more furious tempests were unknown to human breasts, which now cause such uproar and engender such confusion. Avarice, ambition, cruelty, selfishness, were never heard of. Cordial affection, compassion, sympathy, were the only movements with which the mind was yet acquainted. Even the punctilious distinction of *mine* and *thine* was banished from among the happy race of mortals, and carried with it the very notion of property and obligation, justice and injustice.

This *poetical* fiction of the *golden age* is in some respects of a piece with the *philosophical* fiction of the *state of nature*; only that the former is represented as the most charming and most peaceable condition which can possibly be imagined, whereas the latter is painted out as a state of mutual war and violence attended with the most extreme necessity. On the first origin of mankind, we are told, their ignorance and savage nature were so prevalent that they could give no mutual trust, but must each depend upon himself and his own force or cunning for protection and security. No law was heard of; no rule of justice known; no distinction of property regarded. Power was the only measure of right, and a perpetual war of all against all was the result of men's untamed selfishness and barbarity.[1]

Whether such a condition of human nature could ever exist, or if it did, could continue so long as to merit the appellation of a *state*, may justly be doubted. Men are necessarily born in a family-society, at least; and are trained up by their parents to some rule of conduct and behaviour. But this must be admitted that, if such a state of mutual war and violence was ever real, the suspension of all laws of justice, from their absolute inutility, is a necessary and infallible consequence.

The more we vary our views of human life, and the newer and more unusual the lights are in which we survey it, the more shall we be convinced that the origin here assigned for the virtue of justice is real and satisfactory.

Were there a species of creatures intermingled with men, which, though rational, were possessed of such inferior strength, both of body and mind, that they were incapable of all resistance, and could never, upon the highest provocation, make us feel the effects of their resentment, the necessary consequence, I think, is that we should be bound by the laws of humanity to give gentle usage

[1] This fiction of a state of nature, as a state of war, was not first started by Mr. Hobbes, as is commonly imagined. Plato endeavours to refute an hypothesis very like it in the second, third, and fourth books *De Republica*. Cicero, on the contrary, supposes it certain and universally acknowledged.

to these creatures, but should not, properly speaking, lie under any restraint of justice with regard to them, nor could they possess any right or property, exclusive of such arbitrary lords. Our intercourse with them could not be called society—which supposes a degree of equality—but absolute command on the one side, and servile obedience on the other. Whatever we covet, they must instantly resign. Our permission is the only tenure by which they hold their possessions; our compassion and kindness the only check by which they curb our lawless will; and as no inconvenience ever results from the exercise of a power so firmly established in nature, the restraints of justice and property, being totally *useless*, would never have place in so unequal a confederacy.

This is plainly the situation of men with regard to animals; and how far these may be said to possess reason, I leave it to others to determine. The great superiority of civilized Europeans above barbarous Indians tempted us to im-agine ourselves on the same footing with regard to them, and made us throw off all restraints of justice and even of humanity, in our treatment of them. In many nations the female sex are reduced to like slavery, and are rendered incapable of all property, in opposition to their lordly masters. But though the males, when united, have in all countries bodily force sufficient to maintain this severe tyranny, yet such are the insinuation, address, and charms of their fair compan-ions that women are commonly able to break the confederacy and share with the other sex in all the rights and privileges of society.

Were the human species so framed by nature as that each individual possessed within himself every faculty requisite both for his own preservation and for the propagation of his kind, were all society and intercourse cut off between man and man by the primary intention of the supreme Creator, it seems evident that so solitary a being would be as much incapable of justice as of social discourse and conversation. Where mutual regards and forbearance serve to no manner of purpose, they would never direct the conduct of any reasonable man. The headlong course of the passions would be checked by no reflection on future consequences. And as each man is here supposed to love himself alone, and to depend only on himself and his own activity for safety and happiness, he would, on every occasion, to the utmost of his power, challenge the preference above every other being, to none of which he is bound by any ties, either of nature or of interest.

But suppose the conjunction of the sexes to be established in nature, a family immediately arises; and particular rules being found requisite for its subsistence, these are immediately embraced, though without comprehending the rest of mankind within their prescriptions. Suppose that several families unite together into one society which is totally disjoined from all others, the rules which preserve peace and order enlarge themselves to the utmost extent of that society; but becoming then entirely useless, lose their force when carried one step farther. But again suppose that several distinct societies maintain a kind of intercourse for mutual convenience and advantage; the boundaries of justice still grow larger, in proportion to the largeness of men's views and the force of their mutual connexions. History, experience, reason sufficiently instruct us in this natural progress of human sentiments and the gradual enlargement of our regards to justice, in proportion as we become acquainted with the extensive utility of that virtue.

Part II

If we examine the *particular* laws by which justice is directed and property determined, we shall still be presented with the same conclusion. The good of mankind is the only object of all these laws and regulations. Not only is it requisite for the peace and interest of society that men's possessions should be separated, but the rules which we follow in making the separation are such as can best be contrived to serve futher the interests of society.

We shall suppose that a creature, possessed of reason, but unacquainted with human nature, deliberates with himself what rules of justice or property would best promote public interest and establish peace and security among mankind. His most obvious thought would be to assign the largest possessions to the most extensive virtue, and give every one the power of doing good, proportioned to his inclination. In a perfect theocracy, where a being, infinitely intelligent, governs by particular volitions, this rule would certainly have place and might serve to the wisest purposes. But were mankind to execute such a law, so great is the uncertainty of merit, both from its natural obscurity and from the self-conceit of each individual, that no determinate rule of conduct would ever result from it; and the total dissolution of society must be the immediate consequence. Fanatics may suppose *that dominion is founded on grace*, and *that saints alone inherit the earth*; but the civil magistrate very justly puts these sublime theorists on the same footing with common robbers, and teaches them by the severest discipline that a rule, which in speculation may seem the most advantageous to society, may yet be found, in practice, totally pernicious and destructive. . . .

It must, indeed, be confessed that nature is so liberal to mankind that, were all her presents equally divided among the species and improved by art and industry, every individual would enjoy all the necessaries and most of the comforts of life, nor would ever be liable to any ills but such as might accidentally arise from the sickly frame and constitution of his body. It must also be confessed that, wherever we depart from this equality, we rob the poor of more satisfaction than we add to the rich, and that the slight gratification of a frivolous vanity in one individual frequently costs more than bread to many families and even provinces. It may appear withal that the rule of equality, as it would be highly *useful*, is not altogether *impracticable*, but has taken place, at least in an imperfect degree, in some republics, particularly that of Sparta, where it was attended, it is said, with the most beneficial consequences. Not to mention that the Agrarian laws, so frequently claimed in Rome, and carried into execution in many Greek cities, proceeded, all of them, from a general idea of the utility of this principle.

But historians, and even common sense, may inform us that, however specious these ideas of *perfect* equality may seem, they are really at bottom *impracticable*; and were they not so, would be extremely *pernicious* to human society. Render possessions ever so equal, men's different degrees of art, care, and industry will immediately break that equality. Or if you check these virtues, you reduce society to the most extreme indigence; and instead of preventing want and beggary in a few, render it unavoidable to the whole community. The most rigorous inquisition too is requisite to watch every inequality on its first appearance; and the most severe jurisdiction, to punish and redress it. But besides that so much authority must soon degenerate into tyranny and be exerted with great partialities, who can possibly be possessed of it in such a situation as is here supposed? Perfect equality of possessions, destroying all subordination, weakens extremely the authority of magistracy, and must reduce all power nearly to a level, as well as property.

We may conclude, therefore, that, in order to establish laws for the regulation of property, we must be acquainted with the nature and situation of man, must reject appearances which may be false though specious, and must search for those rules which are on the whole most *useful* and *beneficial.* Vulgar sense and slight experience are sufficient for this purpose, where men give not way to too selfish avidity or too extensive enthusiasm,

Who sees not, for instance, that whatever is produced or improved by a man's art or industry ought, for ever, to be secured to him, in order to give encouragement to such *useful* habits and accomplishments? That the property ought also to descend to children and relations for the same *useful* purpose? That it may be alienated by consent in order to beget that commerce and intercourse which is so *beneficial* to human society? And that all contracts and promises ought carefully to be fulfilled in order to secure mutual trust and confidence by which the general *interest* of mankind is so much promoted?

Examine the writers on the laws of nature, and you will always find that, whatever principles they set out with, they are sure to terminate here at last, and to assign as the ultimate reason for every rule which they establish, the convenience and necessities of mankind. A concession thus extorted in opposition to systems has more authority than if it had been made in prosecution of them.

What other reason, indeed, could writers ever give why this must be *mine* and that *yours,* since uninstructed nature surely never made any such distinction? The objects which receive those appellations are of themselves foreign to us; they are totally disjoined and separated from us, and nothing but the general interests of society can form the connexion.

Sometimes the interests of society may require a rule of justice in a particular case, but may not determine any particular rule among several, which are all equally beneficial. In that case the slightest *analogies* are laid hold of, in order to prevent that indifference and ambiguity, which would be the source of perpetual dissension. Thus possession alone, and first possession, is supposed to convey property, where nobody else has any preceding claim and pretension. Many of the reasonings of lawyers are of this analogical nature, and depend on very slight connexions of the imagination.

Does any one scruple, in extraordinary cases, to violate all regard to the private property of individuals, and sacrifice to public interest a distinction which had been established for the sake of that interest? The safety of the people is the supreme law. All other particular laws are subordinate to it and dependent on it. And if, in the *common* course of things, they be followed and regarded, it is only because the public safety and interest *commonly* demand so equal and impartial an administration.

Sometimes both *utility* and *analogy* fail and leave the laws of justice in total uncertainty. Thus it is highly requisite that prescription or long possession should convey property; but what number of days or months or years should be sufficient for that purpose, is it impossible for reason alone to determine. *Civil laws* here supply the place of the natural *code,* and assign different terms for prescription, according to the different *utilities* proposed by the legislator. Bills of exchange and promissory notes, by the laws of most countries, prescribe sooner than bonds, and mortgages, and contracts of a more formal nature.

In general we may observe that all questions of property are subordinate to the authority of civil laws, which extend, restrain, modify, and alter the rules of natural justice, according to the particular *convenience* of each community. The laws have or ought to have a constant reference to the constitution of government, the manners, the climate, the religion, the commerce, the situation of each society. A late author of genius as well as learning has prosecuted this subject at large, and has established from these principles a system of political knowledge which abounds in ingenious and brilliant thoughts and is not wanting in solidity.

What is a man's property? Anything which it is lawful for him, and for him alone, to use. *But what rule have we by which we can distinguish these objects?* Here we must have recourse to statutes, customs, precedents, analogies, and a hundred other circumstances, some of which are constant and inflexible, some variable and arbitrary. But the ultimate point, in which they all professedly terminate, is the interest and happiness of human society. Where this enters not into consideration, nothing can appear more whimsical, unnatural, and even superstitious, than all or most of the laws of justice and of property. . . .

What alone will beget a doubt concerning the theory on which I insist is the influence of education and acquired habits, by which we are so accustomed to blame injustice that we are not in every instance conscious of any immediate reflection on the pernicious consequences of it. The views the most familiar to us are apt, for that very reason, to escape us; and what we have very frequently performed from certain motives, we are apt likewise to continue mechanically without recalling on every occasion the reflections which first determined us. The convenience or rather necessity which leads to justice is so universal and everywhere points so much to the same rules that the habit takes place in all societies; and it is not without some scrutiny that we are able to ascertain its true origin. The matter, however, is not so obscure, but that even in common life we have every moment recourse to the principle of public utility, and ask, *What must become of the world, if such practices prevail? How could society subsist under such disorders?* Were the distinction or separation of possessions entirely useless, can any one conceive that it ever should have obtained in society?

Thus we seem, upon the whole, to have attained a knowledge of the force of that principle here insisted on, and can determine what degree of esteem or moral approbation may result from reflections on public interest and utility. The necessity of justice to the support of society is the sole foundation of that virtue; and since no moral excellence is more highly esteemed, we may conclude that this circumstance of usefulness has, in general, the strongest energy and most entire command over our sentiments. It must, therefore, be the source of a considerable part of the merit ascribed to humanity, benevolence, friendship, public spirit, and other social virtues of that stamp; as it is the sole source of the moral approbation paid to fidelity, justice, veracity, integrity, and those other estimable and useful qualities and principles. It is entirely agreeable to the rules of philosophy and even of common reason, where any principle has been found to have a great force and energy in one instance, to ascribe to it a like energy in all similar instances. This indeed is Newton's chief rule of philosophizing.

Of the Original Contract

As no party, in the present age, can well support itself without a philosophical or speculative system of principles annexed to its political or practical one, we accordingly find that each of the factions into which this nation is divided has reared up a fabric of the former kind, in order to protect and cover that scheme of actions which it pursues. The people being commonly very rude builders, especially in this speculative way, and more especially still when actuated by party zeal, it is natural to imagine that their workmanship must be a little unshapely, and discover evident marks of that violence and hurry in which it was raised. The one party, by tracing up government to the Deity, endeavour to render it so sacred and inviolate that it must be little less than sacrilege, however tyrannical it may become, to touch or invade it in the smallest article. The other party, by founding government altogether on the consent of the people, suppose that there is a kind of *original contract* by which the subjects have tacitly reserved the power of resisting their sovereign, whenever they find themselves aggrieved by that authority with which they have, for certain purposes, voluntarily entrusted him. These are the speculative principles of the two parties, and these, too, are the practical consequences deduced from them.

I shall venture to affirm *that both these systems of speculative principles are just, though not in the sense intended by the parties*, and *that both the schemes of practical consequences are prudent, though not in the extremes to which each party, in opposition to the other, has commonly endeavoured to carry them.*

That the Deity is the ultimate author of all government will never be denied by any who admit a general providence and allow that all events in the universe are conducted by an uniform plan and directed to wise purposes. As it is impossible for the human race to subsist, at least in any comfortable or secure state, without the protection of government, this institution must certainly have been intended by that beneficent Being who means the good of all his creatures. And as it has universally, in fact, taken place in all countries and all ages, we may conclude, with still greater certainty, that it was intended by that omniscient Being who can never be deceived by any event or operation. But since he gave rise to it, not by any particular or miraculous interposition, but by his concealed and universal efficacy, a sovereign cannot, properly speaking, be called his viceregent in any other sense than every power or force, being derived from him, may be said to act by his commission. Whatever actually happens is comprehended in the general plan or intention of Providence; nor has the greatest and most lawful prince any more reason, upon that account, to plead a peculiar sacredness or inviolable authority than an inferior magistrate, or even an usurper, or even a robber and a pirate. The same Divine Superintendent who, for wise purposes, invested a Titus or a Trajan with authority, did also, for purposes no doubt equally wise though unknown, bestow power on a Borgia or an Angria. The same causes which gave rise to the sovereign power in every state established

David Hume, *Essays, Moral and Political,* vol. II, London, 1742.

likewise every petty jurisdiction in it, and every limited authority. A constable, therefore, no less than a king, acts by a divine commission and possesses an indefeasible right.

When we consider how nearly equal all men are in their bodily force, and even in their mental powers and faculties, till cultivated by education, we must necessarily allow that nothing but their own consent could at first associate them together and subject them to any authority. The people, if we trace government to its first origin in the woods and deserts, are the source of all power and jurisdiction, and voluntarily, for the sake of peace and order, abandoned their native liberty and received laws from their equal and companion. The conditions upon which they were willing to submit were either expressed or were so clear and obvious that it might well be esteemed superfluous to express them. If this, then, be meant by the *original contract*, it cannot be denied that all government is, at first, founded on a contract, and that the most ancient rude combinations of mankind were formed chiefly by that principle. In vain are we asked in what records this charter of our liberties is registered. It was not written on parchment, nor yet on leaves or barks of trees. It preceded the use of writing, and all the other civilized arts of life. But we trace it plainly in the nature of man, and in the equality, or something approaching equality, which we find in all the individuals of that species. The force which now prevails, and which is founded on fleets and armies, is plainly political, and derived from authority, the effect of established government. A man's natural force consists only in the vigour of his limbs and the firmness of his courage, which could never subject multitudes to the command of one. Nothing but their own consent and their sense of the advantages resulting from peace and order could have had that influence.

Yet even this consent was long very imperfect, and could not be the basis of a regular administration. The chieftain, who had probably acquired his influence during the continuance of war, ruled more by persuasion than command; and till he could employ force to reduce the refractory and disobedient, the society could scarcely be said to have attained a state of civil government. No compact or agreement, it is evident, was expressly formed for general submission, an idea far beyond the comprehension of savages. Each exertion of authority in the chieftain must have been particular, and called forth by the present exigencies of the case. The sensible utility resulting from his interposition made these exertions become daily more frequent; and their frequency produced an habitual and, if you please to call it so, a voluntary and therefore precarious acquiescence in the people.

But philosophers who have embraced a party—if that be not a contradiction in terms—are not contented with these concessions. They assert not only that government in its earliest infancy arose from consent, or rather the voluntary acquiescence of the people, but also that, even at present, when it has attained its full maturity, it rests on no other foundation. They affirm that all men are still born equal, and owe allegiance to no prince or government unless bound by the obligation and sanction of a *promise*. And as no man, without some equivalent, would forego the advantages of his native liberty and subject himself to the will of another, this promise is always understood to be conditional, and imposes on him no obligation, unless he meet with justice and protection from his sovereign. These advantages the sovereign promises him in return; and if he fail in the execution, he has broken on his part the articles of engagement, and has thereby freed his subject from all obligations to allegiance. Such, according to these philosophers, is the foundation of authority in every government, and such the right of resistance possessed by every subject.

But would these reasoners look abroad into the world, they would meet with nothing that in the least corresponds to their ideas, or can warrant so refined and philosophical a system. On the contrary, we find everywhere princes who claim their subjects as their property, and assert their independent right of sovereignty from conquest or succession. . . .

Were you to preach, in most parts of the world, that political connexions are founded altogether on voluntary consent or a mutual promise, the magistrate would soon imprison you as seditious for loosening the ties of obedience, if your friends did not before shut you up as delirious for advancing such absurdities. It is strange that an act of the mind, which every individual is supposed to have formed, and after he came to the use of reason too, otherwise it could have no authority—that this act, I say, should be so much unknown to all of them that over the face of the whole earth there scarcely remain any traces or memory of it.

But the contract on which government is founded is said to be the *original contract*; and consequently may be supposed too old to fall under the knowledge of the present generation. If the agreement by which savage men first associated and conjoined their force be here meant, this is acknowledged to be real; but being so ancient, and being obliterated by a thousand changes of government and princes, it cannot now be supposed to retain any authority. If we would say anything to the purpose, we must assert that every particular government which is lawful, and which imposes any duty of allegiance on the subject, was at first founded on consent and a voluntary compact. But, besides that this supposes the consent of the fathers to bind the children, even to the most remote generations—which republican writers will never allow—besides this, I say, it is not justified by history or experience in any age or country of the world.

Almost all the governments which exist at present, or of which there remains any record in story, have been founded originally either on usurpation or conquest or both, without any pretence of a fair consent or voluntary subjection of the people. When an artful and bold man is placed at the head of an army or faction, it is often easy for him, by employing sometimes violence, sometimes false pretences, to establish his dominion over a people a hundred times more numerous than his partisans. He allows no such open communication that his enemies can know with certainty their number or force. He gives them no leisure to assemble together in a body to oppose him. Even all those who are the instruments of his usurpation may wish his fall; but their ignorance of each other's intention keeps them in awe, and is the sole cause of his security. By such arts as these many governments have been established; and this is all the *original contract* which they have to boast of. . . .

But would we have a more regular, at least a more philosophical, refutation of this principle of an original contract or popular consent, perhaps the following observations may suffice.

All *moral* duties may be divided into two kinds. The *first* are those to which men are impelled by a natural instinct or immediate propensity which operates on them, independent of all ideas of obligation and of all views either to public or private utility. Of this nature are love of children, gratitude to benefactors, pity to the unfortunate. When we reflect on the advantage which results to society from such humane instincts, we pay them the just tribute of moral approbation and esteem. But the person actuated by them feels their power and influence antecedent to any such reflection.

The *second* kind of moral duties are such as are not supported by any original instinct of nature, but are performed entirely from a sense of obligation, when we consider the necessities of human society and the impossibility of supporting it if these duties were neglected. It is thus *justice*, or a regard to the property of others, *fidelity*, or the observance of promises, become obligatory and acquire an authority over mankind. For as it is evident that every man loves himself better than any other person, he is naturally impelled to extend his acquisitions as much as possible; and nothing can restrain him in this propensity but reflection and experience, by which he learns the pernicious effects of that license and the total dissolution of society which must ensue from it. His original inclination, therefore, or instinct, is here checked and restrained by a subsequent judgment or observation.

The case is precisely the same with the political or civil duty of *allegiance* as with the natural duties of justice and fidelity. Our primary instincts lead us either to indulge ourselves in unlimited freedom, or to seek dominion over others; and it is reflection only which engages us to sacrifice such strong passions to the interests of peace and public order. A small degree of experience and observation suffices to teach us that society cannot possibly be maintained without the authority of magistrates, and that this authority must soon fall into contempt where exact obedience is not paid to it. The observation of these general and obvious interests is the source of all allegiance and of that moral obligation which we attribute to it.

What necessity, therefore, is there to found the duty of *allegiance*, or obedience to magistrates, on that of *fidelity*, or a regard to promises, and to suppose that it is the consent of each individual which subjects him to government, when it appears that both allegiance and fidelity stand precisely on the same foundation and are both submitted to by mankind on account of the apparent interests and necessities of human society? We are bound to obey our sovereign, it is said, because we have given a tacit promise to that purpose. But why are we bound to observe our promise? It must here be asserted that the commerce and intercourse of mankind, which are of such mighty advantage, can have no security where men pay no regard to their engagements. In like manner may it be said that men could not live at all in society, at least in a civilized society, without laws and magistrates and judges to prevent the encroachments of the strong upon the weak, of the violent upon the just and equitable. The obligation to allegiance being like force and authority with the obligation to fidelity, we gain nothing by resolving the one into the other. The general interests or necessities of society are sufficient to establish both.

If the reason be asked of that obedience which we are bound to pay to government, I readily answer, *because society could not otherwise subsist*; and this answer is clear and intelligible to all mankind. Your answer is, *because we should keep our word.* But besides that nobody, till trained in a philosophical system, can either comprehend or relish this answer—besides this, I say, you find yourself embarrassed when it is asked, *why are we bound to keep our word?* Nor can you give any answer but what would immediately, without any circuit, have accounted for our obligation to allegiance. . . .

We shall only observe before we conclude that though an appeal to general opinion may justly, in the speculative sciences of metaphysics, natural philosophy, or astronomy, be deemed unfair and inconclusive, yet in all questions with regard to morals, as well as criticism, there is really no other standard by which any controversy can ever be decided. And nothing is a clearer proof that a theory of this kind is erroneous than to find that it leads to paradoxes repugnant to the common sentiments of mankind, and to the practice and opinion of all nations and all ages. The doctrine which founds all lawful government on an *original contract*, or consent of the people, is plainly of this kind; nor has the most noted of its partisans, in prosecution of it, scrupled to affirm *that absolute monarchy is inconsistent with civil society, and so can be no form of civil government at all,* [1] and *that the supreme power in a state cannot take from any man by taxes and impositions any part of his property, without his own consent or that of his representatives.* [2] What authority any moral reasoning can have, which leads into opinions so wide of the general practice of mankind in every place but this single kingdom, it is easy to determine. . . .

Immanuel Kant

Immanuel Kant (1724–1804) lived his whole life in Konigsberg, East Prussia, finally becoming a professor at the university there. His philosophical writings are generally admitted to be among the most significant ever published. His chief work, the *Critique of Pure Reason* lays the foundation in theory of knowledge and metaphysics for his later works including his writings on ethics, law, and political philosophy. Kant's ethical writings place chief emphasis on the call of duty and deny that duty can be discovered in terms of the pleasure or any other good resulting from actions. He is thus a chief philosophical opponent of utilitarians such as Bentham. In the selection printed below Kant presents a retributivist theory of the justification of punishment. His view on punishment provides a good example of the way in which he differs from utilitarians.

[1] See Locke *On Government*, chap. vii. § 90.
[2] Locke *On Government*, chap. xi. § 138, 139, 140.

The Philosophy of Law

ON PUNISHMENT

Judicial or Juridical Punishment (*poena forensis*) is to be distinguished from Natural Punishment (*poena naturalis*), in which Crime as Vice punishes itself, and does not as such come within the cognizance of the Legislator. Juridical Punishment can never be administered merely as a means for promoting another Good either with regard to the Criminal himself or to Civil Society, but must in all cases be imposed only because the individual on whom it is inflicted *has committed a Crime*. For one man ought never to be dealt with merely as a means subservient to the purpose of another, nor be mixed up with the subjects of Real Right. Against such treatment his Inborn Personality has a Right to protect him, even although he may be condemned to lose his Civil Personality. He must first be found guilty and *punishable*, before there can be any thought of drawing from his Punishment any benefit for himself or his fellow-citizens. The Penal Law is a Categorical Imperative; and woe to him who creeps through the serpent-windings of Utilitarianism to discover some advantage that may discharge him from the Justice of Punishment, or even from the due measure of it, according to the Pharisaic maxim: 'It is better that *one* man should die than that the whole people should perish.' For if Justice and Righteousness perish, human life would no longer have any value in the world.—What, then, is to be said of such a proposal as to keep a Criminal alive who has been condemned to death, on his being given to understand that if he agreed to certain dangerous experiments being performed upon him, he would be allowed to survive if he came happily through them? It is argued that Physicians might thus obtain new information that would be of value to the Commonweal. But a Court of Justice would repudiate with scorn any proposal of this kind if made to it by the Medical Faculty; for Justice would cease to be justice, if it were bartered away for any consideration whatever.

But what is the mode and measure of Punishment which Public Justice takes as its Principle and Standard? It is just the Principle of Equality, by which the pointer of the Scale of Justice is made to incline no more to the one side than the other. It may be rendered by saying that the undeserved evil which any one commits on another, is to be regarded as perpetrated on himself. Hence it may be said: 'If you slander another, you slander yourself; if you steal from another, you steal from yourself; if you strike another, you strike yourself; if you kill another, you kill yourself.' This is the Right of Retaliation (*jus talionis*); and properly understood, it is the only Principle which in regulating a Public Court, as distinguished from mere private judgment, can definitely assign both the quality and the quantity of a just penalty. All other standards are wavering and uncertain; and on account of other considerations involved in them, they contain no principle conformable to the sentence of pure and strict Justice. It

From Immanuel Kant, *The Philosophy of Law*, trans. by W. Hastie, F. & F. Clark, Edinburgh, 1887.

may appear, however, that difference of social status would not admit the application of the Principle of Retaliation, which is that of 'Like with Like.' But although the application may not in all cases be possible according to the letter, yet as regards the effect it may always be attained in practice, by due regard being given to the disposition and sentiment of the parties in the higher social sphere. Thus a pecuniary penalty on account of a verbal injury, may have no direct proportion to the injustice of slander; for one who is wealthy may be able to indulge himself in this offence for his own gratification. Yet the attack committed on the honour of the party aggrieved may have its equivalent in the pain inflicted upon the pride of the aggressor, especially if he is condemned by the judgment of the Court, not only to retract and apologize, but to submit to some meaner ordeal, as kissing the hand of the injured person. In like manner, if a man of the highest rank has violently assaulted an innocent citizen of the lower orders, he may be condemned not only to apologize but to undergo a solitary and painful imprisonment, whereby, in addition to the discomfort endured, the vanity of the offender would be painfully affected, and the very shame of his position would constitute an adequate Retaliation after the principle of 'Like with Like.' But how then would we render the statement: 'If you *steal* from another, you steal from yourself? In this way, that whoever steals anything makes the property of all insecure; he therefore robs himself of all security in property, according to the Right of Retaliation. Such a one has nothing, and can acquire nothing, but he has the Will to live; and this is only possible by others supporting him. But as the State should not do this gratuitously, he must for this purpose yield his powers to the State to be used in penal labour; and thus he falls for a time, or it may be for life, into a condition of slavery.—But whoever has committed Murder, must *die*. There is, in this case, no juridical substitute or surrogate, that can be given or taken for the satisfaction of Justice. There is no Likeness or proportion between Life, however painful, and Death; and therefore there is no Equality between the crime of Murder and the retaliation of it but what is judicially accomplished by the execution of the Criminal. His death, however, must be kept free from all maltreatment that would make the humanity suffering in his Person loathsome or abominable. Even if a Civil Society resolved to dissolve itself with the consent of all its members—as might be supposed in the case of a People inhabiting an island resolving to separate and scatter themselves throughout the whole world—the last Murderer lying in the prison ought to be executed before the resolution was carried out. This ought to be done in order that every one may realize the desert of his deeds, and that bloodguiltiness may not remain upon the people; for otherwise they might all be regarded as participators in the murder as a public violation of Justice.

The Equalization of Punishment with Crime, is therefore only possible by the cognition of the Judge extending even to the penalty of Death, according to the Right of Retaliation. This is manifest from the fact that it is only thus that a Sentence can be pronounced over all criminals proportionate to their internal *wickedness*; as may be seen by considering the case when the punishment of Death has to be inflicted, not on account of a murder, but on account of a political crime that can only be punished capitally. A hypothetical case, founded on history, will illustrate this. In the last Scottish Rebellion there were various participators in it—such as Balmerino and others—who believed that in taking part in the Rebellion they were only discharging their duty to the House of

Stuart; but there were also others who were animated only by private motives and interests. Now, suppose that the Judgment of the Supreme Court regarding them had been this: that every one should have liberty to choose between the punishment of Death or Penal Servitude for life. In view of such an alternative, I say that the Man of Honour would choose Death, and the Knave would choose servitude. This would be the effect of their human nature as it is; for the honourable man values his Honour more highly than even Life itself, whereas a Knave regards a Life, although covered with shame, as better in his eyes than not to be. The former is, without gainsaying, less guilty than the other; and they can only be proportionately punished by death being inflicted equally upon them both; yet to the one it is a mild punishment when his nobler temperament is taken into account, whereas it is a hard punishment to the other in view of his baser temperament. But, on the other hand, were they all equally condemned to Penal Servitude for life, the honourable man would be too severely punished, while the other, on account of his baseness of nature, would be too mildly punished. In the judgment to be pronounced over a number of criminals united in such a conspiracy, the best Equalizer of Punishment and Crime in the form of public Justice is Death. And besides all this, it has never been heard of, that a Criminal condemned to death on account of a murder has complained that the Sentence inflicted on him was more than right and just; and any one would treat him with scorn if he expressed himself to this effect against it. Otherwise it would be neccessary to admit that although wrong and injustice are not done to the Criminal by the law, yet the Legislative Power is not entitled to administer this mode of Punishment; and if it did so, it would be in contradiction with itself.

However many they may be who have committed a murder, or have even commanded it, or have been accessories in it, they ought all to suffer death; for so Justice wills it, in accordance with the Idea of the juridical Power as founded on the universal Laws of Reason. But the number of the Accomplices (*correi*) in such a deed might happen to be so great that the State, in resolving to be without such criminals, would be in danger of soon also being deprived of subjects. But it will not thus dissolve itself, neither must it return to the much worse condition of Nature, in which there would be no external Justice. Nor, above all, should it deaden the sensibilities of the People by the spectacle of Justice being exhibited in the mere carnage of a slaughtering bench. In such circumstances the Sovereign must always be allowed to have it in his power to take the part of the Judge upon himself as a case of Necessity,—and to deliver a Judgment which, instead of the penalty of death, shall assign some other punishment to the Criminals, and thereby preserve a multitude of the People. The penalty of Deportation is relevant in this connection. Such a form of Judgment cannot be carried out according to a public law, but only by an authoritative act of the royal Prerogative, and it may only be applied as an act of grace in individual cases.

Thomas Jefferson

Thomas Jefferson (1743–1826), drafter of the Declaration of
Independence, and third president of the United States, was not
only a statesman, but was also a political thinker very much
aware of the theoretical issues of his times in both America and
Europe. He also carried on an extensive correspondence. The
three letters printed below give a sample of his thought on political issues.

Letters

ON REPUBLICAN GOVERNMENT: TO JOHN TAYLOR

Monticello, May 28, 1816

Dear Sir,—On my return from a long journey and considerable absence from
home, I found here the copy of your "Enquiry into the Principles of our
Government," which you had been so kind as to send me; and for which I pray
you to accept my thanks. The difficulties of getting new works in our situation,
inland and without a single bookstore, are such as had prevented my obtaining a
copy before; and letters which had accumulated during my absence, and were
calling for answers, have not yet permitted me to give to the whole a thorough
reading; yet certain that you and I could not think differently on the fundamen-
tals of rightful government, I was impatient, and availed myself of the intervals
of repose from the writing-table, to obtain a cursory idea of the body of the
work.

I see in it much matter for profound reflection; much which should confirm
our adhesion, in practice, to the good principles of our Constitution, and fix our
attention on what is yet to be made good. The sixth section on the good moral
principles of our government, I found so interesting and replete with sound
principles, as to postpone my letter-writing to its thorough perusal and consideration. Besides much other good matter, it settles unanswerably the right of
instructing representatives, and their duty to obey. The system of banking we
have both equally and ever reprobated. I contemplate it as a blot left in all our
Constitutions, which, if not covered, will end in their destruction, which is
already hit by the gamblers in corruption, and is sweeping away in its progress
the fortunes and morals of our citizens. Funding I consider as limited, rightfully,
to a redemption of the debt within the lives of a majority of the generation

From *The Writings of Thomas Jefferson*, The Thomas Jefferson Memorial
Association, Washington, D.C. 1904. Headings added by the editors.

contracting it; every generation coming equally, by the laws of the Creator of the world, to the free possession of the earth He made for their subsistence, unincumbered by their predecessors, who, like them, were but tenants for life. You have successfully and completely pulverized Mr. Adams' system of orders, and his opening the mantle of republicanism to every government of laws, whether consistent or not with natural right. Indeed, it must be acknowledged, that the term *republic* is of very vague application in every language. Witness the self-styled republics of Holland, Switzerland, Genoa, Venice, Poland. Were I to assign to this term a precise and definite idea, I would say, purely and simply, it means a government by its citizens in mass, acting directly and personally, according to rules established by the majority; and that every other government is more or less republican, in proportion as it has in its composition more or less of this ingredient of the direct action of the citizens. Such a government is evidently restrained to very narrow limits of space and population. I doubt if it would be practicable beyond the extent of a New England township. The first shade from this pure element, which, like that of pure vital air, cannot sustain life of itself, would be where the powers of the government, being divided, should be exercised each by representatives chosen either *pro hac vice*, or for such short terms as should render secure the duty of expressing the will of their constituents. This I should consider as the nearest approach to a pure republic, which is practicable on a large scale of country or population. And we have examples of it in some of our State Constitutions, which, if not poisoned by priest-craft, would prove its excellence over all mixtures with other elements; and, with only equal doses of poison, would still be the best. Other shades of republicanism may be found in other forms of government, where the executive, judiciary, and legislative functions, and the different branches of the latter, are chosen by the people more or less directly, for longer terms of years, or for life, or made hereditary; or where there are mixtures of authorities, some dependent on, and others independent of the people. The further the departure from direct and constant control by the citizens, the less has the government of the ingredient of republicanism; evidently none where the authorities are hereditary, as in France, Venice, etc., or self-chosen, as in Holland; and little, where for life, in proportion as the life continues in being after the act of election.

The purest republican feature in the government of our own State, is the House of Representatives. The Senate is equally so the first year, less the second, and so on. The Executive still less, because not chosen by the people directly. The Judiciary seriously anti-republican, because for life; and the national arm wielded, as you observe, by military leaders, irresponsible but to themselves. Add to this the vicious constitution of our county courts (to whom the justice, the executive administration, the taxation, police, the military appointments of the county, and nearly all our daily concerns are confided), self-appointed, self-continued, holding their authorities for life, and with an impossibility of breaking in on the perpetual succession of any faction once possessed of the bench. They are in truth, the executive, the judiciary, and the military of their respective counties, and the sum of the counties makes the State. And add, also, that one-half of our brethren who fight and pay taxes, are excluded, like Helots, from the rights of representation, as if society were instituted for the soil, and not for the men inhabiting it; or one-half of these could dispose of the rights and the will of the other half, without their consent.

What constitutes a State?
Not high-raised battlements, or labor'd mound,
   Thick wall, or moated gate;
Not cities proud, with spires and turrets crown'd;
   No: men, high-minded men;
   Men, who their duties known;
But know their rights; and knowing, dare maintain.
   These constitute a State.

In the General Government, the House of Representatives is mainly republican; the Senate scarcely so at all, as not elected by the people directly, and so long secured even against those who do elect them; the Executive more republican than the Senate, from its shorter term, its election by the people, in *practice*, (for they vote for A only on an assurance that he will vote for B,) and because, *in practice also*, a principle of rotation seems to be in a course of establishment; the judiciary independent of the nation, their coercion by impeachment being found nugatory.

If, then, the control of the people over the organs of their government be the measure of its republicanism, and I confess I know no other measure, it must be agreed that our governments have much less of republicanism than ought to have been expected; in other words, that the people have less regular control over their agents, than their rights and their interests require. And this I ascribe, not to any want of republican dispositions in those who formed these Constitutions, but to a submission of true principle to European authorities, to speculators on government, whose fears of the people have been inspired by the populace of their own great cities, and were unjustly entertained against the independent, the happy, and therefore orderly citizens of the United States. Much I apprehend that the golden moment is past for reforming these heresies. The functionaries of public power rarely strengthen in their dispositions to abridge it, and an unorganized call for timely amendments is not likely to prevail against an organized opposition to it. We are always told that things are going on well; why change them? "*Chi sta bene, non si muove,*" said the Italian, "let him who stands well, stand still." This is true; and I verily believe they would go on well with us under an absolute monarch, while our present character remains, of order, industry and love of peace, and restrained, as he would be, by the proper spirit of the people. But it is while it remains such, we should provide against the consequences of its deterioration. And let us rest in the hope it will yet be done, and spare ourselves the pain of evils which may never happen.

On this view of the import of the term *republic*, instead of saying, as has been said, "that it may mean anything or nothing," we may say with truth and meaning, that governments are more or less republican, as they have more or less of the element of popular election and control in their composition; and believing, as I do, that the mass of the citizens is the safest depository of their own rights and especially, that the evils flowing from the duperies of the people, are less injurious than those from the egoism of their agents, I am a friend to that composition of government which has in it the most of this ingredient. And I sincerely believe, with you, that banking establishments are more dangerous than standing armies; and that the principle of spending money to be paid by posterity, under the name of funding, is but swindling futurity on a large scale.

I salute you with constant friendship and respect.

ON OBEDIENCE TO LAW: TO J. B. COLVIN

Monticello, September 20, 1810

Sir,—Your favor of the 14th has been duly received, and I have to thank you for the many obliging things respecting myself which are said in it. If I have left in the breasts of my fellow citizens a sentiment of satisfaction with my conduct in the transaction of their business, it will soften the pillow of my repose through the residue of life.

The question you propose, whether circumstances do not sometimes occur, which make it a duty in officers of high trust, to assume authorities beyond the law, is easy of solution in principle, but sometimes embarrassing in practice. A strict observance of the written laws is doubtless *one* of the high duties of a good citizen, but it is not *the highest.* The laws of necessity, of self-preservation, of saving our country when in danger, are of higher obligation. To lose our country by a scrupulous adherence to written law, would be to lose the law itself, with life, liberty, property and all those who are enjoying them with us; thus absurdly sacrificing the end to the means. When, in the battle of Germantown, General Washington's army was annoyed from Chew's house, he did not hesitate to plant his cannon against it, although the property of a citizen. When he besieged Yorktown, he leveled the suburbs, feeling that the laws of property must be postponed to the safety of the nation. While the army was before York, the Governor of Virginia took horses, carriages, provisions and even men by force, to enable that army to stay together till it could master the public enemy; and he was justified. A ship at sea in distress for provisions, meets another having abundance, yet refusing a supply; the law of self-preservation authorizes the distressed to take a supply by force. In all these cases, the unwritten laws of necessity, of self-preservation, and of the public safety, control the written laws of *meum* and *tuum.* Further to exemplify the principle, I will state an hypothetical case. Suppose it had been made known to the Executive of the Union in the autumn of 1805, that we might have the Floridas for a reasonable sum, that that sum had not indeed been so appropriated by law, but that Congress were to meet within three weeks, and might appropriate it on the first or second day of their session. Ought he, for so great an advantage to his country, to have risked himself by transcending the law and making the purchase? The public advantage offered, in this supposed case, was indeed immense; but a reverence for law, and the probability that the advantage might still be *legally* accomplished by a delay of only three weeks, were powerful reasons against hazarding the act. But suppose it foreseen that a John Randolph would find means to protract the proceeding on it by Congress, until the ensuing spring, by which time new circumstances would change the mind of the other party. Ought the Executive, in that case, and with that foreknowledge, to have secured the good to his country, and to have trusted to their justice for the transgression of the law? I think he ought, and that the act would have been approved. After the affair of the Chesapeake, we thought war a very possible result. Our magazines were illy provided with some necessary articles, nor had any appropriations been made for their purchase. We ventured, however, to provide them, and to place our country in safety; and stating the case to Congress, they sanctioned the act.

To proceed to the conspiracy of Burr, and particularly to General Wilkinson's situation in New Orleans. In judging this case, we are bound to consider the state of the information, correct and incorrect, which he then possessed. He expected Burr and his band from above, a British fleet from below, and he knew there was a formidable conspiracy within the city. Under these circumstances, was he justifiable, 1st, in seizing notorious conspirators? On this there can be but two opinions: one, of the guilty and their accomplices; the other, that of all honest men. 2d. In sending them to the seat of government, when the written law gave them a right to trail in the territory? The danger of their rescue, of their continuing their machinations, the tardiness and weakness of the law, apathy of the judges, active patronage of the whole tribe of lawyers, unknown disposition of the juries, an hourly expectation of the enemy, salvation of the city, and of the Union itself, which would have been convulsed to its centre, had that conspiracy succeeded; all these constituted a law of necessity and self-preservation, and rendered the *salus populi* supreme over the written law. The officer who is called to act on this superior ground, does indeed risk himself on the justice of the controlling powers of the Constitution, and his station makes it his duty to incur that risk. But those controlling powers, and his fellow citizens generally, are bound to judge according to the circumstances under which he acted. They are not to transfer the information of this place or moment to the time and place of his action; but to put themselves into his situation. We knew here that there never was danger of a British fleet from below, and that Burr's band was crushed before it reached the Mississippi. But General Wilkinson's information was very different, and he could act on no other.

From these examples and principles you may see what I think on the question proposed. They do not go to the case of persons charged with petty duties, where consequences are trifling, and time allowed for a legal course, nor to authorize them to take such cases out of the written law. In these, the example of overleaping the law is of greater evil than a strict adherence to its imperfect provisions. It is incumbent on those who accept great charges, to risk themselves on great occasions, when the safety of the nation, or some of its very high interests are at stake. An officer is bound to obey orders; yet he would be a bad one who should do it in cases for which they were not intended, and which involved the most important consequences. The line of discrimination between cases may be difficult; but the good officer is bound to draw it at his own peril, and throw himself on the justice of his country and the rectitude of his motives.

I have indulged freer views on this question, on your assurances that they are for your own eye only, and that they will not get into the hands of newswriters. I met their scurrilities without concern, while in pursuit of the great interests with which I was charged. But in my present retirement, no duty forbids my wish for quiet.

Accept the assurances of my esteem and respect.

ON PROGRESS IN THE LAWS: TO SAMUEL KERCHEVAL

Monticello, July 12, 1816

. . . I am not among those who fear the people. They, and not the rich, are our dependence for continued freedom. And to preserve their independence, we must not let our rulers load us with perpetual debt. We must make our election between *economy and liberty*, or *profusion and servitude*. If we run into such debts, as that we must be taxed in our meat and in our drink, in our necessaries and our comforts, in our labors and our amusements, for our callings and our creeds, as the people of England are, our people, like them, must come to labor sixteen hours in the twenty-four, give the earnings of fifteen of these to the government for their debts and daily expenses; and the sixteenth being insufficient to afford us bread, we must live, as they now do, on oatmeal and potatoes; have no time to think, no means of calling the mismanagers to account; but be glad to obtain subsistence by hiring ourselves to rivet their chains on the necks of our fellow sufferers. Our land-holders, too, like theirs, retaining indeed the title and stewardship of estates called theirs, but held really in trust for the treasury, must wander, like theirs, in foreign countries, and be contented with penury, obscurity, exile, and the glory of the nation. This example reads to us the salutary lesson, that private fortunes are destroyed by public as well as by private extravagance. And this is the tendency of all human governments. A departure from principle in one instance becomes a precedent for a second; that second for a third; and so on, till the bulk of the society is reduced to be mere automatons of misery, to have no sensibilities left but for sinning and suffering. Then begins, indeed, the *bellum omnium in omnia*, which some philosophers observing to be so general in this world, have mistaken it for the natural, instead of the abusive state of man. And the fore horse of this frightful team is public debt. Taxation follows that, and in its train wretchedness and oppression.

Some men look at constitutions with sanctimonious reverence, and deem them like the ark of the convenant, too sacred to be touched. They ascribe to the men of the preceiding age a wisdom more than human, and suppose what they did to be beyond amendment. I knew that age well; I belonged to it, and labored with it. It deserved well of its country. It was very like the present, but without the experience of the present; and forty years of experience in government is worth a century of book-reading; and this they would say themselves, were they to rise from the dead. I am certainly not an advocate for frequent and untried changes in laws and constitutions. I think moderate imperfections had better be borne with; because, when once known, we accommodate ourselves to them, and find practical means of correcting their ill effects. But I know also, that laws and institutions must go hand in hand with the progress of the human mind. As that becomes more developed, more enlightened, as new discoveries are made, new truths disclosed, and manners and opinions change with the change of circumstances, institutions must advance also, and keep pace with the times. We might as well require a man to wear still the coat which fitted him when a boy, as civilized society to remain ever under the regimen of their barbarous ancestors. It is this preposterous idea which has lately deluged Europe in blood. Their monarchs, instead of wisely yielding to the gradual change of circumstances, of favoring progressive accommodation to progressive improvement, have clung to old abuses, entrenched themselves behind steady habits, and obliged their subjects to seek through blood and violence rash and ruinous innovations, which, had they been referred to the peaceful deliberations and collected wisdom of the nation, would have been put into acceptable and salutary forms. Let us follow no such examples, nor weakly believe that one generation is not as capable as another of taking care of itself, and of ordering its own affairs. Let us, as our sister States have done, avail ourselves of our reason and experience, to correct the crude essays of our first and unexperienced, although wise, virtuous, and well-meaning councils. And lastly, let us provide in our Constitution for its revision at stated periods. What these periods should be, nature herself indicates. By the European tables of mortality, of the adults living at any one moment of time, a majority will be dead in about nineteen years. At the end of that period then, a new majority is come into place; or, in other words, a new generation. Each generation is as independent of the one preceding, as that was of all which had gone before. It has then, like them, a right to choose for itself the form of government it believes most promotive of its own happiness; consequently, to accommodate to the circumstances in which it finds itself, that received from its predecessors; and it is for the peace and good of mankind, that a solemn opportunity of doing this every nineteen or twenty years, should be provided by the Constitution; so that it may be handed on, with periodical repairs, from generation to generation to the end of time, if anything human can so long endure. It is now forty years since the constitution of Virginia was formed. The same tables inform us, that, within that period, two-thirds of the adults then living are now dead. Have then the remaining third, even if they had the wish, the right to hold in obedience to their will, and to laws heretofore made by them, the other two-thirds, who, with themselves, compose the present mass of adults? If they have not, who has? The dead? But the dead have no rights. They are nothing; and nothing cannot own something. Where there is no substance, there can be no accident. This corporeal globe, and everything upon it, belong to its present corporeal inhabitants, during their generation. They alone have a right to direct what is the concern of themselves alone, and to declare the law of that direction; and this declaration can only be made by their majority. That majority, then, has a right to depute representatives to a convention, and to make the Constitution what they think will be the best for themselves. But how collect their voice? This is the real difficulty. If invited by private authority, or county or district meetings, these divisions are so large that few will attend; and their voice will be imperfectly, or falsely, pronounced. Here, then, would be one of the advantages of the ward divisions I have proposed. The mayor of every ward, on a question like the present, would call his ward together, take the simple yea or nay of its members, convey these to the county court, who would hand on those of all its wards to the proper general authority; and the voice of the whole people would be thus fairly, fully, and peaceably expressed, discussed, and decided by the common reason of the society. If this avenue be shut to the call of sufferance, it will make itself heard through that of force, and we shall go on, as other nations are doing, in the endless circle of oppression, rebellion, reformation; and oppression, rebellion, reformation, again; and so on forever.

Jeremy Bentham

Jeremy Bentham (1748–1832) was born into a wealthy family and was a student at Oxford. His chief interest was in governmental reform and he was led into philosophy in his attempts to justify such reform. He was the leader of a small group known as the Philosophical Radicals which also included James Mill, the father of John Stuart Mill.

Bentham is one of the principal members of the school of moral and political thought known as Utilitarianism, which was mentioned in the Introduction. In the first part of the selection printed below, Bentham explains the principle of utility and how it is to be used in judging actions. The remainder of the selection consists of Bentham's application of his principles to the problem of punishment, which bears on his long-time interest in penal reform.

An Introduction to the Principles of Morals and Legislation

CHAPTER I OF THE PRINCIPLE OF UTILITY

I. Nature has placed mankind under the governance of two sovereign masters, *pain* and *pleasure*. It is for them alone to point out what we ought to do, as well as to determine what we shall do. On the one hand the standard of right and wrong, on the other the chain of causes and effects, are fastened to their throne. They govern us in all we do, in all we say, in all we think: every effort we can make to throw off our subjection, will serve but to demonstrate and confirm it. In words a man may pretend to abjure their empire: but in reality he will remain subject to it all the while. The *principle of utility*[1] recognises this subjection, and assumes it for the foundation of that system, the object of which is to rear

---

[1] Note by the Author, July 1822.

To this denomination has of late been added, or substituted, by the *greatest happiness* or *greatest felicity* principle: this for shortness, instead of saying at length *that principle* which states the greatest happiness of all those whose interest is in question, as being the right and proper, and only right and proper and universally desirable, end of human action: of human action in every situation, and in particular in that of a functionary or set of functionaries exercising the powers of Government. The word *utility* does not so clearly point to the ideas of *pleasure* and *pain* as the words *happiness* and *felicity* do: nor does it lead us to the consideration of the *number*, of the interests affected; to the *number*, as being circum-

Jeremy Bentham, *An Introduction to the Principles of Morals and Legislation*, London 1789, revised edition 1823.

the fabric of felicity by the hands of reason and of law. Systems which attempt to question it, deal in sounds instead of sense, in caprice instead of reason, in darkness instead of light.

But enough of metaphor and declamation: it is not by such means that moral science is to be improved.

II. The principle of utility is the foundation of the present work: it will be proper therefore at the outset to give an explicit and determinate account of what is meant by it. By the principle[2] of utility is meant that principle which approves or disapproves of every action whatsoever, according to the tendency which it appears to have to augment or diminish the happiness of the party whose interest is in question: or, what is the same thing in other words, to promote or to oppose that happiness. I say of every action whatsoever; and therefore not only of every action of a private individual, but of every measure of government.

III. By utility is meant that property in any object, whereby it tends to produce benefit, advantage, pleasure, good, or happiness, (all this in the present case comes to the same thing) or (what comes again to the same thing) to prevent the happening of mischief, pain, evil, or unhappiness to the party whose interest is considered: if that party be the community in general, then the happiness of the community: if a particular individual, then the happiness of that individual.

IV. The interest of the community is one of the most general expressions that can occur in the phraseology of morals: no wonder that the meaning of it is often lost. When it has a meaning, it is this. The community is a fictitious *body*, composed of the individual persons who are considered as constituting as it were its *members.* The interest of the community then is, what?—the sum of the interests of the several members who compose it.

V. It is in vain to talk of the interest of the community, without understanding what is the interest of the individual.[3] A thing is said to promote the interest, or to be *for* the interest, of an individual, when it tends to add to the

---

stance, which contributes, in the largest proportion, to the formation of the standard here in question; the *standard of right and wrong,* by which alone the propriety of human conduct, in every situation, can with propriety be tried. This want of a sufficiently manifest connexion between the ideas of *happiness* and *pleasure* on the one hand, and the idea of *utility* on the other, I have every now and then found operating, and with but too much efficiency, as a bar to the acceptance, that might otherwise have been given, to this principle.

[2] The word principle is derived from the Latin principium: which seems to be compounded of the two words *primus,* first, or chief, and *cipium,* a termination which seems to be derived from *capio,* to take, as in *mancipium, municipium;* to which are analogous, *auceps, forceps,* and others. It is a term of very vague and very extensive signification: it is applied to any thing which is conceived to serve as a foundation or beginning to any series of operations: in some cases, of physical operations; but of mental operations in the present case.

The principle here in question may be taken for an act of the mind; a sentiment; a sentiment of approbation; a sentiment which, when applied to an action, approves of its utility, as that quality of it by which the measure of approbation or disapprobation bestowed upon it ought to be governed.

[3] Interest is one of those words, which not having any superior *genus,* cannot in the ordinary way be defined.

sum total of his pleasures: or, what comes to the same thing, to diminish the sum total of his pain.

VI. An action then may be said to be conformable to the principle of utility, or, for shortness sake, to utility, (meaning with respect to the community at large) when the tendency it has to augment the happiness of the community is greater than any it has to diminish it.

VII. A measure of government (which is but a particular kind of action, performed by a particular person or persons) may be said to be conformable to or dictated by the principle of utility, when in like manner the tendency which it has to augment the happiness of the community is greater than any which it has to diminish it.

VIII. When an action, or in particular a measure of government, is supposed by a man to be conformable to the principle of utility, it may be convenient, for the purposes of discourse, to imagine a kind of law or dictate, called a law or dictate of utility: and to speak of the action in question, as being conformable to such law or dictate.

IX. A man may be said to be a partizan of the principle of utility, when the approbation or disapprobation he annexes to any action, or to any measure, is determined by and proportioned to the tendency which he conceives it to have to augment or to diminish the happiness of the community: or in other words, to its conformity or unconformity to the laws or dictates of utility.

X. Of an action that is conformable to the principle of utility one may always say either that it is one that ought to be done, or at least that it is not one that ought not to be done. One may say also, that it is right it should be done; at least that it is not wrong it should be done: that it is a right action; at least that it is not a wrong action. When thus interpreted, the words *ought*, and *right* and *wrong*, and others of that stamp, have a meaning: when otherwise, they have none.

XI. Has the rectitude of this princple been ever formally contested? It should seem that it had, by those who have not known what they have been meaning. Is it susceptible of any direct proof? it should seem not: for that which is used to prove every thing else, cannot itself be proved: a chain of proofs must have their commencement somewhere. To give such proof is as impossible as it is needless.

XII. Not that there is or ever has been that human creature breathing, however stupid or perverse, who has not on many, perhaps on most occasions of his life, deferred to it. By the natural constitution of the human frame, on most occasions of their lives men in general embrace this principle, without thinking of it: if not for the ordering of their own actions, yet for the trying of their own actions, as well as of those of other men. There have been, at the same time, not many, perhaps, even of the most intelligent, who have been disposed to embrace it purely and without reserve. There are even few who have not taken some occasion or other to quarrel with it, either on account of their not understanding always how to apply it, or on account of some prejudice or other which they were afraid to examine into, or could not bear to part with. For such is the stuff that man is made of: in principle and in practice, in a right track and in a wrong one, the rarest of all human qualities is consistency.

XIII. When a man attempts to combat the principle of utility, it is with reasons drawn, without his being aware of it, from that very principle itself.[4] His arguments, if they prove any thing, prove not that the principle is *wrong*, but that, according to the applications he supposes to be made of it, it is *misapplied.* Is it possible for a man to move the earth? Yes; but he must first find out another earth to stand upon.

XIV. To disprove the propriety of it by arguments is impossible; but, from the causes that have been mentioned, or from some confused or partial view of it, a man may happen to be disposed not to relish it. Where this is the case, if he thinks the settling of his opinions on such a subject worth the trouble, let him take the following steps, and at length, perhaps, he may come to reconcile himself to it.

1. Let him settle with himself, whether he would wish to discard this principle altogether; if so, let him consider what it is that all his reasonings (in matters of politics especially) can amount to?

2. If he would, let him settle with himself, whether he would judge and act without any principle, or whether there is any other he would judge and act by?

3. If there be, let him examine and satisfy himself whether the principle he thinks he has found is really any separate intelligible principle; or whether it be not a mere principle in words, a kind of phrase, which at bottom expresses neither more nor less than the mere averment of his own unfounded sentiments; that is, what in another person he might be apt to call caprice?

4. If he is inclined to think that his own approbation or disapprobation, annexed to the idea of an act, without any regard to its consequences, is a sufficient foundation for him to judge and act upon, let him ask himself whether his sentiment is to be a standard of right and wrong, with respect to every other man, or whether every man's sentiment has the same privilege of being a standard to itself?

5. In the first case, let him ask himself whether his principle is not despotical, and hostile to all the rest of human race?

6. In the second case, whether it is not anarchial, and whether at this rate there are not as many different standards of right and wrong as there are men? and whether even to the same man, the same thing, which is right today, may

---

[4] 'The principle of utility, (I have heard it said) is a dangerous principle: it is dangerous on certain occasions to consult it.' This is as much as to say, what? that it is not consonant to utility, to consult it: in short, that it is *not* consulting it, to consult it.

Addition by the Author, July 1822.

Not long after the publication of the Fragment on Government, anno 1776, in which, in the character of an all-comprehensive and all-commanding principle, the principle of *utility* was brought to view, one person by whom observation to the above effect was made was *Alexander Wedderburn,* at that time Attorney or Solicitor General, afterwards successively Chief Justice of the Common Pleas, and Chancellor of England, under the successive titles of Lord Loughborough and Earl of Rosslyn. It was made—not indeed in my hearing, but in the hearing of a person by whom it was almost immediately communicated to me. So far from being self-contradictory, it was a shrewd and perfectly true one. By that distinguished functionary, the state of the Government was thoroughly understood: by the obscure individual, at that time not so much as supposed to be so: his disquisitions had not been as yet applied, with any thing like a comprehensive view, to the field of Constitutional Law, nor therefore to those features of the English Government, by which the greatest happiness of the ruling *one* with or without that of a favoured few, are now so plainly seen to be the only ends to which the course of it has at any time been directed. The *principle of utility* was an appellative, at that time employed—employed by me, as it had been by others, to

not (without the least change in its nature) be wrong tomorrow? and whether the same thing is not right and wrong in the same place at the same time? and in either case, whether all argument is not at an end? and whether, when two men have said, 'I like this,' and 'I don't like it,' they can (upon such a principle) have any thing more to say?

7. If he should have said to himself, No: for that the sentiment which he proposes as a standard must be grounded on reflection, let him say on what particulars the reflection is to turn? if on particulars having relation to the utility of the act, then let him say whether this is not deserting his own principle, and borrowing assistance from that very one in opposition to which he sets it up: or if not on those particulars, on what other particulars?

8. If he should be for compounding the matter, and adopting his own principle in part, and the principle of utility in part, let him say how far he will adapt it?

9. When he has settled with himself where he will stop, then let him ask himself how he justifies to himself the adopting it so far? and why he will not adopt it any farther?

10. Admitting any other principle than the principle of utility to be a right principle, a principle that it is right for a man to pursue; admitting (what is not true) that the word *right* can have a meaning without reference to utility, let him say whether there is any such thing as a *motive* that man can have to pursue the dictates of it: if there is, let him say what that motive is, and how it is to be distinguished from those which enforce the dictates of utility: if not, then lastly let him say what it is this other principle can be good for?

CHAPTER IV   VALUE OF A LOT OF PLEASURE OR PAIN, HOW TO BE MEASURED

I. Pleasures then, and the avoidance of pains, are the *ends* which the legislator has in view: it behoves him therefore to understand their *value*. Pleasures and pains are the *instruments* he has to work with: it behoves him therefore to understand their force, which is again, in other words, their value.

---

design that which, in a more perspicuous and instructive manner, may as above be designated by the name of the *greatest happiness principle*. 'This principle (said Wedderburn) is a dangerous one. Saying so, he said that which, to a certain extent, is strictly true: a principle, which lays down, as the only *right* and justifiable end of Government, the greatest happiness of the greatest number—how can it be denied to be a dangerous one? dangerous it unquestionably is, to every government which has for its *actual* end or object, the greatest happiness of a certain *one*, with or without the addition of some comparatively small number of others, whom it is matter of pleasure or accommodation to him to admit, each of them, to a share in the concern, on the footing of so many junior partners. *Dangerous* it therefore really was, to the interest—the sinister interest—of all those functionaries, himself included, whose interest it was, to maximize delay, vexation, and expense, in judicial and other modes of procedure, for the sake of the profit, extractible out of the expense. In a Government which had for its end in view the greatest happiness of the greatest number. Alexander Wedderburn might have been Attorney General and then Chancellor: but he would not have been Attorney General with £15,000 a year, nor Chancellor, with a peerage with a veto upon all justice, with £25,000 a year, and with 500 sinecures at his disposal, under the name of Ecclesiastical Benefices, besides *et coeteras*.

II. To a person considered *by himself*, the value of a pleasure or pain considered *by itself*, will be greater or less, according to the four following circumstances:[1]

1. Its *intensity.*
2. Its *duration.*
3. Its *certainty* or *uncertainty.*
4. Its *propinquity* or *remoteness.*

III. These are the circumstances which are to be considered in estimating a pleasure or a pain considered each of them by itself. But when the value of any pleasure or pain is considered for the purpose of estimating the tendency of any *act* by which it is produced, there are two other circumstances to be taken into the account; these are,

5. Its *fecundity*, or the chance it has of being followed by sensations of the *same* kind: that is, pleasures, if it be a pleasure: pains, if it be a pain.

6. Its *purity*, or the chance it has of *not* being followed by sensations of the *opposite* kind: that is, pains, if it be a pleasure: pleasures, if it be a pain.

These two last, however, are in strictness scarcely to be deemed properties of pleasure or the pain itself; they are not, therefore, in strictness to be taken into the account of the value of that pleasure or pain. They are in strictness to be deemed properties only of the act, or other event, by which such pleasure or pain has been produced; and accordingly are only to be taken into the account of the tendency of such act or such event.

IV. To a *number* of persons, with reference to each of whom the value of a pleasure or a pain is considered, it will be greater or less, according to seven circumstances: to wit, the six preceding ones; *viz.*

1. Its *intensity.*
2. Its *duration.*
3. Its *certainty* or *uncertainty.*
4. Its *propinquity* or *remoteness.*
5. Its *fecundity.*
6. Its *purity.*

And one other; to wit:

7. Its *extent*; that is, the number of persons to whom it *extends*; or (in other words) who are affected by it.

V. To take an exact account then of the general tendency of any act, by which the interests of a community are affected, proceed as follows. Begin with any one person of those whose interests seem most immediately to be affected by it: and take an account,

[1] These circumstances have since been denominated *elements* or *dimensions* of *value* in a pleasure or a pain.

Not long after the publication of the first edition, the following memoriter verses were framed, in the view of lodging more effectually, in the memory, these points, on which the whole fabric of morals and legislation may be seen to rest.

 Intense, long, certain, speedy, fruitful, pure—
 Such marks in *pleasure* and in *pains* endure.
 Such pleasures seek of *private* be thy end:
 If it be *public*, wide let them *extend.*
 Such *pains* avoid, whichever be thy view:
 If pains *must* come, let them *extend* to few.

1. Of the value of each distinguishable *pleasure* which appears to be produced by it in the *first* instance.

2. Of the value of each *pain* which appears to be produced by it in the *first* instance.

3. Of the value of each pleasure which appears to be produced by it *after* the first. This constitutes the *fecundity* of the first *pleasure* and the *impurity* of the first *pain.*

4. Of the value of each *pain* which appears to be produced by it after the first. This constitutes the *fecundity* of the first *pain,* and the *impurity* of the first pleasure.

5. Sum up all the values of all the *pleasures* on the one side, and those of all the pains on the other. The balance, if it be on the side of pleasure, will give the *good* tendency of the act upon the whole, with respect to the interests of that *individual* person; if on the side of pain, the *bad* tendency of it upon the whole.

6. Take an account of the *number* of persons whose interests appear to be concerned; and repeat the above process with respect to each. *Sum up* the numbers expressive of the degrees of *good* tendency, which the act has, with respect to each individual, in regard to whom the tendency of it is *good* upon the whole: do this again with respect to each individual, in regard to whom the tendency of it is *good* upon the whole: do this again with respect to each individual, in regard to whom the tendency of it is *bad* upon the whole. Take the *balance;* which, if on the side of *pleasure,* will give the general *good tendency* of the act, with respect to the total number or community of individuals concerned; if on the side of pain, the general *evil tendency,* with respect to the same community.

VI. It is not to be expected that this process should be strictly pursued previously to every moral judgment, or to every legislative or judicial operation. It may, however, be always kept in view: and as near as the process actually pursued on these occasions approaches to it, so near will such process approach to the character of an exact one.

VII. The same process is alike applicable to pleasure and pain, in whatever shape they appear: and by whatever denomination they are distinguished: to pleasure, whether it be called *good* (which is properly the cause or instrument of pleasure) or *profit* (which is distant pleasure, or the cause or instrument of distant pleasure,) or *convenience,* or *advantage, benefit, emolument, happiness,* and so forth: to pain, whether it be called *evil,* (which corresponds to *good*) or *mischief,* or *inconvenience,* or *disadvantage,* or *loss,* or *unhappiness,* and so forth.

VIII. Nor is this a novel and unwarranted, any more than it is a useless theory. In all this there is nothing but what the practice of mankind, wheresoever they have a clear view of their own interest, is perfectly conformable to. An article of property, an estate in land, for instance, is valuable, on what account? On account of the pleasures of all kinds which it enables a man to produce, and what comes to the same thing the pains of all kinds which it enables him to avert. But the value of such an article of property is universally understood to rise or fall according to the length or shortness of the time which a man has in it: the certainty or uncertainty of its coming into possession: and the nearness or remoteness of the time at which, if at all, it is to come into possession. As to the *intensity* of the pleasures which a man may derive from it, this is never thought of, because it depends upon the use which each particular person may come to make of it; which cannot be estimated till the particular pleasures he may come to derive from it, or the particular pains he may come to exclude by means of it, are brought to view. For the same reason, neither does he think of the *fecundity* or *purity* of those pleasures.

Thus much for pleasure and pain, happiness and unhappiness, in *general*. We come now to consider the several particular kinds of pain and pleasure.

CHAPTER VII   OF HUMAN ACTIONS IN GENERAL

I. The business of government is to promote the happiness of the society, by punishing and rewarding. That part of its business which consists in punishing, is more particularly the subject of penal law. In proportion as an act tends to disturb that happiness, in proportion as the tendency of it is pernicious, will be the demand it creates for punishment. What happiness consists of we have already seen: enjoyment of pleasures, security from pains.

II. The general tendency of an act is more or less pernicious, according to the sum total of its consequences: that is, according to the difference between the sum of such as are good, and the sum of such as are evil.

III. It is to be observed, that here, as well as henceforward, wherever consequences are spoken of, such only are meant as are *material*. Of the consequences of any act, the multitude and variety must needs be infinite: but such of them only as are material are worth regarding. Now among the consequences of an act, be they what they may, such only, by one who views them in the capacity of a legislator, can be said to be material,[1] as either consist of pain or pleasure, or have an influence in the production of pain or pleasure.[2]

IV. It is also to be observed, that into the account of the consequences of the act, are to be taken not such only as might have ensued, were intention out of the question, but such also as depend upon the connexion there may be between these first-mentioned consequences and the intention. The connexion there is between the intention and certain consequences is, as we shall see hereafter, a means of producing other consequences. In this lies the difference between rational agency and irrational.

V. Now the intention, with regard to the consequences of an act, will depend upon two things: 1. The state of the will or intention, with respect to the act itself. And, 2. The state of the understanding, or perceptive faculties, with regard to the circumstances which it is, or may appear to be, accompanied with. Now with respect to these circumstances, the perceptive faculty is susceptible of three states: consciousness, unconsciousness, and false consciousness. Consciousness, when the party believes precisely those circumstances, and others, to subsist, which really do subsist: unconsciousness, when he fails of perceiving certain circumstances to subsist, which, however, do subsist: false consciousness, when

---

[1] Or of *importance*.

[2] In certain cases the consequences of an act may be material by serving as evidences indicating the existence of some other material fact, which is even *antecedent* to the act of which they are the consequences: but even here, they are material only because, in virtue of such their evidentiary quality, they have an influence, at a subsequent period of time, in the production of pain and pleasure: for example, by serving as grounds for conviction, and thence for punishment. See tit. [Simple Falsehoods], *verbo* [material].

he believes or imagines certain circumstances to subsist, which in truth do not subsist.

VI. In every transaction, therefore, which is examined with a view to punishment, there are four articles to be considered: 1. The *act* itself, which is done. 2. The *circumstances* in which it is done. 3. The *intentionality* that may have accompanied it. 4. The *consciousness*, unconsciousness, or false consciousness, that may have accompanied it.

What regards the act and the circumstances will be the subject of the present chapter: what regards intention and consciousness, that of the two succeeding.

VII. There are also two other articles on which the general tendency of an act depends: and on that, as well as on other accounts, the demand which it creates for punishment. These are, 1. The particular *motive* or motives which gave birth to it. 2. The general *disposition* which it indicates. These articles will be the subject of two other chapters.

VIII. Acts may be distinguished in several ways, for several purposes.

They may be distinguished, in the first place, into *positive* and *negative*. By positive are meant such as consist in motion or exertion: by negative, such as consist in keeping at rest; that is, in forbearing to move or exert one's self in such and such circumstances. Thus, to strike is a positive act: not to strike on a certain occasion, a negative one. Positive acts are styled also acts of commission; negative, acts of omission or forbearance.[3]

IX. Such acts, again, as are negative, may either be *absolutely* so, or *relatively*: absolutely, when they import the negation of all positive agency whatsoever; for instance, not to strike at all: relatively, when they import the negation of such or such a particular mode of agency; for instance, not to strike such a person or such a thing, or in such a direction.

X. It is to be observed, that the nature of the act, whether positive or negative, is not to be determined immediately by the form of the discourse made use of to express it. An act which is positive in its nature may be characterized by a negative expression: thus, not to be at rest, is as much as to say to move. So also an act, which is negative in its nature, may be characterized by a positive expression: thus, to forbear or omit to bring food to a person in certain circumstances, is signified by the single and positive term *to starve*.

XI. In the second place, acts may be distinguished into *external* and *internal*. By external, are meant corporal acts; acts of the body; by internal, mental acts; acts of the mind. Thus, to strike is an external or exterior[4] act: to intend to strike, an internal or interior one.

[3] The distinction between positive and negative acts runs through the whole system of offences, and sometimes makes a material difference with regard to their consequences. To reconcile us the better to the extensive, and, as it may appear on some occasions, the inconsistent signification here given to the word *act*, it may be considered, 1. That in many cases, where no exterior or overt act is exercised, the state which the mind is in at the time when the supposed act is said to happen, is as truly and directly the result of the will, as any exterior act, how plain and conspicuous soever. The not revealing a conspiracy, for instance, may be as perfectly the act of the will, as the joining in it. In the next place, that even though the mind should never have had the incident in question in contemplation (insomuch that the event of its not happening should not have been so much as obliquely intentional) still the state the person's mind was in at the time when, if he *had* so willed, the incident might have happened, is in many cases productive of as material consequences; and not only as likely, but as fit to call for the interposition of other agents, as the opposite one. Thus, when a tax is imposed, your not paying it is an act which at any rate must be punished in a certain manner, whether you happened to think of paying it or not.

[4] An exterior act is also called by lawyers *overt*.

XII. Acts of *discourse* are a sort of mixture of the two: external acts, which are no ways material, nor attended with any consequences, any farther than as they serve to express the existence of internal ones. To speak to another to strike, to write to him to strike, to make signs to him to strike, are all so many acts of discourse.

XIII. Third, Acts that are external may be distinguished into *transitive* and *intransitive*. Acts may be called transitive, when the motion is communicated from the person of the agent to some foreign body: that is, to such a foreign body on which the effects of it are considered as being *material;* as where a man runs against you, or throws water in your face. Acts may be called intransitive, when the motion is communicated to no other body, on which the effects of it are regarded as material, than some part of the same person in whom it originated: as where a man runs, or washes himself.[5]

XIV. An act of the transitive kind may be said to be in its *commencement*, or in the *first* stage of its progress, while the motion is confined to the person of the agent, and has not yet been communicated to any foreign body, on which the effects of it can be material. It may be said to be in its *termination*, or to be in the last stage of its progress, as soon as the motion or impulse has been communicated to some such foreign body. It may be said to be in the *middle* or intermediate stage or stages of its progress, while the motion, having passed from the person of the agent, has not yet communicated to any such foreign body. Thus, as soon as a man has lifted up his hand to strike, the act he performs in striking you is in its commencement: as soon as his hand has reached you, it is in its termination. If the act be the motion of a body which is separated from the person of the agent before it reaches the object, it may be said, during that interval, to be in its intermediate progress, or in *gradu mediativo:* as in the case where a man throws a stone or fires a bullet at you.

XV. An act of the *in*transitive kind may be said to be in its commencement, when the motion or impulse is as yet confined to the member or organ in which it originated; and has not yet been communicated to any member or organ that is distinguishable from the former. It may be said to be in its termination, as soon as it has been applied to any other part of the same person. Thus, where a man poisons himself, while he is lifting up the poison to his mouth, the act is in its commencement: as soon as it has reached his lips, it is in its termination.

XVI. In the third place, acts may be distinguished into *transient* and *continued*. Thus, to strike is a transient act: to lean, a continued one. To buy, a transient act: to keep in one's possession, a continued one.

XVII. In strictness of speech there is a difference between a *continued* act and a *repetition* of acts. It is a repetition of acts, when there are intervals filled up by acts of different natures: a continued act. when there are no such intervals. Thus, to lean, is one continued act: to keep striking, a repetition of acts.

XVIII. There is a difference, again, between a *repetition* of acts, and a *habit* or *practice*. The term repetition of acts may be employed, let the acts in

---

[5] The distinction is well known to the latter grammarians: it is with them indeed that it took its rise: though by them it has been applied rather to the names than to the things themselves. To verbs, signifying transitive acts, as here described, they have given the name of transitive verbs: those significative of intransitive acts they have termed intransitive. These last are still more frequently called *neuter;* that is, *neither* active nor passive. The appellation seems improper: since, instead of their being *neither,* they are both in one.

question be separated by ever such short intervals, and let the sum total of them occupy ever so short a space of time. The term habit is not employed but when the acts in question are supposed to be separated by long-continued intervals, and the sum total of them to occupy a considerable space of time. It is not (for instance) the drinking ever so many times, nor ever so much at a time, in the course of the same sitting, that will constitute a habit of drunkeness: it is necessary that such sittings themselves be frequently repeated. Every habit is a repetition of acts; or, to speak more strictly, when a man has frequently repeated such and such acts after considerable intervals, he is said to have persevered in or contracted a habit: but every repetition of acts is not a habit.[6]

XIX. Fourth, acts may be distinguished into *indivisible* and *divisible.* Indivisible acts are merely imaginary: they may be easily conceived, but can never be known to be exemplified. Such as are divisble may be so, with regard either to matter or to motion. An act indivisible with regard to matter, is the motion or rest of one single atom of matter. An act indivisible, with regard to motion, is the motion of any body, from one single atom of space to the next to it.

Fifth, acts may be distinguished into *simple* and *complex:* simple, such as the act of striking, the act of leaning, or the act of drinking, above instanced: complex, consisting each of a multitude of simple acts, which, though numerous and heterogeneous, derive a sort of unity from the relation they bear to some common design or end; such as the act of giving a dinner, the act of maintaining a child, the act of exhibiting a triumph, the act of bearing arms, the act of holding a court, and so forth.

XX. It has been every now and then made a question, what it is in such a case that constitutes *one* act: where one act has ended, and another act begun: whether what has happened has been one act or many. These questions, it is now evident, may frequently be answered, with equal propriety, in opposite ways: and if there be any occasions on which they can be answered only in one way, the answer will depend upon the nature of the occasion, and the purpose for which the question is proposed. A man is wounded in two fingers at one stroke—Is it one wound or several? A man is beaten at 12 o'clock, and again at 8 minutes after 12—Is it one beating or several? You beat one man, and instantly in the same breath you beat another—Is this one beating or several? In any of these cases it may be *one*, perhaps, as to some purposes, and *several* as to others. These examples are given, that men may be aware of the ambiguity of language: and neither harass themselves with unsolvable doubts, nor one another with interminable disputes.

XXI. So much with regard to acts considered in themselves: we come to speak of the *circumstances* with which they may have been accompanied. These must necessarily be taken into the account before any thing can be determined relative to the consequences. What the consequences of an act may be upon the whole can never otherwise be ascertained: it can never be known whether it is beneficial, or indifferent, or mischievous. In some circumstances even to kill a man may be a beneficial act: in others, to set food before him may be a pernicious one.

XXII. Now the circumstances of an act, are, what? Any objects whatsoever.

---

[6] A habit, it should seem, can hardly in strictness be termed an aggregate of acts: acts being a sort of real archetypal entities, and habits a kind of fictitious entities or imaginary beings, supposed to be constituted by, or to result as it were out of, the former.

Take any act whatsoever, there is nothing in the nature of things that excludes any imaginable object from being a circumstance to it. Any given object may be a circumstance to any other.[7]

XXIII. We have already had occasion to make mention for a moment of the *consequences* of an act: these were distinguished into material and immaterial. In like manner may the circumstances of it be distinguished. Now *materiality* is a relative term: applied to the consequences of an act, it bore relation to pain and pleasure: applied to the circumstances, it bears relation to the consequences. A circumstance may be said to be material, when it bears a visible relation in point of causality to the consequences: immaterial, when it bears no such visible relation.

XXIV. The consequences of an act are events. A circumstance may be related to an event in point of causality in any one of four ways: 1. In the way of causation or production. 2. In the way of derivation. 3. In the way of collateral connexion. 4. In the way of conjunct influence. It may be said to be related to the event in the way of causation, when it is of the number of those that contribute to the production of such event: in the way of derivation, when it is of the number of the events to the production of which that in question has been contributory: in the way of collateral connexion, where the circumstance in question, and the event in question, without being either of them instrumental in the production of the other, are related, each of them, to some common object, which has been concerned in the production of them both: in the way of conjunct influence, when, whether related in any other way or not, they have both of them concurred in the production of some common consequence.

XXV. An example may be of use. In the year 1628, Villiers, Duke of Buckingham, favourite and minister of Charles I. of England, received a wound and died. The man who gave it him was one Felton, who, exasperated at the mal-administration of which that minister was accused, went down from London to Portsmouth, where Buckingham happened then to be, made his way into his anti-chamber, and finding him busily engaged in conversation with a number of people round him, got close to him, drew a knife and stabbed him. In the effort, the assassin's hat fell off, which was found soon after, and, upon searching him, the bloody knife. In the crown of the hat were found scraps of paper, with sentences expressive of the purpose he was come upon. Here then, suppose the event in question is the wound received by Buckingham: Felton's drawing out his knife, his making his way into the chamber, his going down to Portsmouth, his conceiving an indignation at the idea of Buckingham's administration, that administration itself, Charles's appointing such a minister, and so on, higher and higher without end, are so many circumstances, related to the event of Buckingham's receiving the wound, in the way of causation or production: the bloodiness of the knife, a circumstance related to the same event in the way of derivation: the finding of the hat upon the ground, the finding the sentences in

[7] The etymology of the word circumstance is perfectly characteristic of its import: *circum stantia*, things standing round: objects standing round a given object. I forget what mathematician it was that defined God to be a circle, of which the centre is every where, but the circumference no where. In like manner the field of circumstances, belonging to any act, may be defined a circle, of which the circumference is no where, but of which the act in question is the centre. Now then, as any act may, for the purpose of discourse, be considered as a centre, any other act or object whatsoever may be considered as of the number of those that are standing round it.

the hat, and the writing them, so may circumstances related to it in the way of collateral connexion: and the situation and conversations of the people about Buckingham, were circumstances related to the circumstances of Felton's making his way into the room, going down to Portsmouth, and so forth, in the way of conjunct influence; inasmuch as they contributed in common to the event of Buckingham's receiving the wound, by preventing him from putting himself upon his guard upon the first appearance of the intruder.[8]

XXVI. These several relations do not all of them attach upon an event with equal certainty. In the first place, it is plain, indeed, that every event must have some circumstance or other, and in truth, an indefinite multitude of circumstances, related to it in the way of production: it must of course have a still greater multitude of circumstances related to it in the way of collateral connexion. But it does not appear necessary that every event should have circumstances related to it in the way of derivation: nor therefore that it should have any related to it in the way of conjunct influence. But of the circumstances of all kinds which actually do attach upon an event, it is only a very small number that can be discovered by the utmost exertion of the human faculties: it is a still smaller number that ever actually do attract our notice: when occasion happens, more or fewer of them will be discovered by a man in proportion to the strength, partly of his intellectual powers, partly of his inclination.[9] It appears therefore that the multitude and description of such of the circumstances belonging to an act, as may appear to be material, will be determined by two considerations: 1. By the nature of things themselves. 2. By the strength or weakness of the faculties of those who happen to consider them.

XXVII. Thus much it seemed necessary to premise in general concerning acts, and their circumstances, previously to the consideration of the particular sorts of acts with their particular circumstances, with which we shall have to do in the body of the work. An act of some sort or other is necessarily included in

[8] The division may be farther illustrated and confirmed by the more simple and particular case of animal generation. To production corresponds paternity: to derivation, filiation: to collateral connexion, collateral consanguinity: to conjunct influence, marriage and copulation.

If necessary, it might be again illustrated by the material image of a chain, such as that which, according to the ingenious fiction of the ancients, is attached to the throne of Jupiter. A section of this chain should then be exhibited by way of specimen, in the manner of the *diagram* of a pedigree. Such a figure I should accordingly have exhibited, had it not been for the apprehension that an exhibition of this sort, while it made the subject a small matter clearer to one man out of a hundred, might, like the mathematical formularies we see sometimes employed for the like purpose, make it more obscure and formidable for the other ninety-nine.

[9] The more remote a connexion of this sort is, of course the more obscure. It will often happen that a connexion, the idea of which would at first sight appear extravagant and absurd, shall be rendered highly probable, and indeed indisputable, merely by suggestion of a few intermediate circumstances.

At Rome, 390 years before the Christian era a goose sets up a cackling: two thousand years afterwards a king of France is murdered. To consider these two events, and nothing more, what can appear more extravagant then the notion that the former of them should have had any influence on the production of the latter? Fill up the gap, bring to mind a few intermediate circumstances, and nothing can appear more probable. It was the cackling of a parcel of geese, at the time the Gauls had surprised the Capitol, that saved the Roman commonwealth: had it not been for the ascendancy that commonwealth acquired afterwards over most of the nations of Europe, amongst others over France, the Christian religion, humanly speaking, could not have established itself in the manner it did in that country. Grant then, that such a man as Henry IV. would have existed, no man, however, would have had those motives, by which Ravaillac, misled by a mischievous notion concerning the dictates of that religion, was prompted to assassinate him.

the notion of every offence. Together with this act, under the notion of the same offence, are included certain circumstances: which circumstances enter into the essence of the offence, contribute by their conjunct influence to the production of its consequences, and in conjunction with the act are brought into view by the name by which it stands distinguished. These we shall have occasion to distinguish hereafter by the name of *criminative* circumstances. Other circumstances again entering into combination with the act and the former set of circumstances, are productive of still farther consequences. These additional consequences, if they are of the beneficial kind, bestow, according to the value they bear in that capacity, upon the circumstances to which they owe their birth the appellation of *exculpative* or *extenuative* circumstances: if of the mischievous kind, they bestow on them the appellation of *aggravative* circumstances. Of all these different sets of circumstances, the criminative are connected with the consequences of the original offence, in the way of production; with the act, and with one another, in the way of conjunct influence: the consequences of the original offence with them, and with the act respectively, in the way of derivation: the consequences of the modified offence, with the criminative, exculpative, and extenuative circumstances respectively, in the way also of derivation: these different sets of circumstances, with the consequences of the modified act or offence, in the way of production: and with one another (in respect of the consequences of the modified act or offence) in the way of conjunct influence. Lastly, whatever circumstances can be seen to be connected with the consequences of the offence, whether directly in the way of derivation, or obliquely in the way of collateral affinity (to wit, in virtue of its being connected, in the way of derivation, with some of the circumstances with which they stand connected in the same manner) bear a *material* relation to the offence in the way of evidence, they may accordingly be styled *evidentiary* circumstances, and may become of use, by being held forth upon occasion as so many proofs, indications, or evidence of its having been committed.[10]

CHAPTER XIII   CASES UNMEET FOR PUNISHMENT

1. General View of Cases Unmeet for Punishment

I. The general object which all laws have, or ought to have, in common, is to augment the total happiness of the community; and therefore, in the first place, to exclude, as far as may be, every thing that tends to subtract from that happiness: in other words, to exclude mischief.

II. But all punishment is mischief: all punishment in itself is evil. Upon the principle of utility, if it ought at all to be admitted, it ought only to be admitted in as far as it promises to exclude some greater evil.[1]

---

[10] It is evident that this analysis is equally applicable to incidents of a purely physical nature, as to those in which moral agency is concerned. If therefore it be just and useful here, it might be found not impossible, perhaps, to find some use for it in natural philosophy.

[1] What follows, relative to the subject of punishment, ought regularly to be preceded by a distinct chapter on the ends of punishment. But having little to say on that particular branch of the subject, which has not been said before, it seemed better, in a work, which will at any rate be but too voluminous, to omit this title, reserving it for another, hereafter to be published, entitled *The Theory of Punishment*. To the same work I must refer the

III. It is plain, therefore, that in the following cases punishment ought not to be inflicted.

1. Where it is *groundless:* where there is no mischief for it to prevent; the act not being mischievous upon the whole.

2. Where it must be *inefficacious:* where it cannot act so as to prevent the mischief.

3. Where it is *unprofitable*, or too *expensive:* where the mischief it would produce would be greater than what it prevented.

4. Where it is *needless:* where the mischief may be prevented, or cease of itself, without it: that is, at a cheaper rate.

2. Cases in Which Punishment Is Groundless

These are,

IV. 1. Where there has never been any mischief: where no mischief has been produced to any body by the act in question. Of this number are those in which the act was such as might, on some occasions, be mischievous or disagreeable, but the person whose interest it concerns gave his *consent* to the performance of it. This consent, provided it be free, and fairly obtained, is the best proof that can be produced, that, to the person who gives it, no mischief, at least no immediate mischief, upon the whole, is done. For no man can be so good a judge as the man himself, what it is gives him pleasure or displeasure.

V. 2. Where the mischief was *outweighed:* although a mischief was produced by that act, yet the same act was necessary to the production of a benefit which was of greater value than the mischief. This may be the case with any thing that is done in the way of precaution against instant calamity, as also with any thing that is done in the exercise of the several sorts of powers necessary to be established in every community, to wit, domestic, judicial, military, and supreme.

VI. 3. Where there is a certainty of an adequate compensation: and that in all cases where the offence can be committed. This supposes two things: 1. That the

---

analysis of the several possible modes of punishment, a particular and minute examination of the nature of each, and of its advantages and disadvantages, and various other disquisitions, which did not seem absolutely necessary to be inserted here. A very few words, however, concerning the *ends* of punishment, can scarcely be dispensed with.

The immediate principal end of punishment is to control action. This action is either that of the offender, or of others: that of the offender it controls by its influence, either on his will, in which case it is said to operate in the way of *reformation;* or on his physical power, in which case it is said to operate by *disablement:* that of others it can influence no otherwise than by its influence over their wills; in which case it is said to operate in the way of *example.* A kind of collateral end, which it has a natural tendency to answer, is that of affording a pleasure or satisfaction to the party injured, where there is one, and, in general, to parties whose ill-will, whether on a self-regarding account, or on the account of sympathy or antipathy, has been excited by the offence. This purpose, as far as it can be answered *gratis,* is a beneficial one. But no punishment ought to be allotted merely to this purpose, because (setting aside its effects in the way of control) no such pleasure is ever produced by punishment as can be equivalent to the pain. The punishment, however, which is allotted to the other purpose, ought, as far as it can be done without expense, to be accommodated to this. Satisfaction thus administered to a party injured, in the shape of a dissocial pleasure, may be styled a vindictive satisfaction or compensation: as a compensation, administered in the shape of a self-regarding profit, or stock of pleasure, may be styled a lucrative one. Example is the most important end of all, in proportion as the *number* of the persons under temptation to offend is to *one.*

offence is such as admits of an adequate compensation: 2. That such a compensation is sure to be forthcoming. Of these suppositions, the latter will be found to be a merely ideal one: a supposition that cannot, in the universality here given to it, be verified by fact. It cannot, therefore, in practice, be numbered amongst the grounds of absolute impunity. It may, however, be admitted as a ground for an abatement of that punishment, which other considerations, standing by themselves, would seem to dictate.[2]

3. Cases in Which Punishment Must Be Inefficacious

These are,

VII. 1. Where the penal provision is *not established* until after the act is done. Such are the cases, 1. Of an *ex-post-facto* law; where the legislator himself appoints not a punishment till after the act is done. 2. Of a sentence beyond the law; where the judge, of his own authority, appoints a punishment which the legislator had not appointed.

VIII. 2. Where the penal provision, though established, is *not conveyed* to the notice of the person on whom it seems intended that it should operate. Such is the case where the law has omitted to employ any of the expedients which are necessary, to make sure that every person whatsoever, who is within the reach of the law, be apprized of all the cases whatsoever, in which (being in the station of life he is in) he can be subjected to the penalties of the law.

IX. 3. Where the penal provision, though it were conveyed to a man's notice, *could produce no effect* on him, with respect to the preventing him from engaging in any act of the *sort* in question. Such is the case, 1. In extreme *infancy*; where a man has not yet attained that state or disposition of mind in which the prospect of evils so distant as those which are held forth by the law, has the effect of influencing his conduct. 2. In *insanity*; where the person, if he has attained to that disposition, has since been deprived of it through the influence of some permanent though unseen cause. 3. In *intoxication*; where he has been deprived of it by transient influence of a visible cause: such as the use of wine, or opium, or other drugs, that act in this manner on the nervous system: which condition is indeed neither more nor less than a temporary insanity produced by an assignable cause.[3]

[2] This, for example, seems to have been one ground, at least, of the favour shown by perhaps all systems of laws, to such offenders as stand upon a footing of responsibility: shown, not directly indeed to the persons themselves; but to such offences as none but responsible persons are likely to have the opportunity of engaging in. In particular, this seems to be the reason why embezzlement, in certain cases, has not commonly been punished upon the footing of theft: nor mercantile frauds upon that of common sharping.

[3] Notwithstanding what is here said, the cases of infancy and intoxication (as we shall see hereafter) cannot be looked upon in practice as affording sufficient grounds for absolute impunity. But this is no objection to the propriety of the rule in point of theory. The ground of the exception is neither more nor less than the difficulty there is of ascertaining the matter of fact: viz. whether at the requisite point of time the party was actually in the state in question; that is, whether a given case comes really under the rule. Suppose the matter of fact capable of being perfectly ascertained, without danger or mistake, the impropriety of punishment would be as indubitable in these cases as in any other.

The reason that is commonly assigned for establishing an exemption from punishment in favour of infants, insane persons, and persons under intoxication, is either false in fact, or confusedly expressed. The phrase is, that the will of these persons concurs not with the act; that they have no vicious will; or, that they have not the free use of their will. But suppose all this to be true? What is it to the purpose? Nothing: except in as far as it implies the reason given in the text.

X. 4. Where the penal provision (although, being conveyed to the party's notice, it might very well prevent his engaging in acts of the sort in question, provided he knew that it related to those acts) could not have this effect, with regard to the *individual* act he is about to engage in: to wit, because he knows not that it is of the number of those to which the penal provision relates. This may happen, 1. In the case of *unintentionality*; where he intends not to engage, and thereby knows not that he is about to engage, in the *act* in which eventually he is about to engage. 2. In the case of *unconsciousness*; where, although he may know that he is about to engage in the *act* itself, yet from not knowing all the material *circumstances* attending it, he knows not of the *tendency* it has to produce that mischief, in contemplation of which it has been made penal in most instances. 3. In the case of *missupposal*; where, although he may know of the tendency the act has to produce that degree of mischief, he supposes it, though mistakenly, to be attended with some circumstance, or set of circumstances, which, if it had been attended with, it would either not have been productive of that mischief, or have been productive of such a greater degree of good, as has determined the legislator in such a case not to make it penal.

XI. 5. Where, though the penal clause might exercise a full and prevailing influence, were it to act alone, yet by the *predominant* influence of some opposite cause upon the will, it must necessarily be ineffectual; because the evil which he sets himself about to undergo, in the case of his *not* engaging in the act, is so great, that the evil denounced by the penal clause, in case of his engaging in it, cannot appear greater. This may happen, 1. In the case of *physical danger*; where the evil is such as appears likely to be brought about by the unassisted powers of *nature*. 2. In the case of a *threatened mischief*; where it is such as appears likely to be brought about through the intentional and conscious agency of *man*.[4]

XII. 6. Where (though the penal clause may exert a full and prevailing influence over the *will* of the party) yet his *physical faculties* (owing to the predominant influence of some physical cause) are not in a condition to follow the determination of the will: insomuch that the act is absolutely *involuntary*. Such is the case of physical *compulsion* or *restraint*, by whatever means brought about; where the man's hand, for instance, is pushed against some object which his will disposes him *not* to touch; or tied down from touching some object which his will disposes him to touch.

4. Cases Where Punishment is Unprofitable

These are,

XIII. 1. Where, on the one hand, the nature of the offence, on the other hand, that of the punishment, are, *in the ordinary state of things*, such, that

---

[4] The influences of the *moral* and *religious* sanctions, or, in other words, of the motives of *love of reputation* and *religion*, are other causes, the force of which may, upon particular occasions, come to be greater than that of any punishment which the legislator is *able*, or at least which he will *think proper*, to apply. These, therefore, it will be proper for him to have his eye upon. But the force of these influences is variable and different in different times and places: the force of the foregoing influences is constant and the same, at all times and every where. These, therefore, it can never be proper to look upon as safe grounds for establishing absolute impunity: owing (as in the above-mentioned cases of infancy and intoxication) to the impracticability of ascertaining the matter of fact.

when compared together, the evil of the latter will turn out to be greater than that of the former.

XIV. Now the evil of the punishment divides itself into four branches, by which so many different sets of persons are affected. 1. The evil of *coercion* or *restraint:* or the pain which it gives a man not to be able to do the act, whatever it be, which by the apprehension of the punishment he is deterred from doing. This is felt by those by whom the law is *observed.* 2. The evil of *apprehension:* or the pain which a man, who has exposed himself to punishment, feels at the thoughts of undergoing it. This is felt by those by whom the law has been *broken,* and who feel themselves in *danger* of its being executed upon them. 3. The evil of *sufferance:* or the pain which a man feels, in virtue of the punishment itself, from the time when he begins to undergo it. This is felt by those by whom the law is broken, and upon whom it comes actually to be executed. 4. The pain of sympathy, and the other *derivative* evils resulting to the persons who are in *connection* with the several classes of original sufferers just mentioned. Now of these four lots of evil, the first will be greater or less, according to the nature of the act from which the party is restrained: the second and third according to the nature of the punishment which stands annexed to that offence.

XV. On the other hand, as to the evil of the offence, this will also, of course, be greater or less, according to the nature of each offence. The proportion between the one evil and the other will therefore be different in the case of each particular offence. The cases, therefore, where punishment is unprofitable on this ground, can by no other means be discovered, than by an examination of each particular offence; which is what will be the business of the body of the work.

XVI. 2. Where, although in the *ordinary state* of things, the evil resulting from the punishment is not greater than the benefit which is likely to result from the force with which it operates, during the same space of time, towards the excluding the evil of the offences, yet it may have been rendered so by the influence of some *occasional circumstances.* In the number of these circumstances may be, 1. The multitude of delinquents at a particular juncture; being such as would increase, beyond the ordinary measure, the *quantum* of the second and third lots, and thereby also of a part of the fourth lot, in the evil of the punishment. 2. The extraordinary value of the services of some one delinquent; in the case where the effect of the punishment would be to deprive the community of the benefit of those services. 3. The displeasure of the *people;* that of an indefinite number of the members of the *same* community, in cases where (owing to the influence of some occasional incident) they happen to conceive, that the offence or the offender ought not to be punished at all, or at least ought not to be punished in the way in question. 4. The displeasure of *foreign powers;* that is, of the governing body, or a considerable number of the members of some *foreign* community or communities, with which the community in question is connected.

Cases Where Punishment Is Needless

These are,

XVII. 1. Where the purpose of putting an end to the practice may be attained as effectually at a cheaper rate: by instruction, for instance, as well as by terror: by informing the understanding, as well as by exercising an immediate influence on the will. This seems to be the case with respect to all those offences which consist in the disseminating pernicious principles in matters of *duty;* of whatever kind the duty be; whether political, or moral, or religious. And this, whether such principles be disseminated *under,* or even *without,* a sincere persuasion of their being beneficial. I say, even *without:* for though in such a case it is not instruction that can prevent the writer from endeavouring to inculcate his principles, yet it may keep the readers from adopting them: without which, his endeavouring to inculcate them will do no harm. In such a case, the sovereign will commonly have little need to take an active part: if it be the interest of *one* individual to inculcate principles that are pernicious, it will as surely be the interest of *other* individuals to expose them. But if the sovereign must needs take a part in the controversy, the pen is the proper weapon to combat error with, not the sword.

CHAPTER XIV   OF THE PROPORTION BETWEEN PUNISHMENTS AND OFFENCES

I. We have seen that the general object of all laws is to prevent mischief; that is to say, when it is worth while; but that, where there are no other means of doing this than punishment, there are four cases in which it is *not* worth while.

II. When it *is* worth while, there are four subordinate designs or objects, which, in the course of his endeavours to compass, as far as may be, that one general object, a legislator, whose views are governed by the principle of utility, comes naturally to propose to himself.

III. 1. His first, most extensive, and most eligible object, is to prevent, in as far as it is possible, and worth while, all sorts of offences whatsoever:[1] in other words, so to manage, that no offence whatsoever may be committed.

IV. 2. But if a man must needs commit an offence of some kind or other, the next object is to induce him to commit an offence *less* mischievous, *rather* than one *more* mischievous: in other words, to choose always the *least* mischievous, of two offences that will either of them suit his purpose.

V. 3. When a man has resolved upon a particular offence, the next object is to dispose him to do *no more* mischief than is *necessary* to his purpose: in other words, to do as little mischief as is consistent with the benefit he has in view.

VI. 4. The last object is, whatever the mischief be, which it is proposed to prevent, to prevent it at as *cheap* a rate as possible.

VII. Subservient to these four objects, or purposes, must be the rules or canons by which the proportion of punishment[2] to offences is to be governed.

VIII. Rule 1. 1. The first object, it has been seen, is to prevent, in as far as it

---

[1] By *offences* I mean, at present, acts which appear to him to have a tendency to produce mischief.

[2] The same rules (it is to be observed) may be applied, with little variation, to rewards as well as punishment: in short, to motives in general, which, according as they are of the pleasurable or painful kind, are of the nature of *reward* or *punishment:* and, according as the act they are applied to produce is of the positive or negative kind, are styled impelling or restraining.

is worth while, all sorts of offences; therefore,

The value of the punishment must not be less in any case than what is sufficient to outweigh that of the profit.[3] *of the offence.*

If it be, the offence (unless some other considerations, independent of the punishment, should intervene and operate efficaciously in the character of tutelary motives) will be sure to be committed notwithstanding:[4] the whole lot of punishment will be thrown away: it will be altogether *inefficacious.*

IX. The above rule has been objected, to, on account of its seeming harshness: but this can only have happened for want of its being properly understood. The strength of the temptation, *coeteris paribus,* is as the profit of the offence: the quantum of the punishment must rise with the profit of the offence: *coeteris paribus,* it must therefore rise with the strength of the temptation. This there is no disputing. True it is, that the stronger the temptation, the less conclusive is the indication which the act of delinquency affords of the depravity of the offender's disposition. So far then as the absence of any aggravation, arising from extraordinary depravity of disposition, may operate, or at the utmost, so far as the presence of a ground of extenuation, resulting from the innocence or beneficence of the offender's disposition, can operate, the strength of the temptation may operate in abatement of the demand for punishment. But it can never operate so far as to indicate the propriety of making the punishment ineffectual, which it is sure to be when brought below the level of the apparent profit of the offence.

The partial benevolence which should prevail for the reduction of it below this level, would counteract as well those purposes which such a motive would actually have in view, as those more extensive purposes which benevolence ought to have in view: it would be cruelty not to the public, but to the very persons in whose behalf it pleads: in its effects, I mean, however opposite in its intention. Cruelty to the public, that is cruelty to the innocent, by suffering them, for want of an adequate protection, to lie exposed to the mischief of the offence: cruelty even to the offender himself, by punishing him to no purpose, and without the chance of compassing that beneficial end, by which alone the introduction of the evil of punishment is to be justified.

---

[3] By the profit of an offence, is to be understood, not merely the pecuniary profit, but the pleasure or advantage, of whatever kind it be, which a man reaps, or expects to reap, from the gratification of the desire which prompted him to engage in the offence.

It is the profit (that is, the expectation of the profit) that constitutes the *impelling* motives, or, where there are several, the sum of the impelling motives, by which a man is prompted to engage in the offence. It is the punishment, that is, the expectation of the punishment, that constitutes the *restraining* motive, which either by itself, or in conjunction with others, is to act upon him in a *contrary* direction, so as to induce him to abstain from engaging in the offence. Accidental circumstances apart, the strength of the temptation is as the force of the seducing, that is, of the impelling motive or motives. To say then, as authors of great merit and great name have said, that the punishment ought not to increase with the strength of the temptation, is as much as to say in mechanics, that the moving force or *momentum* of the *power* need not increase in proportion to the momentum of the *burthen.*

[4] It is a well-known adage, though it is to be hoped not a true one, that every man has his price. It is commonly meant of a man's virtue. This saying, though in a very different sense, was strictly verified by some of the Anglo-Saxon laws: by which a fixed price was set, not upon a man's virtue indeed, but upon his life: that of the sovereign himself among the rest. For 200 shillings you might have killed a peasant: for six times as much, a nobleman: for six-and-thirty times as much you might have killed the king. A king in those days was worth exactly 7,200 shillings. If then the heir to the throne, for example, grew weary of waiting for it, he had a secure and legal way of gratifying his impatience: he had but to kill the king with one hand, and pay himself with the other, and all was right. An earl Godwin, or a duke Streon, could have bought the lives of a whole dynasty. It is plain, that if ever a king in

---

X. Rule 2. But whether a given offence shall be prevented in a given degree by a given quantity of punishment, is never any thing better than a chance; for the purchasing of which, whatever punishment is employed, is so much expended in advance. However, for the sake of giving it the better chance of outweighing the profit of the offence,

The greater the mischief of the offence, the greater is the expense, which it may be worth while to be at, in the way of punishment.[5]

XI. Rule 3. The next object is, to induce a man to choose always the least mischievous of two offences; therefore

Where two offences come in competition, the punishment for the greater offence must be sufficient to induce a man to prefer the less.

XII. Rule 4. When a man has resolved upon a particular offence, the next object is, to induce him to do no more mischief than what is necessary for his purpose: therefore

The punishment should be adjusted in such manner to each particular offence, that for every part of the mischief there may be a motive to restrain the offender from giving birth to it.[6]

XIII. Rule 5. The last object is, whatever mischief is guarded against, to guard against it at as cheap a rate as possible: therefore

The punishment ought in no case to be more than what is necessary to bring it into conformity with the rules here given.

XIV. Rule 6. It is further to be observed, that owing to the different manners and degrees in which persons under different circumstances are affected by the same exciting cause, a punishment which is the same in name will not always either really produce, or even so much as appear to others to produce, in two different persons the same degree of pain: therefore

That the quantity actually inflicted on each individual offender may correspond to the quantity intended for similar offenders in general, the several circumstances influencing sensibility ought always to be taken into account.

---

those days died in his bed, he must have had something else, besides this law, to thank for it. This being the production of a remote and barbarous age, the absurdity of it is presently recognized: but, upon examination, it would be found, that the freshest laws of the most civilised nations are continually falling into the same error. This, in short, is the case wheresoever the punishment is fixed while the profit of delinquency is indefinite: or, to speak more precisely, where the punishment is limited to such a mark, that the profit of delinquency may reach beyond it.

[5] For example, if it can ever be worth while to be at the expense of so horrible a punishment as that of burning alive, it will be more so in the view of preventing such a crime as that of murder or incendiarism, than in the view of preventing the uttering of a piece of bad money.

[6] If any one have any doubt of this, let him conceive the offence to be divided into as many separate offences as there are distinguishable parcels of mischief that result from it. Let it consist, for example, in a man's giving you ten blows, or stealing from you ten shillings. If then, for giving you ten blows, he is punished no more than for giving you five, the giving you five of these ten blows is an offence for which there is no punishment at all: which being understood, as often as a man gives you five blows, he will be sure to give you five more, since he may have the pleasure of giving you these five for nothing. In like manner, if for stealing from you ten shillings, he is punished no more than for stealing five, the stealing of the remaining five of those ten shilling is an offence for which there is no punishment at all. This rule is violated in almost every page of every body of laws I have ever seen.

The profit, it is to be observed, though freqently, is not constantly, proportioned to the mischief: for example, where a thief, along with the things he covets, steals others which are of no use to him. This may happen through wantonness, indolence, precipitation, etc., etc.

XV. Of the above rules of proportion, the four first, we may perceive, serve to mark out the limits on the side of diminution; the limits *below* which a punishment ought not to be *diminished:* the fifth, the limits on the side of increase; the limits *above* which it ought not to be *increased.* The five first are calculated to serve as guides to the legislator: the sixth is calculated, in some measure, indeed, for the same purpose; but principally for guiding the judge in his endeavours to conform, on both sides, to the intentions of the legislator.

XVI. Let us look back a little. The first rule, in order to render it more conveniently applicable to practice, may need perhaps to be a little more particularly unfolded. It is to be observed, then, that for the sake of accuracy, it was necessary, instead of the word *quantity* to make use of the less perspicuous term *value.* For the word *quantity* will not properly include the circumstances either of certainty or proximity: circumstances which, in estimating the value of a lot of pain or pleasure, must always be taken into the account. Now, on the one hand, a lot of punishment is a lot of pain; on the other hand, the profit of an offence is a lot of pleasure, or what is equivalent to it. But the profit of the offence *is* commonly more *certain* than the punishment, or, what comes to the same thing, *appears* so at least to the offender. It is at any rate commonly more *immediate.* It follows, therefore, that, in order to maintain its superiority over the profit of the offence, the punishment must have its value made up in some other way, in proportion to that whereby it falls short in two points of *certainty* and *proximity.* Now there is no other way in which it can receive any addition to its *value,* but by receiving an addition in point of *magnitude.* Wherever then the value of the punishment falls short, either in point of *certainty,* or of *proximity,* of that of the profit of the offence, it must receive a proportionable addition in point of *magnitude.*[7]

XVII. Yet farther. To make sure of giving the value of the punishment the superiority over that of the offence, it may be necessary, in some cases, to take into the account the profit not only of the *individual* offence to which the punishment is to be annexed, but also of such *other* offences of the *same sort* as the offender is likely to have already committed without detection. This random mode of calculation, severe as it is, it will be impossible to avoid having recourse to, in certain cases: in such, to wit, in which the profit is pecuniary, the chance of detection very small, and the obnoxious act of such a nature as indicates a habit: for example, in the case of frauds against the coin. If it be *not* recurred to, the practice of committing the offence will be sure to be, upon the balance of the account, a gainful practice. That being the case, the legislator will be absolutely sure of *not* being able to suppress it, and the whole punishment that is bestowed upon it will be thrown away. In a word (to keep to the same expressions we set out with) that whole quantity of punishment will be *ineffica-cious.*

XVIII. Rule 7. These things being considered, the three following rules may be laid down by way of supplement and explanation to Rule 1.

To enable the value of the punishment to outweigh that of the profit of the offence, it must be increased, in point of magnitude, in proportion as it falls short in point of certainty.

[7] It is for this reason, for example, that simple compensation is never looked upon as sufficient punishment for theft or robbery.

XIX. Rule 8. *Punishment must be further increased in point of magnitude, in proportion as it falls short in point of proximity.*

XX. Rule 9. *Where the act is conclusively indicative of a habit, such an increase must be given to the punishment as may enable it to outweigh the profit not only of the individual offence, but of such other like offences as are likely to have been committed with impunity by the same offender.*

XXI. There may be a few other circumstances or considerations which may influence, in some small degree, the demand for punishment: but as the propriety of these is either not so demonstrable, or not so constant, or the application of them not so determinate, as that of the foregoing, it may be doubted whether they be worth putting on a level with the others.

XXII. Rule 10. *When a punishment, which in point of quality is particularly well calculated to answer its intention, cannot exist in less than a certain quantity, it may sometimes be of use, for the sake of employing it, to stretch a little beyond that quantity which, on other accounts, would be strictly necessary.*

XXIII. Rule 11. *In particular, this may sometimes be the case, where the punishment proposed is of such a nature as to be particularly well calculated to answer the purpose of a moral lesson.*[8]

XXIV. Rule 12. The tendency of the above considerations is to dictate an augmentation in the punishment: the following rule operates in the way of diminution. There are certain cases (it has been seen) in which, by the influence of accidental circumstances, punishment may be rendered unprofitable in the whole: in the same cases it may chance to be rendered unprofitable as to a part only. Accordingly,

In adjusting the quantum of punishment, the circumstances, by which all punishment may be rendered unprofitable, ought to be attended to.

XXV. Rule 13. It is to be observed, that the more various and minute any set of provisions are, the greater the chance is that any given article in them will not be borne in mind: without which, no benefit can ensue from it. Distinctions, which are more complex than what the conceptions of those whose conduct it is designed to influence can take in, will even be worse than useless. The whole system will present a confused appearance: and thus the effect, not only to the proportions established by the articles in question, but of whatever is connected with them, will be destroyed. To draw a precise line of direction in such case seems impossible. However, by way of memento, it may be of some use to subjoin the following rule.

Among provisions designed to perfect the proportion between punishments and offences, if any occur, which, by their own particular good effects, would

---

[8] A punishment may be said to be calculated to answer the purpose of a moral lesson, when, by reason of the ignominy it stamps upon the offence, it is calculated to inspire the public with sentiments of aversion towards those pernicious habits and dispositions with which the offence appears to be connected; and thereby to inculcate the opposite beneficial habits and dispositions.

It is this, for example, if any thing, that must justify the application of so severe a punishment as the infamy of a public exhibition, hereinafter proposed, for him who lifts up his hand against a woman, or against his father.

It is partly on this principle, I suppose, that military legislators have justified to themselves the inflicting death on the soldier who lifts up his hand against his superior officer.

not make up for the harm they would do by adding to the intricacy of the Code, they should be omitted.[9]

XXVI. It may be remembered, that the political sanction, being that to which the sort of punishment belongs, which in this chapter is all along in view, is but of four sanctions, which may all of them contribute their share towards producing the same effects. It may be expected, therefore, that in adjusting the quantity of political punishment, allowance should be made for the assistance it may meet with from those other controlling powers. True it is, that from each of these several sources a very powerful assistance may sometimes be derived. But the case is, that (setting aside the moral sanction, in the case where the force of it is expressly adopted into and modified by the political) the force of those other powers is never determinate enough to be depended upon. It can never be reduced, like political punishment, into exact lots, nor meted out in number, quantity, and value. The legislator is therefore obliged to provide the full complement of punishment, as if he were sure of not receiving any assistance whatever from any of those quarters. If he does, so much the better: but lest he should not, it is necessary he should, at all events, make that provision which depends upon himself.

XXVII. It may be of use, in this place, to recapitulate the several circumstances, which, in establishing the proportion betwixt punishments and offences, are to be attended to. These seem to be as follows:

I.   *On the part of the offence:*
1. The profit of the offence;
2. The mischief of the offence;
3. The profit and mischief of other greater or lesser offences, of different sorts, which the offender may have to choose out of;
4 The profit and mischief of other offences, of the same sort, which the same offender may probably have been guilty of already.

II. *On the part of the punishment:*
5. The magnitude of the punishment: composed of its intensity and duration;
6. The deficiency of the punishment in point of certainty;
7. The deficiency of the punishment in point of proximity;
8. The quality of the punishment;
9. The accidental advantage in point of quality of a punishment, not strictly needed in point of quantity;
10. The use of a punishment of a particular quality, in the character of a moral lesson.

III. *On the part of the offender:*
11. The responsibility of the class of persons in a way to offend;
12. The sensibility of each particular offender;
13. The particular merits or useful qualities of any particular offender, in case of a punishment which might deprive the community of the benefit of them;
14. The multitude of offenders on any particular occasion.

[9] Notwithstanding this rule, my fear is, that in the ensuing model, I may be thought to have carried endeavours at proportionality too far. Hitherto scarce any attention has been paid to it. Montesquieu seems to have been almost the first who has had the least idea of any such thing. In such matter, therefore, excess seemed more eligible than defect. The difficulty is to invent: that done, if any thing seems superfluous, it is easy to retrench.

IV. *On the part of the public*, at any particular conjuncture:
  15. The inclinations of the people, for or against any quantity or mode of punishment;
  16. The inclinations of foreign powers.
V. *On the part of the law:* that is, of the public for a continuance:
  17. The necessity of making small sacrifices, in point of proportionality, for the sake of simplicity.

XXVIII. There are some, perhaps, who, at first sight, may look upon the nicety employed in the adjustment of such rules, as so much labour lost: for gross ignorance, they will say, never troubles itself about laws, and passion does not calculate. But the evil of ignorance admits of cure: and as to the proposition that passion does not calculate, this, like most of these very general and oracular propositions, is not true. When matters of such importance as pain and pleasure are at stake, and these in the highest degree (the only matters, in short, that can be of importance) who is there that does not calculate? Men calculate, some with less exactness, indeed, some with more: but all men calculate. I would not say, that even a madman does not calculate.[10] Passion calculates, more or less, in every man: in different men, according to the warmth or coolness of their dispositions: according to the firmness or irritability of their minds: according to the nature of the motives by which they are acted upon. Happily, of all passions, that is the most given to calculation, from the excesses of which, by reason of its strength, constancy, and universality, society has most to apprehend: I mean that which corresponds to the motive of pecuniary interest: so that these niceties, if such they are to be called, have the best chance of being efficacious, where efficacy is of the most importance.

John Stuart Mill

John Stuart Mill (1806–1873) was the son of James Mill, a close associate of Jeremy Bentham. Bentham and the boy's father supervised his education. Mill, himself, reports that by the time he reached twenty-one he was a bottomless pit of learning. He suffered a nervous breakdown, and though he never abondoned the utilitarianism of Bentham, he did make changes in it, partly as a result of experiences during his recovery including the reading of romantic poetry. Mill pursued a successful career with the British East India Company and served one term in Parliament.

The selections printed below from *On Liberty* contain Mill's defense of civil liberties, such as freedom of speech. He attempts

[10] There are few madmen but what are observed to be afraid of the strait waistcoat.

to show that, on the grounds of his utilitarianism, each person has the right to extensive liberty. This essay has been praised by some as the finest defense of liberty ever written, while it has been condemned by others as so confused that its principal thesis cannot even be clearly stated.

On Liberty

CHAPTER 1 INTRODUCTORY

... The object of this Essay is to assert one very simple principle, as entitled to govern absolutely the dealings of society with the individual in the way of compulsion and control, whether the means used be physical force in the form of legal penalties or the moral coercion of public opinion. That principle is, that the sole end for which mankind are warranted, individually or collectively, in interfering with the liberty of action of any of their number, is self-protection. That the only purpose for which power can be rightfully exercised over any member of a civilized community, against his will, is to prevent harm to others. His own good, either physical or moral, is not a sufficient warrant. He cannot rightfully be compelled to do or forbear because it will be better for him to do so, because it will make him happier, because, in the opinions of others, to do so would be wise, or even right. There are good reasons for remonstrating with him, or reasoning with him, or persuading him, or entreating him, but not for compelling him, or visiting him with any evil, in case he do otherwise. To justify that, the conduct from which it is desired to deter him must be calculated to produce evil to some one else. The only part of the conduct of any one, for which he is amenable to society, is that which concerns others. In the part which merely concerns himself, his independence is, of right, absolute. Over himself, over his own body and mind, the individual is sovereign.

It is, perhaps, hardly necessary to say that this doctrine is meant to apply only to human beings in the maturity of their faculties. We are not speaking of children, or of young persons below the age which the law may fix as that of manhood or womanhood. Those who are still in a state to require being taken care of by others, must be protected against their own actions as well as against external injury. For the same reason, we may leave out of consideration those backward states of society in which the race itself may be considered as in its nonage. The early difficulties in the way of spontaneous progress are so great, that there is seldom any choice of means for overcoming them; and a ruler full of the spirit of improvement is warranted in the use of any expedients that will attain an end, perhaps otherwise unattainable. Despotism is a legitimate mode of government in dealing with barbarians, provided the end be their improvement, and the means justified by actually effecting that end. Liberty, as a principle, has no application to any state of things anterior to the time when mankind have

From John Stuart Mill, *On Liberty*, London, 1859.

become capable of being improved by free and equal discussion. Until then, there is nothing for them but implicit obedience to an Akbar or a Charlemagne, if they are so fortunate as to find one. But as soon as mankind have attained the capacity of being guided to their own improvement by conviction or persuasion (a period long since reached in all nations with whom we need here concern ourselves), compulsion, either in the direct form or in that of pains and penalties for non-compliance, is no longer admissible as a means to their own good, and justifiable only for the security of others.

It is proper to state that I forgo any advantage which could be derived to my argument from the idea of abstract right, as a thing independent of utility. I regard utility as the ultimate appeal on all ethical questions; but it must be utility in the largest sense, grounded on the permanent interests of man as a progressive being. Those interests, I contend, authorize the subjection of individual spontaneity to external control, only in respect to those actions of each, which concern the interest of other people. If any one does an act hurtful to others, there is a *prima facie* case for punishing him, by law, or, where legal penalties are not safely applicable, by general disapprobation. There are also many positive acts for the benefit of others, which he may rightfully be compelled to perform; such as, to give evidence in a court of justice; to bear his fair share in the common defence, or in any other joint work necessary to the interest of the society of which he enjoys the protection; and to perform certain acts of individual beneficence, such as saving a fellow creature's life, or interposing to protect the defenceless against ill-usage, things which whenever it is obviously a man's duty to do, he may rightfully be made responsible to society for not doing. A person may cause evil to others not only by his actions but by his inaction, and in either case he is justly accountable to them for the injury. The latter case, it is true, requires a much more cautious exercise of compulsion than the former. To make any one answerable for doing evil to others, is the rule; to make him answerable for not preventing evil, is comparatively speaking, the exception. Yet there are many cases clear enough and grave enough to justify that exception. In all things which regard the external relations of the individual, he is *de jure* amenable to those whose interests are concerned, and if need be, to society as their protector. There are often good reasons for not holding him to the responsibility; but these reasons must arise from the special expediencies of the case: either because it is a kind of case in which he is on the whole likely to act better, when left to his own discretion, than when controlled in any way in which society have it in their power to control him, or because the attempt to exercise control would produce other evils, greater than those which it would prevent. When such reasons as these preclude the enforcement of responsibility, the conscience of the agent himself should step into the vacant judgment-seat, and protect those interests of others which have no external protection; judging himself all the more rigidly, because the case does not admit of his being made accountable to the judgment of his fellow-creatures.

But there is a sphere of action in which society, as distinguished from the individual, has, if any, only an indirect interest; comprehending all that portion of a person's life and conduct which affects only himself, or, if it also affects others, only with their free, voluntary, and undeceived consent and participation. When I say only himself, I mean directly, and in the first instance: for whatever affects himself, may affect others *through* himself; and the objection which may be grounded on this contingency, will receive consideration in the sequel. This, is the appropriate region of human liberty. It comprises, first, the inward domain of consciousness, demanding liberty of conscience, in the most comprehensive sense; liberty of thought and feeling; absolute freedom of opinion and sentiment on all subjects, practical or speculative, scientific, moral, or theological. The liberty of expressing and publishing opinions may seem to fall under a different principle, since it belongs to that part of the conduct of an individual which concerns other people; but, being almost of as much importance as the liberty of thought itself, and resting in great part on the same reasons, is practically inseparable from it. Secondly, the principle requires liberty of tastes and pursuits; of framing the plan of our life to suit our own character; of doing as we like, subject to such consequences as may follow; without impediment from our fellow-creatures, so long as what we do does not harm them, even though they should think our conduct foolish, perverse, or wrong. Thirdly, from this liberty of each individual, follows the liberty, within the same limits, of combination among individuals; freedom to unite, for any purpose not involving harm to others: the persons combining being supposed to be of full age, and not forced or deceived.

No society in which these liberties are not, on the whole, respected, is free, whatever may be its form of government; and none is completely free in which they do not exist absolute and unqualified. The only freedom which deserves the name, is that of pursuing our own way, so long as we do not attempt to deprive others of theirs, or impede their efforts to obtain it. Each is the proper guardian of his own health, whether bodily, or mental and spiritual. Mankind are greater gainers by suffering each other to live as seems good to themselves, than by compelling each to live as seems good to the rest. . . .

It will be convenient for the argument, if, instead of at once entering upon the general thesis, we confine ourselves in the first instance to a single branch of it, on which the principle here stated is, if not fully, yet to a certain point, recognized by the current opinions. This one branch is the Liberty of Thought: from which it is impossible to separate the cognate liberty of speaking and of writing. Although these liberties, to some considerable amount, form part of the political morality of all countries which profess religious toleration and free institutions, the grounds, both philosophical and practical, on which they rest, are perhaps not so familiar to the general mind, nor so thoroughly appreciated by many even of the leaders of opinion, as might have been expected. Those grounds, when rightly understood, are of much wider application than to only one division of the subject, and a thorough consideration of this part of the question will be found the best introduction to the remainder. Those to whom nothing which I am about to say will be new, may therefore, I hope, excuse me, if on a subject which for now three centuries has been so often discussed, I venture on one discussion more.

CHAPTER 2   OF THE LIBERTY OF THOUGHT AND DISCUSSION

The time, it is to be hoped, is gone by when any defence would be necessary of the "liberty of the press" as one of the securities against corrupt or tyrannical government. No argument, we may suppose, can now be needed, against permitting a legislature or an executive, not identified in interest with the people, to prescribe opinions to them, and determine what doctrines or what arguments they shall be allowed to hear. This aspect of the question, besides, has been so often and so triumphantly enforced by preceding writers, that it needs not be specially insisted on in this place. Though the law of England, on the subject of the press, is as servile to this day as it was in the time of the Tudors, there is little danger of its being actually put in force against political discussion, except during some temporary panic, when fear of insurrection drives ministers and judges from their propriety;[1] and, speaking generally, it is not, in constitutional countries, to be apprehended, that the government, whether completely responsible to the people or not, will often attempt to control the expression of opinion, except when in doing so it makes itself the organ of the general intolerance of the public. Let us suppose, therefore, that the government is entirely at one with the people, and never thinks of exerting any power of coercion unless in agreement with what it conceives to be their voice. But I deny the right of the people to exercise such coercion, either by themselves or by their government. The power itself is illegitimate. The best government has no more title to it than the worst. It is as noxious, or more noxious, when exerted in accordance with public opinion, than when in opposition to it. If all mankind minus one, were of one opinion, and only one person were of the contrary opinion, mankind would be no more justified in silencing that one person, than he, if he had the power, would be justified in silencing mankind. Were an opinion a personal possession of no value except to the owner; if to be obstructed in the enjoyment of it were simply a private injury, it would make some difference whether the injury was inflicted only on a few persons or on many. But the peculiar evil of silencing the expression of an opinion is, that it is robbing the human race; posterity as well as the existing generation; those who dissent from the opinion, still more than those who hold it. If the opinion is right, they are deprived of the opportunity of exchanging error for truth: if wrong, they lose, what is almost as great a benefit, the clearer perception and livelier impression of truth, produced by its collision with error.

It is necessary to consider separately these two hypotheses, each of which has a distinct branch of the argument corresponding to it. We can never be sure that the opinion we are endeavoring to stifle is a false opinion; and if we were sure, stifling it would be an evil still.

First: the opinion which it is attempted to suppress by authority may possibly be true. Those who desire to suppress it, of course deny its truth; but they are not infallible. They have no authority to decide the question for all mankind, and exclude every other person from the means of judging. To refuse a hearing to an opinion, because they are sure that it is false, is to assume that *their* certainty is the same thing as *absolute* certainty. All silencing of discussion is an assumption of infallibility. Its condemnation may be allowed to rest on this common argument, not the worse for being common.

[1] These words had scarcely been written, when, as if to give them an emphatic contradiction, occurred the Government Press Prosecutions of 1858. That ill-judged interference with the liberty of public discussion has not, however, induced me to alter a single word in the text, nor has it at all weakened my conviction that, moments of panic excepted, the era of pains and penalties for political discussion has, in our own country, passed away.

Unfortunately for the good sense of mankind, the fact of their fallibility is far from carrying the weight in their practical judgment, which is always allowed to it in theory; for while every one well knows himself to be fallible, few think it necessary to take any precautions against their own fallibility, or admit the supposition that any opinion, of which they feel very certain, may be one of the examples of the error to which they acknowledge themselves to be liable. . . .

Yet it is as evident in itself, as any amount of argument can make it, that ages are no more infallible than individuals; every age having held many opinions which subsequent ages have deemed not only false but absurd; and it is as certain that many opinions, now general, will be rejected by future ages, as it is that many, once general, are rejected by the present.

The objection likely to be made to this argument, would probably take some such form as the following. There is no greater assumption of infallibility in forbidding the propagation of error, than in any other thing which is done by public authority on its own judgment and responsibility. Judgment is given to men that they may use it. Because it may be used erroneously, are men to be told they ought not to use it at all? To prohibit what they think pernicious, is not claiming exemption from error, but fulfilling the duty incumbent on them, although fallible, of acting on their conscientious conviction. If we were never to act on our opinions, because those opinions may be wrong, we should leave all our interests uncared for, and all our duties unperformed. An objection which applies to all conduct, can be no valid objection to any conduct in particular. It is the duty of governments, and of individuals, to form the truest opinions they can; to form them carefully, and never impose them upon others unless they are quite sure of being right. But when they are sure (such reasoners may say), it is not conscientiousness but cowardice to shrink from acting on their opinions, and allow doctrines which they honestly think dangerous to the welfare of mankind, either in this life or in another, to be scattered abroad without restraint, because other people, in less enlightened times, have persecuted opinions now believed to be true. Let us take care, it may be said, not to make the same mistake: but governments and nations have made mistakes in other things, which are not denied to be fit subjects for the exercise of authority: they have laid on bad taxes, made unjust wars. Ought we therefore to lay on no taxes, and, under whatever provocation, make no wars? Men, and governments, must act to the best of their ability. There is no such thing as absolute certainty, but there is assurance sufficient for the purposes of human life. We may, and must, assume our opinion to be true for the guidance of our own conduct: and it is assuming no more when we forbid bad men to pervert society by the propagation of opinions which we regard as false and pernicious.

I answer, that it is assuming very much more. There is the greatest difference between presuming an opinion to be true, because, with every opportunity for contesting it, it has not been refuted, and assuming its truth for the purpose of not permitting its refutation. Complete liberty of contradicting and disproving our opinion, is the very condition which justifies us in assuming its truth for purposes of action; and on no other terms can a being with human faculties have any rational assurance of being right. . . .

Strange it is, that men should admit the validity of the arguments for free discussion, but object to their being "pushed to an extreme;" not seeing that unless the reasons are good for an extreme case, they are not good for any case.

Strange that they should imagine that they are not assuming infallibility, when they acknowledge that there should be free discussion on all subjects which can possibly be *doubtful*, but think that some particular principle or doctrine should be forbidden to be questioned because it is *so certain*, that is, because *they are certain* that it is certain. To call any proposition certain, while there is any one who would deny its certainty if permitted, but who is not permitted, is to assume that we ourselves, and those who agree with us, are the judges of certainty and judges without hearing the other side. . . .

In order more fully to illustrate the mischief of denying a hearing to opinions because we, in our own judgment, have condemned them, it will be desirable to fix down the discussion to a concrete case; and I choose, by preference, the cases which are least favorable to me—in which the argument against freedom of opinion, both on the score of truth and on that of utility, is considered the strongest. Let the opinions impugned be the belief in a God and in a future state, or any of the commonly received doctrines of morality. To fight the battle on such ground, gives a great advantage to an unfair antagonist; since he will be sure to say (and many who have no desire to be unfair will say it internally), Are these the doctrines which you do not deem sufficiently certain to be taken under the protection of law? Is the belief in a God one of the opinions, to feel sure of which, you hold to be assuming infallibility? But I must be permitted to observe, that it is not the feeling sure of a doctrine (be it what it may) which I call an assumption of infallibility. It is the undertaking to decide that question *for others*, without allowing them to hear what can be said on the contrary side. And I denounce and reprobate this pretension not the less, if put forth on the side of my most solemn convictions. However positive any one's persuasion may be, not only of the falsity, but of the pernicious consequences—not only of the pernicious consequences, but (to adopt expressions which I altogether condemn) the immorality and impiety of an opinion; yet if, in pursuance of that private judgment, though backed by the public judgment of his country or his contemporaries, he prevents the opinion from being heard in its defence, he assumes infallibility. And so far from the assumption being less objectionable or less dangerous because the opinion is called immoral or impious, this is the case of all others in which it is most fatal. These are exactly the occasions on which the men of one generation commit those dreadful mistakes, which excite the astonishment and horror of posterity. It is among such that we find the instances memorable in history, when the arm of the law has been employed to root out the best men and the noblest doctrines; with deplorable success as to the men, though some of the doctrines have survived to be (as if in mockery) invoked, in defense of similar conduct towards those who dissent from *them*, or from their received interpretation.

Mankind can hardly be too often reminded, that there was once a man named Socrates, between whom and the legal authorities and public opinion of his time, there took place a memorable collision. Born in an age and country abounding in individual greatness, this man has been handed down to us by those who best knew both him and the age, as the most virtuous man in it; while *we* know him as the head and prototype of all subsequent teachers of virtue, the source equally of the lofty inspiration of Plato and the judicious utilitarianism of Aristotle, "*i maëstri di color che sanno,*" the two headsprings of ethical as of all other philosophy. This acknowledged master of all the eminent thinkers who have since lived—whose fame, still growing after more than two thousand years, all but outweighs the whole remainder of the names which make his native city illustrious—was put to death by his countrymen, after a judicial conviction, for impiety and immorality. Impiety, in denying the gods recognized by the State; indeed his accuser asserted (see the "Apologia") that he believed in no gods at all. Immorality, in being, by his doctrines and instructions, a "corruptor of youth." Of these charges the tribunal, there is every ground for believing, hosestly found him guilty, and condemned the man who probably of all then born had deserved best of mankind, to be put to death as a criminal.

To pass from this to the only other instance of judicial iniquity, the mention of which, after the condemnation of Socrates, would not be an anti-climax: the event which took place on Calvary rather more than eighteen hundred years ago. The man who left on the memory of those who witnessed his life and conversation, such an impression of his moral grandeur, that eighteen subsequent centuries have done homage to him as the Almighty in person, was ignominiously put to death, as what? As a blasphemer. Men did not merely mistake their benefactor; they mistook him for the exact contrary of what he was, and treated him as that prodigy of impiety, which they themselves are now held to be, for their treatment of him. The feelings with which mankind now regard these lamentable transactions, especially the later of the two, render them extremely unjust in their judgment of the unhappy actors. These were, to all appearance, not bad men—not worse than men commonly are, but rather the contrary; men who possessed in a full, or somewhat more than a full measure, the religious, moral, and patriotic feelings of their time and people: the very kind of men who, in all times, our own included, have every chance of passing through life blameless and respected. The high-priest who rent his garments when the words were pronounced, which, according to all the ideas of his country, constituted the blackest guilt, was in all probability quite as sincere in his horror and indignation, as the generality of respectable and pious men now are in the religious and moral sentiments they profess; and most of those who now shudder at his conduct, if they had lived in his time, and been born Jews, would have acted precisely as he did. Orthodox Christians who are tempted to think that those who stoned to death the first martyrs must have been worse men than they themselves are, ought to remember that one of those persecutors was Saint Paul. . . .

But it is not the minds of heretics that are deteriorated most, by the ban placed on all inquiry which does not end in the orthodox conclusions. The greatest harm done is to those who are not heretics, and whose whole mental development is cramped, and their reason cowed, by the fear of heresy. Who can compute what the world loses in the multitude of promising intellects combined with timid characters, who dare not follow out any bold, vigorous, independent train of thought, lest it should land them in something which would admit of being considered irreligious or immoral? Among them we may occasionally see some man of deep conscientiousness, and subtile and refined understanding, who spends a life in sophisticating with an inteleect which cannot silence, and exhausts the resources of ingenuity in attempting to reconcile the promptings of his conscience and reason with orthodoxy, which yet he does not, perhaps, to the end succeed in doing. No one can be a great thinker who does not recognize, that as a thinker it is his first duty to follow his intellect to whatever conclusions it may lead. Truth gains more even by the errors of one who, with due study and preparation, thinks for himself, than by the true opinions of those who only hold them because they do not suffer themselves to think. Not that it is solely, or chiefly, to form great thinkers, that freedom of thinking is required. On the contrary, it is as much, and even more indispensable, to enable average human beings to attain the mental stature which they are capable of. There have been, and may again be, great individual thinkers, in a general atmosphere of mental slavery. But there never has been, nor ever will be, in that atmosphere, an intellectually active people. Where any people has made a temporary approach to such a character, it has been because the dread of heterodox speculation was for a time suspended. Where there is a tacit convention that principles are not to be disputed; where the discussion of the greatest questions which can occupy humanity is considered to be closed, we cannot hope to find that generally high scale of mental activity which has made some periods of history so remarkable. Never when controversy avoided the subjects which are large and important enough to kindle enthusiasm, was the mind of a people stirred up from its foundations, and the impulse given which raised even persons of the most ordinary intellect to something of the dignity of thinking beings. . . .

Let us now pass to the second division of the argument, and dismissing the supposition that any of the received opinons may be false, let us assume them to be true, and examine into the worth of the manner in which they are likely to be held, when their truth is not freely and openly canvassed. However unwillingly a person who has a strong opinion may admit the possibility that his opinion may be false, he ought to be moved by the consideration that however true it may be, if it is not fully, frequently, and fearlessly discussed, it will be held as a dead dogma, not a living truth.

There is a class of persons (happily not quite so numerous as formerly) who think it enough if a person assents undoubtingly to what they think true, though he has no knowledge whatever of the grounds of the opinion, and could not make a tenable defence of it against the most superficial objections. Such persons, if they can once get their creed taught from authority, naturally think that no good, and some harm, comes of its being allowed to be questioned. Where their influence prevails, they make it nearly impossible for the received opinion to be rejected wisely and considerately, though it may still be rejected rashly and ignorantly; for to shut out discussion entirely is seldom possible, and when it once gets in, beliefs not grounded on conviction are apt to give way before the slightest semblance of an argument. Waiving, however, this possibility—assuming that the true opinion abides in the mind, but abides as a prejudice, a belief independent of, and proof against, argument—this is not the way in which truth ought to be held by a rational being. This is not knowing the truth. Truth, thus held is but one superstition the more, accidentally clinging to the words which enunciate a truth.

If the intellect and judgment of mankind ought to be cultivated, a thing which Protestants at least do not deny, on what can these faculties be more appropriately exercised by any one, than on the things which concern him so much that it is considered necessary for him to hold opinions on them? If the cultivation of the understanding consists in one thing more than in another, it is surely in learning the grounds of one's own opinions. Whatever people believe, on subjects on which it is of the first importance to believe rightly, they ought to be able to defend against at least the common objections. But, some one may say, "Let them be *taught* the grounds of their opinions. It does not follow that opinions must be merely parroted because they are never heard controverted. Persons who learn geometry do not simply commit the theorems to memory, but understand and learn likewise the demonstrations; and it would be absurd to say that they remain ignorant of the grounds of geometrical truths, because they never hear any one deny, and attempt to disprove them." Undoubtedly: and such teaching suffices on a subject like mathematics, where there is nothing at all to be said on the wrong side of the question. The peculiarity of the evidence of mathematical truths is, that all the argument is on one side. There are no objections, and no answers to objections. But on every subject on which difference of opinion is possible, the truth depends on a balance to be struck between two sets of conflicting reasons. Even in natural philosophy, there is always some other explanation possible of the same facts: some geocentric theory instead of heliocentric, some phlogiston instead of oxygen; and it has to be shown why that other theory cannot be the true one: and until this is shown, and until we know it is shown, we do not understand the grounds of our opinion. But when we turn to subjects infinitely more complicated, to morals, religion, politics, social relations, and the business of life, three-fourths of the arguments for every disputed opinion consist in dispelling the appearances which favor some opinion different from it. The greatest orator, save one, of antiquity, has left it on record that he always studied his adversary's case with as great, if not with still greater, intensity than even his own. What Cicero practised as the means of forensic success, requires to be imitated by all who study any subject in order to arrive at the truth. He knows only his own side of the case, knows little of that. His reasons may be good, and no one may have been able to refute them. But if he is equally unable to refute the reasons on the opposite side; if he does not so much as know what they are, he has no ground for preferring either opinion. The rational position for him would be suspension of judgment, and unless he contents himself with that, he is either led by authority, or adopts, like the generality of the world, the side to which he feels most inclination. Nor is it enough that he should hear the arguments of adversaries from his own teachers, presented as they state them, and accompanied by what they offer as refutations. That is not the way to do justice to the arguments, or bring them into real contact with his own mind. He must be able to hear them from persons who actually believe them; who defend them in earnest, and do their very utmost for them. He must know them in their most plausible and persuasive form; he must feel the whole force of the difficulty which the true view of the subject has to encounter and dispose of; else he will never really possess himself of the portion of truth which meets and removes that difficulty. Ninety-nine in a hundred of what are called educated men are in this condition; even of those who can argue fluently for their opinions. Their conclusion may be true, but it might be false for anything they know: they have never thrown themselves into the mental position of those who think differently from them, and considered what such persons may have to say; and consequently they do not, in any proper sense of the word, know the doctrine which they themselves profess. They do not know those parts of it which explain and justify the remainder; the considerations which show that a fact which seemingly conflicts with another is reconcilable with it, or that, of two apparently strong reasons, one and not the other ought to be preferred. All that part of the truth which turns the scale, and decides the judgment of a completely informed mind, they are strangers to; nor is it ever really known, but to those who have attended equally and impartially to both sides, and endeavored to see the reasons of both in the strongest light. So essential is this discipline to a real understanding of moral and human subjects, that if opponents of all important truths do not exist, it is indispensable to imagine them, and supply them with the strongest arguments which the most skilful devil's advocate can conjure up.

To abate the force of these considerations, an enemy of free discussion may be supposed to say, that there is no necessity for mankind in general to know and understand all that can be said against or for their opinions by philosophers and theologians. That it is not needful for common men to be able to expose all the misstatements or fallacies of an ingenious opponent. That is enough if there is always somebody capable of answering them, so that nothing likely to mislead uninstructed persons remains unrefuted. That simple minds, having been taught the obvious grounds of the truths inculcated on them, may trust to authority for the rest, and being aware that they have neither knowledge nor talent to resolve every difficulty which can be raised, may repose in the assurance that all those which have been raised have been or can be answered, by those who are specially trained to the task.

Conceding to this view of the subject the utmost that can be claimed for it by those most easily satisfied with the amount of understanding of truth which ought to accompany the belief of it; even so, the argument for free discussion is no way weakened. For even this doctrine acknowledges that mankind ought to have a rational assurance that all objections have been satisfactorily answered; and how are they to be answered if that which requires to be answered is not spoken? or how can the answer be known to be satisfactory, if the objectors have no opportunity of showing that it is unsatisfactory? If not the public, at least the philosophers and theologians who are to resolve the difficulties, must make themselves familiar with those difficulties in their most puzzling form; and this cannot be accomplished unless they are freely stated, and placed in the most advantageous light which they admit of. . . .

If, however, the mischievous operation of the absence of free discussion, when the received opinions are true, were confined to leaving men ignorant of the grounds of those opinions, it might be thought that this, if an intellectual, is not moral evil, and does not affect the worth of the opinions, regarded in their influence on the character. The fact, however, is, that not only the grounds of the opinion are forgotten in the absence of discussion, but too often the meaning of the opinion itself. The words which convey it, cease to suggest ideas, or suggest only a small portion of those they were originally employed to communicate. Instead of a vivid conception and a living belief, there remain only a few phrases retained by rote; or, if any part, the shell and husk only of the meaning is retained, the finer essence being lost. The great chapter in human history which this fact occupies and fills, cannot be too earnestly studied and meditated on.

It is illustrated in the experience of almost all ethical doctrines and religious creeds. They are all full of meaning and vitality to those who originate them, and to the direct disciples of the originators. Their meaning continues to be felt in undiminished strength, and is perhaps brought out into even fuller consciousness, so long as the struggle lasts to give the doctrine or creed an ascendency over other creeds. At last it either prevails, and becomes the general opinion, or its progress stops; it keeps possession of the ground it has gained, but ceases to spread further. When either of these results has become apparent, controversy on the subject flags, and gradually dies away. The doctrine has taken its place, if not as a received opinion, as one of the admitted sects or divisions of opinion: those who hold it have generally inherited, not adopted it; and conversion from one of these doctrines to another, being now an exceptional fact, occupies little place in the thoughts of their professors. Instead of being, as at first, constantly on the alert either to defend themselves against the world, or to bring the world over to them, they have subsided into acquiescence, and neither listen, when they can help it, to arguments against their creed, nor trouble dissentients (if there be such) with arguments in its favor. From this time may usually be dated the decline in the living power of the doctrine. . . .

But what! (it may be asked) Is the absence of unanimity an indispensable condition of true knowledge? Is it necessary that some part of mankind should persist in error, to enable any to realize the truth? Does a belief cease to be real and vital as soon as it is generally received—and is a proposition never thoroughly understood and felt unless some doubt of it remains? As soon as mankind have unanimously accepted a truth, does the truth perish within them? The highest aim and best result of improved intelligence, it has hitherto been thought, is to unite mankind more and more in the acknowledgment of all important truths: and does the intelligence only last as long as it has not achieved its object? Do the fruits of conquest perish by the very completeness of the victory?

I affirm no such thing. As mankind improve, the number of doctrines which are no longer disputed or doubted will be constantly on the increase: and the well-being of mankind may almost be measured by the number and gravity of the truths which have reached the point of being uncontested. The cessation, on one question after another, of serious controversy, is one of the necessary incidents of the consolidation of opinon; a consolidation as salutary in the case of true opinions, as it is dangerous and noxious when the opinions are erroneous. But though this gradual narrowing of the bounds of diversity of opinion is necessary in both senses of the term, being at once inevitable and indispensable, we are not therefore obliged to conclude that all its consequences must be beneficial. The loss of so important an aid to the intelligent and living apprehension of a truth, as is afforded by the necessity of explaining it to, or defending it against, opponents, though most sufficient to outweigh, is no trifling drawback from, the benefit of its universal recognition. Where this advantage can no longer be had, I confess I should like to see the teachers of mankind endeavoring to provide a substitute for it; some contrivance for making the difficulties of the question as present to the learner's consciousness, as if they were pressed upon him by a dissentient champion, eager for his conversion. . . .

It still remains to speak of one of the principal causes which make diversity of opinion advantageous, and will continue to do so until mankind shall have entered a stage of intellectual advancement which at present seems at an incalculable distance. We have hitherto considered only two possibilities: that the received opinion may be false, and some other opinion, consequently, true; or that, the received opinion being true, a conflict with the opposite error is essential to a clear apprehension and deep feeling of its truth. But there is a commoner case than either of these; when the conflicting doctrines, instead of being one true and the other false, share the truth between them; and the nonconforming opinion is needed to supply the remainder of the truth, of which the received doctrine embodies only a part. Popular opinions, on subjects not palpable to sense, are often true, but seldom or never the whole truth. They are a part of the truth; sometimes a greater, sometimes a smaller part, but exaggerated, distorted, and disjoined from the truths by which they ought to be accompanied and limited. Heretical opinions, on the other hand, are generally some of these suppressed and neglected truths, bursting the bonds which kept them down, and either seeking reconciliation with the truth contained in the common opinion, or fronting it as enemies and setting themselves up, with similar exclusiveness, as the whole truth. The latter case is hitherto the most frequent, as in the human mind, one-sidedness has always been the rule, and many-sidedness of exception. Hence, even in revolutions of opinion, one part of the truth usually sets while another rises. Even progress, which ought to superadd, for the most part only substitutes one partial and incomplete truth for another; improvement consisting chiefly in this, that the new fragment of truth is more wanted, more adapted to the needs of the time, than that which it displaces. Such being the partial character of prevailing opinions, even when resting on a true foundation; every opinion which embodies somewhat of the portion of truth which the common opinion omits, ought to be considered precious, with whatever amount of error and confusion that truth may be blended. . . .

We have now recognized the necessity to the mental well-being of mankind (on which all their other well-being depends) of freedom of opinion, and freedom of the expression of opinion, on four distinct grounds; which we will now briefly recapitulate.

First, if any opinion is compelled to silence, that opinion may, for aught we can certainly know, be true. To deny this is to assume our own infallibility.

Secondly, though the silenced opinion be an error, it may, and very commonly does, contain a portion of truth; and since the general or prevailing opinion on any subject is rarely or never the whole truth, it is only by the collision of adverse opinions that the remainder of the truth has any chance of being supplied.

Thirdly, even if the received opinion be not only true, but the whole truth; unless it is suffered to be, and actually is, vigorously and earnestly contested, it will, by most of those who receive it, be held in the manner of a prejudice, with little comprehension or feeling of its rational grounds. And not only this, but, fourthly, the meaning of the doctrine itself will be in danger of being lost, or enfeebled, and deprived of its vital effect on the character and conduct: the dogma becoming a mere formal profession, inefficacious for good, but cumbering the ground, and preventing the growth of any real and heartfelt conviction from reason or personal experience.

CHAPTER 3   OF INDIVIDUALITY, AS ONE OF THE ELEMENTS
             OF WELL-BEING

Such being the reasons which make it imperative that human beings should be free to form opinions, and to express their opinions without reserve; and such the baneful consequences to the intellectual, and through that to the moral nature of man, unless this liberty is either conceded, or asserted in spite of prohibition; let us next examine whether the same reasons do not require that men should be free to act upon their opinions—to carry these out in their lives, without hindrance, either physical or moral, from their fellow-men, so long as it is at their own risk and peril. This last proviso is of course indispensable. No one pretends that actions should be as free as opinions. On the contrary, even opinions lose their immunity, when the circumstances in which they are expressed are such as to constitute their expression a positive instigation to some mischievous act. An opinion that corn-dealers are starvers of the poor, or that private property is robbery, ought to be unmolested when simply circulated through the press, but may justly incur punishment when delivered orally to an excited mob assembled before the house of a corn-dealer, or when handed about among the same mob in the form of a placard. Acts, of whatever kind, which, without justifiable cause, do harm to others, may be, and in the more important cases absolutely require to be, controlled by the unfavorable sentiments, and, when needful, by the active interference of mankind. The liberty of the individual must be thus far limited; he must not make himself a nuisance to other people. But if he refrains from molesting others in what concerns them, and merely acts according to his own inclination and judgment in things which concern himself, the same reasons which show that opinion should be free, prove also that he should be allowed, without molestation, to carry his opinions into practice at his own cost. That mankind are not infallible; that their truths, for the most part, are only half-truths; that unity of opinion, unless resulting from the fullest and freest comparison of opposite opinions, is not desirable, and diversity not an evil, but a good, until mankind are much more capable than at present of recognizing all sides of the truth, are principles applicable to men's modes of action, not less than to their opinions. As it is useful that while mankind are imperfect there should be different opinions, so is it that there should be different experiments of living; that free scope should be given to varieties of character, short of injury to others; and that the worth of different modes of life should be proved practically, when any one thinks fit to try them. It is desirable, in short, that in things which do not primarily concern others, individuality should assert itself. Where, not the person's own character, but the traditions or customs of other people are the rule of conduct, there is wanting one of the principal ingredients of human happiness, and quite the chief ingredient of individual and social progress. . . .

CHAPTER 4   OF THE LIMITS TO THE AUTHORITY OF THE STATE OVER THE INDIVIDUAL

What, then, is the rightful limit to the sovereignty of the individual over himself? Where does the authority of society begin? How much of human life should be assigned to individuality, and how much to society?

Each will receive its proper share, if each has that which more particularly concerns it. To individuality should belong the part of life in which it is chiefly the individual that is interested; to society, the part which chiefly interests society.

Though society is not founded on a contract, and though no good purpose is answered by inventing a contract in order to deduce social obligations from it, every one who receives the protection of society owes a return for the benefit, and the fact of living in society renders it indispensable that each should be bound to observe a certain line of conduct towards the rest. This conduct consists, first, in not injuring the interests of one another; or rather certain interests, which, either by express legal provision or by tacit understanding, ought to be considered as rights; and secondly, in each person's bearing his share (to be fixed on some equitable principle) of the labors and sacrifices incurred for defending the society or its members from injury and molestation. These conditions society is justified in enforcing, at all costs to those who endeavor to withold fulfilment. Nor is this all that society may do. The acts of an individual may be hurtful to others, or wanting in due consideration for their welfare, without going the length of violating any of their constituted rights. The offender may then be justly punished by opinion, though not by law. As soon as any part of a person's conduct affects prejudicially the interests of others, society has jurisdiction over it, and the question whether the general welfare will or will not be promoted by interfering with it, becomes open to discussion. But there is no room for entertaining any such question when a person's conduct affects the interests of no persons besides himself, or needs not affect them unless they like (all the persons concerned being of full age, and the ordinary amount of understanding). In all such cases there should be perfect freedom, legal and social, to do the action and stand the consequences.

It would be a great misunderstanding of this doctrine, to suppose that it is one of selfish indifference, which pretends that human beings have no business with each other's conduct in life, and that they should not concern themselves about the well-doing or well-being of one another, unless their own interest is involved. Instead of any diminution, there is need of a great increase of disinterested exertion to promote the good of others. But disinterested benevolence can find other instruments to persuade people to their good, than whips and scourges, either of the literal or the metaphorical sort. I am the last person to undervalue the self-regarding virtues; they are only second in importance, if even second, to the social. It is equally the business of education to cultivate both. But even education works by conviction and persuasion as well as by compulsion, and it is by the former only that, when the period of education is past, the self-regarding virtues should be inculcated. Human beings owe to each other help to distinguish the better from the worse, and encouragement to choose the former and avoid the latter. They should be forever stimulating each other to increased exercise of their higher faculties, and increased direction of their feelings and aims towards wise instead of foolish, elevating instead of degrading, objects and contemplations. But neither one person, nor any number of persons, is warranted in saying to another human creature of ripe years, that he shall not do with his life for his own benefit what he chooses to do with it. He is the person most interested in his own well-being: the interest which any other person, except in cases of strong personal attachment, can have in it, is trifling, compared with that which he himself has; the interest which society has in him individually (except as to his conduct to others) is fractional, and altogether indirect: while, with respect to his own feelings and circumstances, the most ordinary man or woman has means of knowledge immeasurably surpassing those that can be possessed by anyone else. The interference of society to overrule his judgment and purposes in what only regards himself, must be grounded on general presumptions; which may be altogether wrong, and even if right, are as likely as not to be misapplied to individual cases, by persons no better acquainted with the circumstances of such cases than those are who look at them merely from without. In this department, therefore, of human affairs, Individuality has its proper field of action. In the conduct of human beings towards one another, it is necessary that general rules should for the most part be observed, in order that people may know what they have to expect; but in each person's own concerns, his individual spontaneity is entitled to free exercise. Considerations to aid his judgment, exhortations to strengthen his will, may be offered to him, even obtruded on him, by others; but he, himself, is the final judge. All errors which he is likely to commit against advice and warning, are far outweighed by the evil of allowing others to constrain him to what they deem his good. . . .

What I contend for is, that the inconveniences which are strictly inseparable from the unfavorable judgment of others, are the only ones to which a person should ever be subjected for that portion of his conduct and character which concerns his own good, but which does not affect the interests of others in their relations with him. Acts injurious to others require a totally different treatment. Encroachment on their rights; infliction on them of any loss or damage not justified by his own rights; falsehood or duplicity in dealing with them; unfair or ungenerous use of advantages over them; even selfish abstinence from defending them against injury—these are fit objects of moral reprobation, and, in grave cases, of moral retribution and punishment. And not only these acts, but the dispositions which lead to them, are properly immoral, and fit subjects of disapprobation which may rise to abhorrence. Cruelty of disposition; malice and ill-nature; that most anti-social and odious of all passions, envy; dissimulation and insincerity; irascibility on insufficient cause, and resentment disproportioned to the provocation; the love of domineering over others; the desire to engross more than one's share of advantages (the πλεονεξία of the Greeks); the pride which derives gratification from the abasement of others; the egotism which thinks self and its concerns more important than everything else, and decides all doubtful questions in his own favor—these are moral vices, and constitute a bad and odious moral character: unlike the self-regarding faults previously mentioned, which are not properly immoralities, and to whatever pitch they may be carried, do not constitute wickedness. They may be proofs of any amount of folly, or want of personal dignity and self-respect; but they are only a subject of moral reprobation when they involve a breach of duty to others, for whose sake the individual is bound to have care for himself. What are called duties to ourselves are not socially obligatory, unless circumstances render them at the same time duties to others. The term duty to oneself, when it means anything more than prudence, means self-respect or self-development; and for none of these is any one accountable to his fellow-creatures, because for none of them is it for the good of mankind that he be held accountable to them. . . .

The distinction here pointed out between the part of a person's life which concerns only himself, and that which concerns others, many persons will refuse to admit. How (it may be asked) can any part of the conduct of a member of society be a matter of indifference to the other members? No person is an entirely isolated being; it is impossible for a person to do anything seriously or permanently hurtful to himself, without mischief reaching at least to his near connections, and often far beyond them. If he injures his property, he does harm to those who directly or indirectly derived support from it, and usually diminishes, by a greater or less amount, the general resources of the community. If he deteriorates his bodily or mental faculties, he not only brings evil upon all who depended on him for any portion of their happiness, but disqualifies himself for rendering the services which he owes to his fellow-creatures generally; perhaps becomes a burden on their affection or benevolence; and if such conduct were very frequent, hardly any offence that is committed would detract more from the general sum of good. Finally, if by his vices or follies a person does no direct harm to others, he is nevertheless (it may be said) injurious by his example; and ought to be compelled to control himself, for the sake of those whom the sight or knowledge of his conduct might corrupt or mislead.

And even (it will be added) if the consequences of misconduct could be confined to the vicious or thoughtless individual, ought society to abandon to their own guidance those who are manifestly unfit for it? If protection against themselves is confessedly due to children and persons under age, is not society equally bound to afford it to persons of mature years who are equally incapable of self-government? If gambling, or drunkenness, or incontinence, or idleness, or uncleanliness, are as injurious to happiness, and as great a hindrance to improvement, as many or most of the acts prohibited by law, why (it may be asked) should not law, so far as is consistent with practicability and social convenience, endeavor to repress these also? And as a supplement to the unavoidable imperfections of law, ought not opinion at least to organize a powerful police against these vices, and visit rigidly with social penalties those who are known to practice them? There is no question here (it may be said) about restricting individuality, or impeding the trial of new and original experiments in living. The only thing it is sought to prevent are things which have been tried and condemned from the beginning of the world until now; things which experience has shown not to be useful or suitable to any person's individuality. There must be some length of time and amount of experience, after which a moral or prudential truth may be regarded as established: and it is merely desired to prevent generation after generation from falling over the same precipice which has been fatal to their predecessors.

I fully admit that the mischief which a person does to himself, may seriously affect, both through their sympathies and their interests, those nearly connected with him, and in a minor degree, society at large. When, by conduct of this sort, a person is led to violate a distinct and assignable obligation to any other person or persons, the case is taken out of the self-regarding class, and becomes amenable to moral disapprobation in the proper sense of the term. If, for example, a man, through intemperance or extravagance, becomes unable to pay his debts, or, having undertaken the moral responsibility of a family, becomes from the same cause incapable of supporting or educating them, he is deservedly reprobated, and might be justly punished; but it is for the breach of duty to his family or creditors, not for the extravagance. If the resources which ought to have been devoted to them, had been diverted from them for the most prudent investment, the moral culpability would have been the same. George Barnwell murdered his uncle to get money for his mistress, but if he had done it to set himself up in business, he would equally have been hanged. Again, in the frequent case of a man who causes grief to his family by addiction to bad habits, he deserves reproach for his unkindness or ingratitude; but so he may for cultivating habits not in themselves vicious, if they are painful to those with whom he passes his life, or who from personal ties are dependent on him for their comfort. Whoever fails in the consideration generally due to the interests and feelings of others, not being compelled by some more imperative duty, or justified by allowable self-preference, is a subject of moral disapprobation for that failure, but not for the cause of it, nor for the errors, merely personal to himself, which may have remotely led to it. In like manner, when a person disables himself, by conduct purely self-regarding, from the performance of some definite duty incumbent on him to the public, he is guilty of a social offence. No person ought to be punished simply for being drunk; but a soldier or a policeman should be punished for being drunk on duty. Whenever, in short, there is a definite damage, or a definite risk of damage, either to an individual or to the public, the case is taken out of the province of liberty, and placed in that of morality or law.

But with regard to the merely contingent, or, as it may be called, constructive injury which a person causes to society, by conduct which neither violates any specific duty to the public, nor occasions perceptible hurt to any assignable individual except himself; the inconvenience is one which society can afford to bear, for the sake of the greater good of human freedom. If grown persons are to be punished for not taking proper care of themselves, I would rather it were for their own sake, than under pretence of preventing them from impairing their capacity of rendering to society benefits which society does not pretend it has a right to exact. But I cannot consent to argue the point as if society had no means of bringing its weaker members up to its ordinary standard of rational conduct, except waiting till they do something irrational, and then punishing them, legally or morally, for it. Society has had absolute power over them during all the early portion of their existence: it has had the whole period of childhood and nonage in which to try whether it could make them capable of rational conduct in life. The existing generation is master both of the training and the entire circumstances of the generation to come; it cannot indeed make them perfectly wise and good, because it is itself so lamentably deficient in goodness and wisdom; and its best efforts are not always, in individual cases, its most successful ones; but it is perfectly well able to make the rising generation, as a whole, as good as, and a little better than, itself. If society lets any considerable number of its members grow up mere children, incapable of being acted on by rational consideration of distant motives, society has itself to blame for the consequences. . . .

But the strongest of all the arguments against the interference of the public with purely personal conduct, is that when it does interfere, the odds are that it interferes wrongly, and in the wrong place. On questions of social morality, of duty to others, the opinion of the public, that is, of an overruling majority, though often wrong, is likely to be still oftener right; because on such questions they are only required to judge of their own interests; of the manner in which some mode of conduct, if allowed to be practised, would affect themselves. But the opinion of a similar majority, imposed as a law on the minority, on questions of self-regarding conduct, is quite as likely to be wrong as right; for in these cases public opinion means, at the best, some people's opinion of what is good or bad for other people; while very often it does not even mean that; the public, with the most perfect indifference, passing over the pleasure or convenience of those whose conduct they censure, and considering only their own preference. There are many who consider as an injury to themselves any conduct which they have a distaste for, and resent it as an outrage to their feelings; as a religious bigot, when charged with disregarding the religious feelings of others, has been known to retort that they disregard his feelings, by persisting in their abominable worship or creed. But there is no parity between the feeling of a person for his own opinion, and the feeling of another who is offended at his holding it; no more than between the desire of a thief to take a purse, and the desire of the right owner to keep it. And a person's taste is as much his own peculiar concern as his opinion or his purse. It is easy for any one to imagine an ideal public, which leaves the freedom and choice of individuals in all uncertain matters undisturbed, and only requires them to abstain from modes of conduct which universal experience has condemned. But where has there been seen a public which set any such limit to its censorship? or when does the public trouble itself about universal experience? In its interferences with personal conduct it is seldom thinking of anything but the enormity of acting or feeling differently from itself; and this standard of judgment, thinly disguised, is held up to mankind as the dictate of religion and philosophy, by nine tenths of all moralists and speculative writers. These teach that things are right because they are right; because we feel them to be so. They tell us to search in our own minds and hearts for laws of conduct binding on ourselves and on all others. What can the poor public do but apply these instructions, and make their own personal feelings of good and evil, if they are tolerably unanimous in them, obligatory on all the world? . . .

Georg Wilhelm Friedrich Hegel

The following selection from *Introduction to the Philosophy of History* by Georg Wilhelm Friederich Hegel (1770–1831) serves as a good summary of Hegel's conception of the relationship between freedom and the state. In explaining what he believes genuine freedom to be, Hegel brings out many of the aspects of his organic theory of the state. Some see in this conception of the state many elements of fascism; others see only a recognition of the necessarily close relationship of the individual and the state. At least one thing is clear: it was against this conception of the state that Karl Marx reacted (though it is not obvious that the young Marx did not actually adopt something like this conception after all). And Hegel's organicism helped spawn the individualistic reactions of existentialists.

Introduction to the Philosophy of History

3. THE STATE

(a) The State as Realization of the Idea

... What is the material in which the final end of Reason is to be realized? It is first of all the subjective agent itself, human desires, subjectivity in general. In human knowledge and volition, as its material basis, the rational attains existence. We have considered subjective volition with its purpose, namely, the truth of reality, insofar as moved by a great world-historical passion. As a subjective will in limited passions it is dependent; it can gratify its particular desires only within this dependence. But the subjective will has also a substantial life, a reality where it moves in the region of essential being and has the essential itself as the object of its existence. This essential being is the union of the subjective with the rational will; it is the moral whole, the *State*. It is that actuality in which the individual has and enjoys his freedom, but only as knowing, believing, and willing the universal. This must not be understood as if the subjective will of the individual attained its gratification and enjoyment through the common will and the latter were a means for it—as if the individual limited his freedom among the other individuals, so that this common limitation, the mutal constraint of all, might secure a small space of liberty for each. (This would only be negative freedom.) Rather, law, morality, the State, and they alone, are the positive reality and satisfaction of freedom. The caprice of the individual is not freedom. It is this caprice which is being limited, the license of particular desires.

The subjective will, passion, is the force which actualizes and realizes. The Idea is the interior; the State is the externally existing, genuinely moral life. It is the union of the universal and essential with the subjective will, and as such it is *Morality*. The individual who lives in this unity has a moral life, a value which

From G. W. F. Hegel: *Reason in History: A General Introduction to the Philosophy of History*, translated by Robert S. Hartman, copyright © 1953 by the Liberal Arts Press, Inc., reprinted by permission of The Liberal Arts Press Division of The Bobbs-Merrill Company, Inc. The footnotes are those of the translator. Brackets and italics represent interpolations from the third edition and are based on notes from lectures.

consists in this substantiality alone.[1] Sophocles' Antigone says: "The divine commands are not of yesterday nor of today; no, they have an infinite existence, and no one can say whence they came."[2] The laws of ethics are not accidental, but are rationality itself. It is the end of the State to make the substantial prevail and maintain itself in the actual doings of men and in their convictions. It is the absolute interest of Reason that this moral whole exist; and herein lies the justification and merit of heroes who have founded states, no matter how crude.

[*What counts in a state is the practice of acting according to a common will and adopting universal aims. Even in the crude state there is subjection of one will under another; but this does not mean that the individual does not have a will of his own. It means that his particular will has no validity. Whims, lusts are not valid. The particularity of the will is being renounced already in such crude political formations. What counts is the common will. In thus being suppressed the individual will retires into itself. And this is the first condition necessary for the existence of the universal, the condition, namely, of knowledge, of thought —for it is thought that man has in common with the divine.[3] It thus makes its appearance in the state. Only on this soil, that is, in the state, can art and religion exist. The objects of our considerations are peoples that have organized themselves rationally.*] In world history only those peoples that form states can come to our notice. [*One must not imagine that such organizations could appear on a desert island or in isolation. Although it is true that all great men have formed themselves in solitude, they have done so only by assimilating what the state had already created. The universal must be not only something which the individual merely intends, but which is in existence. As such it is present in the state; it is that which is valid in it. Here inwardness is at the same time actuality. It is but actuality of an external manifold, yet comprehended here in universality.*

The universal Idea manifests itself in the state. The term "manifestation" has here a meaning different from the usual one. Usually we distinguish between power (potentiality) and manifestation, as if the former were the essential, the latter the unessential or external. But no concrete determination lies as yet in the category of power itself, while where Spirit is, or the concrete concept, manifestation itself is the essential. The criterion of Spirit is its action, its active essence. Man is his own action, the sequence of his actions, that into which he has been making himself. Thus Spirit is essentially Energy; and in regard to Spirit one cannot set aside its manifestation. The manifestation of Spirit is its actual self-determination, and this is the element of its concrete nature. Spirit which does not determine itself is an abstraction of the intellect. The manifestation of Spirit is its self-determination, and it is this manifestation that we have to investigate in the form of states and individuals.

The spiritual individual, the people, insofar as it is organized in itself, an

---

[1] Social institutions, originally extrinsic to the individual and his intrinsic morality, grow up to complete this morality in the course of their development. Their totality, the State, thus becomes itself intrinsic morality, both with respect to the individual, as completion of his intrinsic freedom, and to the World Spirit, as concretion of its universal Freedom.

[2] This seems an unfortunate reference, for Antigone *opposes* the eternal laws of the gods to the temporal commands of a state—thus making a point opposed to the one here being made by Hegel.

[3] This clause is restored from the first edition.

organic whole, is what we call the State. This designation is ambiguous in that by "state" and "constitutional law" one usually means the simple political aspect as distinct from religion, science, and art. But when we speak of the manifestation of the spiritual we understand the term "state" in a more comprehensive sense, similar to the term Reich *(empire, realm). For us, then, a people is primarily a spiritual individual. We do not emphasize the external aspects but concentrate on what has been called the spirit of a people. We mean its consciousness of itself, of its own truth, its own essence, the spiritual powers which live and rule in it. The universal which manifests itself in the State and is known in it—the* form *under which everything that is, is subsumed—is that which constitutes the* culture *of a nation. The definite* content *which receives this universal form and is contained in the concrete actuality of the state is the* spirit of the people. *The actual state is animated by this spirit in all its particular affairs, wars, institutions, etc. This spiritual content is something definite, firm, solid, completely exempt from caprice, the particularities, the whims of individuality, of change. That which is subject to the latter is not the nature of the people: it is like the dust playing over a city or a field, which does not essentially transform it. This spiritual content then constitutes the essence of the individual as well as that of the people. It is the holy bond that ties the men, the spirits together. It is one life in all, a grand object, a great purpose and content on which depend all individual happiness and all private decisions.*] [*The state does not exist for the citizens; on the contrary, one could say that the state is the end and they are its means. But the means-end relation is not fitting here. For the state is not the abstract confronting the citizens; they are parts of it, like members of an organic body, where no member is end and none is means.*] It is the realization of Freedom, of the absolute, final purpose, and exists for its own sake. All the value man has, all spiritual reality, he has only through the state. For his spiritual reality is the knowing presence to him of his own essence, of rationality, of its objective, immediate actuality present in and for him. Only thus is he truly a consciousness, only thus does he partake in morality, in the legal and moral life of the state. For the True is the unity of the universal and particular will. And the universal in the state is in its laws, its universal and rational provisions. The state is the divine Idea as it exists on earth.

Thus the State is the definite object of world history proper. In it freedom achieves its objectivity and lives in the enjoyment of this objectivity. For law is the objectivity of Spirit; it is will in its true form. Only the will that obeys the law is free, for it obeys itself and, being in itself, is free. In so far as the state, our country, constitutes a community of existence, and as the subjective will of man subjects itself to the laws, the antithesis of freedom and necessity disappears. The rational, like the substantial, is necessary. We are free when we recognize it as law and follow it as the substance of our own being. The objective and the subjective will are then reconciled and form one and the same harmonious whole. For the ethos of the state is not of the moral, the reflective kind in which one's own conviction rules supreme. This latter is rather the peculiarity of the modern world. The true and antique morality is rooted in the principle that everybody stands in his place of duty. An Athenian citizen did what was required of him, as it were from instinct. But if I reflect on the object of my activity, I must have the consciousness that my will counts. Morality, however, is the duty, the substantial law, the second nature, as it has been rightly called; for the first nature of man is his immediate, animalic existence.

(b) Law as Realization of Freedom

The detailed development of the state is the subject of legal philosophy. But it must be observed that in present-day theories various errors are current respecting the state, which pass for established truths and have become prejudices. We will mention only a few of them, particularly those which refer to the subject of history.

The first error that we encounter is the direct contradiction of our principle that the State is the realization of freedom: the view, namely, that man is free by nature but that in society and in the state, to which he necessarily belongs, he must limit this natural freedom. That man is free "by nature" is quite correct in the sense that he is free according to the very concept of man, that is, in his *destination* only, as he is, in himself; the "nature" of a thing is indeed tantamount to its concept. But the view in question also introduces into the concept of man his immediate and natural way of *existence*. In this sense a state of nature is assumed in which man is imagined in the possession of his natural rights and the unlimited exercise and enjoyment of his freedom. This assumption is not presented as a historical fact; it would indeed be difficult, were the attempt seriously made, to detect any such condition anywhere, either in the present or the past. Primitive conditions can indeed be found, but they are marked by brute passions and acts of violence. Crude as they are, they are at the same time connected with social institutions which, to use the common expression, restrain freedom. The assumption (of the noble savage) is one of those nebulous images which theory produces, an idea which necessarily flows from that theory and to which it ascribes real existence without sufficient historical justification.

Such a state of nature is in theory exactly as we find it in practice. Freedom as the *ideal* of the original state of nature does not *exist* as original and natural. It must first be acquired and won, and that is possible only through an infinite process of the discipline of knowledge and will power. The state of nature, therefore, is rather the state of injustice, violence, untamed natural impulses, of inhuman deeds and emotions. There is, it is true, a limitation by society and the state, but it is a limitation of the brute emotions and rude instincts, as well as (in a more advanced stage of culture) of self-reflecting caprice and passion. This constraint is part of the process through which is first produced the consciousness of and the desire for freedom in its true, that is, rational and ideal form. The idea of freedom necessarily implies law and morality. These are in and for themselves universal essences, objects, and aims, to be discovered only by the activity of thought, emancipating itself from, and developing itself in opposition to, the merely sensuous; it must be assimilated to and incorporated with the originally sensuous will against its natural inclination. The perpetual misunderstanding of freedom is this: that one knows it only in its formal subjective sense, abstracted from its essential objects and aims. Thus the limitation of impulse, desire, passion—pertaining merely to the particular individual as such—of caprice and willfullness, is taken as a limitation of freedom. On the contrary, such limitation is the very condition leading to liberation; and society and the state are the very conditions in which freedom is realized.

Secondly, there is another theory that objects to the development of morality into legal form. The *patriarchal* state is viewed, either in relation to the whole or to some branches (of the human family), as that condition in which, together with the legal element, the moral and emotional find their fulfillment. Hence justice, it is believed, can be truly carried out only through the union of its content with the moral and emotional elements. The basis of the patriarchal condition is the family relation. It develops as the first phase of conscious morality, to be followed by that of the state as its second phase. The patriarchal condition is one of transition, in which the family has already advanced to a race or people. The union, therefore, has already ceased to be simply a bond of love and confidence and has become one of service. To understand this transition we must first examine the ethical principle of the family. The family is a single person; its members have either, as parents, mutually surrendered their individuality—and consequently their legal relations to one another, as well as their particular interests and desires—or have not yet attained individuality, as children, who are at first in the merely natural condition already mentioned. They live therefore in a unity of feeling, love, confidence, and faith in each other. In love, the one individual has the consciousness of himself in the consciousness of the other; he lives selflessly. In this mutual self-renunciation each gains the life of the other, as well as his own which is one with the other. All other interests of life, its necessities and external concerns, education of the children, form a common purpose for the members of the family. The spirit of the family—the Penates—are as much one substantial being as the spirit of a people in the State. Morality in both cases consists in a feeling, a consciousness, and a will not of the individual personality and its interests but of the common personality, the interest of all members as such. But this unity is in the case of the family essentially one of feeling, remaining within the limits of the natural. The sacredness of the family relation should be respected in the highest degree by the state. Through it the state has as members individuals who are already, as such and in themselves, moral—for as mere persons they are not; and who, in uniting to form a state, bring with them the sound basis of a political edifice, the capacity of feeling one with a whole. But the expansion of the family to a patriarchal whole extends beyond the ties of blood relationship, the simple, natural basis of the state. Beyond that the individuals must acquire the status of personality. A detailed review of the patriarchal condition would lead us to the discussion of theocracy. The head of the patriarchal clan is also its priest. When the family is not yet distinct from civil society and the state, the separation of religion from it has not yet taken place either; and so much the less since its piety is itself (like religion) an inwardness of feeling.

(c) The Legal Foundation of the State   (the Constitution)

We have discussed two aspects of freedom, the objective and the subjective. If freedom implies the consent of each individual, then of course only the subjective aspect is meant. From this principle follows as a matter of course that no law is valid except by agreement of all. This implies that the majority decides; hence the minority must yield to the majority. But already Rousseau has remarked that this means the absence of freedom, for the will of the minority is disregarded. In the Polish diet all decisions had to be unanimous, and it was from this kind of freedom that the state perished. Moreover, it is a dangerous and false presupposition that the people *alone* has reason and insight and knows what is right; for each popular faction can set itself up as the People. What constitutes the state is a matter of trained intelligence, not a matter of "the people."

If the principle of individual will and consent of all is laid down as the only basis of constitutional freedom, then actually there is no *Constitution*. The only institution necessary would be a neutral, centrally located observer who would announce what in his opinion were the needs of the state, a mechanism of assembling the individuals, casting their vote, and the arithmetical counting and comparison of the votes on the various propositions—and this would already be the decision. The state is an abstract entity which has its—merely general—reality in the citizens. But it is real, and the merely general existence must be translated into individual will and activity. Thus arises the necessity of government and administration, the selection of individuals who have to take the helm of political administration, decide its execution, and command the citizens entrusted with it. Thus, even in a democracy the people's decision on a war requires a general as leader of the army. Only in the constitution does the abstract entity of the state assume life and reality; but this involves a distinction between those who command and those who obey. Yet, it does not seem to be in accordance with freedom to obey, and those who command seem to act in opposition to the concept of freedom, the very basis of the state.

Thus the distinction between commanding and obeying seems necessary for the very function of the state. Hence one recommends—as a matter of purely external necessity, which is in opposition to the nature of freedom in its abstract aspect—that the constitution should at least be so framed that the citizens have to obey as little as possible and the authorities are allowed to command as little as possible. The nature and degree of whatever authority is necessary should be determined and decided in large measure by the people, that is to say, by the will of the majority; yet at the same time the state, as reality, as individual unit, should have power and strength.

The primary distinction to be made is, then, between the governing and the governed. Constitutions have rightly been classified as monarchic, aristocratic, and democratic; the monarchy proper, however, must be distinguished again from despotism. Also, it must be understood that such classifications are drawn from abstract concepts so as to emphasize the fundamental differences only. They are types of genera or species which cannot exhaustively account for the concrete realities. Particularly, they admit of a great number of special modifications, not only within the types but also among the types; even though such fusions or mixtures of type conduce to misshapen, unstable, and inconsistent forms. The problem, in such collisions, therefore is to determine the *best constitution*, namely, the institution, organization, or mechanism of government which most securely guarantees the purpose of the state. This goal can of course be considered in various ways, for example, as the quiet enjoyment of life, as universal happiness. Such aims have brought about the so-called ideals of government and, particularly, the ideals of the education of princes, as in Fénolon,[4] or of the rulers or the aristocracy in general, as in Plato. The emphasis is here put on the nature of the ruling individuals; the content of the organic institutions of the state is not at all considered. It is often thought that the question of the best or a better constitution is not only in theory a matter of

---

[4] In his *Télémague* (1699), written after Fénelon's tutorship of the Duke of Burgundy, who for a year (1711-1712) was heir-apparent to the throne of Louis XIV. Fénelon (1651-1715) also wrote a *Treatise on the Education of Girls*, which for a century became the standard handbook on the subject. In 1695 he became archbishop of Cambrai. His writings form the transition from absolutism to enlightenment.

free individual conviction, but that its actual introduction could also be only a matter of purely theoretical decisions; so that the constitution would be a matter of free choice, determined by nothing but reflection. In this quite naive sense the Persian magnates—though not the Persian people—deliberated upon the constitution which they wanted to introduce in Persia, after their conspiracy against the pseudo-Smerdis and the Magi had succeeded and there was no royal heir. And the account that Herodotus gives this deliberation is equally naïve.

Today the constitution of a country and people is not regarded as so entirely dependent upon free choice. The underlying, but abstractly entertained conception of freedom has resulted in the Republic's being quite universally regarded—in theory—as the only just and true constitution. Many of those who even have high official positions under monarchical constitutions do not resist but rather incline toward such views. They understand, however, that such a constitution, though ideal, cannot be realized under all circumstances. People being what they are, one has to be content with less freedom, so that the monarchical constitution, under the given circumstances and the moral condition of the people, is regarded the most useful. Even in this view the actual condition on which the constitution is thought to depend is regarded as a merely external accident. This opinion is based on the separation which reflection and understanding make between the concept and its reality. Holding to an abstract and hence untrue concept they do not grasp the idea; or—which comes to the same thing insofar as the content, though not the form, is concerned—they have no concrete view of a people and a state. We shall show later that the constitution of a people is of the same substance, the same spirit as its art and philosophy, or at least its imagination, its thoughts, and its general culture—not to mention the additional, external influences of climate, neighbors, and global position. A state is an individual totality from which no particular aspect, not even one as highly important as the constitution, can be separated and considered by itself alone. Nor can this constitution be considered, discussed, and selected in isolation. Not only is the constitution intimately connected with those other spiritual forces and dependent on them, but the determination of the whole spiritual individuality, including all its forces, is only a moment in the history of the whole and predetermined in its course. It is this that gives to the constitution its highest sanction and necessity. The origin of the state is domination on the one hand, instinctive obedience on the other. But obedience and force, fear of a ruler, is already a connection of wills. Already in primitive states we found that the will of the individual does not count, that particularity is renounced and the universal will is the essential. This unity of the universal and the particular is the Idea itself, present as the State and as such developing itself further. The abstract but necessary course of the development of truly independent states begins then with royal power, either patriarchal or military. After that, individuality and particularity must assert themselves in aristocracy and democracy. The end is the subjection of this particularity under one power which must be absolutely of such a nature that the two spheres have their independence outside of it: it must be monarchical. Thus we must distinguish a first (or original) and a second phase of royalty. This course is a necessary one; each concrete constitution must enter it. A constitution is therefore not a matter of choice but depends on the stage of the people's spiritual development.

What is important in a constitution is the internal development of the rational, that is, the political condition, the setting free of the successive moments of the concept. The particular powers must become distinct, each one completing itself, but at the same time they must freely cooperate for one purpose and be held together by it, thus forming an organic whole. Thus the State is rational and self-conscious freedom, objectively knowing itself. For its objectivity resides precisely in the fact that its moments are not merely ideally present but actualized in their particularity; that they pass over from their own self-related activity into that activity from which results the whole, the soul, the individual unity.

The State is the idea of Spirit in the externality of human will and its freedom. It therefore is essentially the medium of historical change, and the stages of the Idea represent in it various *principles.* The constitutions wherein world-historical peoples have reached their flowering are peculiar to them, hence give us no universally valid basis. Their differences consist not in the individual manners of elaboration and development, but rather in the differences of principles. Thus we can learn little for the political principle of our time, as the last constitutional principle, from a comparison with the constitutions of earlier world-historical peoples. It is different with science and art. The philosophy of the ancients, for example, is so much the basis of modern philisophy that it must be contained in the latter as its fundament. The relation is here one of uninterrupted development of an identical structure, whose foundations, walls, and roof are still the same. In art that of the Greeks is the highest model. But in respect to the constitution it is different; here the old and the new do not have the essential principle in common, although we do have in common abstract speculations and doctrines of just government, of insight and virtue of the ruler. Yet, nothing is so inappropriate as to use as models for our constitutional institutions examples from Greece, Rome, or the Orient. From the Orient we can take agreeable pictures of patriarchal conditions, fatherly government, popular devotion; from Greeks and Romans descriptions of popular liberty. The Greeks and Romans understood the concept of a free constitution as granting all citizens a share in the council and decisions of communal affairs and laws. Also in our times this is the general opinion, but with one modification: our states are so big and their people so many, that they cannot directly, but only indirectly through representatives, contribute their will to political decisions. For purposes of legislation the people must be represented by deputies. A free constitution is for us dependent upon the idea of representative government, and this has become a firm prejudice. Thus people and government are separated. But there is something malicious in this opposition, a trick of bad will, as if the people were the whole. Also, at the bottom of this idea lies the principle of individuality, the absoluteness of the subjective will of which we spoke above. The main thing is that freedom, as it is determined by the concept, is *not* based on the subjective will and caprice but on the understanding of the general will, and that the system of freedom is the free development of its stages. The subjective will is a purely formal concept which does not say at all *what* it wills. Only the rational will is the universal which determines and develops itself in itself and unfolds its successive moments in an organic manner. Of such Gothic cathedral architecture the ancients knew nothing.

(d) The Religious Foundation of the State

We have established as the two points of our discussion, first, the idea of Freedom as absolute final aim, and, secondly, the means of its realization, the subjective side of knowledge and volition with their vitality, mobility, and activity. We then discussed the State as the moral whole and the reality of freedom, and thus as the objective unity of the two preceding factors. Although for analysis we separated the two elements, it must be well remembered that they are closely connected and that this connection is within each of them when we examine them singly. On the one hand we recognized the Idea in its determination, as self-knowing and self-willing freedom which has only itself as its aim. As such, it is at the same time the simple idea of reason and likewise that which we have called subject, the consciousness of self, the Spirit existing in the world. On the other hand, in considering this subjectivity, we find that subjective knowing and willing are Thinking. But in thoughtful knowing and willing I will the universal object, the substance of actualized rationality (of what is in and for itself rational). We thus observe a union which is in itself, between the objective element, the concept, and the subjective element. The objective existence of this unity is the State. The State, thus, is the foundation and center of the other concrete aspects of national life, of art, law, morality, religion, science. All spiritual activity, then, has the aim of becoming conscious of this union, that is, of its freedom. Among the forms of these conscious unions *religion* is the highest. In it the spirit existing in the world becomes conscious of absolute Spirit. In this consciousness of actualized ("being-in-and-for-itself") essence the will of man renounces particular interest; it puts it aside in devotion in which he is not concerned any more with particulars. Through sacrifice man expresses his renunciation of property, his will, his private feelings. The religious concentration of the mind appears as emotion, but passes also into contemplation; ritual is an expression of contemplation. The second form of the spiritual union between the objective and the subjective is *Art:* it appears more in sensible reality than does religion; in its most noble attitude it has to represent, not indeed the spirit of God but the form of the God—and then the divine, the spiritual in general. It renders the divine visible to imagination and the senses. The True, however, not only achieves representation and feeling, as in religion, and for the senses, as in art, but also for thinking spirit; this leads to the third form of the union, *Phisosophy.* It is in this respect the highest, freest, and wisest product. We cannot here discuss these three forms in any detail. They had to be mentioned only because they occupy the same ground as the object of our study, the *State.*

The universal which appears and becomes known in the state, the form into which is cast all reality, constitutes what is generally called the *culture* of a nation. The definite content, however, which receives the form of universality and is contained in the concrete reality of the State, is the *spirit of the people.* The true State is animated by this spirit in all its affairs, wars, institutions, etc. But man must himself know of this—his own—spirit and essence and give himself the consciousness of his original union with it. For we said that all morality is the unity of subjective and general will. The spirit, then, must give itself an express consciousness of this unity, and the center of this knowledge is religion. Art and science are only different aspects of this very same content.

In discussing religion it is important to ask whether it recognizes truth, or the

Idea, only in its separation or in its true unity. In its separation: when God is conceived as the abstract highest Being, Lord of Heaven and Earth, transcending the world, beyond, and excluded from, human reality—or in its unity: God as unity of the universal and particular, in Whom even the particular is positively regarded, in the idea of incarnation. Religion is the sphere where a people gives itself the definition of what it regards as the True. Such a definition contains everything which belongs to the essence of the object, reducing its nature to a simple fundamental characteristic as focus for all other characteristics—the universal soul of all particulars. The idea of God thus is the general fundament of a people.

In this respect religion stands in closest connection with the principle of the State. Freedom can only exist where individuality is known as positive in the divine Being. There is a further connection between religion and the state: secular existence is temporal and moves within private interest. Hence it is relative and unjustified. Its justification can only be derived from the absolute justification of its universal soul, its principle. And this is justified only as determination and existence of the essence of God. For this reason the State is based on religion. We hear this often repeated in our time. But mostly nothing more is meant than that individuals should be pious in order to be more willing and prepared to do their duty; for obedience to prince and law is so easily connected with reverence toward God. It is true that reverence toward God, in elevating the universal over the particular, can turn against the particular in fanaticism, and work against the State, burning and destroying its buildings and institutions. Hence reverence for God, it is believed, should be temperate and kept in a certain degree of coolness, lest it storm against and destroy that which ought to be protected and preserved by it. The possibility of such disaster is at least latent in it.

The correct conviction that the State rests on religion may give religion a position which presupposes the existence of the State. Then, in order to preserve the State, religion must be carried into it, in buckets and bushels, in order to impress it upon people's minds. It is quite correct that man must be educated to religion, but not as to something which does not yet exist. For, when we say that the State is based on religion and that it has its roots in it, we mean essentially that it has arisen from it and now and always continues to arise out of it. That is, the principles of the State must be regarded as valid in and for themselves, which they can only insofar as they are known to be determinations of divine nature itself. The nature of its religion, therefore, determines that of the State and its constitution. It actually has originated from it: the Athenian and the Roman states were possible only through the specific paganism of these peoples, just as a Catholic state has a spirit and constitution different from a Protestant one.

It would be bad if this appeal, this urge and drive to implant religion, were a call of anguish and distress, as it looks so often—as if it expressed the danger that religion were about to disappear or already had disappeared from the State. Indeed, it would be worse than this appeal assumes; for it assumes it can still implant and inculcate religion as a means against this evil. But religion is not such an artifact. Its self-production is a much more profound process. Another and opposite folly which we meet in our time is the tendency to invent and institute constitutions independently from religion. The Catholic religion, although, like the Protestant, part of Christianity, does not concede to the State the inner justice and morality which follows from the inwardness of the Protestant principle. This separation of constitutional law and of constitutions themselves from morality is necessary because of the peculiarity of that religion; it does not regard law and morality as independent and substantial. But thus torn away from inwardness, from the last sanctuary of conscience, from the quiet corner where religion has its abode, the constitutional principles and institutions lack a real center and remain abstract and indeterminate.

In summary, the vitality of The State in individuals is what we call Morality. The State, its laws, its institutions are the rights of the citizens; its nature, its soil, its mountains, airs, and waters are their land, their country, their external property. The history of the State are their deeds, and what their ancestors have accomplished belongs to them and lives in their memory. Everything is their possession just as they are possessed by it, for it constitutes their substance and being.

Their minds are full of it and their wills are their willing of these laws and of their country. It is this temporal totality which is One Being, the spirit of One People. To it the individuals belong; each individual is the son of his people and, at the same time, insofar as his state is in development, the son of his age. No one remains behind it, no one can leap ahead of it. This spiritual being is his—he is one of its representatives--it is that from which he arises and wherein he stands. For the Athenians Athens had a double meaning, the totality of their institutions as well as the goddess which represented the spirit and the unity of the people.

This spirit of a people is a *definite* spirit and, as was just said, is also determined according to the historical state of its development. This spirit, then, is the basis and content of the other forms of consciousness which have been mentioned. For the spirit in its consciousness of itself must be concrete to itself. Its objectivity immediately contains the origin of differences, which in their totality are the various spheres of the objective spirit itself—just as the soul exists only as the organization of its members which constitute it by combining themselves into simple unity. Thus it is one individuality. Its essence is represented, revered, and enjoyed as God, in religion; presented as image and intuition, in art; apprehended cognitively and conceived as thought, in philosophy. Because of the original identity of their substance, their content, and their subject matter with that of the State these products are inseparably united with the spirit of the State. Only with such a religion can there be such a form of the State, and only with such a State such art and such philosophy.

Furthermore, the definite national spirit itself is only one individual in the course of world history. For world history is the manifestation of the Divine, the absolute process of Spirit in its highest forms. It is this development wherein it achieves its truth and the consciousness of itself. The products of its stages are the world-historical national spirits, the definiteness of their moral lives, their constitution, art, religion, and science. To realize these stages in the infinite élan of the World Spirit, its irresistible urge; for this differentiation and its realization constitute its concept. World history only shows how the World Spirit gradually attains the consciousness and willing of truth. Dawn rises in the Spirit; it discovers focal points; and finally, it attains full consciousness.

Karl Marx

Of the following three selections from the writings of Karl Marx (1818–1883), the best known is *The Communist Manifesto*, written with Engels. This is a fairly popular work, specifically designed to raise support and present a definite program of action.

The other two selections are both Marx's own work, and both aim at more technical philosophical issues. The *Theses on Feuerbach* are a connected series of statements intended to explain how Marx's position differed from that of Feuerbach, another prominent anti-Hegelian philosopher and sociologist. The idealist referred to in the *Theses* is Hegel. The *Theses* give a fairly clear explanation of what Marx means by 'materialism'.

The final selection is from Marx's *Economic and Philosophical Manuscripts.* The *Manuscripts* represent an early stage in Marx's thinking, and the influence of Hegelian modes of thinking is still obvious here. The *Manuscripts* only recently became generally available, which explains in part a resurgence of interest in Marx; for Marx's early writings show an ethical concern which appeared to be lost in his later work, particularly in *Das Kapital.* In fact, there is a continuity between Marx's earlier and later writings, but Marx's emphasis in his later period was on action rather than theory—hence the apparent change. In any case, the selection presented here is particularly useful in explaining a key term in Marx's terminology, 'alienation'.

The Communist Manifesto

A specter is haunting Europe—the specter of communism. All the powers of old Europe have entered into a holy alliance to exorcise this specter: Pope and Czar, Metternich and Guizot, French Radicals and German police-spies.

Where is the party in opposition that has not been decried as communistic by its opponents in power? Where the opposition that has not hurled the branding reproach of communism, against the more advanced opposition parties, as well as against its reactionary adversaries?

From *The Communist Manifesto,* Karl Marx and Friedrich Engels, 1848.

Two things result from this fact.

I. Communism is already acknowledged by all European powers to be itself a power.

II. It is high time that Communists should openly, in the face of the whole world, publish their views, their aims, their tendencies, and meet this nursery tale of the specter of communism with a Manifesto of the party itself.

To this end, Communists of various nationalities have assembled in London, and sketched the following Manifesto, to be published in the English, French, German, Italian, Flemish, and Danish languages.

II Proletarians and Communists

In what relation do the Communists stand to the proletarians as a whole?

The Communists do not form a separate party opposed to other working-class parties.

They have no interests separate and apart from those of the proletariat as a whole.

They do not set up any sectarian principles of their own, by which to shape and mold the proletarian movement.

The Communists are distinguished from the other working-class parties by this only: 1. In the national struggles of the proletarians of the different countries, they point out and bring to the fore the common interests of the entire proletariat, independent of all nationality. 2. In the various stages of development through which the struggle of the working class against the bourgeoisie has to pass, they always and everywhere represent the interests of the movement as a whole.

The Communists, therefore, are on the one hand, in the sphere of practice, the most advanced and resolute action of the working-class parties of every country, that section which pushes forward all others; and on the other hand, in the realm of theory, they have over the great mass of the proletariat the advantage of clearly understanding the line of march, the conditions, and the ultimate general results of the proletarian movement.

The immediate aim of the Communists is the same as that of all the other proletarian parties: the formation of the proletariat into a class; the overthrow of the bourgeois supremacy; and the conquest of political power by the proletariat.

The theoretical conclusions of the Communists are in no way based on ideas or principles that have been invented or discovered by this or that would-be universal reformer.

They merely express, in general terms, actual relations springing from an existing class struggle, from a historical movement going on under our very eyes. The abolition of existing property relations is not at all a distinctive feature of Communism.

All property relations in the past have continually been subject to historical change resulting from the change in historical conditions.

The French Revolution, for example, abolished feudal property in favor of bourgeois property.

The distinguishing feature of Communism is not the abolition of property generally, but the abolition of bourgeois property. But modern bourgeois private property is the final and most complete expression of the system of producing and appropriating products, that is based on class antagonisms, on the exploitation of the many by the few.

In this sense, the theory of the Communists may be summed up in the single sentence: the abolition of private property.

We Communists have been reproached with the desire of abolishing the right of personally acquiring property as the fruit of a man's own labor, the property that is alleged to be the foundation of all personal freedom, activity and independence.

Hard-won, self-acquired, self-earned property! Do you mean the property of the petty artisan and of the small peasant, a form of property that preceded the bourgeois form? There is no need to abolish that: the development of industry has to a great extent already destroyed it and is still destroying it daily.

Or do you mean modern bourgeois private property?

But does wage labor create any property for the laborer? Not a bit. It creates capital, *i.e.*, that kind of property which exploits wage labor, and which cannot increase except upon condition of begetting a new supply of wage labor for fresh exploitation. Property, in its present form, is based on the antagonism of capital and wage labor. Let us examine both sides of this antagonism.

To be a capitalist, is to have not only a purely personal, but also social *status* in production. Capital is a collective product, and only by the united action of many members, nay, in the last resort, only by the united action of all members of society, can it be set in motion.

Capital is, therefore, not a personal but a social power.

When, therefore, capital is converted into common property, into the property of all members of society, personal property is not thereby transformed into social property. It is only the social character of the property that is changed. It loses its class character.

Let us now take wage labor.

The average price of wage labor is the minimum wage, *i.e.*, that quantity of the means of subsistence, which is absolutely requisite to keep the laborer in bare existence as a laborer. What, therefore, the wage-laborer appropriates by means of his labor, merely suffices to prolong and reproduce a bare existence. We by no means intend to abolish this personal appropriation of the products of labor, an appropriation that is made for the maintenance and reproduction of human life and that leaves no surplus wherewith to command the labor of others. All that we want to do away with is the miserable character of this appropriation, under which the laborer lives merely to increase capital and is allowed to live only in so far as the interest of the ruling class requires it.

In bourgeois society, living labor is but a means to increase accumulated labor. In Communist society, accumulated labor is but a means to widen, to enrich, to promote the existence of the laborer.

In bourgeois society, therefore, the past dominates the present; in Communist society, the present dominates the past. In bourgeois society capital is independent and has individuality, while the living person is dependent and has no individuality.

And the abolition of this state of things is called by the bourgeois abolition of individuality and freedom! And rightly so. The abolition of bourgeois individuality, bourgeois independence, and bourgeois freedom is undoubtedly aimed at.

By freedom is meant, under the present bourgeois conditions of production, free trade, free selling and buying.

But if selling and buying disappears, free selling and buying disappears also. This talk about free selling and buying, and all the other "brave words" of our bourgeoisie about freedom in general, have a meaning, if any, only in contrast with restricted selling and buying, with the fettered traders of the Middle Ages, but have no meaning when opposed to the Communistic abolition of buying and selling, of the bourgeois conditions of production, and of the bourgeoisie itself.

You are horrified at our intending to do away with private property. But in your existing society, private property is already done away with for nine tenths of the population; its existence for the few is solely due to its nonexistence in the hands of those nine tenths. You reproach us, therefore, with intending to do away with a form of property, the necessary condition for whose existence is, the nonexistence of any property for the immense majority of society.

In one word, you reproach us with intending to do away with your property. Precisely so; that is just what we intend.

From the moment when labor can no longer be converted into capital, money, or rent, into a social power capable of being monopolized, *i.e.*, from the moment when individual property can no longer be transformed into bourgeois property, into capital, from that moment, you say, individuality vanishes.

You must, therefore, confess that by "individual" you mean no other person than the bourgeois, than the middle-class owner of property. This person must, indeed, be swept out of the way, and made impossible.

Communism deprives no man of the power to appropriate the products of society; all that it does is to deprive him of the power to subjugate the labor of others by means of such appropriation.

It has been objected that upon the abolition of private property all work will cease, and universal laziness will overtake us.

According to this, bourgeois society ought long ago to have gone to the dogs through sheer idleness; for those of its members who work, acquire nothing, and those who acquire anything, do not work. The whole of this objection is but another expression of tautology: that there can no longer be any wage labor when there is no longer any capital.

All objections urged against the Communistic mode of producing and appropriating material products, have, in the same way, been urged against the Communistic modes of producing and appropriating intellectual products. Just as, to the bourgeois, the disappearance of class property is the disappearance of production itself, so the disappearance of class culture is to him identical with the disappearance of all culture.

That culture, the loss of which he laments, is for the enormous majority a mere training to act as a machine.

But don't wrangle with us so long as you apply to our intended abolition of bourgeois property the standard of your bourgeois notions of freedom, culture, law, etc. Your very ideas are but the outgrowth of the conditions of your bourgeois production and bourgeois property, just as your jurisprudence is but the will of your class made into a law for all, a will, whose essential character and direction are determined by the economic conditions of existence of your class.

The selfish misconception that induces you to transform into eternal laws of nature and of reason, the social forms springing from your present mode of production and form of property—historical relations that rise and disappear in the progress of production—this misconception you share with every ruling class that has preceded you. What you see clearly in the case of ancient property, what you admit in the case of feudal property, you are of course forbidden to admit in the case of your own bourgeois form of property.

Abolition of the family! Even the most radical flare up at this infamous proposal of the Communists.

On what foundation is the present family, the bourgeois family, based? On capital, on private gain. In its completely developed form this family exists only among the bourgeoisie. But this state of things finds its complement in the practical absence of the family among the proletarians and in public prostitution.

The bourgeois family will vanish as a matter of course when its complement vanishes, and both will vanish with the vanishing of capital.

Do you charge us with wanting to stop the exploitation of children by their parents? To this crime we plead guilty.

But, you will say, we destroy the most hallowed of relations, when we replace home education by social.

And your education! Is not that also social and determined by the social conditions under which you educate, by the intervention, direct or indirect, of society, by means of schools, etc? The Communists have not invented the intervention of society in education; they only seek to alter the character of that intervention and to rescue education from the influence of the ruling class.

The bourgeois claptrap about the family and education, about the hallowed relationship between parent and child, becomes all the more disgusting, the more that, as a result of modern industry, all family ties among the proletarians are torn asunder and their children transformed into simple articles of commerce and instruments of labor.

But you Communists would introduce community of women, screams the whole bourgeoisie in chorus.

The bourgeois sees in his wife a mere instrument of production. He hears that the instruments of production are to be exploited in common, and, naturally, can come to no other conclusion than that the lot of being common to all will likewise fall to the women.

He has not even a suspicion that the real point aimed at is to do away with the status of women as mere instruments of production.

For the rest, nothing is more ridiculous than the virtuous indignation of our bourgeois at the community of women which, they pretend, is to be openly and officially established by the Communists. The Communists have no need to introduce community of women; it has existed almost from time immemorial.

Our bourgeois, not content with having the wives and daughters of their proletarians at their disposal, not to speak of common prostitutes, take the greatest pleasure in seducing each others' wives.

Bourgeois marriage is in reality a system of wives in common and thus, at the most, what the Communists might possibly be reproached with is that they desire to introduce, in place of a hypocritically concealed community of women, an openly legalized one. For the rest, it is self-evident that the abolition of the present system of production must bring with it the abolition of the community of women springing from that system, *i.e.*, of prostitution both public and private.

The Communists are further reproached with desiring to abolish countries and nationality.

The working men have no country. We cannot take from them what they have not got. Since the proletariat must first of all acquire political supremacy, must rise to be the leading class of the nation, must constitute itself *the* nation, it is to this extent itself national, though not in the bourgeois sense of the word.

National differences and antagonisms between peoples are daily more and more vanishing, owing to the development of the bourgeoisie, to freedom of commerce, to the world market, to uniformity in the mode of production and in the conditions of life corresponding thereto.

The supremacy of the proletariat will cause them to vanish still faster. United action, at least of the leading civilized countries, is one of the first conditions of the emancipation of the proletariat.

To the extent that the exploitation of one individual by another is put to an end, the exploitation of one nation by another will also be put to an end. To the extent that the antagonism between classes within the nation vanishes, the hostility of one nation to another will come to an end.

The charges against Communism made from a religious, a philosophical, and, generally, from an ideological standpoint, are not deserving of serious examination.

Does it require deep intuition to comprehend that man's ideas, views and conceptions, in one word, man's consciousness, changes with every change in the conditions of his material existence, in his social relations and in his social life?

What else does the history of ideas prove than that intellectual production changes its character to the extent that material production is changed? The ruling ideas of each age have always been the ideas of its ruling class.

When people speak of ideas that revolutionize society, they only express the fact, that within the old society, the elements of a new one have been created, and that the dissolution of the old ideas keeps pace with the dissolution of the old conditions of existence.

When the ancient world was in its last throes, the ancient religions were overcome by Christianity. When Christian ideas succumbed in the eighteenth century to rationalist ideas, feudal society fought its death battle with the then revolutionary bourgeoisie. The ideas of religious liberty and freedom of conscience merely gave expression to the sway of free competition within the domain of knowledge.

"Undoubtedly," it will be said, "religious, moral, philosophical and juridical ideas have been modified in the course of historical development. But religion, morality, philosophy, political science, and law constantly survived this change."

"There are, besides, eternal truths, such as Freedom, Justice, etc., that are common to all states of society. But Communism abolishes eternal truths; it abolishes all religion, and all morality, instead of constituting them on a new basis; it therefore acts in contradiction to all past historical experience."

To what does this accusation reduce itself? The history of all past society has consisted in the development of class antagonisms, antagonisms that assumed different forms at different epochs.

But whatever form they may have taken, one fact is common to all past ages, *viz.*, the exploitation of one part of society by the other. No wonder, then, that the social consciousness of past ages, despite all the multiplicity and variety it displays, moves within certain common forms, or general ideas, which cannot completely vanish except with the total disappearance of class antagonisms.

The Communist revolution is the most radical rupture with traditional property relations; no wonder that its development involves the most radical rupture with traditional ideas.

But let us be done with the bourgeois objections to Communism.

We have seen above that the first step in the revolution by the working class is to raise the proletariat to the position of ruling class, to win the battle of democracy.

The proletariat will use its political supremacy to wrest, by degrees, all capital from the bourgeoisie, to centralize all instruments of production in the hands of the State (*i.e.*, the proletariat organized as the ruling class), and to increase the total of productive forces as rapidly as possible.

Of course, in the beginning, this cannot be effected except by means of despotic inroads on the rights of property and on the conditions of bourgeois production; by means of measures, therefore, which appear economically insufficient and untenable, but which, in the course of the movement, outstrip themselves, necessitate further inroads upon the old social order, and are unavoidable as a means of entirely revolutionizing the mode of production.

These measures will of course be different in different countries.

Nevertheless in the most advanced countries, the following will be pretty generally applicable.

1. Abolition of property in land and application of all rents of land to public purposes.
2. A heavy progressive or graduated income tax.
3. Abolition of all right of inheritance.
4. Confiscation of the property of all emigrants and rebels.
5. Centralization of credit in the hands of the State, by means of a national bank with State capital and an exclusive monopoly.
6. Centralization of the means of communication and transport in the hands of the State.
7. Extension of factories and instruments of production owned by the State; cultivation of waste-lands; and improvement of the soil generally in accordance with a common plan.
8. Equal liability of all to labor. Establishment of industrial armies, especially for agriculture.
9. Combination of agriculture with manufacturing industries; and gradual abolition of the distinction between town and country by a more equable distribution of the population over the country.
10. Free education for all children in public schools. Abolition of children's factory labor in its present form. Combination of education with industrial production, etc.

When, in the course of development, class distinctions have disappeared and all production has been concentrated in the hands of a vast association of the whole nation, the public power will lose its political character. Political power, properly so called, is merely the organized power of one class for oppressing another. If the proletariat during its contest with the bourgeoisie is compelled, by the force of circumstances, to organize itself as a class, if, by means of a revolution, it makes itself the ruling class and as such sweeps away by force the old conditions of production, then it will have swept away, along with these conditions, the conditions for the existence of class antagonisms and classes generally and will thereby have abolished its own supremacy as a class.

In place of the old bourgeois society, with its classes and class antagonisms, we shall have an association in which the free development of each is the condition for the free development of all.

Theses on Feuerbach

I

The chief defect of all hitherto existing materialism—that of Feuerbach included—is that the thing, reality, sensuousness, is conceived only in the form of the *object* or of *contemplation,* but not as *human sensuous activity, practice,* not subjectively. Hence it happened that the *active* side, in contradistinction to materialism, was developed by idealism—but only abstractly, since, of course, idealism does not know real, sensuous activity as such. Feuerbach wants sensuous objects, really differentiated from the thought-objects, but he does not conceive human activity itself as *objective* activity. Hence, in the *Essence of Christianity,* he regards the theoretical attitude as the only genuinely human attitude, while practice is conceived and fixed only in its dirty-judaical form of appearance. Hence he does not grasp the significance of "revolutionary," of "practical-critical," activity.

II

The question whether objective truth can be attributed to human thinking is not a question of theory but a *practical* question. In practice man must prove the truth, that is, the reality and power, the this-sidedness of his thinking. The dispute over the reality or non-reality of thinking which is isolated from practice is a purely *scholastic* question.

III

The materialist doctrine that men are products of circumstances and upbringing, and that, therefore, changed men are products of other circumstances and changed upbringing, forgets that it is men that change circumstances and that the educator himself needs educating. Hence, this doctrine necessarily arrives at dividing society into two parts, of which one is superior to society (in Robert Owen, for example).

These theses were found by Engels in one of Marx's notebooks from 1845.

The coincidence of the changing of circumstances and of human activity can be conceived and rationally understood only as *revolutionizing practice.*

IV

Feuerbach starts out from the fact of religious self-alienation, the duplication of the world into a religious, imaginary world and a real one. His work consists in the dissolution of the religious world into its secular basis. He overlooks the fact that after this work is completed the chief thing still remains to be done. For the fact that the secular foundation detaches itself from itself and establishes itself in the clouds as an independent realm is really only to be explained by the self-cleavage and self-contradictoriness of this secular basis. The latter must itself, therefore, first be understood in its contradiction, and then revolutionized in practice by the removal of the contradiction. Thus, for instance, once the earthly family is discovered to be the secret of the holy family, the former must then itself be criticized in theory and revolutionized in practice.

V

Feuerbach, not satisfied with *abstract thinking,* apppeals to *sensuous contemplation;* but he does not conceive sensuousness as *practical,* human-sensuous activity.

VI

Feuerbach resolves the religious essence into the *human* essence. But the human essence is no abstraction inherent in each single individual. In its reality it is the ensemble of the social relations.

Feuerbach, who does not enter upon a criticism of this real essence, is consequently compelled:

1. To abstract from the historical process and to fix the religious sentiment as something by itself and to presuppose an abstract—*isolated*—human individual.

2. The human essence, therefore, can with him be comprehended only as "genus," as an internal, dumb generality which merely *naturally* unites the many individuals.

VII

Feuerbach, consequently, does not see that the "religious sentiment" is itself a *social product,* and that the abstract individual whom he analyzes belongs in reality to a particular form of society.

VIII

Social life is essentially *practical.* All mysteries which mislead theory to mysticism find their rational solution in human practice and in the comprehension of this practice.

IX

The highest point attained by *contemplative* materialism, that is, materialism which does not understand sensuousness as practical activity, is the contemplation of single individuals in "civil society."

X

The standpoint of the old materialism is "civil" society; the standpoint of the new is *human* society, or socialized humanity.

XI

The philosophers have only *interpreted* the world in various ways; the point, however, is to *change* it.

Economic and Philosophical Manuscripts

ALIENATED LABOUR

... We shall begin from a *contemporary* economic fact. The worker becomes poorer the more wealth he produces and the more his production increases in power and extent. The worker becomes an ever cheaper commodity the more goods he creates. The *devaluation* of the human world increases in direct relation with the *increase in value* of the world of things. Labour does not only create goods; it also produces itself and the worker as a *commodity*, and indeed in the same proportion as it produces goods.

This fact simply implies that the object produced by labour, its product, now stands opposed to it as an *alien being*, as a *power independent* of the producer. The product of labour is labour which has been embodied in an object and turned into a physical thing; this product is an *objectification* of labour. The performance of work is at the same time its objectification. The performance of work appears in the sphere of political economy as a *vitiation* of the worker, objectification as a *loss* and as *servitude to the object*, and appropriation as *alienation*.

So much does the performance of work appear as vitiation that the worker is vitiated to the point of starvation. So much does objectification appear as loss of the object that the worker is deprived of the most essential things not only of

From *Karl Marx: Early Writings*, Translated and edited by T. B. Bottomore. © T. B. Bottomore, 1963. Used by permission of McGraw-Hill Book Company and C. A. Watts and Company, Ltd. The editors have changed the order of the text in one place.

life but also of work. Labour itself becomes an object which he can acquire only by the greatest effort and with unpredictable interruptions. So much does the appropriation of the object appear as alienation that the more objects the worker produces the fewer he can possess and the more he falls under the domination of his product, of capital.

All these consequences follow from the fact that the worker is related to the *product of his labour* as to an *alien* object. For it is clear on this presupposition that the more the worker expends himself in work the more powerful becomes the world of objects which he creates in face of himself, the poorer he becomes in his inner life, and the less he belongs to himself. It is just the same as in religion. The more of himself man attributes to God the less he has left in himself. The worker puts his life into the object, and his life then belongs no longer to himself but to the object. The greater his activity, therefore, the less he possesses. What is embodied in the product of his labour is no longer his own. The greater this product is, therefore, the more he is diminished. The *alienation* of the worker in his product means not only that his labour becomes an object, assumes an *external* existence, but that it exists independently, *outside himself*, and alien to him, and that it stands opposed to him as an autonomous power. The life which he has given to the object sets itself against him as an alien and hostile force. . . .

So far we have considered the alienation of the worker only from one aspect; namely, *his relationship with the products of his labour.* However, alienation appears not merely in the result but also in the *process* of *production*, within *productive activity* itself. How could the worker stand in an alien relationship to the product of his activity if he did not alienate himself in the act of production itself? The product is indeed only the *résumé* of activity, of production. Consequently, if the product of labour is alienation, production itself must be active alienation—the alienation of activity and the activity of alienation. The alienation of the object of labour merely summarizes the alienation in the work activity itself.

What constitutes the alienation of labour? First, that the work is *external* to the worker, that it is not part of his nature; and that, consequently, he does not fulfil himself in his work but denies himself, has a feeling of misery rather than well-being, does not develop freely his mental and physical energies but is physically exhausted and mentally debased. The worker, therefore, feels himself at home only during his leisure time, whereas at work he feels homeless. His work is not voluntary but imposed, *forced labour.* It is not the satisfaction of a need, but only a *means* for satisfying other needs. Its alien character is clearly shown by the fact that as soon as there is no physical or other compulsion it is avoided like the plague. External labour, labour in which man alienates himself, is a labour of self-sacrifice, of mortification. Finally, the external character of work for the worker is shown by the fact that it is not his own work but work for someone else, that in work he does not belong to himself but to another person. . . .

We arrive at the result that man (the worker) feels himself to be freely active only in his animal functions—eating, drinking and procreating, or at most also in his dwelling and in personal adornment—while in his human functions he is reduced to an animal. The animal becomes human and the human becomes animal.

Eating, drinking and procreating are of course also genuine human functions. But abstractly considered, apart from the environment of human activities, and turned into final and sole ends, they are animal functions.

We have now considered the act of alienation of practical human activity, labour, from two aspects: (a) the relationship of the worker to the *product of labour* as an alien object which dominates him. This relationship is at the same time the relationship to the sensuous external world, to natural objects, as an alien and hostile world; (2) the relationship of labour to the *act of production* within *labour*. This is the relationship of the worker to his own activity as something alien and not belonging to him, activity as suffering (passivity), strength as powerlessness, creation as emasculation, the *personal* physical and mental energy of the worker, his personal life (for what is life but activity?), as an activity which is directed against himself, independent of him and not belonging to him. This is *self-alienation* as against the above-mentioned alienation of the *thing*.

We have now to infer a third characteristic of *alienated labour* from the two we have considered.

Man is a species-being not only in the sense that he makes the community (his own as well as those of other things) his object both practically and theoretically, but also (and this is simply another expression for the same thing) in the sense that he treats himself as the present, living species, as a *universal* and consequently free being.

Species-life, for man as for animals, has its physical basis in the fact that man (like animals) lives from inorganic nature, and since man is more universal than an animal so the range of inorganic nature from which he lives is more universal. Plants, animals, minerals, air, light, etc. constitute, from the theoretical aspect, a part of human consciousness as objects of natural science and art; they are man's spiritual inorganic nature, his intellectual means of life, which he must first prepare for enjoyment and perpetuation. So also, from the practical aspect, they form a part of human life and activity. In practice man lives only from these natural products, whether in the form of food, heating, clothing, housing, etc. The universality of man appears in practice in the universality which makes the whole of nature into his inorganic body: (1) as a direct means of life; and equally (2) as the material object and instrument of his life activity. Nature is the inorganic body of man; that is to say nature, excluding the human body itself. To say that man *lives* from nature means that nature is his *body* with which he must remain in a continuous interchange in order not to die. The statement that the physical and mental life of man, and nature, are interdependent means simply that nature is interdependent with itself, for man is a part of nature.

Since alienated labour: (1) alienates nature from man; and (2) alienates man from himself, from his own active function, his life activity; so it alienates him from the species. It makes *species-life* into a means of individual life. In the first place it alienates species-life and individual life, and secondly, it turns the latter, as an abstraction, into the purpose of the former, also in its abstract and alienated form.

For labour, *life activity*, *productive life*, now appear to man only as *means* for the satisfaction of a need, the need to maintain his physical existence. Productive life is, however, species-life. It is life creating life. In the type of life activity resides the whole character of a species, its species-character; and free, conscious activity is the species-character of human beings. Life itself appears only as a *means of life.*

The animal is one with its life activity. It does not distinguish the activity from itself. It is *its activity.* But man makes his life activity itself an object of his will and consciousness. He has a conscious life activity. It is not a determination with which he is completely identified. Conscious life activity distinguishes man from the life activity of animals. Only for this reason is he a species-being. Or rather, he is only a self-conscious being, i.e. his own life is an object for him, because he is a species-being. Only for this reason is his activity free activity. Alienated labour reverses the relationship, in that man because he is a self-conscious being makes his life activity, his *being,* only a means for his *existence.*

The practical construction of an *objective world,* the *manipulation* of inorganic nature, is the confirmation of man as a conscious species-being, i.e. a being who treats the species as his own being or himself as a species-being. Of course, animals also produce. They construct nests, dwellings, as in the case of bees, beavers, ants, etc. But they only produce what is strictly necessary for themselves or their young. They produce only in a single direction, while man produces universally. They produce only under the compulsion of direct physical needs, while man produces when he is free from physical need and only truly produces in freedom from such need. Animals produce only themselves, while man reproduces the whole of nature. The products of animal production belong directly to their physical bodies, while man is free in face of his product. Animals construct only in accordance with the standards and needs of the species to which they belong, while man knows how to produce in accordance with the standards of every species and knows how to apply the appropriate standard to the object. Thus man constructs also in accordance with the laws of beauty.

It is just in his work upon the objective world that man really proves himself as a *species-being.* This production is his active species-life. By means of it nature appears as *his* work and his reality. The object of labour is, therefore, the *objectification of man's species-life;* for he no longer reproduces himself merely intellectually, as in consciousness, but actively and in a real sense, and he sees his own reflection in a world which he has constructed. While, therefore, alienated labour takes away the object of production from man, it also takes away his *species-life,* his real objectivity as a species-being, and changes his advantage over animals into a disadvantage in so far as his inorganic body, nature, is taken from him.

Just as alienated labour transforms free and self-directed activity into a means, so it transforms the species-life of man into a means of physical existence.

Consciousness, which man has from his species, is transformed through alienation so that species-life becomes only a means for him. (3) Thus alienated labour turns the *species-life of man,* and also nature as his mental species-property, into an *alien* being and into a *means* for his *individual existence.* It alienates from man his own body, external nature, his mental life and his *human* life. (4) A direct consequence of the alienation of man from the product of his labour, from his life activity and from his species-life, is that *man* is *alienated* from other *men.* When man confronts himself he also confronts *other* men. What is true of man's relationship to his work, to the product of his work and to himself, is also true of his relationship to other men, to their labour and to the objects of their labour.

In general, the statement that man is alienated from his species-life means that each man is alienated from others, and that each of the others is like-wise alienated from human life.

Human alienation, and above all the relation of man to himself, is first realized and expressed in the relationship between each man and other man. Thus in the relationship of alienated labour every man regards other men according to the standards and relationships in which he finds himself placed as a worker.

We began with an economic fact, the alienation of the worker and his production. We have expressed this fact in cenceptual terms as *alienated labour*, and in analysing the concept we have merely analysed an economic fact.

Let us now examine further how this concept of alienated labour must express and reveal itself in reality. If the product of labour is alien to me and confronts me as an alien power, to whom does it belong? If my own activity does not belong to me but is an alien, forced activity, to whom does it belong? To a being *other* than myself. And who is this being? The *gods?* It is apparent in the earlier stages of advanced production, e.g. temple building, etc. in Egypt, India, Mexico, and in the service rendered to gods, that the product belonged to the gods. But the gods alone were never the lords of labour. And no more was *nature*. What a contradiction it would be if the more man subjugates nature by his labour, and the more the marvels of the gods are rendered superfluous by the marvels of industry, the more he should abstain from his joy in producing and his enjoyment of the product for love of these powers.

The *alien* being to whom labour and the product of labour belong, to whose service labour is devoted, and to whose enjoyment the product of labour goes, can only be *man* himself. If the product of labour does not belong to the worker, but confronts him as an alien power, this can only be because it belongs to *a man other than the worker*. If his activity is a torment to him it must be a source of *enjoyment* and pleasure to another. Not the gods, nor nature, but only man himself can be this alien power over men.

Consider the earlier statement that the relation of man to himself is first *realized, objectified*, through his relation to other men. If he is related to the product of his labour, his objectified labour, as to an *alien*, hostile, powerful and independent object, he is related in such a way that another alien, hostile, powerful and independent man is the lord of this object. If he is related to his own activity as to unfree activity, then he is related to it as activity in the service, and under the domination, coercion and yoke, of another man.

Every self-alienation of man, from himself and from nature, appears in the relation which he postulates between other men and himself and nature. Thus religious self-alienation is necessarily exemplified in the relation between laity and priest, or, since it is here a question of the spiritual world, between the laity and a mediator. In the real world of practice this self-alienation can only be expressed in the real, practical relation of man to his fellow men. The medium through which alienation occurs is itself a *practical* one. Through alienated labour, therefore, man not only produces his relation to the object and to the process of production as to alien and hostile men; he also produces the relation of other men to his production and his product, and the relation between himself and other men. Just as he creates his own production as a vitiation, a punishment, and his own product as a loss, as a product which does not belong to him, so he creates the domination of the non-producer over production and its product. As he alienates his own activity, so he bestows upon the stranger an activity which is not his own. . . .

Thus, through alienated labour the worker creates the relation of another man, who does not work and is outside the work process, to this labour. The relation of the worker to work also produces the relation of the capitalist (or whatever one likes to call the lord of labour) to work. *Private property* is, therefore, the product, the necessary result, of *alienated labour*, of the external relation of the worker to nature and to himself.

Private property is thus derived from the analysis of the concept of *alienated labour*; that is, alienated man, alienated labour, alienated life, and estranged man.

PRIVATE PROPERTY AND COMMUNISM

. . . Labour, the subjective essence of private property as the exclusion of property, and capital, objective labour as the exclusion of labour, constitute *private property* as the developed relation of the contradiction and thus a dynamic relation which drives towards its resolution. . . .

[*C*]*ommunism* is the positive expression of the abolition of private property, and in the first place of universal private property. In taking this relation in its *universal aspect* communism is, in its first form, only the generalization and fulfilment of the relation. As such it appears in a double form; the domination of material property looms so large that it aims to destroy everything which is incapable of being possessed by everyone as private property. It wishes to eliminate talent, etc, by *force*. Immediate physical possession seems to it the unique goal of life and existence. The role of *worker* is not abolished, but is extended to all men. The relation of private property remains the relation of the community to the world of things. Finally, this tendency to oppose general private property to private property is expressed in an animal form; *marriage* (which is incontestably a form of *exclusive private property*) is contrasted with the community of women, in which women become communal and common property. One may say that this idea of the *community of women* is the *open secret* of this entirely crude and unreflective communism. Just as women are to pass from marriage to universal prostitution, so the whole world of wealth (i.e. the objective being of man) is to pass from the relation of exclusive marriage with the private owner to the relation of universal prostitution with the community. This communism, which negates the *personality* of man in every sphere, is only the logical expression of private property, which is this negation. Universal *envy* setting itself up as a power is only a camouflaged form of cupidity which re-establishes itself and satisfies itself in a different way. The thoughts of every individual private property are *at least* directed against any *wealthier* private property, in the form of envy and the desire to reduce everything to a common level; so that this envy and levelling in fact constitute the essence of competition. Crude communism is only the culmination of such envy and levelling-down on the basis of a *preconceived* minimum. How little this abolition of private property represents a genuine appropriation is shown by the abstract negation of the whole world of culture and civilization, and the regression to the *unnatural* simplicity of the poor and wantless individual who has not only not surpassed private property but has not yet even attained to it.

The community is only a community of *work* and of *equality of wages* paid out by the communal capital, by the *community* as universal capitalist. . . . Communism is the phase of negation of the negation and is, consequently, for the next stage of historical development, a real and necessary factor in the emancipation and rehabilitation of man. Communism is the necessary form and the dynamic principle of the immediate future, but communism is not itself the goal of human development—the form of human society. . . .

Communism (*a*) still political in nature, democratic or despotic; (*b*) with the abolition of the state, yet still incomplete and influenced by private property, that is, by the alienation of man. In both forms communism is already aware of being the reintegration of man, his return to himself, the supression of man's self-alienation. But since it has not yet grasped the positive nature of private property, or the *human* nature of needs, it is still captured and contaminated by private property. It has well understood the concept, but not the essence.

Communism is the *positive* abolition of *private property*, of *human self-alienation*, and thus the real *appropriation* of *human* nature through and for man. It is, therefore, the return of man himself as a *social*, i.e. really human, being, a complete and conscious return which assimilates all the wealth of previous development. Communism as a fully developed naturalism is humanism and as a fully developed humanism is naturalism. It is the *definitive* resolution of the antagonism between man and nature, and between man and man. It is the true solution of the conflict between existence and essence, between objectification and self-affirmation, between freedom and necessity, between individual and species. It is the solution of the riddle of history and knows itself to be this solution. . . .

[O]n the assumption that private property has been positively superseded, man produces man, himself and then other men; how the object which is the direct activity of his personality is at the same time his existence for other men and their existence for him. Similarly, the material of labour and man himself as a subject are the starting-point as well as the result of this movement (and because there must be this starting-point private property is a historical necessity). Therefore, the *social* character is the universal character of the whole movement; *as* society itself produces *man* as *man*, so it is *produced* by him. Activity and mind are social in their content as well as in their *origin;* they are *social* activity and social mind. The *human* significance of nature only exists for *social* man because only in this case is nature a *bond* with other *men*, the basis of his existence for others and of their existence for him. Only then is nature the *basis* of his own *human* experience and a vital element of human reality. The *natural* existence of man has here become his *human* existence and nature itself has become human for him. Thus *society* is the accomplished union of man with nature, the veritable resurrection of nature, the realized naturalism of man and the realized humanism of nature.

Social activity and social mind by no means exist *only* in the form of activity or mind which is directly communal. Nevertheless, communal activity and mind, i.e. activity and mind which express and confirm themselves directly in a *real association* with other men, occur everywhere where this direct expression of sociability arises from the content of the activity or corresponds to the nature of mind.

Even when I carry out *scientific* work, etc., an activity which I can seldom conduct in direct association with other men, I perform a *social*, because *human*, act. It is not only the material of my activity—such as the language itself which the thinker uses—which is given to me as a social product. My *own existence* is a social activity. For this reason, what I myself produce I produce for society, and with the consciousness of acting as a social being.

My universal consciousness is only the *theoretical* form of that whose *living* form is the real community, the social entity, although at the present day this universal consciousness is an abstraction from real life and is opposed to it as an enemy. That is why the *activity* of my universal consciousness as such is my *theoretical* existence as a social being.

It is above all necessary to avoid postulating "society" once again as an abstraction confronting the individual. The individual *is* the *social being*. The manifestation of his life—even when it does not appear directly in the form of a communal manifestation, accomplished in association with other men—is, therefore, a manifestation and affirmation of *social life*. Individual human life and species-life are not different things, even though the mode of existence of individual life is necessarily either a more *specific* or a more *general* mode of species-life, or that of species-life a *specific* or more *general* mode of individual life.

In his *species-consciousness* man confirms his real *social life*, and reproduces his real existence in thought; while conversely, species-life confirms itself in species-consciousness and exists for itself in its universality as a thinking being. Though man is a unique individual—and it is just his particularity which makes him an individual, a really *individual* communal being—he is equally the *whole*, the ideal whole, the subjective existence of society as thought and experience. He exists in reality as the representation and the real mind of social existence, and as the sum of human manifestations of life.

Thought and being are indeed *distinct* but they also form a unity. *Death* seems to be a harsh victory of the species over the individual and to contradict their unity; but the particular individual is only a *determinate species-being* and as such he is mortal. . . .

Private property has made us so stupid and partial that an object is only *ours* when we have it, when it exists for us as capital or when it is directly eaten, drunk, worn, inhabited, etc., in short, *utilized* in some way. But private property itself only conceives these various forms of possession as *means of life*, and the life for which they serve as means is the *life* of *private property*—labour and creation of capital.

Thus *all* the physical and intellectual senses have been replaced by the simple alienation of *all* these senses; the sense of *having*. The human being had to be reduced to this absolute poverty in order to be able to give birth to all his inner wealth. . . .

Fyodor Dostoyevsky

Fyodor Dostoyevsky (1821–1881) was a novelist of such depth and insight that his works continue to attract the attention of psychologists and philosophers. His *Notes from Underground* is often regarded as a precursor of later existentialist themes and was read by Nietzsche as the work of a kindred spirit. But far from sharing in Nietzsche's rejection of Christianity, Dostoyevsky was a Christian and a fervent Russian nationalist. His best-known novels are *Crime and Punishment* and *The Brothers Karamazov,* from which the selection printed below is taken.

In "The Grand Inquisitor" Ivan, a westernized agnostic, relates a story to Alyosha, his deeply Christian brother. The story can be interpreted in many ways, but it is clearly concerned with many issues which a political philosopher must face. Few philosophers could manage to put the issue so dramatically or so powerfully.

The Grand Inquisitor

"He comes on the scene in my poem, but He says nothing, only appears and passes on. Fifteen centuries have passed since He promised to come in His glory, fifteen centuries since His prophet wrote, 'Behold, I come quickly'; 'Of that day and that hour knoweth no man, neither the Son, but the Father,' as He Himself predicted on earth. But humanity awaits him with the same faith and with the same love. Oh, with greater faith, for it is fifteen centuries since man has ceased to see signs from Heaven.

No signs from Heaven come today
To add to what the heart doth say.

There was nothing left but faith in what the heart doth say. It is true there were many miracles in those days. There were saints who performed miraculous cures; some holy people, according to their biographies, were visited by the Queen of Heaven herself. But the devil did not slumber, and doubts were already arising among men of the truth of these miracles. And just then there appeared in the north of Germany a terrible new heresy. 'A huge star like to a torch' (that is, to a church) 'fell on the sources of the waters and they became bitter.' These heretics began blasphemously denying miracles. But those who remained faithful were all the more ardent in their faith. The tears of humanity rose up to Him as

From *The Brothers Karamazov,* trans. Constance Garnett. Modern Library, New York, 1929.

before, awaited His coming, loved Him, hoped for Him, yearned to suffer and die for Him as before. And so many ages mankind had prayed with faith and fervour, 'O Lord our God, hasten Thy coming,' so many ages called upon Him, that in His infinite mercy He deigned to come down to His servants. Before that day He had come down, He had visited some holy men, martyrs and hermits, as is written in their 'Lives.' Among us, Tyutchev, with absolute faith in the truth of his words, bore witness that

> Bearing the Cross, in slavish dress,
> Weary and worn, the Heavenly King
> Our mother, Russia, came to bless,
> And through our land went wandering.

And that certainly was so, I assure you.

"And behold, He deigned to appear for a moment to the people, to the tortured, suffering people, sunk in iniquity, but loving Him like children. My story is laid in Spain, in Seville, in the most terrible time of the Inquisition, when fires were lighted every day to the glory of God, and 'in the splendid *auto da fé* the wicked heretics were burnt.' Oh, of course, this was not the coming in which He will appear according to His promise at the end of time in all His heavenly glory, and which will be sudden 'as lightning flashing from east to west.' No, He visited His children only for a moment, and there where the flames were crackling round the heretics. In His infinite mercy He came once more among men in that human shape in which He walked among men for three years fifteen centuries ago. He came down to the 'hot pavement' of the southern town in which on the day before almost a hundred heretics had, *ad majorem gloriam Dei*, been burnt by the cardinal, the Grand Inquisitor, in a magnificent *auto da fé*, in the presence of the king, the court, the knights, the cardinals, the most charming ladies of the court, and the whole population of Seville.

"He came softly, unobserved, and yet, strange to say, every one recognised Him. That might be one of the best passages in the poem. I mean, why they recognised Him. The people are irresistibly drawn to Him, they surround Him, they flock about Him, follow Him. He moves silently in their midst with a gentle smile of infinite compassion. The sun of love burns in His heart, light and power shine from His eyes, and their radiance, shed on the people, stirs their hearts with responsive love. He holds out His hands to them, blesses them, and a healing virtue comes from contact with Him, even with His garments. An old man in the crowd, blind from childhood, cries out, 'O Lord, heal me and I shall see Thee!' and, as it were, scales fall from his eyes and the blind man sees Him. The crowd weeps and kisses the earth under His feet. Children throw flowers before Him, sing, and cry hosannah. 'It is He—it is He!' all repeat. 'It must be He, it can be no one but Him!' He stops at the steps of the Seville cathedral at the moment when the weeping mourners are bringing in a little open white coffin. In it lies a child of seven, the only daughter of a prominent citizen. The dead child lies hidden in flowers. 'He will raise your child,' the crowd shouts to the weeping mother. The priest, coming to meet the coffin, looks perplexed, and frowns, but the mother of the dead child throws herself at His feet with a wail. 'If it is Thou, raise my child!' she cries, holding out her hands to Him. The procession halts, the coffin is laid on the steps at His feet. He looks with compassion, and His lips once more softly pronounce, 'Maiden, arise!' and the maiden arises. The little girl sits up in the coffin and looks round, smiling with wide-open wondering eyes, holding a bunch of white roses they had put in her hand.

"There are cries, sobs, confusion among the people, and at that moment the cardinal himself, the Grand Inquisitor, passes by the cathedral. He is an old man, almost ninety, tall and erect, with a withered face and sunken eyes, in which there is still a gleam of light. He is not dressed in his gorgeous cardinal's robes, as he was the day before, when he was burning the enemies of the Roman Church—at that moment he was wearing his coarse, old, monk's cassock. At a distance behind him come his gloomy assistants and slaves and the 'holy guard.' He stops at the sight of the crowd and watches it from a distance. He sees everything; he sees them set the coffin down at His feet, sees the child rise up, and his face darkens. He knits his thick grey brows and his eyes gleam with a sinister fire. He holds out his finger and bids the guards take Him. And such is his power, so completely are the people cowed into submission and trembling obedience to him, that the crowd immediately make way for the guards, and in the midst of deathlike silence they lay hands on Him and lead Him away. The crowd instantly bows down to the earth, like one man, before the old inquisitor. He blesses the people in silence and passes on. The guards lead their prisoner to the close, gloomy vaulted prison in the ancient palace of the Holy Inquisition and shut Him in it. The day passes and is followed by the dark, burning 'breathless' night of Seville. The air is 'fragrant with laurel and lemon.' In the pitch darkness the iron door of the prison is suddenly opened and the Grand Inquisitor himself comes in with a light in his hand. He is alone; the door is closed at once behind him. He stands in the doorway and for a minute or two gazes into His face. At last he goes up slowly, sets the light on the table and speaks.

" 'Is it Thou? Thou?' but receiving no answer, he adds at once, 'Don't answer, be silent. What canst Thou say, indeed? I know too well what Thou wouldst say. And Thou hast no right to add anything to what Thou hadst said of old. Why, then, art Thou come to hinder us? For Thou hast come to hinder us, and Thou knowest that. But dost Thou know what will be tomorrow? I know not who Thou art and care not to know whether it is Thou or only a semblance of Him, but tomorrow I shall condemn Thee and burn Thee at the stake as the worst of heretics. And the very people who have today kissed Thy feet, tomorrow at the faintest sign from me will rush to heap up the embers of Thy fire. Knowest Thou that? Yes, maybe Thou knowest it,' he added with thoughtful penetration, never for a moment taking his eyes off the Prisoner."

"I don't quite understand, Ivan. What does it mean?" Alyosha, who had been listening in silence, said with a smile, "Is it simply a wild fantasy, or a mistake on the part of the old man—some impossible *quid pro quo*?"

"Take it as the last," said Ivan, laughing, "if you are so corrupted by modern realism and can't stand anything fantastic. If you like it to be a case of mistaken identity, let it be so. It is true," he went on, laughing, "the old man was ninety, and he might well be crazy over his set idea. He might have been struck by the appearance of the Prisoner. . . .

" 'Hast Thou the right to reveal to us one of the mysteries of that world from which Thou hast come?' my old man asks Him, and answers the question for Him. 'No, Thou hast not; that Thou mayest not add to what has been said of old, and mayest not take from men the freedom which Thou didst exalt when Thou wast on earth. Whatsoever Thou revealest anew will encroach on men's freedom of faith; for it will be manifest as a miracle, and the freedom of their faith was dearer to Thee than anything in those days fifteen hundred years ago. Didst Thou not often say then, "I will make you free"? But now Thou hast seen these "free" men,' the old man adds suddenly, with a pensive smile. 'Yes, we've paid dearly for it,' he goes on, looking sternly at Him, 'but at last we have completed that work in Thy name. For fifteen centuries we have been wrestling with Thy freedom, but now it is ended and over for good, Dost Thou not believe that it's over for good? Thou lookest meekly at me and deignest not even to be wroth with me. But let me tell Thee that now, today, people are more persuaded than ever that they have perfect freedom, yet they have brought their freedom to us and laid it humbly at our feet. But that has been our doing. Was this what Thou didst? Was this Thy freedom?' "

"I don't understand again," Alyosha broke in. "Is he ironical, is he jesting?"

"Not a bit of it! He claims it as a merit for himself and his Church that at last they have vanquished freedom and have done so to make men happy. 'For now' (he is speaking of the Inquisition, of course) 'for the first time it has become possible to think of the happiness of men. Man was created a rebel; and how can rebels be happy? Thou wast warned,' he says to Him. 'Thou hast had no lack of admonitions and warnings, but Thou didst not listen to those warnings; Thou didst reject the only way by which men might be made happy. But, fortunately, departing Thou didst hand on the work to us. Thou hast promised, Thou hast established by Thy word, Thou hast given to us the right to bind and to unbind, and now, of course, Thou canst not think of taking it away. Why, then, hast Thou come to hinder us?' "

"And what's the meaning of 'no lack of admonitions and warnings'?" asked Alyosha.

"Why, that's the chief part of what the old man must say.

" 'The wise and dread spirit, the spirit of self-destruction and non-existence,' the old man goes on, 'the great spirit talked with Thee in the wilderness, and we are told in the books that he "tempted" Thee. Is that so? And could anything truer be said than what he revealed to Thee in three questions and what Thou didst reject, and what in the books is called "the temptation"? And yet if there has ever been on earth a real stupendous miracle, it took place on that day, on the day of the three temptations. The statement of those three questions was itself the miracle. If it were possible to imagine simply for the sake of argument that those three questions of the dread spirit had perished utterly from the books, and that we had to restore them and to invent them anew, and to do so had gathered together all the wise men of the earth--rulers, chief priests, learned men, philosophers, poets—and had set them the task to invent three questions, such as would not only fit the occasion, but express in three words, three human phrases, the whole future history of the world and of humanity—dost Thou believe that all the wisdom of the earth united could have invented anything in depth and force equal to the three questions which were actually put to Thee then by the wise and mighty spirit in the wilderness? From those questions alone, from the miracle of their statement, we can see that we have here to do not with the fleeting human intelligence, but with the absolute and eternal. For in those three questions the whole subsequent history of mankind is, as it were, brought together into one whole, and foretold, and in them are united all the unsolved historical contradictions of human nature. At the time it could not be so clear, since the future was unknown; but now that fifteen hundred years have passed, we see that everything in those three questions was so justly divined and foretold, and has been so truly fulfilled, that nothing can be added to them or taken from them.

" 'Judge Thyself who was right—Thou or he who questioned Thee then? Remember the first question; its meaning, in other words, was this: "Thou wouldst go into the world, and art going with empty hands, with some promise of freedom which men in their simplicity and their natural unruliness cannot even understand, which they fear and dread—for nothing has ever been more insupportable for a man and a human society than freedom. But seest Thou these stones in this parched and barren wilderness? Turn them into bread, and mankind will run after Thee like a flock of sheep, grateful and obedient, though for ever trembling, lest Thou withdraw Thy hand and deny them Thy bread." But Thou wouldst not deprive man of freedom and didst reject the offer, thinking, what is that freedom worth, if obedience is bought with bread? Thou didst reply that man lives not by bread alone. But dost Thou know that for the sake of that earthly bread the spirit of the earth will rise up against Thee and will strive with Thee and overcome Thee, and all will follow him, crying, "Who can compare with this beast? He has given us fire from heaven!" Dost Thou know that the ages will pass, and humanity will proclaim by the lips of their sages that there is no crime, and therefore no sin; there is only hunger? "Feed men, and then ask of them virtue!" that's what they'll write on the banner, which they will raise against Thee, and with which they will destroy Thy temple. Where Thy temple stood will rise a new building; the terrible tower of Babel will be built again, and though, like the one of old, it will not be finished, yet Thou mightest have prevented that new tower and have cut short the sufferings of men for a thousand years; for they will come back to us after a thousand years of agony with their tower. They will seek us again, hidden underground in the catacombs, for we shall be again persecuted and tortured. They will find us and cry to us, "Feed us, for those who have promised us fire from heaven haven't given it!" And then we shall finish building their tower, for he finishes the building who feeds them. And we alone shall feed them in Thy name, declaring falsely that it is in Thy name. Oh, never, never can they feed themselves without us! No science will give them bread so long as they remain free. In the end they will lay their freedom at our feet, and say to us, "Make us your slaves, but feed us." They will understand themselves, at last, that freedom and bread enough for all are inconceivable together, for never, never will they be able to share between them! They will be convinced, too, that they can never be free, for they are weak, vicious, worthless and rebellious. Thou didst promise them the bread of Heaven, but, I repeat again, can it compare with earthly bread in the eyes of the weak, ever sinful and ignoble race of man? And if for the sake of the bread of Heaven thousands and tens of thousands shall follow Thee, what is to become of the millions and tens of thousands of millions of creatures who will not have the strength to forego the earthly bread for the sake of the heavenly? Or dost Thou care only for the tens of thousands of the great and strong, while the millions, numerous as the sands of the sea, who are weak but love Thee, must exist only for the sake of the great and strong? No, we care for the weak too. They are sinful and rebellious, but in the end they too will become obedient. They will marvel at us and look on us as gods, because we are ready to endure the freedom which they have found so dreadful and to rule over them—so awful it will seem to them to be free. But we shall tell them that we are Thy servants and rule them in Thy name. We shall deceive them again, for we will not let Thee come to us again. That deception will be our suffering, for we shall be forced to lie.

" 'This is the significance of the first question in the wilderness, and this is what Thou has rejected for the sake of that freedom which Thou hast exalted above everything. Yet in this question lies hid the great secret of this world. Choosing "bread," Thou wouldst have satisfied the universal and everlasting craving of humanity—to find some one to worship. So long as man remains free he strives for nothing so incessantly and so painfully as to find some one to worship. But man seeks to worship what is established beyond dispute, so that all men would agree at once to worship it. For these pitiful creatures are concerned not only to find what one or the other can worship, but to find something that all would believe in and worship; what is essential is that all may be *together* in it. This craving for *community* of worship is the chief misery of every man individually and of all humanity from the beginning of time. For the sake of common worship they've slain each other with the sword. They have set up gods and challenged one another, "Put away your gods and come and worship ours, or we will kill you and your gods!" And so it will be to the end of the world, even when gods disappear from the earth; they will fall down before idols just the same. Thou didst know, Thou couldst not but have known, this fundamental secret of human nature, but Thou didst reject the one infallible banner which was offered Thee to make all men bow down to Thee alone—the banner of earthly bread; and Thou hast rejected it for the sake of freedom and the bread of Heaven. Behold what Thou didst further. And all again in the name of freedom! I tell Thee that man is tormented by no greater anxiety than to find some one quickly to whom he can hand over that gift of freedom with which the ill-fated creature is born. But only one who can appease their conscience can take over their freedom. In bread there was offered Thee an invincible banner; give bread, and man will worship Thee, for nothing is more certain than bread. But if some one else gains possession of his conscience—oh! then he will cast away Thy bread and follow after him who has ensnared his conscience. In that Thou wast right. For the secret of man's being is not only to live but to have something to live for. Without a stable conception of the object of life, man would not consent to go on living, and would rather destroy himself than remain on earth, though he had bread in abundance. That is true. But what happened? Instead of taking men's freedom from them, Thou didst make it greater than ever! Didst Thou forget that man prefers peace, and even death, to freedom of choice in the knowledge of good and evil? Nothing is more seductive for man than his freedom of conscience, but nothing is a greater cause of suffering. And behold, instead of giving a firm foundation for setting the conscience of man at rest for ever, Thou didst choose all that is exceptional, vague and enigmatic; Thou didst choose what was utterly beyond the strength of men, acting as though Thou didst not love them at all—Thou who didst come to give Thy life for them! Instead of taking possession of men's freedom, Thou didst increase it, and burdened the spiritual kingdom of mankind with its sufferings for ever. Thou didst desire man's free love, that he should follow Thee freely, enticed and taken captive by Thee. In place of the rigid ancient law, man must hereafter with free heart decide for himself what is good and what is evil, having only Thy image before him as his guide. But didst Thou not know he would at last reject even Thy image and Thy truth, if he is weighed down with the fearful burden of free choice? They will cry aloud at last that the truth is not in Thee, for they could not have been left in greater confusion and suffering than Thou hast caused, laying upon them so many cares and unanswerable problems.

" 'So that, in truth, Thou didst Thyself lay the foundation for the destruction of Thy kingdom, and no one is more to blame for it. Yet what was offered Thee? There are three powers, three powers alone, able to conquer and to hold captive for ever the conscience of these impotent rebels for their happiness—those forces are miracle, mystery and authority. Thou hast rejected all three and hast set the example for doing so. When the wise and dread spirit set Thee on the pinnacle of the temple and said to Thee, "If Thou wouldst know whether Thou art the Son of God then cast Thyself down, for it is written: the angels shall hold him up lest he fall and bruise himself, and Thou shalt know then whether Thou art the Son of God and shalt prove then how great is Thy faith in Thy Father." But Thou didst refuse and wouldst not cast Thyself down. Oh! of course, Thou didst proudly and well, like God; but the weak, unruly race of men, are they gods? Oh, Thou didst know then that in taking one step, in making one movement to cast Thyself down, Thou wouldst be tempting God and have lost all Thy faith in Him, and wouldst have been dashed to pieces against that earth which Thou didst come to save. And the wise spirit that tempted Thee would have rejoiced. But I ask again, are there many like Thee? And couldst Thou believe for one moment that men, too, could face such a temptation? Is the nature of men such, that they can reject miracle, and at the great moments of their life, the moments of their deepest, most agonising spiritual difficulties, cling only to the free verdict of the heart? Oh, Thou didst know that Thy deed would be recorded in books, would be handed down to remote times and the utmost ends of the earth, and Thou didst hope that man, following Thee, would cling to God and not ask for a miracle. But Thou didst not know that when man rejects miracle he rejects God too; for man seeks not so much God as the miraculous. And as man cannot bear to be without the miraculous, he will create new miracles of his own for himself, and will worship deeds of sorcery and witchcraft, though he might be a hundred times over a rebel, heretic and infidel. Thou didst not come down from the Cross when they shouted to Thee, mocking and reviling Thee, "Come down from the cross and we will believe that Thou art He." Thou didst not come down, for again Thou wouldst not enslave man by a miracle, and didst crave faith given freely, not based on miracle. Thou didst crave for free love and not the base raptures of the slave before the might that has overawed him for ever. But Thou didst think too highly of men therein, for they are slaves, of course, though rebellious by nature. Look round and judge; fifteen centuries have passed, look upon them. Whom hast Thou raised up to Thyself? I swear, man is weaker and baser by nature than Thou hast believed him! Can he, can he do what Thou didst? By showing him so much respect, Thou didst, as it were, cease to feel for him, for Thou didst ask far too much from him—Thou who hast loved him more than Thyself! Respecting him less, Thou wouldst have asked less of him. That would have been more like love, for his burden would have been lighter. He is weak and vile. What though he is everywhere now rebelling against our power, and proud of his rebellion? It is the pride of a child and a schoolboy. They are little children rioting and barring out the teacher at school. But their childish delight will end; it will cost them dear. They will cast down temples and drench the earth with blood. But they will see at last, the foolish children, that, though they are rebels, they are impotent rebels, unable to keep up their own rebellion. Bathed in their foolish tears, they will recognise at last that He who created them rebels must have meant to mock at them. They will say this in despair, and their utterance will be a blasphemy which will make them more unhappy still, for man's nature cannot bear blasphemy, and in the end always avenges it on itself. And so unrest, confusion and unhappiness—that is the present lot of man after Thou didst bear so much for their freedom! Thy great prophet tells in vision and in image, that he saw all those who took part in the first resurrection and that there were of each tribe twelve thousand. But if there were so many of them, they must have been not men but gods. They had borne Thy cross, they had endured scores of years in the barren, hungry wilderness, living upon locusts and roots—and Thou mayest indeed point with pride at those children of freedom, of free love, of free and splendid sacrifice for Thy name. But remember that they were only some thousands; and what of the rest? And how are the other weak ones to blame, because they could not endure what the strong have endured? How is the weak soul to blame that it is unable to receive such terrible gifts? Canst Thou have simply come to the elect and for the elect? But if so, it is a mystery and we cannot understand it. And if it is a mystery, we too have a right to preach a mystery, and to teach them that it's not the free judgment of their hearts, not love that matters, but a mystery which they must follow blindly, even against their conscience. So we have done. We have corrected Thy work and have founded it upon *miracle, mystery* and *authority.* And men rejoiced that they were again led like sheep, and that the terrible gift that had brought them such suffering, was, at last, lifted from their hearts. Were we right teaching them this? Speak! Did we not love mankind, so meekly acknowledging their feebleness, lovingly lightening their burden, and permitting their weak nature even sin with our sanction? Why hast Thou come now to hinder us? And why dost Thou look silently and searchingly at me with Thy mild eyes? Be angry. I don't want Thy love, for I love Thee not. And what use is it for me to hide anything from Thee? Don't I know to Whom I am speaking? All that I can say is known to Thee already. And is it for me to conceal from Thee our mystery? Perhaps it is Thy will to hear it from my lips. Listen, then. We are not working with Thee, but with *him*—that is our mystery. It's long—eight centuries—since we have been on *his* side and not on Thine. Just eight centuries ago, we took from him what Thou didst reject with scorn, that last gift he offered Thee, showing Thee all the kingdoms of the earth. We took from him Rome and the sword of Cæsar, and proclaimed ourselves sole rulers of the earth, though hitherto we have not been able to complete our work. But whose fault is that? Oh, the work is only beginning, but it has begun. It has long to await completion and the earth has yet much to suffer, but we shall triumph and shall be Cæsars, and then we shall plan the universal happiness of man. But Thou mightest have taken even then the sword of Cæsar. Why didst Thou reject that last gift? Hadst Thou accepted that last counsel of the mighty spirit, Thou wouldst have accomplished all that man seeks on earth—that is, some one to worship, some one to keep his conscience, and some means of uniting all in one unanimous and harmonious ant-heap, for the craving for universal unity is the third and last anguish of men. Mankind as a whole has always striven to organise a universal state. There have been many great nations with great histories, but the more highly they were developed the more unhappy they were, for they felt more acutely than other people the craving for worldwide union. The great conquerors, Timours and Ghenghis-Khans, whirled like hurricanes over the face of the earth striving to subdue its people, and they too were but the unconscious expression of the same craving for universal unity. Hadst Thou taken the world and Cæsar's purple, Thou wouldst have founded the universal state and have given universal peace. For who can rule men if not he who holds their conscience and their bread in his hands? We have taken the sword of Cæsar, and in taking it, of course, have rejected Thee and followed *him*. Oh, ages are yet to come of the confusion of free thought, of their science and cannibalism. For having begun to build their tower of Babel without us, they will end, of course, with cannibalism. But then the beast will crawl to us and lick our feet and spatter them with tears of blood. And we shall sit upon the beast and raise the cup, and on it will be written, "Mystery." But then, and only then, the reign of peace and happiness will come for men. Thou art proud of Thine elect, but Thou hast only the elect, while we give rest to all. And besides, how many of those elect, those mighty ones who could become elect, have grown weary waiting for Thee, and have transferred and will transfer the powers of their spirit and the warmth of their heart to the other camp, and end by raising their *free* banner against Thee. Thou didst Thyself lift up that banner. But with us all will be happy and will no more rebel nor destroy one another as under Thy freedom. Oh, we shall persuade them that they will only become free when they renounce their freedom to us and submit to us. And shall we be right or shall we be lying? They will be convinced that we are right, for they will remember the horrors of slavery and confusion to which Thy freedom brought them. Freedom, free thought and science, will lead them into such straits and will bring them face to face with such marvels and insoluble mysteries, that some of them, the fierce and rebellious, will destroy themselves, others, rebellious but weak, will destroy one another, while the rest, weak and unhappy, will crawl fawning to our feet and whine to us: "Yes, you were right, you alone possess His mystery, and we come back to you, save us from ourselves!"

" 'Receiving bread from us, they will see clearly that we take the bread made by their hands from them, to give it to them, without any miracle. They will see that we do not change the stones to bread, but in truth they will be more thankful for taking it from our hands than for the bread itself! For they will remember only too well that in old days, without our help, even the bread they made turned to stones in their hands, while since they have come back to us, the very stones have turned to bread in their hands. Too, too well they know the value of complete submission! And until men know that, they will be unhappy. Who is most to blame for their not knowing it, speak? Who scattered the flock and sent it astray on unknown paths? But the flock will come together again and will submit once more, and then it will be once for all. Then we shall give them the quiet humble happiness of weak creatures such as they are by nature. Oh, we shall persuade them at last not to be proud, for Thou didst lift them up and thereby taught them to be proud. We shall show them that they are weak, that they are only pitiful children, but that childlike happiness is the sweetest of all.

They will become timid and will look to us and huddle close to us in fear, as chicks to the hen. They will marvel at us and will be awe-stricken before us, and will be proud at our being so powerful and clever, that we have been able to subdue such a turbulent flock of thousands of millions. They will tremble impotently before our wrath, their minds will grow fearful, they will be quick to shed tears like women and children, but they will be just as ready at a sign from us to pass to laughter and rejoicing, to happy mirth and childish song. Yes, we shall set them to work, but in their leisure hours we shall make their life like a child's game, with children's songs and innocent dance. Oh, we shall allow them even sin, they are weak and helpless, and they will love us like children because we allow them to sin. We shall tell them that every sin will be expiated, if it is done with our permission, that we allow them to sin because we love them, and the punishment for these sins we take upon ourselves. And we shall take it upon ourselves, and they will adore us as their saviours who have taken on themselves their sins before God. And they will have no secrets from us. We shall allow or forbid them to live with their wives and mistresses, to have or not to have children—according to whether they have been obedient or disobedient—and they will submit to us gladly and cheerfully. The most painful secrets of their conscience, all, all they will bring to us, and we shall have an answer for all. And they will be glad to believe our answer, for it will save them from the great anxiety and terrible agony they endure at present in making a free decision for themselves. And all will be happy, all the millions of creatures except the hundred thousand who rule over them. For only we, we who guard the mystery, shall be unhappy. There will be thousands of millions of happy babes, and a hundred thousand sufferers who have taken upon themselves the curse of the knowledge of good and evil. Peacefully they will die, peacefully they will expire in Thy name, and beyond the grave they will find nothing but death. But we shall keep the secret, and for their happiness we shall allure them with the reward of heaven and eternity. Though if there were anything in the other world, it certainly would not be for such as they. It is prophesied that Thou wilt come again in victory, Thou wilt come with Thy chosen, the proud and strong, but we will say that they have only saved themselves, but we have saved all. We are told that the harlot who sits upon the beast, and holds in her hand the *mystery*, shall be put to shame, that the weak will rise up again, and will rend her royal purple and will strip naked her loathsome body. But then I will stand up and point out to Thee the thousand millions of happy children who have known no sin. And we who have taken their sins upon us for their happiness will stand up before Thee and say: "Judge us if Thou canst and darest." Know that I fear Thee not. Know that I too have been in the wilderness, I too have lived on roots and locusts, I too prized the freedom with which Thou hast blessed men, and I too was striving to stand among Thy elect, among the strong and powerful, thirsting "to make up the number." But I awakened and would not serve madness. I turned back and joined the ranks of those *who have corrected Thy work.* I left the proud and went back to the humble, for the happiness of the humble. What I say to Thee will come to pass, and our dominion will be built up. I repeat, tomorrow Thou shalt see that obedient flock who at a sign from me will hasten to heap up the hot cinders about the pile on which I shall burn Thee for coming to hinder us. For if any one has ever deserved our fires, it is Thou. Tomorrow I shall burn Thee. Dixi.' "

Ivan stopped. He was carried away as he talked and spoke with excitement; when he had finished, he suddenly smiled.

Alyosha had listened in silence; towards the end he was greatly moved and seemed several times on the point of interrupting, but restrained himself. Now his words came with a rush.

"But . . . that's absurd!" he cried, flushing. "Your poem is in praise of Jesus, not in blame of Him—as you mean it to be. And who will believe you about freedom? Is that the way to understand it? That's not the idea of it in the Orthodox Church . . . That's Rome, and not even the whole of Rome, it's false—those are the worst of the Catholics, the Inquisitors, the Jesuits! . . . And there could not be such a fantastic creature as your Inquisitor. What are these sins of mankind they take on themselves? Who are these keepers of the mystery who have taken some curse upon themselves for the happiness of mankind? When have they been seen? We know the Jesuits, they are spoken ill of, but surely they are not what you describe? They are not that at all, not at all. . . . They are simply the Romish army for the earthly sovereignty of the world in the future, with the Pontiff of Rome for Emperor . . . that's their ideal, but there's no sort of mystery or lofty melancholy about it. . . . It's simple lust of power, of filthy earthly gain, of domination—something like a universal serfdom with them as masters—that's all they stand for. They don't even believe in God perhaps. Your suffering inquisitor is a mere fantasy."

"Stay, stay," laughed Ivan. "how hot you are! A fantasy you say, let it be so! Of course it's a fantasy. But allow me to say: do you really think that the Roman Catholic movement of the last centuries is actually nothing but the lust of power, of filthy earthly gain? Is that Father Païssy's teaching?"

"No, no, on the contrary, Father Païssy did once say something rather the same as you . . . but of course it's not the same, not a bit the same," Alyosha hastily corrected himself.

"A precious admission, in spite of your 'not a bit the same.' I ask you why your Jesuits and Inquisitors have united simply for vile material gain? Why can there not be among them one martyr oppressed by great sorrow and loving humanity? You see, only suppose that there was one such man among all those who desire nothing but filthy material gain—if there's only one like my old inquisitor, who had himself eaten roots in the desert and made frenzied efforts to subdue his flesh to make himself free and perfect. But yet all his life he loved humanity, and suddenly his eyes were opened, and he saw that it is no great moral blessedness to attain perfection and freedom, if at the same time one gains the conviction that millions of God's creatures have been created as a mockery, that they will never be capable of using their freedom, that these poor rebels can never turn into giants to complete the tower, that it was not for such geese that the great idealist dreamt his dream of harmony. Seeing all that he turned back and joined—the clever people. Surely that could have happened?"

"Joined whom, what clever people?" cried Alyosha, completely carried away. "They have no such great cleverness and no mysteries and secrets. . . . Perhaps nothing but Atheism, that's all their secret. Your inquisitor does not believe in God, that's his secret!"

"What if it is so! At last you have guessed it. It's perfectly true that that's the whole secret, but isn't that suffering, at least for a man like that, who has wasted his whole life in the desert and yet could not shake off his incurable love of humanity? In his old age he reached the clear conviction that nothing but the advice of the great dread spirit could build up any tolerable sort of life for the feeble, unruly, 'incomplete, empirical creatures created in jest.' And so, convinced of this, he sees that he must follow the counsel of the wise spirit, the dread spirit of death and destruction, and therefore accept lying and deception, and lead men consciously to death and destruction, and yet deceive them all the way so that they may not notice where they are being led, that the poor blind creatures may at least on the way think themselves happy. And note, the deception is in the name of Him in Whose ideal the old man had so fervently believed all his life long. Is not that tragic? And if only one such stood at the head of the whole army 'filled with the lust of power only for the sake of filthy gain'—would not one such be enough to make a tragedy? More than that, one such standing at the head is enough to create the actual leading of the Roman Church with all its armies and Jesuits, its highest idea. I tell you frankly that I firmly believe that there has always been such a man among those who stood at the head of the movement. Who knows, there may have been some such even among the Roman Popes. Who knows, perhaps the spirit of the accursed old man who loves mankind so obstinately in his own way, is to be found even now in a whole multitude of such old men, existing not by change but by agreement, as a secret league formed long ago for the guarding of the mystery, to guard it from the weak and the unhappy, so as to make them happy. No doubt it is so, and so it must be indeed. I fancy that even among the Masons there's something of the same mystery at the bottom, and that that's why the Catholics so detest the Masons as their rivals breaking up the unity of the idea, while it is so essential that there should be one flock and one shepherd. . . . But from the way I defend my idea I might be an author impatient of your criticism. Enough of it."

"You are perhaps a Mason yourself!" broke suddenly from Alyosha. "You don't believe in God," he added, speaking this time very sorrowfully. He fancied besides that his brother was looking at him ironically. "How does your poem end?" he asked, suddenly looking down. "Or was it the end?"

"I meant to end it like this. When the Inquisitor ceased speaking he waited some time for his Prisoner to answer him. His silence weighed down upon him. He saw that the Prisoner had listened intently all the time, looking gently in his face and evidently not wishing to reply. The old man longed for Him to say something, however bitter and terrible. But He suddenly approached the old man in silence and softly kissed him on his bloodless aged lips. That was all his answer. The old man shuddered. His lips moved. He went to the door, opened it, and said to Him: 'Go, and come no more. . . . Come not at all, never, never!' And he let Him out into the dark alleys of the town. The Prisoner went away."

"And the old man?"

"The kiss glows in his heart, but the old man adheres to his idea."

Henry David Thoreau

Henry David Thoreau (1817–1862), essayist, poet, and philosopher, dissented from the public policies of his day in ways and over principles which sound very familiar in contemporary America. Thoreau was passionately opposed to racial injustice and slavery, to the Mexican War, and to the destruction of natural beauty. In the famous essay, "Civil Disobedience," printed below, he recommends several kinds of resistance to the government and its policies.

Civil Disobedience

I heartily accept the motto—"That government is best which governs least;" and I should like to see it acted up to more rapidly and systematically. Carried out, it finally amounts to this, which also I believe,—"That government is best which governs not at all;" and when men are prepared for it, that will be the kind of government which they will have. Government is at best but an expedient; but most governments are usually, and all governments are sometimes, inexpedient. The objections which have been brought against a standing army, and they are many and weighty, and deserve to prevail, may also at last be brought against a standing government. The standing army is only an arm of the standing government. The government itself, which is only the mode which the people have chosen to execute their will, is equally liable to be abused and perverted before the people can act through it. Witness the present Mexican war, the work of comparatively a few individuals using the standing government as their tool; for, in the outset, the people would not have consented to this measure.

This American government—what is it but a tradition, though a recent one, endeavoring to transmit itself unimpaired to posterity, but each instant losing some of its integrity? It has not the vitality and force of a single living man; for a single man can bend it to his will. It is a sort of wooden gun to the people themselves; and, if ever they should use it in earnest as a real one against each other, it will surely split. But it is not the less necessary for this; for the people must have some complicated machinery or other, and hear its din, to satisfy that idea of government which they have. Governments show thus how successfully men can be imposed on, even impose on themselves, for their own advantage. It is excellent, we must all allow; yet this government never of itself furthered any enterprise, but by the alacrity with which it got out of its way. *It* does not keep

This essay was published in *Aesthetic Papers*, ed. by Elizabeth Peabody, Boston, 1849 under the title "Resistance to Civil Government." It, was originally a lecture delivered to the Concord Lyceum in January, 1848.

the country free. *It* does not settle the West. *It* does not educate. The character inherent in the American people has done all that has been accomplished; and it would have done somewhat more, if the government had not sometimes got in its way. For government is an expedient by which men would fain succeed in letting one another alone; and, as has been said, when it is most expedient, the governed are most let alone by it. Trade and commerce, if they were not made of India rubber, would never manage to bounce over the obstacles which legislators are continually putting in their way; and, if one were to judge these men wholly by the effects of their actions, and not partly by their intentions, they would deserve to be classed and punished with those mischievous persons who put obstructions on the railroads.

But, to speak practically and as a citizen, unlike those who call themselves no-government men, I ask for, not at once no government, but *at once* a better government. Let every man make known what kind of government would command his respect, and that will be one step toward obtaining it.

After all, the practical reason why, when the power is once in the hands of the people, a majority are permitted, and for a long period continue, to rule, is not because they are most likely to be in the right, nor because this seems fairest to the minority, but because they are physically the strongest. But a government in which the majority rule in all cases cannot be based on justice, even as far as men understand it. Can there not be a government in which majorities do not virtually decide right and wrong, but conscience?—in which majorities decide only those questions to which the rule of expediency is applicable? Must the citizen ever for a moment, or in the least degree, resign his conscience, to the legislator? Why has every man a conscience, then? I think that we should be men first, and subjects afterward. It is not desirable to cultivate a respect for the law, so much as for the right. The only obligation which I have a right to assume, is to do at any time what I think right. It is truly enough said, that a corporation has no conscience; but a corporation of conscientious men is a corporation *with* a conscience. Law never made men a whit more just; and, by means of their respect for it, even the well-disposed are daily made the agents of injustice. A common and natural result of an undue respect for law is, that you may see a file of soldiers, colonel, captain, corporal, privates, powder-monkeys and all, marching in admirable order over hill and dale to the wars, against their wills, aye, against their common sense and consciences, which makes it very steep marching indeed, and produces a palpitation of the heart. They have no doubt that it is a damnable business in which they are concerned; they are all peaceably inclined. Now, what are they? Men at all? or small moveable forts and maga-zines, at the service of some unscrupulous man in power? Visit the Navy Yard, and behold a marine, such a man as an American government can make, or such as it can make a man with its black arts, a mere shadow and reminiscence of humanity, a man laid out alive and standing, and already, as one may say, buried under arms with funeral accompaniments, though it may be

> Not a drum was heard, nor a funeral note,
>   As his corpse to the ramparts we hurried;
> Not a soldier discharged his farewell shot
>   O'er the grave where our hero we buried.

The mass of men serve the State thus, not as men mainly, but as machines, with their bodies. They are the standing army, and the militia, jailers, constables, *posse comitatus*, &c. In most cases there is no free exercise whatever of the judgment or of the moral sense; but they put themselves on a level with wood and earth and stones; and wooden men can perhaps be manufactured that will serve the purpose as well. Such command no more respect than men of straw, or a lump of dirt. They have the same sort of worth only as horses and dogs. Yet such as these even are commonly esteemed good citizens. Others, as most legislators, politicians, lawyers, ministers, and office-holders, serve the State chiefly with their heads; and, as they rarely make any moral distinctions, they are as likely to serve the devil, without intending it, as God. A very few, as heroes, patriots, martyrs, reformers in the great sense, and *men*, serve the State with their consciences also, and so necessarily resist it for the most part; and they are commonly treated by it as enemies. A wise man will only be useful as a man, and will not submit to be "clay," and "stop a hole to keep the wind away," but leave that office to his dust at least:—

> I am too high-born to be propertied,
> To be a secondary at control,
> Or useful serving-man and instrument
> To any sovereign state throughout the world.

He who gives himself entirely to his fellow-men appears to them useless and selfish; but he who gives himself partially to them is pronounced a benefactor and philanthropist.

How does it become a man to behave toward this American government today? I answer that he cannot without disgrace be associated with it. I cannot for an instant recognize that political organization as *my* government which is the *slave's* government also.

All men recognize the right of revolution; that is, the right to refuse allegiance to and to resist the government, when its tyranny or its inefficiency are great and unendurable. But almost all say that such is not the case now. But such was the case, they think, in the Revolution of '75. If one were to tell me that this was a bad government because it taxed certain foreign commodities brought to its ports, it is most probable that I should not make an ado about it, for I can do without them: all machines have their friction; and possibly this does enough good to counterbalance the evil. At any rate, it is a great evil to make a stir about it. But when the friction comes to have its machine, and oppression and robbery are organized, I say, let us not have such a machine any longer. In other words, when a sixth of the population of a nation which has undertaken to be the refuge of liberty are slaves, and a whole country is unjustly overrun and conquered by a foreign army, and subjected to military law, I think that it is not too soon for honest men to rebel and revolutionize. What makes this duty the more urgent is the fact, that the country so overrrun is not our own, but ours is the invading army.

Paley, a common authority with many on moral questions, in his chapter on the "Duty of Submission to Civil Government," resolves all civil obligation into expediency; and he proceeds to say, "that so long as the interest of the whole society requires it, that is, so long as the established government cannot be resisted or changed without public inconveniency, it is the will of God, that the established government be obeyed, and no longer."—"This principle being admitted, the justice of every particular case of resistance is reduced to a computation of the quantity of the danger and grievance on the one side, and of the probability and expense of redressing it on the other." Of this, he says, every man shall judge for himself. But Paley appears never to have contemplated those cases to which the rule of expediency does not apply, in which a people, as well as an individual, must do justice, cost what it may. If I have unjustly wrested a plank from a drowning man, I must restore it to him though I drown myself. This, according to Paley, would be inconvenient. But he that would save his life, in such a case, shall lose it. This people must cease to hold slaves, and to make war on Mexico, though it cost them their existence as a people.

In their practice, nations agree with Paley; but does any one think that Massachusetts does exactly what is right at the present crisis?

A drab of state, a cloth-o'-silver slut,
To have her train borne up, and her soul trail in the dirt.

Practically speaking, the opponents to a reform in Massachusetts are not a hundred thousand politicians at the South, but a hundred thousand merchants and farmers here, who are more interested in commerce and agriculture than they are in humanity, and are not prepared to do justice to the slave and to Mexico, *cost what it may.* I quarrel not with far-off foes, but with those who, near at home, co-operate with, and do the bidding of those far away, and without whom the latter would be harmless. We are accustomed to say, that the mass of men are unprepared; but improvement is slow, because the few are not materially wiser or better than the many. It is not so important that many should be as good as you, as that there be some absolute goodness somewhere; for that will leaven the whole lump. These are thousands who are *in opinion* opposed to slavery and to the war, who yet in effect do nothing to put an end to them; who, esteeming themselves children of Washington and Franklin, sit down with their hands in their pockets, and say that they know not what to do, and do nothing; who even postpone the question of freedom to the question of free-trade, and quietly read the prices-current along with the latest advices from Mexico, after dinner, and, it may be, fall asleep over them both. What is the price-current of an honest man and patriot today? They hesitate, and they regret, and sometimes they petition; but they do nothing in earnest and with effect. They will wait, well disposed, for others to remedy the evil, that they may no longer have it to regret. At most, they give only a cheap vote, and a feeble countenance and Godspeed, to the right, as it goes by them. There are nine hundred and ninety-nine patrons of virtue to one virtuous man; but it is easier to deal with the real possessor of a thing than with the temporary guardian of it.

All voting is a sort of gaming, like chequers or backgammon, with a slight moral tinge to it, a playing with right and wrong, with moral questions; and betting naturally accompanies it. The character of the voters is not staked. I cast my vote, perchance, as I think right; but I am not vitally concerned that that right should prevail. I am willing to leave it to the majority. Its obligation, therefore, never exceeds that of expediency. Even voting *for the right* is *doing* nothing for it. It is only expressing to men feebly your desire that it should prevail. A wise man will not leave the right to the mercy of chance, nor wish it to prevail through the power of the majority. There is but little virtue in the action of masses of men. When the majority shall at length vote for the abolition of slavery, it will be because they are indifferent to slavery, or because there is but little slavery left to be abolished by their vote. *They* will then be the only slaves. Only *his* vote can hasten the abolition of slavery who asserts his own freedom by his vote.

I hear of a convention to be held at Baltimore, or elsewhere, for the selection of a candidate for the Presidency, made up chiefly of editors, and men who are politicians by profession; but I think, what is it to any independent, intelligent, and respectable man what decision they may come to, shall we not have the advantage of his wisdom and honesty, nevertheless? Can we not count upon some independent votes? Are there not many individuals in the country who do not attend conventions? But no: I find that the respectable man, so called, has immediately drifted from his position, and despairs of his country, when his country has more reason to despair of him. He forthwith adopts one of the candidates thus selected as the only *available* one, thus proving that he is himself *available* for any purposes of the demagogue. His vote is of no more worth than that of any unprincipled foreigner or hireling native, who may have been bought. Oh for a man who is a *man*, and, as my neighbor says, has a bone in his back which you cannot pass your hand through! Our statistics are at fault: the population has been returned too large. How many *men* are there to a square thousand miles in this country? Hardly one. Does not America offer any inducement for men to settle here? The American has dwindled into an Odd Fellow,—one who may be known by the development of his organ of gregariousness, and a manifest lack of intellect and cheerful self-reliance; whose first and chief concern, on coming into the world, is to see that the alms-houses are in good repair; and, before yet he has lawfully donned the virile garb, to collect a fund for the support of the widows and orphans that may be; who, in short, ventures to live only by aid of the mutual insurance company, which has promised to bury him decently.

It is not a man's duty, as a matter of course, to devote himself to the eradication of any, even the most enormous wrong; he may still properly have other concerns to engage him; but it is his duty, at least, to wash his hands of it, and if he gives it no thought longer, not to give it practically his support. If I devote myself to other pursuits and contemplations, I must first see, at least, that I do not pursue them sitting upon another man's shoulders. I must get off him first, that he may pursue his contemplations too. See what gross inconsistency is tolerated. I have heard some of my townsmen say, "I should like to have them order me out to help put down an insurrection of the slaves, or too march to Mexico—see if I would go;" and yet these very men have each, directly by their allegiance, and so indirectly, at least, by their money, furnished a substitute. The soldier is applauded who refuses to serve in an unjust war by those who do not refuse to sustain the unjust government which makes the war; is applauded by those whose own act and authority he disregards and sets at nought; as if the State were penitent to that degree that it hired one to scourge it while it sinned, but not to that degree that it left off sinning for a moment. Thus, under the name of order and civil government, we are all made at last to pay homage to and support our own meanness. After the first blush of sin, comes its indifference; and from immoral it becomes, as it were, *un*moral, and not quite unnecessary to that life which we have made.

The broadest and most prevalent error requires the most disinterested virtue to sustain it. The slight reproach to which the virtue of patriotism is commonly liable, the noble are most likely to incur. Those who, while they disapprove of the character and measure of a government, yield to it their allegiance and support, are undoubtedly its most conscientious supporters, and so frequently the most serious obstacles to reform. Some are petitioning the State to dissolve the Union, to disregard the requisitions of the President. Why do they not dissolve it themselves—the union between themselves and the State—and refuse to pay their quota into its treasury? Do not they stand in the same relation to the State, that the State does to the Union? And have not the same reasons prevented the State from resisting the Union, which have prevented them from resisting the State?

How can a man be satisfied to entertain an opinion merely, and enjoy *it*? Is there any enjoyment in it, if his opinions is that he is aggrieved? If you are cheated out of a single dollar by your neighbor, you do not rest satisfied with knowing that you are cheated or with saying that you are cheated, or even with petitioning him to pay you your due; but you take effectual steps at once to obtain the full amount, and see that you are never cheated again. Action from principle,—the perception and the performance of right,—changes things and relations; it is essentially revolutionary, and does not consist wholly with any thing which was. It not only divides states and churches, it divides families, aye, it divides the *individual*, separating the diabolical in him from the divine.

Unjust laws exist; shall we be content to obey them, or shall we endeavor to amend them, and obey them until we have succeeded, or shall we transgress them at once? Men generally, under such a government as this, think that they ought to wait until they have persuaded the majority to alter them. They think that, if they should resist, the remedy would be worse than the evil. But it is the fault of the government itself that the remedy *is* worse than the evil. *It* makes it worse. Why is it not more apt to anticipate and provide for reform? Why does it not cherish its wise minority? Why does it cry and resist before it is hurt? Why does it not encourage its citizens to be on the alert to point out its faults, and *do* better that it would have them? Why does it always crucify Christ, and excommunicate Copernicus and Luther, and pronounce Washington and Franklin rebels?

One would think, that a deliberate and practical denial of its authority, was the only offense never contemplated by government; else, why has it not assigned its definite, its suitable and proportionate penalty? If a man who has no property refuses but once to earn nine shillings for the State, he is put in prison for a period unlimited by any law that I know, and determined only by the discretion of those who placed him there; but if he should steal ninety times nine shillings from the State, he is soon permitted to go at large again.

If the injustice is part of the necessary friction of the machine of government, let it go, let it go; perchance it will wear smooth—certainly the machine will wear out. If the injustice has a spring, or a pulley, or a rope, or a crank, exclusively for itself, then perhaps you may consider whether the remedy will not be worse than the evil; but if it is of such a nature that it requires you to be the agent of injustice to another, then, I say, break the law. Let your life be a counter friction to stop the machine. What I have to do is to see, at any rate, that I do not lend myself to the wrong which I condemn.

As for adopting the ways which the State has provided for remedying the evil,

I know not of such ways. They take too much time, and a man's life will be gone. I have other affairs to attend to. I came into this world, not chiefly to make this a good place to live in, but to live in it, be it good or bad. A man has not every thing to do, but something; and because he cannot do *every thing*, it is not necessary that he should do *something* wrong. It is not my business to be petitioning the governor or the legislature any more than it is theirs to petition me; and, if they should not hear my petition, what should I do then? But in this case the State has provided no way: its very constitution is the evil. This may seem to be harsh and stubborn and unconciliatory; but it is to treat with the utmost kindness and consideration the only spirit that can appreciate or deserve it. So is all change for the better, like birth and death which convulse the body.

I do not hesitate to say, that those who call themselves abolitionists should at once effectually withdraw their support, both in person and property, from the government of Massachusetts, and not wait till they constitute a majority of one, before they suffer the right to prevail through them. I think that it is enough if they have God on their side, without waiting for that other one. Moreover, any man more right than his neighbors, constitutes a majority of one already.

I meet this American government, or its representative the State government, directly, and face to face, once a year, no more, in the person of its tax-gatherer; this is the only mode in which a man situated as I am necessarily meets it; and it then says distinctly, recognize me; and the simplest, the most effectual, and, in the present posture of affairs, the indispensable mode of treating with it on this head, of expressing your little satisfaction with and love for it, is to deny it then. My civil neighbor, the tax-gatherer, is the very man I have to deal with—for it is, after all, with men and not with parchment that I quarrel,—and he has voluntarily chosen to be an agent of the government. How shall he ever know well what he is and does as an officer of the government, or as a man, until he is obliged to consider whether he shall treat me, his neighbor, for whom he has respect, as a neighbor and well-disposed man, or as a maniac and disturber of the peace, and see if he can get over this obstruction to his neighborliness without a ruder and more impetuous thought or speech corresponding with his action? I know this well, that if one thousand, if one hundred, if ten men whom I could name,—if ten *honest* men only,—aye, if *one* HONEST man, in this State of Massachusetts, *ceasing to hold slaves*, were actually to withdraw from this copartnership, and be locked up in the county jail therfor, it would be the abolition of slavery in America. For it matters not how small the beginning may seem to be: what is once well done is done for ever. But we love better to talk about it: that we say in our mission. Reform keeps many scores of newspapers in its service, but not one man. If my esteemed neighbor, the State's ambassador, who will devote his days to the settlement of the question of human rights in the Council Chamber, instead of being threatened with the prisons of Carolina, were to sit down the prisoner of Massachusetts, that State which is so anxious to foist the sin of slavery upon her sister,—though at present she can discover only an act of inhospitality to be the ground of a quarrel with her,—the Legislature would not wholly waive the subject the following winter.

Under a government which imprisons any unjustly, the true place for a just man is also a prison. The proper place today, the only place which Massachusetts has provided for her freer and less despondent spirits, is in her prisons, to be put out and locked out of the State by her own act, as they have already put themselves out by their principles. It is there that the fugitive slave, and the Mexican prisoner on parole, and the Indian come to plead the wrongs of his race, should find them; on that separate, but more free and honorable ground, where the State places those who are not *with* her but *against* her,—the only house in a slave-state in which a free man can abide with honor. If any think that their influence would be lost there, and their voices no longer afflict the ear of the State, that they would not be as an enemy within its walls, they do not know by how much truth is stronger than error, nor how much more eloquently and effectively he can combat injustice who has experienced a little in his own person. Cast your whole vote, not a strip of paper merely, but your whole influence. A minority is powerless while it conforms to the majority; it is not even a minority then; but it is irresistible when it clogs by its whole weight. If the alternative is to keep all just men in prison, or give up war and slavery, the State will not hesitate which to choose. If a thousand men were not to pay their tax-bills this year, that would not be a violent and bloody measure, as it would be to pay them, and enable the State to commit violence and shed innocent blood. This is, in fact, the definition of a peaceable revolution, if any such is possible. If the tax-gatherer, or any other public officer, asks me, as one has done, "But what shall I do?" my answer is, "If you really wish to do any thing, resign your office." When the subject has refused allegiance, and the officer has resigned his office, then the revolution is accomplished. But even suppose blood should flow. Is there not a sort of blood shed when the conscience is wounded? Through this wound a man's real manhood and immortality flow out, and he bleeds to an everlasting death. I see this blood flowing now.

I have contemplated the imprisonment of the offender, rather than the seizure of his goods,—though both will serve the same purpose,—because they who assert the purest right, and consequently are most dangerous to a corrupt State, commonly have not spent much time in accumulating property. To such the State renders comparatively small service, and a slight tax is wont to appear exorbitant, particularly if they are obliged to earn it by special labor with their hands. If there were one who lived wholly without the use of money, the State itself would hesitate to demand it of him. But the rich man—not to make any invidious comparison—is always sold to the institution which makes him rich. Absolutely speaking, the more money, the less virtue; for money comes between a man and his objects, and obtains them for him; and it was certainly no great virtue to obtain it. It puts to rest many questions which he would otherwise be taxed to answer; while the only new question which it puts is the hard but superfluous one, how to spend it. Thus his moral ground is taken from under his feet. The opportunities of living are diminished in proportion as what are called the "means" are increased. The best thing a man can do for his culture when he is rich is to endeavor to carry out those schemes which he entertained when he was poor. Christ answered the Herodians according to their condition. "Show me the tribute-money," said he;—and one took a penny out of his pocket;—if you use money which has the image of Caesar on it, and which he has made current and valuable, that is, *if you are men of the State*, and gladly enjoy the advantages of Caesar's government, then pay him back some of his own when he demands it; "Render therefore to Caesar that which is Caesar's, and to God those things which are God's,"—leaving them no wiser than before as to which was which; for they did not wish to know.

When I converse with the freest of my neighbors, I perceive that, whatever they may say about the magnitude and seriousness of the question, and their regard for the public tranquillity, the long and the short of the matter is, that they cannot spare the protection of the existing government, and they dread the consequences of disobedience to it to their property and families. For my own part, I should not like to think that I ever rely on the protection of the State. But, if I deny the authority of the State when it presents its tax-bill, it will soon take and waste all my property, and so harass me and my children without end. This is hard. This makes it impossible for a man to live honestly and at the same time comfortably in outward respects. It will not be worth the while to accumulate property; that would be sure to go again. You must hire or squat somewhere, and raise but a small crop, and eat that soon. You must live within yourself, and depend upon yourself, always tucked up and ready for a start, and not have many affairs. A man may grow rich in Turkey even, if he will be in all respects a good subject of the Turkish government. Confucius said,—"If a State is governed by the principles of reason, poverty and misery are subjects of shame; if a State is not governed by the principles of reason, riches and honors are the subjects of shame." No: until I want the protection of Massachusetts to be extended to me in some distant southern port, where my liberty is endangered, or until I am bent solely on building up an estate at home by peaceful enterprise, I can afford to refuse allegiance to Massachusetts, and her right to my property and life. It costs me less in every sense to incur the penalty of disobedience to the State, than it would to obey. I should feel as if I were worth less in that case.

Some years ago, the State met me in behalf of the church, and commanded me to pay a certain sum toward the support of a clergyman whose preaching my father attended, but never I myself. "Pay it," it said, "or be locked up in the jail." I declined to pay. But, unfortunately another man saw fit to pay it. I did not see why the schoolmaster should be taxed to support the priest, and not the priest the schoolmaster: for I was not the State's schoolteacher, but I supported myself by voluntary subscription. I did not see why the lyceum should not present its tax-bill, and have the State to back its demand, as well as the church. However, at the request of the selectmen, I condescended to make some such statement as this in writing:—"Know all men by these presents, that I, Henry Thoreau, do not wish to be regarded as a member of any incorporated society which I have not joined." This I gave to the town-clerk; and he has it. The State, having thus learned that I did not wish to be regarded as a member of that church, has never made a like demand on me since; though it said that it must adhere to its original presumption that time. If I had known how to name them, I should then have signed off in detail from all the societies which I never signed on to; but I did not know where to find a complete list.

I have paid no poll-tax for six years. I was put into a jail once on this account, for one night; and, as I stood considering the walls of solid stone, two or three feet thick, the door of wood and iron, a foot thick, and the iron grating which strained the light, I could not help being struck with the foolishness of that institution which treated me as if I were mere flesh and blood and bones, to be locked up. I wondered that it should have concluded at length that this was the best use it could put me to, and had never thought to avail itself of my services in some way. I saw that, if there was a wall of stone between me and my townsmen, there was a still more difficult one to climb or break through, before they could get to be as free as I was. I did not for a moment feel confined, and the walls seemed a great waste of stone and mortar. I felt as if I alone of all my townsmen had paid my tax. They plainly did not know how to treat me, but behaved like persons who are underbred, In every threat and in every compliment there was a blunder; for they thought that my chief desire was to stand the other side of that stone wall. I could not but smile to see how industriously they locked the door on my meditations, which followed them out again without let or hinderance, and *they* were really all that was dangerous. As they could not reach me, they had resolved to punish my body; just as boys, if they cannot come at some person against whom they have a spite, will abuse his dog. I saw that the State was half-witted, that it was timid as a lone woman with her silver spoons, and that it did not know its friends from its foes, and I lost all my remaining respect for it, and pitied it.

Thus the State never intentionally confronts a man's sense, intellectual or moral, but only his body, his senses. It is not armed with superior wit or honesty, but with superior physical strength. I was not born to be forced. I will breathe after my own fashion. Let us see who is the strongest. What force has a multitude? They only can force me who obey a higher law than I. They force me to become like themselves. I do not hear of *men* being *forced* to live this way or that by masses of men. What sort of life were that to live? When I meet a government which says to me, "Your money or your life," why should I be in haste to give it my money? It may be in a great strait, and not know what to do: I cannot help that. It must help itself: do as I do. It is not worth the while to snivel about it. I am not responsible for the successful working of the machinery of society. I am not the son of the engineer. I perceive that, when an acorn and a chestnut fall side by side, the one does not remain inert to make way for the other, but both obey their own laws, and spring and grow and flourish as best they can, till one, perchance, over-shadows and destroys the other. If a plant cannot live according to its nature, it dies; and so a man. . . .

When I came out of prison—for some one interfered, and paid the tax—I did not perceive that great changes had taken place on the common, such as he observed who went in a youth, and emerged a tottering and gray-headed man; and yet a change had to my eyes come over the scene,—the town, and State, and country,—greater than any that mere time could effect. I saw to what extent the people among whom I lived could be trusted as good neighbors and friends; that their friendship was for summer weather only; that they did not greatly purpose to do right; that they were a distinct race from me by their prejudices and superstitions. . . .

I have never declined paying the highway tax, because I am as desirous of being a good neighbor as I am of being a bad subject; and, as for supporting schools, I am doing my part to educate my fellow-countrymen now. It is for no particular item in the tax-bill that I refuse to pay it. I simply wish to refuse allegiance to the State, to withdraw and stand aloof from it effectually. I do not care to trace the course of my dollar, if I could, till it buys a man, or a musket to shoot one with,—the dollar is innocent,—but I am concerned to trace the effects of my allegiance. In fact, I quietly declare war with the State, after my fashion, though I will still make what use and get what advantage of her I can, as is usual in such cases.

If others pay the tax which is demanded of me, from a sympathy with the State, they do but what they have already done in their own case, or rather they abet injustice to a greater extent than the State requires. If they pay a tax from a mistaken interest in the individual taxed, to save his going to jail, it is because they have not considered wisely how far they let their private feelings interfere with the public good.

This, then, is my position at present. But one cannot be too much on his guard in such a case, lest his action be biased by obstinacy, or an undue regard for the opinions of men. Let him see that he does only what belongs to himself and to the hour.

I think sometimes, Why, this people mean well; they are only ignorant; they would do better if they knew how; why give your neighbors this pain to treat you as they are not inclined to? But I think, again, this is no reason why I should do as they do, or permit others to suffer much greater pain of a different kind. Again, I sometimes say to myself, when many millions of men, without heat, without ill-will, without personal feeling of any kind, demand of you a few shillings only, without the possibility, such is their constitution, of retracting or altering their present demand, and without the possibility, on your side, of appeal to any other millions, why expose yourself to this overwhelming brute force? You do not resist cold and hunger, the winds and the waves, thus obstinately; you quietly submit to a thousand similar necessities. You do not put your head into the fire. But just in proportion as I regard this as not wholly a brute force, but partly a human force, and consider that I have relations to those millions as to so many millions of men, and not of mere brute or inanimate things, I see that appeal is possible, first and instantaneously, from them to the Maker of them, and, secondly, from them to themselves. But, if I put my head deliberately into the fire, there is no appeal to fire or to the Maker of fire, and I have only myself to blame. If I could convince myself that I have any right to be satisfied with men as they are, and to treat them accordingly, and not according, in some respects, to my requisitions and expectations of what they and I ought to be, then, like a good Mussulman and fatalist, I should endeavor to be satisfied with things as they are, and say it is the will of God. And, above all, there is this difference between resisting this and a purely brute or natural force, that I can resist this with some effect; but I cannot expect, like Orpheus, to change the nature of the rocks and trees and beasts.

I do not wish to quarrel with any man or nation. I do not wish to split hairs, to make fine distinctions, or set myself up as better than my neighbors. I seek rather, I may say, even an excuse for conforming to the laws of the land. I am but too ready to conform to them. Indeed I have reason to suspect myself on this head; and each year, as the tax-gatherer comes around, I find myself disposed to review the acts and position of the general and state governments, and the spirit of the people, to discover a pretext for conformity. I believe that the State will soon be able to take all my work of this sort out of my hands, and then I shall be no better a patriot than my fellow-country-men. Seen from a lower point of view, the Constitution, with all its faults, is very good; the law and the courts are very respectable; even this State and this American government are, in many respects, very admirable and rare things, to be thankful for, such as a great many have described them; but seen from a point of view a little higher, they are what I have described them; seen from a higher still, and the highest, who shall say what they are, or that they are worth looking at or thinking of at all?

However, the government does not concern me much, and I shall bestow the fewest possible thoughts on it. It is not many moments that I live under a government, even in this world. If a man is thought-free, fancy-free, imagination-free, that which *is not* never for a long time appearing *to be* to him, unwise rulers or reformers cannot fatally interrupt him.

I know that most men think differently from myself; but those whose lives are by profession devoted to the study of these or kindred subjects, content me as little as any. Statesmen and legislators, standing so completely within the institution, never distinctly and nakedly behold it. They speak of moving society, but have no resting-place without it. They may be men of a certain experience and discrimination, and have no doubt invented ingenious and even useful systems, for which we sincerely thank them; but all their wit and usefulness lie within certain not very wide limits. They are wont to forget that the world is not governed by policy and expediency. . . .

They who know of no purer sources of truth, who have traced up its stream no higher, stand, and wisely stand, by the Bible and the Constitution, and drink at it there with reverence and humility, but they who behold where it comes trickling into this lake or that pool, gird up their loins once more, and continue their pilgrimage toward its fountain-head.

No man with a genius for legislation has appeared in America. They are rare in the history of the world. There are orators, politicians, and eloquent men, by the thousand; but the speaker has not yet opened his mouth to speak, who is capable of settling the much-vexed questions of the day. We love eloquence for its own sake, and not for any truth which it may utter, or any heroism it may inspire. . . .

The authority of government, even such as I am willing to submit to,—for I will cheerfully obey those who know and can do better than I, and in many things even those who neither know nor can do so well,—is still an impure one: to be strictly just, it must have the sanction and consent of the governed. It can have no pure right over my person and property but what I concede to it. The progress from an absolute to a limited monarchy, from a limited monarchy to a democracy, is a progress toward a true respect for the individual. Is a democracy, such as we know it, the last improvement possible in government? Is it not possible to take a step further towards recognizing and organizing the rights of man? There will never be a really free and enlightened State, until the State comes to recognize the individual as a higher and independent power, from which all its own power and authority are derived, and treats him accordingly. I please myself with imagining a State at last which can afford to be just to all men, and to treat the individual with respect as a neighbor; which even would not think it inconsistent with its own repose, if a few were to live aloof from it, not meddling with it, nor embraced by it, who fulfilled all the duties of neighbors and fellow-men. A State which bore this kind of fruit, and suffered it to drop off as fast as it ripened, would prepare the way for a still more perfect and glorious State, which also I have imagined, but not yet anywhere seen.

Friedrich Nietzsche

Friedrich Nietzsche (1844–1900), a German philosopher, was one
of the most brilliant and influential thinkers of the nineteenth
century. He was not really a political philosopher, but he had
important things to say about several issues in political philosophy. The first selection below deals primarily with the question
of punishment; the second, from *Thus Spake Zarathustra*, reveals
Nietzsche's view of the state.

On the Genealogy of Morals

PUNISHMENT AND CONSCIENCE

12

Yet a word on the origin and the purpose of punishment—two problems that
are separate, or ought to be separate: unfortunately, they are usually confounded. How have previous genealogists of morals set about solving these
problems? Naïvely, as has always been their way: they seek out some "purpose"
in punishment, for example, revenge or deterrence, then guilelessly place this
purpose at the beginning as *causa fiendi*[1] of punishment, and—have done. The
"purpose of law," however, is absolutely the last thing to employ in the history
of the origin of law: on the contrary, there is for historiography of any kind no
more important proposition than the one it took such effort to establish but
which really *ought to be* established now: the cause of the origin of a thing and
its eventual utility, its actual employment and place in a system of purposes, lie
worlds apart; whatever exists, having somehow come into being, is again and
again reinterpreted to new ends, taken over, transformed, and redirected by
some power superior to it; all events in the organic world are a subduing, a
becoming master, and all subduing and becoming master involves a fresh interpretation, an adaptation through which any previous "meaning" and "purpose"
are necessarily obscured or even obliterated. However well one has understood
the *utility* of any physiological organ (or of a legal institution, a social custom, a
political usage, a form in art or in a religious cult), this means nothing regarding
its origin: however uncomfortable and disagreeable this may sound to older
ears—for one had always believed that to understand the demonstrable purpose,

[1] The cause of the origin.

the utility of a thing, a form, or an institution, was also to understand the reason why it originated—the eye being made for seeing, the hand being made for grasping.

Thus one also imagined that punishment was devised for punishing. But purposes and utilities are only *signs* that a will to power has become master of something less powerful and imposed upon it the character of a function; and the entire history of a "thing," an organ, a custom can in this way be a continuous sign-chain of ever new interpretations and adaptations whose causes do not even have to be related to one another but, on the contrary, in some cases succeed and alternate with one another in a purely chance fashion. The "evolution" of a thing, a custom, an organ is thus by no means its *progressus* toward a goal, even less a logical *progressus* by the shortest route and with the smallest expenditure of force—but a succession of more or less profound, more or less mutually independent processes of subduing, plus the resistances they encounter, the attempts at transformation for the purpose of defense and reaction, and the results of successful counteractions. The form is fluid, but the "meaning" is even more so.

The case is the same even within each individual organism: with every real growth in the whole, the "meaning" of the individual organs also changes; in certain circumstances their partial destruction, a reduction in their numbers (for example, through the disappearance of intermediary members) can be a sign of increasing strength and perfection. It is not too much to say that even a partial *diminution of utility*, an atrophying and degeneration, a loss of meaning and purposiveness—in short, death—is among the conditions of an actual *progressus*, which always appears in the shape of a will and way to *greater power* and is always carried through at the expense of numerous smaller powers. The magnitude of an "advance" can even be measured by the mass of things that had to be sacrificed to it; mankind in the mass sacrificed to the prosperity of a single *stronger* species of man—that *would* be an advance.

I emphasize this major point of historical method all the more because it is in fundamental opposition to the now prevalent instinct and taste which would rather be reconciled even to the absolute fortuitousness, even the mechanistic senselessness of all events than to the theory that in all events a *will to power* is operating. The democratic idiosyncracy which opposes everything that dominates and wants to dominate, the modern *misarchism*[2] (to coin an ugly word for an ugly thing) has permeated the realm of the spirit and disguised itself in the most spiritual forms to such a degree that today it has forced its way, has acquired the *right* to force its way into the strictest, apparently most objective sciences; indeed, it seems to me to have already taken charge of all physiology and theory of life—to the detriment of life, as goes without saying, since it has robbed it of a fundamental concept, that of *activity*. Under the influence of the above-mentioned idiosyncracy, one places instead "adaptation" in the foreground, that is to say, an activity of the second rank, a mere reactivity; indeed, life itself has been defined as a more and more efficient inner adaptation to external conditions (Herbert Spencer). Thus the essence of life, its *will to power*, is ignored; one overlooks the essential priority of the spontaneous, aggressive, expansive, form-giving forces that give new interpretations and directions, although "adaptation" follows only after this; the dominant role of the highest

[2] Hatred of rule or government.

functionaries within the organism itself in which the will to life appears active and form-giving is denied. One should recall what Huxley[3] reproached Spencer with—his "administrative nihilism": but it is a question of rather *more* than mere "administration."

13

To return to our subject, namely *punishment*, one must distinguish two aspects: on the one hand, that in it which is relatively *enduring*, the custom, the act, the "drama," a certain strict sequence of procedures; on the other, that in it which is *fluid*, the meaning, the purpose, the expectation associated with the performance of such procedures. In accordance with the previously developed major point of historical method, it is assumed without further ado that the procedure itself will be something older, earlier than its employment in punishment, that the latter is *projected* and interpreted *into* the procedure (which has long existed but been employed in another sense), in short, that the case is *not* as has hitherto been assumed by our naïve genealogists of law and morals, who have one and all thought of the procedure as *invented* for the purpose of punishing, just as one formerly thought of the hand as invented for the purpose of grasping.

As for the other element in punishment, the fluid element, its "meaning," in a very late condition of culture (for example, in modern Europe) the concept "punishment" possesses in fact not *one* meaning but a whole synthesis of "meanings": the previous history of punishment in general, the history of its employment for the most various purposes, finally crystallizes into a kind of unity that is hard to disentangle, hard to analyze and, as must be emphasized especially, totally *indefinable*. (Today it is impossible to say for certain *why* people are really punished: all concepts in which an entire process is semiotically concentrated elude definition; only that which has no history is definable.) At an earlier stage, on the contrary, this synthesis of "meanings" can still be disentangled, as well as changed; one can still perceive how in each individual case the elements of the synthesis undergo a shift in value and rearrange themselves accordingly, so that now this, now that element comes to the fore and dominates at the expense of the others; and under certain circumstances one element (the purpose of deterrence perhaps) appears to overcome all the remaining elements.

To give at least an idea of how uncertain, how supplemental, how accidental "the meaning" of punishment is, and how one and the same procedure can be employed, interpreted, adapted to ends that differ fundamentally, I set down here the pattern that has emerged from consideration of relatively few chance instances I have noted. Punishment as a means of rendering harmless, of preventing further harm. Punishment as recompense to the injured party for the harm done, rendered in any form (even in that of a compensating affect). Punishment as the isolation of a disturbance of equilibrium, so as to guard against any further spread of the disturbance. Punishment as a means of inspiring

---

[3] Thomas Henry Huxley (1825—95), the English biologist and writer, fought tirelessly for the acceptance of Darwinism. In 1869 he coined the word *agnosticism*, which Spencer took over from him. Aldous Huxley (1894—1963), the author of *Brave New World* (1932), and Julian Huxley (born 1897), the biologist, are T. H. Huxley's grandsons.

fear of those who determine and execute the punishment. Punishment as a kind of repayment for the advantages the criminal has enjoyed hitherto (for example, when he is employed as a slave in the mines). Punishment as the expulsion of a degenerate element (in some cases, of an entire branch, as in Chinese law: thus as a means of preserving the purity of a race or maintaining a social type). Punishment as a festival, namely as the rape and mockery of a finally defeated enemy. Punishment as the making of a memory, whether for him who suffers the punishment—so-called "improvement"—or for those who witness its execution. Punishment as payment of a fee stipulated by the power that protects the wrongdoer from the excesses of revenge. Punishment as a compromise with revenge in its natural state when the latter is still maintained and claimed as a privilege by powerful clans. Punishment as a declaration of war and a war measure against an enemy of peace, of the law, of order, of the authorities, whom, as a danger to the community, as one who has broken the contract that defines the conditions under which it exists, as a rebel, a traitor, and breaker of the peace, one opposes with the means of war.—

14

This list is certainly not complete; it is clear that punishment is overdetermined by utilities of all kinds. All the more reason, then, for deducting from it a *supposed* utility that, to be sure, counts in the popular consciousness as the most essential one—belief in punishment, which for several reasons is tottering today, always finds its strongest support in this. Punishment is supposed to possess the value of awakening the *feeling of guilt* in the guilty person; one seeks in it the actual *instrumentum* of that psychical reaction called "bad conscience," "sting of conscience." Thus one misunderstands psychology and the reality of things even as they apply today: how much more as they applied during the greater part of man's history, his prehistory!

It is precisely among criminals and convicts that the sting of conscience is extremely rare; prisons and penitentiaries are *not* the kind of hotbed in which this species of gnawing worm is likely to flourish: all conscientious observers are agreed on that, in many cases unwillingly enough and contrary to their own inclinations. Generally speaking, punishment makes men hard and cold; it concentrates; it sharpens the feeling of alienation; it strengthens the power of resistance. If it happens that punishment destroys the vital energy and brings about a miserable prostration and self-abasement, such a result is certainly even less pleasant than the usual effects of punishment—characterized by dry and gloomy seriousness.

If we consider those millennia *before* the history of man, we may unhesitatingly assert that it was precisely through punishment that the development of the feeling of guilt was most powerfully *hindered*—at least in the victims upon whom the punitive force was vented. For we must not underrate the extent to which the sight of the judicial and executive procedures prevents the criminal from considering his deed, the type of his action *as such*, reprehensible: for he sees exactly the same kind of actions practiced in the service of justice and approved of and practiced with a good conscience: spying, deception, bribery, setting traps, the whole cunning and underhand art of police and prosecution, plus robbery, violence, defamation, imprisonment, torture, murder, practiced as a matter of principle and without even emotion to excuse them, which are pronounced characteristics of the various forms of punishment—all of them therefore actions which his judges in no way condemn and repudiate *as such*, but only when they are applied and directed to certain particular ends.

The "bad conscience," this most uncanny and most interesting plant of all our earthly vegetation, did *not* grow on this soil; indeed, during the greater part of the past the judges and punishers themselves were *not at all* conscious of dealing with a "guilty person." But with an instigator of harm, with an irresponsible piece of fate. And the person upon whom punishment subsequently descended, again like a piece of fate, suffered no "inward pain" other than that induced by the sudden appearance of something unforeseen, a dreadful natural event, a plunging, crushing rock that one cannot fight.

15

This fact once came insidiously into the mind of Spinoza (to the vexation of his interpreters, Kuno Fischer,[4] for example, who make a real *effort* to misunderstand him on this point), when one afternoon, teased by who knows what recollection, he mused on the question of what really remained to him of the famous *morsus conscientiae*[5]—he who had banished good and evil to the realm of human imagination and had wrathfully defended the honor of his "free" God against those blasphemers who asserted that God effected all things *sub ratione boni*[6] ("but that would mean making God subject to fate and would surely be the greatest of all absurdities"). The world, for Spinoza, had returned to that state of innocence in which it had lain before the invention of the bad conscience: what then had become of the *morsus conscientiae*?

"The opposite of *gaudium*,"[7] he finally said to himself—"a sadness accompanied by the recollection of a past event that flouted all of our expectations." *Eth. III, propos. XVIII, schol. I. II.* Mischief-makers overtaken by punishments have for thousands of years felt in respect of their "transgressions" *just as Spinoza did*: "here something has unexpectedly gone wrong," *not*: "I ought not to have done that." They submitted to punishment as one submits to an illness or to a misfortune or to death, with that stout-hearted fatalism without rebellion through which the Russians, for example, still have an advantage over us Westerners in dealing with life.

If there existed any criticism of the deed in those days, it was prudence that criticized the deed: the actual *effect* of punishment must beyond question be sought above all in a heightening of prudence, in an extending of the memory, in a will henceforth to go to work more cautiously, mistrustfully, secretly, in the insight that one is definitely too weak for many things, in a kind of improvement in self-criticism. That which can in general be attained through punishment, in men and in animals, is an increase of fear, a heightening of prudence, mastery of the desires: thus punishment *tames* men, but it does not make them

---

[4] Kuno Fischer (1824–1907), professor at Heidelberg, made a great reputation with a ten-volume history of modern philosophy that consists of imposing monographs on selected modern philosophers. One of the volumes is devoted to Spinoza.

[5] Sting of conscience.

[6] For a good reason.

[7] Joy.

"better"—one might with more justice assert the opposite ("Injury makes one prudent," says the proverb: insofar as it makes one prudent it also makes one bad. Fortunately, it frequently makes people stupid.)

16

At this point I can no longer avoid giving a first, provisional statement of my own hypothesis concerning the origin of the "bad conscience": it may sound rather strange and needs to be pondered, lived with, and slept on for a long time. I regard the bad conscience as the serious illness that man was bound to contract under the stress of the most fundamental change he ever experienced—that change which occurred when he found himself finally enclosed within the walls of society and of peace. The situation that faced sea animals when they were compelled to become land animals or perish was the same as that which faced these semi-animals, well adapted to the wilderness, to war, to prowling, to adventure: suddenly all their instincts were disvalued and "suspended." From now on they had to walk on their feet and "bear themselves" whereas hitherto they had been borne by the water: a dreadful heaviness lay upon them. They felt unable to cope with the simplest undertakings; in this new world they no longer possessed their former guides, their regulating, unconscious and infallible drives: they were reduced to thinking, inferring, reckoning, co-ordinating cause and effect, these unfortunate creatures; they were reduced to their "consciousness," their weakest and most fallible organ! I believe there has never been such a feeling of misery on earth, such a leaden discomfort—and at the same time the old instincts had not suddenly ceased to make their usual demands! Only it was hardly or rarely possible to humor them: as a rule they had to seek new and, as it were, subterranean gratifications.

All instincts that do not discharge themselves outwardly *turn inward*—this is what I call the *internalization* of man: thus it was that man first developed what was later called his "soul." The entire inner world, originally as thin as if it were stretched between two membranes, expanded and extended itself, acquired depth, breath, and height, in the same measure as outward discharge was *inhibited*. Those fearful bulwarks with which the political organization protected itself against the old instincts of freedom—punishments belong among these bulwarks—brought about that all those instincts of wild, free, prowling man turned backward *against man himself*. Hostility, cruelty, joy in persecuting, in attacking, in change, in destruction—all this turned against the possessors of such instincts: *that* is the origin of the "bad conscience."

The man who, from lack of external enemies and resistances and forcibly confined to the oppressive narrowness and punctiliousness of custom, impatiently lacerated, persecuted, gnawed at, assaulted, and maltreated himself; this animal that rubbed itself raw against the bars of its cage as one tried to "tame" it; this deprived creature, racked with homesickness for the wild, who had to turn himself into an adventure, a torture chamber, an uncertain and dangerous wilderness—this fool, this yearning and desperate prisoner became the inventor of the "bad conscience." But thus began the gravest and uncanniest illness, from which humanity has not yet recovered, man's suffering *of man, of himself*—the result of a forcible sundering from his animal past, as it were a leap and plunge into new surroundings and conditions of existence, a declaration of war against the old instincts upon which his strength, joy, and terribleness had rested hitherto.

Let us add at once that, on the other hand, the existence on earth of an animal soul turned against itself, taking sides against itself, was something so new, profound, unheard of, enigmatic, contradictory, *and pregnant with a future* that the aspect of the earth was essentially altered. Indeed, divine spectators were needed to do justice to the spectacle that thus began and the end of which is not yet in sight—a spectacle too subtle, too marvelous, too paradoxical to be played senselessly unobserved on some ludicrous planet! From now on, man is *included* among the most unexpected and exciting lucky throws in the dice game of Heraclitus' "great child," be he called Zeus or chance; he gives rise to an interest, a tension, a hope, almost a certainty, as if with him something were announcing and preparing itself, as if man were not a goal but only a way, an episode, a bridge, a great promise.—

17

Among the presuppositions of this hypothesis concerning the origin of the bad conscience is, first, that the change referred to was not a gradual or voluntary one and did not represent an organic adaptation to new conditions but a break, a leap, a compulsion, an ineluctable disaster which precluded all struggle and even all *ressentiment.* Secondly, however, that the welding of a hitherto unchecked and shapeless populace into a firm form was not only instituted by an act of violence but also carried to its conclusion by nothing but acts of violence—that the oldest "state" thus appeared as a fearful tyranny, as an oppressive and remorseless machine, and went on working until this raw material of people and semi-animals was at last not only thoroughly kneaded and pliant but also *formed.*

I employed the word "state": it is obvious what is meant—some pack of blond beasts of prey, a conqueror and master race which, organized for war and with the ability to organize, unhesitatingly lays its terrible claws upon a populace perhaps tremendously superior in numbers but still formless and nomad. That is after all how the "state" began on earth: I think that sentimentalism which would have it begin with a "contract" has been disposed of. He who can command, he who is by nature "master," he who is violent in act and bearing—what has he to do with contracts! One does not reckon with such natures; they come like fate, without reason, consideration, or pretext; they appear as lightning appears, too terrible, too sudden, too convincing, too "different" even to be hated. Their work is an instinctive creation and imposition of forms; they are the most involuntary, unconscious artists there are—wherever they appear something new soon arises, a ruling structure that *lives,* in which parts and functions are delimited and coordinated, in which nothing whatever finds a place that has not first been assigned a "meaning" in relation to the whole. They do not know what guilt, responsibility, or consideration are, these born organizers; they exemplify that terrible artists' egoism that has the look of bronze and knows itself justified to all eternity in its "work," like a mother in her child. It is not in *them* that the "bad conscience" developed, that goes without saying—but it would not have developed *without them,* this ugly growth, it would be lacking if a tremendous quantity of freedom had not been expelled from the world, or at least from the visible world, and made as it were *latent* under their hammer blows and artists' violence. This *instinct for freedom* forcibly made latent—we have seen it already—this instinct for freedom pushed back and repressed, incarcerated within and finally able to discharge and vent itself only on itself: that, and that alone, is what the *bad conscience* is in its beginnings.

18

One should guard against thinking lightly of this phenomenon merely on account of its initial painfulness and ugliness. For fundamentally it is the same active force that is at work on a grander scale in those artists of violence and organizers who build states, and that here, internally, on a smaller and pettier scale, directed backward, in the "labyrinth of the breast," to use Goethe's expression, creates for itself a bad conscience and builds negative ideals—namely, the *instinct for freedom* (in my language: the will to power); only here the material upon which the form-giving and ravishing nature of this force vents itself is man himself, his whole ancient animal self—and *not*, as in that greater and more obvious phenomenon, some *other* man, *other* men. This secret self-ravishment, this artists' cruelty, this delight in imposing a form upon oneself as a hard, recalcitrant, suffering material and in burning a will, a critique, a contradiction, a contempt, a No into it, this uncanny, dreadfully joyous labor of a soul voluntarily at odds with itself that makes itself suffer out of joy in making suffer—eventually this entire *active* "bad conscience"—you will have guessed it—as the womb of all ideal and imaginative phenomena, also brought to light an abundance of strange new beauty and affirmation, and perhaps beauty itself.— After all, what would be "beautiful" if the contradiction had not first become conscious of itself, if the ugly had not first said to itself: "I am ugly"?

This hint will at least make less enigmatic the enigma of how contradictory concepts such as *selflessness, self-denial, self-sacrifice* can suggest an ideal, a kind of beauty; and one thing we know henceforth—I have no doubt of it—and that is the nature of the *delight* that the selfless man, the self-denier, the self-sacrificer feels from the first: this delight is tied to cruelty.

So much for the present about the origin of the moral value of the "unegoistic," about the soil from which this value grew: only the bad conscience, only the will to self-maltreatment provided the conditions for the *value* of the unegoistic.—

19

The bad conscience is an illness, there is no doubt about that, but an illness as pregnancy is an illness. Let us seek out the conditions under which this illness has reached its most terrible and most sublime height; we shall see what it really was that thus entered the world. But for that one needs endurance—and first of all we must go back again to an earlier point of view.

The civil-law relationship between the debtor and his creditor, discussed above, has been interpreted in an, historically speaking, exceedingly remarkable and dubious manner into a relationship in which to us modern men it seems perhaps least to belong: namely into the relationship between the present generation and its ancestors.

Within the original tribal community—we are speaking of primeval times—the living generation always recognized a juridical duty toward earlier generations, and especially toward the earliest, which founded the tribe (and by no means a merely sentimental obligation: there are actually reasons for denying the existence of the latter for the greater part of human history). The conviction reigns that it is only through the sacrifices and accomplishments of the ancestors that the tribe *exists*—and that one has to *pay them back* with sacrifices and accomplishments: one thus recognizes a *debt* that constantly grows greater, since these forebears never cease, in their continued existence as powerful spirits, to accord the tribe new advantages and new strength. In vain, perhaps? But there is no "in vain" for these rude and "poor-souled" ages. What can one give them in return? Sacrifices (initially as food in the coarsest sense), feasts, music, honors; above all, obedience—for all customs, as works of the ancestors, are also their statutes and commands: can one ever give them enough? This suspicion remains and increases; from time to time it leads to a wholesale sacrifice, something tremendous in the way of repayment to the "creditor" (the notorious sacrifice of the first-born, for example; in any case blood, human blood).

The *fear* of the ancestor and his power, the consciousness of indebtedness to him, increases, according to this kind of logic, in exactly the same measure as the power of the tribe itself increases, as the tribe itself grows ever more victorious, independent, honored, and feared. By no means the other way round! Every step toward the decline of a tribe, every misfortune, every sign of degeneration, of coming disintegration always *diminishes* fear of the spirit of its founder and produces a meaner impression of his cunning, foresight, and present power. If one imagines this rude kind of logic carried to its end, then the ancestors of the *most powerful* tribes are bound eventually to grow to monstrous dimensions through the imagination of growing fear and to recede into the darkness of the divinely uncanny and unimaginable: in the end the ancestor must necessarily be transfigured into a *god.* Perhaps this is even the origin of gods, an origin therefore out of *fear!* ... And whoever should feel obliged to add, "but out of piety also!" would hardly be right for the greater part of the existence of man, his prehistory. To be sure, he would be quite right for the *intermediate* age, in which the noble tribes developed—who indeed paid back their originators, their ancestors (heroes, gods) with interest all the qualities that had become palpable in themselves, the *noble* qualities. We shall take another look later at the ennoblement of the gods (which should not be confused with their becoming "holy"); let us first of all follow to its end the course of this whole development of the consciousness of guilt.

20

History shows that the consciousness of being in debt to the deity did not by any means come to an end together with the organization of communities on the basis of blood relationship. Even as mankind inherited the concepts "good and bad" from the tribal nobility (along with its basic psychological propensity to set up orders of rank), it also inherited, along with the tribal and family divinities, the burden of still unpaid debts and of the desire to be relieved of them. (The transition is provided by those numerous slave and dependent populations who, whether through compulsion or through servility and mimicry, adapted themselves to their masters' cult of the gods: this inheritance then overflows from them in all directions.) The guilty feeling of indebtedness to the divinity continued to grow for several millennia—always in the same measure as the concept of God and the feeling for divinity increased on earth and was carried to the heights. (The entire history of ethnic struggle, victory, reconciliation, fusion, everything that precedes the definitive ordering of rank of the different national elements in every great racial synthesis, is reflected in the confused genealogies of their gods, in the sagas of the gods' struggles, victories, and reconciliations; the advance toward universal empires is always also an advance toward universal divinities; despotism with its triumph over the independent nobility always prepares the way for some kind of monotheism.)

The advent of the Christian God, as the maximum god attained so far, was therefore accompanied by the maximum feeling of guilty indebtedness on earth. Presuming we have gradually entered upon the *reverse* course, there is no small probability that with the irresistible decline of faith in the Christian God there is now also a considerable decline in mankind's feeling of guilt; indeed, the prospect cannot be dismissed that the complete and definitive victory of atheism might free mankind of this whole feeling of guilty indebtedness toward its origin, its *causa prima.*[8] Atheism and a kind of *second innocence* belong together.—

21

So much for a first brief preliminary on the connection of the concepts "guilt" and "duty" with religious presuppositions: I have up to now deliberately ignored the moralization of these concepts (their pushing back into the conscience; more precisely, the involvement of the *bad* conscience with the concept of god); and at the end of the last section I even spoke as if this moralization had not taken place at all, and as if these concepts were now necessarily doomed since their presupposition, the faith in our "creditor." in God, had disappeared. The reality is, to a fearful degree, otherwise.

The moralization of the concepts guilt and duty, their being pushed back into the *bad* conscience, actually involves an attempt to *reverse* the direction of the development described above, or at least to bring it to a halt: the *aim* now is to preclude pessimistically, once and for all, the prospect of a final discharge; the *aim* now is to make the glance recoil disconsolately from an iron impossibility; the *aim* now is to turn back the concepts "guilt" and "duty"—back against whom? There can be no doubt: against the "debtor" first of all, in whom from now on the bad conscience is firmly rooted, eating into him and spreading within him like a polyp, until at last the irredeemable debt gives rise to the conception of irredeemable penance, the idea that it cannot be discharged ("*eternal* punishment"). Finally, however, they are turned back against the "creditor," too: whether we think of the *causa prima* of man, the beginning of the human race, its primal ancestor who is from now on burdened with a curse ("Adam," original sin," "unfreedom of the will"), or of nature from whose womb mankind arose and into whom the principle of evil is projected from now on ("the diabolizing of nature"), or of existence in general, which is now

[8] First cause.

considered *worthless as such* (nihilistic withdrawal from it, a desire for nothingness or a desire for its antithesis, for a different mode of being, Buddhism and the like)—suddenly we stand before the paradoxical and horrifying expedient that afforded temporary relief for tormented humanity, that stroke of genius on the part of Christianity: God himself sacrifices himself for the guilt of mankind, God himself makes payment to himself, God as the only being who can redeem man from what has become unredeemable for man himself—the creditor sacrifices himself for his debtor, out of *love* (can one credit that?), out of love for his debtor!—

You will have guessed *what* has really happened here, *beneath* all this: that will to self-tormenting, that repressed cruelty of the animal-man made inward and scared back into himself, the creature imprisoned in the "state" so as to be tamed, who invented the bad conscience in order to hurt himself after the *more natural* vent for this desire to hurt had been blocked—this man of the bad conscience has seized upon the presupposition of religion so as to drive his self-torture to its most gruesome pitch of severity and rigor. Guilt before *God:* this thought becomes an instrument of torture to him. He apprehends in "God" the ultimate antithesis of his own ineluctable animal instincts; he reinterprets these animal instincts themselves as a form of guilt before God (as hostility, rebellion, insurrection against the "Lord," the "father," the primal ancestor and origin of the world); he stretches himself upon the contradiction "God" and "Devil"; he ejects from himself all his denial of himself, of his nature, naturalness, and actuality, in the form of an affirmation, as something existent, corporeal, real, as God, as the holiness of God, as God the Judge, as God the Hangman, as the beyond, as eternity, as torment without end, as hell, as the immeasurability of punishment and guilt.

In this psychical cruelty there resides a madness of the will which is absolutely unexampled: the *will* of man to find himself guilty and reprehensible to a degree that can never be atoned for; his *will* to think himself punished without any possibility of the punishment becoming equal to the guilt; his *will* to infect and poison the fundamental ground of things with the problem of punishment and guilt so as to cut off once and for all his own exit from this labyrinth of "fixed ideas"; his *will* to erect an ideal—that of the "holy God"—and in the face of it to feel the palpable certainty of his own absolute unworthiness. Oh this insane, pathetic beast—man! What ideas he has, what unnaturalness, what paroxysms of nonsense, what *bestiality of thought* erupts as soon as he is prevented just a little from being a *beast in deed*!

All this is interesting, to excess, but also of a gloomy, black, unnerving sadness, so that one must forcibly forbid oneself to gaze too long into these abysses. Here is *sickness*, beyond any doubt, the most terrible sickness that has ever raged in man; and whoever can still bear to hear (but today one no longer has ears for this!) how in this night of torment and absurdity there has resounded the cry of *love*, the cry of the most nostalgic rapture, of redemption through *love*, will turn away, seized by invincible horror.—There is so much in man that is hideous!—Too long, the earth has been a madhouse!—

Thus Spake Zarathustra

On the New Idol

Somewhere there are still peoples and herds, but not where we live, my brothers: here there are states. State? What is that? Well then, open your ears to me, for now I shall speak to you about the death of peoples.

State is the name of the coldest of all cold monsters. Coldly it tells lies too; and this lie crawls out of its mouth: "I, the state, am the people." That is a lie! It was creators who created peoples and hung a faith and a love over them: thus they served life.

It is annihilators who set traps for the many and call them "state": they hang a sword and a hundred appetites over them.

Where there is still a people, it does not understand the state and hates it as the evil eye and the sin against customs and rights.

This sign I give you: every people speaks its tongue of good and evil, which the neighbor does not understand. It has invented its own language of customs and rights. But the state tells lies in all the tongues of good and evil; and whatever it says it lies—and whatever it has it has stolen. Everything about it is false; it bites with stolen teeth, and bites easily. Even its entrails are false. Confusion of tongues of good and evil: this sign I give you as the sign of the state. Verily, this sign signifies the will to death. Verily, it beckons to the preachers of death.

All-too-many are born: for the superfluous the state was invented.

Behold, how it lures them, the all-too-many—and how it devours them, chews them, and ruminates!

"On earth there is nothing greater than I: the ordering finger of God am I"—thus roars the monster. And it is not only the long-eared and shortsighted who sink to their knees. Alas, to you too, you great souls, it whispers its dark lies. Alas, it detects the rich hearts which like to squander themselves. Indeed, it detects you too, you vanquishers of the old god. You have grown weary with fighting, and now your weariness still serves the new idol. With heroes and honorable men it would surround itself, the new idol! It likes to bask in the sunshine of good consciences—the cold monster!

It will give you everything if you will adore it, this new idol: thus it buys the splendor of your virtues and the look of your proud eyes. It would use you as bait for the all-too-many.

Indeed, a hellish artifice was invented there, a horse of death, clattering in the finery of divine honors. Indeed, a dying for many was invented there, which praises itself as life: verily, a great service to all preachers of death!

State I call it where all drink poison, the good and the wicked; state, where all lose themselves, the good and the wicked, state, where the slow suicide of all is called "life."

Behold the superfluous! They steal the works of the inventors and the treasures of the sages for themselves; "education" they call their theft—and everything turns to sickness and misfortune for them.

Behold the superfluous! They are always sick; they vomit their gall and call it a newspaper. They devour each other and cannot even digest themselves.

Behold the superfluous! They gather riches and become poorer with them. They want power and first the lever of power, much money—the impotent paupers!

Watch them clamber, these swift monkeys! They clamber over one another and thus drag one another into the mud and the depth. They all want to get to the throne: that is their madness—as if happiness sat on the throne. Often mud sits on the throne—and often also the throne on mud. Mad they all appear to me, clambering monkeys and overardent. Foul smells their idol, the cold monster: foul they smell to me altogether, these idolators.

My brothers, do you want to suffocate in the fumes of their snouts and appetites? Rather break the windows and leap to freedom.

Escape from the bad smell! Escape from the idolatry of the superfluous!

Escape from the bad smell! Escape from the steam of these human sacrifices!

The earth is free even now for great souls. There are still many empty seats for the lonesome and the twosome, fanned by the fragrance of silent seas.

A free life is still free for great souls. Verily, whoever possesses little is possessed that much less: praised be a little poverty!

Only where the state ends, there begins the human being who is not superfluous: there begins the song of necessity, the unique and inimitable tune.

Where the state *ends*—look there, my brothers! Do you not see it, the rainbow and the bridges of the overman?

Thus spoke Zarathustra.

Peter Kropotkin

Peter Kropotkin (1842–1921) was born in Moscow of noble parents, but he early rejected his title and rebuked those who called him "Prince." He became involved in revolutionary activity and was forced into exile in England, where he lived for over forty years pursuing scientific research and writing in support of anarchism. He returned to Russia after the revolution, but was not pleased that the revolution had led only to a new government rather than the abolition of government. As an anarchist he is best known for his insistence that anarchy could be supported by scientific research and that the path of evolution is leading to the abolition of government. He was, however, a revolutionary anarchist who wished to help speed this evolutionary process.

The essay "Law and Authority" from which the selection printed here is taken is an attack upon all laws and punishment.

Law and Authority

Section I

"When ignorance reigns in society and disorder in the minds of men, laws are multiplied, legislation is expected to do everything, and each fresh law being a fresh miscalculation, men are continually led to demand from it what can proceed only from themselves, from their own education and their own morality." It is no revolutionist who says this, not even a reformer. It is the jurist, Dalloy, author of the collection of French law knows as *Repertoire de la Législation.* And yet, though these lines were written by a man who was himself a maker and admirer of law, they perfectly represent the abnormal condition of our society.

In existing States a fresh law is looked upon as a remedy for evil. Instead of themselves altering what is bad, people begin by demanding a *law* to alter it. If the road between two villages is impassable, the peasant says:—"There should be a law about parish roads." If a park-keeper takes advantage of the want of spirit in those who follow him with servile observance and insults one of them, the insulted man says, "There should be a law to enjoin more politeness upon park-keepers." If there is stagnation in agriculture or commerce, the husbandman, cattle-breeder, or corn speculator argues, "It is protective legislation that we require." Down to the old clothesman there is not one who does not demand a law to protect his own little trade. If the employer lowers wages or increases the hours of labor, the politician in embryo exclaims, "We must have a law to put all that to rights." In short, a law everywhere and for everything! A law about fashions, a law about mad dogs, a law about virtue, a law to put a stop to all the vices and all the evils which result from human indolence and cowardice.

We are so perverted by an education which from infancy seeks to kill in us the spirit of revolt, and to develop that of submission to authority; we are so perverted by this existence under the ferrule of a law, which regulates every event in life—our birth, our education, our development, our love, our friendship—that, if this state of things continues, we shall lose all initiative, all habit of thinking for ourselves. Our society seems no longer able to understand that it is possible to exist otherwise than under the reign of law, elaborated by a representative government and administered by a handful of rulers. And even when it has gone so far as to emancipate itself from the thralldom, its first care has been to reconstitute it immediately. "The Year I of Liberty" has never lasted more than a day, for after proclaiming it men put themselves the very next morning under the yoke of law and authority.

Indeed, for some thousands of years, those who govern us have done nothing but ring the changes upon "Respect for law, obedience to authority." This is the moral atmosphere in which parents bring up their children, and school only

Reprinted from *Kropotkin's Revolutionary Pamphlets,* ed. Roger N. Baldwin. Vanguard Press, New York, 1927. Originally published London, 1886.

serves to confirm the impression. Cleverly assorted scraps of spurious science are inculcated upon the children to prove necessity of law; obedience to the law is made a religion; moral goodness and the law of the masters are fused into one and the same divinity. The historical hero of the schoolroom is the man who obeys the law, and defends it against rebels.

Later when we enter upon public life, society and literature, impressing us day by day and hour by hour as the water drop hollows the stone, continue to inculate the same prejudice. Books of history, of political science, of social economy, are stuffed with this respect for law. Even the physical sciences have been pressed into the service by introducing artificial modes of expression, borrowed from theology and arbitrary power, into knowledge which is purely the result of observation. Thus our intelligence is successfully befogged, and always to maintain our respect for law. The same work is done by newspapers. They have not an article which does not preach respect for law, even where the third page proves every day the imbecility of that law, and shows how it is dragged through every variety of mud and filth by those charged with its administration. Servility before the law has become a virtue, and I doubt if there was ever even a revolutionist who did not begin in his youth as the defender of law against what are generally called "abuses," although these last are inevitable consequences of the law itself.

Art pipes in unison with would-be science. The hero of the sculptor, the painter, the musician, shields Law beneath his buckler, and with flashing eyes and distended nostrils stands ever ready to strike down the man who would lay hands upon her. Temples are raised to her; revolutionists themselves hesitate to touch the high priests consecrated to her service, and when revolution is about to sweep away some ancient institution, it is still by law that it endeavors to sanctify the deed.

The confused mass of rules of conduct called law, which has been bequeathed to us by slavery, serfdom, feudalism, and royalty, has taken the place of those stone monsters, before whom human victims used to be immolated, and whom slavish savages dared not even touch lest they should be slain by the thunderbolts of heaven.

This new worship has been established with especial success since the rise to supreme power of the middle class—since the great French Revolution. Under the ancient régime, men spoke little of laws; unless, indeed, it were, with Montesquieu, Rousseau and Voltaire, to oppose them to royal caprice. Obedience to the good pleasure of the king and his lackeys was compulsory on pain of hanging or imprisonment. But during and after the revolutions, when the lawyers rose to power, they did their best to strengthen the principle upon which their ascendancy depended. The middle class at once accepted it as a dyke to dam up the popular torrent. The priestly crew hastened to sanctify it, to save their bark from foundering amid the breakers. Finally the people received it as an improvement upon the arbitrary authority and violence of the past.

To understand this, we must transport ourselves in imagination into the eighteenth century. Our hearts must have ached at the story of the atrocities committed by the all-powerful nobles of that time upon the men and women of the people before we can understand what must have been the magic influence upon the peasant's mind of the words, "Equality before the law, obedience to the law without distinction of birth or fortune." He who until then had been treated more cruelly than a beast, he who had never had any rights, he who had never obtained justice against the most revolting actions on the part of a noble, unless in revenge he killed him and was hanged—he saw himself recognized by this maxim, at least in theory, at least with regard to his personal rights, as the equal of his lord. Whatever this law might be, it promised to affect lord and peasant alike; it proclaimed the equality of rich and poor before the judge. The promise was a lie, and today we know it; but at that period it was an advance, a homage to justice, as hypocrisy is a homage rendered to truth. This is the reason that when the saviors of the menaced middle class (the Robespierres and the Dantons) took their stand upon the writings of the Rousseaus and the Voltaires, and proclaimed "respect for law, the same for every man," the people accepted the compromise; for their revolutionary impetus had already spent its force in the contest with a foe whose ranks drew closer day by day; they bowed their neck beneath the yoke of law to save themselves from the arbitrary power of their lords.

The middle class has ever since continued to make the most of this maxim, which with another principle, that of representative government, sums up the whole philosophy of the bourgeois age, the nineteenth century. It has preached this doctrine in its schools, it has propagated it in its writings, it has moulded its art and science to the same purpose, it has thrust its beliefs into every hole and corner—like a pious Englishwoman, who slips tracts under the door—and it has done all this so successfully that today we behold the issue in the detestable fact that men who long for freedom begin the attempt to obtain it by entreating their masters to be kind enough to protect them by modifying the laws which these masters themselves have created!

But times and tempers are changed. Rebels are everywhere to be found who no longer wish to obey the law without knowing whence it comes, what are its uses, and whither arises the obligation to submit to it, and the reverence with which it is encompassed. The rebels of our day are criticizing the very foundations of society which have hitherto been held sacred, and first and foremost amongst them that fetish, law.

The critics analyze the sources of law, and find there either a god, product of the terrors of the savage, and stupid, paltry and malicious as the priests who vouch for its supernatural origin, or else, bloodshed, conquest by fire and sword. They study the characteristics of law, and instead of perpetual growth corresponding to that of the human race, they find its distinctive trait to be immobility, a tendency to crystallize what should be modified and developed day by day. They ask how law has been maintained, and in its service they see the atrocities of Byzantinism, the cruelties of the Inquisition, the tortures of the middle ages, living flesh torn by the lash of the executioner, chains, clubs, axes, the gloomy dungeons of prisons, agony, curses and tears. In our own days they see, as before, the axe, the cord, the rifle, the prison; on the one hand, the brutalized prisoner, reduced to the condition of a caged beast by the debasement of his whole moral being, and on the other, the judge, stripped of every feeling which does honor to human nature, living like a visionary in a world of legal fictions, revelling in the infliction of imprisonment and death, without even suspecting, in the cold malignity of his madness, the abyss of degradation into which he has himself fallen before the eyes of those whom he condemns.

They see a race of law-makers legislating without knowing what their laws are about; today voting a law on the sanitation of towns, without the faintest notion of hygiene, tomorrow making regulations for the armament of troops, without so much as understanding a gun; making laws about teaching and education without ever having given a lesson of any sort, or even an honest education to their own children; legislating at random in all directions, but never forgetting the penalties to be meted out to ragamuffins, the prison and the galleys, which are to be the portion of men a thousand times less immoral than these legislators themselves.

Finally, they see the jailer on the way to lose all human feeling, the detective trained as a blood-hound, the police spy despising himself; "informing," metamorphosed into a virtue; corruption, erected into a system; all the vices, all the evil qualities of mankind countenanced and cultivated to insure the triumph of law.

All this we see, and, therefore, instead of inanely repeating the old formula, "Respect the law," we say, "Despise law and all its attributes!" In place of the cowardly phrase, "Obey the law," our cry is "Revolt against all laws!"

Only compare the misdeeds accomplished in the name of each law with the good it has been able to effect, and weigh carefully both good and evil, and you will see if we are right.

Section IV

The millions of laws which exist for the regulation of humanity appear upon investigation to be divided into three principal categories: protection of property, protection of persons, protection of government. And by analyzing each of these three categories, we arrive at the same logical and necessary conclusion: *the uselessness and hurtfulness of law.*

Socialists know what is meant by protection of property. Laws on property are not made to guarantee either to the individual or to society the enjoyment of the produce of their own labor. On the contrary, they are made to rob the producer of a part of what he has created, and to secure to certain other people that portion of the produce which they have stolen either from the producer or from society as a whole. When, for example, the law establishes Mr. So-and-So's right to a house, it is not establishing his right to a cottage he has built for himself, or to a house he has erected with the help of some of his friends. In that case no one would have disputed his right. On the contrary, the law is establishing his right to a house which is *not* the product of his labor; first of all because he has had it built for him by others to whom he has not paid the full value of their work, and next because that house represents a social value which he could not have produced for himself. The law is establishing his right to what belongs to everybody in general and to nobody in particular. The same house built in the midst of Siberia would not have the value it possesses in a large town, and, as we know, that value arises from the labor of something like fifty generations of men who have built the town, beautified it, supplied it with water and gas, fine promenades, colleges, theatres, shops, railways and roads leading in all directions. Thus, by recognizing the right of Mr. So-and-So to a particular house in Paris, London or Rouen, the law is unjustly appropriating to him a certain portion of the produce of the labor of mankind in general. And it is precisely because this appropriation and all other forms of property bearing the same character are a crying injustice, that a whole arsenal of laws and a whole army of soldiers, policemen and judges are needed to maintain it against the good sense and just feeling inherent in humanity.

Half our laws,—the civil code in each country,—serves no other purpose than to maintain this appropriation, this monopoly for the benefit of certain individuals against the whole of mankind. Three-fourths of the causes decided by the tribunals are nothing but quarrels between monopolists—two robbers disputing over their booty. And a great many of our criminal laws have the same object in view, their end being to keep the workman in a subordinate position towards his employer, and thus afford security for exploitation.

As for guaranteeing the product of his labor to the producer, there are no laws which even attempt such a thing. It is so simple and natural, so much a part of the manners and customs of mankind, that law has not given it so much as a thought. Open brigandage, sword in hand, is no feature of our age. Neither does one workman ever come and dispute the produce of his labor with another. If they have a misunderstanding they settle it by calling in a third person, without having recourse to law. The only person who exacts from another what that other has produced, is the proprietor, who comes in and deducts the lion's share. As for humanity in general, it everywhere respects the right of each to what he has created, without the interposition of any special laws.

As all the laws about property which make up thick volumes of codes and are the delight of our lawyers have no other object than to protect the unjust appropriation of human labor by certain monopolists, there is no reason for their existence, and, on the day of the revolution, social revolutionists are thoroughly determined to put an end to them. Indeed, a bonfire might be made with perfect justice of all laws bearing upon the so-called rights of property, all title-deeds, all registers, in a word, of all that is in any way connected with an institution which will soon be looked upon as a blot in the history of humanity, as humiliating as the slavery and serfdom of past ages.

The remarks just made upon laws concerning property are quite as applicable to the second category of laws; those for the maintenance of government, i.e., constitutional law.

It again is a complete arsenal of laws, decrees, ordinances, orders in council, and what not, all serving to protect the diverse forms of representative government, delegated or usurped, beneath which humanity is writhing. We know very well—anarchists have often enough pointed out in their perpetual criticism of the various forms of government—that the mission of all governments, monarchical, constitutional, or republican, is to protect and maintain by force the privileges of the classes in possession, the aristocracy, clergy and traders. A good third of our laws—and each country possesses some tens of thousands of them—the fundamental laws on taxes, excise duties, the organization of ministerial departments and their offices, of the army, the police, the church, etc., have no other end than to maintain, patch up, and develop the administrative machine. And this machine in its turn serves almost entirely to protect the privileges of the possessing classes. Analyze all these laws, observe them in action day by day, and you will discover that not one is worth preserving.

About such laws there can be no two opinions. Not only anarchists, but more or less revolutionary radicals also, are agreed that the only use to be made of laws concerning the organization of government is to fling them into the fire.

The third category of law still remains to be considered; that relating to the protection of the person and the detection and prevention of "crime." This is the most important because most prejudices attach to it; because, if law enjoys a certain amount of consideration, it is in consequence of the belief that this species of law is absolutely indispensable to the maintenance of security in our societies. These are laws developed from the nucleus of customs useful to human communities, which have been turned to account by rulers to sanctify their own domination. The authorithy of the chiefs of tribes, of rich families in towns, and of the king, depended upon their judicial functions, and even down to the present day, whenever the necessity of government is spoken of, its function as supreme judge is the thing implied. "Without a government men would tear one another to pieces," argues the village orator. "The ultimate end of all government is to secure twelve honest jurymen to every accused person," said Burke.

Well, in spite of all the prejudices existing on this subject, it is quite time that anarchists should boldly declare this category of laws as useless and injurious as the preceding ones.

First of all, as to so-called crimes—assaults upon persons—it is well known that two-thirds, and often as many as three-fourths, of such "crimes" are instigated by the desire to obtain possession of someone's wealth. This immense class of so-called crimes and misdemeanors will disappear on the day on which private property ceases to exist. "But," it will be said, "there will always be brutes who will attempt the lives of their fellow citizens, who will lay their hands to a knife in every quarrel, and revenge the slightest offense by murder, if there are no laws to restrain and punishments to withhold them." This refrain is repeated every time the right of society *to punish* is called in question.

Yet there is one fact concerning this head which at the present time is thoroughly established; the severity of punishment does not diminish the amount of crime. Hang, and, if you like, quarter murderers, and the number of murders will not decrease by one. On the other hand, abolish the penalty of death, and there will not be one murder more; there will be fewer. Statistics prove it. But if the harvest is good, and bread cheap, and the weather fine, the number of murders immediately decreases. This again is proved by statistics. The amount of crime always augments and diminishes in proportion to the price of provisions and the state of the weather. Not that all murderers are actuated by hunger. That is not the case. But when the harvest is good, and provisions are at an obtainable price, and when the sun shines, men, lighter-hearted and less miserable than usual, do not give way to gloomy passions, do not from trivial motives plunge a knife into the bosom of a fellow creature.

Moreover, it is also a well known fact that the fear of punishment has never stopped a single murderer. He who kills his neighbor from revenge or misery does not reason much about consequences; and there have been few murderers who were not firmly convinced that they should escape prosecution.

Without speaking of a society in which a man will receive a better education, in which the development of all his faculties, and the possibility of exercising them, will procure him so many enjoyments that he will not seek to poison them by remorse—even in our society, even with those said products of misery whom we see today in the public houses of great cities—on the day when no punishment is inflicted upon murderers, the number of murders will not be augmented by a single case. And it is extremely probable that it will be, on the contrary, diminished by all those cases which are due at present to habitual criminals, who have been brutalized in prisons.

We are continually being told of the benefits conferred by law, and the beneficial effect of penalties, but have the speakers ever attempted to strike a balance between the benefits attributed to laws and penalties, and the degrading effect of these penalties upon humanity? Only calculate all the evil passions awakened in mankind by the atrocious punishments formerly inflicted in our streets! Man is the cruelest animal upon earth. And who has pampered and developed the cruel instincts unknown, even among monkeys, if it is not the king, the judge, and the priests, armed with law, who caused flesh to be torn off in strips, boiling pitch to be poured into wounds, limbs to be dislocated, bones to be crushed, men to be sawn asunder to maintain their authority? Only estimate the torrent of depravity let loose in human society by the "informing" which is countenanced by judges, and paid in hard cash by governments, under pretext of assisting in the discovery of "crime." Only go into the jails and study what man becomes when he is deprived of freedom and shut up with other depraved beings, steeped in the vice and corruption which oozes from the very walls of our existing prisons. Only remember that the more these prisons are reformed, the more detestable they become. Our model modern penitentiaries are a hundred-fold more abominable than the dungeons of the middle ages. Finally, consider what corruption, what depravity of mind is kept up among men by the idea of obedience, the very essence of law; of chastisement; of authority having the right to punish, to judge irrespective of our conscience and the esteem of our friends; of the necessity for executioners, jailers, and informers—in a word, by all the attributes of law and authority. Consider all this, and you will assuredly agree with us in saying that a law inflicting penalties is an abomination which should cease to exist.

Peoples without political organization, and therefore less depraved than ourselves, have perfectly understood that the man who is called "criminal" is simply unfortunate; that the remedy is not to flog him, to chain him up, or to kill him on the scaffold or in prison, but to help him by the most brotherly care, by treatment based on equality, by the usages of life among honest men. In the next revolution we hope that this cry will go forth:

"Burn the guillotines; demolish the prisons; drive away the judges, policemen and informers—the impurest race upon the face of the earth; treat as a brother the man who has been led by passion to do ill to his fellow; above all, take from the ignoble products of middle-class idleness the possibility of displaying their vices in attractive colors; and be sure that but few crimes will mar our society."

The main supports of crime are idleness, law and authority; laws about property, laws about government, laws about penalties and misdemeanors; and authority, which takes upon itself to manufacture these laws and to apply them.

No more laws! No more judges! Liberty, equality. and practical human sympathy are the only effectual barriers we can oppose to the anti-social instincts of certain among us.

Part II
Contemporary
Political
Thought

Section I
Theoretical
Concerns

Brian Barry

> Brian Barry is a Fellow of Nuffield College, Oxford. As Barry
> points out in the essay "The Public Interest," printed below, in
> the actual give and take of political debate over concrete issues
> one finds the public interest appealed to much more often than
> justice, equality, freedom, or fairness. Many political thinkers
> would, of course, argue that this is true because the public
> interest is a vacuous concept which allows politicians and bureau-
> crats to avoid giving any concrete defense of their policies. Barry
> argues, on the contrary, that the public interest is not a vacuous
> term, but that it points to considerations particularly relevant to
> problems faced in most Western industrial nations, and thus is a
> popular consideration in political debate.

The Public Interest

I

A Tribunal of Enquiry claims that the public interest requires journalists to
disclose their sources of information; the Restrictive Practices Court invalidates
an agreement among certain manufacturers as contrary to the Restrictive Practices Act and therefore contrary to the public interest; the National Incomes
Commission says that a proposed rise for the workers in an industry would be
against the public interest. These examples could be multiplied endlessly. Each
day's newspaper brings fresh ones. In arguments about concrete issues (as
opposed to general rhetoric in favour of political parties or entire societies) 'the
public interest' is more popular than 'justice', 'fairness', 'equality', or 'freedom'.

Why is this? Roughly, there are two possible answers. One is that 'the public
interest' points to a fairly clearly definable range of considerations in support of
a policy and if it is a very popular concept at the moment all this shows is that
(for better or worse) these considerations are highly valued by many people at
the moment. This is my own view. The other answer is that politicians and civil
servants find it a handy smoke-screen to cover their decisions, which are actually
designed to conciliate the most effectively deployed interest.

These sceptics often buttress their arguments by pointing out that most
theoretical writing about 'the public interest' is vague and confused. This theme
is copiously illustrated by Frank J. Sorauf in his article 'The Public Interest
Reconsidered', *Journal of Politics*, XIX (Nov. 1957) and by Glendon Schubert in
his book *The Public Interest: Critique of a Concept*. But it is a familiar idea that

From *Proceedings of the Aristotelian Society*, Supp. Vol. 38, 1964. Copyright 1964 The Aristotelian Society. Reprinted by Courtesy of the Editor of the
Aristotelian Society.

people who are perfectly well able to *use* a concept may nevertheless talk rubbish *about* it, so even if many of the writings about the concept are confused it does not follow that the concept itself is. A more cogent line of argument is to construct a definition of 'the public interest' and then show that, so defined, nothing (or not much) satisfies it. From this, it can be deduced that most uses of the phrase in political discussion must be either fraudulent or vacuous. Like Sorauf and Schubert, the best known expositors of the view are Americans—one may mention A. F. Bentley's *The Process of Government* and D. B. Truman's *The Governmental Process.* But the most succinct and recent treatment is to be found in Chapters Three and Four of *The Nature of Politics* by J. D. B. Miller, and it is to a criticism of these chapters that I now turn.

II

Miller defines 'interest' as follows: 'we can say that an interest exists when we see some body of persons showing a *common concern* about particular matters' (p. 39). On the basis of this he later puts forward two propositions. First, one is not 'justified in going beyond people's own inclinations in order to tell them that their true interest lies somewhere else' (p. 41), It 'seems absurd' to suppose that an interest can exist if those whose interest it is are not aware of it (p. 40). And secondly, a 'common concern ... must be present if we are to say that a general interest exists'. 'A common concern will sometimes be found in the society at large, and sometimes not. More often it will not be there' (p. 54).

Apart from the last point, which is a statement of fact and one I shall not query here, these propositions follow analytically from the original definition of 'interest', though Miller does not see this clearly. Everything hinges on that slippery word 'concern' which plays such a crucial part in the definition. One can be concerned *at* (a state of affairs) or concerned *about* (an issue) or concerned *with* (an organization or activity) or, finally, concerned *by* (an action, policy, rule, *etc.*). The noun, as in 'so-and-so's concerns' can correspond to any of the first three constructions, and it seems plain enough that in these three kinds of use nobody can be concerned without knowing it. In the fourth use, where 'concerned by' is roughly equivalent to 'affected by', this is not so: someone might well be affected by an economic policy of which he had never heard. But the noun 'concern' does not have a sense corresponding to this nor does Miller stretch it to cover it. Naturally, if 'interest' is understood in terms of actual striving, no sense can be given to the idea of someone's having an interest but not pursuing it. Similarly, if 'interest' is defined as 'concern' it hardly needs several pages of huffing and puffing against rival conceptions (pp. 52-54) to establish that 'common or general interest' must be equivalent to 'common or general concern'.

Since, then, Miller's conclusions follow analytically from his definition of 'interest', with the addition of a factual premise which I am not here disputing. I must, if I am to reject his conclusions, reject his definition. Miller can, of course, define 'interest' any way he likes; but if he chooses a completely idiosyncratic definition he can hardly claim to have proved much if it turns out that most of the things that people have traditionally said about interests then become false or meaningless. He clearly believes himself to be taking part in a debate with previous writers and it is because of this that he is open to criticism.

Let us start from the other end. Let us begin by considering the things we normally want to say about interests, the distinctions which we normally want to draw by using the concept, and then see whether it is not possible to construct a definition of 'interest' which will make sense of these ordinary speech habits.

The first part of Miller's definition, which makes interests *shared* concerns, conflicts with our normal wish to draw a distinction between someone's private or personal interests on the one hand and the interests which he shares with various groups of people on the other hand. Simply to rule out the former by fiat as Miller does seems to have nothing to recommend it. It might perhaps be argued in defence of the limitation that only interests shared among a number of people are politically important, but it can surely be validly replied that this is neither a necessary nor a sufficient condition.

The second part of the definition equates a man's interests with his concerns. This conflict with a great many things we ordinarily want to say about interests. We want to say that people can mistake their interests, and that while some conflicts are conflicts of interests, others (e.g. 'conflicts of principle') are not. We distinguish between 'disinterested' concern and 'interested' concern in a particular matter; we find it convenient to distinguish 'interest groups' (e.g. The National Farmers' Union) from 'cause' or 'promotional' groups (e.g., The Abortion Law Reform Association). 'They co-operate because they have a common interest' is ordinarily taken as a genuine explanation, rather than a pseudo-explanation of the *'vis dormitiva'* type, as it would be if co-operation were identified with (or regarded as a direct manifestation of) a common interest. We allow that one can recognize something as being in one's interest without pursuing it. Finally, we do not regard it as a contradiction in terms to say, 'I realize that so-and-so would be in my interests but nevertheless I am against it'. These points are all inconsistent with Miller's definition, and in addition the last of them is inconsistent with any attempt such as that of S. I. Benn to define a man's interests as 'something he thought he could *reasonably* ask for' (' "Interest" in Politics', *Proceedings of the Aristotelian Society*, 1960, p. 127).

Can a definition be found which will make sense of all these uses of 'interest'? I suggest this: a policy, a law or institution is in someone's interest if it increases his opportunities to get what he wants—whatever that may be. Notice that this is a definition of '*in* so-and-so's interests'. Other uses of 'interest' all seem to me either irrelevant or reducible to sentences with this construction. Thus, the only unforced sense that one can give to 'What are your interests?', which Benn imagines being put seriously to a farmer, is that it is an enquiry into his favorite intellectual preoccupations or perhaps into his leisure activities—applications of 'interest' whose irrelevance Benn himself affirms. Otherwise, it has no normal application, though a 'plain man' with an analytical turn of mind (such as John Locke) might reply:

> Civil interest I call life, liberty, health and indolency of body; and the possession of outward things, such as money, lands, houses, furniture and the like. (*Letter Concerning Toleration.*)

This might be regarded as a specification of the kinds of ways in which a policy, law or institution must impinge on someone before it can be said to be 'in his interests'. Unpacked into more logically transparent (if more long-winded) terms it might read: 'A policy, law or institution may be said to be in someone's interests if it satisfies the following conditions. . . .'

The main point about my proposed definition, however, is that it is always a *policy* that is said to be 'in so-and-so's interest'--not the actual manner in which he is impinged upon. (From now on I shall use 'policy' to cover 'policy, law or institution'.) There are straightforward criteria specifying the way in which someone has to be affected by a policy before that policy can be truly described as being 'in his interests'; but whether or not a given policy will bring about such results may quite often be an open question.

It is this feature of 'interest' which explains how people can 'mistake their interests'—item number one on the list of 'things we want to say about interests'. The stock argument against this possibility is that if you assert it you must commit yourself to the view that 'some people know what's good for other people better than they do themselves'. But this can now be seen to rest on a gross equivocation. The presumably illiberal, and therefore damaging, view to be saddled with would be the view that policies which impinge on people in ways which they dislike may nevertheless be said to be 'in their interests'. But this is not entailed by the statement that people may 'mistake their interests'. All that one has to believe is that they may think a policy will impinge upon them in a way which will increase their opportunities to get what they want when in fact it will do the opposite. Whether his opportunities are increased or narrowed by being unemployed is something each man may judge for himself; but it is surely only sensible to recognize that most people's opinions about the most effective economic policies for securing given ends are likely to be worthless. In his Fireside Chat on June 28, 1934, President Roosevelt said:

> The simplest way for each of you to judge recovery lies in the plain facts of your own individual situation. Are you better off than you were last year? Are your debts less burdensome? Is your bank account more secure? Are your working conditions better? Is your faith in your own individual future more firmly grounded?

It is quite consistent to say that people can 'judge recovery for themselves' without respecting their opinions about the efficacy of deficit financing.

The other 'things we normally want to say' also fit the proposed definition. People may want policies other than those calculated to increase their opportunities--hence the possibility of 'disinterested action' and 'promotional groups'. Similarly, a man may definitely not want a policy which will increase his opportunities (perhaps because he thinks that the policy is unfair and that others should get the increase instead). Hence the possibility of someone's not wanting something that he acknowledges would be in his interests. Finally, nothing is more common than for someone to agree that a policy would increase his opportunities if adopted, and to want it to be adopted, but at the same time to say that the addition of his own efforts to the campaign to secure its adoption would have such a small probability of making the decisive difference between success and failure for the campaign that it is simply not worth making the effort; and of course if everyone is in the habit of reasoning like this a policy which is in the interests of a great many people, but not greatly in the interest of any of them, may well fail to receive any organized support at all.

No doubt there is room for amplification of my definition of what it is for a policy to be in someone's interest. In particular the phrase 'opportunities to get what he wants' needs closer analysis, and account should be taken of the expression 'so-and-so's *best* interests' which tends to be used where it is thought that the person in question would make such an unwise use of increased opportunities that he would be better off without them (e.g., a heavy drinker winning a first dividend on the football pools). However, I doubt whether refinements in the definition of 'interest' would alter the correctness or incorrectness of what I have to say about 'the public interest', so I turn now to that expression.

III

If 'interest' is defined in such a way that 'this policy is in A's interest' is equivalent to 'A is trying to get this policy adopted' it is decisive evidence against there being in any but a few cases a 'public interest' that there is conflict over the adoption of nearly all policies in a state. But on the definition of 'interest' I have proposed this would no longer be so. A policy might be truly describable as 'in the public interest' even though some people opposed it. This could come about in a way already mentioned: those who oppose the policy might have 'mistaken their interests'. In other words, they may think the policy in question is not in their interests when it really is. Most opposition in the U.S.A. to unbalanced budgets can be explained in this way, for example. Disagreements about defence and disarmament policy are also largely disagreements about the most effective means to fairly obvious common goals such as national survival and (if possible) independence.

There are two other possibilities. One is that the group opposing the measure is doing so in order to further a different measure which is outside the range of relevant comparisons. The other possibility is that the opposing group have a special interest in the matter which counteracts their interest as members of the public. I do not expect these two descriptions to be clear; I shall devote the remainder of the paper to trying to make them so, taking up the former in this section and IV, and the latter in V.

Comparison enters into any evaluation in terms of interests. To say that a policy would be in someone's interests is implicitly to compare it with some other policy—often simply the continuance of the *status quo*. So if you say that a number of people have a common interest in something you must have in mind some alternative to it in a certain industry. If each kind of employee had a separate trade union one might expect as many incompatible claims as there were unions, each seeking to appropriate most of the increase for its own members. If for example there were a hundred unions with a thousand members apiece each employee might have a thousand pounds (a thousandth of the total) claimed on his behalf, and the total claims would add up to a hundred million pounds. At the other extreme if there were only one union, there would be no point in its putting in a claim totalling more than a million pounds (we assume for convenience that the union accepts the unalterability of this amount) and if it made an equal claim on behalf of each of its members this would come to only ten pounds a head. Intermediate numbers of unions would produce intermediate results.

Rousseau's distinction between the 'will of all' and the 'general will' now fits in neatly. The 'will of all' is simply shorthand for 'the policy most in A's interests, taking A in isolation; the policy most in B's interests, taking B in isolation; and so on'. (These will of course normally be different policies for A, B and the rest.) The 'general will' is a *single* policy which is equally in the interests of all the members of the group. It will usually be different from any of the policies mentioned before, and less beneficial to anyone than the policy most beneficial to himself alone.

We can throw light on some of the other things Rousseau says in the one-page chapter II.iii. of the *Social Contract* by returning to the trade union example. Suppose now that the leaders of the hundred trade unions are told that the money will be forthcoming only if a majority of them can reach agreement on a way of dividing it up. A possible method would be for each leader to write down his preferred solution on a slip of paper, and for these to be compared, the process continuing until a requisite number of papers have the same proposal written on them. If each started by writing down his maximum demand there would be as many proposals as leaders—the total result would be the 'will of all'. This is obviously a dead end, and if no discussion is allowed among the leaders, there is a good chance that they would all propose, as a second best, an equal division of the money. (There is some experimental evidence for this, presented in Chapter 3 of Thomas Schelling's *The Strategy of Conflict.*) Such a solution would be in accordance with the 'general will' and represents a sort of highest common factor of agreement. As Rousseau puts it, it arises when the pluses and minuses of the conflicting first choices are cancelled out.

If instead of these arrangements communication is allowed, and even more if the groups are fewer and some leaders control large block votes, it becomes less likely that an equal solution will be everyone's second choice. It will be possible for some leaders to agree together to support a proposal which is less favourable to any of their members than each leader's first choice was to his own members, but still more favourable than any solution equally beneficial to all the participants. Thus, as Rousseau says, a 'less general will' prevails.

In II.iii. Rousseau suggests that this should be prevented by not allowing groups to form or, if they do form, by seeing that they are many and small. In the less optimistic mood of IV.i., when he returns to the question, he places less faith in mechanical methods and more in widespread civic virtue. He now says that the real answer is for everyone to ask himself 'the right question', i.e., 'What measure will benefit me in common with everyone else, rather than me at the expense of everyone else?' (I have never seen attention drawn to the fact that this famous doctrine is something of an afterthought whose first and only occurrence in the *Social Contract* is towards the end.) However, this is a difference only about the most effective means of getting a majority to vote for what is in the common interest of all. The essential point remains the same: that only where all are equally affected by the policy adopted can an equitable solution be expected.

> The undertakings which bind us to the social body are obligatory only because they are mutual; and their nature is such that in fulfilling them we cannot work for others without working for ourselves. . . . What makes the will general is less the number of voters than the common interest uniting them; for, under this system, each necessarily submits to the conditions he imposes on others: and this admirable agreement between interest and

justice gives to the common deliberations an equitable character which at once vanishes when any particular question is discussed, in the absence of a common interest to unite and identify the ruling of the judge with that of the party.

(II.iv. Cole's translation.)

Provided this condition is met, nobody will deliberately vote for a burdensome law because it will be burdensome to him too: this is why no *specific* limitations on 'the general will' are needed. Disagreements can then be due only to conflicts of opinion—not to conflicts of interest. Among the various policies which would affect everyone in the same way, each person has to decide which would benefit himself most—and, since everyone else is similarly circumstanced, he is automatically deciding at the same time which would benefit everyone else most. Thus, to go back to our example of a law prohibiting assault: disagreement will arise, if at all, because some think they (in common with everyone else) would make a net gain of opportunities from the absence of any law against assault, while others think the opposite. This is, in principle, a dispute with a right and a wrong answer; and everyone benefits from the right answer's being reached rather than the wrong one. Rousseau claims that a majority is more likely to be right than any given voter, so that someone in the minority will in fact gain from the majority's decision carrying the day. This has often been regarded as sophistical or paradoxical, but it is quite reasonable once one allows Rousseau his definition of the situation as one in which everyone is co-operating to find a mutually beneficial answer, for so long as everyone is taken as having an equal, better than even chance of giving the right answer, the majority view will (in the long run) be right more often than that of any given voter. (Of course, the same thing applies in reverse: if each one has on average a *less* than even chance of being right, the majority will be *wrong* more often than any given voter.) The formula for this was discovered by Condorcet and has been presented by Duncan Black on page 164 of his *Theory of Committees and Elections*. To illustrate its power, here is an example: if we have a voting body of a thousand, each member of which is right on average fifty-one percent of the time, what is the probability in any particular instance that a fifty-one percent majority has the right answer? The answer, rather surprisingly perhaps, is: better than two to one (69%). Moreover, if the required majority is kept at fifty-one percent and the number of voters raised to ten thousand, or if the number of voters stays at one thousand and the required majority is raised to sixty percent, the probability that the majority (5,100 to 4,900 in the first case or 600 to 400 in the second) has the right answer rises virtually to unity (99.97%). None of this, of course, shows that 'Rousseau was right' but it does suggest that he was no simpleton.

To sum up, Rousseau calls for the citizen's deliberations to comprise two elements: (a) the decision to forgo (either as unattainable or as immoral) policies which would be in one's own personal interest alone, or in the common interest of a group smaller than the whole, and (b) the attempt to calculate which, of the various lines of policy that would affect oneself equally with all others, is best for him (and, since others are like him, for others). This kind of two-step deliberation is obviously reminiscent of the method recommended in Mr. Hare's *Freedom and Reason*, with the crucial difference that whereas Mr. Hare will settle for a willingness to be affected by the policy in certain hypothetical circumstances, Rousseau insists that my being affected by the policy must actually be in prospect. There is no need to construct a special planet to test my good faith—my bluff is called every time. By the same token, the theory I have attributed to Rousseau requires far more stringent conditions to be met before something can be said to be in the common interest of all than the vague requirement of 'equal consideration' put forward by Benn and Peters in their *Social Principles and the Democratic State.*

V

Even if Rousseau can be shown to be consistent it does not follow that the doctrine of the *Social Contract* has wide application. Rousseau himself sets out a number of requirements that have to be met before it applies at all: political virtue (reinforced by a civil religion), smallness of state, and rough economic equality among the citizens. And even then, as he points out plainly, it is only a few questions which allow solutions that touch all in the same way. If only some are affected by a matter the 'general will' cannot operate. It is no longer a case of each man legislating for himself *along with others*, but merely one of some men legislating *for* others. It is fairly obvious that Rousseau's requirements are not met in a great modern nation state—a conclusion that would not have worried him. But since I am trying to show that 'the public interest' is applicable in just such a state it does have to worry me. It is here that I must introduce my remaining explanation of the way in which something can be 'in the public interest' while still arousing opposition from some.

Think again of the examples with which I began this paper. The thing that is claimed to be 'in the public interest' is not *prima facie* in the interests of the journalist whose sources may dry up, the workers whose rise is condemned or the businessmen whose restrictive practices are outlawed. But do first appearances mislead? After all, the journalist along with the rest gains from national security, and workers or industrialists gain along with the rest from lower prices. To avoid a flat contradiction we need more refined tools; and they exist in ordinary speech. Instead of simply saying that some measure is 'in his interests' a man will often specify some role or capacity in which it is favourable to him: 'as a parent', as a businessman', 'as a house owner' and so on. One of the capacities in which everyone finds himself is that of 'a member of the public'. Some issues allow a policy to be produced which will affect everyone in his capacity as a 'member of the public' and nobody in any other capacity. This is the pure 'Rousseau' situation. Then there are other issues which lack this simplicity but still do not raise any problems because those who are affected in a capacity other than that of 'member of the public' are either affected in that capacity in the same direction as they are in their other capacity of 'member of the public' or at least are not affected so strongly in the contrary direction as to tip the overall balance of their interest (what I shall call their 'net interest') that way. Although this is not quite what I have called the 'Rousseau' situation, the 'Rousseau' formula still works. Indeed, Rousseau sometimes seems explicitly to accept this kind of situation as satisfactory, as when he says (III.xv.) that in a well-ordered state 'the aggregate of the common happiness furnishes a greater proportion of that of each individual'.

Finally, we have the familiar case where for some people a special interest outweighs their share in the public interest. The journalist may think, for example, that compulsory disclosure of sources would indeed be in the public interest but at the same time conclude that his own special interest as a journalist in getting information from people who want to stay anonymous is more important to him than the marginal gain in security that is at stake. In such cases as this Rousseau's formula will not work, for although everyone still has a common interest in the adoption of a certain policy *qua* 'member of the public', some have a net interest in opposing it.

To adopt the policy which is 'in the public interest' in such a case is still different from deliberately passing over an available policy which would treat everyone equally, for in the present case there *is* no such policy available. Even so, it involves favouring some at the expense of others, which makes it reasonable to ask whether it is justifiable to recommend it. Various lines of justification are possible. Bentham seems to have assumed that in most matters there was a public interest on one side (e.g., in cheap and speedy legal procedures) and on the other side the 'sinister' interest of those who stood to gain balance from abuses (e.g., 'Judge & Co.') and to have believed (what is surely not unreasonable) that a utilitarian calculation would generally give the verdict to the policy favouring 'the public'. On a different tack, it might be argued that it is inequitable for anyone to benefit from 'special privileges' at the expense of the rest of the community. But unfortunately neither of these is as clear as it looks because a hidden process of evaluation has already gone on to decide at what point an interest becomes 'sinister' and how well placed someone must be to be 'privileged'. The cheapest and speediest dispensation of law could be obtained by conscripting the legal profession and making them work twelve hours a day for subsistence rations; but this would no doubt be ruled out by a utilitarian as imposing 'hardship' and by the believer in distributive justice as not giving a 'just reward' for the work done. Thus, by the time one has fixed the level of rewards beyond which one is going to say that 'privilege' and 'sinister interest' lie it is virtually analytic that one has defined a 'good' solution (whether the criteria be utilitarian or those of distributive justice).

It is clearer to say that in these 'non-Rousseauan' situations the public interest has to be balanced against the special interests involved and cannot therefore be followed exclusively. But 'the public interest' remains of prime importance *in politics*, even when it runs against the net interest of some, because interests which are shared by few can be promoted by them whereas interests shared by many have to be furthered by the state if they are to be furthered at all. Only the state has the universality and the coercive power necessary to prevent people from doing what they want to do when it harms the public and to raise money to provide benefits for the public which cannot, or cannot conveniently, be sold on the market: and these are the two main ways in which 'the public interest' is promoted. This line of thought brings us into touch with the long tradition that finds in the advancement of the interests common to all one of the main tasks of the state. The peculiarity of the last two centuries or so has lain in the widespread view that the other traditional candidates—the promotion of True Religion or the enforcement of the Laws of Nature and God—should be eliminated. This naturally increases the relative importance of 'the public interest'.

A contributory factor to this tendency is the still continuing process of social and economic change which one writer has dubbed the 'organizational revolu-tion'. These developments have in many ways made for a more humane society than the smaller-scale, more loosely articulated, nineteenth-century pattern of organization could provide. But they have had the incidental result of making obsolete a good deal of our inherited conceptual equipment. Among the victims of this technological unemployment are 'public opinion' and 'the will of the people'. On most of the bills, statutory instruments and questions of administra-tive policy which come before Parliament there is little corresponding to the nineteenth-century construct of 'public opinion': the bulk of the electorate holding well-informed, principled, serious views. Even when an issue is sufficient-ly defined and publicized for there to be a widespread body of 'opinion' about it these opinions are likely to be based on such a small proportion of the relevant data that any government which conceived its job as one of automatically implementing the majority opinion would be inviting disaster.

This does not entail that voting with universal suffrage is not a better way of choosing political leaders than any alternative; but if 'public opinion' is not a horse that won't run this means that 'public interest' has to run all the harder to make up, since we have seen it has the advantage of operating where those affected by the policy in question have not even heard of it and would not understand it if they did. Consider for example the arrangements which enable the staffs of organizations whose members are affected by impending or existing legislation to consult with their opposite numbers in government departments about its drafting and administration. This system of 'functional representation', which now has almost constitutional status, would not get far if each side tried to argue from the *opinions* of its clients (the organization members and 'the public' respectively) on the matter; but their *interests* do provide a basis for dicussion, a basis which leaves room for the uncomfortable fact that in a large organization (whether it be a trade union, a limited company or a state) information and expertise are just as likely to be concentrated in a few hands as is the formal power to make decisions.

VI

At the beginning of this paper I suggested that the popularity of 'the public interest' as a political justification could be attributed either to its vacuity or to its being used to adduce in support of policies definite considerations of a kind which are as a matter of fact valued by many people. If my analysis of 'the public interest' is correct, it may be expected to flourish in a society where the state is expected to produce affluence and maintain civil liberties but not virtue or religious conformity, a society which has no distinction between different grades of citizen, and a society with large complex organizations exhibiting a high degree of rank and file apathy. I do not think it is necessary to look any further for an explanation of the concept's present popularity.

H. L. A. Hart

H. L. A. Hart (b. 1907), is a Research Fellow of University College, Oxford, and was for a number of years Professor of Jurisprudence at Oxford. He is one of the most widely read contemporary philosophers of law. In addition to numerous articles, he has published such influential works as *The Concept of Law; Law, Liberty, and Morality; Punishment and Responsibility;* and (with A. M. Honore) *Causation in the Law.*

In the first selection printed below, the essay "Are There Any Natural Rights?," he considers the vexing question of supporting the claim that men have certain rights by nature and argues that if there are any moral rights at all there is at least one natural right—the equal right of all men to be free. The second selection is his analysis of the concept of justice taken from his book *The Concept of Law.*

Are There Any Natural Rights?

I shall advance the thesis that if there are any moral rights at all, it follows that there is at least one natural right, the equal right of all men to be free. By saying that there is this right, I mean that in the absence of certain special conditions which are consistent with the right being an equal right, any adult human being capable of choice (1) has the right to forbearance on the part of all others from the use of coercion or restraint against him save to hinder coercion or restraint and (2) is at liberty to do (i.e., is under no obligation to abstain from) any action which is not one coercing or restraining or designed to injure other persons.[1]

I have two reasons for describing the equal right of all men to be free as a

[1] Further explanation of the perplexing terminology of freedom is, I fear, necessary. *Coercion* includes, besides preventing a person from doing what he chooses, making his choice less eligible by threats; *restraint* includes any action designed to make the exercise of choice impossible and so includes killing or enslaving a person. But neither coercion nor restraint includes *competition.* In terms of the distinction between "having a right to" and "being at liberty to," used above and further discussed in Section I, B, all men may have, consistently with the obligation to forbear from coercion, the *liberty* to satisfy if they can such at least of their desires as are not designed to coerce or injure others, even though in fact, owing to scarcity, one man's satisfaction causes another's frustration. In conditions of extreme scarcity this distinction between competition and coercion will not be worth drawing; natural rights are only of importance "where peace is possible" (Locke). Further, freedom (the absence of coercion) can be *valueless* to those victims of unrestricted competition too poor to make use of it; so it will be pedantic to point out to them that though starving they are free. This is the truth exaggerated by the Marxists whose *identification* of poverty with lack of freedom confuses two different evils.

Reprinted from *The Philosophical Review,* Vol. XLIV, 1955 with the permission of the Editor and the author.

natural right; both of them were always emphasized by the classical theorists of natural rights. (1) This right is one which all men have if they are capable of choice; they have it *qua* men and not only if they are members of some society or stand in some special relation to each other. (2) This right is not created or conferred by men's voluntary action; other moral rights are.[2] Of course, it is quite obvious that my thesis is not as ambitious as the traditional theories of natural rights; for although on my view all men are *equally* entitled to be free in the sense explained, no man has an absolute or unconditional right to do or not to do any particular thing or to be treated in any particular way; coercion or restraint of any action may be justified in special conditions consistently with the general principle. So my argument will not show that men have any right (save the equal right of all to be free) which is "absolute," "indefeasible," or "imprescriptible." This may for many reduce the importance of my contention, but I think that the principle that all men have an equal right to be free, meager as it may seem, is probably all that the political philosophers of the liberal tradition need have claimed to support any program of action even if they have claimed more. But my contention that there is this one natural right may appear unsatisfying in another respect; it is only the conditional assertion that *if* there are any moral rights then there must be this one natural right. Perhaps few would now deny, as some have, that there are moral rights; for the point of that denial was usually to object to some philosophical claim as to the "ontological status" of rights, and this objection is now expressed not as a denial that there are any moral rights but as a denial of some assumed logical similarity between sentences used to assert the existence of rights and other kinds of sentences. But it is still important to remember that there may be codes of conduct quite properly termed moral codes (though we can of course say they are "imperfect") which do not employ the notion of *a* right, and there is nothing contradictory or otherwise absurd in a code or morality consisting wholly of prescriptions or in a code which prescribed only what should be done for the realization of happiness or some ideal of personal perfection. Human actions in such systems would be evaluated or criticised as compliances with prescriptions or as *good* or *bad*, *right* or *wrong*, *wise* or *foolish*, *fitting*, or *unfitting*, but no one in such a system would have, exercise, or claim rights, or violate or infringe them. So those who lived by such systems could not of course be committed to the recognition of the equal right of all to be free; nor, I think (and this is one respect in which the notion of a right differs from other moral notions), could any parallel argument be constructed to show that, from the bare fact that actions were recognized as ones which ought or ought not to be done, as right, wrong, good or bad, it followed that some specific kind of conduct fell under these categories.

I

(A) Lawyers have for their own purposes carried the dissection of the notion of a legal right some distance, and some of their results are of value in the elucidation of statements of the form "X has a right to . . ." outside legal contexts. There is of course no simple identification to be made between moral and legal rights, but there is an intimate connection between the two, and this

---

[2] Save those general rights (cf. Section II, B) which are particular exemplifications of the right of all men to be free.

itself is one feature which distinguishes a moral right from other fundamental moral concepts. It is not merely that as a matter of fact men speak of their moral rights mainly when advocating their incorporation in a legal system, but that the concept of a right belongs to that branch of morality which is specifically concerned to determine when one person's freedom may be limited by another's and so to determine what actions may appropriately be made the subject of coercive legal rules. The words *"droit," "diritto,"* and *"Recht,"* used by continental jurists, have no simple English translation and seem to English jurists to hover uncertainly between law and morals, but they do in fact mark off an area of morality (the morality of law) which has special characteristics. It is occupied by the concepts of justice, fairness, rights, and obligation (if this last is not used as it is by many moral philosophers as an obscuring general label to cover every action that morally we ought to do or forbear from doing). The most important common characteristic of this group of moral concepts is that there is no incongruity, but a special congruity in the use of force or the threat of force to secure that what is just or fair or someone's right to have done shall in fact be done; for it is in just these circumstances that coercion of another human being is legitimate. Kant, in the *Rechtslehre*, discussed the obligations which arise in this branch of morality under the title of *officia juris*, "which do not require that respect for duty shall be of itself the determining principle of the will," and contrasts them with *officia virtutis*, which have no moral worth unless done for the sake of the moral principle. His point is, I think, that we must distinguish from the rest of morality those principles regulating the proper distribution of human freedom which alone make it morally legitimate for one human being to determine by his choice how another should act; and a certain specific moral value is secured (to be distinguished from moral virtue in which the good will is manifested) if human relationships are conducted in accordance with these principles even though coercion has to be used to secure this, for only if these principles are regarded will freedom be distributed among human beings as it should be. And it is I think a very important feature of a moral right that the possessor of it is conceived as having a moral justification for limiting the freedom of another and that he has this justification not because the action he is entitled to require of another has some moral quality but simply because in the circumstances a certain distribution of human freedom will be maintained if he by his choice is allowed to determine how that other shall act.

(B) I can best exhibit this feature of a moral right by reconsidering the question whether moral rights and "duties"[3] are correlative. The contention that they are means, presumably, that every statement of the form "X has a right to . . ." entails and is detailed by "Y has a duty (not) to . . . ," and at this stage we must not assume that the values of the name-variables "X" and "Y" must be different persons. Now there is certainly one sense of "a right" (which I have already mentioned) such that it does not follow from X's having a right that X

---

[3] I write " 'duties' " here because one factor obscuring the nature of a right is the philosophical use of "duty" and "obligation" for all cases where there are moral reasons for saying an action ought to be done or not done. In fact "duty," "obligations," "right," and "good" come from different segments of morality, concern different types of conduct, and make different types of moral criticism or evaluation. Most important are the points (1) that obligations may be voluntarily incurred or created, (2) that they are *owed to* special persons (who have rights), (3) that they do not arise out of the character of the actions which are obligatory but out of the relationship of the parties. Language roughly though not consistently confines the use of "having an obligation" to such cases.

or someone else has any duty. Jurists have isolated rights in this sense and have referred to them as "liberties" just to distinguish them from rights in the centrally important sense of "right" which has "duty" as a correlative. The former sense of "right" is needed to describe those areas of social life where competition is at least morally unobjectionable. Two people walking along both see a ten-dollar bill in the road twenty yards away, and there is no clue as to the owner. Neither of the two are under a "duty" to allow the other to pick it up; each has in this sense a right to pick it up. Of course there may be many things which each has a "duty" not to do in the course of the race to the spot—neither may kill or wound the other—and corresponding to these "duties" there are rights to forbearances. The moral propriety of all economic competition implies this minimum sense of "a right" in which to say that "X has a right to" means merely that X is under no "duty" not to. Hobbes saw that the expression "a right" could have this sense but he was wrong if he thought that there is no sense in which it does follow from X's having a right that Y has a duty or at any rate an obligation.

(C) More important for our purpose is the question whether for all moral "duties" there are correlative moral rights, because those who have given an affirmative answer to this question have usually assumed without adequate scrutiny that to have a right is simply to be capable of benefiting by the performance of a "duty"; whereas in fact this is not a sufficient condition (and probably not a necessary condition) of having a right. Thus animals and babies who stand to benefit by our performance of our "duty" not to ill-treat them are said *therefore* to have rights to proper treatment. The full consequence of this reasoning is not usually followed out; most have shrunk from saying that we have rights against ourselves because we stand to benefit from our performance of our "duty" to keep ourselves alive or develop our talents. But the moral situation which arises from a promise (where the legal-sounding terminology of rights and obligations is most appropriate) illustrates most clearly that the notion of having a right and that of benefiting by the performance of a "duty" are not identical. X promises Y in return for some favor that he will look after Y's aged mother in his absence. Rights arise out of this transaction, but it is surely Y to whom the promise has been made and not his mother who *has* or *possesses* these rights. Certainly Y's mother is a person concerning whom X has an obligation and a person who will benefit by its performance, but the person *to whom* he has an obligation to look after her is Y. This is something *due* or *owed to* Y, so it is Y, not his mother, whose right X will disregard and to whom X will have done *wrong* if he fails to keep his promise, though the mother may be physically injured. And it is Y who has a moral *claim* upon X, is *entitled* to have his mother looked after, and who can *waive* the claim and *release* Y from the obligation. Y is, in other words, morally in a position to determine by his choice how X shall act and in this way to limit X's freedom of choice; and it is this fact, not the fact that he stands to benefit, that makes it appropriate to say that he has *a right*. Of course often the person to whom a promise has been made will be the only person who stands to benefit by its performance, but this does not justify the identification of "having a right" with "benefiting by the performance of a duty." It is important for the whole logic of rights that, while the person who stands to benefit by the performance of a duty is discovered by considering what will happen if the duty is not performed, the person who has right (to whom performance is *owed* or *due*) is discovered by examining the transaction or antecedent situation or relations of the parties out of which the "duty" arises. These considerations should incline us not to extend to animals and babies whom it is wrong to ill-treat the notion of a right to proper treatment, for the moral situation can be simply and adequately described here by saying that it is wrong or that we ought not to ill-treat them or, in the philosopher's generalized sense of "duty," that we have a duty not to ill-treat them. If common usage sanctions talk of the rights of animals or babies it makes an idle use of the expression "a right," which will confuse the situation with other different moral situations where the expression "a right" has a specific force and cannot be replaced by the other moral expressions which I have mentioned. Perhaps some clarity on this matter is to be gained by considering the force of the preposition "to" in the expression "having a duty to Y" or "being under an obligation to Y" (where "Y" is the name of a person); for it is significantly different from the meaning of "to" in "doing something to Y" or "doing harm to Y," where it indicates the person affected by some action. In the first pair of expressions, "to" obviously does not have this force, but indicates the person to whom the person morally bound is bound. This is an intelligible development of the figure of a bond (*vinculum juris: obligare*); the precise figure is not that of two persons bound by a chain, but of *one* person bound, the other end of the chain lying in the hands of another to use if he chooses. So it appears absurd to speak of having duties or owing obligations to ourselves—of course we may have "duties" not to do harm to ourselves, but what could be meant (once the distinction between these different meanings of "to" has been grasped) by insisting that we have duties or obligations *to* ourselves not to do harm to ourselves?

(D) The essential connection between the notion of a right and the justified limitation of one person's freedom by another may be thrown into relief if we consider codes of behavior which do not purport to confer rights but only to prescribe what shall be done. Most natural law thinkers down to Hooker conceived of natural law in this way: there were natural duties compliance with which would certainly benefit man—things to be done to achieve man's natural end—but not natural rights. And there are of course many types of codes of behavior which only prescribe what is to be done, e.g., those regulating certain ceremonies. It would be absurd to regard these codes as conferring rights, but illuminating to contrast them with rules of games, which often create rights, though not, of course, moral rights. But even a code which is plainly a moral code need not establish rights; the Decalogue is perhaps the most important example. Of course, quite apart from heavenly rewards human beings stand to benefit by general obedience to the Ten Commandments: disobedience is wrong and will certainly harm individuals. But it would be a surprising interpretation of them that treated them as conferring rights. In such an interpretation obedience to the Ten Commandments would have to be conceived as due to individuals, not merely to God, and disobedience not merely as wrong but *as a wrong to* (as well as harm to) individuals. The Commandments would cease to read like penal statutes designed only to rule out certain types of behavior and would have to be thought of as rules placed at the disposal of individuals and regulating the extent to which *they* may demand certain behavior from others. Rights are typically conceived of as *possessed* or *owned by* or *belonging to* individuals, and these expressions reflect the conception of moral rules as not only prescribing conduct but as forming a kind of moral property of individuals to which they are as individuals entitled; only when rules are conceived in this way can we speak of *rights* and *wrongs* as well as right and wrong actions.[4]

II

So far I have sought to establish that to have a right entails having a moral justification for limiting the freedom of another person and for determining how he should act; it is now important to see that the moral justification must be a special kind if it is to constitute a right, and this will emerge most clearly from an examination of the circumstances in which rights are asserted with the typical expression "I have a right to. . . ." It is I think the case that this form of words is used in two main types of situations: (A) when the claimant has some special justification for interference with another's freedom which other persons do not have ("I have a right to be paid what you promised for my services"); (B) when the claimant is concerned to resist or object to some interference by another person as having no justification ("I have a right to say what I think").

(A) *Special rights.* When rights arise out of special transactions between individuals or out of some special relationship in which they stand to each other, both the persons who have the right and those who have the corresponding obligation are limited to the parties to the special transaction or relationship. I call such rights special rights to distinguish them from those moral rights which are thought of as rights against (i.e., as imposing obligations upon) everyone, such as those that are asserted when some unjustified interference is made or threatened as in (B) above.

(i) The most obvious cases of special rights are those that arise from promises. By promising to do or not to do something, we voluntarily incur obligations and create or confer rights on those to whom we promise; we alter the existing moral independence of the parties' freedom of choice in relation to some action and create a new moral relationship between them, so that it becomes morally legitimate for the person to whom the promise is given to determine how the promisor shall act. The promisee has a temporary authority or sovereignty in relation to some specific matter over the other's will which we express by saying that the promisor is under an obligation *to* the promisee to do what he has promised. To some philosophers the notion that moral phenomena—rights and duties or obligations—can be brought into existence by the voluntary action of individuals has appeared utterly mysterious; but this I think has been so because they have not clearly seen how special the moral notions of a right and an obligation are, nor how peculiarly they are connected with the distribution of freedom of choice; it would indeed be mysterious if we could make actions morally good or bad by voluntary choice. The simplest case of promising illustrates two points characteristic of all special rights: (1) the right and obligation arise not because the promised action has itself any particular moral quality, but just because of the voluntary transaction between the parties; (2) the identity of the parties concerned is vital—only *this* person (the promisee) has

---

[4] Continental jurists distinguish between *"subjektives"* and *"objektives Recht,"* which corresponds very well to the distinction between *a* right, which an individual has, and what it is right to do.

the moral justification for determining how the promisor shall act. It is *his* right; only in relation to him is the promisor's freedom of choice diminished, so that if he chooses the release to promisor no one else can complain.

(ii) But a promise is not the only kind of transaction whereby rights are conferred. They may be *accorded* by a person consenting or authorizing another to interfere in matters which but for this consent or authorization he would be free to determine for himself. If I consent to your taking precautions for my health or happiness or authorize you to look after my interests, then you have a right which others have not, and I cannot complain of your interference if it is within the sphere of your authority. This is what is meant by a person surrendering his rights to another; and again the typical characteristics of a right are present in this situation; the person authorized has the right to interfere not because of its intrinsic character but because *these* persons have stood in *this* relationship. No one else (not similarly authorized) has any *right* to interfere in theory even if the person authorized does not excercise his right.

(iii) Special rights are not only those created by the deliberate choice of the party on whom the obligation falls, as they are when they are accorded or spring from promises, and not all obligations to other persons are deliberately incurred, though I think it is true of all special rights that they arise from previous voluntary actions. A third very important source of special rights and obligations which we recognize in many spheres of life is what may be termed mutuality of restrictions, and I think political obligation is intelligible only if we see what precisely this is and how it differs from the other right-creating transactions (consent, promising) to which philosophers have assimilated it. In its bare schematic outline it is this: when a number of persons conduct any joint enterprise according to rules and thus restrict their liberty, those who have submitted to these restrictions when required have a right to a similar submission from those who have benefited by their submission. The rules may provide that officials should have authority to enforce obedience and make further rules, and this will create a structure of legal rights and duties, but the moral obligation to obey the rules in such circumstances is *due to* the co-operating members of the society, and they have the correlative moral right to obedience. In social situations of this sort (of which political society is the most complex example) the obligation to obey the rules is something distinct from whatever other moral reasons there may be for obedience in terms of good consequences (e.g., the prevention of suffering); the obligation is due to the co-operating members of the society as such and not because they are human beings on whom it would be wrong to inflict suffering. The utilitarian explanation of political obligation fails to take account of this feature of the situation both in its simple version that the obligation exists because and only if the direct consequences of a particular act of disobedience are worse than obedience, and also in its more sophisticated version that the obligation exists even when this is not so, if disobedience increases the probability that the law in question or other laws will be disobeyed on other occasions when the direct consequences of obedience are better than those of disobedience.

Of course to say that there is such a moral obligation upon those who have benefited by the submission of other members of society to restrictive rules to obey these rules in their turn does not entail either that this is the only kind of moral reason for obedience or that there can be no cases where disobedience will be morally justified. There is no contradiction or other impropriety in saying "I have an obligation to do X, someone has a right to ask me to, but I now see I ought not to do it." It will in painful situations sometimes be the lesser of two moral evils to disregard what really are people's rights and not perform our obligations to them. This seems to me particularly obvious from the case of promises: I may promise to do something and thereby incur an obligation just because that is one way in which obligations (to be distinguished from other forms of moral reasons for acting) are created; reflection may show that it would in the circumstances be wrong to keep this promise because of the suffering it might cause, and we can express this by saying "I *ought not* to do it though I *have an obligation to him* to do it" just because the italicized expressions are not synonyms but come from different dimensions of morality. The attempt to explain this situation by saying that our real obligation here is to avoid the suffering and that there is only a prima facie obligation to keep the promise seems to me to confuse two quite different kinds of moral reason, and in practice such a terminology obscures the precise character of what is at stake when "for some greater good" we infringe people's right or do not perform our obligations to them.

The social-contract theorists rightly fastened on the fact that the obligation to obey the law is not merely a special case of benevolence (direct or indirect), but something which arises between members of a particular political society out of their mutual relationship. Their mistake was to identify *this* right-creating situation of mutual restrictions with the paradigm case of promising; there are of course important similarities, and these are just the points which all special rights have in common, viz., that they arise out of special relationships between human beings and not out of the character of the action to be done or its effects.

(iv) There remains a type of situation which may be thought of as creating rights and obligations: where the parties have a special natural relationship, as in the case of parent and child. The parent's moral right to obedience from his child would I suppose now be thought to terminate when the child reaches the age "of discretion," but the case is worth mentioning because some political philosophies have had recourse to analogies with this case as an explanation of political obligation, and also because even this case has some of the features we have distinguished in special rights, viz., the right arises out of the special relationship of the parties (though it is in this case a natural relationship) and not out of the character of the actions to the performance of which there is a right.

(v) To be distinguished from special rights, of course, are special liberties, where, exceptionally, one person is *exempted* from obligations to which most are subject but does not thereby acquire a *right* to which there is a correlative obligation. If you catch me reading your brother's diary, you say, "You have no right to read it." I say, "I have a right to read it—your brother said I might unless he told me not to, and he has not told me not to." Here I have been specially *licensed* by your brother who had a right to require me not to read his diary, so I am exempted from the moral obligation not to read it, but your brother is under no obligation to let me go on reading it. Cases where *rights*, not liberties, are accorded to manage or interfere with another person's affairs are those where the license is not revocable at will by the person according the right.

(B) *General rights*. In contrast with special rights, which constitute a justification peculiar to the holder of the right for interfering with another's freedom, are general rights, which are asserted defensively, when some unjustified interference is anticipated or threatened, in order to point out that the interference is unjustified. "I have the right to say what I think." "I have the right to worship as I please." Such rights share two important characteristics with special rights. (1) To have them is to have a moral justification for determining how another shall act, viz., that he shall not interfere. (2) The moral justification does not arise from the character of the particular action to the performance of which the claimant has a right; what justifies the claim is simply—there being no special relation between him and those who are threatening to interfere to justify that interference—that this is a particular exemplification of the equal right to be free. But there are of course striking differences between such defensive general rights and special rights. (1) General rights do not arise out of any special relationship or transaction between men. (2) They are not rights which are peculiar to those who have them but are rights which all men capable of choice have in the absence of those special conditions which give rise to special rights. (3) General rights have as correlatives obligations not to interfere to which everyone else is subject and not merely the parties to some special relationship or transaction, though of course they will often be asserted when some particular persons threaten to interfere as a moral objection to that interference. To assert a general right is to claim relation to some particular action the equal right of all men to be free in the absence of any of those special conditions which constitute a special right to limit another's freedom; to assert a special right is to assert in relation to some particular action a right constituted by such special conditions to limit another's freedom. The assertion of general rights directly invokes the principle that all men equally have the right to be free; the assertion of a special right (as I attempt to show in Section III) invokes it indirectly.

III

It is, I hope, clear that unless it is recognized that interference with another's freedom requires a moral justification the notion of a right could have no place in morals; for to assert a right is to assert that there is such a justification. The characteristic function in moral discourse of those sentences in which the meaning of the expression "a right" is to be found—"I have a right to . . . ." "You have no right to . . .," "What right have you to . . .?"—is to bring to bear on interferences with another's freedom, or on claims to interfere, a type of moral evaluation or criticism specially appropriate to interference with freedom and characteristically different from the moral criticism of actions made with the use of expressions like "right," "wrong," "good," and "bad." And this is only one of many different types of moral ground for saying "You ought . . ." or "You ought not. . . ." The use of the expression "What right have you to . . .?" shows this more clearly, perhaps, than the others; for we use it, just at the point where interference is actual or threatened, to call for the moral *title* of the person addressed to interfere; and we do this often without any suggestion at all that what he proposes to do is otherwise wrong and sometimes with the implication that the same interference on the part of another person would be unobjectionable.

But though our use in moral discourse of "a right" does presuppose the recognition that interference with another's freedom requires a moral justification, this would not itself suffice to establish, except in a sense easily trivialized, that in the recognition of moral rights there is implied the recognition that all men have a right to equal freedom; for unless there is some restriction inherent in the meaning of "a right" on the type of moral justification for interference which can constitute a right, the principle could be made wholly vacuous. It would, for example, be possible to adopt the principle and then assert that some characteristic or behavior of some human beings (that they are improvident, or atheists, or Jews, or Negroes) constitutes a moral justification for interfering with their freedom; *any* differences between men could, so far as my argument has yet gone, be treated as a moral justification for interference and so constitute a right, so that the equal right of all men to be free would be compatible with gross inequality. It may be that the expression "moral" itself imports some restriction on what can constitute a moral justification for interference which would avoid this consequence, but I cannot myself yet show that this is so. It is, on the other hand clear to me that the moral justification for interference which is to constitute a *right* to interfere (as distinct from merely making it morally good or desirable to interfere) is restricted to certain special conditions and that this is inherent in the meaning of "a right" (unless this is used so loosely that it could be replaced by the other moral expressions mentioned). Claims to interfere with another's freedom based on the general character of the activities interfered with (e.g., the folly or cruelty of "native" practices) or the general character of the parties ("We are Germans; they are Jews") even when well founded are not matters of moral right or obligation. Submission in such cases even where proper is not *due to* or *owed to* the individuals who interfere; it would be equally proper whoever of the same class of persons interfered. Hence other elements in our moral vocabulary suffice to describe this case, and it is confusing here to talk of rights. We saw in Section II that the types of justification for interference involved in special rights was independent of the character of the action to the performance of which there was a right but depended upon certain previous transactions and relations between individuals (such as promises, consent, authorization, submission to mutal restrictions). Two questions here suggest themselves: (1) On what intelligible principle could these bare forms of promising, consenting, submission to mutual restrictions, be either necessary or sufficient, irrespective of their content, to justify interference with another's freedom? (2) What characteristics have these types of transaction or relationship in common? The answer to both these questions is I think this: If we justify interference on such grounds as we give when we claim a moral right, we are in fact indirectly invoking as our justification the principle that all men have an equal right to be free. For we are in fact saying in the case of promises and consents or authorizations that this claim to interfere with another's freedom is justified because he has, in exercise of his equal right to be free, freely chosen to create this claim; and in the case of mutual restrictions we are in fact saying that this claim to interfere with another's freedom is justified because it is fair; and it is fair because only so will there be an equal distribution of restrictions and so of freedom among this group of men. So in the case of special rights as well as of general rights recognition of them implies the recognition of the equal right of all men to be free.

The Concept of Law

PRINCIPLES OF JUSTICE

The terms most frequently used by lawyers in the praise or condemnation of law or its administration are the words 'just' and 'unjust' and very often they write as if the ideas of justice and morality were coextensive. There are indeed very good reasons why justice should have a most prominent place in the criticism of legal arrangements; yet it is important to see that it is a distinct segment of morality, and that laws and the administration of laws may have or lack excellences of different kinds. Very little reflection on some common types of moral judgment is enough to show this special character of justice. A man guilty of gross cruelty to his child would often be judged to have done something morally *wrong, bad,* or even *wicked* or to have disregarded his moral *obligation* or duty to his child. But it would be strange to criticize his conduct as *unjust.* This is not because the word 'unjust' is too weak in condemnatory force, but because the point of moral criticism in terms of justice or injustice is usually different from, and more specific than, the other types of general moral criticism which are appropriate in this particular case and are expressed by words like 'wrong', 'bad', or 'wicked'. 'Unjust' would become appropriate if the man had arbitrarily selected one of his children for severer punishment than those given to others guilty of the same fault, or if he had punished the child for some offence without taking steps to see that he really was the wrongdoer. Similarly, when we turn from the criticism of individual conduct to the criticism of law, we might express our approval of a law requiring parents to send their children to school, by saying that it was a good law and our disapproval of a law forbidding the criticism of the Government, as by calling it a bad law. Such criticisms would not normally be couched in terms of 'justice' and 'injustice'. 'Just" on the other hand, would be the appropriate expression of approval of a law distributing the burden of taxation according to wealth; so 'unjust' would be appropriate for the expression of disapproval of a law which forbade coloured people to use the public means of transport or the parks. That just and unjust are more specific forms of moral criticism than good and bad or right and wrong, is plain from the fact that we might intelligibly claim that a law was good because it was just, or that it was bad because it was unjust, but not that it was just because good, or unjust because bad.

The distinctive features of justice and their special connexion with law begin to emerge if it is observed that most of the criticisms made in terms of just and unjust could almost equally well be conveyed by the words 'fair' and 'unfair'. Fairness is plainly not coextensive with morality in general; references to it are mainly relevant in two situations in social life. One is when we are concerned not with a single individual's conduct but with the way in which *classes* of individu-

From H. L. A. Hart, *The Concept of Law.* By permission of the Clarendon Press, Oxford.

als are treated, when some burden or benefit falls to be distributed among them. Hence what is typically fair or unfair is a 'share'. The second situation is when some injury has been done and compensation or redress is claimed. These are not the only contexts where appraisals in terms of justice or fairness are made. We speak not only of distributions or compensations as just or fair but also of a judge as just or unjust; a trial as fair or unfair; and a person as justly or unjustly convicted. These are derivative applications of the notion of justice which are explicable once the primary application of justice to matters of distribution and compensation is understood.

The general principle latent in these diverse applications of the idea of justice is that individuals are entitled in respect of each other to a certain relative position of equality or inequality. This is something to be respected in the vicissitudes of social life when burdens or benefits fall to be distributed; it is also something to be restored when it is disturbed. Hence justice is traditionally thought of as maintaining or restoring a *balance* or *proportion*, and its leading precept is often formulated as 'Treat like cases alike'; though we need to add to the latter 'and treat different cases differently'. So when, in the name of justice, we protest against a law forbidding coloured people the use of the public parks, the point of such criticism is that such a law is bad, because in distributing the benefits of public amenities among the population it discriminates between persons who are, in all relevant respects, alike. Conversely, if a law is praised as just because it withdraws from some special section some privilege or immunity, e.g., in taxation, the guiding thought is that there is no such relevant difference between the privileged class and the rest of the community as to entitle them to the special treatment. These simple examples are, however, enough to show that, though 'Treat like cases alike and different cases differently' is a central element in the idea of justice, it is by itself incomplete and, until supplemented, cannot afford any determinate guide to conduct. This is so because any set of human beings will resemble each other in some respect and differ from each other in others and, until it is established what resemblance and differences are relevant, 'Treat like cases alike' must remain an empty form. To fill it we must know when, for the purposes in hand, cases are to be regarded as alike and what differences are relevant. Without this further supplement we cannot proceed to criticize laws or other social arrangements as unjust. It is not unjust for the law when it forbids homicide to treat the red-haired murderers in the same way as others; indeed it would be as unjust if it treated them differently, as it would be if it refused to treat differently the sane and the insane.

There is therefore a certain complexity in the structure of the idea of justice. We may say that it consists of two parts: a uniform or constant feature, summarized in the precept 'Treat like cases alike' and a shifting or varying criterion used in determining when, for any given purpose, cases are alike or different. In this respect justice is like the notion of what is genuine, or tall, or warm, which contain an implicit reference to a standard which varies with the classification of the thing to which they are applied. A tall child may be the same height as a short man, a warm winter the same temperature as a cold summer, and a fake diamond may be a genuine antique. But justice is far more complicated than these notions because the shifting standard of relevant resemblance between different cases incorporated in it not only varies with the type of subject to which it is applied, but may often be open to challenge even in relation to a single type of subject.

In certain cases, indeed, the resemblances and differences between human beings which are relevant for the criticism of legal arrangements as just or unjust are quite obvious. This is pre-eminently the case when we are concerned not with the justice or injustice of the *law* but of its *application* in particular cases. For here the relevant resemblances and differences between individuals, to which the person who administers the law must attend, are determined by the law itself. To say that the law against murder is justly applied is to say that it is impartially applied to all those and only those who are alike in having done what the law forbids; no prejudice or interest has deflected the administrator from treating them 'equally'. Consistently with this the procedural standards such as *'audi alteram partem'* 'let no one be a judge in his own cause' are thought of as requirements of justice, and in England and America are often referred to as principles of Natural Justice. This is so because they are guarantees of impartiality or objectivity, designed to secure that the law is applied to all those and only to those who are alike in the relevant respect marked out by the law itself.

The connexion between this aspect of justice and the very notion of proceeding by rule is obviously very close. Indeed, it might be said that to apply a law justly to different cases is simply to take seriously the assertion that what is to be applied in different cases is the same general rule, without prejudice, interest, or caprice. This close connexion between justice in the administration of the law and the very notion of a rule has tempted some famous thinkers to identify justice with conformity to law. Yet plainly this is an error unless 'law' is given some specially wide meaning; for such an account of justice leaves unexplained the fact that criticism in the name of justice is not confined to the administration of the law in particular cases, but the laws themselves are often criticized as just or unjust. Indeed there is no absurdity in conceding that an unjust law forbidding the access of coloured persons to the parks has been justly administered, in that only persons genuinely guilty of breaking the law were punished under it and then only after a fair trail.

When we turn from the justice or injustice of the administration of the law to the criticism of the law itself in these terms, it is plain that the law itself cannot now determine what resemblances and differences among individuals the law must recognize if its rules are to treat like cases alike and so be just. Here accordingly there is much room for doubt and dispute. Fundamental differences, in general moral and political outlook, may lead to irreconcilable differences and disagreement as to what characteristics of human beings are to be taken as relevant for the criticism of law as unjust. Thus, when in the previous example we stigmatized as unjust a law forbidding coloured people access to the parks, this was on the footing that, at least in the distribution of such amenities, differences of colour are irrelevant. Certainly in the modern world, the fact that human beings, of whatever colour, are capable of thought, feeling, and self-control, would be generally though not universally accepted as constituting crucial resemblances between them to which the law should attend. Hence, in most civilized countries there is a great measure of agreement that both the criminal law (conceived not only as restricting liberty but as providing protection from various sorts of harm) and the civil law (conceived as offering redress for harm), would be unjust if in the distribution of these burdens and benefits they discriminated between persons, by reference to such characteristics as colour or religious belief. And if, instead of these well-known *foci* of human prejudice, the law discriminated by reference to such obvious irrelevancies as height, weight, or beauty it would be both unjust and ludicrous. If murderers belonging to the established church were exempt from capital punishment, if only members of the peerage could sue for libel, if assaults on coloured persons were punished less severely than those on whites, the laws would in most modern communities be condemned as unjust on the footing that *prima facie* human beings should be treated alike and these privileges and immunities rested on no relevant ground.

Indeed so deeply embedded in modern man is the principle that *prima facie* human beings are entitled to be treated alike that almost universally where the laws do discriminate by deference to such matters as colour and race, lip service at least is still widely paid to this principle. If such discriminations are attacked they are often defended by the assertion that the class discriminated against lack, or have not yet developed, certain essential human attributes; or it may be said that, regrettable though it is, the demands of justice requiring their equal treatment must be overridden in order to preserve something held to be of greater value, which would be jeopardized if such discriminations were not made. Yet though lip service is now general, it is certainly possible to conceive of a morality which did not resort to these often disingenuous devices to justify discrimination and inequalities, but openly rejected the principle that *prima facie* human beings were to be treated alike. Instead, human beings might be thought of as falling naturally and unalterably into certain classes, so that some were naturally fitted to be free and others to be their slaves or, as Aristotle expressed it, the living instruments of others. Here the sense of *prima facie* equality among men would be absent. Something of this view is to be found in Aristotle and Plato, though even there, there is more than a hint that any full defence of slavery would involve showing that those enslaved lacked the capacity for independent existence or differed from the free in their capacity to realize some ideal of the good life.

It is therefore clear that the criteria of relevant resemblances and differences may often vary with the fundamental moral outlook of a given person or society. Where this is so, assessments of the justice or injustice of the law may be met with counter-assertions inspired by a different morality. But sometimes a consideration of the object which the law in question is admittedly designed to realize may make clear the resemblances and differences which a just law should recognize and they may then be scarcely open to dispute. If a law provides for the relief of poverty then the requirement of the principle that 'Like cases be treated alike' would surely involve attention to the *need* of different claimants for relief. A similar criterion of need is implicitly recognized when the burden of taxation is adjusted by a graded income tax to the wealth of the individuals taxed. Sometimes what is relevant are the *capacities* of persons for a specific function with which the exercise of the law in question may be concerned. Laws which exclude from the franchise, or withhold the power to make wills or contracts from children, or the insane, are regarded as just because such persons lack the capacity, which sane adults are presumed to have, to make a rational use of these facilities. Such discriminations are made on grounds which are obviously relevant, whereas discriminations in these matters between the sexes or between persons of different colour are not; though of course it has been argued in defence of the subjection of women, or coloured people, that women or coloured people lack the white male's capacity for rational thought and decision.

To argue thus is of course to admit that equal capacity for a particular function is the criterion of justice in the case of such law, though in the absence of any evidence that such capacity is lacking in women or coloured persons, again only lip service is paid to this principle.

So far we have considered the justice or injustice of laws which may be viewed as *distributing* among individuals burdens and benefits. Some of the benefits are tangible, like poor relief, or food rations; others are intangible, like the protection from bodily harm given by the criminal law, or the facilities afforded by laws relating to testamentary or contractual capacity, or the right to vote. From distribution in this wide sense, we must distinguish *compensation* for injury done by one person to another. Here the connexion between what is just and the central precept of justice 'Treat like cases alike and different cases differently' is certainly less direct. Yet it is not too indirect to be traced and may be seen in the following way. The laws which provide for the compensation by one person of another for torts or civil injuries might be considered unjust for two different reasons. They might, on the one hand, establish unfair privileges or immunities. This would be so if only peers could sue for libel, or if no white person were liable to a coloured person for trespass or assault. Such laws would violate, in a straightforward way, principles of fair distribution of the rights and duties of compensation. But such laws might also be unjust in a quite different way: for while making no unfair discriminations they might fail altogether to provide for certain types of injury inflicted by one person on another, even though morally compensation would be thought due. In this matter the law might be unjust while treating all alike.

The vice of such laws would then not be the maldistribution, but the refusal to all alike, of compensation for injuries which it was morally wrong to inflict on others. The crudest case of such unjust refusal of redress would be a system in which no one could obtain damages for physical harm wantonly inflicted. It is worth observing that *this* injustice would still remain even if the criminal law prohibited such assaults under penalty. Few instances of anything so crude can be found, but the failure of English law to provide compensation for invasions of privacy, often found profitable by advertisers, has often been criticized in this way. Failure to provide compensation where morally it is held due is, however, also the gravamen of the charge of injustice against technicalities of the law of tort or contract which permit 'unjust enrichment' at the expense of another by some action considered morally wrong.

The connexion between the justice and injustice of the compensation for injury, and the principle 'Treat like cases alike and different cases differently', lies in the fact that outside the law there is a moral conviction that those with whom the law is concerned have a right to mutual forbearance from certain kinds of harmful conduct. Such a structure of reciprocal rights and obligations proscribing at least the grosser sorts of harm, constitutes the basis though not the whole, of the morality of every social group. Its effect is to create among individuals a moral and, in a sense, an artificial equality to offset the inequalities of nature. For when the moral code forbids one man to rob or use violence on another even when superior strength or cunning would enable him to do so with impunity, the strong and cunning are put on a level with the weak and simple. Their cases are made morally alike. Hence the strong man who disregards morality and takes advantage of his strengths to injure another is conceived as upsetting this equilibrium, or order of equality, established by morals; justice then requires that this moral *status quo* should as far as possible be restored by the wrongdoer. In simple cases of theft this would simply involve giving back the thing taken; and compensation for other injuries is an extension of this primitive notion. One who has physically injured another either intentionally or through negligence is thought of as having taken something from his victim; and though he has not literally done this, the figure is not too far fetched: for he has profited at his victim's expense, even if it is only by indulging his wish to injure him or not sacrificing his ease to the duty taking adequate precautions. Thus when laws provide compensation where justice demands it, they recognize indirectly the principle 'Treat like cases alike' by providing for the restoration, after disturbance, of the moral *status quo* in which victim and wrongdoer are on a footing of equality and so alike. Again, it is conceivable that there might be a moral outlook which did not put individuals on a footing of reciprocal equality in these matters. The moral code might forbid Barbarians to assault Greeks but allow Greeks to assault Barbarians. In such cases a Barbarian may be thought morally bound to compensate a Greek for injuries done though entitled to no such compensation himself. The moral order here would be one of inequality in which victim and wrongdoer were treated differently. For such an outlook, repellent though it may be to us, the law would be just only if it reflected this difference and treated different cases differently.

In this brief outline of justice we have considered only some of its simpler applications in order to show the specific form of excellence attributed to laws which are appraised as just. Not only is this distinct from other values which laws may have or lack, but sometimes the demands of justice may conflict with other values. This may occur, when a court, in sentencing a particular offender for a crime which has become prevalent, passes a severer sentence than that passed in other similar cases, and avowedly does this 'as a warning'. There is here a sacrifice of the principle 'Treat like cases alike' to the general security or welfare of society. In civil cases, a similar conflict between justice and the general good is resolved in favour of the latter, when the law provides no remedy for some moral wrong because to enforce compensation in such cases might involve great difficulties of proof, or overburden the courts, or unduly hamper enterprise. There is a limit to the amount of law enforcement which any society can afford, even when moral wrong has been done. Conversely the law, in the name of the general welfare of society, may enforce compensation from one who has injured another, even where morally, as a matter of justice, it might not be thought due. This is often said to be the case when liability in tort is strict, i.e., independent of the intention to injure or failure to take care. This form of liability is sometimes defended on the ground that it is in the interest of 'society' that those accidentally injured should be compensated; and it is claimed that the easiest way of doing this is to place the burden on those whose activities, however carefully controlled, result in such accidents. They commonly have deep pockets and opportunities to insure. When this defence is made, there is in it an implicit appeal to the general welfare of society which, though it may be morally acceptable and sometimes even called '*social* justice', differs from the primary forms of justice which are concerned simply to redress, as far as possible, the *status quo* as between two individuals.

An important juncture point between ideas of justice and social good or welfare should be noticed. Very few social changes or laws are agreeable to or advance the welfare of all individuals alike. Only laws which provide for the most elementary needs, such as police protection or roads, come near to this. In most cases the law provides benefits for one class of the population only at the cost of depriving others of what they prefer. Provision for the poor can be made only out of the goods of others; compulsory school education for all may mean not only loss of liberty for those who wish to educate their children privately, but may be financed only at the cost of reducing or sacrificing capital invest-ment in industry or old-age pensions or free medical services. When a choice has been made between such competing alternatives it may be defended as proper on the ground that it was for the 'public good' or the 'common good'. It is not clear what these phrases mean, since there seems to be no scale by which contribu-tions of the various alternatives to the common good can be measured and the greater identified. It is, however, clear that a choice, made without prior consideration of the interests of all sections of the community would be open to criticism as merely partisan and unjust. It would, however, be rescued from *this* imputation if the claims of all had been impartially considered before legislation, even though in the result the claims of one section were subordinated to those of others.

Some might indeed argue that all that in fact could be meant by the claim that a choice between the competing claims of different classes or interests was made 'for the common good', was that the claims of all had been thus impar-tially surveyed before decision. Whether this is true or not, it seems clear that justice in this sense is at least a necessary condition to be satisfied by any legislative choice which purports to be for the common good. We have here a further aspect of distributive justice, differing from those simple forms which we have discussed. For here what is justly 'distributed' is not some specific benefit among a class of claimants to it, but impartial attention to and consideration of of competing claims to different benefits.

Gregory Vlastos

Gregory Vlastos (b. 1907) is Professor of Philosophy at Princeton University. Professor Vlastos is known not only for his work in political philosophy, but also as a distinguished classical scholar.

The selection printed below is the second section of his article "Justice and Equality." In the first section of his article Professor Vlastos has pointed out that while justice is almost always in some way tied to equality, most of the usual maxims of distributive justice, such as "to each according to his need" or "to each according to his merit," seem to sanction unequal distribution. He points out that an equalitarian conception of justice can admit that there are just inequalities if and only if the grounds it gives for equal human rights can also be grounds for unequal rights of other sorts. In the selection printed below he offers an account of the basis of equal human rights which he thinks will allow an equalitarian theory of justice to meet this condition. In the later sections of the article, on the basis of his account of equal rights, Professor Vlastos defines a just act as one which is prescribed exclusively by regard for the rights of all whom it affects substantially. He then goes on to show how his conception of justice can cover within its equalitarian framework the various maxims of distributive justice he has discussed earlier.

Justice and Equality

SECTION II JUSTICE, EQUALITY, AND HUMAN WORTH

Let me begin with the first on my list of maxims of distributive justice: "To each according to his need." Since needs are often unequal, this looks like a precept of unequal distribution. But this is wrong. It is in fact *the most perfect form of equal distribution.* To explain this let me take one of the best established rights in the natural law tradition: the right to the security of life and person. Believing that this is an equal right, what do we feel this means in cases of special need?

Suppose, for instance, New Yorker X gets a note from Murder, Inc., that looks like business. To allocate several policemen and plainclothesmen to guard him over the next few weeks at a cost a hundred times greater than the per capita cost of security services to other citizens during the same period, is surely *not* to make an exception to the equal distribution required by the equal right of all citizens to the security of their life and person; it is not done on the assumption that X has a greater right to security or a right to greater security. If the visitor from Mars drew this conclusion from the behavior of the police, he would be told that he was just mistaken. The greater allocation of community resources in X's favor, we would have to explain, is made precisely *because* X's security rights are equal to those of other people in New York. This means that X is entitled to the same level of police-made security as is maintained for other New Yorkers. Hence in these special circumstances, where his security level would drop to zero without extra support, he should be given this to bring his

Gregory Vlastos, "Justice and Equality" in Richard B. Brandt, Ed., *Social Justice,* © 1962, pp. 40-53. Reprinted by permission of Prentice-Hall Inc., Englewood Cliffs, New Jersey.

security level nearer the normal. I say "nearer," not "up to" the normal, because I am talking of New York as of 1961. If I were thinking of New York with an ideal municipal government, ideally supplied with police resources, I *would* say "up to the normal," because that is what equality of right would ideally mean. But as things are, perhaps the best that can be done for X without disrupting the general level of security maintained for all the other New Yorkers is to decrease his chances of being bumped off in a given week to, say, one to ten thousand, while those of ordinary citizens, with ordinary protection are, say, one to ten million—no small difference.[1] Now if New York were more affluent, it would be able to buy more equality[2] of security for its citizens (as well as more security): by getting more, and perhaps also better paid, policemen, it would be able to close the gap between security maintained for people in ordinary circumstances and that supplied in cases of special need, like that of X in his present jam. Here we stumble on something of considerable interest: that approximation to the goal of completely equal security benefits for all citizens is a function of two variables: first, and quite obviously, of the pattern of distribution of the resources; second, and less obviously, of their size. If the distributable resources are so meager that they are all used up to maintain a general level barely sufficient for ordinary needs, their reallocation to meet exceptional need will look too much like robbing Peter to pay Paul. In such conditions there is likely to be little, if any, provision for extremity of need and, what is more, the failure to meet the extremity will not be felt as a social injustice but as a calamity of fate. And since humanity has lived most of its life under conditions of general indigence, we can understand why it has been so slow to connect provision for special need with the notion of justice, and has so often made it a matter of charity; and why "to each according to his need" did not become popularized as a precept of justice until the first giant increase in the productive resources, and then only by men like Blanc and Marx, who projected an image of a super-affluent, machine-run society on the grid of an austerely equalitarian conception of justice.[3]

So we can see why distribution according to personal need, far from conflicting with the equality of distribution required by a human right, is so linked with its very meaning that under ideal conditions equality of right would coincide with distribution according to personal need. Our visitor misunderstood the sudden mobilization of New York policemen in favor of Mr. X, because he failed to understand that it is benefits to persons, not allocation of resources as such, that are meant to be made equal; for then he would have seen at once that unequal distribution of resources would be required to equalize benefits in cases of

[1] These figures, needless to say, are "pulled out of a hat."
[2] This point was first suggested to me by Professor Kenneth Boulding's striking remark that "only a rich society can afford to be equalitarian," *The Economics of Peace* (Englewood Cliffs, N.J.: Prentice-Hall, 1945), p. 111. The more guarded form in which I am stating the point will protect it against apparent counter-examples to Boulding's remark, e.g., the astonishing equalitarianism that was still practiced by the Eskimos of the Coronation Gulf and the Mackenzie River earlier in this century (see V. Stefansson's essay in *Freedom*, Ruth N. Anshen, ed., [New York: Harcourt, Brace and World, 1940]).
[3] The well-known maxim, "from each according to his ability, to each according to his need" (Karl Marx, *Critique of the Gotha Programme*, 1875), echoes, without acknowledgment, a remark in the 9th edition of Louis Blanc's *L'Organization du travail* (Paris, 1850) that "true equality" is that "which apportions work to ability and recompense to needs" (cited in D. O. Wagner, *Social Reformers* [New York: The Macmillan Co., 1946], p. 248).

unequal need. But if he saw this he might then ask, "But why do you want this sort of equality?" My answer would have to be: Because the human worth of all persons is equal, however unequal may be their merit. To the explanation of this proposition I shall devote the balance of this Section.

By "merit" I shall refer throughout this essay to all the kinds of valuable qualities or performances in respect of which persons may be graded.[4] The concept will not be restricted to moral actions or dispositions.[5] Thus wit, grace of manner, and technical skill count as meritorious qualities fully as much as sincerity, generosity, or courage. Any valuable human characteristic, or cluster of characteristics, will qualify, provided only it is "acquired," i.e., represents what its possessor has himself made of his natural endowments and environmental opportunities. Given the immense variety of individual differences, it will be commonly the case that of any two persons either may excel the other in respect of different kinds or sub-kinds of merit. Thus if A and B are both clever and brave men, A may be much the cleverer as a business man, B as a literary critic, and A may excel in physical, B in moral, courage. It should be clear from just this that to speak of "a person's merit" will be strictly senseless except insofar as this is an elliptical way of referring to that person's merits, i.e., to those specifiable qualities or activities in which he rates well. So if there is a value attaching to the person himself as an integral and unique individual, *this* value will not fall under merit or be reducible to it. For it is of the essence of merit, as here defined, to be a grading concept; and there is no way of grading individuals as such. We can only grade them with respect to their qualities, hence only by abstracting from their individuality. If A is valued for some meritorious quality, m, his individuality does not enter into the valuation. As an individual he is then dispensable; his place could be taken without loss of value by any other individual with as good an m-rating. Nor would matters change by multiplying and diversifying the meritorious qualities with which A is endowed. No matter how enviable a package of well-rounded excellence A may represent, it would still follow that, if he is valued only for his merit, he is not being valued as an individual. To be sure individuals *may* be valued only for their merits. This happens all too commonly. A might be valued in just this way by P, the president of his company, for whom A, highly successful vice-president in charge of sales, amusing dinner-guest, and fine asset to the golf club, is simply high-grade equipment in various complexes of social machinery which P controls or patronizes. On the other hand, it is possible that, much as P prizes this conjunct of qualities (M), he values A also as an individual. A may be his son, and he may be genuinely fond of him. If so, his affection will be for A, not for his M-qualities. The latter P approves, admires, takes pride in, and the like. But his affection and good will are for A, and *not only because*, or *insofar as*, A has the M-qualities. For P may be equally fond of another son who rates well below A in P's scoring system. Moreover, P's affection for A, as distinct from his approval or admiration of him, need not fluctuate with the ups and downs in A's achieve-

---

[4] This is only one of the senses recognized by the dictionary (*The Shorter Oxford English Dictionary*, s.v., 4 and 6): "Excellence," "An Excellence," the latter being illustrated by "Would you ask for his merits? Alas! he has none" (from Goldsmith). In the other senses listed by the dictionary the word either *means* "desert" or at least includes this in its meaning. On the present use of "merit" the connection with "desert" is synthetic.

[5] As is done by some philosophical moralists, e.g., Sir David Ross, *op. cit.*, pp. 135ff., where "merit" and (moral) "virtue" are co-extensive.

ments. Perhaps *A* had some bad years after graduating from college, and it looked then as though his brilliant gifts would be wasted. It does not follow that *P*'s love for *A* then lapsed or even ebbed. Constancy of affection in the face of variations of merit is one of the surest tests of whether or not a parent does love a child. If he feels fond of it only when it performs well, and turns coldly indifferent or hostile when its achievements slump, then his feeling for the child can scarcely be called *love*. There are many relations in which one's liking or esteem for a person are strictly conditional on his measuring up to certain standards. But convincing evidence that the relation is of this type is no evidence that the relation is one of parental love or any other kind of love. It does nothing to show that one has this feeling, or any feeling, for an *individual*, rather than for a place-holder of qualities one likes to see instantiated by somebody or other close about one.

Now if this concept of value attaching to a person's individual existence, over and above his merit—"individual worth,"[6] let me call it—were applicable *only* in relations of personal love, it would be irrelevant for the analysis of justice. To serve our purpose its range of application must be coextensive with that of justice. It must hold in all human relations, including (or rather, especially in) the most impersonal of all, those to total strangers, fellow-citizens or fellow-men. I must show that the concept of individual worth does meet this condition.

Consider its role in our political community, taking the prescriptions of our laws for the treatment of persons as the index to our valuations. For merit (among other reasons) persons may be appointed or elected to public office or given employment by state agencies. For demerit they may lose licences, jobs, offices; they may be fined, jailed, or even put to death. But in a large variety of law-regulated actions directed to individuals, either by private persons or by organs of the state, the question of merit and demerit does not arise. The "equal protection of the laws" is due to persons not to meritorious ones, or to them in some degree above others.[7] So too for the right to vote. One does not have it for being intelligent and public-spirited, or lose it for being lazy, ignorant, or viciously selfish. One is entitled to exercise it as long as, having registered, one manages to keep out of jail. This kind of arrangement would look like whimsy or worse, like sheer immoralism, if the only values recognized in our political community were those of merit. For obviously there is nothing compulsory about our political system; we could certainly devise, if we so wished, workable alternatives which would condition fundamental rights on certain kinds of merit. For example, we might have three categories of citizenship. The top one might be for those who meet high educational qualifications and give definite evidence of responsible civic interest, e.g., by active participation in political functions, tenure of public office, record of leadership in civic organizations and support to them, and the like. People in this *A*-category might have multiple votes in all elections and exclusive eligibility for the more important political offices; they might also be entitled to a higher level of protection by the police and to a

---

[6] That this is *intrinsic* worth goes without saying. But I do not put this term into my label, since I want to distinguish this kind of value as sharply as possible from that of merit, and I include under "merit" not only extrinsically, but also intrinsically, valuable qualities.

[7] A modicum of merit by way of self-help and law-obedience is generally presupposed. But it would be a mistake to think of the protection of the laws as a reward for good behavior. Thus many legal protections are due as much to those who will not look out for themselves as to those who do, and to lawbreakers as much as to law-observers.

variety of other privileges and immunities. At the other end there would be a *C*-category, disfranchised and legally underpriviliged, for those who do not meet some lower educational test or have had a record of law-infraction or have been on the relief rolls for over three months. In between would be the *B*'s with ordinary suffrage and intermediate legal status.

This "*M*-system" would be more complicated and cumbersome than ours. But something like it could certainly be made to work if we were enamoured of its peculiar scheme of values. Putting aside the question of efficiency, it gives us a picture of a community whose political valuations, conceived entirely in terms of merit, would never be grounded on individual worth, so that this notion would there be politically useless.[8] For us, on the other hand, it is indispensable.[9] We have to appeal to it when we try to make sense of the fact that our legal system accords to all citizens an identical status, carrying with it rights such as the *M*-system reserves to the *B*'s or the *A*'s and some which (like suffrage or freedom of speech) have been denied even to the nobility in some caste-systems of the past. This last comparison is worth pressing: it brings out the illuminating fact that in one fundamental respect our society is much more like a caste society (with a *unique* caste) than like the *M*-system. The latter has no place for a rank of dignity which descends on an individual by the purely existential circumstance (the "accident") of birth and remains his unalterably for life. To reproduce this feature of our system we would have to look not only to caste-societies, but to extremely rigid ones, since most of them make some provision for elevation in rank for rare merit or degradation for extreme demerit. In our legal system no such thing can happen: even a criminal may not be sentenced to second-class citizenship.[10] And the fact that first-class citizenship, having been made common, is no longer a mark of distinction does not trivialize the privileges it entails. It is the simple truth, not declamation, to speak of it, as I have done, as a "rank of dignity" in some ways comparable to that enjoyed by hereditary nobilities of the past. To see this one need only think of the position of groups in our society who have been cheated out of this status by the subversion of their constitutional rights. The difference in social position between Negroes and whites described in Dollard's classic[11] is not smaller than that between, say bourgeoisie and aristocracy in the *ancien régime* of France. It might well be greater.

Consider finally the role of the same value in the moral community. Here differences of merit are so conspicuous and pervasive that we might even be tempted to *define* the moral response to a person in terms of moral approval or disapproval of his acts or disposition, i.e., in terms of the response to his moral merit. But there are many kinds of moral response for which a person's merit is as irrelevant as is that of New Yorker *X* when he appeals to the police for help. If I see someone in danger of drowning I will not need to satisfy myself about his moral character before going to his aid. I owe assistance to any man in such

[8] Though it might have uses in the family or other relations.
[9] Even where a purely pragmatic justification is offered for democracy (e.g., Pendleton Herring, *Politics of Democracy* [New York: W. W. Norton & Co., 1940]) equality of worth must still be acknowledged, if only as a popular "myth" or "dogma."
[10] No one, I trust, will confuse second-class citizenship with extreme punishments, such as the death-penalty or a life-sentence, or, for that matter, with *any* legal punishment in a democratic society. Second-class citizens are those deprived of rights without any presumption of legal guilt.
[11] John Dollard, *Caste and Class in a Southern Town* (New Haven: Yale Univ. Press, 1937).

circumstances, nor merely to good men. Nor is it only in rare and exceptional cases, as this example might suggest, that my obligations to others are independent of their moral merit. To be sincere, reliable, fair, kind, tolerant, unintrusive, modest in my relations with my fellows is not due them because they have made brilliant or even passing moral grades, but simply because they happen to be fellow-members of the moral community. It is not necessary to add, "members in good standing." The moral community is not a club from which members may be dropped for delinquency. Our morality does not provide for moral outcasts or half-castes. It does provide for punishment. But this takes place *within* the moral community and under its rules. It is for this reason that, for example, one has no right to be cruel to a cruel person. His offense against the moral law has not put him outside the law. He is still protected by its prohibition of cruelty—as much so as are kind persons. The pain inflicted on him as punishment for his offense does not close out the reserve of good will on the part of all others which is his birthright as a human being: it is a limited withdrawal from it. Capital punishment, if we believe in it, is no exception. The fact that a man has been condemned to death does not license his jailors to beat him or virtuous citizens to lynch him.

Here, then, as in the single-status political community, we acknowledge personal rights which are not proportioned to merit and could not be justified by merit. Their only justification could be the value which persons have simply because they are persons: their "intrinsic value as individual human beings," as Frankena calls it; the "infinite value" or the "sacredness" of their individuality, as others have called it. I shall speak of it as "individual human worth"; or "human worth," for short. What these expressions stand for is also expressed by saying that men are "ends in themselves." This latter concept is Kant's. Some of the kinks in his formulation of it[12] can be straightened out by explaining it as follows: Everything other than a person can only have value *for* a person. This applies not only to physical objects, natural or manmade, which have only instrumental value, but also to those products of the human spirit which have also intrinsic, no less than extrinsic, value: an epic poem, a scientific theory, a legal system, a moral disposition. Even such things as these will have value only because they can be (a) experienced or felt to be valuable by human beings and (b) chosen by them from competing alternatives. Thus of everything without exception it will be true to say: if x is valuable and is not a person, then x will have value for some individual other than itself. Hence even a musical composition or a courageous deed, valued for their own sake, as "ends" not as means to anything else, will still fall into an entirely different category from that of the *valuers*, who do not need to be valued as "ends" by someone else[13] in order to have value. In just this sense persons, and only persons, are "ends in themselves."

[12] See, e.g., H. Sidgwick, *Methods of Ethics* (London, 1874), p. 363. For a parallel objection see the next note. Still another is that Kant, using the notion of *intrinsic worth* (*Würde* in contrast to *Preis*) to define *end in itself*, and hence as its sufficient condition, tends to conflate the value of *persons* as ends in themselves with that of their *moral merit*. Thus, though he says that "Respect [the attitude due to a being which is an end in itself] always applies to persons only" (*Critique of Practical Reason*, trans. L. W. Beck [New York, 1956], p. 79) he illustrates by respect for a person's "righteousness" (l.c.) and remarks: "Respect is a tribute we cannot refuse to pay to merit . . ." (p. 80).

[13] Though, of course, they may be (if they are loved or respected as persons). In that case it will not be, strictly, the persons, but their welfare or freedom, which will be the "end" of those who so love or respect them: since only that which can be realized by action can be an end, to speak of another *person* as my end is bad logical grammar.

The two factors in terms of which I have described the value of the valuer—the capacities answering to (a) and (b) above—may not be exhaustive. But their conjunction offers a translation of "individual human worth" whose usefulness for working purposes will speak for itself. To (a) I might refer as "happiness," if I could use this term as Plato and Aristotle use *eudaimonia*, i.e., without the exclusively hedonistic connotations which have since been clamped on it. It will be less misleading to use "well-being" or "welfare" for what I intend here; that is, the enjoyment of value in all the forms in which it can be experienced by human beings. To (b) I shall refer as "freedom," bringing under this term not only conscious choices and deliberate decisions but also those subtler modulations and more spontaneous expressions of individual preference which could scarcely be called "choices" or "decisions" without some forcing of language. So understood, a person's well-being and freedom are aspects of his individual existence as unique and unrepeatable as is that existence itself: If *A* and *B* are listening to the same symphony with similar tastes and dispositions, we may speak of their enjoying the "same" good, or having the "same" enjoyment, and say that each has made the "same" choice for this way of spending his time and money. But here "same" will mean no more than "very similar"; the two enjoyments and choices, occurring in the consciousness of *A* and *B* respectively, are absolutely unique. So in translating "*A*'s human worth" into "the worth of *A*'s well-being and freedom" we are certainly meeting the condition that the former expression is to stand for whatever it is about *A* which, unlike his merit, has *individual* worth.

We are also meeting another condition: that the equality of human worth be justification, or ground, of equal human rights. I can best bring this out by reverting to the visitor from Mars who had asked a little earlier why we want equalization of security benefits. Let us conjure up circumstances in which his question would spring, not from idle curiosity, but from a strong conviction that this, or any other, right entailing such undiscriminating equality of benefits, would be entirely *un*reasonable. Suppose then that he hails from a strict meritarian community, which maintains the *M*-system in its political life and analogous patterns in other associations. And to make things simpler, let us also suppose that he is shown nothing in New York or elsewhere that is out of line with our formal professions of equality, so that he imagines us purer, more strenuous, equalitarians than we happen to be. The pattern of valuation he ascribes to us then seems to him fantastically topsy-turvy. He can hardly bring himself to believe that rational human beings should want equal personal rights, legal and moral, for their "riff-raff" and their élites. Yet neither can he explain away our conduct as pure automatism, a mere fugue of social habit. "These people, or some of them," he will be saying to himself, "must have some reasons for this incredible code. What could these be?" If we volunteered an answer couched in terms of human worth, he might find it hard to understand us. Such an answer, unglossed, would convey to him no more than that we recognize something which is highly and equally valuable in all persons, but has nothing to do with their merit, and constitutes the ground of their equal rights. But this might start him hunting—snark-hunting—for some special quality named by "human worth" as honesty is named by "honesty" and kindness by "kindness," wondering all the while how it could have happened that he and all his tribe have had no inkling of it, if all of them have always had it.[14]

But now suppose that we avail ourselves of the aforesaid translation. We could then tell him: "To understand our code you should take into account how very different from yours is our own estimate of the relative worth of the welfare and freedom of different individuals. We agree with you that not all persons are capable of experiencing the same values. But there is a wide variety of cases in which persons are capable of this. Thus, to take a perfectly clear case, no matter how A and B might differ in taste and style of life, they would both crave relief from acute physical pain. In that case we would put the same value on giving this to either of them, regardless of the fact that A might be a talented, brilliantly successful person, B 'a mere nobody.' On this we would disagree sharply. You would weigh the welfare of members of the élite more highly than that of that of 'riff-raff,' as you call them. We would not. If A were a statesman, and giving him relief from pain enabled him to conclude an agreement that would benefit millions, while B, an unskilled laborer, was himself the sole beneficiary of the like relief, we would, of course, agree that the *instrumental* value of the two experiences would be vastly different—but not their *intrinsic* value. In all cases where human being are capable of enjoying the same goods, we feel that the intrinsic value of their enjoyment is the same. In just this sense we hold that (1) *one man's well-being is as valuable as any other's*. And there is a parallel difference in our feeling for freedom. You value it only when exercised by good persons for good ends. We put no such strings on its value. We feel that choosing for oneself what one will do, believe, approve, say, see, read, worship, has its own intrinsic value, the same for all persons, and quite independently of the value of the things they happen to choose. Naturally, we hope that all of them will make the best possible use of their freedom of choice. But we value their exercise of that freedom, regardless of the outcome; and we value it equally for all. For us (2) *one man's freedom is as valuable as any other's.*"

This sort of explanation, I submit, would put him in a position to resolve his dilemma. For just suppose that, taking this homily at face-value, he came to think of us as believing (1) and (2).[15] No matter how unreasonable he might think of us he would feel it entirely reasonable that, since we do believe in equal *value* of human well-being and freedom, we should also believe in the *prima facie* equality of men's *right* to well-being and to freedom. He would see the former as a good reason for the latter; or, more formally, he could think of (1) and (2) respectively as crucial premises in justification arguments whose respective conclusions would be: (3) One man's (*prima facie*) right to well-being is equal to that of any other, and (4) One man's (*prima facie*) right to freedom is equal to that of any other. Then given (4), he could see how this would serve as the basis for a great variety of rights to specific kinds of freedom: freedom of movement, of association, of suffrage, of speech, of thought, of worship, of choice of employment, and the like. For each of these can be regarded as simply a

[14] Cf.Melden, *Rights and Right Conduct*, p. 80.
[15] I am bypassing the factual question of the extent to which (1) and (2) are generally believed.

specification of the general right to freedom, and would thus be covered by the justification of the latter. Moreover, given (3), he could see in it the basis for various welfare-rights, such as the right to education, medical care, work under decent conditions, relief in periods of unemployment, leisure, housing, etc.[16] Thus to give him (1) and (2) as justification for (3) and (4) would be to give him a basis for every one of the rights which are mentioned in the most complete of currently authoritative declarations of human rights, that passed by the Assembly of the United Nations in 1948. Hence to tell him that we believe in the equal worth of individual freedom and happiness would be to answer, in terms he can understand, his question, "What is your reason for your equalitarian code?"[17]

Nowhere in this defense of the translation of "equal human worth" into "equal worth of human well-being and freedom" have I claimed that the former can be *reduced* to the latter. I offered individual well-being and freedom simply as two things which do satisfy the conditions defined by individual human worth. Are there others? For the purposes of this essay this may be left an open question. For if there are, they would provide, at most, additional grounds for human rights. The ones I have specified are grounds enough. They are all I need for the analysis of equalitarian justice as, I trust, will appear directly.

[16]I am well aware of the incompleteness of this highly schematic account. It does not pretend to give the full argument for the justification of (3) and (4) (and see next note) or of their "specifications." Among other omissions, it fails to make allowance for the fact that the complex inter-relations of these various rights would affect the justification of each.

[17]On p. 19 Frankena writes as though his own answer to the same question would be, "because 'all men are similarly capable of enjoying a good life' "; this, he says, is what "justifies the *prima facie* requirement that they be treated as equals." But that A and B are similarly capable of enjoying respectively good lives $G(A)$ and $G(B)$ is not a compelling reason for saying that A and B have equal right respectively to $G(A)$ and $G(B)$. The Brahmin who held (Sir Henry Maine, *Early History of Institutions* [New York, 1875], p. 399) that "a Brahmin was entitled to 20 times as much happiness as anyone else" need not have held that the Brahmin's *capacity* for happiness (or, for "enjoying a good life") differs in the same ratio from that of others. All he would have to deny would be the equal *value* of the happiness of Brahmins and of others. It is some such premise as this that Frankena must affirm to bring off his justification-argument. I might add that I am not objecting to listing capacity among the premises. The only reason I did not is that I was only citing the "crucial" premise, the one that would be normally decisive for the acceptance or rejection of the justificandum. A reference to capacity would also be necessary, and I would follow Frankena in conceding that "men may well be different in such a way that the best life of which one is capable simply is not as good as that of which another is capable" (p. 20), adding a like concession in the case of freedom. A's and B's *prima facie* equal rights to well-being and to freedom are in effect equal rights to that well-being and freedom of which A and B are equally capable. Thus where the capacity for freedom is severely limited (e.g., that of an idiot or anyone else in the *non compos mentis* class), the right to freedom would be correspondingly limited.

John Rawls

John Rawls (b. 1921) is Professor of Philosophy at Harvard University. Since 1958 he has published a series of interrelated articles dealing with philosophical problems concerning justice. His resulting view of justice is systematically developed in his book, *A Theory of Justice.*

"Justice As Fairness," the first article printed here, contains the foundations of Rawls's later work. In this article he presents an analysis of the concept of justice and a derivation of its associated principles. Rawls's view of justice is basically contractarian in nature, falling in the tradition linked with Rousseau and Locke, but it is important to notice that he uses the concept of an original agreement or position only as a conceptual tool in analyzing the concept of justice and deriving its associated principles. He does not view the original position as an historical event, nor does he derive the authority of law from any implicit promise or contract on the part of the citizen.

Justice as Fairness

1. It might seem as first sight that the concepts of justice and fairness are the same, and that there is no reason to distinguish them, or to say that one is more fundamental than the other. I think that this impression is mistaken. In this paper I wish to show that the fundamental idea in the concept of justice is fairness; and I wish to offer an analysis of the concept of justice from this point of view. To bring out the force of this claim, and the analysis based upon it, I shall then argue that it is this aspect of justice for which utilitarianism, in its classical form, is unable to account, but which is expressed, even if misleadingly, by the idea of the social contract.

To start with I shall develop a particular conception of justice by stating and commenting upon two principles which specify it, and by considering the circumstances and conditions under which they may be thought to arise. The principles defining this conception, and the conception itself, are, of course, familiar. It may be possible, however, by using the notion of fairness as a framework, to assemble and to look at them in a new way. Before stating this conception, however, the following preliminary matters should be kept in mind.

Throughout I consider justice only as a virtue of social institutions, or what I

Reprinted from *The Philosophical Review,* Vol. LXVII, 1958 by permission of the author and the Editor. The last paragraph of Section 3 has been revised.

shall call practices.[1] The principles of justice are regarded as formulating restrictions as to how practices may define positions and offices, and assign thereto powers and liabilities, rights and duties. Justice as a virtue of particular actions or of persons I do not take up at all. It is important to distinguish these various subjects of justice, since the meaning of the concept varies according to whether it is applied to practices, particular actions, or persons. These meanings are, indeed, connected, but they are not identical. I shall confine my discussion to the sense of justice as applied to practices, since this sense is the basic one. Once it is understood, the other senses should go quite easily.

Justice is to be understood in its customary sense as representing but *one* of the many virtues of social institutions, for these may be antiquated, inefficient, degrading, or any number of other things, without being unjust. Justice is not to be confused with an all inclusive vision of a good society; it is only one part of any such conception. It is important, for example, to distinguish that sense of equality which is an aspect of the concept of justice from that sense of equality which belongs to a more comprehensive social ideal. There may well be inequalities which one concedes are just, or at least not unjust, but which, nevertheless, one wishes, on other grounds, to do away with. I shall focus attention, then, on the usual sense of justice in which it is essentially the elimination of arbitrary distinctions and the establishment, within the structure of a practice, of a proper balance between competing claims.

Finally, there is no need to consider the principles discussed below as *the* principles of justice. For the moment it is sufficient that they are typical of a family of principles normally associated with the concept of justice. The way in which the principles of this family resemble one another, as shown by the background against which they may be thought to arise, will be made clear by the whole of the subsequent argument.

2. The conception of justice which I want to develop may be stated in the form of two principles as follows: first, each person participating in a practice, or affected by it, has an equal right to the most extensive liberty compatible with a like liberty for all; and second, inequalities are arbitrary unless it is reasonable to expect that they will work out for everyone's advantage, and provided the positions and offices to which they attach, or from which they may be gained, are open to all. These principles express justice as a complex of three ideas: liberty, equality, and reward for services contributing to the common good.[2]

[1] I use the word "practice" throughout as a sort of technical term meaning any form of activity specified by a system of rules which defines offices, roles, moves, penalties, defenses, and so on, and which gives the activity its structure. As examples one may think of games and rituals, trials and parliaments, markets and systems of property. I have attempted a partial analysis of the notion of a practice in a paper "Two Concepts of Rules," *Philosophical Review*, LXIV (1955), 3-32.

[2] These principles are, of course, well-known in one form or another and appear in many analyses of justice even where the writers differ widely on other matters. Thus if the principle of equality is commonly associated with Kant (see *The Philosophy of Law*, tr. by W. Hastie, Edingburgh, 1887, pp. 56 f), it may be claimed that it can also be found in J. S. Mill's *On Liberty* and elsewhere, and in many other liberal writers. Recently H. L. A. Hart has argued for something like it in his paper "Are There Any Natural Rights?," *Philosophical Review*, LXIV (1955), 175-191. The injustice of inequalities which are not won in return for a contribution to the common advantage is, of course, widespread in political writings of all sorts. The conception of justice here discussed is distinctive, if at all, only in selecting these two principles in this form; but for another similar analysis, see the discussion by W. D. Lamont, *The Principles of Moral Judgment* (Oxford, 1946), ch. v.

The term "person" is to be construed variously depending on the circumstances. On some occasions it will mean human individuals, but in others it may refer to nations, provinces, business firms, churches, teams, and so on. The principles of justice apply in all these instances, although there is a certain logical priority to the case of human individuals. As I shall use the term "person," it will be ambiguous in the manner indicated.

The first principle holds, of course, only if other things are equal: that is, while there must always be a justification for departing from the initial position of equal liberty (which is defined by the pattern of rights and duties, powers and liabilities, established by a practice), and the burden of proof is placed on him who would depart from it, nevertheless, there can be, and often there is, a justification for doing so. Now, that similar particular cases, as defined by a practice, should be treated similarly as they arise, is part of the very concept of a practice; it is involved in the notion of an activity in accordance with rules.[3] The first principle expresses an analogous conception, but as applied to the structure of practices themselves. It holds, for example, that there is a presumption against the distinctions and classifications made by legal systems and other practices to the extent that they infringe on the original and equal liberty of the persons participating in them. The second principle defines how this presumption may be rebutted.

It might be argued at this point that justice requires only an equal liberty. If, however, a greater liberty were possible for all without loss or conflict, then it would be irrational to settle on a lesser liberty. There is no reason for circumscribing rights unless their exercise would be incompatible, or would render the practice defining them less effective. Therefore no serious distortion of the concept of justice is likely to follow from including within it the concept of the greatest equal liberty.

The second principle defines what sorts of inequalities are permissible; it specifies how the presumption laid down by the first principle may be put aside. Now by inequalities it is best to understand not *any* differences between offices and positions, but differences in the benefits and burdens attached to them either directly or indirectly, such as prestige and wealth, or liability to taxation and compulsory services. Players in a game do not protest against there being different positions, such as batter, pitcher, catcher, and the like, nor to there being various privileges and powers as specified by the rules; nor do the citizens of a country object to there being the different offices of government such as president, senator, governor, judge, and so on, each with their special rights and duties. It is not differences of this kind that are normally thought of as inequalities, but differences in the resulting distribution established by a practice, or made possible by it, of the things men strive to attain or avoid. Thus they may complain about the pattern of honors and rewards set up by a practice (e.g., the privileges and salaries of government officials) or they may object to the distribution of power and wealth which results from the various ways in which men avail themselves of the opportunities allowed by it (e.g., the concentration of wealth which may develop in a free price system allowing large entrepreneurial or speculative gains).

[3] This point was made by Sidgwick, *Methods of Ethics,* 6th ed. (London, 1901), Bk. III, ch. v. sec. 1. It has recently been emphasized by Sir Isaiah Berlin in a Symposium, "Equality," *Proceedings of the Aristotelian Society,* n.s. LVI (1955-56), 305 f.

It should be noted that the second principle holds that an inequality is allowed only if there is reason to believe that practice with the inequality, or resulting in it, will work for the advantage of *every* party engaging in it. Here it is important to stress that *every* party must gain from the inequality. Since the principle applies to practices, it implies that the representative man in every office or position defined by a practice, when he views it as a going concern, must find it reasonable to prefer his condition and prospects with the inequality to what they would be under the practice without it. The principle excludes, therefore, the justification of inequalities on the grounds that the disadvantages of those in one position are outweighed by the greater advantages of those in another position. This rather simple restriction is the main modification I wish to make in the utilatarian principle as usually understood. When coupled with the notion of a practice, it is a restriction of consequence,[4] and one which some utilitarians, e.g., Hume and Mill, have used in their discussions of justice without realizing apparently its significance, or at least without calling attention to it.[5] Why it is a significant modification of principle, changing one's conception of justice entirely, the whole of my argument will show.

Further, it is also necessary that the various offices to which special benefits or burdens attach are open to all. It may be, for example, to the common advantage, as just defined, to attach special benefits to certain offices. Perhaps by doing so the requisite talent can be attracted to them and encouraged to give its best efforts. But any offices having special benefits must be won in a fair competition in which contestants are judged on their merits. If some offices were not open, those excluded would normally be justified in feeling unjustly treated, even if they benefited from the greater efforts of those who were allowed to compete for them. Now if one can assume that offices are open, it is necessary only to consider the design of practices themselves and how they

[4] In the paper referred to above, footnote 2, I have tried to show the importance of taking practices as the proper subject of the utilitarian principle. The criticisms of so-called restricted utilitarianism by J. J. C. Smart, "Extreme and Restricted Utilitarianism," *Philosophical Quarterly*, VI (1956), 344-354, and by H. J. McCloskey, "An Examination of Restricted Utilitarianism," *Philosophical Review*, LXVI (1957), 466-485, do not affect my argument. These papers are concerned with the very general proposition, which is attributed (with what justice I shall not consider) to S. E. Toulmin and P. H. Nowell-Smith (and in the case of the latter paper, also apparently, to me); namely, the proposition that particular moral actions are justified by appealing to moral rules, and moral rules in turn by reference to utility. But clearly I meant to defend no such view. My discussion of the concept of rules as maxims is an explicit rejection of it. What I did argue was that, in the *logically special* case of practices (although actually quite a common case) where the rules have special features and are not moral rules at all but legal rules or rules of games and the like (except, perhaps, in the case of promises), there is a peculiar force to the distinction between justifying particular actions and justifying the system of rules themselves. Even then I claimed only that restricting the utilitarian principle to practices as defined strengthened it. I did not argue for the position that this amendment alone is sufficient for a complete defense of utilitarianism as a general theory of morals. In this paper I take up the question as to how the utilitarian principle itself must be modified, but here, too, the subject of inquiry is not all of morality at once, but a limited topic, the concept of justice.

[5] It might seem as if J. S. Mill, in paragraph 36 of Chapter v of *Utilitarianism*, expressed the utilitarian principle in this modified form, but in the remaining two paragraphs of the chapter, and elsewhere, he would appear not to grasp the significance of the change. Hume often emphasizes that *every* man must benefit. For example, in discussing the utility of general rules, he holds that they are requisite to the "well-being of every individual"; from a stable system of property "every individual person must find himself a gainer in balancing the account...." "Every member of society is sensible of this interest; everyone expresses this sense to his fellows along with the resolution he has taken of squaring his actions by it, on the conditions that others will do the same." *A Treatise of Human Nature*, Bk. III, Pt. II, Section II, paragraph 22.

jointly, as a system, work together. It will be a mistake to focus attention on the varying relative positions of particular persons, who may be known to us by their proper names, and to require that each such change, as a once for all transaction viewed in isolation, must be in itself just. It is the system of practices which is to be judged from a general point of view: unless one is prepared to criticize it from the standpoint of a representative man holding some particular office, one has no complaint against it.

3. Given these principles one might try to derive them from a priori principles of reason, or claim that they were known by intuition. These are familiar enough steps and, at least in the case of the first principle, might be made with some success. Usually, however, such arguments, made at this point, are unconvincing. They are not likely to lead to an understanding of the basis of the principles of justice, not at least as principles of justice. I wish, therefore, to look at the principle in a different way.

Imagine a society of persons amongst whom a certain system of practices is *already* well established. Now suppose that by and large they are mutually self-interested; their allegiance to their established practices is normally founded on the prospect of self-advantage. One need not assume that, in all senses of the term "person," the persons in this society are mutually self-interested. If the characterization as mutually self-interested applies when the line of division is the family, it may still be true that members of families are bound by ties of sentiment and affection and willingly acknowledge duties in contradiction to self-interest. Mutual self-interestedness in the relations between families, nations, churches, and the like, is commonly associated with intense loyalty and devotion on the part of individual members. Therefore, one can form a more realistic conception of this society if one thinks of it as consisting of mutually self-interested families, or some other association. Further, it is not necessary to suppose that these persons are mutually self-interested under all circumstances, but only in the usual situations in which they participate in their common practices.

Now suppose also that these persons are rational: they know their own interests more or less accurately; they are capable of tracing out the likely consequences of adopting one practice rather than another; they are capable of adhering to a course of action once they have decided upon it; they can resist present temptations and the enticements of immediate gain; and the bare knowledge or perception of the difference between their condition and that of others is not, within certain limits and in itself, a source of great dissatisfaction. Only the last point adds anything to the usual definition of rationality. This definition should allow, I think, for the idea that a rational man would not be greatly downcast from knowing, or seeing, that others are in a better position than himself, unless he thought their being so was the result of injustice, or the consequence of letting chance work itself out for no useful common purpose, and so on. So if these persons strike us as unpleasantly egoistic, they are at least free in some degree from the fault of envy.[6]

---

[6] It is not possible to discuss here this addition to the usual conception of rationality. If it seems peculiar, it may be worth remarking that it is analogous to the modification of the utilitarian principle which the argument as a whole is designed to explain and justify. In the same way that the satisfaction of interests, the representative claims of which violate the principles of justice, is not a reason for having a practice (see sec. 7), unfounded envy, within limits, need not be taken into account.

Finally, assume that these persons have roughly similar needs and interests, or needs and interests in various ways complementary, so that fruitful cooperation amongst them is possible; and suppose that they are sufficiently equal in power and ability to guarantee that in normal circumstances none is able to dominate the others. This condition (as well as the others) may seem excessively vague; but in view of the conception of justice to which the argument leads, there seems no reason for making it more exact here.

Since these persons are conceived as engaging in their common practices, which are already established, there is no question of our supposing them to come together to deliberate as to how they will set these practices up for the first time. Yet we can imagine that from time to time they discuss with one another whether any of them has a legitimate complaint against their established institutions. Such discussions are perfectly natural in any normal society. Now suppose that they have settled on doing this in the following way. They first try to arrive at the principles by which complaints, and so practices themselves, are to be judged. Their procedure for this is to let each person propose the principles upon which he wishes his complaints to be tried with the understanding that, if acknowledged, the complaints of others will be similarly tried, and that no complaints will be heard at all until everyone is roughly of one mind as to how complaints are to be judged. They each understand further that the principles proposed and acknowledged on this occasion are binding on future occasions. Thus each will be wary of proposing a principle which would give him a peculiar advantage, in his present circumstances, supposing it to be accepted. Each person knows that he will be bound by it in future circumstances the peculiarities of which cannot be known, and which might well be such that the principle is then to his disadvantage. The idea is that everyone should be required to make *in advance* a firm commitment, which others also may reasonably be expected to make, and that no one be given the opportunity to tailor the canons of a legitimate complaint to fit his own special condition, and then to discard them when they no longer suit his purpose. Hence each person will propose principles of a general kind which will, to a large degree, gain their sense from the various applications to be made of them, the particular circumstances of which being as yet unknown. These principles will express the conditions in accordance with which each is the least unwilling to have his interests limited in the design of practices, given the competing interests of the others, on the supposition that the interests of others will be limited likewise. The restrictions which would so arise might be thought of as those a person would keep in mind if he were designing a practice in which his enemy were to assign him his place.

The two main parts of this conjectural account have a definite significance. The character and respective situations of the parties reflect the typical circumstances in which questions of justice arise. The procedure whereby principles are proposed and acknowledged represents constraints, analogous to those of having a morality, whereby rational and mutually self-interested persons are brought to act reasonably. Thus the first part reflects the fact that questions of justice arise when conflicting claims are made upon the design of a practice and where it is taken for granted that each person will insist, as far as possible, on what he considers his rights. It is typical of cases of justice to involve persons who are pressing on one another their claims, between which a fair balance or equilibrium must be found. On the other hand, as expressed by the second part, having a morality must at least imply the acknowledgment of principles as impartially applying to one's own conduct as well as to another's and moreover principles which may constitute a constraint, or limitation, upon the pursuit of one's own interests. There are, of course, other aspects of having a morality: the acknowledgment of moral principles must show itself in accepting a reference to them as reasons for limiting one's claims, in acknowledging the burden of providing a special explanation, or excuse, when one acts contrary to them, or else in showing shame and remorse and a desire to make amends, and so on. It is sufficient to remark here that having a morality is analogous to having made a firm commitment in advance; for one must acknowledge the principles of morality even when to one's disadvantage.[7] A man whose moral judgments always coincided with his interests could be suspected of having no morality at all.

Thus the two parts of the foregoing account are intended to mirror the kinds of circumstances in which questions of justice arise and the constraints which having a morality would impose upon persons so situated. In this way one can see how the acceptance of the principles of justice might come about, for given all these conditions as described, it would be natural if the two principles of justice were to be acknowledged. Since there is no way for anyone to win special advantages for himself, each might consider it reasonable to acknowledge equality as an initial principle. There is, however, no reason why they should regard this position as final; for if there are inequalities which satisfy the second principle, the immediate gain which equality would allow can be considered as intelligently invested in view of its future return. If, as is quite likely, these inequalities work as incentives to draw out better efforts, the members of this society may look upon them as concessions to human nature: they, like us, may think that people ideally should want to serve one another. But as they are mutually self-interested, their acceptance of these inequalities is merely the acceptance of the relations in which they actually stand, and a recognition of the motives which lead them to engage in their common practices. *They* have no title to complain of one another. And so provided that the conditions of the principle are met, there is no reason why they should not allow such inequalities. Indeed, it would be short-sighted of them not to do so, and could result, in most cases, only from their being dejected by the bare knowledge, or perception, that others are better situated. Each person will however, insist on an advantage to himself, and so on a common advantage, for none is willing to sacrifice anything for the others.

These remarks are not offered as a rigorous proof that persons conceived and situated as the conjectural account supposes, and required to adopt the procedure described, would settle on the two principles of justice. For such a proof a more elaborate and formal argument would have to be given; there remain certain details to be filled in, and various alternatives to be ruled out. The argument should, however, be taken as a proof, or as a sketch of a proof; for the

[7] The idea that accepting a principle as a moral principle implies that one generally acts on it, failing a special explanation, has been stressed by R. M. Hare, *The Language of Morals* (Oxford, 1952). His formulation of it needs to be modified, however, along the lines suggested by P. L. Gardiner, "On Assenting to a Moral Principle," *Proceedings of the Aristotelian Society*, n.s. LV (1955), 23-44. See also C. K. Grant, "Akrasia and the Criteria of Assent to Practical Principles," *Mind*, LXV (1950), 400-407, where the complexity of the criteria for assent is discussed.

proposition I seek to establish is a necessary one, that is, it is intended as a theorem: namely, that when mutually self-interested and rational persons confront one another in typical circumstances of justice, and when they are required by a procedure expressing the constraints of having a morality to jointly acknowledge principles by which their claims on the design of their common practices are to be judged, they will settle on these two principles as restrictions governing the assignment of rights and duties, and thereby accept them as limiting their rights against one another. It is this theorem which accounts for these principles as principles of justice, and explains how they come to be associated with this moral concept. Moreover this theorem is analogous to those about human conduct in other branches of social thought. That is, a simplified situation is described in which rational persons pursuing certain ends and related to one another in a definite way, are required to act subject to certain limitations; then, given this situation, it is shown that they will act in a certain manner. Failure to so act would imply that one or more of the assumptions does not obtain. The foregoing account aims to establish, or to sketch, a theorem in this sense; the aim of the argument is to show the basis for saying that the principles of justice may be regarded as those principles which arise when the constraints of having a morality are imposed upon rational persons in typical circumstances of justice.

4. These ideas are, of course, connected with a familiar way of thinking about justice which goes back at least to the Greek Sophists, and which regards the acceptance of the principles of justice as a compromise between persons of roughly equal power who would enforce their will on each other if they could, but who, in view of the equality of forces amongst them and for the sake of their own peace and security, acknowledge certain forms of conduct insofar as prudence seems to require. Justice is thought of as a pact between rational egoists the stability of which is dependent on a balance of power and a similarity of circumstances.[8] While the previous account is connected with this tradition, and with its most recent variant, the theory of games,[9] it differs from it in

[8] Perhaps the best known statement of this conception is that given by Glaucon at the beginning of Book II of Plato's *Republic*. Presumably it was, in various forms, a common view among the Sophists; but that Plato gives a fair representation of it is doubtful. See K. R. Popper, *The Open Society and Its Enemies*, rev. ed. (Princeton, 1950), pp. 112-118. Certainly Plato usually attributes to it a quality of manic egoism which one feels must be an exaggeration; on the other hand, see the Melian Debate in Thucydides, *The Peloponnesian War*, Book V, ch. vii, although it is impossible to say to what extent the views expressed there reveal any current philosophical opinion. Also in this tradition are the remarks of Epicurus on justice in *Principal Doctrines*, XXXI-XXXVIII. In modern times elements of the conception appear in a more sophisticated form in Hobbes, *The Leviathan* and in Hume *A Treatise of Human Nature*, Book III, Pt. II, as well as in the writings of the school of natural law such as Pufendorf's *De jure naturae et gentium*. Hobbes and Hume are especially instructive. For Hobbes's argument see Howard Warrender's *The Political Philosophy of Hobbes* (Oxford, 1957). W. J. Baumol's *Welfare Economics and the Theory of the State* (London, 1952), is valuable in showing the wide applicability of Hobbes's fundamental idea (interpreting his natural law as principles of prudence), although in this book it is traced back only to Hume's *Treatise*.

[9] See J. von Neumann and O. Morgenstern, *The Theory of Games and Economic Behavior*, 2nd ed. (Princeton, 1947). For a comprehensive and not too technical discussion of the developments since, see R. Duncan Luce and Howard Raiffa, *Games and Decisions: Introduction and Critical Survey* (New York, 1957). Chs. vi and xiv discuss the developments most obviously related to the analysis of justice.

several important respects which, to forestall misinterpretations, I will set out here.

First, I wish to use the previous conjectural account of the background of justice as a way of analyzing the concept. I do not want, therefore, to be interpreted as assuming a general theory of human motivation: when I suppose that the parties are mutually self-interested, and are not willing to have their (substantial) interests sacrificed to others, I am referring to their conduct and motives as they are taken for granted in cases where questions of justice ordinarily arise. Justice is the virtue of practices where there are assumed to be competing interests and conflicting claims, and where it is supposed that persons will press their rights on each other. That persons are mutually self-interested in certain situations and for certain purposes is what gives rise to the question of justice in practices covering those circumstances. Amongst an association of saints, if such community could really exist, the disputes about justice could hardly occur; for they would all work selflessly together for one end, the glory of God as defined by their common religion, and reference to this end would settle every question of right. The justice of practices does not come up until there are several different parties (whether we think of these as individuals, associations, or nations and so on, is irrelevant) who do press their claims on one another, and who do regard themselves as representatives of interests which deserve to be considered. Thus the previous account involves no general theory of human motivation. Its intent is simply to incorporate into the conception of justice the relations of men to one another which set the stage for questions of justice. It makes no difference how wide or general these relations are, as this matter does not bear on the analysis of the concept.

Again, in contrast to the various conceptions of the social contract, the several parties do not establish any particular society or practice; they do not covenant to obey a particular sovereign body or to accept a given constitution.[10] Nor do they, as in the theory of games (in certain respects a marvelously sophisticated development of this tradition), decide on individual strategies adjusted to their circumstances in the game. What the parties do is to *jointly* acknowledge certain *principles* of appraisal relating to their common *practices* either as already established or merely proposed. They accede to standards of judgment, not to a given practice; they do not make any specific agreement, or bargain, or adopt a particular strategy. The subject of their acknowledgment is, therefore, very general indeed; it is simply the acknowledgment of certain principles of judgment, fulfilling certain general conditions, to be used in criticizing the arrangement of their common affairs. The relations of mutual self-interest between the parties who are similarly circumstanced mirror the conditions under which questions of justice arise, and the procedure by which the principles of judgment are proposed and acknowledged reflects the constraints of having a morality. Each aspect, then, of the preceding hypothetical account serves the purpose of bringing out a feature of the notion of justice. One could, if one liked, view the principles of justice as the "solution" of this highest order "game" of adopting, subject to the procedure described, principles of

[10] For a general survey see J. W. Gough, *The Social Contract*, 2nd ed. (Oxford, 1957), and Otto von Gierke, *The Development of Political Theory*, tr. by B. Freyd (London, 1939), Pt. II, ch. ii.

argument for all coming particular "games" whose peculiarities one can in no way foresee. But this comparison, while no doubt helpful, must not obscure the fact that this highest order "game" is of a special sort.[11] Its significance is that its various pieces represent aspects of the concept of justice.

Finally, I do not, of course, conceive the several parties as necessarily coming together to establish their common practices for the first time. Some institutions may, indeed, be set up *de novo;* but I have framed the preceding account so that it will apply when the full complement of social institutions already exists and represents the result of a long period of development. Nor is the account in any way fictitious. In any society where people reflect on their institutions they will have an idea of what principles of justice would be acknowledged under the conditions described, and there will be occasions when questions of justice are actually discussed in this way. Therefore if their practices do not accord with these principles, this will affect the quality of their social relations. For in this case there will be some recognized situations wherein the parties are mutually aware that one of them is being forced to accept what the other would concede is unjust. The foregoing analysis may then be thought of as representing the actual quality of relations between persons as defined by practices accepted as just. In such practices the parties acknowledge the principles on which it is constructed, and the general recognition of this fact shows itself in the absence of resentment and in the sense of being justly treated. Thus one common objection to the theory of the social contract, its apparently historical and fictitious character, is avoided.

5. That the principles of justice may be regarded as arising in the manner described illustrates an important fact about them. Not only does it bring out the idea that justice is a primitive moral notion in that it arises once the concept of morality is imposed on mutually self-interested agents similarly circum-stanced, but it emphasizes that, fundamental to justice, is the concept of fairness which relates to right dealing between persons who are cooperating with or

[11]The difficulty one gets into by a mechanical application of the theory of games to moral philosophy can be brought out by considering among several possible examples, R. B. Braithwaite's study, *Theory of Games as a Tool for the Moral Philosopher* (Cambridge, 1955). On the analysis there given, it turns out that the fair division of playing time between Matthew and Luke depends on their preferences, and these in turn are connected with the instruments they wish to play. Since Matthew has a threat advantage over Luke, arising purely from the fact that Matthew, the trumpeter, prefers both of them playing at once to neither of them playing, whereas Luke, the pianist, prefers silence to cacophony, Matthew is alloted 26 evenings of play to Luke's 17. If the situation were reversed, the threat advantage would be with Luke. See pp. 36 f. But now we have only to suppose that Matthew is a jazz enthusiast who plays the drums, and Luke a violinist who plays sonatas, in which case it will be fair, on this analysis, for Matthew to play whenever and as often as he likes, assuming, of course, as it is plausible to assume, that he does not care whether Luke plays or not. Certainly something has gone wrong. To each according to his threat advantage is hardly the principle of fairness. What is lacking is the concept of morality, and it must be brought into the conjectural account in some way or other. In the text this is done by the form of the procedure whereby principles are proposed and acknowledged (Section 3). If one starts directly with the particular case as known, and if one accepts as given and definitive the preferences and relative positions of the parties, whatever they are, it is impossible to give an analysis of the moral concept of fairness. Braithwaite's use of the theory of games, insofar as it is intended to analyze the concept of fairness, is, I think, mistaken. This is not, of course, to criticize in any way the theory of games as a mathematical theory, to which Braithwaite's book certainly contributes, nor as an analysis of how rational (and amoral) egoists might behave (and so as an analysis of how people sometimes actually do behave). But it is to say that if the theory of games is to be used to analyze moral concepts, its formal structure must be interpreted in a special and general manner as indicated in the text. Once we do this though, we are in touch again with a much older tradition.

competing agianst one another, as when one speaks of fair games, fair competition, and fair bargains. The question of fairness arises when free persons, who have no authority over one another, are engaging in a joint activity and amongst themselves settling or acknowledging the rules which define it and which determine the respective shares in its benefits and burdens. A practice will strike the parties as fair if none feels that, by participating in it, they or any of the others are taken advantage of, or forced to give in to claims which they do not regard as legitimate. This implies that each has a conception of legitimate claims which he thinks it reasonable for others as well as himself to acknowledge. If one thinks of the principles of justice as arising in the manner described, then they do define this sort of conception. A practice is just or fair, then, when it satisfies the principles which those who participate in it could propose to one another for mutual acceptance under the afore-mentioned circumstances. Persons engaged in a just, or fair, practice can face one another openly and support their respective positions, should they appear questionable, by reference to principles which it is reasonable to expect each to accept.

It is this notion of the possibility of mutual acknowledgment of principles by free persons who have no authority over one another which makes the concept of fairness fundamental to justice. Only if such acknowledgment is possible can there by true community between persons in their common practices; otherwise their relations will appear to them as founded to some extent on force. If, in ordinary speech, fairness applies more particularly to practices in which there is a choice whether to engage or not (e.g., in games, business competition), and justice to practices in which there is no choice (e.g., in slavery), the element of necessity does not render the conception of mutual acknowledgment inapplicable, although it may make it much more urgent to change unjust than unfair institutions. For one activity in which one can always engage is that of proposing and acknowledging principles to one another supposing each to be similarly circumstanced; and to judge practices by the principles so arrived at is to apply the standard of fairness to them.

Now if the participants in a practice accept its rules as fair, and so have no complaint to lodge against it, there arises a prima facie duty (and a corresponding prima facie right) of the parties to each other to act in accordance with the practice when it falls upon them to comply. When any number of persons engage in a practice, or conduct a joint undertaking according to rules, and thus restrict their liberty, those who have submitted to these restrictions when required have the right to a similar acquiescence on the part of those who have benefited by their submission. These conditions will obtain if a practice is correctly acknowledged to be fair, for in this case all who participate in it will benefit from it. The rights and duties so arising are special rights and duties in that they depend on previous actions voluntarily undertaken, in this case on the parties having engaged in a common practice and knowingly accepted its benefits.[12] It is not, however, an obligation which presupposes a deliberate performative act in the sense of a promise, or contract, and the like.[13] An unfortunate

---

[12] For the definition of this prima facie duty, and the idea that it is a special duty, I am indebted to H. L. A. Hart. See his paper "Are There Any Natural Rights?," *Philosophical Review*, LXIV (1955), 185 f.

[13] The sense of "performative" here is to be derived from J. L. Austin's paper in the symposium, "Other Minds," *Proceedings of the Aristotelian Society*, Supplementary Volume (1946), pp. 170-174.

mistake of proponents of the idea of the social contract was to suppose that political obligation does require some such act, or at least to use language which suggests it. It is sufficient that one has knowingly participated in and accepted the benefits of a practice acknowledged to be fair. This prima facie obligation may, of course, be overridden: it may happen, when it comes one's turn to follow a rule, that other considerations will justify not doing so. But one cannot, in general, be released from this obligation by denying the justice of the practice only when it falls on one to obey. If a person rejects a practice, he should, so far as possible, declare his intention in advance, and avoid participating in it or enjoying its benefits.

This duty I have called that of fair play, but it should be admitted that to refer to it in this way is, perhaps, to extend the ordinary notion of fairness. Usually acting unfairly is not so much the breaking of any particular rule, even if the infraction is difficult to detect (cheating), but taking advantage of loop-holes or ambiguities in rules, availing oneself of unexpected or special circumstances which make it impossible to enforce them, insisting that rules be enforced to one's advantage when they should be suspended, and more generally, acting contrary to the intention of a practice. It is for this reason that one speaks of the sense of fair play: acting fairly requires more than simply being able to follow rules; what is fair must often be felt, or perceived, one wants to say. It is not, however, an unnatural extension of the duty of fair play to have it include the obligation which participants who have knowingly accepted the benefits of their common practice owe to each other to act in accordance with it when their performance falls due; for it is usually considered unfair if someone accepts the benefits of a practice but refuses to do his part in maintaining it. Thus one might say of the tax-dodger that he violates the duty of fair play: he accepts the benefits of government but will not do his part in releasing resources to it; and members of labor unions often say that fellow workers who refuse to join are being unfair: they refer to them as "free-riders," as persons who enjoy what are the supposed benefits of unionism, higher wages, shorter hours, job security, and the like, but who refuse to share in its burdens in the form of paying dues, and so on.

The duty of fair play stands beside other prima facie duties such as fidelity and gratitude as a basic moral notion; yet it is not to be confused with them.[14] These duties are all clearly distinct, as would be obvious from their definitions. As with any moral duty, that of fair play implies a constraint on self-interest in particular cases; on occasion it enjoins conduct which a rational egoist strictly defined would not decide upon. So while justice does not require of anyone that he sacrifice his interests in that *general position* and procedure whereby the

---

[14] This, however, commonly happens. Hobbes, for example, when invoking the notion of a "tacit convenant," appeals not to the natural law that promises should be kept but to his fourth law of nature, that of gratitude. On Hobbes's shift from fidelity to gratitude, see Warrender, *op cit.*, pp. 51-52, 233-237. While it is not a serious criticism of Hobbes, it would have improved his argument had he appealed to the duty of fair play. On his premises he is perfectly entitled to do so. Similarly Sidgwick thought that a principle of justice, such as every man ought to receive adequate requital for his labor, is like gratitude universalized. See *Methods of Ethics*, Bk. III, ch v, Sec. 5. There is a gap in the stock of moral concepts used by philosophers into which the concept of the duty of fair play fits quite naturally.

principles of justice are proposed and acknowledged, it may happen that in particular situations, arising in the context of engaging in a practice, the duty of fair play will often cross his interests in the sense that he will be required to forego particular advantages which the peculiarities of his circumstances might permit him to take. There is, of course, nothing surprising in this. It is simply the consequence of the firm commitment which the parties may be supposed to have made, or which they would make, in the general position, together with the fact that they have participated in and accepted the benefits of a practice which they regard as fair.

Now the acknowledgment of this constraint in particular cases, which is manifested in acting fairly or wishing to make amends, feeling ashamed, and the like, when one has evaded it, is one of the forms of conduct by which participants in a common practice exhibit their recognition of each other as persons with similar interests and capacities. In the same way that, failing a special explanation, the criterion for the recognition of suffering is helping one who suffers, acknowledging the duty of fair play is a necessary part of the criterion for recognizing another as a person with similar interests and feelings as oneself.[15] A person who never under any circumstances showed a wish to help others in pain would show, at the same time, that he did not recognize that they were in pain; nor could he have any feelings of affection or friendship for anyone; for having these feelings implies, failing special circumstances, that he comes to their aid when they are suffering. Recognition that another is a person in pain shows itself in sympathetic action; this primitive natural response of compassion is one of those responses upon which the various forms of moral conduct are built.

Similarly, the acceptance of the duty of fair play by participants in a common practice is a reflection in each person of the recognition of the aspirations and interests of the others to be realized by their joint activity. Failing a special explanation, their acceptance of it is a necessary part of the criterion for their recognizing one another as persons with similar interests and capacities, as the conception of their relations in the general position suppose them to be. Otherwise they would show no recognition of one another as persons with similar capacities and interests, and indeed, in some case perhaps hypothetical, they would not recognize one another as persons at all, but as complicated objects involved in a complicated activity. To recognize another as a person one must respond to him and act towards him in certain ways; and these ways are intimately connected with the various prima facie duties. Acknowledging these duties in *some* degree, and so having the elements of morality, is not a matter of choice, or of intuiting moral qualities, or a matter of the expression of

[15]I am using the concept of criterion here in what I take to be Wittgenstein's sense. See *Philosophical Investigations* (Oxford, 1953); and Norman Malcolm's review, "Wittgenstein's *Philosophical Investigations,*" *Philosophical Review,* LXIII (1954), 543-547. That the response of compassion, under appropriate circumstances, is part of the criterion for whether or not a person understands what "pain" means, is, I think, in the *Philosophical Investigations.* The view in the text is simply an extension of this idea. I cannot, however, attempt to justify it here. Similar thoughts are to be found, I think, in Max Scheler, *The Nature of Sympathy,* tr. by Peter Heath (New Haven, 1954). His way of writing is often so obscure that I cannot be certain.

feeling or attitudes (the three interpretations between which philosophical opinion frequently oscillates); it is simply the possession of one of the forms of conduct in which the recognition of others as persons is manifested.

These remarks are unhappily obscure. Their main purpose here, however, is to forestall, together with the remarks in Section 4, the misinterpretation that on the view presented, the acceptance of justice and the acknowledgment of the duty of fair play depends in every day life solely on there being a *de facto* balance of forces between the parties. It would indeed be foolish to underestimate the importance of such a balance in securing justice; but it is not the only basis thereof. The recognition of one another as persons with similar interests and capacities engaged in a common practice must, failing a special explanation, show itself in the acceptance of the principles of justice and the acknowledgment of the duty of fair play.

The conception at which we have arrived, then, is that the principles of justice may be thought of as arising once the constraints of having a morality are imposed upon rational and mutually self-interested parties who are related and situated in a special way. A practice is just if it is in accordance with the principles which all who participate in it might reasonably be expected to propose or to acknowledge before one another when they are similarly circumstanced and required to make a firm commitment in advance without knowledge of what will be their peculiar condition, and thus when it meets standards which the parties could accept as fair should occasion arise for them to debate its merits. Regarding the participants themselves, once persons knowingly engage in a practice which they acknowledge to be fair and accept the benefits of doing so, they are bound by the duty of fair play to follow the rules when it comes their turn to do so, and this implies a limitation on their pursuit of self-interest in particular cases.

Now one consequence of this conception is that, where it applies, there is no moral value in the satisfaction of a claim incompatible with it. Such a claim violates the conditions of reciprocity and community amongst persons, and he who presses it, not being willing to acknowledge it when pressed by another, has no grounds for complaint when it is denied; whereas he against whom it is pressed can complain. As it cannot be mutually acknowledged it is a resort to coercion; granting the claim is possible only if one party can compel acceptance of what the other will not admit. But it makes no sense to concede claims the denial of which cannot be complained of in preference to claims the denial of which can be objected to. Thus in deciding on the justice of a practice it is not enough to ascertain that it answers to wants and interests in the fullest and most effective manner. For if any of these conflict with justice, they should not be counted, as their satisfaction is no reason at all for having a practice. It would be irrelevant to say, even if true, that it resulted in the greatest satisfaction of desire. In tallying up the merits of a practice one must toss out the satisfaction of interests the claims of which are incompatible with the principles of justice.

6. The discussion so far has been excessively abstract. While this is perhaps unavoidable, I should now like to bring out some of the features of the conception of justice as fairness by comparing it with the conception of justice in classical utilitarianism as represented by Bentham and Sidgwick, and its counterpart in welfare economics. This conception assimilates justice to benevol-

ence and the latter in turn to the most efficient design of institutions to promote the general welfare. Justice is a kind of efficiency.[16]

Now it is said occasionally that this form of utilitarianism puts no restrictions on what might be a just assignment of rights and duties in that there might be circumstances which, on utilitarian grounds, would justify institutions highly offensive to our ordinary sense of justice. But the classical utilitarian conception is not totally unprepared for this objection. Beginning with the notion that the general happiness can be represented by a social utility function consisting of a sum of individual utility functions with identical weights (this being the meaning of the maxim that each counts for one and no more than one),[17] it is commonly assumed that the utility functions of individuals are similar in all essential respects. Differences between individuals are ascribed to accidents of education and upbringing, and they should not be taken into account. This assumption, coupled with that of diminishing marginal utility, results in a prima facie case for equality, e.g., of equality in the distribution of income during any given period of time, laying aside indirect effects on the future. But even if utilitarianism is interpreted as having such restrictions built into the utility function, and even if it is supposed that these restrictions have in practice much the same result as the application of the principles of justice (and appear, perhaps, to be ways of expressing these principles in the language of mathematics and psychology), the fundamental idea is very different from the conception of justice as fairness. For one thing, that the principles of justice should be accepted is interpreted as the contingent result of a higher order administrative decision. The form of this decision is regarded as being similar to that of an entrepreneur deciding how much to produce of this or that commodity in view of its marginal revenue, or to that of someone distributing goods to needy persons according to the relative urgency of their wants. The choice between practices is thought of as being made on the basis of the allocation of benefits and burdens to individuals (these

[16]While this assimilation is implicit in Bentham's and Sidgwick's moral theory, explicit statements of it as applied to justice are relatively rare. One clear instance in *The Principles of Morals and Legislation* occurs in ch. x, footnote 2 to section XL: ".... justice, in the only sense in which it has a meaning, is an imaginary personage, feigned for the convenience of discourse, whose dictates are the dictates of utility, applied to certain particular cases. Justice, then, is nothing more than an imaginary instrument, employed to forward on certain occasions, and by certain means, the purposes of benevolence. The dictates of justice are nothing more than a part of the dictates of benevolence, which, on certain occasions, are applied to certain subjects. ...." Likewise in *The Limits of Jurisprudence Defined*, ed. by C. W. Everett (New York, 1945), pp. 117 f., Bentham criticizes Grotius for denying that justice derives from utility; and in *The Theory of Legislation*, ed. by C. K. Ogden (London, 1931), p. 3, he says that he uses the words "just" and "unjust" along with other words "simply as collective terms including the ideas of certain pains or pleasures." That Sidgwick's conception of justice is similar to Bentham's is admittedly not evident from his discussion of justice in Book III, ch. v of *Methods of Ethics*. But it follows, I think, from the moral theory he accepts. Hence C. D. Broad's criticisms of Sidgwick in the matter of distributive justice in *Five Types of Ethical Theory* (London, 1930), pp. 249-253, do not rest on a misinterpretation.

[17]This maxim is attributed to Bentham by J. S. Mill in *Utilitarianism*, ch. v, paragraph 36. I have not found it in Bentham's writings, nor seen such a reference. Similarly James Bonar, *Philosophy and Political Economy* (London, 1893), p. 234n. But it accords perfectly with Bentham's ideas. See the hitherto unpublished manuscript in David Baumgardt, *Bentham and the Ethics of Today* (Princeton, 1952), Appendix IV. For example, "the total value of the stock of pleasure belonging to the whole community is to be obtained by multiplying the number expressing the value of it as respecting any one person, by the number expressing the multitude of such individuals" (p. 556).

being measured by the present capitalized value of their utility over the full period of the practice's existence), which results from the distribution of rights and duties established by a practice.

Moreover, the individuals receiving these benefits are not conceived as being related in any way: they represent so many different directions in which limited resources may be allocated. The value of assigning resources to one direction rather than another depends solely on the preferences and interests of individuals as individuals. The satisfaction of desire has its value irrespective of the moral relations between persons, say as members of a joint undertaking, and of the claims which, in the name of these interests, they are prepared to make on one another;[18] and it is this value which is to be taken into account by the (ideal) legislator who is conceived as adjusting the rules of the system from the center so as to maximize the value of the social utility function.

It is thought that the principles of justice will not be violated by a legal system so conceived provided these executive decisions are correctly made. In this fact the principles of justice are said to have their derivation and explanation; they simply express the most important general features of social institutions in which the administrative problem is solved in the best way. These principles have, indeed, a special urgency because, given the facts of human nature, so much depends on them; and this explains the peculiar quality of the moral feelings associated with justice.[19] This assimilation of justice to a higher order executive decision, certainly a striking conception, is central to classical utilitarianism; and it also brings out its profound individualism, in one sense of this ambiguous word. It regards persons as so many *separate* directions in which benefits and burdens may be assigned; and the value of the satisfaction or dissatisfaction of desire is not thought to depend in any way on the moral relations in which individuals stand, or on the kinds of claims which they are willing, in the pursuit of their interests, to press on each other.

7. Many social decisions are, of course, of an administrative nature. Certainly this is so when it is a matter of social utility in what one may call its ordinary sense: that is, when it is a question of the efficient design of social institutions

---

[18] An idea essential to the classical utilitarian conception of justice. Bentham is firm in his statement of it: "It is only upon that principle [the principle of asceticism], and not from the principle of utility, that the most abominable pleasure which the vilest of malefactors ever reaped from his crime would be reprobated, if it stood alone. The case is, that it never does stand alone; but is necessarily followed by such a quantity of pain (or, what comes to the same thing, such a chance for a certain quantity of pain) that the pleasure in comparison of it, is as nothing: and this is the true and sole, but perfectly sufficient, reason for making it a ground for punishment" (*The Principles of Morals and Legislation*, ch. ii, sec. iv. See also ch. x, footnote 1). The same point is made in *The Limits of Jurisprudence Defined*, pp. 115 f. Although much recent welfare economics, as found in such important works as I. M. D. Little, *A Critique of Welfare Economics*, 2nd ed. (Oxford, 1957) and K. J. Arrow, *Social Choice and Individual Values* (New York, 1951), dispenses with the idea of cardinal utility, and uses instead the theory of ordinal utility as stated by J. R. Hicks, *Value and Capital*, 2nd ed. (Oxford, 1946), Pt. I, it assumes with utilitarianism that individual preferences have value as such, and so accepts the idea being criticized here. I hasten to add, however, that this is no objection to it as a means of analyzing economic policy, and for that purpose it may, indeed, be a necessary simplifying assumption. Nevertheless it is an assumption which cannot be made in so far as one is trying to analyze moral concepts, especially the concept of justice, as economists would, I think, agree. Justice is usually regarded as a separate and distinct part of any comprehensive criterion of economic policy. See, for example, Tibor Scitovsky, *Welfare and Competition* (London, 1952), pp. 59-69, and Little, *op cit.*, ch. vii.

[19] See J. S. Mill's argument in *Utilitarianism*, ch. v. pars. 16-25.

for the use of common means to achieve common ends. In this case either the benefits and burdens may be assumed to be impartially distributed, or the question of distribution is misplaced, as in the instance of maintaining public order and security or national defense. But as an interpretation of the basis of the principles of justice, classical utilitarianism is mistaken. It *permits* one to argue, for example, that slavery is unjust on the grounds that the advantages to the slaveholder as slaveholder do not counterbalance the disadvantages to the slave and to society at large burdened by a comparatively inefficient system of labor. Now the conception of justice as fairness, when applied to the practice of slavery with its offices of slaveholder and slave, would not allow one to consider the advantages of the slaveholder in the first place. As that office is not in accordance with principles which could be mutually acknowledged, the gains accruing to the slaveholder, assuming them to exist, cannot be counted as in *any* way mitigating the injustice of the practice. The question whether these gains outweigh the disadvantages to slave and to society cannot arise, since in considering the justice of slavery these gains have no weight at all which requires that they be overridden. Where the conception of justice as fairness applies, slavery is *always* unjust.

I am not, of course, suggesting the absurdity that the classical utilitarians approved of slavery. I am only rejecting a type of argument which their view allows them to use in support of their disapproval of it. The conception of justice as derivative from efficiency implies that judging the justice of a practice is always, in principle at least, a matter of weighing up advantages and disadvantages, each having an intrinsic value or disvalue as the satisfaction of interests, irrespective of whether or not these interests necessarily involve acquiescence in principles which could not be mutually acknowledged. Utilitarianism cannot account for the fact that slavery is always unjust, nor for the fact that it would be recognized as irrelevant in defeating the accusation of injustice for one person to say to another, engaged with him in a common practice and debating its merits, that nevertheless it allowed of the greatest satisfaction of desire. The charge of injustice cannot be rebutted in this way. If justice were derivative from a higher order executive efficiency, this would not be so.

But now, even if it is taken as established that, so far as the ordinary conception of justice goes, slavery is always unjust (that is, slavery by definition violates commonly recognized principles of justice), the classical utilitarian would surely reply that these principles, as other moral principles subordinate to that of utility, are only generally correct. It is simply for the most part true that slavery is less efficient than other institutions; and while common sense may define the concept of justice so that slavery is unjust, nevertheless, where slavery would lead to the greatest satisfaction of desire, it is not wrong. Indeed, it is then right, and for the very same reason that justice, as ordinarily understood, is usually right. If, as ordinarily understood, slavery is always unjust, to this extent the utilitarian conception of justice might be admitted to differ from that of common moral opinion. Still the utilitarian would want to hold that as a matter of moral principle, his view is correct in giving no special weight to considerations of justice beyond that allowed for by the general presumption of effectiveness. And this, he claims, is as it should be. The every day opinion is morally in error, although, indeed, it is a useful error, since it protects rules of generally high utility.

The question, then, relates not simply to the analysis of the concept of justice as common sense defines it, but the analysis of it in the wider sense as to how much weight considerations of justice, as defined, are to have when laid against other kinds of moral considerations. Here again I wish to argue that reasons of justice have a *special* weight for which only the conception of justice as fairness can account. Moreover, it belongs to the concept of justice that they do have this special weight. While Mill recognized that this was so, he thought that it could be accounted for by the special urgency of the moral feelings which naturally support principles of such high utility. But it is a mistake to resort to the urgency of feeling; as with the appeal to intuition, it manifests a failure to pursue the question far enough. The special weight of considerations of justice can be explained from the conception of justice as fairness. It is only necessary to elaborate a bit what has already been said as follows.

If one examines the circumstances in which a certain tolerance of slavery is justified, or perhaps better, excused, it turns out that these are of a rather special sort. Perhaps slavery exists as an inheritance from the past and it proves necessary to dismantle it piece by piece; at times slavery may conceivably be an advance on previous institutions. Now while there may be some excuse for slavery in special conditions, it is never an excuse for it that it is sufficiently advantageous to the slaveholder to outweigh the disadvantages to the slave and to society. A person who argues in this way is not perhaps making a wildly irrelevant remark; but he is guilty of a moral fallacy. There is disorder in his conception of the ranking of moral principles. For the slaveholder, by his own admission, has no moral title to the advantages which he receives as a slave-holder. He is no more prepared than the slave to acknowledge the principle upon which is founded the respective positions in which they both stand. Since slavery does not accord with principles which they could mutually acknowledge, they each may be supposed to agree that it is unjust: it grants claims which it ought not to grant and in doing so denies claims which it ought not to deny. Amongst persons in a general position who are debating the form of their common practices, it cannot, therefore, be offered as a reason for a practice that, in conceding these very claims that ought to be denied, it nevertheless meets existing interests more effectively. By their very nature the satisfaction of these claims is without weight and cannot enter into any tabulation of advantages and disadvantages.

Furthermore, it follows from the concept of morality that, to the extent that the slaveholder recognizes his position vis-a-vis the slave to be unjust, he would not choose to press his claims. His not wanting to receive his special advantages is one of the ways in which he shows that he thinks slavery is unjust. It would be fallacious for the legislator to suppose, then, that it is a ground for having a practice that it brings advantages greater than disadvantages, if those for whom the practice is designed, and to whom the advantages flow, acknowledge that they have no moral title to them and do not wish to receive them.

For these reasons the principles of justice have a special weight; and with respect to the principle of the greatest satisfaction of desire, as cited in the general position amongst those discussing the merits of their common practices, the principles of justice have an absolute weight. In this sense they are not contingent; and this is why their force is greater than can be accounted for by the general presumption (assuming that there is one) of the effectiveness, in the utilitarian sense, of practices which in fact satisfy them.

If one wants to continue using the concepts of classical utilitarianism, one will have to say, to meet this criticism, that at least the individual or social utility functions must be so defined that no value is given to the satisfaction of interests the representative claims of which violate the principles of justice. In this way it is no doubt possible to include these principles within the form of the utilitarian conception; but to do so is, of course, to change its inspiration altogether as a moral conception. For it is to incorporate within it principles which cannot be understood on the basis of a higher order executive decision aiming at the greatest satisfaction of desire.

It is worth remarking, perhaps, that this criticism of utilitarianism does not depend on whether or not the two assumptions, that of individuals having similar utility functions and that of diminishing marginal utility, are interpreted as psychological propositions to be supported or refuted by experience, or as moral and political principles expressed in a somewhat technical language. There are, certainly, several advantages in taking them in the latter fashion.[20] For one thing, one might say that this is what Bentham and others really meant by them, at least as shown by how they were used in arguments for social reform. More importantly, one could hold that the best way to defend the classical utilitarian view is to interpret these assumptions as moral and political principles. It is doubtful whether, taken as psychological propositions, they are true of men in general as we know them under normal conditions. On the other hand, utilitarians would not have wanted to propose them merely as practical working principles of legislation, or as expedient maxims to guide reform, given the egalitarian sentiments of modern society.[21] When pressed they might well have invoked the idea of a more or less equal capacity of men in relevant respects if given an equal chance in a just society. But if the argument above regarding slavery is correct, then granting these assumptions as moral and political principles makes no difference. To view individuals as equally fruitful lines for the allocation of benefits, even as a matter of moral principle, still leaves the mistaken notion that the satisfaction of desire has value in itself irrespective of the relations between persons as members of a common practice, and irrespective of the claims upon one another which the satisfaction of interests represents. To see the error of this idea one must give up the conception of justice as an executive decision altogether and refer to the notion of justice as fairness: that participants in a common practice be regarded as having an original and equal liberty and that their common practices be considered unjust unless they accord with principles which persons so circumstanced and related could freely acknowledge before one another, and so could accept as fair. Once the emphasis is put upon the concept of the mutual recognition of principles by participants in a common practice the rules of which are to define their several relations and give form to their claims on one another, then it is clear that the granting of a claim the principle of which could not be acknowledged by each in the general position (that is, in the position in which the parties propose and acknowledge principles before one another) is not a reason for adopting a practice. Viewed in

[20] See D. G. Ritchie, *Natural Rights* (London, 1894), pp. 95 ff., 249 ff. Lionel Robbins has insisted on this point on several occasions. See *An Essay on the Nature and Significance of Economic Science,* 2nd ed. (London, 1935), pp. 134-43, "Interpersonal Comparisons of Utility: A Comment," *Economic Journal,* XLVIII (1938), 635-41, and more recently, "Robertson on Utility and Scope," *Economica,* n.s. XX (1953), 108f.

[21] As Sir Henry Maine suggested Bentham may have regarded them. See *The Early History of Institutions* (London, 1875), pp. 398 ff.

this way, the background of the claim is seen to exclude it from consideration; that it can represent a value in itself arises from the conception of individuals as separate lines for the assignment of benefits, as isolated persons who stand as claimants on an administrative or benevolent largesse. Occasionally persons do so stand to one another; but this is not the general case, nor, more importantly, is it the case when it is a matter of the justice of practices themselves in which participants stand in various relations to be appraised in accordance with standards which they may be expected to acknowledge before one another. Thus however mistaken the notion of the social contract may be as history, and however far it may overreach itself as a general theory of social and political obligation, it does express, suitably interpreted, an essential part of the concept of justice.[22]

8. By way of conclusion I should like to make two remarks: first, the original modification of the utilitarian principle (that it require of practices that the offices and positions defined by them be equal unless it is reasonable to suppose that the representative man in *every* office would find the inequality to his advantage), slight as it may appear at first sight, actually has a different conception of justice standing behind it. I have tried to show how this is so by developing the concept of justice as fairness and by indicating how this notion involves the mutual acceptance, from a general position, of the principles on which a practice is founded, and how this in turn requires the exclusion from consideration of claims violating the principles of justice. Thus the slight alteration of principle reveals another family of notions, another way of looking at the concept of justice.

Second, I should like to remark also that I have been dealing with the *concept* of justice. I have tried to set out the kinds of principles upon which judgments concerning the justice of practices may be said to stand. The analysis will be successful to the degree that it expresses the principles involved in these judgments when made by competent persons upon deliberation and reflection.[23] Now every people may be supposed to have the concept of justice, since in the life of every society there must be at least some relations in which the parties consider themselves to be circumstanced and related as the concept of justice as fairness requires. Societies will differ from one another not in having or in failing to have this notion but in the range of cases to which they apply it and in the emphasis which they give to it as compared with other moral concepts.

[22] Thus Kant was not far wrong when he interpreted the original contract merely as an "Idea of Reason"; yet he still thought of it as a *general* criterion of right and as providing a general theory of political obligation. See the second part of the essay, "On the Saying 'That may be right in theory but has no value in practice' " (1793), in *Kant's Principles of Politics,* tr. by W. Hastie (Edinburgh, 1891). I have drawn on the contractarian tradition not for a general theory of political obligation but to clarify the concept of justice.

[23] For a further discussion of the idea expressed here, see my paper, "Outline of a Decision Procedure for Ethics," in the *Philosophical Review,* LX (1951), 177-197. For an analysis, similar in many respects but using the notion of the ideal observer instead of that of considered judgment of a competent person, see Roderick Firth, "Ethical Absolutism and the Ideal Observer," *Philosophy and Phenomenological Research,* XII (1952), 317-345. While the similarities between these two discussions are more important than the differences, an analysis based on the notion of a considered judgment of a competent person, as it is based on a kind of judgment, may prove more helpful in understanding the features of moral judgment than an analysis based on the notion of an ideal observer, although this remains to be shown. A man who rejects the conditions imposed on a considered judgment of a competent person could do no longer profess to *judge* at all. This seems more fundamental than his rejecting the conditions of observation, for these do not seem to apply, in an ordinary sense, to making a moral judgment.

A firm grasp of the concept of justice itself is necessary if these variations, and the reasons for them, are to be understood. No study of the development of moral ideas and of the differences between them is more sound than the analysis of the fundamental moral concepts upon which it must depend. I have tried, therefore, to give an analysis of the concept of justice which should apply generally, however large a part the concept may have in a given morality, and which can be used in explaining the course of men's thoughts about justice and its relations to other moral concepts. How it is to be used for this purpose is a large topic which I cannot, of course, take up here. I mention it only to emphasize that I have been dealing with the concept of justice itself and to indicate what use I consider such an analysis to have.

Isaiah Berlin

Sir Isaiah Berlin (b. 1909), President of Wolfson College, Oxford, has written respected works in philosophy, intellectual history, and political theory. In "Two Concepts of Liberty" he analyzes two differing conceptions of freedom which he thinks have played important and often conflicting roles in political thought.

Two Concepts of Liberty

I

To coerce a man is to deprive him of freedom—freedom from what? Almost every moralist in human history has praised freedom. Like happiness and goodness, like nature and reality, the meaning of this term is so porous that there is little interpretation that it seems able to resist. I do not propose to discuss either the history or the more than two hundred senses of this protean word recorded by historians of ideas. I propose to examine no more than two of these senses—but those central ones, with a great deal of human history behind them, and, I dare say, still to come. The first of these political senses of freedom or liberty (I shall use both words to mean the same), which (following much

By permission. From "Two Concepts of Liberty" in *Four Essays on Liberty* by Sir Isaiah Berlin published by Oxford University Press.

precedent) I shall call the 'negative' sense, is involved in the answer to the question 'What is the area within which the subject—a person or group of persons—is or should be left to do or be what he is able to do or be, without interference by other persons?' The second, which I shall call the positive sense, is involved in the answer to the question 'What, or who, is the source of control or interference that can determine someone to do, or be, this rather than that?' The two questions are clearly different, even though the answers to them may overlap.

The Notion of 'Negative' Freedom

I am normally said to be free to the degree to which no man or body of men interferes with my activity. Political liberty in this sense is simply the area within which a man can act unobstructed by others. If I am prevented by others from doing what I could otherwise do, I am to that degree unfree; and if this area is contracted by other men beyond a certain minimum, I can be described as being coerced, or, it may be, enslaved. Coercion is not, however, a term that covers every form of inability. If I say that I am unable to jump more than ten feet in the air, or cannot read because I am blind, or cannot understand the darker pages of Hegel, it would be eccentric to say that I am to that degree enslaved or coerced. Coercion implies the deliberate interference of other human beings within the area in which I could otherwise act. You lack political liberty or freedom only if you are prevented from attaining a goal by human beings.[1] Mere incapacity to attain a goal is not lack of political freedom.[2] This is brought out by the use of such modern expressions as 'economic freedom' and its counterpart, 'economic slavery'. It is argued, very plausibly, that if a man is too poor to afford something on which there is no legal ban—a loaf of bread, a journey round the world, recourse to the law courts—he is as little free to have it as he would be if it were forbidden him by law. If my poverty were a kind of disease, which prevented me from buying bread, or paying for the journey round the world or getting my case heard, as lameness prevents me from running, this inability would not naturally be described as a lack of freedom, least of all political freedom. It is only because I believe that my inability to get a given thing is due to the fact that other human beings have made arrangements whereby I am, whereas others are not, prevented from having enough money with which to pay for it, that I think myself a victim of coercion or slavery. In other words, this use of the term depends on a particular social and economic theory about the causes of my poverty or weakness. If my lack of material means is due to my lack of mental or physical capacity, then I begin to speak of being deprived of freedom (and not simply about poverty) only if I accept the theory.[3] If, in addition, I believe that I am being kept in want by a specific arrangement which I consider unjust or unfair, I speak of economic slavery or oppression. 'The nature of things does not madden us, only ill will does', said Rousseau. The criterion of oppression is the part that I believe to be played by

[1] I do not, of course, mean to imply the truth of the converse.

[2] Helvétius made this point very clearly: 'The free man is the man who is not in irons, nor imprisoned in a gaol, nor terrorized like a slave by the fear of punishment . . . it is not lack of freedom not to fly like an eagle or swim like a whale.'

[3] The Marxist conception of social laws is, of course, the best-known version of this theory, but it forms a large element in some Christian and utilitarian, and all socialist, doctrines.

other human beings, directly or indirectly, with or without the intention of doing so, in frustrating my wishes. By being free in this sense I mean not being interfered with by others. The wider the area of non-interference the wider my freedom.

This is what the classical English political philosophers meant when they used this word.[4] They disagreed about how wide the area could or should be. They supposed that it could not, as things were, be unlimited, because if it were, it would entail a state in which all men could boundlessly interfere with all other men; and this kind of 'natural' freedom would lead to social chaos in which men's minimum needs would not be satisfied; or else the liberties of the weak would be suppressed by the strong. Because they perceived that human purposes and activities do not automatically harmonize with one another, and because (whatever their official doctrines) they put high value on other goals, such as justice, or happiness, or culture, or security, or varying degrees of equality, they were prepared to curtail freedom in the interests of other values and, indeed, of freedom itself. For, without this, it was impossible to create the kind of association that they thought desirable. Consequently, it is assumed by these thinkers that the area of men's free action must be limited by law. But equally it is assumed, especially by such libertarians as Locke and Mill in England, and Constant and Tocqueville in France, that there ought to exist a certain minimum area of personal freedom which must on no account be violated; for if it is overstepped, the individual will find himself in an area too narrow for even that minimum development of his natural faculties which alone makes it possible to pursue, and even to conceive, the various ends which men hold good or right or sacred. It follows that a frontier must be drawn between the area of private life and that of public authority. Where it is to be drawn is a matter of argument, indeed of haggling. Men are largely interdependent, and no man's activity is so completely private as never to obstruct the lives of others in any way. 'Freedom for the pike is death for the minnows'; the liberty of some must depend on the restraint of others. 'Freedom for an Oxford don', others have been known to add, 'is a very different thing from freedom for an Egyptian peasant.'

This proposition derives its force from something that is both true and important, but the phrase itself remains a piece of political claptrap. It is true that to offer political rights, or safeguards against intervention by the state, to men who are half-naked, illiterate, underfed, and diseased is to mock their condition; they need medical help or education before they can understand, or make use of, an increase in their freedom. What is freedom to those who cannot make use of it? Without adequate conditions for the use of freedom, what is the value of freedom? First things come first: there are situations, as a nineteenth-century Russian radical writer declared, in which boots are superior to the works of Shakespeare; individual freedom is not everyone's primary need. For freedom is not the mere absence of frustration of whatever kind; this would inflate the meaning of the word until it meant too much or too little. The Egyptian peasant needs clothes or medicine before, and more than, personal liberty, but the minimum freedom that he needs today, and the greater degree that he may need

---

[4] 'A free man', said Hobbes, 'is he that . . . is not hindered to do what he hath the will to do.' Law is always a 'fetter', even if it protects you from being bound in chains that are heavier than those of the law, say, some more repressive law or custom, or arbitrary despotism or chaos. Bentham says much the same.

tomorrow, is not some species of freedom peculiar to him, but identical with that of professors, artists, and millionaires.

What troubles the consciences of Western liberals is not, I think, the belief that the freedom that men seek differs according to their social or economic conditions, but that the minority who possess it have gained it by exploiting, or, at least, averting their gaze from, the vast majority who do not. They believe, with good reason, that if individual liberty is an ultimate end for human beings, none should be deprived of it by others; least of all that some should enjoy it at the expense of others. Equality of liberty; not to treat others as I should not wish them to treat me; repayment of my debt to those who alone have made possible my liberty or prosperity or enlightenment; justice, in its simplest and most universal sense—these are the foundations of liberal morality. Liberty is not the only goal of men. I can, like the Russian critic Belinsky, say that if others are to be deprived of it—if my brothers are to remain in poverty, squalor, and chains—then I do not want it for myself, I reject it with both hands and infinitely prefer to share their fate. But nothing is gained by a confusion of terms. To avoid glaring inequality or widespread misery I am ready to sacrifice some, or all, of my freedom: I may do so willingly and freely: but it is freedom that I am giving up for the sake of justice or equality or the love of my fellow men. I should be guilt-stricken, and rightly so, if I were not, in some circumstances, ready to make this sacrifice. But a sacrifice is not an increase in what is being sacrificed, namely freedom, however great the moral need or the compensation for it. Everything is what it is: liberty is liberty, not equality or fairness or justice or culture, or human happiness or a quiet conscience. If the liberty of myself or my class or nation depends on the misery of a number of other human beings, the system which promotes this is unjust and immoral. But if I curtail or lose my freedom, in order to lessen the shame of such inequality, and do not thereby materially increase the individual liberty of others, an absolute loss of liberty occurs. This may be compensated for by a gain in justice or in happiness or in peace, but the loss remains, and it is a confusion of values to say that although my 'liberal', individual freedom may go by the board, some other kind of freedom—'social' or 'economic'—is increased. Yet it remains true that the freedom of some must at times be curtailed to secure the freedom of others. Upon what principle should this be done? If freedom is a sacred, untouchable value, there can be no such principle. One or other of these conflicting rules or principles must, at any rate in practice, yield: not always for reasons which can be clearly stated, let alone generalized into rules or universal maxims. Still, a practical compromise has to be found.

Philosophers with an optimistic view of human nature and a belief in the possibility of harmonizing human interests, such as Locke or Adam Smith and, in some moods, Mill, believed that social harmony and progress were compatible with reserving a large area for private life over which neither the state nor any other authority must be allowed to trespass. Hobbes, and those who agreed with him, especially conservative or reactionary thinkers, argued that if men were to be prevented from destroying one another and making social life a jungle or a wilderness, greater safeguards must be instituted to keep them in their places; he wished correspondingly to increase the area of centralized control and decrease that of the individual. But both sides agreed that some portion of human existence must remain independent of the sphere of social control. To invade that preserve, however small, would be despotism. The most eloquent of all defenders of freedom and privacy, Benjamin Constant, who had not forgotten the Jacobin dictatorship, declared that at the very least the liberty of religion, opinion, expression, property, must be guaranteed against arbitrary invasion. Jefferson, Burke, Paine, Mill, compiled different catalogues of individual liberties, but the argument for keeping authority at bay is always substantially the same. We must preserve a minimum area of personal freedom if we are not to 'degrade or deny our nature'. We cannot remain absolutely free, and must give up some of our liberty to preserve the rest. But total self-surrender is self-defeating. What then must the minimum be? That which a man cannot give up without offending against the essence of his human nature. What is this essence? What are the standards which it entails? This has been, and perhaps always will be, a matter of infinite debate. But whatever the principle in terms of which the area of non-interference is to be drawn, whether it is that of natural law or natural rights, or of utility or the pronouncements of categorical imperative, or the sancity of the social contract, or any other concept with which men have sought to clarify and justify their convictions, liberty in this sense means liberty *from*; absence of interference beyond the shifting, but always recognizable, frontier. 'The only freedom which deserves the name is that of pursuing our own good in our own way', said the most celebrated of its champions. If this is so, is compulsion ever justified? Mill had no doubt that it was. Since justice demands that all individuals be entitled to a minimum of freedom, all other individuals were of necessity to be restrained, if need be by force, from depriving anyone of it. Indeed, the whole function of law was the prevention of just such collisions: the state was reduced to what Lassalle contemptuously described as the functions of a night watchman or traffic policeman.

What made the protection of individual liberty so sacred to Mill? In his famous essay he declares that, unless men are left to live as they wish 'in the path which merely concerns themselves', civilization cannot advance; the truth will not, for lack of a free market in ideas, come to light; there will be no scope for spontaneity, originality, genius, for mental energy, for moral courage. Society will be crushed by the weight of 'collective mediocrity'. Whatever is rich and diversified will be crushed by the weight of custom, by men's constant tendency to conformity, which breeds only 'withered capacities', 'pinched and hidebound', cramped and warped' human beings. 'Pagan self-assertion is as worthy as Christian self-denial,' 'All the errors which a man is likely to commit against advice and warning are far outweighed by the evil of allowing others to constrain him to what they deem is good.' The defence of liberty consists in the 'negative' goal of warding off interference. To threaten a man with persecution unless he submits to a life in which he exercises no choices of his goals; to block before him every door but one, no matter how noble the prospect upon which it opens, or how benevolent the motives of those who arrange this, is to sin against the truth that he is a man, a being with a life of his own to live. This is liberty as it has been conceived by liberals in the modern world from the days of Erasmus (some would say of Occam) to our own. Every plea for civil liberties and individual rights, every protest against exploitation and humiliation, against the encroachment of public authority, or the mass hypnosis of custom or organized propaganda, springs from this individualistic, and much disputed, conception of man.

Three facts about this position may be noted. In the first place Mill confuses two distinct notions. One is that all coercion is, in so far as it frustrates human desires, bad as such, although it may have to be applied to prevent other, greater evils; while non-interference, which is the opposite of coercion, is good as such, although it is not the only good. This is the 'negative' conception of liberty in its classical form. The other is that men should seek to discover the truth, or to develop a certain type of character of which Mill approved—critical, original, imaginative, independent, non-conforming to the point of eccentricity, and so on—and that truth can be found, and such character can be bred, only in conditions of freedom. Both these are liberal views, but they are not identical, and the connexion between them is, at best, empirical. No one would argue that truth or freedom of self-expression could flourish where dogma crushes all thought. But the evidence of history tends to show (as, indeed, was argued by James Stephen in his formidable attack on Mill in his *Liberty, Equality, Fraternity*) that integrity, love of truth, and fiery individualism grow at least as often in severely disciplined communities among, for example, the puritan Calvinists of Scotland or New England, or under military discipline, as in more tolerant or indifferent societies; and if this is so, Mill's argument for liberty as a necessary condition for the growth of human genius falls to the ground. If his two goals proved incompatible, Mill would be faced with a cruel dilemma, quite apart from the further difficulties created by the inconsistency of his doctrines with strict utilitarianism, even in his own humane version of it.[5]

In the second place, the doctrine is comparatively modern. There seems to be scarcely any discussion of individual liberty as a conscious political ideal (as opposed to its actual existence) in the ancient world. Condorcet had already remarked that the notion of individual rights was absent from the legal conceptions of the Romans and Greeks; this seems to hold equally of the Jewish, Chinese, and all other ancient civilizations that have since come to light.[6] The domination of this ideal has been the exception rather than the rule, even in the recent history of the West. Nor has liberty in this sense often formed a rallying cry for the great masses of mankind. The desire not to be impinged upon, to be left to oneself, had been a mark of high civilization both on the part of individuals and communities. The sense of privacy itself, of the area of personal relationships as something sacred on its own right, derives from a conception of freedom which, for all its religious roots, is scarcely older, in its developed state, than the Renaissance or the Reformation.[7] Yet its decline would mark the death of civilization, of an entire moral outlook.

The third characteristic of this notion of liberty is of greater importance. It is that liberty in this sense is not incompatible with some kinds of autocracy, or at

[5] This is but another illustration of the natural tendency of all but a very few thinkers to believe that all the things they hold good must be intimately connected, or at least compatible, with one another. The history of thought, like the history of nations, is strewn with examples of inconsistent, or at least disparate, elements artificially yoked together in a despotic system, or held together by the danger of some common enemy. In due course the danger passes, and conflicts between the allies arise, which often disrupt the system, sometimes to the great benefit of mankind.

[6] See the valuable discussion of this in Michel Villey, *Leçons d'histoire de la philosophie du droit*, who traces the embryo of the notion of subjective rights to Occam.

[7] Christian (and Jewish or Moslem) belief in the absolute authority of divine or natural laws, or in the equality of all men in the sight of God, is very different from belief in freedom to live as one prefers.

any rate with the absence of self-government. Liberty in this sense is principally concerned with the area of control, not with its source. Just as a democracy may, in fact, deprive the individual citizen of a great many liberties which he might have in some other form of society, so it is perfectly conceivable that a liberal-minded despot would allow his subjects a large measure of personal freedom. The despot who leaves his subjects a wide area of liberty may be unjust, or encourage the wildest inequalities, care little for order, or virtue, or knowledge; but provided he does not curb their liberty, or at least curbs it less than many other régimes, he meets with Mill's specification.[8] Freedom in this sense is not, at any rate logically, connected with democracy or self-government. Self-government may, on the whole, provide a better guarantee of the preservation of civil liberties than other régimes, and has been defended as such by libertarians. But there is no necessary connexion between individual liberty and democratic rule. The answer to the question 'Who governs me?' is logically distinct from the question 'How far does government interfere with me?' It is in this difference that the great contrast between the two concepts of negative and positive liberty, in the end, consists.[9] For the 'positive' sense of liberty comes to light if we try to answer the question, not 'What am I free to do or be?', but 'By whom am I ruled?' or 'Who is to say what I am, and what I am not, to be or do?' The connexion between democracy and individual liberty is a good deal more tenuous than it seemed to many advocates of both. The desire to be governed by myself, or at any rate to participate in the process by which my life is to be controlled, may be as deep a wish as that of a free area for action, and perhaps historically older. But it is not a desire for the same thing. So different is it,

---

[8] Indeed, it is arguable that in the Prussia of Frederick the Great or in the Austria of Josef II men of imagination, originality, and creative genius, and, indeed, minorities of all kinds, were less persecuted and felt the pressure, both of institutions and custom, less heavy upon them than in many an earlier or later democracy.

[9] 'Negative liberty' is something the extent of which, in a given case, it is difficult to estimate. It might, prima facie, seem to depend simply on the power to choose between at any rate two alternatives. Nevertheless, not all choices are equally free, or free at all. If in a totalitarian state I betray my friend under threat of torture, perhaps even if I act from fear of losing my job, I can reasonably say that I did not act freely. Nevertheless, I did, of course, make a choice, and could, at any rate in theory, have chosen to be killed or tortured or imprisoned. The mere existence of alternatives is not, therefore, enough to make my action free (although it may be voluntary) in the normal sense of the word. The extent of my freedom seems to depend on (a) how many possibilities are open to me (although the method of counting these can never be more than impressionistic. Possibilities of action are not discrete entities like apples, which can be exhaustively enumerated); (b) how easy or difficult each of these possibilities is to actualize; (c) how important in my plan of life, given my character and circumstances, these possibilities are when compared with each other; (d) how far they are closed and opened by deliberate human acts; (e) what value not merely the agent, but the general sentiment of the society in which he lives, puts on the various possibilities. All these magnitudes must be 'integrated', and a conclusion, necessarily never precise, or indisputable, drawn from this process. It may well be that there are many incommensurable kinds and degrees of freedom, and that they cannot be drawn up on any single scale of magnitude. Moreover, in the case of societies, we are faced by such (logically absurd) questions as 'Would arrangement X increase the liberty of Mr. A more than it would that of Messrs. B, C, and D between them, added together?' The same difficulties arise in applying utilitarian criteria. Nevertheless, provided we do not demand precise measurement, we can give valid reasons for saying that the average subject of the King of Sweden is, on the whole, a good deal freer today than the average citizen of Spain or Albania. Total patterns of life must be compared directly as wholes, although the method by which we make the comparison, and the truth of the conclusions, are difficult or impossible to demonstrate. But the vagueness of the concepts, and the multiplicity of the criteria involved, is an attribute of the subject-matter itself, not of our imperfect methods of measurement, or incapacity for precise thought.

indeed, as to have led in the end to the great clash of ideologies that dominates our world. For it is this—the 'positive' conception of liberty: not freedom from, but freedom to—to lead one prescribed form of life—which the adherents of the 'negative' notion represent as being, at times, no better than a specious disguise for brutal tyranny.

II   The Notion of Positive Freedom

The 'positive' sense of the word 'liberty' derives from the wish on the part of the individual to be his own master. I wish my life and decisions to depend on myself, not on external forces of whatever kind. I wish to be the instrument of my own, not of other men's, acts of will. I wish to be a subject, not an object; to be moved by reasons, by conscious purposes, which are my own, not by causes which affect me, as it were, from outside. I wish to be somebody, not nobody; a doer—deciding, not being decided for, self-directed and not acted upon by external nature or by other men as if I were a thing, or an animal, or a slave incapable of playing a human role, that is, of conceiving goals and policies of my own and realizing them. This is at least part of what I mean when I say that I am rational, and that it is my reason that distinguishes me as a human being from the rest of the world. I wish, above all, to be conscious of myself as a thinking, willing, active being, bearing responsibility for my choices and able to explain them by references to my own ideas and purposes. I feel free to the degree that I believe this to be true, and enslaved to the degree that I am made to realize that it is not.

The freedom which consists in being one's own master, and the freedom which consists in not being prevented from choosing as I do by other men, may, on the face of it, seem concepts at no great logical distance from each other—no more than negative and positive ways of saying much the same thing. Yet the 'positive' and 'negative' notions of freedom historically developed in divergent directions not always by logically reputable steps, until, in the end, they came into direct conflict with each other.

One way of making this clear is in terms of the independent momentum which the, initially perhaps quite harmless, metaphor of self-mastery acquired. 'I am my own master'; 'I am slave to no man'; but may I not (as Platonists or Hegelians tend to say) be slave to nature? Or to my own 'unbridled' passions? Are these not so many species of the identical genus 'slave'—some political or legal, others moral or spiritual? Have not men had the experience of liberating themselves from spiritual slavery, or slavery to nature, and do they not in the course of it become aware, on the one hand, of a self which dominates, and, on the other, of something in them which is brought to heel? This dominant self is then variously identified with reason, with my 'higher nature', with the self which calculates and aims at what will satisfy it in the long run, with my 'real', or 'autonomous' self, or with my self 'at its best'; which is then contrasted with irrational impulse, uncontrolled desires, my 'lower' nature, the pursuit of imme-diate pleasures, my 'empirical' or 'heteronomous' self, swept by every gust of desire and passion, needing to be rigidly disciplined if it is ever to rise to the full height of its 'real' nature. Presently the two selves may be represented as divided by an even larger gap: the real self may be conceived as something wider than the individual (as the term is normally understood), as a social 'whole' of which the individual is an element or aspect: a tribe, a race, a church, a state, the great society of the living and the dead and the yet unborn. This entity is then identified as being the 'true' self which, by imposing its collective, or 'organic', single will upon its recalcitrant 'members', achieves its own, and therefore their, 'higher' freedom. The perils of using organic metaphors to justify the coercion of some men by others in order to raise them to a 'higher' level of freedom have often been pointed out. But what gives such plausibility as it has to this kind of language is that we recognize that it is possible, and at times justifiable, to coerce men in the name of some goal (let us say, justice or public health) which they would, if they were more enlightened, themselves pursue, but do not, because they are blind or ignorant or corrupt. This renders it easy for me to conceive of myself as coercing others for their own sake, in their, not my, interest. I am then claiming that I know what they truly need better than they know it themselves. What, at most, this entails is that they would not resist me if they were rational and as wise as I and understood their interests as I do. But I may go on to claim a good deal more than this. I may declare that they are actually aiming at what in their benighted state they consciously resist, because there exists within them an occult entity—their latent rational will, or their 'true' purpose—and that this entity, although it is belied by all that they overtly feel and do and say, is their 'real' self, of which the poor empirical self in space and time may know nothing or little; and that this inner spirit is the only self that deserves to have its wishes taken into account.[10] Once I take this view, I am in a position to ignore the actual wishes of men or societies, to bully, oppress, torture them in the name, and on behalf, of their 'real' selves, in the secure knowledge that whatever is the true goal of man (happiness, performance of duty, wisdom, a just society, self-fulfillment) must be identical with his freedom—the free choice of his 'true', albeit often submerged and inarticulate, self.

This paradox has been often exposed. It is one thing to say that I know what is good for X, while he himself does not; and even to ignore his wishes for its—and his—sake; and a very different one to say that he has *eo ipso* chosen it, not indeed consciously, not as he seems in everyday life, but in his role as a rational self which his empirical self may not know—the 'real' self which discerns the good, and cannot help it once it is revealed. This monstrous impersonation, which consists in equating what X would choose if he were something he is not, or at least not yet, with what X actually seeks and chooses, is at the heart of all political theories of self-realization. It is one thing to say that I may be coerced for my own good which I am too blind to see: this may, on occasion, be for my benefit; indeed it may enlarge the scope of my liberty. It is another to say that if it is my good, then I am not being coerced, for I have willed it, whether I know this or not, and am free (or 'truly' free) even while my poor earthly body and foolish mind bitterly reject it, and struggle against those who seek however benevolently to impose it, with the greatest desperation.

This magical transformation, or sleight of hand (for which William James so

[10] 'The ideal of true freedom is the maximum of power for all the members of human society alike to make the best of themselves', said T. H. Green in 1881. Apart from the confusion of freedom with equality, this entails that if a man chose some immediate pleasure—which (in whose view?) would not enable him to make the best of himself (what self?)—what he was exercising was not 'true' freedom: and if deprived of it, would not lose anything that mattered. Green was a genuine liberal: but many a tyrant could use this formula to justify his worst acts of oppression.

justly mocked the Hegelians), can no doubt be perpetrated just as easily with the 'negative' concept of freedom, where the self that should not be interfered with is no longer the individual with his actual wishes and needs as they are normally conceived, but the 'real' man within, identified with the pursuit of some ideal purpose not dreamed of by his empirical self. And, as in the case of the 'positively' free self, this entity may be inflated into some super-personal entity—a state, a class, a nation, or the march of history itself, regarded as a more 'real' subject of attributes than the empirical self. But the 'positive' conception of freedom as self-mastery, with its suggestion of a man divided against himself, has, in fact, and as a matter of history, of doctrine and of practice, lent itself more easily to this splitting of personality into two: the transcendent, dominant controller, and the empirical bundle of desires and passions to be disciplined and brought to heel. It is this historical fact that has been influential. This demonstrates (if demonstration of so obvious a truth is needed) that conceptions of freedom directly derive from views of what constitutes a self, a person, a man. Enough manipulation with the definition of man, and freedom can be made to mean whatever the manipulator wishes. Recent history has made it only too clear that the issue is not merely academic. . . .

VIII   The One and the Many

One belief, more than any other, is responsible for the slaughter of individuals on the altars of the great historical ideals—justice or progress or the happiness of future generations, or the sacred mission or emancipation of a nation or race or class, or even liberty itself, which demands the sacrifice of individuals for the freedom of society. This is the belief that somewhere, in the past or in the future, in divine revelation or in the mind of an individual thinker, in the pronouncements of history or science, or in the simple heart of an uncorrupted good man, there is a final solution. This ancient faith rests on the conviction that all the positive values in which men have believed must, in the end, be compatible, and perhaps even entail one another. 'Nature binds truth, happiness, and virtue together as by an indissoluble chain', said one of the best men who ever lived, and spoke in similar terms of liberty, equality, and justice.[11] But is this true? It is a commonplace that neither political equality nor efficient organization nor social justice is compatible with more than a modicum of individual liberty, and certainly not with unrestricted *laissez-faire;* that justice and generosity, public and private loyalties, the demands of genius and the claims of society, can conflict violently with each other. And it is no great way from that to the generalization that not all good things are compatible, still less all the ideals of mankind. But somewhere, we shall be told, and in some way, it must be possible for all these values to live together, for unless this is so, the

[11] Condorcet, from whose *Esquisse* these words are quoted, declares that the task of social science is to show 'by what bonds Nature has united the progress of enlightenment with that of liberty, virtue, and respect for the natural rights of man; how these ideals, which alone are truly good, yet so often separated from each other that they are even believed to be incompatible, should, on the contrary, become inseparable, as soon as enlightment has reached a certain level simultaneously among a large number of nations'. He goes on to say that: 'Men still preserve the errors of their childhood, of their country, and of their age long after having recognized all the truths needed for destroying them.' Ironically enough, his belief in the need and possibility of uniting all good things may well be precisely the kind of error he himself so well described.

universe is not a cosmos, not a harmony; unless this is so, conflicts of values may be an intrinsic, irremovable element in human life. To admit that the fulfilment of some of our ideals may in principle make the fulfilment of others impossible is to say that the notion of total human fulfilment is a formal contradiction, a metaphysical chimaera. For every rationalist metaphysician, from Plato to the last disciples of Hegel or Marx, this abandonment of the notion of a final harmony in which all riddles are solved, all contradictions reconciled, is a piece of crude empiricism, abdication before brute facts, intolerable bankruptcy of reason before things as they are, failure to explain and to justify, to reduce everything to a system, which 'reason' indignantly rejects. But if we are not armed with an *a priori* guarantee of the proposition that a total harmony of true values is somewhere to be found—perhaps in some ideal realm the characteristics of which we can, in our finite state, not so much as conceive—we must fall back on the ordinary resources of empirical observation and ordinary human knowledge. And these certainly give us no warrant for supposing (or even understanding what would be meant by saying) that all good things, or all bad things for that matter, are reconcilable with each other. The world that we encounter in ordinary experience is one in which we are faced with choices between ends equally ultimate, and claims equally absolute, the realization of some of which must inevitably involve the sacrifice of others. Indeed, it is because this is their situation that men place such immense value upon the freedom to choose; for if they had assurance that in some perfect state, realizable by men on earth, no ends pursued by them would ever be in conflict, the necessity and agony of choice would disappear, and with it the central importance of the freedom to choose. Any method of bringing this final state nearer would then seem fully justified, no matter how much freedom were sacrificed to forward its advance. It is, I have no doubt, some such dogmatic certainty that has been responsible for the deep, serene, unshakeable conviction in the minds of some of the most merciless tyrants and persecutors in history that what they did was fully justified by its purpose. I do not say that the ideal of self-perfection—whether for individuals or nations or churches or classes—is to be condemned in itself, or that the language which was used in its defence was in all cases the result of a confused or fraudulent use of words, or of moral or intellectual perversity. Indeed, I have tried to show that it is the notion of freedom in its 'positive' sense that is at the heart of the demands for national or social self-direction which animate the most powerful and morally just public movements of our time, and that not to recognize this is to misunderstand the most vital facts and ideas of our age. But equally it seems to me that the belief that some single formula can in principle be found whereby all the diverse ends of men can be harmoniously realized is demonstrably false. If, as I believe, the ends of men are many, and not all of them are in principle compatible with each other, then the possibility of conflict—and of tragedy—can never wholly be eliminated from human life, either personal or social. The necessity of choosing between absolute claims is then an inescapable characteristic of the human condition. This gives its value to freedom as Acton had conceived of it—as an end in itself, and not as a temporary need, arising out of our confused notions and irrational and disordered lives, a predicament which a panacea could one day put right.

I do not wish to say that individual freedom is, even in the most liberal societies, the sole, or even the dominant, criterion of social action. We compel children to be educated, and we forbid public executions. These are certainly curbs to freedom. We justify them on the ground that ignorance, or a barbarian upbringing, or cruel pleasures and excitements are worse for us than the amount of restraint needed to repress them. This judgment in turn depends on how we determine good and evil, that is to say, on our moral, religious, intellectual, economic, and aesthetic values; which are, in their turn, bound up with our conception of man, and of the basic demands of his nature. In other words, our solution of such problems is based on our vision, by which we are consciously or unconsciously guided, of what constitutes a fulfilled human life, as contrasted with Mill's 'cramped and warped', 'pinched and hidebound' natures. To protest against the laws governing censorship or personal morals as intolerable infringements of personal liberty presupposes a belief that the activities which such laws forbid are fundamental needs of men as men, in a good (or, indeed, any) society. To defend such laws is to hold that these needs are not essential, or that they cannot be satisfied without sacrificing other values which come higher—satisfy deeper needs—than individual freedom, determined by some standard that is not merely subjective, a standard for which some objective status—empirical or *a priori*—is claimed.

The extent of a man's, or a people's, liberty to choose to live as they desire must be weighed against the claims of many other values, of which equality, or justice, or happiness, or security, or public order are perhaps the most obvious examples. For this reason, it cannot be unlimited. We are rightly reminded by R. H. Tawney that the liberty of the strong, whether their strength is physical or economic, must be restrained. This maxim claims respect, not as a consequence of some *a priori* rule, whereby the respect for the liberty of one man logically entails respect for the liberty of others like him; but simply because respect for the principles of justice, or shame at gross inequality of treatment, is as basic in men as the desire for liberty. That we cannot have everything is a necessary, not a contingent, truth. Burke's plea for the constant need to compensate, to reconcile, to balance; Mill's plea for novel 'experiments in living' with their permanent possibility of error, the knowledge that it is not merely in practice but in principle impossible to reach clear-cut and certain answers, even in an ideal world of wholly good and rational men and wholly clear ideas—may madden those who seek for final solutions and single, all-embracing systems, guaranteed to be eternal. Nevertheless, it is a conclusion that cannot be escaped by those who, with Kant, have learnt the truth that out of the crooked timber of humanity no straight thing was ever made.

There is little need to stress the fact that monism, and faith in a single criterion, has always proved a deep source of satisfaction both to the intellect and to the emotions. Whether the standard of judgment derives from the vision of some future perfection, as in the minds of the *philosophes* in the eighteenth century and their technocratic successors in our own day, or is rooted in the past—*la terre et les morts*—as maintained by German historicists or French theocrats, or neo-Conservatives in English-speaking countries, it is bound, provided it is inflexible enough, to encounter some unforeseen and unforeseeable human development, which it will not fit; and will then be used to justify the *a priori* barbarities of Procrustes—the vivisection of actual human societies into some fixed pattern dictated by our fallible understanding of a largely imaginary past or a wholly imaginary future. To preserve our absolute categories or ideals at the expense of human lives offends equally against the principles of science and of history; it is an attitude found in equal measure on the right and left wings in our days, and is not reconcilable with the principles accepted by those who respect the facts.

Pluralism, with the measure of 'negative' liberty that it entails, seems to me a truer and more humane ideal than the goals of those who seek in the great, disciplined, authoritarian structures the ideal of 'positive' self-mastery by classes, or peoples, or the whole of mankind. It is truer, because it does, at least, recognize the fact that human goals are many, not all of them commensurable, and in perpetual rivalry with one another. To assume that all values can be graded on one scale, so that it is a mere matter of inspection to determine the highest, seems to me to falsify our knowledge that men are free agents, to represent moral decision as an operation which a slide-rule could, in principle, perform. To say that in some ultimate, all-reconciling, yet realizable synthesis, duty *is* interest, or individual freedom *is* pure democracy or an authoritarian state, is to throw a metaphysical blanket over either self-deceit or deliberate hypocrisy. It is more humane because it does not (as the system builders do) deprive men, in the name of some remote, or incoherent, ideal, of much that they have found to be indispensable to their life as unpredictably self-transforming human beings.[12] In the end, men choose between ultimate values; they choose as they do, because their life and thought are determined by fundamental moral categories and concepts that are, at any rate over large stretches of time and space, a part of their being and thought and sense of their own identity; part of what makes them human.

It may be that the ideal of freedom to choose ends without claiming eternal validity for them, and the pluralism of values connected with this, is only the late fruit of our declining capitalist civilization: an ideal which remote ages and primitive societies have not recognized, and one which posterity will regard with curiosity, even sympathy, but little comprehension. This may be so; but no sceptical conclusions seem to me to follow. Principles are not less sacred because their duration cannot be guaranteed. Indeed, the very desire for guarantees that our values are eternal and secure in some objective heaven is perhaps only a craving for the certainties of childhood or the absolute values of our primitive past. 'To realise the relative validity of one's convictions', said an admirable writer of our time, 'and yet stand for them unflinchingly, is what distinguishes a civilised man from a barbarian.' To demand more than this is perhaps a deep and incurable metaphysical need; but to allow it to determine one's practice is a symptom of an equally deep, and more dangerous, moral and political immaturity.

---

[12]On this also Bentham seems to me to have spoken well: 'Individual interests are the only real interests . . . can it be conceived that there are men so absurd as to . . . prefer the man who is not to him who is; to torment the living, under pretence of promoting the happiness of them who are not born, and who may never be born?' This is one of the infrequent occasions when Burke agrees with Bentham; for this passage is at the heart of the empirical, as against the metaphysical, view of politics.

Ronald Dworkin

Ronald Dworkin (b. 1931), has been Professor of Jurisprudence
at Yale University and is now Professor of Jurisprudence at
Oxford University. In the article printed below Professor
Dworkin is concerned with the question of the proper limits of
the law in relation to personal activities, particularly sexual activities. This question has been the subject of a well-known disagreement between Lord Devlin and Professor H. L. A. Hart. Professor
Dworkin's article is particularly useful in that he states clearly the
positions and main arguments of both Devlin and Hart, as well as
making a valuable contribution to the debate.

Lord Devlin and the
Enforcement of Morals

No doubt most Americans and Englishmen think that homosexuality, prostitution, and the publication of pornography are immoral. What part should this
fact play in the decision whether to make them criminal? This is a tangled
question, full of issues with roots in philosophical and sociological controversy.
It is a question lawyers must face, however, and two recent controversial
events—publication of the Wolfenden Report in England,[1] followed by a public
debate on prostitution and homosexuality, and a trio of obscenity decisions in
the United States Supreme court[2]—press it upon us.

Several positions are available, each with its own set of difficulties. Shall we
say that public condemnation is sufficient, in and of itself, to justify making an
act a crime? This seems inconsistent with our traditions of individual liberty, and
our knowledge that the morals of even the largest mob cannot come warranted
for truth. If public condemnation is not sufficient, what more is needed? Must
there be some demonstration of present harm to particular persons directly
affected by the practice in question? Or is it sufficient to show some effect on
social customs and institutions which alters the social environment, and thus
affects all members of society indirectly? If the latter, must it also be demonstrated that these social changes threaten long-term harm of some standard sort,
like an increase in crime or a decrease in productivity? Or would it be enough to
show that the vast bulk of the present community would deplore the change? If

[1] Report of the Committee on Homosexual Offenses and Prostitution, Cmd. No. 247
(1957).
[2] Memoirs v. Massachusetts (Fanny Hill), 383 U.S. 413 (1966), Ginzburg v. United
States, 383 U.S. 463 (1966), Mishkin v. New York, 383 U.S. 502 (1966).

Reprinted by permission of the author, The Yale Law Journal Company and
Fred B. Rothman and Company from *The Yale Law Journal,* Vol. 75, pp. 986-
1005.

so, does the requirement of harm add much to the bare requirement of public comdemnation?

In 1958 Lord Devlin delivered the second Maccabaean Lecture to the British Academy. He called his lecture "The Enforcement of Morals," and devoted it to these issues of principle.[3] His conclusions he summarized in these remarks about the practice of homosexuality: "We should ask ourselves in the first instance whether, looking at it calmly and dispassionately, we regard it as a vice so abominable that its mere presence is an offense. If that is the genuine feeling of the society in which we live, I do not see how society can be denied the right to eradicate it."[4]

The lecture, and in particular this hypothetical position on punishing homosexuals, provoked a tide of rebuttal that spilled over from academic journals into the radio and the almost-popular press.[5] Lord Devlin has now republished the Maccabaean Lecture, together with six further essays developing and defending the views there expressed, a preface to the whole, and some important new footnotes to the original lecture.[6]

American lawyers ought to attend to Lord Devlin's arguments. His conclusions will not be popular, although the swaggering insensitivity some of his critics found disappears with careful reading. Popular or not, we have no right to disregard them until we are satisfied that his arguments can be met. One of these arguments—the second of the two I shall discuss—has the considerable merit of focusing our attention on the connection between democratic theory and enforcement of morals. It provokes us to consider, more closely than we have, the crucial concept upon which this connection depends—the concept of a public morality.

Lord Devlin's Disenchantment

The preface to the new book contains a revealing account of how Lord Devlin came to his controversial opinions. When he was invited to prepare his Maccabaean Lecture the celebrated Wolfenden Committee had recently published its recommendation that homosexual practices in private between consenting adults no longer be criminal. He had read with complete approval the Committee's expression of the proper division between crime and sin:

> In this field, its [the law's] function, as we see it, is to preserve public order and decency, to protect the citizen from what is offensive or injurious, and to provide sufficient safeguards against exploitation and corruption of others. . . . It is not, in our view, the function of the law to intervene in the private lives of citizens, or to seek to enforce any particular pattern of behavior, further than is necessary to carry out the purposes which we have outlined. . . .
>
> [T]here must remain a realm of private morality and immorality which is, in brief and crude terms, not the law's business.[7]

[3] Devlin, *The Enforcement of Morals* (Oxford University Press 1959). Reprinted in Devlin, *The Enforcement of Morals* (Oxford University Press 1965). [The latter is hereinafter cited as Devlin.]

[4] Devlin 17. This position was carefully stated as hypothetical. Apparently Lord Devlin does not now think that the condition is met, because he has publically urged modification of the laws on homosexuality since the book's publication.

[5] Lord Devlin includes references to these comments in a bibliography. Devlin xiii.

[6] Devlin.

[7] Report of the Committee on Homosexual Offenses and Prostitution, *supra* note 1, at 9-10, 24.

Lord Devlin believed that these ideals, which he recognized as derived from the teachings of Jeremy Bentham and John Stuart Mill, were unquestionable. He decided to devote his lecture to a painstaking consideration of what further changes, beyond the changes in the crime of homosexuality that the Committee recommended, would be necessary to make the criminal law of England conform to them. But study, in his words, "destroyed instead of confirming the simple faith in which I had begun my task"[8] and he ended in the conviction that these ideals were not only questionable, but wrong.

The fact of his disenchantment is clear, but the extent of his disenchantment is not. He seems sometimes to be arguing the exact converse of the committee's position, namely that society has a right to punish conduct of which its members strongly disapprove, even though that conduct has no effects which can be deemed injurious to others, on the ground that the state has a role to play as moral tutor and the criminal law is its proper tutorial technique. Those readers who take this to be his position are puzzled by the fact that distinguished philosophers and lawyers have concerned themselves to reply, for this seems a position that can safely be regarded as eccentric. In fact he is arguing not this position, but positions which are more complex and neither so eccentric nor so flatly at odds with the Wolfenden ideals. They are nowhere summarized in any crisp form (indeed the statement on homosexuality I have already quoted is as good a summary as he gives) but must be taken from the intricate arguments he develops.

There are two chief arguments. The first is set out in structured form in the Maccabaean Lecture. It argues from society's right to protect its own existence. The second, a quite different and much more important argument, develops in disjointed form through various essays. It argues from the majority's right to follow its own moral convictions in defending its social environment from change it opposes. I shall consider these two arguments in turn, but the second at greater length.

The First Argument: Society's Right to Protect Itself

The first argument—and the argument which has received by far the major part of the critics' attention—is this:[9]

(1) In a modern society there are a variety of moral principles which some men adopt for their own guidance and do not attempt to impose upon others. There are also moral standards which the majority places beyond toleration and imposes upon those who dissent. For us, the dictates of particular religion are an example of the former class, and the practice of monogamy an example of the latter. A society cannot survive unless some standards are of the second class, because some moral conformity is essential to its life. Every society has a right to preserve its own existence, and therefore the right to insist on some such conformity.

(2) If society has such a right, then it has the right to use the institutions and sanctions of its criminal law to enforce the right—"[S]ociety may use the law to preserve morality in the same way it uses it to safeguard anything else if it is

[8] Devlin vii.
[9] It is developed chiefly in Devlin 7-25.

essential to its existence."[10] Just as society may use its law to prevent treason, it may use it to prevent a corruption of that conformity which ties it together.

(3) But society's right to punish immorality by law should not necessarily be exercised against every sort and on every occasion of immorality—we must recognize the impact and the importance of some restraining principles. There are several of these, but the most important is that there "must be toleration of the maximum individual freedom that is consistent with the integrity of society."[11] These restraining principles, taken together, require that we exercise caution in concluding that a practice is considered profoundly immoral. The law should stay its hand if it detects any uneasiness or half-heartedness or latent toleration in society's condemnation of the practice. But none of these restraining principles apply, and hence society is free to enforce its rights, when public feeling is high, enduring and relentless, when, in Lord Devlin's phrase, it rises to "intolerance, indignation and disgust."[12] Hence the summary conclusion about homosexuality: if it is genuinely regarded as an abominable vice, society's right to eradicate it cannot be denied.

We must guard against a possible, indeed tempting, misconception of this argument. It does not depend upon any assumption that when the vast bulk of a community thinks a practice is immoral they are likely right. What Lord Devlin thinks is at stake, when our public morality is challenged, is the very survival of society, and he believes that society is entitled to preserve itself without vouching for the morality that holds it together.

Is this argument sound? Professor H. L. A. Hart, responding to its appearance at the heart of the Maccabaean lecture,[13] thought that it rested upon a confused conception of what a society is. If one holds anything like a conventional notion of a society, he said, it is absurd to suggest that every practice the society views as profoundly immoral and disgusting threatens its survival. This is as silly as arguing that society's existence is threatened by the death of one of its members or the birth of another, and Lord Devlin, he reminds us, offers nothing by way of evidence to support any such claim. But if one adopts an artificial definition of a society, such that a society consists of that particular complex of moral ideas and attitudes which its members happen to hold at a particular moment in time, it is intolerable that each such moral status quo should have the right to preserve its precarious existence by force. So, Professor Hart argued, Lord Devlin's argument fails whether a conventional or an artificial sense of "society" is taken.

Lord Devlin replies to Professor Hart in a new and lengthy footnote. After summarizing Hart's criticism he comments, "I do not assert that *any* deviation from a society's shared morality threatens its existence any more than I assert that *any* subversive activity threatens its existence. I assert that they are both activities which are capable in their nature of threatening the existence of society so that neither can be put beyond the law."[14] This reply exposes a serious flaw in the architecture of the argument.

It tells us that we must understand the second step of the argument—the

[10] *Id.* at 11
[11] *Id.* at 16
[12] *Id.* at 17.
[13] H. L. A. Hart, *Law, Liberty and Morality* 51 (1963).
[14] Devlin 13.

crucial claim that society has a right to enforce its public morality by law—as limited to a denial of the proposition that society never has such a right. Lord Devlin apparently understood the Wolfenden Report's statement of a "realm of private morality ... not the law's business" to assert a fixed jurisdictional barrier placing private sexual practices forever beyond the law's scrutiny. His arguments, the new footnote tells us, are designed to show merely that no such constitutional barrier should be raised, because it is possible that the challenge to established morality might be so profound that the very existence of a conformity in morals, and hence of the society itself, would be threatened.[15]

We might well remain unconvinced, even of this limited point. We might believe that the danger which any unpopular practice can present to the existence of society is so small that it would be wise policy, a prudent protection of individual liberty from transient hysteria, to raise just this sort of constitutional barrier and forbid periodic reassessments of the risk.

But if we were persuaded to forego this constitutional barrier we would expect the third step in the argument to answer the inevitable next question: Granted that a challenge to deep-seated and genuine public morality may conceivably threaten society's existence, and so must be placed above the threshold of the law's concern, how shall we know when the danger is sufficiently clear and present to justify not merely scrutiny but action? What more is needed beyond the fact of passionate public disapproval to show that we are in the presence of an actual threat?

The rhetoric of the third step makes it seem responsive to this question—there is much talk of "freedom" and "toleration" and even "balancing." But the argument is not responsive, for freedom, toleration and balancing turn out to be appropriate only when the public outrage diagnosed at the second step shown is to be overstated, when the fever, that is, turns out to be feigned. When the fever is confirmed, when the intolerance, indignation and disgust are genuine, the

[15]This reading had great support in the text even without the new footnote:

> I think, therefore, that it is not possible to set theoretical limits to the power of the State to legislate against immorality. It is not possible to settle in advance exceptions to the general rule or to define inflexibly areas of morality into which the law is in no circumstances to be allowed to enter. (Devlin 12-13.)

The arguments presented bear out this construction. They are of the *reductio ad absurdum* variety, exploiting the possibility that what is immoral can in theory become subversive of society.

> But suppose a quarter or a half of the population got drunk every night, what sort of society would it be? You cannot set a theoretical limit to the number of people who can get drunk before society is entitled to legislate against drunkenness. The same may be said of gambling. (*Id.* at 14.)

Each example argues that no jurisdictional limit may be drawn, not that every drunk or every act of gambling threatens society. There is no suggestion that society is entitled actually to make drunkenness or gambling crimes if the practice in fact falls below the level of danger. Indeed Lord Devlin quotes the Royal Commission on Betting, Lotteries, and Gambling to support his example on gambling:

> If we were convinced that whatever the degree of gambling this effect [on the character of the gambler as a member of society] must be harmful we should be inclined to think that it was the duty of the state to restrict gambling to the greatest extent practicable. (Cmd. No. 8190 at para. 159 (1951), quoted in Devlin 14).

The implication is that society may scrutinize and be ready to regulate, but should not actually do so until the threat of harm in fact exists.

principle that calls for "the maximum individual freedom consistent with the integrity of society" no longer applies. But this means that nothing more than passionate public disapproval is necessary after all.

In short, the argument involves an intellectual sleight of hand. At the second step public outrage is presented as a threshold criterion, merely placing the practice in a category which the law is not forbidden to regulate. But offstage, somewhere in the transition to the third step, this threshold criterion becomes itself a dispositive affirmative reason for action, so that when it is clearly met the law may proceed without more. The power of this manoeuvre is proved by the passage on homosexuality. Lord Devlin concludes that if our society hates homosexuality enough it is justified in outlawing it, and forcing human beings to choose between the miseries of frustration and persecution, because of the danger the practice presents to society's existence. He manages this conclusion without offering evidence that homosexuality presents any danger at all to society's existence, beyond the naked claim that all "deviations from a society's shared morality . . . are capable in their nature of threatening the existence of society" and so "cannot be put beyond the law."[16]

The Second Argument: Society's Right to Follow Its Own Lights

We are therefore justified in setting aside the first argument and turning to the second. My reconstruction includes making a great deal explicit which I believe implicit, and so involves some risk of distortion, but I take the second argument to be this:[17]

(1) If those who have homosexual desires freely indulged them, our social environment would change. What the changes would be cannot be calculated with any precision, but it is plausible to suppose, for example, that the position of the family, as the assumed and natural institution around which the educational, economic and recreational arrangements of men center, would be undermined, and the further ramifications of that would be great. We are too sophisticated to suppose that the effects of an increase in homosexuality would be confined to those who participate in the practice alone, just as we are too sophisticated to suppose that prices and wages affect only those who negotiate them. The environment in which we and our children must live is determined, among other things, by patterns and relationships formed privately by others than ourselves.

(2) This in itself does not give society the right to prohibit homosexual practices. We cannot conserve every custom we like by jailing those who do not want to preserve it. But it means that our legislators must inevitably decide some moral issues. They must decide whether the institutions which seem threatened are sufficiently valuable to protect at the cost of human freedom. And they must decide whether the practices which threaten that institution are immoral, for if they are then the freedom of an individual to pursue them counts for less. We do not need so strong a justification, in terms of the social importance of the institutions being protected, if we are confident that no one has a moral right to do what we want to prohibit. We need less of a case, that is, to abridge

[16]Devlin 13, n.1.
[17]Most of the argument appears in Devlin chapters V, VI and VII. See also an article published after the book: Law and Morality, 1 *Manitoba L.S.J.* 243 (1964/65).

someone's freedom to lie, cheat or drive recklessly, than his freedom to choose his own jobs or to price his own goods. This does not claim that immorality is sufficient to make conduct criminal; it argues, rather, that on occasion it is necessary.

(3) But how shall a legislator decide whether homosexual acts are immoral? Science can give no answer, and a legislator can no longer properly turn to organized religion. If it happens, however, that the vast bulk of the community is agreed upon an answer, even though a small minority of educated men may dissent, the legislator has a duty to act on the consensus. He has such a duty for two closely connected reasons: (a) In the last analysis the decision must rest on some article of moral faith, and in a democracy this sort of issue, above all others, must be settled in accordance with democratic principles. (b) It is, after all, the community which acts when the threats and sanctions of the criminal law are brought to bear. The community must take the moral responsibility, and it must therefore act on its own lights—that is, on the moral faith of its members.

This, as I understand it, is Lord Devlin's second argument. It is complex, and almost every component invites analysis and challenge. Some readers will dissent from its central assumption, that a change in social institutions is the sort of harm a society is entitled to protect itself against. Others who do not take this strong position (perhaps because they approve of laws which are designed to protect economic institutions) will nevertheless feel that society is not entitled to act, however immoral the practice, unless the threatened harm to an institution is demonstrable and imminent rather than speculative. Still others will challenge the thesis that the morality or immorality of an act ought even to count in determining whether to make it criminal (though they would no doubt admit that it does count under present practice), and others still will argue that even in a democracy legislators have the duty to decide moral questions for themselves, and must not refer such issues to the community at large. I do not propose to argue now for or against any of these positions. I want instead to consider whether Lord Devlin's conclusions are valid on his own terms, on the assumption, that is, that society does have a right to protect its central and valued social institutions against conduct which the vast bulk of its members disapproves on moral principle.

I shall argue that his conclusions are not valid, even on these terms, because he misunderstands what it is to disapprove on moral principle. I might say a cautionary word about the argument I shall present. It will consist in part of reminders that certain types of moral language (terms like "prejudice" and "moral position," for example) have standard uses in moral argument. My purpose is not to settle issues of political morality by the fiat of a dictionary, but to exhibit what I believe to be mistakes in Lord Devlin's moral sociology. I shall try to show that our conventional moral practices are more complex and more structured than he takes them to be, and that he consequently misunderstands what it means to say that the criminal law should be drawn from public morality. This is a popular appealing thesis, and it lies near the core not only of Lord Devlin's, but of many other, theories about law and morals. It is crucial that its implications be understood.

The Concept of a Moral Position

We might start with the fact that terms like "moral position" and "moral conviction" function in our conventional morality as terms of justification and criticism, as well as of description. It is true that we sometimes speak of a group's "morals," or "morality," or "moral beliefs," or "moral positions" or "moral convictions," in what might be called an anthropological sense, meaning to refer to whatever attitudes the group displays about the propriety of human conduct, qualities or goals. We say, in this sense, that the morality of Nazi Germany was based on prejudice, or was irrational. But we also use some of these terms, particularly "moral position" and "moral conviction," in a discriminatory sense, to contrast the positions they describe with prejudices, rationalizations, matters of personal aversion or taste, arbitrary stands, and the like. One use—perhaps the most characteristic use—of this discriminatory sense is to offer a limited but important sort of justification for an act, when the moral issues surrounding that act are unclear or in dispute.

Suppose I tell you that I propose to vote against a man running for a public office of trust because I know him to be a homosexual and because I believe that homosexuality is profoundly immoral. If you disagree that homosexuality is immoral, you may accuse me of being about to cast my vote unfairly, acting on prejudice or out of a personal repugnance which is irrelevant to the moral issue. I might then try to convert you to my position on homosexuality, but if I fail in this I shall still want to convince you of what you and I will both take to be a separate point—that my vote was based upon *a* moral position, in the discriminatory sense, even though one which differs from yours. I shall want to persuade you of this, because if I do I am entitled to expect that you will alter your opinion of me and of what I am about to do. Your judgment of my character will be different—you might still think me eccentric (or puritanical or unsophisticated) but these are types of character and not faults of character. Your judgment of my act will also be different, in this respect. You will admit that so long as I hold my moral position, I have a moral right to vote against the homosexual, because I have a right (indeed a duty) to vote my own convictions. You would not admit such a right (or duty) if you were still persuaded that I was acting out of a prejudice or a personal taste.

I am entitled to expect that your opinion will change in these ways, because these distinctions are a part of the conventional morality you and I share, and which forms the background for our discussion. They enforce the difference between positions we must respect, although we think them wrong, and positions we need not respect because they offend some ground rule of moral reasoning. A great deal of debate about moral issues (in real life, although not in philosophy texts) consists of arguments that some position falls on one or the other side of this crucial line.

It is this feature of conventional morality that animates Lord Devlin's argument that society has the right to follow its own lights. We must therefore examine that discriminatory concept of a moral position more closely, and we can do so by pursuing our imaginary conversation. What must I do to convince you that my position is a moral position?

(a) I must produce some reasons for it. This is not to say that I have to articulate a moral principle I am following or a general moral theory to which I subscribe. Very few people can do either, and the ability to hold a moral position is not limited to those who can. My reason need not be a principle or theory at all. It must only point out some aspect or feature of homosexuality which moves me to regard it as immoral: the fact that the Bible forbids it, for example, or that one who practices homosexuality becomes unfit for marriage and parenthood. Of course, any such reason would presuppose my acceptance of some general principle or theory, but I need not be able to state what it is, or realize that I am relying upon it.

Not every reason I might give will do, however. Some will be excluded by general criteria stipulating sorts of reasons which do not count. We might take note of four of the most important such criteria:

(i) If I tell you that homosexuals are morally inferior because they do not have heterosexual desires, and so are not "real men," you would reject that reason as showing one type of prejudice. Prejudices, in general, are postures of judgment that take into account considerations our conventions exclude. In a structured context, like a trial or a contest, the ground rules exclude all but certain considerations, and a prejudice is a basis of judgment which violates these rules. Our conventions stipulate some ground rules of moral judgment which obtain even apart from such special contexts, the most important of which is that a man must not be held morally inferior on the basis of some physical, racial or other characteristic he cannot help having. Thus a man whose moral judgments about Jews, or Negroes, or Southerners, or women, or effeminate men are based on his belief that any member of these classes automatically deserves less repect, without regard to anything he himself has done, is said to be prejudiced against that group.

(ii) If I base my view about homosexuals on a personal emotional reaction ("they make me sick") you would reject that reason as well. We distinguish moral positions from emotional reactions, not because moral positions are supposed to be unemotional or dispassionate—quite the reverse is true—but because the moral position is supposed to justify the emotional reaction, and not vice versa. If a man is unable to produce such reasons, we do not deny the fact of his emotional involvement, which may have important social or political consequences, but we do not take this involvement as demonstrating his moral conviction. Indeed, it is just this sort of position—a severe emotional reaction to a practice or a situation for which one cannot account—that we tend to describe, in lay terms, as a phobia or an obsession.

(iii) If I base my position on a proposition of fact ("homosexual acts are physically debilitating") which is not only false, but is so implausible that it challenges the minimal standards of evidence and argument I generally accept and impose upon others, then you would regard my belief, even though sincere, as a form of rationalization, and disqualify my reason on that ground. (Rationalization is a complex concept, and also includes, as we shall see, the production of reasons which suggest general theories I do not accept.)

(iv) If I can argue for my own position only by citing the beliefs of others ("everyone knows homosexuality is a sin") you will conclude that I am parroting and not relying on a moral conviction of my own. With the possible (though complex) exception of a deity, there is no moral authority to which I can appeal and so automatically make my position a moral one. I must have my own reasons, though of course I may have been taught these reasons by others.

No doubt many readers will disagree with these thumbnail sketches of prejudice, mere emotional reaction, rationalization and parroting. Some may have their own theories of what these are. I want to emphasize now only that these are distinct concepts, whatever the details of the differences might be, and that they have a role in deciding whether to treat another's position as a moral conviction. They are not merely epithets to be pasted on positions we strongly dislike.

(b) Suppose I do produce a reason which is not disqualified on one of these (or similar) grounds. That reason will presuppose some general moral principle or theory, even though I may not be able to state that principle or theory, and do not have it in mind when I speak. If I offer, as my reason, the fact that the Bible forbids homosexual acts, or that homosexual acts make it less likely that the actor will marry and raise children, I suggest that I accept the theory my reason presupposes, and you will not be satisfied that my position is a moral one if you believe that I do not. It may be a question of my sincerity—do I in fact believe that injunctions of the Bible are morally binding as such, or that all men have a duty to procreate? Sincerity is not, however, the only issue, for consistency is also in point. I may believe that I accept one of these general positions, and be wrong, because my other beliefs, and my own conduct on other occasions, may be inconsistent with it. I may reject certain Biblical injunctions, or I may hold that men have a right to remain bachelors if they please or use contraceptives all their lives.

Of course, my general moral positions may have qualifications and exceptions. The difference between an exception and an inconsistency is that the former can be supported by reason which presuppose other moral positions I can properly claim to hold. Suppose I condemn all homosexuals on Biblical authority, but not all fornicators. What reason can I offer for the distinction? If I can produce none which supports it, I cannot claim to accept the general position about Biblical authority. If I do produce a reason which seems to support the distinction, the same sorts of question may be asked about that reason as were asked about my original reply. What general position does the reason for my exception presuppose? Can I sincerely claim to accept that further general position? Suppose my reason, for example, is that fornication is now common, and has been sanctioned by custom. Do I really believe that what is immoral becomes moral when it becomes popular? If not, and if I can produce no other reason for the distinction, I cannot claim to accept the general position that what the Bible condemns is immoral. Of course, I may be persuaded, when this is pointed out, to change my views on fornication. But you would be alert to the question of whether this is a genuine change of heart, or only a performance for the sake of the argument.

In principle there is no limit to these ramifications of my original claim, though of course, no actual argument is likely to pursue very many of them.

(c) But do I really have to have a reason to make my position a matter of moral conviction? Most men think that acts which cause unnecessary suffering, or break a serious promise with no excuse, are immoral, and yet they could give no reason for these beliefs. They feel that no reason is necessary, because they take it as axiomatic or self-evident that these are immoral acts. It seems contrary to common sense to deny that a position held in this way can be a moral position.

Yet there is an important difference between believing that one's position is self-evident and just not having a reason for one's position. The former presupposes a positive belief that no further reason is necessary, that the immorality of the act in question does not depend upon its social effects, or its effects on the character of the actor, or its proscription by a deity, or anything else, but follows from the nature of the act itself. The claim that a particular position is axiomatic, in other words, does supply a reason of a special sort, namely that the act is immoral in and of itself, and this special reason, like the others we considered, may be inconsistent with more general theories I hold.

The moral arguments we make presuppose not only moral principles, but also more abstract positions about moral reasoning. In particular, they presuppose positions about what kinds of acts can be immoral in and of themselves. When I criticize your moral opinions, or attempt to justify my own disregard of traditional moral rules I think are silly, I will likely proceed by denying that the act in question has any of the several features that can make an act immoral— that it involves no breach of an undertaking or duty, for example, harms no one including the actor, is not proscribed by any organized religion, and is not illegal. I proceed in this way because I assume that the ultimate grounds of immorality are limited to some such small set of very general standards. I may assert this assumption directly or it may emerge from the pattern of my argument. In either event, I will enforce it by calling positions which can claim no support from any of these ultimate standards *arbitrary* as I should certainly do if you said that photography was immoral, for instance, or swimming. Even if I cannot articulate this underlying assumption, I shall still apply it, and since the ultimate criteria I recognize are among the most abstract of my moral standards, they will not vary much from those my neighbors recognize and apply. Although many who despise homosexuals are unable to say why, few would claim affirmatively that one needs no reason, for this would make their position, on their own standards, an arbitrary one.

(d) This anatomy of our argument could be continued, but it is already long enough to justify some conclusions. If the issue between us is whether my views on homosexuality amount to a moral position, and hence whether I am entitled to vote against a homosexual on that ground, I cannot settle the issue simply by supporting my feelings. You will want to consider the reasons I can produce to support my belief, and whether my other views and behavior are consistent with the theories these reasons presuppose. You will have, of course, to apply your own understanding, which may differ in detail from mine, of what a prejudice or a rationalization is, for example, and of when one view is inconsistent with another. You and I may end in disagreement over whether my position is a moral one, partly because of such differences in understanding, and partly because one is less likely to recognize these illegitimate grounds in himself than in others.

We must avoid the sceptical fallacy of passing from these facts to the conclusion that there is no such thing as a prejudice or a rationalization or an inconsistency, or that these terms mean merely that the one who uses them strongly dislikes the positions he describes this way. That would be like arguing that because different people have different understandings of what jealousy is, and can in good faith disagree about whether one of them is jealous, there is no such thing as jealousy, and one who says another is jealous merely means he dislikes him very much.

Lord Devlin's Morality

We may now return to Lord Devlin's argument. He argues that when legislators must decide a moral issue (as by his hypothesis they must when a practice threatens a valued social arrangement), they must follow any consensus of moral position which the community at large has reached, because this is required by the democratic principle, and because a community is entitled to follow its own lights. The argument would have some plausibility if Lord Devlin meant, in speaking of the moral consensus of the community, those positions which are moral positions in the discriminatory sense we have been exploring.

But he means nothing of the sort. His definition of a moral position shows he is using it in what I called the anthropological sense. The ordinary man whose opinions we must enforce, he says, "... is not expected to reason about anything and his judgment may be largely a matter of feeling."[18] "If the reasonable man believes," he adds, "that a practice is immoral and believes also—no matter whether the belief is right or wrong, so be it that it is honest and dispassionate—that no right-minded member of his society could think otherwise, then for the purpose of the law it is immoral."[19] Elsewhere he quotes with approval Dean Rostow's attribution to him of the view that "the common morality of a society, at any time is a blend, of custom and conviction, of reason and feeling, of experience and prejudice."[20] His sense of what a moral conviction is emerges most clearly of all from the famous remark about homosexuals. If the ordinary man regards homosexuality "as a vice so abominable that its mere presence is an offense,"[21] this demonstrates for him that the ordinary man's feelings about homosexuals are a matter of moral conviction.[22]

His conclusions fail because they depend upon using "moral position" in this anthropological sense. Even if it is true that most men think homosexuality an abominable vice and cannot tolerate its pressence, it remains possible that this common opinion is a compound of prejudice (resting on the assumption that homosexuals are morally inferior creatures because they are effeminate), rationalization (based on assumptions of fact so unsupported that they challenge the community's own standards of rationality), and personal aversion (representing no conviction but merely blind hate rising from unacknowledged self-suspicion).

[18] Devlin 15.
[19] Id. at 22-23.
[20] Rostow, The Enforcement of Morals, 1960 Camb. L.J. 174, 197; reprinted in E. V. Rostow, The Sovereign Prerogative 45, 78 (1962). Quoted in Devlin 95.
[21] Id. at 17.
[22] In the preface (Id. at viii) Lord Devlin acknowledges that the language of the original lecture might have placed "too much emphasis on feeling and too little on reason," and he states that the legislator is entitled to disregard "irrational" beliefs. He gives as an example of the latter the belief that homosexuality causes earthquakes, and asserts that the exclusion of irrationality "is usually an easy and comparatively unimportant process." I think it fair to conclude that this is all Lord Devlin would allow him to exclude. If I am wrong, and Lord Devlin would ask him to exclude prejudices, personal aversions, arbitrary stands and the rest as well, he should have said so, and attempted to work some of these distinctions out. If he had, his conclusions would have been different and would no doubt have met with a different reaction.

It remains possible that the ordinary man could produce no reason for his view, but would simply parrot his neighbor who in turn parrots him, or that he would produce a reason which presupposes a general moral position he could not sincerely or consistently claim to hold. If so, the principles of democracy we follow do not call for enforcement of the consensus, for the belief that prejudices, personal aversions and rationalizations do not justify restricting another's freedom itself occupies a critical and fundamental position in our popular morality. Nor would the bulk of the community then be entitled to follow its own lights, for the community does not extend that privilege to one who acts on the basis of prejudice, rationalization, or personal aversion. Indeed, the distinction between these and moral convictions, in the discriminatory sense, exists largely to mark off the former as the sort of positions one is not entitled to pursue.

A conscientious legislator who is told a moral consensus exists must test the credentials of that consensus. He cannot, of course, examine the beliefs or behavior of individual citizens; he cannot hold hearings on the Clapham omnibus. That is not the point.

The claim that a moral consensus exists is not itself based on a poll. It is based on an appeal to the legislator's sense of how his community reacts to some disfavored practice. But this same sense includes an awareness of the grounds on which that reaction is generally supported. If there has been a public debate involving the editorial columns, speeches of his colleagues, the testimony of interested groups, and his own correspondence, these will sharpen his awareness of what arguments and positions are in the field. He must sift these arguments and positions, trying to determine which are prejudices or rationalizations, which presuppose general principles or theories vast parts of the population could not be supposed to accept, and so on. It may be that when he has finished this process of reflection he will find that the claim of a moral consensus has not been made out. In the case of homosexuality, I expect, it would not be, and that is what makes Lord Devlin's undiscriminating hypothetical so serious a misstatement. What is shocking and wrong is not his idea that the community's morality counts, but his idea of what counts as the community's morality.

Of course the legislator must apply these tests for himself. If he shares the popular views he is less likely to find them wanting, though if he is self-critical the exercise may convert him. His answer, in any event, will depend upon his own understanding of what our shared morality requires. That is inevitable, for whatever criteria we urge him to apply, he can apply them only as he understands them.

A legislator who proceeds in this way, who refuses to take popular indignation, intolerance and disgust as the moral conviction of his community, is not guilty of moral elitism. He is not simply setting his own educated views against those of a vast public which rejects them. He is doing his best to enforce a distinct, and fundamentally important, part of his community's morality, a consensus more essential to society's existence in the form we know it than the opinion Lord Devlin bids him follow.

No legislator can afford to ignore the public's outrage. It is a fact he must reckon with. It will set the boundaries of what is politically feasible, and it will determine his strategies of persuasion and enforcement within these boundaries. But we must not confuse strategy with justice, nor facts of political life with principles of political morality. Lord Devlin understands these distinctions, but his arguments will appeal most, I am afraid, to those who do not.

Postcript on Pornography

I have been discussing homosexuality because that is Lord Devlin's example. I should like to say a word about pornography, if only because it is, for the time being, more in the American legal headlines than homosexuality. This current attention is due to the Supreme Court's decisions and opinions in three recent cases: *Ginzburg*, *Mishkin* and *Fanny Hill*. In two of these, convictions (and jail sentences) for the distribution of pornography were upheld, and in the third, while the Court reversed a state ban on an allegedly obscene novel, three justices dissented.

Two of the cases involved review of state procedures for constitutionality, and the third the interpretation and application of a federal statute. The Court therefore had to pass on the constitutional question of how far a state or the nation may legally restrict the publication of erotic literature, and on questions of statutory construction. But each decision nevertheless raises issues of political principle of the sort we have been considering.

A majority of the Court adheres to the constitutional test laid down some years ago in *Roth*.[23] As that test now stands, a book is obscene, and as such not protected by the first amendment, if: "(a) the dominant theme of the material taken as a whole appeals to a prurient interest in sex; (b) the material is patently offensive because it affronts contemporary community standards relating to the description or representation of sexual matters; and (c) the material is utterly without redeeming social value."[24] We might put the question of political principle this way: What gives the federal government, or any state, the moral right to prohibit the publication of books which are obscene under the *Roth* test?

Justice Brennan's opinion in *Mishkin* floated one answer: erotic literature, he said, incites some readers to crime. If this is true, if in a significant number of such cases the same readers would not have been incited to the same crime by other stimuli, and if the problem cannot effectively be handled in other ways, this might give society a warrant to ban these books. But these are at least speculative hypotheses, and in any event are not pertinent to a case like *Ginzburg*, in which the Court based its decision not on the obscene character of the publications themselves, but on the fact that they were presented to the public as salacious rather than enlightening. Can any other justification be given for the prohibition of obscene books?

An argument like Lord Devlin's second argument can be constructed, and many of those who feel society is entitled to ban pornography are in fact moved by some such argument. It might take this form:

(1) If we permit obscene books freely to be sold, to be delivered as it were with the morning milk, the whole tone of the community will eventually change. That which is now thought filthy and vulgar in speech and dress, and in public behavior, will become acceptable. A public which could enjoy pornography

[23] *Roth v. United States*, 354 U.S. 476 (1957).
[24] *Memoirs v. Massachusetts (Fanny Hill)*, 383 U.S. 413, 418 (1966).

legally would soon settle for nothing very much tamer, and all forms of popular culture would inevitably move closer to the salacious. We have seen these forces at work already—the same relaxations in our legal attitudes which enabled books like *Tropic of Cancer* to be published have already had an effect on what we find in movies and magazines, on beaches and on the city streets. Perhaps we must pay that price for what many critics plausibly consider works of art, but we need not pay what would be a far greater price for trash—mass-manufactured for profit only.

(2) It is not a sufficient answer to say that social practices will not change unless the majority willingly participates in the change. Social corruption works through media and forces quite beyond the control of the mass of the people, indeed quite beyond the control of any conscious design at all. Of course, pornography attracts while it repels, and at some point in the deterioration of community standards the majority will not object to further deterioration, but that is a mark of the corruption's success, not proof that there has been no corruption. It is precisely that possibility which makes it imperative that we enforce our standards while we still have them. This is an example—it is not the only one—of our wishing the law to protect us from ourselves.

(3) Banning pornography abridges the freedom of authors, publishers and would-be readers. But if what they want to do is immoral, we are entitled to protect ourselves at that cost. Thus we are presented with a moral issue: does one have a moral right to publish or to read "hard-core" pornography which can claim no value or virtue beyond its erotic effect? This moral issue should not be solved by fiat, nor by self-appointed ethical tutors, but by submission to the public. The public at present believes that hard-core pornography is immoral, that those who produce it are panderers, and the protection of the community's sexual and related mores is sufficiently important to justify restricting their freedom.

But surely it is crucial to this argument, whatever else one might think of it, that the consensus described in the last sentence be a consensus of moral conviction. It it should turn out that the ordinary man's dislike of pornographers is a matter of taste, or an arbitrary stand, the argument would fail because these are not satisfactory reasons for abridging freedom.

It will strike many readers as paradoxical even to raise the question whether the average man's views on pornography are moral convictions. For most people the heart of morality is a sexual code, and if the ordinary man's views on fornication, adultery, sadism, exhibitionism and the other staples of pornography are not moral positions, it is hard to imagine any beliefs he is likely to have that are. But writing and reading about these adventures is not the same as performing in them, and one may be able to give reasons for condemning the practices (that they cause pain, or are sacrilegious, or insulting, or cause public annoyance) which do not extend to producing or savoring fantasies about them.

Those who claim a consensus of moral conviction on pornography must provide evidence that this exists. They must provide moral reasons or arguments which the average member of society might sincerely and consistently advance in the manner we have been describing. Perhaps this can be done, but it is no substitute simply to report that the ordinary man—within or without the jury box—turns his thumb down on the whole business.

A. R. Louch

A. R. Louch (b. 1927) is Professor of Philosophy at Claremont Graduate School. In the article printed below, "Scientific Discovery and Legal Change," Professor Louch criticizes the claim that traditional legal models of punishment should give way to therapy or treatment by psychiatrists and psychologists. He does not, of course, defend the barbarous conditions usually found in prisons, but argues that in replacing these with therapy in the attempt to be scientific and humane we would succeed only in being less humane than ever. Professor Louch is not concerned here to advocate any one of the traditional justifications of punishment mentioned in our Introduction, but only to argue against an alternative to punishment which he thinks robs a man of his humanity.

Scientific Discovery and Legal Change

I

In contemporary law the sentencing of criminals is often thought to be a hit or miss affair, a jumble of legal, moral and factual considerations brought together by the primitive desire to punish lawbreakers. Moreover, jailing offenders fails to do the job of deterring crime or reforming criminals. We charge society for the support of men and women in enforced unproductivity and reap only the reward of increased recidivism. It is not surprising that it seems obvious to many that we should seek a more intelligent and humane policy.

Psychologists, psychiatrists, sociologists and many jurists have suggested that that policy is to be found in modern behavioral science. What we need, so the argument goes, is a method for discovering the causes of crime—in the physical constitution, the environment or the personality of the offender. It will then be possible to remove these causes or control their effects upon behavior by suitable therapy, whether surgery, medicine, psychoanalysis or social engineering. By such proper use of scientific know-how we will reduce crime, and recidivism, resolve rationally the vexing issue of responsibility, and do away with the method of punishment, providing in its place a more humane way of dealing with offenders.

These are large claims. I want to go a small way toward challenging them.

Reprinted from *The Monist*, Volume 49, Number 3 (July, 1965) La Salle, Illinois with the permission of the publishers.

This is not easy to do, for one must overcome the double barreled polemic that the proposed reforms are both scientific and humane. To object to the psychiatric argument (as I shall call it, for the sake of a convenient label) is thus to appear unscientific, irrational, primitive and vindictive all at once. No wonder so many have fallen victims to its blandishments.

Nevertheless there are serious difficulties with the psychiatric argument. To approach the problem of criminal law holding that scientific method is applicable to every problem and that punishment is an unmixed evil is to miss, it seems to me, the essence of the legal process. To carry through these beliefs into policy threatens the existence of a society based on law and civil procedure. I shall explore this general theme by arguing, first, that scientific findings about the causes of behavior cannot determine responsibility or identify the criminal act; second, that the diagnosis of mental illness in criminal offenders confuses scientific and moral categories and so advances the aims of moral coercion under the guise of scientific control; and finally that punishment is in fact more humane than therapy. From these deliberations we may draw the more general moral, that legal problems do not admit of scientific resolution. If this is so we should be even more on our guard against the interference in legal questions of the pseudoscientific polemic of psychiatrists.

II

How first do supposed scientific discoveries bear upon the question of responsibility? The psychiatrist wishes to offer his evidence as decisive on this question just in the way that other experts—the fingerprint, clothing-fragment, bloodstain and ballistics men—offer evidence that can be decisive on the question of guilt. But does the analogy hold? Let us suppose, for the moment, a thesis that we will challenge later, that the criminal act can be traced to, say, sugar deficiency. I choose this as against the psychoanalytic story, for example, because it makes for the strongest possible defense for the psychiatric argument. It must always be borne in mind how important it is for the psychiatrist to advance his views as deterministic hypotheses.[1] In the first place, deterministic hypotheses give his claim the appearance of scientific authority; in the second, they make it seem obvious that, if determined, a criminal is not responsible for his acts. How, then, are judge and jury to act on the evidence that the crime was caused by sugar deficiency in the brain of the accused? It looks as if they must bow to scientific fact: this is the cause, therefore the individual is not responsible; and to the recommendations that seem to follow from the fact, that the accused requires therapy, not punishment.

There are many ways in which facts bear on the question of responsibility. Circumstances may show that a man was entitled to defend himself; other circumstances that, given his justifiable actions, the offending act was unavoidable. Often, too, facts about the individual bear on the issue. He may be a child or, in the words of the much despised M'Naghten Rules (despised, it seems, because they allow too many to escape the therapeutic net), he may be

[1] Cf. Edward Sachar, "Behavioral Science and Criminal Law," *Scientific American*, **209**, No. 5 (Nov., 1963), the most dogmatic statement I know of the claim that scientific discoveries call for changes in the criminal law, and the most blindly enthusiastic propaganda for the scientific status of psychiatry. It is a scandal that a journal devoted to reports of scientific findings should print such a piece of pure polemic.

incapable of understanding what he did, or its moral significance. In all these cases responsibility is assessed by answering the question: does some circumstance excuse the act? Sometimes a causal relationship hangs from the issue of responsibility. If we formulate the general rule that the damage done by a defendant as a result of bodily movements caused by some external agency, like the hand of another, is an excused action, testimony to that effect in a particular case will determine the degree of responsibility. But in such a case the causal claim determines responsibility only because it has already been decided that a person should not be blamed for such an act. Similarly in the case of childhood or madness one says: a person is not responsible for antisocial acts when he is incapable, by reasons of age, mental deficiency or distraction, of learning correct social behavior. Now this is an exceedingly delicate point, for it is the beachhead of the psychiatrist's advance into the hinterland of antisocial behavior. But the question is still not one that admits of a factual, scientific answer. We must first decide that specified states of mind qualify as grounds excusing behavior before we can admit expert testimony identifying those states. In section III we shall see that ambiguity shrouds the psychiatrist's means of identifying those further mental states that he wishes to exempt from responsibility. Here we need only see that the relevance of such expert, quasi-expert or, for that matter, on-the-scene testiomy, depends on a prior determination of what counts as a case of diminished or absolved responsibility. This is a moral and legal matter; it is a business of deciding how we want things to be, not a matter of discovering what in fact is the case.

It is surely not evident, without the prior moral deliberations, why a person whose actions are caused by one set of circumstances is not, while a person whose actions are caused by some other set is, responsible for his actions. If in the courtroom we bow to causal testimony on its own account, we must draw the conclusion that, if the accused is not responsible, nor is the judge, jury or psychiatrist. For the deterministic point of view that backs up the psychiatrist's claim to expertise demands that all actions be thought of as caused. In consequence when the psychiatrist delivers his testimony as expert on the subject of responsibility he is not deciding on the facts of the particular case that the accused is or is not responsible. He is not claiming that A is *not* responsible in a way in which it would make sense to claim that B *is* responsible. The concept of responsibility simply has no place in a causal account. Taken in this spirit, psychiatric testimony does not refine and settle the issue of responsibility, it bypasses it, and so leads to a major overhauling of legal attitudes and procedures. For law sets standards for performance, a code to live up to; and this can often be done only with effort, sometimes with skill. But it must insist that it can be lived up to, otherwise the notion of life governed by law becomes meaningless.[2] The decision of responsibility is the judgment that the law can be lived up to. Thus to exclude the notion of responsibility is to exclude the method of law. On this score, at least, the psychiatrist cannot claim to improve a method which in fact he proposes to overthrow.

If there are difficulties in getting the gears of causal determinism and legal responsibility to mesh, so there are difficulties in fitting the concept of crime

[2] A viewpoint taken, e.g., by the court in a decision quoting Justices Cardozo, Jackson and Thurman Arnold, *Dusky v. U.S.* 295 F 2n 743, 753-754 (8th Circ., 1961). Cf. also the statement of O. W. Holmes, Jr. that the law requires a person "at his own peril to come up to a certain height." *The Common Law* (Boston: Little Brown & Co., 1881), pp. 50-51.

into the determinist's picture of human behavior. Crimes are untoward acts, wrong, violations of accepted or stated rules. We could not identify or label an act as criminal without benefit of moral and legal categories. It might, however, seem feasible to correlate a set of legally defined acts with particular physical or environmental antecedents, and thus allow the plausibility, at least, of giving a causal explanation of crime. The difficulty is that laws and customs, and so definitions of criminal acts, change. Are we to suppose that the use of contraceptives in Massachusetts is caused by sugar deficiency, but not in other places? Or that, with the framing of new laws, those who had habitually acted contrary to their intent come to do so now by reason of sugar deficiency? It would be absurd to suppose so.

It is clear that the relation of the psychiatrist to the criminal must be framed in some more modest way. Perhaps this: the psychiatrist is concerned only with criminal acts that can be defined without reference to particular legal enactments, e.g., violent actions. But the distinction needed here is an exceedingly difficult one to give, for it cannot be based simply on a description of the act, e.g., one that results in death or injury. A man may kill for gain or to escape detection or to resolve an impasse between wife and mistress, but these are not crimes that call for special attention beyond the determination of guilt. The psychiatrist's foothold in crime comes instead through cases like killing for pleasure or for no reason at all, rape of children or aged grandmothers, torture, or less savage, the constant theft of worthless trinkets. Thus the distinction depends on the shifty ground of intention and rationality. We understand many of the actions of which we disapprove, but some remain opaque, and it is these that seem to require a rather different attention than that involved in sentencing those convicted of crime. Oddity is thus the defining mark of the cases we want singled out. A case seems odd because the action does not appear to be justifiable by the rules we apply to the circumstances open to our inspection. Once more it is a moral point of view that allows us to single out these cases, and as our customs may change so may the kinds of actions we single out for special causal analysis. The absurd consequence of a general causal explanation of crime is thus not avoided in the more modest case.

Moreover the ways we do have of resolving the oddity of these special cases are infinitely various. We may discover that the agent held false beliefs about the circumstances in which he acted, or lacked crucial information; we may discover the same difficulties in our surmises as observers. We may also appeal to intoxication, hypnosis, extreme anger, mental deficiency, and so on and on. There is clearly no particular cause that singles out the odd criminal any more than there is any single reason behind crimes of the more rational variety. Part of the evidence that helps dispel the oddity can it is true be given by a psychiatrist, but not as an expert on the causes of certain actions, but rather as the citizen who finds himself in a privileged position to obtain the needed facts about the agent's thoughts and circumstances. His testimony helps judge and jury put together a consistent picture of the crime; it is thus exactly like the testimony of a good friend or colleague. They are all privileged spectators, on-the-scene witnesses, so to speak, of facts not immediately available to the court. The relevance of the psychiatrist's evidence is determined by prior judicial reflections on the nature of responsibility and criminality; it is neither an answer to nor a substitute for that question. So far in our argument, at least, we must insist that sentencing procedures remain with the court; there is no justification for turning these tasks over to panels of psychiatrists, social workers and judges favorably disposed to the psychiatric reform of criminal law.[3]

New moral sensitivities, of course, may open the door to the psychiatrist and social workers as advisors to political and judicial projects. Once we think of slums as an unmitigated evil we need to get all the information we can about the slum background of criminal offenders. But it is the moral significance of the slum that makes the sociologist's findings, the psychiatrist's biographical details and the social worker's recommendations relevant to the proceedings of the court. Statistics that show a high correlation between slums and crime no doubt add fuel to the moral argument. But if such a correlation were to be found to hold instead between crime and an upper middle-class, white Protestant environment we should not find in this statistic welcome support for arguments attempting to excuse actions. It is the evil of the slum that gives these statistics and the biographical and social facts of slum careers their importance to judicial consideration. In a sense it is society's guilt in allowing such conditions that mitigate the responsibility of the slum product. The connection between the psychiatrist's or sociologist's evidence and the matter of sentencing cannot be expressed by the formula: "Don't punish him, his actions are causally determined"; but rather by the formula: "Don't punish him, what has happened is punishment enough." Admittedly the second formula is little more than a caricature of the complicated arguments of the courtroom; but I venture to say that it is closer to the truth than the first.

III

The first psychiatric gambit is the attack on responsibility, using for this maneuver the quite inappropriate tools of causal analysis. The focus is on the cause of the particular act. The second gambit focuses attention instead upon the general state of illness from which the criminal supposedly suffers. The psychiatric examination is designed to reveal mental illness in the criminal, quite apart from the fact that he has committed a criminal act. But the trouble is, if he really does succeed in doing so, he has the problem of showing that "but for the disease the act would not have been committed."[4] For the connection between disease and act is surely not self-evident. If, on the other hand, the diagnosis includes specification of the criminal act, the psychiatrist is in danger of judging the accused to be mentally ill simply because of his criminal act.

Take the first alternative. We may discover a low sugar level, schizophrenic reaction, or anxiety syndrome, but by what authority do we move directly to the claim that such a condition caused the criminal act? Such conditions are

[3] A procedure advocated by jurists and psychiatrists alike. See especially, Sheldon Glueck, *Law and Psychiatry* (Baltimore: Johns Hopkins University Press, 1962), p. 152.

[4] The words quoted are from *Carter v. U.S.*, 252 F 2nd 608 (D.C. Circ., 1957), in a case in which the court was trying to carry out the intent of the Durham case. (*Durham v. U.S.*, 214 F 2d 862 (D.C. Circ., 1954). In that case Judge Bazelon laid it down that the "accused is not responsible if his unlawful act was the product of mental disease or mental defect." It was a decision applauded by most psychiatrists.

surely often present in individuals who commit no crimes. The psychiatrist is put in the position of arguing *post hoc:* the accused did have a low sugar level *and* he did the old vicar in, therefore, the sugar level was responsible for his deed. At best a statistical connection might be drawn between diagnostic categories and criminal acts, evidence that might be useful to law-enforcement officials in watching out for likely suspects—a crime-index, so to speak. Mere statistical connection, even if established, would not automatically excuse offenders, however. We might find a high correlation between crime and height or rate of hair growth. This fact too would be useful (conceivably) in forecasting behavior, but we should probably not think of hair growth as the cause and certainly not regard it as the mitigating circumstance in the commission of crimes.

There may be exceptions in which the diagnosis of illness and the commission of the criminal act seem more intimately connected. A murder might be explained in terms of the delusions of the murderer, another murder by the murderer's tendency to uncontrollable rages. In the first case, if we say that A killed B because he thought B was messing about by remote control with his liver, the 'because' has a logical sense; A's beliefs are his *reasons* for murder. But then we must suppose that in some sense the murder was a rational consequence of the beliefs, and no evidence of 'disease' can be worked out of that connection. The problem of establishing mental illness now begins all over again, presumably by suggesting that beliefs so bizarre must be an indication of mental illness. But this method leads nowhere; the psychiatrist never establishes the disease, but only alleged symptoms of it. He, and anyone, might say that A would not have killed B except for his delusions, but his only authority for calling the beliefs indications of mental disorder is that they are bizarre. We are no closer by such diagnoses to a causal explanation of the criminal act, for the diagnosis is no more than an appraisal of a man's beliefs according to some conventions regarded by the psychiatrist as governing matters of evidence, proof, and fact. Far from giving an account of a criminal act in terms of a disease he has simply pushed that question back another stage, leaving it unanswered. In its place he has simply passed judgment on the beliefs of the accused.

The second case is like the first. Modern habits tempt us to say that fits of rage *indicate* mental illness. Do we mean 'indicate', 'symptoms of'? If so, it is an odd use of 'disease' that identifies a disease with symptoms of it. Or do we mean to define mental illness in this way (among others)? If so a psychiatrist might tell us, or a man's wife might tell us, that the accused is sick, having seen him in his rages. But there is nothing explanatory in saying so, and no particular expertise would be required to identify illness, once we had learned the use of the term. As in the first case, insufficient attention is paid to the meaning of 'because' in such contexts. In 'He killed only because he was angry', *what* he did is one of the things that count as being angry. Smothering Desdemona was the form of Othello's jealous rage, not the effect of it. Moreover established tendencies do not establish incapacity to resist; they only serve to warn us to be on our guard against men of such tendencies. Once more, the question of disease is pushed a step back, and left unanswered.

The fact is, I suggest, that the mental examination and subsequent diagnosis of mental illness is a piece of theater designed to give an aura of a causal explanation by dredging up any further idiosyncracy of thought or behavior.[5] It is the criminal act itself, or its special quality, that brings forth the diagnosis of mental illness. The criminal act is recognizable only on moral and legal grounds; to redescribe such findings in the language of medicine is thus at the minimum confusing, and is more apt to threaten the legal rights of those accused of crimes. For now the psychiatrist becomes our moral watchdog, but on the unchallengeable pedestal of scientific expertise. If his talents were to extend to positive means for 'redeeming' the fallen, the situation would be even worse. He would have the right to decide what behavior is truly morally reprehensible and the power to change deviants into decent citizens according to his lights. Perhaps this right may extend only over a special segment of those apprehended for crimes, perhaps it may include all crimes; but given the rather more flexible possibilities in the term 'mental illness' lacking to 'criminal offense' it is quite conceivable that his deviant hunt may extend quite beyond the bounds of criminal law.[6]

The results are in the first place dictatorial. Moral judgments are announced as the claims of scientific experts, and are thus protected from the kind of debate and criticism they deserve—the argument in the courtroom and the deliberation of juries. In the second place the results are capricious. Instead of laying down fixed rules for dealing with criminal offenders (and ultimately those defining offenses), the psychiatrist will decide in each case what is to be done. This is not a legal procedure at all. Finally, a point that we must amplify in the next section, the scientist's method alters our entire attitude toward the offender. He is no longer a person who could have lived up to a code but didn't;[7] he is instead an object to be manipulated in such a way as to produce desired behavior. On none of these counts, surely, can the psychiatrist's claim to scientific expertise be construed as a way of improving the muddled and ancient procedures of the law; it is rather a recommendation for eliminating legal procedure altogether. If this method is as efficient as its advocates claim for it, we may indeed reduce the crime-rate, but at the cost of losing civil society to an

[5]Thomas Szasz, one psychiatrist who sees through the maneuver by which those whose beliefs and actions are disapproved of are called mentally ill, has many instructive cases of it. For example, a Mr. Rosario who, because he insisted that his wife's lover drew blood from his arms and drank it in beer to prove his vigor, was solemnly declared paranoid by four psychiatrists who, on discovering that Mr. Rosario's claims were true, reversed themselves and found him sane and ready to stand trial. *Law, Liberty and Psychiatry* (New York: Macmillan, 1963), pp. 166-7.

[6]G. B. Chisholm in "The Psychiatry of Enduring Peace and Progress," *Psychiatry* 9, No. 3 (1946), thinks that all difficulties in living are neurotic, thus neatly converting all moral into pseudo-scientific questions. Cf. Szasz, *op. cit.,* p. 3.

[7]I do not wish to minimize the difficulties in assigning responsibility; only that there are clearly cases we are able to contrast. My handwriting is terrible, and I can't be held responsible at this date for improving it. But it is possible to print a message when legibility is crucial, and I should be held accountable if I failed to do so. This contrast is important to keep in mind when approaching some of the most formidable arguments against the possibility of assessing responsibility for criminal acts. Cf., e.g., H. L. A. Hart, "Legal Responsibility and Excuses," in Sidney Hook, ed., *Determinism and Freedom in the Age of Modern Science* (New York: New York University Press and Collier Books, 1958), pp. 81-104; "Prolegomena to the Theory of Punishment," *Aristotelian Society Proceedings,* 60 (1959-1960); and *Punishment and the Elimination of Responsibility* (London: Athlone Press, 1962).

efficient, scientific dictatorship. These are consequences that require more in their defense than the claim to scientific efficiency alone.

IV

The final gambit is the claim that therapy is more humane than punishment. Lady Wootton, for example, thinks psychiatry has had an overwhelming humanizing influence on the law because it is concerned with the health rather than the morals of the offender.[8] This is a popular view, perhaps because the only option to therapy seems to be imprisonment, and jails do not prompt thoughts of humanitarian care.[9] It is not clear that mental hospitals are much of an improvement, but present conditions are not as important for our argument as possible conditions. Imagine, then, that we take our convicts gently by the hand and lead them toward productive, nondeviant lives through a pleasant environment with sunny rooms, flowers on the sill, pretty nurses and steak every Saturday. I would still want to argue that the idea of humane therapy is so elastic and so potentially misleading that we cannot have the slightest idea what we are getting into in basing our hopes upon it. Secondly, the psychiatrist's claim completely misconceives, to my mind, the meaning and purpose of punishment.

First, our 'humane'—i.e., our pleasant, bland or agreeable—environment could very well be used for quite inhumane purposes. It is not clear, for example, why B. F. Skinner's schedules of positive reinforcement should be regarded as humane simply because his subjects are conditioned by rewards rather than punishment. The point is that the conditioner treats the individual, not as a person entitled to his views and attitudes, but as an object whose sole function is to be made to perform just those tasks its master asks of it. It may be a balm to our consciences to know that we can coerce by rewards and other pleasantries more effectively than by whips and scourges, but there is nothing particularly humane about it. To act humanely requires not just an environment or method of a certain kindliness, it requires also a special attitude on the part of the judge, jailor, or therapist. A person must be thought to be in rightful possession of his desires, needs and beliefs, however much we may wish him to change them or give them up, or however deeply we feel them wrong or bad. We may attempt to argue and persuade; and with major breaches of the legal code we may be forced to confine him for his actions. But we do not subject him to devices that will insure that his actions will be no more than automatic responses to our commands. This, however, is the promise of a truly scientific therapy. It must rest its case on the proven possibility of employing techniques that will insure predicted results, whether the subject is a salivating dog or a murderous one.

Thus it appears that at the heart of the psychiatric polemic lies a basic inconsistency between the scientifically efficient and the humane connotations of the therapeutic approach. So long as we think of the counsellor paying heed to his patient's problems and gently encouraging him toward more positive and

[8] Barbara Wootton, *Social Science and Social Pathology* (New York: Macmillan, 1959), p. 206.

[9] Once again, Szasz' *Law, Liberty and Psychiatry*, along with Ervine Goffman's *Asylums: Essays on the Social Situation of Mental Patients and other Inmates* (New York: Doubleday, 1961), is the place to go for a corrective to the view that hospitals must be humane simply because they are not jails.

resourceful attitudes toward his social obligations, or of the social worker seeking to provide the probationer with a job that suits his talents and an environment that will release him from old criminal ties it is easy enough to applaud the therapeutic option to imprisonment as more humane. It is not so easy when the concept of therapy is expanded to include shock treatment, tranquilizing drugs, surgery, or reconditioning. Humane treatment is not just in fact but by definition inefficient, for it leaves open to the individual the capacity to reject our arguments, ignore our recommendations, and resist our exhortations. Treatment which might in principle be efficient, on the other hand, is quite indifferent to the objective of agreement, and must seek always to limit the individual's capacity to reject, ignore or resist the attempts to change him. It may be clear why the psychiatrist should seek to exploit the claims, both to efficiency and humanity. He appeals to scientific efficiency in order to usurp, as qualified expert, the place formerly occupied by untutored judges and juries; and then justifies the change as more civilized by conjuring up pictures of talking-out and social aid which unfortunately do not qualify as instances of his scientifically efficient procedures. But it is equally clear that the two barrels of his argument cannot be fired together.

But the fact is that the humane virtues of therapy are rarely urged on their own account, but only against the contrasting and supposedly inhumane disabilities of the method of punishment. Thus it appears that any alternative must be an improvement. Lady Wootton, once again, sees punishment in one of its guises, playing hob with civilized behavior by allowing feelings of revulsion and the excesses they beget to be reinforced by legal powers. These anxieties ought to lead instead to reaffirm the crucial role of legal powers and procedures. For the force of moral sentiment is best diluted and dissipated by having to surmount and survive legal protocols. To turn the job over to the psychiatrist is to substitute *ad hoc* judgments for rules, and thus allow the force of moral revulsion to express itself more directly, if hypocritically, as a concern for health. For notice that in calling a man mentally sick we exempt ourselves from the requirement of defending our charges against his beliefs and behavior. We do not, in such circumstances, challenge his beliefs or actions on their merits; but, by assuming these beliefs and actions to be the expressions of a sick mind, assume without reflection or defense, the propriety of our own moral convictions. This is moral judgment disguised so as to sneak by its own appropriate customs of moral defense.

It is perhaps true that punishment gives vent to "the revulsion felt by the great majority of citizens" for criminal acts.[10] It may even prove to be a useful safety-valve to such feelings. But surely this is but a small part of a very complex social institution. Punishment needs to be thought of first of all as a way of penalizing infractions of the rules of the social game. Penalties are exacted, not so much to deter players from breaking the rules or as a means of reforming those who have broken them, but to insure that the game continues under conditions of fair play. No game can withstand indefinitely an excess of unpunished infractions. Those handicapped by the violations of others must lose interest; they have set out to play by the rules only to discover that rule-breaking brings even greater rewards. And so the game becomes meaningless. In civil

[10]The words are Lord Denning's in *The Royal Commission on Capital Punishment, 1949-1953, Report,* Cmd. 8932 (Her Majesty's Stationery Office, 1953), para. 53.

society numbers of infractions can be penalized through restitution, a device that illustrates the objective of social balance to be achieved by penalties. But restitution is not always possible, and especially not in just those acts of violence that form one preoccupation of criminal law. Here something needs to be done to stand in place of restitution, something that will restore fair conditions of play. It is not easy, of course, to find the punishment that fits the crime, or to create an institution serving the ends of punishment that is not of dubious moral qualifications. But these difficulties, vexing though they may be, should not lead us to embrace the psychiatric alternative, whether in the name of science or humanity. For the object of punishment is not vengeance but the preservation of social order; its target is not the individual offender, but the social system affected by the offense. The psychiatric argument fails to see the way in which the concept of punishment is entangled in the very idea of a civil society. The essence of that society is that rules should show us how to play; the psychiatric alternative advertises itself as guaranteeing that those treated cannot help but act according to their demands. It is a consequence of the notion of a game that its rules can be broken, otherwise we do not have players. Conditioned behavior on the other hand, is not rule-following; and rules that cannot be broken are not rules.

V

The method of civil society suffers from severe disabilities. It practically guaranteeds lawbreaking, and so the problems of punishment. We are at times so oppressed by these vexations that we are prepared to embrace utopian alternatives that guarantee, as in the conditioned citizens of *Walden II*, that people will be good. That frame of mind usually lasts only so long as we think of ourselves as the conditioners; as the subjects conditioned the value of civil society reasserts itself.

In any case I do not wish to argue the much larger case for civil as against utopian society. Mine is the more limited aim of showing that the psychiatric argument, under the guise of scientific expertise, in fact proposes an end to criminal law, and eventually to a society based on the notion of law. Before we succumb to the blandishments of a polemic aimed at one of our most vulnerable points, respect for science, we ought at least to reflect on the kind of society we want. This reflection is moral, legal, political; it cannot be brought to conclusion by scientific methods or discoveries, even when these are brought forth in a humane disguise. In heeding the psychiatrist's call we are, so to speak, engaging him to repair the cracks in the foundation of our home, but find that he plans to redesign the whole edifice as a modern laboratory. As our architect and contractor he assures us that there is nothing to worry about; after all, he is the expert on matters of construction. Moreover, he will make things as convenient and as comfortable as could be wished.

We should not be bullied by his credentials into accepting his plans. We know what sort of building we want. The house, it's true, is settling, and someone could in all probability hurt himself tripping over uneven places in the floor. Still, it's a house, and that's what we wanted when we called the architect. The laboratory is grand, terribly scientific, and convenient—for a laboratory. But living in it means we must cook all our meals over bunsen burners, and shower at the YMCA.

There are also cracks in our social system, prisons among them. But we should think awhile before turning over the problem to the psychiatrist. For it may turn out that, in his attitude toward the problem, and his advertised scientific efficiency in dealing with it, he will tear down the edifice of society and build a different one less to our liking.

J. D. Mabbott

J. D. Mabbott (b. 1898) has been Fellow, Tutor, and President of St. Johns College, Oxford. He is the author of *The State and the Citizen,* an excellent introduction to political philosophy. In the article "Punishment" printed below he defends a retributive theory of punishment. Such a theory rejects the claim that punishment is to be justified by its deterrent effect, its reformative effect, or any other utilitarian consideration.

Punishment

I propose in this paper to defend a retributive theory of punishment and to reject absolutely all utilitarian considerations from its justification. I feel sure that this enterprise must arouse deep suspicion and hostility both among philosophers (who must have felt that the retributive view is the only moral theory except perhaps psychological hedonism which has been definitely destroyed by criticism) and among practical men (who have welcomed its steady decline in our penal practice).

The question I am asking is this. Under what circumstances is the punishment of some particular person justified and why? The theories of reform and deterrence which are usually considered to be the only alternatives to retribution involve well-known difficulties. These are considered fully and fairly in Dr.

Reprinted from *Mind,* 1939, by permission of the author and the Editor of *Mind.*

Ewing's book, *The Morality of Punishment*, and I need not spend long over them. The central difficulty is that both would on occasion justify the punishment of an innocent man, the deterrent theory if he were believed to have been guilty by those likely to commit the crime in future, and the reformatory theory if he were a bad man though not a criminal. To this may be added the point against the deterrent theory that it is the threat of punishment and not punishment itself which deters, and that when deterrence seems to depend on actual punishment, to implement the threat, it really depends on publication and may be achieved if men believe that punishment has occurred even if in fact it has not. As Bentham saw, for a Utilitarian apparent justice is everything, real justice is irrelevant.

Dr. Ewing and other moralists would be inclined to compromise with retribution in the face of the above difficulties. They would admit that one fact and one fact only can justify the punishment of this man, and that is a *past* fact, that he has committed a crime. To this extent reform and deterrence theories, which look only to the consequences, are wrong. But they would add that retribution can determine only *that* a man should be punished. It cannot determine how or how much, and here reform and deterrence may come in. Even Bradley, the fiercest retributionist of modern times, says "Having once the right to punish we may modify the punishment according to the useful and the pleasant, but these are external to the matter; they cannot give us a right to punish and nothing can do that but criminal desert." Dr. Ewing would maintain that the whole estimate of the amount and nature of a punishment may be effected by considerations of reform and deterrence. It seems to me that this is a surrender which the upholders of retribution dare not make. As I said above, it is publicity and not punishment which deters, and the publicity though often spoken of as "part of a man's punishment" is no more part of it than his arrest or his detention prior to trial, though both these may be also unpleasant and bring him into disrepute. A judge sentences a man to three years' imprisonment not to three years *plus* three columns in the press. Similarly with reform. The visit of the prison chaplain is not part of a man's punishment nor is the visit of Miss Fields or Mickey Mouse.

The truth is that while punishing a man and punishing him justly, it is possible to deter others, and also to attempt to reform him, and if these additional goods are achieved the total state of affairs is better than it would be with the just punishment alone. But reform and deterrence are not modifications of the punishment, still less reasons for it. A parallel may be found in the case of tact and truth. If you have to tell a friend an unpleasant truth you may do all you can to put him at his ease and spare his feelings as much as possible, while still making sure that he understands your meaning. In such a case no one would say that your offer of a cigarette beforehand or your apology afterwards are modifications of the truth still less reasons for telling it. You do not tell the truth in order to spare his feelings, but having to tell the truth you also spare his feelings. So Bradley was right when he said that reform and deterrence were "external to the matter," but therefore wrong when he said that they may "modify the punishment." Reporters are admitted to our trials so that punishments may become public and help to deter others. But the punishment would be no less just were reporters excluded and deterrence not achieved. Prison authorities may make it possible that a convict may become physically or morally better. They cannot ensure either result; and the punishment would still be just if the criminal took no advantage of their arrangements and their efforts failed. Some moralists see this and exclude these "extra" arrangements for deterrence and reform. They say that it must be the punishment *itself* which reforms and deters. But it is just my point that the punishment *itself* seldom reforms the criminal and never deters others. It is only "extra" arrangements which have any chance of achieving either result. As this is the central point of my paper, at the cost of laboured repetition I would ask the upholders of reform and deterrence two questions. Suppose it could be shown that a particular criminal had not been improved by a punishment and also that no other would-be criminal had been deterred by it, would that prove that the punishment was unjust? Suppose it were discovered that a particular criminal had lived a much better life after his release and that many would-be criminals believing him to have been guilty were influenced by his fate, but yet that the "criminal" was punished for something he had never done, would these excellent results prove the punishment just?

It will be observed that I have throughout treated punishment as a purely legal matter. A "criminal" means a man who has broken a law, not a bad man; an "innocent" man is a man who has not broken the law in connection with which he is being punished, though he may be a bad man and have broken other laws. Here I dissent from most upholders of the retributive theory—from Hegel, from Bradley, and from Dr. Ross. They maintain that the essential connection is one between punishment and moral or social wrong-doing.

My fundamental difficulty with their theory is the question of *status*. It takes two to make a punishment, and for a moral or social wrong I can find no punisher. We may be tempted to say when we hear of some brutal action "that ought to be punished"; but I cannot see how there can be duties which are nobody's duties. If I see a man ill-treating a horse in a country where cruelty to animals is not a legal offence, and I say to him "I shall now punish you," he will reply, rightly, "What has it to do with you? Who made you a judge and a ruler over me?" I may have a duty to try to stop him and one way of stopping him may be to hit him, but another way may be to buy the horse. Neither the blow nor the price is a punishment. For a moral offence, God alone has the *status* necessary to punish the offender; and the theologians are becoming more and more doubtful whether even God has a duty to punish wrong-doing.

Dr. Ross would hold that not all wrong-doing is punishable, but only invasion of the rights of others; and in such a case it might be thought that the injured party had a right to punish. His right, however, is rather a right to reparation and should not be confused with punishment proper.

This connection, on which I insist, between punishment and crime, not between punishment and moral or social wrong, alone accounts for some of our beliefs about punishment, and also meets many objections to the retributive theory as stated in its ordinary form. The first point on which it helps us is with regard to retrospective legislation. Our objection to this practice is unaccountable on reform and deterrence theories. For a man who commits a wrong before the date on which a law against it is passed, is as much in need of reform as a man who commits it afterwards; nor is deterrence likely to suffer because of additional punishments for the same offence. But the orthodox retributive theory is equally at a loss here, for if punishment is given for moral wrong-doing or for invasion of the rights of others, that immorality or invasion existed as certainly before the passing of the law as after it.

My theory also explains, where it seems to me all others do not, the case of punishment imposed by an authority who believes the law in question is a bad law. I was myself for some time disciplinary officer of a college whose rules included a rule compelling attendance at chapel. Many of those who broke this rule broke it on principle. I punished them. I certainly did not want to reform them; I respected their characters and their views. I certainly did not want to drive others into chapel through fear of penalties. Nor did I think there had been a wrong done which merited retribution. I wished I could have believed that I would have done the same myself. My position was clear. They had broken a rule; they knew it and I knew it. Nothing more was necessary to make punishment proper.

I know that the usual answer to this is that the judge enforces a bad law because otherwise law in general would suffer and good laws would be broken. The effect of punishing good men for breaking bad laws is that fewer bad men break good laws.

[*Excursus on Indirect Utilitarianism.* The above argument is a particular instance of a general utilitarian solution of all similar problems. When I am in funds and consider whether I should pay my debts or give the same amount to charity, I must choose the former because repayment not only benefits my creditor (for the benefit to him might be less than the good done through charity) but also upholds the general credit system. I tell the truth when a lie might do more good to the parties directly concerned, because I thus increase general trust and confidence. I keep a promise when it might do more immediate good to break it, because indirectly I bring it about that promises will be more readily made in future and this will outweigh the immediate loss involved. Dr. Ross has pointed out that the effect on the credit system of my refusal to pay a debt is greatly exaggerated. But I have a more serious objection of principle. It is that in all these cases the indirect effects do not result from my wrong action—my lie or defalcation or bad faith—but from the publication of these actions. If in any instance the breaking of the rule were to remain unknown then I could consider only the direct or immediate consequences. Thus in my "compulsory chapel" case I could have considered which of my culprits were law-abiding men generally and unlikely to break any other college rule. Then I could have sent for each of these separately and said "I shall let you off if you will tell no one I have done so." By these means the general keeping of rules would not have suffered. Would this course have been correct? It must be remembered that the proceedings need not deceive everybody. So long as they deceive would-be law-breakers the good is achieved.

As this point is of crucial importance and as it has an interest beyond the immediate issue, and gives a clue to what I regard as the true general nature of law and punishment, I may be excused for expanding and illustrating it by an example or two from other fields. Dr. Ross says that two men dying on a desert island would have duties to keep promises to each other even though their breaking them would not affect the future general confidence in promises at all. Here is certainly the same point. But as I find that desert-island morality always rouses suspicion among ordinary men I should like to quote two instances from my own experience which also illustrate the problem.

(i) A man alone with his father at his death promises him a private and quiet funeral. He finds later that both directly and indirectly the keeping of this promise will cause pain and misunderstanding. He can see no particular positive good that the quiet funeral will achieve. No one yet knows that he has made the promise nor need anyone ever know. Should he therefore act as though it had never been made?

(ii) A college has a fund given to it for the encouragement of a subject which is now expiring. Other expanding subjects are in great need of endowment. Should the authorities divert the money? Those who oppose the diversion have previously stood on the past, the promise. But one day one of them discovers the "real reason" for this slavery to a dead donor. He says "We must consider not only the value of this money for these purposes, since on all direct consequences it should be diverted at once. We must remember the effect of this diversion on the general system of benefactions. We know that benefactors like to endow special objects, and this act of ours would discourage such benefactors in future and leave learning worse off." Here again is the indirect utilitarian reason for choosing the alternative which direct utilitarianism would reject. But the immediate answer to this from the most ingenious member of the opposition was crushing and final. He said, "Divert the money but keep it dark." This is obviously correct. It is not the act of diversion which would diminish the stream of benefactions but the news of it reaching the ears of benefactors. Provided that no possible benefactor got to hear of it no indirect loss would result. But the justification of our action would depend entirely on the success of the measures for "keeping it dark." I remember how I felt and how others felt that whatever answer was right this result was certainly wrong. But it follows that indirect utilitarianism is wrong in all such cases. For its argument can always be met by "Keep it dark."]

The view, then, that a judge upholds a bad law in order that law in general should not suffer is indefensible. He upholds it simply because he has no right to dispense from punishment.

The connection of punishment with law-breaking and not with wrong-doing also escapes moral objections to the retributive theory as held by Kant and Hegel or by Bradley and Ross. It is asked how we can measure moral wrong or balance it with pain, and how pain can wipe out moral wrong. Retributivists have been pushed into holding that pain *ipso facto* represses the worse self and frees the better, when this is contrary to the vast majority of observed cases. But if punishment is not intended to measure or balance or negate moral wrong then all this is beside the mark. There is the further difficulty of reconciling punishment with repentance and with forgiveness. Repentance is the reaction morally appropriate to moral wrong and punishment added to remorse is an unnecessary evil. But if punishment is associated with law-breaking and not with moral evil the punisher is not entitled to consider whether the criminal is penitent any more than he may consider whether the law is good. So, too, with forgiveness. Forgiveness is not appropriate to law-breaking. (It is noteworthy that when, in divorce cases, the law has to recognize forgiveness it calls it "condonation," which is symptomatic of the difference of attitude.) Nor is forgiveness appropriate to moral evil. It is appropriate to personal injury. No one has any right to forgive me except the person I have injured. No judge or jury can do so. But the person I have injured has no right to punish me. Therefore there is no clash between punishment and forgiveness since these two duties do not fall on the same person nor in connection with the same characteristic of my act. (It is the weakness of vendetta that it tends to confuse this clear line, though even there it is only by personifying the family that the injured party and the avenger are identified. Similarly we must guard against the plausible fallacy of personifying society and regarding the criminal as "injuring society," for then once more the old dilemma about forgiveness would be insoluble.) A clergyman friend of mine catching a burglar red-handed was puzzled about his duty. In the end he ensured the man's punishment by information and evidence, and at the same time showed his own forgiveness by visiting the man in prison and employing him when he came out. I believe any "good Christian" would accept this as representing his duty. But obviously if the punishment is thought of as imposed *by* the victim or *for* the injury or immorality then the contradiction with forgiveness is hopeless.

So far as the question of the actual punishment of any individual is concerned this paper could stop here. No punishment is morally retributive or reformative or deterrent. Any criminal punished for any one of these reasons is certainly unjustly punished. The only justification for punishing any man is that he has broken a law.

In a book which has already left its mark on prison administration I have found a criminal himself confirming these views. *Walls Have Mouths*, by W. F. R. Macartney, is prefaced, and provided with appendices to each chapter, by Compton Mackenzie. It is interesting to notice how the novelist maintains that the proper object of penal servitude should be reformation,[1] whereas the prisoner himself accepts the view I have set out above. Macartney says "To punish a man is to treat him as an equal. To be punished *for an offence against rules* is a sane man's right."[2] It is striking also that he never uses "injustice" to describe the brutality or provocation which he experienced. He makes it clear that there were only two types of prisoner who were *unjustly* imprisoned, those who were insane and not responsible for the acts for which they were punished[3] and those who were innocent and had broken no law.[4] It is irrelevant, as he rightly observes, that some of these innocent men were, like Steinie Morrison, dangerous and violent characters, who on utilitarian grounds might well have been restrained. That made their punishment no whit less unjust.[5] To these general types may be added two specific instances of injustice. First, the sentences on the Dartmoor mutineers. "The Penal Servitude Act . . . lays down specific punishments for mutiny and incitement to mutiny, which include flogging. . . . Yet on the occasion of the only big mutiny in an English prison, men are not dealt with by the Act specially passed to meet mutiny in prison, but are taken out of gaol and tried under an Act expressly passed to curb and curtail the Chartists—a revolutionary movement."[6] Here again the injustice does not lie in the actual effect the sentences are likely to have on the prisoners (though Macartney has some searching suggestions about that also) but in condemning men for breaking a law they did not break and not for breaking the law they did break. The second specific instance is that of Coulton, who served his twenty years and then was brought back to prison to do another eight years and to die. This is due to the "unjust order that no lifer shall be released unless he has either relations or a job to whom he can go: and it is actually suggested that this is really for the lifer's own good. Just fancy, you admit that the man is doing years upon years in prison had expiated his crime: but, instead of releasing him, you

---

[1] p. 97.   [2] p. 165. My italics.   [3] pp. 165-166.   [4] p. 298.   [5] p. 301.
[6] p. 255.

keep him a further time—perhaps another three years—because you say he has nowhere to go. Better a ditch and hedge than prison! True, there are abnormal cases who want to stay in prison, but Lawrence wanted to be a private soldier, and men go into monasteries. Because occasionally a man wants to stay in prison, must every lifer who has lost his family during his sentence (I was doing only ten years and I lost all my family) be kept indefinitely in gaol after he has paid his debt?"[7] Why is it unjust? Because he has paid his debt. When that is over it is for the man himself to decide what is for his own good. Once again the reform and utilitarian arguments are summarily swept aside. Injustice lies not in bad treatment or treatment which is not in the man's own interest, but in restriction which, according to the law, he has not merited.

It is true that Macartney writes, in one place, a paragraph of general reflection on punishment in which he confuses, as does Compton Mackenzie, retribution with revenge and in which he seems to hold that the retributive theory has some peculiar connection with private property. "Indeed it is difficult to see how, in society as it is today constituted, a humane prison system could function. All property is sacred, although the proceeds of property may well be reprehensible, therefore any offence against property is sacrilege and must be punished. Till a system eventuates which is based not on exploitation of man by man and class by class, prisons must be dreadful places, but at least there might be an effort to ameliorate the more savage side of the retaliation, and this could be done very easily."[8] The alternative system of which no doubt he is thinking is the Russian system described in his quotations from *A Physician's Tour in Soviet Russia*, by Sir James Purves-Stewart, the system of "correctional colonies" providing curative "treatment" for the different types of criminal.[9] There are two confusions here, to one of which we shall return later. First, Macartney confuses the retributive system with the punishment of one particular type of crime, offences against property, when he must have known that the majority of offenders against property do not find themselves in Dartmoor or even in Wandsworth. After all his own offence was not one against property—it was traffic with a foreign Power—and it was one for which in the classless society of Russia the punishment is death. It is surely clear that a retributive system may be adopted for any class of crime. Secondly, Macartney confuses injustice within a penal system with the wrongfulness of a penal system. When he pleads for "humane prisons" as if the essence of the prison should be humanity, or when Compton Mackenzie says the object of penal servitude should be reform, both of them are giving up punishment altogether, not altering it. A Russian "correctional colony," if its real object is curative treatment, is no more a "prison" than is an isolation hospital or a lunatic asylum. To this distinction between abolishing injustice in punishment and abolishing punishment altogether we must now turn.

It will be objected that my original question "Why ought X to be punished?" is an illegitimate isolation of the issue. I have treated the whole set of circumstances as determined. X is a citizen of a state. About his citizenship, whether willing or unwilling, I have asked no questions. About the government, whether it is good or bad, I do not enquire. X has broken a law. Concerning the law, whether it is well-devised or not, I have not asked. Yet all these questions are surely relevant before it can be decided whether a particular punishment is just.

[7] p. 400.   [8] pp. 166, 167.   [9] p. 229.

It is the essence of my position that none of these questions is relevant. Punishment is a corollary of law-breaking by a member of the society whose law is broken. This is a static and an abstract view but I see no escape from it. Considerations of utility come in on two quite different issues. Should there be laws, and what laws should there be? As a legislator I may ask what general types of action would benefit the community, and, among these, which can be "standardized" without loss, or should be standardized to achieve their full value. This, however, is not the primary question since particular laws may be altered or repealed. The choice which is the essential *prius* of punishment is the choice that there should be laws. The choice is not Hobson's. Other methods may be considered. A government might attempt to standardize certain modes of action by means of advice. It might proclaim its view and say "Citizens are requested" to follow this or that procedure. Or again it might decide to deal with each case as it arose in the manner most effective for the common welfare. Anarchists have wavered between these two alternatives and a third—that of doing nothing to enforce a standard of behaviour but merely giving arbitrational decisions between conflicting parties, decisions binding only by consent

I think it can be seen without detailed examination of particular laws that the method of law-making has its own advantages. Its orders are explicit and general. It makes behaviour reliable and predictable. Its threat of punishment may be so effective as to make punishment unneccessary. It promises to the good citizen a certain security in his life. When I have talked to business men about some inequity in the law of liability they have usually said "Better a bad law than no law, for then we know where we are."

Someone may say I am drawing an impossible line. I deny that punishment is utilitarian; yet now I say that punishment is a corollary of law and we decide whether to have laws and which laws to have on utilitarian grounds. And surely it is only this corollary which distinguishes law from good advice or exhortation. This is a misunderstanding. Punishment is a corollary not of law but of law-breaking. Legislators do not choose to punish. They hope no punishment will be needed. Their laws would succeed even if no punishment occurred. The criminal makes the essential choice: he "brings it on himself." Other men obey the law because they see its order is reasonable, because of inertia, because of fear. In this whole area, and it may be the major part of the state, law achieves its ends without punishment. Clearly, then, punishment is not a corollary of law.

We may return for a moment to the question of amount and nature of punishment. It may be thought that this also is automatic. The law will include its own penalties and the judge will have no option. This, however, is again an initial choice of principle. If the laws do include their own penalties then the judge has no option. But the legislature might adopt a system which left complete or partial freedom to the judge, as we do except in the case of murder. Once again, what are the merits (regardless of particular laws, still more of particular cases) of fixed penalties and variable penalties? At first sight it would seem that all the advantages are with the variable penalties; for men who have broken the same law differ widely in degree of wickedness and responsibility. When, however, we remember that punishment is not an attempt to balance moral guilt this advantage is diminished. But there are still degrees of responsibility; I do not mean degrees of freedom of will but, for instance, degrees of complicity in a crime. The danger of allowing complete freedom to the judicature in fixing penalties is not merely that it lays too heavy a tax on human nature but that it would lead to the judge expressing in his penalty the degree of his own moral aversion to the crime. Or he might tend on deterrent grounds to punish more heavily a crime which was spreading and for which temptation and opportunity were frequent. Or again on deterrent grounds he might "make examples" by punishing ten times as heavily those criminals who are detected in cases in which nine out of ten evade detection. Yet we should revolt from all such punishments if they involved punishing theft more heavily than blackmail or negligence more heavily than premeditated assault. The death penalty for sheep-stealing might have been defended on such deterrent grounds. But we should dislike equating sheep-stealing with murder. Fixed penalties enable us to draw these distinctions between crimes. It is not that we can say how much imprisonment is right for a sheep-stealer. But we can grade crimes in a rough scale and penalties in a rough scale, and keep our heaviest penalties for what are socially the most serious wrongs regardless of whether these penalties will reform the criminal or whether they are exactly what deterrence would require. The compromise of laying down maximum penalties and allowing judges freedom below these limits allows for the arguments on both sides.

To return to the main issue, the position I am defending is that it is essential to a legal system that the infliction of a particular punishment should *not* be determined by the good *that particular punishment* will do either to the criminal or to "society." In exactly the same way it is essential to a credit system that the repayment of a particular debt should not be determined by the good that particular payment will do. One may consider the merits of a legal system or of a credit system, but the acceptance of either involves the surrender of utilitarian considerations in particular cases as they arise. This is in effect admitted by Ewing in one place where he says "It is the penal system as a whole which deters and not the punishment of any individual offender."[10]

To show that the choice between a legal system and its alternatives is one we do and must make, I may quote an early work of Lenin in which he was defending the Marxist tenet that the state is bound to "wither away" with the establishment of a classless society. He considers the possible objection that some wrongs by man are not economic and therefore that the abolition of classes would not *ipso facto* eliminate crime. But he sticks to the thesis that these surviving crimes should not be dealt with by law and judicature. "We are not Utopians and do not in the least deny the possibility and inevitability of excesses by *individual persons*, and equally the need to suppress such excesses. But for this no special machine, no special instrument of repression is needed. This will be done by the armed nation itself as simply and as readily as any crowd of civilized people even in modern society parts a pair of combatants or does not allow a woman to be outraged."[11] This alternative to law and punishment has obvious demerits. Any injury not committed in the presence of the crowd, any wrong which required skill to detect or pertinacity to bring home would go untouched. The lynching mob, which is Lenin's instrument of justice, is liable to error and easily deflected from its purpose or driven to extremes. It must be a mob, for there is to be no "machine." I do not say that no alternative

[10] A. C. Ewing, *The Morality of Punishment* (London: Routledge and Kegan Paul, Ltd., 1929), p. 66.
[11] *The State and Revolution* (Eng. Trans.), p. 93. Original italics.

machine to ours could be devised but it does seem certain that the absence of all "machines" would be intolerable. An alternative machine might be based on the view that "society" is responsible for all criminality, and a curative and protective system developed. This is the system of Butler's "Erewhon" and something like it seems to be growing up in Russia except for cases of "sedition."

We choose, then, or we acquiesce in and adopt the choice of others of, a legal system as one of our instruments for the establishment of the conditions of a good life. This choice is logically prior to and independent of the actual punishment of any particular persons or the passing of any particular laws. The legislators choose particular laws within the framework of this predetermined system. Once again a small society may illustrate the reality of these choices and the distinction between them. A Headmaster launching a new school must explicitly make both decisions. First, shall we have any rules at all? Second, what rules shall we have? The first decision is a genuine one and one of great importance. Would it not be better to have an "honour" system, by which public opinion in each house or form dealt with any offence? (This is the Lenin method.) Or would complete freedom be better? Or should he issue appeals and advice? Or should he personally deal with each malefactor individually, as the case arises, in the way most likely to improve his conduct? I can well imagine an idealistic Headmaster attempting to run a school with one of these methods or with a combination of several of them and therefore without punishment. I can even imagine that with a small school of, say, twenty pupils all open to direct personal psychological pressure from authority and from each other, these methods involving no "rules" would work. The pupils would of course grow up without two very useful habits, the habit of having some regular habits and the habit of obeying rules. But I suspect that most Headmasters, especially those of large schools, would either decide at once, or quickly be driven, to realize that some rules were necessary. This decision would be "utilitarian" in the sense that it would be determined by consideration of consequences. The question "what rules?" would then arise and again the issue is utilitarian. What action must be regularized for the school to work efficiently? The hours of arrival and departure, for instance, in a day school. But the one choice which is now no longer open to the Headmaster is whether he shall punish those who break the rules. For if he were to try to avoid this he would in fact simply be returning to the discarded method of appeals and good advice. Yet the Headmaster does not decide to punish. The pupils make the decision there. He decides actually to have rules and to threaten, but only hypothetically, to punish. The one essential condition which makes actual punishment just is a condition he *cannot* fulfil—namely that a rule should be broken.

I shall add a final word of consolation to the practical reformer. Nothing that I have said is meant to counter any movement for "penal reform" but only to insist that none of these reforms have anything to do with punishment. The only type of reformer who can claim to be reforming the system of punishment is a follower of Lenin or of Samuel Butler who is genuinely attacking the *system* and who believes there should be no laws and no punishments. But our great British reformers have been concerned not with punishment but with its accessories. When a man is sentenced to imprisonment he is not sentenced also to partial starvation, to physical brutality, to pneumonia from damp cells and so on. And any movement which makes his food sufficient to sustain health, which counters the permanent tendency to brutality on the part of his warders, which gives him a dry or even a light and well-aired cell, is pure gain and does not touch the theory of punishment. Reformatory influences and prisoners' aid arrangements are also entirely unaffected by what I have said. I believe myself that it would be best if all such arrangements were made optional for the prisoners, so as to leave him in these cases a freedom of choice which would make it clear that they are not part of his punishment. If it is said that every such reform lessens a man's punishment, I think that is simply muddled thinking which, if it were clear, would be mere brutality. For instance, a prisoners' aid society is said to lighten his punishment, because otherwise he would suffer not merely imprisonment but also unemployment on release. But he was sentenced to imprisonment, not imprisonment *plus* unemployment. If I promise to help a friend and through special circumstances I find that keeping my promise will involve upsetting my day's work, I do not say that I really promised to help him and to ruin my day's work. And if another friend carries on my work for me I do not regard him as carrying out part of my promise, nor as stopping me from carrying it out myself. He merely removes an indirect and regrettable consequence of my keeping my promise. So with punishment. The Prisoners' Aid Society does not alter a man's punishment nor diminish it, but merely removes an indirect and regrettable consequence of it. And anyone who thinks that a criminal cannot make this distinction and will regard all the inconvenience that comes to him as punishment, need only talk to a prisoner or two to find how sharply they resent wanton additions to a punishment which by itself they will accept as just. Macartney's chapter on "Food" in the book quoted above is a good illustration of this point, as are also his comments on Clayton's administration. "To keep a man in prison for many years at considerable expense and then to free him charged to the eyes with uncontrollable venom and hatred generated by the treatment he has received in gaol, does not appear to be sensible." Clayton "endeavoured to send a man out of prison in a reasonable state of mind. 'Well. I've done my time. They were not too bad to me. Prison is prison and not a bed of roses. Still they didn't rub it in. . . .' "[12] This "reasonable state of mind" is one in which a prisoner on release feels he has been punished but not *additionally* insulted or ill-treated. I fell convinced that penal reformers would meet with even more support if they were clear that they were *not* attempting to alter the system of punishment but to give its victims "fair play." We have no more right to starve a convict that to starve an animal. We have no more right to keep a convict in a Dartmoor cell "down which the water trickles night and day" than we have to keep a child in such a place. If our reformers really want to alter the system of punishment, let them come out clearly with their alternative and preach, for instance, that no human being is responsible for any wrong-doing, that all the blame is on society, that curative or protective measures should be adopted, forcibly if necessary, as they are with infection or insanity. Short of this let them admit that the essence of prison is deprivation of liberty for the

[12] p. 152.

breaking of law, and that deprivation of food or of health or of books is unjust. And if our sentimentalists cry "coddling of prisoners," let us ask them also to come out clearly into the open and incorporate whatever starvation and disease and brutality they think necessary *into the sentences they propose.*[13] If it is said that some prisoners will prefer such reformed prisons, with adequate food and aired cells, to the outer world, we may retort that their numbers are probably not greater than those of the masochists who like to be flogged. Yet we do not hear the same "coddling" critics suggest abolition of the lash on the grounds that some criminals may like it. Even if the abolition from our prisons of all maltreatment other than that imposed by law results in a few down-and-outs breaking a window (as O. Henry's hero did) to get a night's lodging, the country will lose less than she does by her present method of sending out her discharged convicts "charged with venom and hatred" because of the additional and uncovenanted "rubbing it in" which they have received.

I hope I have established both the theoretical importance and the practical value of distinguishing between penal reform as we know and approve it— that reform which alters the accompaniments of punishment without touching its essence—and those attacks on punishment itself which are made not only by reformers who regard criminals as irresponsible and in need of treatment, but also by every judge who announces that he is punishing a man to deter others or to protect society, and by every juryman who is moved to his decision by the moral baseness of the accused rather than by his legal guilt.

Edmund L. Pincoffs

Edmund L. Pincoffs (b. 1919) is Professor of Philosophy at the University of Texas. In his book *The Rationale of Legal Punishment,* Professor Pincoffs presents a careful analysis of traditional justifications of punishment and attempts to clarify the issues with which the traditional theories dealt. The selection reprinted below is the final chapter of his book and presents his conclusions concerning the justification of legal punishment.

[13] "One of the minor curiosities of jail life was that they quickly provided you with a hundred worries which left you no time or energy for worrying about your sentence, long or short. . . . Rather as if you were thrown into a fire with spikes in it, and the spikes hurt you so badly that you forget about the fire. But then your punishment would *be* the spikes not the fire. Why did they pretend it was only the fire, when they knew very well about the spikes?" (From *Lifer* by Jim Phelan, p. 40.)

The Rationale of
Legal Punishment

THE JUSTIFICATION OF PUNISHMENT

By what right do some people punish others?   Tolstoy

No one can know how many reasons there are or might be for wishing to modify or reject punishment. And as we offer the case for the institution of legal punishment, we wish to reveal as candidly as possible the vulnerable underpinnings on which the argument rests. For it is not a justification for all space and time, but one which applies only under certain conditions. These conditions are not local or peculiar, but it is easy to conceive of a world in which they did not obtain.

I

What, in principle, would constitute an adequate defense of the institution of legal punishment? Before attempting an answer we must raise a prior question: What kind of undertaking *is* a "defense" or "justification" of an institution or practice?[1] Not, how do we go about it? But, what is it we are going about?

We are offering reasons for the conclusion that punishment should be retained not abolished. In doing so, we are thinking of the practice of punishment not as a rib of the universe, but as a device which serves certain purposes well or ill. It is not a device in the sense that it is a "dodge" or "gadget" which can be used today and abandoned tomorrow. But it is something which has been devised—not all at once, or consciously, perhaps; but it is an invention of man. It is an arrangement which we (the writer and most of the readers of this book) find already present in the culture of which we become bearers; but our culture could have been otherwise. There are cultures in which there is no legal punishment. To justify legal punishment is, then, to show that there are better reasons for retaining than for abolishing it.

Strictly speaking, if we subscribe to the principle that the burden of proof is on him who would institute a change; all that is necessary in the defense of a going practice is to show that no adequate grounds for changing it have been brought forward. But it is not merely because it is there, and change always makes difficulties, that punishment should be retained. A positive case can be made out for it which would warrant instituting legal punishment if it were not already the practice.

How, then, should we go about offering a justification of legal punishment? What, in principle, would constitute an adequate general defense or justification of punishment or of any social practice? To justify a practice is to show two things: that under the circumstances, *a* practice is necessary, called for, or would

---

[1] We will settle here on the wider term, "practice," since we wish to compare punishment with possible alternatives which would qualify as practices but not as institutions.

New York, Humanities Press Inc. 1966. By permission of the publisher and the author.

be useful; and that of the alternatives available and acceptable, the practice in question would likely be the most effective. We will refer to the reason why some practice must be instituted as the "guiding principle" of justification; and to the considerations by reference to which the practice is rejected as nonacceptable even though it seems the best of the available alternatives, in the light of the guiding principle, as the "limiting principles" of justification. It is with respect to the guiding principle that a proposed practice can be more or less effective; but it may be rejected, even though effective, by a limiting principle.

These are general formal conditions of the justification of a practice. It is a necessary condition of an adequate justification of a practice that of the available alternatives it most efficiently serves the purpose for which a practice is needed; it is a necessary condition that the practice not be ruled out by a limiting principle; and it is a necessary and sufficient condition that the practice serve the purpose as well as possible within the bounds set by the limiting principles.[2] This schema is at least useful in approaching the problem of the justification of a specific practice. It forces us to distinguish between the questions whether *a* practice is necessary; whether the practice in question best fills the need; and if, even so, it must be rejected.

But Tolstoy's question, with which we wish to come to grips in this chapter, concerns the right to punish. It requests a specifically moral justification. Like an economic or aesthetic justification of a practice, a moral justification will have guiding and limiting principles. But whatever principles we accept must be shown to be *morally* defensible. This may seem to present insuperable difficulties, for there are apparently irreconcilable differences over the ultimate principles of morality. Hence, what is morally defensible to one school will not be so to another. Utilitarians, self-realizationalists, intuitionists might fail to agree on the moral defensibility of the guiding and limiting principles by which punishment must be morally assessed as a practice. It may come out this way. But it may not. What is morally defensible from one point of view need not be indefensible from another. And it may be that the schema we use will point up the complementarity rather than the incompatibility of the leading moral views. For who wishes to deny that a practice must be shown to serve some purpose? The retributivist can, as we have seen, argue with real plausibility, that particular decisions concerning punishments should not be made on the ground that some

---

[2] The general view of the justification of punishment presented here is perhaps closer to Ross' than to any other traditional view. The distinctions made here, however, give us certain advantages over Ross' account. Ross speaks of the balance between the *prima facie* duty of "injuring wrong-doers only to the extent that they have injured others," and the *prima facie* duty of "promoting the general interest." (*The Right and The Good*, Oxford, 1930, Ch. II, Appendix II, "Punishment".) In the first place, our account avoids the implication that we simply balance these considerations one against the other like weights on a scale (*op. cit.*, pp. 63 and 41). It is not a question of choosing either justice or utility or a balance between, but of finding the most useful social device consistent with the demands of justice. Secondly (though Ross might well not agree that this is an advantage) the emphasis is more on standing on, or holding a principle, than on knowing that something is true. Third, our account is not open, as Ross' is, to the kind of objection raised by J. S. Mill (in *Hamilton*) to the effect that we cannot very well balance the maxims of justice against those of utility, since what one maxim of justice demands may be incompatible with what another maxim of justice demands. On the present account, such conflicts, which I believe are real, need not concern us; since if the practice in question conflicts with any maxim which we adhere to, then it is ruled out; and we must look about for one which is acceptable. But, like Ross, we are able to avoid the charge that, by setting in motion an utilitarian engine of justification uncurbed, we are likely to justify too much.

supposedly good purpose would be served by punishing. And the retributivist can argue (less plausibly I believe) that all penal laws should be passed solely on the ground that justice demands them.

But is it really plausible to argue that justice demands *a* practice? Is it not more plausible to argue that when a practice can be shown to be necessary on utilitarian grounds, it should meet the demands of justice? Does justice demand the institution or practice of law, or marriage, or private property, or coined money? Or, at least, that there should be *an* institution which serves the purposes served by these? To say Yes, is to say that there are burdens and privileges existing prior to an institution or practice, which the practice should be invented and adopted to protect. But then the question is how we can know what these burdens and privileges are, prior to any practice within which they operate. To say that the institution should be invented and adopted to protect these burdens and privileges is like saying that basketball should be invented so that fouls and points for goals can be recognized and penalized or rewarded. But, outside of basketball there are no fouls and points for goals. What would it mean to say that there are burdens and privileges which persons have, to protect which it is essential that we adopt the practice of marriage?

This might seem more plausible with respect to punishment. Is punishment as an institution justified because justice demands that there should be an institution which accords punishment to ill desert? The ill desert must then be supposed to exist independently of any practice in terms of which it can be defined. The crucial point here is that it is impossible to account for the *existence* of desert in the absence of a practice in terms of which desert can be assigned. What may lead us to think that desert can exist independently of a given punishment-practice is that desert is a concept in not one but several practices: legal punishment being merely the most clearly articulated of them. But if we stop to think of it we would realize that we could not speak, for example, of what Johnny deserves for pouring ink on the oriental rug were it not for *some* prior understanding of a practice. According to this practice, those persons playing the role of parent are given the authority to assign penalties not only for certain kinds of acts in advance, but also for acts adjudged "bad" or "naughty" after the fact: like pouring ink on rugs or putting glue in the seats. Punishment of such acts is justified, even though there is no rule promulgated in advance against them. But whence do parents derive the moral authority to identify and punish such acts? Surely not from some table beyond the tables of rules. Then we would simply have to ask for the credentials of that table, and of any table from which it was derived, and so on. It is not that the ill desert exists prior to the role of parent, but that parents are persons who are given discretion, according to a practice, to make decisions concerning ill desert.

It might seem that, nevertheless, there is ill desert independent of the practices of punishment, because the decisions of parents or judges are not merely arbitrary: decisions concerning desert are not right simply by virtue of being made by the proper authorities, but by virtue of being made in accordance with standards which the authorities should observe. We can criticize the authority's decisions on rational grounds. But the analogous point holds for fouls in basketball, or balls and strikes in baseball. Here too we can criticize the decision of the umpire by reference to the criteria by which he should be governed. But it does not follow that there could be balls and strikes were there no game of baseball. The assertion that a person deserves severe punishment is significant if and only if there is some practice according to which some authority could, by discoverable criteria, rightly award severe punishment. To say that justice is a limiting principle of possible practices of punishment is not to say that practices should somehow meet the requirement that some abstract, extra-practice "desert" should be given its due. It is but to say that the practice must, in virtue of its arrangements, give everyone concerned a fair shake. This point will be expanded below.

II

Let us now turn to the question what the circumstances are which give rise to the need for some practice, be it legal punishment, or an alternative. Here we will list certain very general assumptions of fact which, taken together, give rise to the problem. To the extent that these assumptions of fact are shaky, the justification of punishment totters; for the problem punishment and its competing practices are designed to meet alters or disappears. The assumptions of fact in question fall naturally into three different categories: assumptions concerning human nature, human society, and nature or "supernature."

Concerning human nature, we assume that humans are non-ant-like in that they do not order their affairs by instinct: *i.e.*, without rules. We assume also that whatever rules or regulations men set for themselves, there will be tension between the rules and the private interests, desires, or passions of persons falling under these rules: that there will not be automatic submission.

Concerning human society we assume that it is necessary to set some rules if men wish to survive, simply because human beings, being without enough instinctual equipment, are incapable of carrying on common activities necessary for their survival unless they are shown, told, taught, how to conduct themselves, what to do, and what to refrain from doing. And we assume that it is *desirable* to set *other* rules if the common life is to enhance the well-being (however that is defined) and reduce the misery and unhappiness (easier to agree upon) of all.

Concerning nature or "supernature," we assume that no natural or supernatural forces either compel action in accordance with the rules, or counter each violation with retribution. Lightning does not, as matter of course, strike down either the man whose hand is raised with murderous intention or the murderer whose intention has been fulfilled. If lightning, pestilence, or tornado operated in either of these ways, social arrangements to ensure compliance with rules would be redundant.

To these factual assumptions we must now add a moral one. We assume that survival in conditions not merely miserable, and with some hope of happiness, is a value worthy of protection. We shall assume, indeed, that to interfere with these modest prospects and possibilities is morally wrong; and that each community has a collective moral right to prevent such interference.

Granting, then, that men wish to survive, and to decrease their misery and enhance their well-being there must be rules; and some social arrangement must be found which will counter the tendency to violate rules. Two points should be noted here. The arrangement in question is not required to be one which equally discourages the violation of all rules; some rules are more important for survival and well-being than others; and the effectiveness needed in the prevention of some rule-violations is not demanded for the prevention of all rule-violations. And, whatever practice may be instituted, its application in the prevention of rule-violations will be justified only to the extent that the rule and/or rule-set is justified. This latter point must be expanded.

Legislators may be in a position to enact any rules they choose. In enacting rules, they may or may not have sufficiently in mind the survival or well-being of the citizens. Their laws may be designed to enhance their own well-being. The state may be administered like the legislators' private plantation, the citizens regarded as serfs—and it may be badly administered even on these terms. Can any practice designed to encourage compliance with the rules of such a legislature be justified? The alternative practices in question are not designed to encourage compliance with any particular set of rules, but are devices to encourage compliance with *rules*. To show that there may be bad rules is not to show that the practices are bad practices. The practices are *needed* to counter the tendency to violate rules which for our survival and well-being we must have; but this, unfortunately, does not prevent their *being used* to enforce rules which may even go against the ends of survival and well-being. To reject them on this account is like rejecting hammers because they may be used by murderers, or representative government because we disapprove of the Senator from Mississippi.

There is a limit beyond which this argument should not be pressed. For telling counter-examples can be given. Should we not reject the practice of carrying hand-guns, *e.g.*, even though it arose for a defensible set of purposes: to provide a light gun, capable of being carried on long trips, which can be used for small game and, in wild country, for self-defense? Should we not have rejected duelling, even though it may originally have been a desirable substitute for simple unorganized mayhem? But the analogous argument in the present discussion would have to show that the conditions which gave rise to the demand for a practice designed to encourage compliance with rules are now so changed that practices originally meeting that need are not now needed and are used for unjustifiable ends. While this does not now seem a plausible pair of contentions. it should be conceded that they could be, under circumstances now hard to foresee. If the great majority of human beings were in some way transformed so that the tension between rules and personal interests, passions, and desires disappeared; then the circumstances which gave rise to the need for a practice would have disappeared. And it could be that, under those circumstances, the practices originally designed to encourage compliance with rules, and now no longer necessary, were being used instead merely as instruments of oppression.

III

Suppose it be granted that, conditions being what they are, some practice to encourage compliance with rules is needed. Should punishment be preferred to other possible practices? Before attempting to assess the relative merits and demerits of punishment and its competitors, we must discuss the grounds of comparison. These, as we have noted, concern effectiveness and acceptability.

Punishment is *not* the most effective possible method for discouraging crime. Probably the most effective way to discourage—better, abolish—crime is to annihilate the human race. Or if this seems a little extreme, no doubt we could go a long way toward the elimination of crime by the use of drugs: the tranquilization of the human race. These possibilities are mentioned to point up the absurdity of arguing solely on grounds of effectiveness in the reduction of crime. Even though the procedures mentioned would work to eliminate crime, they would not be acceptable. What are the boundaries of acceptability? To what limiting principles may we appeal in rejecting an effective practice?[3]

Above, we mentioned not only justice but also humanity. By denominating humanity a limiting principle, we mean that one possible ground for refusal to accept an effective practice is that it is inhumane. It is apparently usually assumed in theoretical writing that any practice which is inhumane is by the same token unjust, since humanity as a separate limiting principle is not discussed. Yet it is not absurd to suppose that a given practice could be just but inhumane: that it might violate none of the maxims of justice and still demand treatment of individuals which we would agree is cruel or degrading. The "solution" of the problem of crime by annihilation or drugging could be not only effective, but just—in that it did not violate any of the maxims of justice by discriminating between persons: drugging or annihilating everyone impartially. This possibility gives rise to the maxim that justice should be "tempered with mercy"—and to a certain confusion attending this maxim. For justice is not inherently opposed to mercy: what is just may be humane enough; but it need not be humane at all.

How is it to be decided whether a proposed practice is inhumane? It will not do to speak briskly of setting up cardinal or ordinal scales on which there is a zero mark between minus-inhumane degrees and positive-humane ones. The question would then be how we know where to place any practice on the scale. Is it possible to find a purely formal criterion of inhumanity in a practice? It may be, but if so it would have to be developed in conjunction with a criterion of the justice of a practice, to which problem we now turn.

What is it for a practice to be just?[4] We shall take it that a practice is just if,

[3] How many limiting principles are there? This is like asking how many ways there are for an effective practice to go awry. Limiting principles reject the proposed practice because it can be seen in advance that once this device is set in motion there are ways in which it would operate which we could never accept. But because the demand for *a* practice is sometimes very great, the grounds on which a candidate may be ruled out as nonacceptable are naturally very much curtailed. Justice and humanity, in that order, seem to be the limiting principles which bind with the greatest stringency; but for less important practice-choices, many more limiting principles can enter in. Compare the choice of a practice for assigning responsibility for the rearing of the young, to the choice of a practice by which recipients of the "keys of the city" are to be designated.

[4] The definition of and test for justice in a practice are topics which lead way beyond the scope of the present discussion. What is offered here is merely an approach which seems to me promising. One might agree that justice is a limiting principle even though one disagreed that it could be defined as it is defined here. Much of what I have to say here has been suggested by John Rawls' article, "Justice as Fairness" (*Philosophical Review*, 1958, pp. 164-194). For a more complete discussion, the reader is referred to the whole of this article. I do not adopt Rawls' device of positing that the uncommitted individual we must picture is completely self-interested. He is but a construct, and we can do with him what we please, but to require that he be merely self-interested is to risk misleading comparison with Hobbes, and to make him more artificial that is necessary for my purpose. His recognition that *a* practice is needed may be based in part on altruism: a regard for the well-being of (even remote) others. But he would not likely join that society which would not give him, or anyone, a fair shake.

knowing that it is necessary that there should be *a* practice and that this one would be effective, each of us would be willing to accept the practice not knowing in advance what role we would play. To expand: the assessment of the justice of a practice involves the conception of a particular view of the practice. It is the view taken of it by a person who realizes that a practice is necessary, and that this one will fulfill the need; who also realizes that in any practice there are going to be burdens and privileges;[5] and who must decide whether these privileges and burdens are fairly apportioned in view of what the practice is designed to accomplish. The test of fairness of apportionment of burdens and privileges is whether the person contemplating the practice would be willing to commit himself to it not knowing which role he might play; not from benevolence or self-sacrifice, but because he, along with everyone else, needs the practice.

Our hypothetical uncommitted person might be unwilling to commit himself to a proposed practice for fear of discrimination, not only within, but in assignment to the roles of the practice; and these two types of discrimination are worth distinguishing here. I might be able to predict now that I would (because of the color of my skin, say) be more likely than other persons to be assigned a given burdened role in a proposed practice (criminal, defendant). Or the role itself (slave) might be such that whoever has to play it is the victim of discrimination, no matter how effective the practice may seem for no matter what good purposes. Slavery, then, may doubly discriminate: in its choice of persons to play the burdened role, and in its allocation of burdens and privileges between roles. It is with discrimination in the second sense that the justice of practices is, strictly speaking, concerned. But by thinking whether a person situated as described could agree to the practice; we will not lose sight of the first form of discrimination either.

We may now return to the question of the criterion of humanity. More accurately, what is wanted is a criterion or criteria by reference to which it can be determined whether a practice is inhumane. Duelling may be a useful example. It is one of the several alternative practices by which quarrels can be settled.[6] A practice was needed. Whether it was a just practice may be questioned. That it was inhumane to cause a man to lose his life as the price of losing an argument, seems clear—to us, here, now. Why, on what ground, would we call it inhumane? It was not inhumane in that it resulted in the loss of life. Lives were lost in the transportation of freight from harbor to harbor; and the practice of exchanging goods was not on that account inhumane. Duelling was inhumane because it resulted in *unnecessary* mutilation, suffering, degradation, and loss of life: unnecessary because there were available equally efficient and just ways of settling quarrels.

There is another way in which a practice can impose unnecessary, and thus inhumane, degradation, suffering, or death: it can be, unlike duelling, a practice which serves no necessary purpose at all. It is hard to think of examples, partly because when a practice becomes a part of the way of life of a people it begins

[5] Compare "burdened" and "privileged" vessels in the International Rules of the Road.

[6] This, of course, is over-simple. The quarrels in question often arose out of supposed insults which, according to the code of honor, could only be expunged by duelling; so that it was the code of honor as a whole which had to give way, not duelling alone.

to play roles not originally envisaged for it, even if it ceases to be needed for the original purposes. But unless we are willing to subscribe to the thesis, so far as practices are concerned, that whatever is is right, there will be ritual and other practices which because of the degradation and suffering they cause individuals falling under them are inhumane and hence no longer acceptable. Examples might be the *suttee*, and the taking of heads as trophies.

If the criterion of inhumanity in a practice is to be that suffering, misery, death or degradation are imposed unnecessarily; then what is a test by which we can know that a given practice is inhumane? Analogously to the test for injustice of a practice, we can ask whether a person, acknowledging the need for practice, acknowledging that this practice would be efficient in fulfilling that need, acknowledging that the practice in question fairly distributes the burdens and privileges it creates, would nevertheless not want to commit himself to the practice on the ground that there are other equally efficient and fair practices which do not (as this one does) impose suffering, misery, degradation or death.[7]

IV

We may now return to the justification of legal punishment. We have tried to show that *a* practice is needed, and we have tried to specify criteria of comparison between punishment and alternative practices. What alternative practices are available, and how do they compare to punishment in the light of these criteria?

We will not here attempt to cover all the kinds of practice which would be used to encourage compliance with rules, but will limit ourselves to those which presuppose a system of law.[8] We are thus taking it for granted that it is not only advantageous to have rules but to have legal rules. Our only excuse for such a leap is that to do more than sketch, as we have done, the general justification of rules, is to embark on a question, the justification of law, which cannot be handled within the scope of this book. A full answer to Owen and Tolstoy, who attack the system of law as well as punishment, would require a very much larger book than this one.

There is in principle no limit to the devices which human imagination could create for encouraging compliance with legal rules. Some of these we have noted

---

[7] The discussion here is admittedly, barely opened. How, by what test, do we decide that degradation, misery, or death are *unnecessary*? And, even more difficult, what is to *count as* misery, suffering, and (most difficult) degradation? But even though the theoretical explication of our test for humanity of a practice may be difficult, still the test can be used prior to explication; for, by and large and never-mind-how, we do agree on what is unnecessary, and on whether suffering, misery, and degradation (to say nothing of death) are imposed. Or, if we do not agree, we know how to go about discussing the point. Explication could only start from the considerations we take as relevant in such discussion.

[8] Justice may be thought of as a virtue of practices, or actions, or of men. If we start from justice as a virtue of practices we will tend to think of acts and men as just insofar as they conform to the practices; and if we start from justice as a virtue of acts we will tend to think of practices as just insofar as they require the kinds of acts, which we already, prior to the practice, consider just. But there is something odd in the notion that there can be justice of actions prior to justice of practices (though there is nothing odd about the notion of justice of actions prior to justice of institutions), and that the justice of practices consists in making these, prior, just, actions possible. Does punishment, as a practice, exist to make possible that balance of punishment and desert which is known, independently of the practice, to be what justice demands? This is not at all plausible if we think in wide, generic, terms of the "practice of punishment." It becomes more plausible as we confine ourselves to particular practices or those formal practices we call institutions.

(and rejected) in passing, such as telishment, the practices which would make of judges or legislators mere social engineers or mere balancers of the scales of justice, and "treatment." There are at least four remaining general sorts of practice which should be mentioned: 1) Practices which punish failure to comply with the law by informal means rather than the formal procedure of legal punishment involving legislators, judges, and jailers. Varieties of social suasion other than punishment have been described for us by cultural anthropologists; and while (is this analytic?) there will be no statutes in preliterate tribes, it is conceivable that social suasion could be relied upon to enforce statutes. For example, it might be the practice that if a man commits incest, he is shamed in public by anyone knowing of the deed; or if he fails to support his in-laws his wife will leave him. 2) Practices according to which compliance with the law is rewarded. 3) Practices according to which men are persuaded to abide by the law. 4) Practices according to which men are conditioned (drugs, neo-Pavlovian techniques) to obey the law. Of these, all are really consistent with legal punishment. And "adequate" is to be understood in terms of the criteria already mentioned.

Social suasion is perhaps the strongest candidate of the four. What is envisaged is the possibility that criminal statutes should be enacted with no penalty attached; that courts should decide guilt but not sentence; that, instead, suitable publicity should be given the crime, and the criminal returned to home and community. The assumption is that the public opinion of the home and immediate community would prove a stronger deterrent and reformative agent than the formal and more impersonal workings of a penal system.

This is a topic as large as the varieties of social suasion and the experience of the human race in their application. It is eminently worthy of research by social scientists, and, so far, little developed. The practice of leaving the punishment to the community has in its favor the point that for any individual the most meaningful punishment is that which is inflicted by those closest to him. It is the opinion of his peers that he values far more than the opinion of some vast and faceless "general public" represented by the sentencing judge. It is a point in its favor, also, that it makes for no discontinuity between the legal and moral community in the way that legal punishment does, in setting off some offences as subject to the sway of jails and jailers while other offences, morally as heinous, are not so subject.

There are, on the other hand, serious disadvantages in social suasion as compared to legal punishment. These turn largely around in the concept of "community." In the first place, there can be not only deviant persons, but deviant communities; and where this is so we cannot rely upon the opinion of peers to enforce laws which are for the public good. The deviant community may not regard laws necessary for the well-being of the larger community as incumbent upon it. Perhaps the term "deviant" should not be overstressed. It has inevitable connotations of criminality; and while we wish to include gangs and mobs in these remarks, we wish also to include any community insofar as it pursues its own (supposed) interests to the exlusion of the interests of the larger community, in survival, avoidance of suffering, and enhancement of well-being. If we leave the sanctions of laws designed to further these ends of the larger community up to any smaller community, the system may not be viable, since with respect to the purposes of the laws in question, the smaller community may be deviant. And to rely on the social pressure of the larger community is to weaken the claim of social suasion to operate with the force of the judgment of peers—since the most effective peer-judgment comes from the most immediate communities.

Secondly, were the sanctions left up to the community, the same crime would be punished in many different ways rather than in the one way set by the legal penalty; but this would be unjust. It might be answered that the crime would still be punished in accordance with its seriousness, since in communities where it is a heinous offense it would be punished severely, but where it is only a venal offense it would be punished lightly. But this answer only begs the question, raised in the previous paragraph, whether the smaller community may not be deviant in regarding as venal, *e.g.*, what would be inimical to the well-being of the larger group.

Bearing in mind these reasons for rejecting social suasion as a substitute for punishment, we may without contradiction acknowledge its importance for legal punishment. The force of the threat contained in the penal clause of a criminal law is great not merely because the person contemplating crime fears the pain or suffering the penalty would impose if inflicted. Perhaps it is not even mainly this; for he also greatly fears the judgment of his peers symbolized by this official pronouncement of guilt and sentence. In fact, distinctions are made in everyday life and in legal debate between those penalties (*e.g.* fines) which do not necessarily carry this public disapprobation with them, and those (imprisonment, execution) which do. Justice Brandeis is quoted by Hall[9] as saying "It is . . . imprisonment in a penitentiary which now renders a crime infamous." But it is a necessary condition of this disapprobration, or infamy, that the criminal has been sentenced to a penitentiary; so the disapprobation is not here to be considered a substitute for punishment.[10]

Let us turn to the practice of rewarding rather than punishing crime. It is not clear how such a practice would operate. Would there be a reward for each person who goes through a year without breaking a law? A reward for each person who, though severely tempted in given circumstances, refrains from violating the law? Such practices are indeed conceivable, but would be subject to grave objections. Those laws which it is most important to enforce are often those there is the greatest temptation to violate. How could we prevent by means of rewards those crimes which in their nature are extremely profitable, such as embezzlement, or forgery? And would the prospect of reward deter a man about to commit a crime of violence? More importantly, would it be morally defensible to reward a person abiding by (presumable necessary and just) laws?

There *is* a sense of the word "reward" in which it is used synonymously with "positive reinforcement." In this sense, reward provides indispensable support

[9] *Op. cit.*, p. 327.

[10] The question, presently much discussed, whether or not a given piece of legislation is punitive in intent, is likely to turn on the question not merely what suffering it imposes but also on the way in which the suffering is imposed will be generally regarded. A suggested test for legislation punitive in intent is to determine "whether the legislative concern underlying the statute was to regulate 'the activity or status from which the individual is barred' or whether the statute is evidently 'aimed at the person or class or persons disqualified' ". (*Fleming v. Nestor*, 363 U.S. 603, 1960.)

for legal punishment. For here reward is indistinguishable from social suasion, the reinforcement in question consisting in the repeated approval of one's abiding by the law under temptation to violate it.

Concerning the possibility of substituting of persuasion for punishment, we would follow Aristotle in his assessment of human nature when he says "... most people obey necessity rather than argument, and punishments rather than the sense of what is noble."[11] This should be immediately qualified (as Aristotle qualified it) by our assertion that we would much prefer to use persuasion rather than punishment, since punishment is a practice forced on us by the "human condition" rather than chosen as something positively desirable on its own account. It should also be said that persuasion may have a kind of pyramiding effect with respect to building respect for rules. That is, to the extent that we risk persuasion rather than punishment, we help develop people amenable to persuasion and not needing fear of punishment as a motive for abiding by the rules. Unlike some other alternatives, then, the side-effects of persuasion as a practice are good: better than the side-effects of punishment.

The cause of persuasion is one open to the advocate of punishment, Aristotle's assessment of human nature being granted as a generalization, but not taken to imply that any given person may not change in his amenability to persuasion. Persuasion as a means of encouraging compliance with the laws should clearly be promoted. This means that the rationale of laws should be the subject of public discussion, that only demonstrably necessary or desirable legal rules be enacted, and that some attempt be made to render the body of law intelligible. If persuasion must be rejected, it is not as an adjunct but as a substitute for punishment. And it is not by virtue of its running afoul of the limiting principles that we must reject it as a substitute for punishment, but as failing to measure up to the demands of the guiding principle.

The achievement of a law-abiding community by the use of drugs or Pavlovian conditioning seems in principle perfectly possible, but the side-effects of such procedures we would not, on grounds of humanity, be willing to accept. We would not accept them because they are unnecessarily degrading: unnecessarily, because law-abidingness can be attained at lower cost in human degradation. Thus, as opposed to persuasion, we would accept conditioning so far as the guiding principle is concerned, but reject it for violating the limiting principles.

The case for punishment so far is that, granting certain very general assumptions of fact, the disvalue of misery, and the consequent needs for rules, *a* practice is needed to encourage compliance with rules. And of the alternative practices some (*i.e.*, rewarding, persuading) fail to measure up to the guiding principle as well as punishment, and others (*i.e.*, conditioning, social suasion) are ruled out on the ground that they conflict with justice or humanity. This argument is deficient in two respects. It is not conclusive; since there may be alternatives not taken into account which would compete more successfully with punishment. If this is the case, then it is open to the opponents of punishments to propose these alternatives and compare them to punishment by the criteria of efficiency and acceptabilty. It is also deficient in that it offers no positive justification of punishment. It says only, so far, that punishment is the least undesirable of the alternatives.

[11] *Ethica Nichomachea*, 118a, 3-13.

V

There is much to be said for the thesis that punishment is just that: not anything we would want to have in the best of all possible words, but something we must accept for lack of something better in the world in which we live. Yet it may be well to note how it measures up to the criteria of efficiency in encouraging compliance with rules, of justice, and of humanity. But before turning to these, we should note that there are some very general assumptions of fact, beyond those which give rise to the need for *a* practice, upon which any justification of the practice of punishment must rest.

The first of these assumptions is that men are capable of calculating their own interest; and that in general they will. Obviously the efficacy of the threat contained in a criminal law rests on this assumption. If a man is unable or unwilling to look ahead to the probable consequences for him of bank robbery then of course the possibility of a prison sentence is no deterrent.

Zilboorg tells us that "The indifference of the criminal to the penalty that is ahead of him, even if this penalty is death, is more the rule than the exception."[12] Bentham, on the other hand, argues

> When matters of such importance as pain and pleasure are at stake, and these in the highest degree (the only matters in short that can be of importance) who is there that does not calculate? Men calculate, some with less exactness, indeed, some with more: but all men calculate. I would not say, that even a mad man does not calculate.[13]

The case seems to me to be overstated on both sides. Bentham does not need to claim that everybody calculates. Even if the percentage of people who calculate is relatively small, punishment would so far be worthwhile; for by the threat of punishment crime could be reduced. And more moderate psychiatrists do not accept such conclusions as Zilboorg's. Robert Waelder, for example, tells us that the claim of "a very small but articulate number of psychiatrists" that punishment does not deter is "a radical contention in view of everybody's daily experience in office and shop."[14]

The second assumption is that, in general, men are able to govern present impulses by the thought of future consequences. If they were not, the threat of punishment would be useless. This, so far as it applies to criminals, is also challenged by some of the more extreme psychiatrists. Third, it is assumed that it is possible to find "evils" which are more or less universally dreaded. If there were no general desire to avoid fines or jail, then these "evils" would not be eligible as punishment. But unless the legislator can find some "evil" which qualifies, the institution of punishment fails; or is modified to allow judges complete discretion in the choice of punishment. Whether this would still be punishment and this "judge" a judge are open questions. Certainly a door would be left ajar for radical abuse of power. There are advocates of the "individualization of punishment" who would be willing to take this risk for the supposed gain

[12] Gregory Zilboorg, *The Psychology of the Criminal Act and Punishment,* York, 1954, p. 32.

[13] *Principles of Morals and Legislation,* XIV, 28

[14] "Psychiatry and the Problem of Criminal Responsibility," *University of Pennsylvania Law Review,* 1952, p. 383.

in reformatory effectiveness. But what is gained here may well be lost on the side of deterrence of would-be offenders, who could never know what the penalty is, for the crime they contemplate.

To turn to assumptions concerning human society, we assume, first, that there is a virtual monopoly of coercive power in the state. Suppose that each man has an H-bomb which he threatens to explode if molested. Then force could be used on a man only by his consent, and legal punishment would break down. Secondly, we assume that the culture is such that it is possible for people to grasp what it is to be an official in a legal system. If not, sentencing and the execution of sentences will be understood as moves made by particular persons against particular persons; and deterrence will give way to cycles of retaliation. This may help explain why for Tolstoy, who refused on principle to allow the distinction between what is permissible for an official of a system and for an individual falling under the system, punishment was a moral nightmare.

To the extent that any of these assumptions, or the assumptions on which the need for *a* practice is predicated, are false, the case for legal punishment breaks down. We shall not argue for them, but simply assume their truth. Assuming them true, it seems *a priori* likely that punishment would be effective in encouraging compliance with legal rules. More than this: the experience of centuries of civilization constitutes evidence that it is effective. But not very conclusive evidence. We do not know to what extent social suasion and intellectual conviction have been responsible for the tendency of the masses to abide by the law. We do not have controlled social experiments in which punishment is compared in point of efficacy to treatment, or social suasion, or persuasion. In those chaotic revolutionary situations in which the recent history of the human race abounds, we would hardly have dared rely on less than the strong medicine of legal punishment. Yet perhaps in more orderly times, less drastic practices can be encouraged.

Under the heading of the effectiveness of punishment as a practice we should note (what has sometimes been recognized) that punishment is at least more ingenious than its alternatives in that it works like a pricing system in reverse. Whereas the store keeper tries to price his wares in such a way that there will be as many purchasers as possible; the legislator tries (or should try) to "price" crimes in such a way that there will be as few takers-of-the-risk of criminal behavior as possible. And—as we realize from our survey of Bentham—it is more subtle than this. It is not merely that we want few takers, but that we want less takers of the worst crimes. So on these we put the highest price and our "pricing" can—on the practice of punishment—be carefully adjusted to the disvalue of the crimes: just as (inversely) the storekeeper can progressively encourage the taking of his wares by lowering the price.

What must be borne in mind is that if the evidence for the effectiveness of punishment in encouraging compliance with legal rules is less than satisfactory, the evidence for the comparatively untried alternatives is even less satisfactory. But the burden of proof is on him who would make a change, on the principle that we should change only where there is a likely advantage in doing so. And this principle seems worth defending, since changes, in deep-rooted practices especially, inevitably involve difficult readjustments, and sometimes involve consequences not foreseen.

What is also required in justification is that punishment should be shown as acceptable, *i.e.*, as not violating the limiting principles of justice and humanity. Is the practice of punishment, as such, unjust or inhumane? To say that it is, is to say that a person so far uncommitted to a society, recognizing the need in any society for an effective practice to encourage compliance with rules, recognizing that there must be burdens and privileges under whatever practice is chosen, would be willing to enter that society and fall under that practice, even though he does not know in advance and from this uncommitted standpoint what role he might have to play and what burdens or privileges would fall to his lot. To say that he would not commit himself to the society on the ground that he might through no fault of his own fall into a role which is at a disadvantage in the distribution of burdens and privileges, receiving, compared to other roles, most of the burdens and none of the privileges, is to say that the practice is unjust. To say that he would not commit himself to the society on the ground that the burdens which must be carried by the players of some roles (even though they may be fairly distributed) are at the same time very heavy and not necessary for the attainment of the purposes of the practice, is to say that the practice is inhumane.

Is the practice of punishment unjust? There is a heavily burdened role, criminal, into which any of us might fall; but not, we may assume, without fault. The proper answer to the person who refuses to commit himself to the society containing this practice, on the ground that he might fall into the unfavored role of criminal, is that once he commits himself to society and practice, whether he then plays or avoids the role of criminal is still open. He *can* have the advantages of the practice, and at the same time avoid the burdens of the unfavored role. And should he fall into the role of criminal, there is nothing inherent in the practice which would make the burden borne by one category of criminal out of proportion to that borne by others, granted the need to distinguish between more and less dangerous crimes.

Is it inhumane? Since, as practice, it does not specify the burdens to be borne, but only that they shall be adequate to the purpose of discouraging crime, the practice does not *as such* demand that there should be burdens not warranted by its purpose. It does not follow from the fact that there may be "cruel and unusual" punishments that the practice of punishment is therefore inhumane. Contrast the practice whereby the rulers administer drugs to the population at large which ensure that whatever laws are enacted will not be violated. This could work only if the critical faculties were so deadened that the individual could no longer distinguish between good and bad laws, and between occasions on which even good laws should and should not be violated. But, since there are alternative ways of encouraging compliance with the laws, which do not involve these consequences, they are unneccessary, and the practice is inhumane.

Morally speaking, if our very general assumptions of fact be granted, and our judgement that widespread misery is a disvalue, then rules are necessary, and some way must be found to make them effective. But if the best and most acceptable way is the practice of legal punishment, then those persons who find themselves playing the roles of judge and jailer have the moral right to sentence and carry out sentences. They have this right as officials of a practice which is, by hypothesis, for the good of everyone alike.

VI

So much, then, for the justification of the practice of legal punishment. It may be well to point out some things this justification does *not* pretend to do. 1) It does not pretend to offer a conclusive argument for punishment, whatever that would be. It presents the case for punishment: a case which must be compared with the case which can be made out for available alternative practices. 2) It does not, as we have noted, claim to warrant punishment as preferable to other practices regardless of context. It could well be that, for example, in a simple, stable, closely interdependent society, where there is more emphasis on character than on rules, punishment would be out of place. 3) It does not justify any particular mode of punishment, such as capital punishment or imprisonment.

The objection that capital punishment or imprisonment are inhumane does not, even if accepted, necessarily weigh against the practice of legal punishment; since there are other modes of punishment which can be used. However, there is a finite number of modes, and if we were unable to find effective and acceptable modes, this would undercut the case for legal punishment.

The argument over capital punishment tends to turn in the wrong gimbals. Even if it should be shown that capital punishment is more effective than some other mode of punishment in discouraging certain sorts of crime, this would not be sufficient to justify its use; for it might be ruled out as acceptable by justice or humanity as limiting principles. So far as justice is concerned, capital punishment can be as impartially administered as any other mode of punishment. It is argued, with great force, that it is not in fact impartially administered, and that those executed tend to be the poor and the ignorant. This would not make any great difference, unfortunately, between capital punishment and imprisonment, were it not for the important point that there is no way of rectifying a judicial error arising from inadequate legal representation, once a man has been executed. Since there is the possibility of an irreversible error stemming from inadequate representation, it seems clear that our uncommitted individual, contemplating societies with varying modes of punishment, and not knowing whether he would play the role of rich or poor man, should he join the society, would prefer a society which did not have capital punishment to one which did. On this test, capital punishment is unjust.

But the capital punishment society may fail the test of humanity as well. For if our uncommitted onlooker can see no clear case for the thesis that capital punishment is necessary for the encouragement of compliance with the law, and is aware of alternative less cruel modes of punishment which singly or together are as effective, then he will naturally avoid the capital punishment society, even though he may think sentences to capital punishment are nondiscriminatory. And this much is clear: that no clear-cut case showing the necessity of capital punishment as a means of discouraging crime has been brought forward.

It might be argued that it is an unfair burden of proof to place upon the advocate of capital punishment to require him to show that his mode of punishment is necessary for the discouragement of crime, whereas the same burden is not placed upon the advocates of imprisonment and fines. But the difference is that capital punishment is admittedly more cruel than imprisonment[15] and fines and therefore should, upon the principle of humanity, be ruled out if it can be dispensed with. And, we may add, there is ample evidence that capital punishment can be abolished without an advance in the rate of crimes it purportedly discouraged.

There are some persons who argue that life imprisonment is more cruel than capital punishment, and there is much to be said for this thesis, but there seems to be no way of deciding *in general* which is more cruel. Our test would have to be the same; namely to ask ourselves whether an uncommitted outsider would choose a capital punishment society in preference to a life-imprisonment society. And (granting for the moment that "life-imprisonment" really means imprisonment for life) we cannot be certain how he would answer, since we do not know whether he would be young or old, well or ill, disdainful or not of the prudent preservation of mere existence. However, the choice fortunately does not have to be made, since the sentence of life imprisonment today rarely means that in fact the criminal will remain in prison for the rest of his life.[16]

What, then, of imprisonment as a punishment? The live question here is not whether imprisonment, which unlike capital punishment admits of degrees, is justifiable, but what kind and how much imprisonment is justifiable. What has not been sufficiently recognized by the general public, in spite of the writings of G. B. Shaw,[17] Galsworthy,[18] John Barlow Martin[19] and others is that imprisonment can be a kind of torture worse than mutilation or the rack. Whether it is will depend upon the conditions and duration of imprisonment, and, inevitably, upon the character and personality of the offender. It is clear that from the standpoint of justice and humanity, to say nothing of efficiency, imprisonment as a mode of punishment should receive careful scrutiny. It is by and large only by the latter criterion that it tends to be measured. Here the argument sometimes slides from the inefficiency of a given penitentiary system to the undesirability of imprisonment as a mode of punishment (or even to the undesirability of punishment as a practice.) Yet it does not follow that because a given mode of imprisonment is inefficient that imprisonment as a mode of punishment is inefficient; and, since efficiency is a comparative criterion, it must be shown that there are more efficient modes of punishment which can replace imprisonment. And of course even if imprisonment were the most efficient mode of punishment available, it would not follow that, by the same token, it should be accepted.

The careful scrutiny of imprisonment as a mode of punishment not only from the standpoint of efficiency (here excellent work has already been done) but also of humanity and justice would result, I believe, in a radical reappraisal of

[15] See qualifications below.

[16] "Life Imprisonment means, on the average, only about ten years." (H. E. Barnes and N. K. Teeters, *New Horizons in Criminology*, 3rd ed., Englewood Cliffs, N.J., 1959, p. 59.)

[17] *Imprisonment*, New York, 1924.

[18] John Galsworthy, *The Silver Box*, New York & London, 1909; and *Justice*, New York, 1913.

[19] "Prison: The Enemy of Society," *Harpers*, April, 1954, pp. 29-38; and many other articles and books.

the conditions and duration of imprisonment: in bold experiments, at least, in the shortening of legal penalties. For without such probing experiments the burden of proof, which humanity requires, that the penalties presently in force are necessary for the discouragement of crime, will not have been shouldered.

What we say here implies, correctly, that we believe that the schema of guiding and limiting principles can be applied not only to the justification of the practice of punishment but also to the justification of penal legislation. This we will not undertake here, but the main lines of the venture should be clear. Here the questions would be, first, whether a law is necessary, and second, whether the proposed law would be the most efficient of the acceptable alternatives. But justice and humanity as limiting principles of legislation cannot be defined or applied in the same way as they are above. The uncommitted bystander must have committed himself to the practice of punishment, and must now consider alternative laws under that practice. Should we then attempt to apply our schema to the justification of sentences? If so, our uncommitted bystander must have accepted not only the practice but the law violated, along with its attached range of penalties.

Whether the distinction between guiding and limiting principles can be maintained in the justification of sentences is a difficult question not to be undertaken here. It is enough, for our purposes, if the conclusion of Chapter IV be allowed to stand: that the judge cannot be reduced either to a social engineer, or to a balancer of the scales.

The short answer to Tolstoy's question, "By what right do some people punish others?" is that, needing a practice, we do not know any better one than legal punishment. The long answer would begin with this chapter and move back to the justification of legislation, penalties, and sentences. This book may provide an outline and some material for that venture.

Reinhold Niebuhr

Reinhold Niebuhr, (1892-1971) twentieth-century Christian theologian, wrote a great deal on topics in political philosophy. Of particular interest are his views on power, love, justice, and the relationship of the individual to the state. The following selection from *Moral Man and Immoral Society* deals primarily with the latter issue. In it, Niebuhr defends his theory that the ethical resources of the state are small, and that one cannot expect too much of organized men's moral resources—though it is possible to expect a great deal from individuals.

Moral Man and Immoral Society

MAN AND SOCIETY: THE ART OF LIVING TOGETHER

Though human society has roots which lie deeper in history than the beginning of human life, men have made comparatively but little progress in solving the problem of their aggregate existence. Each century originates a new complexity and each new generation faces a new vexation in it. For all the centuries of experience, men have not yet learned how to live together without compounding their vices and covering each other "with mud and with blood." The society in which each man lives is at once the basis for, and the nemesis of, that fulness of life which each man seeks. However much human ingenuity may increase the treasures which nature provides for the satisfaction of human needs, they can never be sufficient to satisfy all human wants; for man, unlike other creatures, is gifted and cursed with an imagination which extends his appetites beyond the requirements of subsistence. Human society will never escape the problem of the equitable distribution of the physical and cultural goods which provide for the preservation and fulfillment of human life.

Unfortunately the conquest of nature, and the consequent increase in nature's beneficences to man, have not eased, but rather accentuated, the problem of justice. The same technology, which drew the fangs of nature's enmity of man, also created a society in which the intensity and extent of social cohesion has been greatly increased, and in which power is so unevenly distributed, that justice has become a more difficult achievement. Perhaps it is man's sorry fate, suffering from ills which have their source in the inadequacies of both nature and human society, that the tools by which he eliminates the former should become the means of increasing the latter. That, at least, has been his fate up to the present hour; and it may be that there will be no salvation for the human spirit from the more and more painful burdens of social injustice until the ominous tendency in human history has resulted in perfect tragedy.

Human nature is not wanting in certain endowments for the solution of the problem of human society. Man is endowed by nature with organic relations to his fellowmen; and natural impulse prompts him to consider the needs of others even when they compete with his own. With the higher mammals man shares concern for his offspring; and the long infancy of the child created the basis for an organic social group in the earliest period of human history. Gradually intelligence, imagination, and the necessities of social conflict increased the size of this group. Natural impulse was refined and extended until a less obvious type of consanguinity than an immediate family relationship could be made the basis of social solidarity. Since those early days the units of human co-operation have constantly grown in size, and the areas of significant relationships between the units have likewise increased. Nevertheless conflict between the national units remains as a permanent rather than a passing characteristic of their relations to each other; and each national unit finds it increasingly difficult to maintain either peace or justice within its common life.

While it is possible for intelligence to increase the range of benevolent impulse, and thus prompt a human being to consider the needs and rights of other than those to whom he is bound by organic and physical relationship, there are definite limits in the capacity of ordinary mortals which makes it impossible for them to grant to others what they claim for themselves. Though educators ever since the eighteenth century have given themselves to the fond illusion that justice through voluntary co-operation waited only upon a more universal or a more adequate educational enterprise, there is good reason to believe that the sentiments of benevolence and social goodwill will never be so pure or powerful, and the rational capacity to consider the rights and needs of others in fair competition with our own will never be so fully developed as to create the possibility for the anarchistic millennium which is the social utopia, either explicit or implicit, of all intellectual or religious moralists.

All social co-operation on a larger scale than the most intimate social group requires a measure of coercion. While no state can maintain its unity purely by coercion neither can it preserve itself without coercion. Where the factor of mutual consent is strongly developed, and where standardised and approximately fair methods of adjudicating and resolving conflicting interests within an organised group have been established, the coercive factor in social life is frequently covert, and becomes apparent only in moments of crisis and in the group's policy toward recalcitrant individuals. Yet it is never absent. Divergence of interest, based upon geographic and functional differences within a society, is bound to create different social philosophies and political attitudes which goodwill and intelligence may partly, but never completely, harmonise. Ultimately, unity within an organised social group, or within a federation of such groups, is created by the ability of a dominant group to impose its will. Politics will, to the end of history, be an area where conscience and power meet, where the ethical and coercive factors of human life will interpenetrate and work out their tentative and uneasy compromises. The democratic method of resolving social conflict, which some romanticists hail as a triumph of the ethical over the coercive factor, is really much more coercive than at first seems apparent. The majority has its way, not because the minority believes that the majority is right (few minorities are willing to grant the majority the moral prestige of such a concession), but because the votes of the majority are a symbol of its social strength. Whenever a minority believes that it has some strategic advantage which outweighs the power of numbers, and whenever it is sufficiently intent upon its ends, or desperate enough about its position in society, it refuses to accept the dictates of the majority. Military and economic overlords and revolutionary zealots have been traditionally contemptuous of the will of majorities. Recently Trotsky advised the German communists not to be dismayed by the greater voting strength of the fascists since in the inevitable revolution the power of industrial workers, in charge of the nation's industrial process, would be found much more significant than the social power of clerks and other petty bourgeoisie who comprised the fascist movement.

There are, no doubt, rational and ethical factors in the democratic process. Contending social forces presumably use the forum rather than the battleground to arbitrate their differences in the democratic method, and thus differences are resolved by moral suasion and a rational adjustment of rights to rights. If political issues were really abstract questions of social policy upon which unbiased citizens were asked to commit themselves, the business of voting and the debate which precedes the election might actually be regarded as an educational programme in which a social group discovers its common mind. But the fact is that political opinions are inevitably rooted in economic interests of some kind or other, and only comparatively few citizens can view a problem of social policy without regard to their interest. Conflicting interests therefore can never be completely resolved; and minorities will yield only because the majority has come into control of the police power of the state and may, if the occasion arises, augment that power by its own military strength. Should a minority regard its own strength, whether economic or martial, as strong enough to challenge the power of the majority, it may attempt to wrest control of the state apparatus from the majority, as in the case of the fascist movement in Italy. Sometimes it will resort to armed conflict, even if the prospects of victory are none too bright, as in the instance of the American Civil War, in which the Southern planting interests, outvoted by a combination of Eastern industrialists and Western agrarians, resolved to protect their peculiar interests and privileges by a forceful dissolution of the national union. The coercive factor is, in other words, always present in politics. If economic interests do not conflict too sharply, if the spirit of accommodation partially resolves them, and if the democratic process has achieved moral prestige and historic dignity, the coercive factor in politics may become too covert to be visible to the casual observer. Nevertheless, only a romanticist of the purest water could maintain that a national group ever arrives at a "common mind" or become conscious of a "general will' without the use of either force or the threat of force. This is particularly true of nations, but it is also true, though in a slighter degree, of other social groups. Even religious communities, if they are sufficiently large, and if they deal with issues regarded as vital by their members, resort to coercion to preserve their unity. Religious organisations have usually availed themselves of a covert type of coercion (excommunication and the interdict) or they have called upon the police power of the state.

The limitations of the human mind and imagination, the inability of human beings to transcend their own interests sufficiently to envisage the interests of their fellowmen as clearly as they do their own makes force an inevitable part of the process of social cohesion. But the same force which guarantees peace also makes for injustice. "Power," said Henry Adams, "is poison"; and it is a poison which blinds the eyes of moral insight and lames the will of moral purpose. The individual or the group which organises any society, however social its intentions or pretensions, arrogates an inordinate portion of social privilege to itself. The two most obvious types of power are the military and the economic, though in primitive society the power of the priest, partly because he dispenses supernatural benefits and partly because he establishes public order by methods less arduous than those of the soldier, vies with that of the soldier and the landlord. The chief difference between the agrarian civilisations, which lasted from the rise of ancient Babylon and Egypt to the fall of European feudalism, and the commercial and industrial civilisations of today is that in the former the military power is primary, and in the latter it has become secondary, to economic power. In agrarian civilisations the soldier becomes the landlord. In more primitive periods he may claim the land by his own military prowess. In later periods a grateful sovereign bestowed land upon the soldiers who defended his realm and consolidated his dominion. The soldier thus gained the economic security and the social prestige which could be exploited in further martial service to his sovereign. The business man and industrial overlord are gradually usurping the position of eminence and privilege once held by the soldier and the priest. In most European nations their ascendancy over the landed aristocrat of military traditions is not as complete as in America, which has no feudal traditions. . . .

On the pre-eminence of economic power in an industrial civilisation and its ability to make the military power its tool we shall have more to say later. Our interest at the moment is to record that any kind of significant social power develops social inequality. Even if history is viewed from other than equalitarian perspectives, and it is granted that differentials in economic rewards are morally justified and socially useful, it is impossible to justify the degree of inequality which complex societies inevitably create by the increased centralisation of power which develops with more elaborate civilisations. The literature of all ages is filled with rational and moral justifications of these inequalities, but most of them are specious. If superior abilities and services to society deserve special rewards it may be regarded as axiomatic that the rewards are always higher than the services warrant. No impartial society determines the rewards. The men of power who control society grant these perquisites to themselves. Whenever special ability is not associated with power, as in the case of the modern professional man, his excess of income over the average is ridiculously low in comparison with that of the economic overlords, who are the real centres of power in an industrial society. Most rational and social justifications of unequal privilege are clearly afterthoughts. The facts are created by the disproportion of power which exists in a given social system. The justifications are usually dictated by the desire of the men of power to hide the nakedness of their greed, and by the inclination of society itself to veil the brutal facts of human life from itself. This is a rather pathetic but understandable inclination; since the facts of man's collective life easily rob the average individual of confidence in the human enterprise. The inevitable hypocrisy, which is associated with all of the collective activities of the human race, springs chiefly from this source: that individuals have a moral code which makes the actions of collective man an outrage to their conscience. They therefore invent romantic and moral interpretations of the real facts, preferring to obscure rather than reveal the true character of their collective behavior. Sometimes they are as anxious to offer moral justifications for the brutalities from which they suffer as for those which they commit. The fact that the hypocrisy of man's group behavior expresses itself not only in terms of self-justification but in terms of moral justification of human behavior in general, symbolises one of the tragedies of the human spirit: its inability to conform its collective life to its individual ideals. As individuals, men believe that they ought to love and serve each other and establish justice between each other. As racial, economic and national groups they take for themselves, whatever their power can command.

The disproportion of power in a complex society which began with the transmutation of the pastoral to the agrarian economy, and which destroyed the simple equalitarianism and communism of the hunting and nomadic social organisation, has perpetuated social injustice in every form through all the ages. Types of power have changed, and gradations of social inequality have varied, but the essential facts have remained unchanged. In Egypt the land was divided into three parts, respectively claimed by the king, the soldiers and the priests.

The common people were landless. In Peru, where a rather remarkable despotic communism developed, the king owned all the land but gave use of one third to the people, another third to the priests and kept one third for himself and his nobles. Needless to say, the commoners were expected to till not only their third but the other two thirds of the lands. In China, where the emperor maintained the right of eminent domain for many centuries, defeating the experiment in feudalism in the third century A.D., and giving each family inalienable rights in the soil which nominally belonged to him, there has probably been less inequality than in any other ancient empire. Nevertheless slavery persisted until a very recent day. In Japan the emperor gave the land to feudal princes, who again sublet it to the inferior nobility. The power of the feudal clans, originating in martial prowess and perpetuated through land ownership, has remained practically unbroken to this day, though the imperial power was ostensibly restored in the latter part of the last century, and growing industry has developed a class of industrial overlords who were partly drawn from the landed aristocracy. In Rome the absolute property rights of the *pater familias* of the patrician class gave him power which placed him on top of the social pyramid. All other classes, beginning with his own women and children, then the plebeians and finally the slaves, took their places in the various lower rungs of the social ladder. The efforts of the Gracchi to destroy the ever growing inequality, which resulted from power breeding more power, proved abortive, as did the land reforms of Solon and Lycurgus in Greece. Military conquest gave the owners of the Roman *latifundia* hundreds of slaves by the labor of which they reduced the small freeholders to penury. Thus the decay of the Roman Empire was prepared; for a state which has only lords and slaves lacks the social cement to preserve it from internal disintegration and the military force to protect it from external aggression.

All through history one may observe the tendency of power to destroy its very *raison d'être*. It is suffered because it achieves internal unity and creates external defenses for the nation. But it grows to such proportions that it destroys the social peace of the state by the animosities which its exactions arouse, and it enervates the sentiment of patriotism by robbing the common man of the basic privileges which might bind him to his nation. The words attributed by Plutarch to Tiberius Gracchus reveal the hollowness of the pretensions by which the powerful classes enlist their slaves in the defense of their dominions: "The wild beasts in Italy had at least their lairs, dens and caves whereto they might retreat; whereas the men who fought and died for that land had nothing in it save air and light, but were forced to wander to and fro with their wives and children, without resting place or house wherein they might lodge. . . . The poor folk go to war, to fight and to die for the delights, riches and superfluities of others."[1] In the long run these pretensions are revealed and the sentiment of patriotism is throttled in the breasts of the disinherited. The privileged groups who are outraged by the want of patriotism among modern proletarians could learn the cause of proletarian internationalism by a little study of history. "It is absurd," says Diodorus Siculus, speaking of Egypt, "to entrust the defence of a country to people who own nothing in it," a reflection which has applicability to other ages and other nations than his own. Russian

---

[1] Plutarch, *The Parallel Lives,* see "Tiberius Gracchus," *Loeb Classical Library,* Vol. X.

communists of pure water pour their scorn upon European socialists, among whom patriotism outweighed class loyalty in the World War. But there is a very simple explanation for the nationalism of European socialists. They were not as completely, or at least not as obviously, disinherited as their Russian comrades.

The history of slavery in all ancient civilisations offers an interesting illustration of the development of social injustice with the growing size and complexity of the social unit. In primitive tribal organisation rights are essentially equal within the group, and no rights, or only very minimum rights are recognised outside of the group. The captives of war are killed. With the growth of agriculture the labor of captives becomes useful, and they are enslaved rather than destroyed. Since rightless individuals are introduced into the intimate life of the group, equality of rights disappears; and the inequality remains even after the slaves are no longer regarded as enemies and have become completely organic to the life of the group. The principle of slavery once established, is enlarged to include debt slaves, victims of the growing property system. The membership of the debt slaves in the original community at first guarantees them rights which the captive slaves do not enjoy. But the years gradually wipe out these distinctions and the captive slaves are finally raised to the status of debtor slaves. Thus the more humane attitudes which men practice within their social groups gains a slight victory over the more brutal attitudes towards individuals in other groups. But the victory is insignificant in comparison with the previous introduction of the morals of inter-group relations into the intimate life of the group by the very establishment of slavery. Barbarism knows little or nothing of class distinctions. These are created and more and more highly elaborated by civilisation. The social impulses, with which men are endowed by nature are not powerful enough, even when they are extended by a growing intelligence, to apply with equal force toward all members of a large community. The distinction between slave and freeman is only one of the many social gradations which higher societies develop. They are determined in every case by the disproportion of power, military and economic, which develops in the more complex civilisations and in the larger social units. A growing social intelligence may be affronted by them and may protest against them, but it changes them only slightly. Neither the prophets of Israel nor the social idealists of Egypt and Babylon, who protested against social injustice, could make their version of a just society effective. The man of power, though humane impulse may awaken in him, always remains something of the beast of prey. He may be generous within his family, and just within the confines of the group which shares his power and privilege. With only rare exceptions, his highest moral attitude toward members of other groups is one of warlike sportsmanship toward those who equal his power and challenge it, and one of philanthropic generosity toward those who possess less power and privilege. His philanthrophy is a perfect illustration of the curious compound of the brutal and the moral which we find in all human behavior; for his generosity is at once a display of his power and an expression of his pity. His generous impulses freeze within him if his power is challenged or his generosities are accepted without grateful humility. If individual men of power should achieve more ethical attitudes than the one described, it remains nevertheless typical for them as a class; and is their practically unvarying attitude when they express themselves not as individuals but as a group.

The rise of modern democracy, beginning with the Eighteenth Century, is sometimes supposed to have substituted the consent of the governed for the power of royal families and aristocratic classes as the cohesive force of national society. This judgment is partly true, but not nearly as true as the uncritical devotees of modern democracy assume. The doctrine that government exists by the consent of the governed, and the democratic technique by which the suffrage of the governed determines the policy of the state, may actually reduce the coercive factor in national life, and provide for peaceful and gradual methods of resolving conflicting social interests and changing political institutions. But the creeds and institutions of democracy have never become fully divorced from the special interests of the commercial classes who conceived and developed them. It was their interest to destroy political restraint upon economic activity, and they therefore weakened the authority of the state and made it more pliant to their needs. With the increased centralisation of economic power in the period of modern industrialism, this development merely means that society as such does not control economic power as much as social well-being requires; and that the economic, rather than the political and military, power has become the significant coercive force of modern society. Either it defies the authority of the state or it bends the institutions of the state to its own purposes. Political power has been made responsible, but economic power has become irresponsible in society. The net result is that political power has been made more responsible to economic power. It is, in other words, again the man of power or the dominant class which binds society together, regulates its processes, always paying itself inordinate rewards for its labors. The difference is that owners of factories, rather than owners of land, exert the power, and that it is more purely economic and less military than that which was wielded by the landed aristocrats. Needless to say, it is not completely divorced from military power. It may on occasion appropriate the police and the army of the state to defend its interests against internal and external foes. The military power has become the hired servant and is no longer the progenitor of economic ownership. . . .

Society is perennially harassed not only by the fact that the coercive factors in social life (which the limitations of human intelligence and imagination make inevitable) create injustice in the process of establishing peace; but also the tendency of the same factors, which make for an uneasy peace within a social group, to aggravate intergroup conflict. Power sacrifices justice to peace within the community and destroys peace between communities. It is not true that only kings make war. The common members of any national community, while sentimentally desiring peace, nevertheless indulge impulses of envy, jealousy, pride, bigotry, and greed which make for conflict between communities. Neither is it true that modern wars are caused solely by the modern capitalistic system with its disproportion of economic power and privilege. Without an almost miraculous increase in human intelligence it will not be easy to resolve the conflicts of interest between various national communities even after the special privilege and the unequal power, which now aggravate international conflicts, have been destroyed. Nevertheless the whole history of mankind bears testimony to the fact that the power which prevents anarchy in intra-group relations encourages anarchy in intergroup relations. The kings of old claimed the loyalty and sacrifices of their subjects in conflicts with other tyrants, in which the interests of the state and the welfare of the people were completely subordinated to the capricious purpose of the monarch. No personal whim, which a human being might indulge, is excluded from the motives, which have prompted monarchs to shed the blood of their unhappy subjects. Pride, jealousy, disappointed love, hurt vanity, greed for greater treasures, lust for power over larger dominions, petty animosities between royal brothers or between father and son, momentary passions and childish whims, these all have been, not the occasional but the perenially recurring, causes and occasions of international conflict. The growing intelligence of mankind and the increased responsibility of monarchs to their people have placed a check upon the caprice, but not upon the self-interest, of the men of power. They may still engage in social conflict for the satisfaction of their pride and vanity provided they can compound their personal ambitions with, and hallow them by, the ambitions of their group, and the pitiful vanities and passions of the individuals who compose the group. The story of Napoleon belongs to modern and not to ancient history. He could bathe Europe in blood for the sake of gratifying his overweening lust for power, as long as he could pose as the tool of French patriotism and as the instrument of revolutionary fervor. The fact that the domocratic sentiment, opposed to the traditional absolutisms of Europe, could be exploited to create a tyranny more sanguinary and terrible than those which it sought ostensibly to destroy; and that the dream of equality, liberty and fraternity of the French Revolution could turn so quickly into the nightmare of Napoleonic imperialism is a tragic revelation of the inadequacies of the human resources with which men must try to solve the problem of their social life. The childish vanity of the German Emperor, who wanted a large navy so that he could stand on equal footing with his royal English uncle at naval manueuvers, helped to make the World War inevitable.[2] He would not have been permitted to indulge this vanity however had it not seemed compatible with the prejudices of his people and the economic necessities of a growing empire. Theodore Roosevelt belonged to a little junta which foisted the Spanish-American War upon the American people. The ambition and vanity which prompted him could be veiled and exalted because the will-to-power of an adolescent nation and the frustrated impulses of pugnacity and martial ardor of the pitiful little "men in the street" could find in him symbolic expression and vicarious satisfaction. The need of the modern industrial overlord for raw materials and markets, and rivalry over control of the undeveloped and unexploited portions of the earth are the occasion of modern wars. Yet the ambitions and greed of dominant economic groups within each nation are not the only cause of international conflict. Every social group tends to develop imperial ambitions which are aggravated, but not caused solely, by the lusts of its leaders and privileged groups. Every group, as every individual, has expansive desires which are rooted in the instinct of survival and soon extend beyond it. The will-to-live becomes the will-to-power. Only rarely does nature provide armors of defense which cannot be transmuted into instruments of aggression. The frustrations of the average man, who can never realise the power and the glory which his imagination sets as the ideal, makes him the more willing tool and victim of the imperial ambitions of his group. His frustrated individual ambitions gain a measure of satisfaction in the power and the aggrandisement of his nation. The will-to-power of competing national groups is the cause of the international anarchy which the moral sense of mankind has thus far vainly striven to overcome. Since some nations are more powerful than others, they

[2] See *Memoirs of Prince Von Bülow*, Vol. III, p. 204.

will at times prevent anarchy by effective imperialism, which in our industrial period has become more covert than overt. But the peace is gained by force and is always an uneasy and an unjust one. As powerful classes organise a nation, so powerful nations organise a crude society of nations. In each case the peace is a tentative one because it is unjust. It has been achieved only partially by a mutual accommodation of conflicting interests and certainly not by a rational and moral adjustment of rights. It will last only until those, who feel themselves too weak to challenge strength, will become, or will feel themselves, powerful enough to do so. It is not necessary to discount the moral influence of the League of Nations completely or to deny that it represents certain gains in the rational and moral organisation of society, to recognise that the peace of contemporary Europe is maintained by the force of French arms and that it will last only as long as the ingenuities of French statesmanship can maintain the combination of political and military forces which holds the people, who feel themselves defrauded by the Versailles Treaty, in check. Significantly the same power, which prompts the fear that prevents immediate action, also creates the mounting hatred which guarantees ultimate rebellion.

Thus society is in a perpetual state of war. Lacking moral and rational resources to organise its life, without resort to coercion, except in the most immediate and intimate social groups, men remain the victims of the individuals, classes and nations by whose force a momentary coerced unity is achieved, and further conflicts are as certainly created. The fact that the coercive factor in society is both necessary and dangerous seriously complicates the whole task of securing both peace and justice. History is a long tale of abortive efforts toward the desired end of social cohesion and justice in which failure was usually due either to the effort to eliminate the factor of force entirely or to an undue reliance upon it. Complete reliance upon it means that new tyrants usurp the places of eminence from which more traditional monarchs are cast down. Tolstoian pacifists and other advocates of non-resistance, noting the evils which force introduces into society, give themselves to the vain illusion that it can be completely eliminated, and society organised upon the basis of anarchistic principles. Their conviction is an illusion, because there are definite limits of moral goodwill and social intelligence beyond which even the most vital religion and the most astute educational programme will not carry a social group, whatever may be possible for individuals in an intimate society. The problem which society faces is clearly one of reducing force by increasing the factors which make for a moral and rational adjustment of life to life; of bringing such force as is still necessary under responsibility of the whole of society; of destroying the kind of power which cannot be made socially responsible (the power which resides in economic ownership for instance); and of bringing forces of moral self-restraint to bear upon types of power which can never be brought completely under social control. Every one of these methods has its definite limitations. Society will probably never be sufficiently intelligent to bring all power under its control. The stupidity of the average man will permit the oligarch, whether economic or political, to hide his real purposes from the scrutiny of his fellows and to withdraw his activities from effective control. Since it is impossible to count on enough moral goodwill among those who possess irresponsible power to sacrifice it for the good of the whole, it must be destroyed by coercive methods and these will always run the peril of introducing new forms of injustice in place of those abolished. There is, for instance, as yet no clear proof that the power of economic overlords can be destroyed by means less rigorous than communism has employed; but there is also no proof that communistic oligarchs, once the idealistic passion of a revolutionary period is spent, will be very preferable to the capitalistic oligarchs, whom they are to displace. Since the increasing complexity of society makes it impossible to bring all those who are in charge of its intricate techniques and processes, and who are therefore in possession of social power, under complete control, it will always be necessary to rely partly upon the honesty and self-restraint of those who are not socially restrained. But here again, it will never be possible to insure moral antidotes sufficiently potent to destroy the deleterious effects of the poison of power upon character. The future peace and justice of society therefore depend upon, not one but many social strategies, in all of which moral and coercive factors are compounded in varying degrees. So difficult is it to avoid the Scylla of despotism and the Charybdis of anarchy that it is safe to hazard the prophecy that the dream of perpetual peace and brotherhood for human society is one which will never be fully realised. It is a vision prompted by the conscience and insight of individual man, but incapable of fulfillment by collective man. It is like all true religious visions, possible of approximation but not of realisation in actual history. The vitality of the vision is the measure of man's rebellion against the fate which binds his collective life to the world of nature from which his soul recoils. The vision can be kept alive only by permitting it to overreach itself. But meanwhile collective man, operating on the historic and mundane scene, must content himself with a more modest goal. His concern for some centuries to come is not the creation of an ideal society in which there will be uncoerced and perfect peace and justice, but a society in which there will be enough justice, and in which coercion will be sufficiently non-violent to prevent his common enterprise from issuing into complete disaster. That goal will seem too modest for the romanticists; but the romanticists have so little understanding for the perils in which modern society lives, and overestimate the moral resources at the disposal of the collective human enterprise so easily, that any goal regarded as worthy of achievement by them must necessarily be beyond attainment.

Gajo Petrovic

Gajo Petrovic (b. 1927) is Associate Professor of Philosophy at Zagreb University, Yugoslavia. His writings on Marxist philosophy have emphasized the interpretation and development of the views of Marx himself rather than the later additions by Lenin and Stalin. The essay printed below, "Man and Freedom," presents a Marxist view of freedom heavily influenced by the more humanistic outlook of early Marx.

Man and Freedom

1. What makes man man is not some property or activity peculiar to him (or a sum of all such properties or activities), but a structure of being peculiar to him which is common to all really human properties and activities—that is, praxis. Man is the being that exists through and as praxis.

2. Praxis is a mode of being essentially different from any other mode of being. Freedom is one of the essential constituents of that mode. As the being of praxis man is the being of freedom. There is no freedom without man and no humanity without freedom.

3. Freedom is the essence of man, but that does not mean that man is always and everywhere free. The "escape from freedom" is widespread in the contemporary world. However, this does not refute the thesis that man is the being of freedom; it only confirms that contemporary man alienates himself from his essence, from what he as man can and ought to be.

4. There are various "kinds," "forms," and "aspects" of freedom. One speaks of metaphysical, ethical, psychological, economic, political, national, religious freedom; of freedom of the spirit, of the will, of thought, of conscience, of movement, of action; of freedom of the press, of radio and television, of assembly, of speech, of association; of freedom from exploitation, oppression, hunger, war, and fear; of freedom from tradition, convention, vice, passion, weakness, prejudice; of freedom of art, science, education, teaching; of free behavior, free love, free time, etc. But listing various kinds or forms of freedom does not solve the question, What is freedom? Before we answer this question we cannot be sure whether the kinds of freedom mentioned are really freedoms, or only pseudo-freedoms.

5. If freedom is understood as the nonexistence of external obstacles to movement, then it is nothing specifically human; such freedom can appertain to a beast, bird, fish, even to water or a stone. But freedom is not the absence of external obstacles or, more generally, the sum of the external conditions under which something exists; freedom is a specific mode of being peculiar to man.

6. If freedom is conceived as the knowledge and acceptance of fate, destiny, universal necessity, then freedom is only another name for voluntary slavery. But freedom is not passive submission or adaptation to "external" or "internal" necessity. A free action can only be one by which a man changes his world and himself.

7. Mere intensity of activity or the degree to which activity has proved successful is by no means a measure of freedom. Even the most intensive and successful activity, if it is determined from the outside, is not free. Disciplined soldiers, obedient employees, well-paid policemen may be extraordinarily active and successful, nevertheless their activity is anything but free. An action is free only when a man determines his deed by himself.

8. However, not every activity which is determined "from within" is free. Spontaneous activity in which a man's needs, inclinations, desires, or passions

From *SOCIALIST HUMANISM: An International Symposium*, edited by Erich Fromm Copyright © 1965 by Doubleday & Company, Inc. Reprinted by permission of Doubleday & Company, Inc.

directly determine his acts is very often not free. Only that self-determined activity in which a man acts as an integral many-sided personality, in which he is not a slave of one or another individual thought, feeling, or aspiration, is truly free.

9. Those who are seemingly freest are really furthest from free activity. Tyrannical dictators, ruthless conquerors, insatiable exploiters are all slaves of their inhuman fixed ideas and ambitions. Their activity is the destruction of humaneness; a man is really free only when what is human in him determines his actions, and when he, by his deeds, contributes to humanity.

10. The theory according to which knowledge of necessity is a precondition of free activity is, at best, incomplete. If everything were necessary, human activity would not be free either. The knowledge of necessity (if by this word we mean that which is outside human power) is only a recognition of the limits of freedom. A positive condition of freedom is the knowledge of the limits of necessity, the awareness of human creative possibilities.

11. The ingenious but contradictory definition of freedom as control over nature founded on the knowledge of natural necessity is an adequate expression of the basic orientation of modern man, who is interested in something only as a possible object of subjection and exploitation. However, freedom does not consist in the reckless exploitation of nature, but in the ability of man to humanize it and to participate in its blessings in a human way.

12. The concept of freedom as control over oneself presupposes the split of man into one part which controls and another part which is controlled. But domination is a negation of freedom. The idea of freedom as control over oneself serves frequently as a disguise for efforts to repress man's aspiration for freedom and to justify reconciliation with "external" unfreedom.

13. The above two conceptions and their synthesis, the idea of freedom as the control of man over external nature and over himself, presuppose that man and nature are a sum of ready-made forces which one only has to harness, subject, and use. However, the essence of freedom is not in the subjection of the given, but in the creation of something new, in the development of man's creative abilities, in the broadening and enriching of humanity.

14. The being of freedom (man) is never absolutely free (a complete unalienated man) or absolutely unfree (a completely inhuman being). Man is always, to a greater or lesser degree, free. Hence freedom is "relative," but this relativity does not form the essence of freedom.

15. The aim of human freedom is a free person in a free society. This "ideal" has not been thought up arbitrarily. There can be no free society without free persons, or any free person outside a social community. But this does not mean that in a free society all are free, or that in an unfree society all are unfree.

16. Even in a free society an individual may not be free. Society can be so organized as to enable and encourage the development of free personalities, but freedom cannot be given as a gift to or forced upon anyone. An individual becomes a free human person only through his own free activity.

17. Even in an unfree society an individual can be more or less free. The external obstacles erected by an unfree society may make free human activity more difficult or limit it, but they cannot prevent it entirely. An unwavering revolutionary in chains is freer than the jailer who guards him, or the torturer who tries in vain to break him.

18. An unfree society strives to crush and destroy free personality; a free

society enables and helps its blossoming. Hence the struggle for a free society is a component part of the struggle for the freeing of personality. When this part wants to become the whole of it, it becomes the reverse of what it ought to be. The struggle for a free society is not a struggle for a free society unless through it an ever greater degree of individual freedom is created.

19. The problem of freedom is "eternal," but in every epoch it assumes a different form. In our time it has been shown, for example, that a free society is not created merely by the "expropriation of the expropriators," or merely by the raising of living standards, or by a combination of the two. In a society from which exploiters have been eliminated, man's freedom is threatened by the means by which he communicates with nature and with other men (technology) and by the social forms in which that communication takes place (social organizations and institutions). The question of freedom faces us today primarily as a question of freedom with socialism, and as a question of freedom with technology.

The above theses can be divided into three groups: theses 1 to 4 are introductory—they try to explain and to locate the question concerning the essence of freedom; theses 5 to 14 are central—they attempt to answer the question raised; those in the third group (15 to 19) are perhaps the most important—they discuss an essential aspect of the question, an aspect with far-reaching consequences.

I begin with a few summary statements on man and praxis. The first two theses are very incomplete; I have said more about the subject elsewhere.[1] That I start from man and praxis is to show how the question of freedom inevitably emerges when one wants to solve the question of man. In trying to elucidate the sense of the question of freedom, I criticize the view that the question can be answered by a classification of the forms of freedom, or by a description of the development of freedom. I also reject the view that it can be solved by a linguistic study, or simply by preaching. The question of freedom is first and above all the question of the essence of freedom. So what is most important in theses 1 to 4 can be expressed briefly: the question of freedom is an essential part of the question of man, and the question of the essence of freedom is the central part of the question of freedom.

It is impossible to say what freedom is without saying what it is not. Therefore, in discussing the question of the essence of freedom (theses 5 to 14), I criticize some of the unacceptable theories of freedom. First is the theory— advocated by Hobbes in the seventeenth century and still held by a number of philosophers (including some "Marxists") even in the twentieth century—according to which freedom is something outside the free man, namely, the mere absence of external impediments to motion. The second is the theory which regards freedom as something "external" which has become "internal," as an external "necessity" known and accepted, or somehow used, by the free person. Found in ancient Greeks, Spinoza, Hegel, Engels, it is a theory developed in several variants which, at first glance, might seem quite different. Compare, for

---

[1] "Pitanje o covjeku i Karl Marx," *Nase teme* (Zagreb), No. 4, 1961, pp. 536-76; "El Concepto del hombre en Marx," *Cuadernos Americanos* (Mexico D.F.), No. 4, 1962, pp. 112-32; "Marx's Theory of Alienation," *Philosophy and Phenomenological Research* (Philadelphia), No. 3, 1963, pp. 419-26; "Man as Economic Animal and Man as Praxis," *Inquiry* (Oslo), Vol. 6, 1963, pp. 35-56.

example: "freedom is the knowledge of necessity," "freedom is adjustment to a known necessity," "freedom is power over nature and over oneself based on the knowledge of the external and internal necessity." The third main theory which I briefly touch and criticize reduces freedom to a pure internal self-determination, to a mere "precondition" of free activity, a theory which has also been developed in many different variants (compare, for example, Kant and Sartre). In criticizing the above three theories, I try to state and explain different aspects of a theory the core of which is the view that freedom is something "internal" becoming also "external," namely the self-determining creative activity, the creative deed of enlarging and enriching humaneness. A possible misunderstanding concerning the "absolute" and the "relative" character of freedom is dispelled in thesis 14.

Although the question of the essence of freedom is the major question about freedom, it is not the only one which can be raised. To ask about the different forms or aspects of freedom is not only legitimate; it is indispensable. In theses 15 to 18 I restricted myself to only one part of the question about the forms of freedom: the relationship between the free person and the free society. What is perhaps most important in these theses is to understand the asymmetrical character of the relationship between "personal" and "social" freedom: there can be no free society without free persons (which does not mean that *all* individuals in a free society are free persons), but there *can* be a free person without a free society (which does not mean that a person can be free outside any social community, or that the degree of the achieved social freedom is irrelevant to personal freedom). If one grasps the exact character of that fundamental asymmetry, which has important consequences both for personal responsibility and for social action, the rest of the theses on free person and free society become easy to understand.

The concluding thesis (19) touches the difficult aspect of freedom as an "eternal" and "historical" problem. It serves as a concluding remark here; it could serve as an introductory remark elsewhere (for example, in a text on freedom today).

There is no mention in the theses of the thinker who mainly inspired them. This is not in order to conceal the origin, but simply because it is not difficult to see that they were inspired by the man who wrote: *"Die Lebensgefahr für jedes Wesen besteht darin, sich selbst zu verlieren. Die Unfreiheit ist daher die eigentliche Todesgefahr für den Menschen."*[2] ("The mortal danger for each person consists in the danger of losing himself. Hence, lack of freedom is the true mortal danger for man.")

I subscribe to most of Marx's theses on freedom such as they stand, or with certain corrections. As concerns the one just quoted, I am inclined to correct it slightly: Un-freedom is not merely the death-*danger* for man, it is man's *death*.

[2] Karl Marx: "Debatten über die Pressfreiheit," *Rheinische Zeitung*, No. 135 (May 15, 1842). In Karl Marx and Friedrich Engels, *Werke* (Berlin, 1957), Vol. 1, p. 60.

Herbert Marcuse

Herbert Marcuse (b. 1898), Professor of Philosophy at the University of California, San Diego, has written a number of works dealing with issues in political philosophy. Of particular interest are *Reason and Revolution*, a critical study of Hegel and Marx, and *One-Dimensional Man*, a radical critique of Western industrial society which has found favor with some segments of the New Left. In the essay "Ethics and Revolution," printed below, he considers the conditions necessary to justify revolution.

Ethics and Revolution

I propose to discuss the relation between ethics and revolution by taking as guidance the following question: Can a revolution be justified as right, as good, perhaps even as necessary, and justified not merely in political terms (as expedient for certain interests) but in ethical terms, that is to say, justified with respect to the human condition as such, to the potential of man in a given historical situation? This means that ethical terms such as "right" or "good" will be applied to political and social movements, with the hypothesis that the moral evaluation of such movements is (in a sense to be defined) more than subjective, more than a matter of preference. Under this hypothesis, "good" and "right" would mean serving to establish, to promote, or to extend human freedom and happiness in a commonwealth, regardless of the form of government. This preliminary definition combines individual and personal, private and public welfare. It tries to recapture a basic concept of classical political philosophy which has been all too often repressed, namely, that the end of government is not only the greatest possible freedom, but also the greatest possible happiness of man, that is to say, a life without fear and misery, and a life in peace.

Here we encounter the first vexing question, namely, who determines, who can and by what right determine the general interest of a commonwealth, and thereby determine the range and limits of individual freedom and happiness, and the sacrifices imposed upon individual freedom and happiness in the name and on behalf of the commonwealth? For as long as the general and individual welfare do not immediately coincide, the latter will be *made* to conform with the former. And if we ask this question we are at once confronted with an equally serious and embarrassing problem: granted even that freedom is not only an individual and private affair, that it is rather determined by the society, by the state in which we live, what about happiness? Is the happiness of an individual his own private affair, or is it too, in a very definite sense, subject to the limitations and even the definitions imposed upon it by a commonwealth? The extreme position that human happiness is and must remain individual and the individual's own affair cannot be defended if we give it only a few minutes' thought. There are certainly modes and types of individual happiness which cannot be tolerated by any kind of commonwealth. It is perfectly possible—as a matter of fact we know it to be the fact—that the people who were the master torturers in the Hitler concentration camps were often quite happy doing their job. This is one of the many cases of individual happiness where we do not hesitate to say that it is not merely the individual himself who can be and who can remain the judge of his own happiness. We assume a tribunal which is (actually or morally) entitled to "define" individual happiness.

Now after these preliminary clarifications, let me define what I mean by "revolution." By "revolution" I understand the overthrow of a legally established government and constitution by a social class or movement with the aim of altering the social as well as the political structure. This definition excludes all military coups, palace revolutions, and "preventive" counterrevolutions (such as Fascism and Nazism) because they do not alter the basic social structure. If we define revolution in this way we can move one step forward by saying that such a radical and qualitative change implies violence. Peaceful revolutions, if there are such things, if there can be such things, do not present any problem. We can therefore reformulate the initial question by asking: Is the revolutionary use of violence justifiable as a means for establishing or promoting human freedom and happiness? The question implies a very important assumption, namely, that there are rational criteria for determining the possibilities of human freedom and happiness available to a society in a specific historical situation. If there are no such rational criteria, it would be impossible to evaluate a political movement in terms of its chances to attain a greater extent or a higher degree of freedom and happiness in society.

But postulating the availability of rational standards and criteria for judging the given possibilities of human freedom and happiness means assuming that the ethical, moral standards are *historical* standards. If they are not, they remain meaningless abstractions. Applied to our question, this means that to claim an ethical and moral right a revolutionary movement must be able to give rational grounds for its chances to grasp real possibilities of human freedom and happiness, and it must be able to demonstrate the adequacy of its means for obtaining this end. Only if the problem is placed in such a historical context, is it susceptible to rational discussion. Otherwise, only two positions remain open, namely, to reject *a priori* or to endorse *a priori* all revolution and revolutionary violence. Both positions, the affirmative as well as the negative one, offend against historical facts. It is, for example, meaningless to say that modern society *could* have come about without the English, American, and French Revolutions. It is also meaningless to say that all revolutionary violence had the same social function and consequences. The violence of the Civil Wars in seventeenth century England, the violence of the first French Revolution certainly had effects and consequences very different from those of the Bolshevik Revolution, and very different from the counterrevolutionary violence perpetrated by the Nazi and Fascist regimes. Moreover, the positions of *a priori* rejecting or *a priori* approving social and political violence would amount to sanctioning any change brought about in history, regardless of whether it would be in a progressive or regressive, liberating or enslaving direction.

A very brief glance at the historical development of our problem may facilitate the discussion. In classical political philosophy, revolutions were not considered as breaks of the historical continuum. Plato as well as Aristotle believed that revolutions were built into the very dynamic of politics, that they belonged to the historical and at the same time natural cycle of birth, growth and decay of political forms. In medieval and early modern philosophy the idea of a natural and divine order either outlawed all resistance to established government or made resistance against tyranny not only a right but a moral duty and obligation. Then, in the sixteenth and seventeenth centuries, the practically unlimited right to resist a government, even to overthrow a government, was normally claimed by Protestant against Catholic, and by Catholic against Protestant regimes. A most characteristic reaction against these doctrines may be seen in the attitude towards revolution which we find in such different figures as Hobbes and Descartes, namely that change is always to the worst. Leave the established social and political institutions as they are, for, no matter how bad they may be, the risk of overthrowing them is too great. Descartes, the great revolutionary in thought, was extremely conservative with respect to the "great public bodies." To them, doubt is not supposed to be extended, they are supposed to be left alone. At the same time, philosophers are strongly inclined to endorse a revolution once it has proved to be successful. Representative of this attitude is the case of Kant—certainly not a paragon of opportunism and expediency—who rejected the right of resistance and condemned revolt against established government, but added that, once a revolution has succeeded, a new legal government is established, and man owes obedience to the new revolutionary government just as he owed it to the government which was overthrown by the revolution.

On the other side of the fence, political theory and practice recognize historical situations in which violence becomes the necessary and essential element of progress. This concept is instrumental in the political theory and practice of totalitarian democracy. Robespierre calls for the "despotism of liberty" against the despotism of tyranny: in the fight for freedom, in the interest of the whole against the particular interests of oppression, terror may become a necessity and an obligation. Here, violence, revolutionary violence, appears not only as a political means but as a moral duty. The terror is defined as *counter*violence: it is "legitimate" only in defense against the oppressors and until they are defeated. Similarly, the Marxian concept of proletarian dictatorship is that of a transitional self-cancelling dictatorship: self-cancelling because it is supposed to last only as long as the power of the old ruling classes still combats the construction of the socialist society; after their defeat, the engines of repression were to be stopped. Here too, revolutionary violence is defined as counterviolence. The Marxian concept assumes that the old ruling classes would never voluntarily abdicate their position, that they would be the first to use violence against the revolution, and that revolutionary violence would be the defense against counterrevolutionary violence.

The theory of an educational, transitional dictatorship implies the paradoxical proposition that man must be "forced to be free." Political philosophy has always recognized the moral function of coercion (the coercive power of law, either above the sovereign or identical with the sovereign), but Rousseau pro-vides a radically new justification. Coercion is necessitated by the immoral, repressive conditions under which men live. The basic idea is: how can slaves who do not even know they are slaves free themselves? How can they liberate themselves by their own power, by their own faculties? How can they spontane-ously accomplish liberation? They must be taught and must be led to be free, and this the more so the more the society in which they live uses all available means in order to shape and preform their consciousness and to make it immune against possible alternatives. This idea of an educational, preparatory dictator-ship has today become an integral element of revolution and of the justification of the revolutionary oppression. The dictatorships which began as revolutionary dictatorships and then perpetuated themselves claim to be in their very essence and structure transitional and preparatory for a stage at which they can be abolished by virtue of their own achievements.

The main argument against the notion of the transitional dictatorship is usually condensed in the question: who educates the educators? By what right do those who actually exercise the dictatorship speak in the name of freedom and happiness as general conditions? This argument by itself is not sufficient, because in a lesser degree it applies even to non-authoritarian societies, where the policy-making top layer is not constantly and effectively controlled from below. However, even if we concede that the majority of men are not yet free today, and that their liberation cannot be spontaneous, the question still remains whether the dictatorial means are adequate to attain the end, namely, liberation. In other words the question of a transitional dictatorship cannot be separated from the general question of whether there can be such a thing as a moral justification of suppression and violence in a revolution. I shall now briefly discuss this question.

The historical revolutions were usually advocated and started in the name of freedom, or rather in the name of greater freedom for more strata of the population. We must first examine this claim strictly on empirical grounds. Human freedom is not and never has been a static condition but an historical condition, a process which involves the radical alteration, and even negation, of established ways of life. The form and content of freedom change with every new stage in the development of civilization, which is man's increasing mastery of man and nature. In both modes, mastery means domination, control; more effective control of nature makes for more effective control of man. Obviously, the possibilities of human freedom and happiness in advanced industrial society today are in no way comparable with those available, even theoretically avail-able, at preceding stages of history. Thus, with respect to the form, extent, degree and content of human freedom, we deal with strictly historical and changing conditions. We can say even more. Measured against the real possibili-ties of freedom, we always live in a state of relative unfreedom. The wide gap between real possibility and actuality, between the rational and the real has never been closed. Freedom always presupposes liberation, or a step from one state of freedom and unfreedom to a subsequent state. With the advance of technical progress, the later state is *potentially* (but by no means actually!) a *higher* stage, that is, quantitatively and qualitatively. But if this is the case, if freedom always presupposes liberation from unfree and unhappy conditions, it means that this liberation always offends against and ultimately subverts established and sanctioned institutions and interests. In history, they never abdicated voluntarily. Consequently, if and when freedom is a process of liberation, a transition from lower, more restricted forms of freedom to higher forms of freedom, then it always, no matter how, offends against the existing and established state of affairs. And precisely on this ground revolutionary violence has been most effectively justified as counterviolence, that is, as violence necessary in order to secure higher forms of freedom against the resistance of the established forms.

The ethics of revolution thus testifies to the clash and conflict of two historical rights: on the one side, the right of that which *is*, the established commonwealth on which the life and perhaps even the happiness of the individuals depend; and on the other side, the right of that which *can* be and perhaps even *ought* to be because it may reduce toil, misery, and injustice, provided always that this chance can be demonstrated as a real possibility. Such a demonstration must provide rational criteria; we can now add: these must be *historical* criteria. As such, they amount to an "historical calculus," namely, calculation of the chances of a future society as against the chances of the existing society with respect to human progress, that is to say, technical and material progress used in such a way that it increases individual freedom and happiness. Now if such an historical calculus is to have any rational basis, it must, on the one side, take into account the sacrifices exacted from the living generations on behalf of the established society, the established law and order, the number of victims made in defense of this society in war and peace, in the struggle for existence, individual and national. The calculus would further have to take into account the intellectual and material resources available to the society and the manner in which they are actually used with respect to their full capacity of satisfying vital human needs and pacifying the struggle for existence. On the other side, the historical calculus would have to project the chances of the contesting revolutionary movement of improving the prevailing conditions, namely, whether the revolutionary plan or program demonstrates the technical, material, and mental possibility of reducing the sacrifices and the number of victims. Even prior to the question as to the possibility of such a calculus (which, I believe, does exist), its inhuman quantifying character is evident. But its inhumanity is that of history itself, token of its empirical, rational foundation. No hypocrisy should from the beginning distort the examination. Nor is this brutal calculus an empty intellectual abstraction; in fact, at its decisive turns, history became such a calculated experiment.

The ethics of revolution, if there is such a thing, will therefore be in accordance not with absolute, but with historical standards. They do not cancel the validity of those general norms which formulate requirements for the progress of mankind toward humanity. No matter how rationally one may justify revolutionary means in terms of the demonstrable chance of obtaining freedom and happiness for future generations, and thereby justify violating existing rights and liberties and life itself, there are forms of violence and suppression which no revolutionary situation can justify because they negate the very end for which the revolution is a means. Such are arbitrary violence, cruelty, and indiscriminate terror. However, within the historical continuum, revolutions establish a moral and ethical code of their own and in this way become the origin, the fountainhead and source of new general norms and values. In fact some of today's most generally-professed values originated in revolutions, for example, the value of tolerance in the English Civil Wars, the inalienable rights of man in the American and French Revolutions. These ideas become an historical force, first as partial ideas, instruments of a revolutionary movement for specific political ends. Their realization originally involved violence; they then assumed not only partial political but general ethical validity and rejected violence. In this way, revolutions place themselves under ethical standards.

Violence *per se* has never been made a revolutionary value by the leaders of the historical revolutions. His contemporaries rejected Georges Sorel's attempt to cut the link between violence and reason, which was at the same time the attempt to free the class struggle from all ethical considerations. In comparing the violence of the class struggle in its revolutionary phase with the violence of military operations in war, he made the former subject to strategic calculations only: the end was the total defeat of the enemy; violence a means to attain this end—the relation between means and end was a technical one. Sorel's defense of violence this side of good and evil remained isolated from the revolutionary reality of his time; if he had any influence, it was on the side of the counter-revolution. Otherwise, violence was defended, not *per se*, but as part of rational suppression, suppression of counterrevolutionary activity, of established rights and privileges, and, for the society at large, of material and intellectual needs, that is, enforcement of austerity, rationing, censorship.

Now this suppression which includes violence is practiced in the interest of the objectives of the revolution, and these objectives are presented not only as political but also as moral values, ethical imperatives, namely greater freedom for the greater number of people. And in this sense the objectives and the ends of the revolution itself claim general validity and become subject to moral standards and evaluation.

Here we are confronted with the problem of all ethics, namely, the question as to the ultimate sanction of moral values. Or, in plain language, who or what determines the validity of ethical norms? The question becomes acute only with the secularization of the West; it was no problem in the Middle Ages as long as a transcendent sanction of ethics was accepted. The infidels could justly be exterminated, heretics could justly be burned—in spite of all protest. This was justice in terms of the prevailing values, which in turn were those of transcendent ethics. But today, where is the sanction of ethical values—sanction not in terms of the enforcement but in terms of the acceptance of ethical values, the proof of their validity? Sanction today, it seems, rests mainly in a precarious and flexible syndrome of custom, fear, utility, and religion; flexible because, within the syndrome, there is a large range of change. I refer, for example, to the high degree of liberalization in sexual morality which we have witnessed during the last thirty years, or, to the easy suspension of practically all ethical values in so-called emergency situations. The sanction and validity of ethical norms is thus restricted to the normal state of affairs in social and political relations.

Now in terms of the normal established state of affairs, a revolution is by definition immoral; it offends against the right of the existing commonwealth; it permits and even demands deception, cunning, suppression, destruction of life and property, and so on. But a judgment by definition is an inadequate judgment. Ethical standards by virtue of their imperative claim transcend any given state of affairs, and they transcend it, not to any metaphysical entities but to the historical continuum in which every given state of affairs has emerged, by which every given state of affairs is defined, and in which every given state of affairs will be altered and surpassed by other states. And in the historical continuum which defines its place and function, the ethics of revolution appeal to an historical calculus. Can the intended new society, the society intended by the revolution, offer better chances for progress in freedom than the existing society? In the historical continuum, these chances can only be measured by going beyond the given state of affairs, going beyond it not simply into an abstract vacuum of speculation, but going beyond it by calculating the resources, intellectual as well as material, scientific as well as technical, available to a given society, and projecting the most rational ways of utilizing these resources. Now if such projection is possible, then it can yield objective criteria for judging revolutions as to their historical function in terms of progress or regression, in terms of the development of *humanitas.*

A preliminary answer is suggested by a glance at the historical process itself. Historically, the objective tendency of the great revolutions of the modern period was the enlargement of the social range of freedom and the enlargement of the satisfaction of needs. No matter how much the social interpretations of the English and French Revolutions may differ, they seem to agree in that a redistribution of the social wealth took place, so that previously less privileged or under-privileged classes were the beneficiaries of this change, economically and/or politically. In spite of subsequent periods of reaction and restoration, the result and objective function of these revolutions was the establishment of more liberal governments, a gradual democratization of society, and technical progress. I said "objective function" because this evaluation of the revolution is obviously a judgment *ex post facto.* The intention and ideology of the leaders of the revolution, and the drives of the masses may have had quite different aims and motives. By virtue of their objective function, these revolutions attained progress in the sense defined, namely a demonstrable enlargement of the range of human freedom; they thus established, in spite of the terrible sacrifices exacted by them, an ethical right over and above all political justification.

But if such ethical right and its criteria are always and necessarily after the fact, it serves for nought and leaves us with the irrational choice of either *a priori* accepting or *a priori* rejecting all revolution. Now I submit that, while the historical function of a revolution becomes identifiable only after the fact, its prospective direction, progressive or regressive is, with the certainty of a reasonable *chance,* demonstrable *before* the fact—to the same degree to which the historical conditions of progress are demonstrable. For example, it could be demonstrated—and it was demonstrated before the fact—that the French Revolution of 1789 would give, in terms of the historical calculus, a better chance for the development of human freedom than the Ancien Régime. Contrariwise, it could be demonstrated, and was demonstrated long before the fact, that Fascist and National-Socialist regimes would do the exact opposite, namely, necessarily restrict the range of human freedom. Moreover, and I think this is a very important point, such demonstration of the historical *chances* before the fact becomes increasingly rational with the development of our scientific, technical, and material resources and capabilities, with our progress in the scientific mastery of man and nature. The possibilities and contents of freedom today are coming more and more under the control of man: they are becoming increasingly calculable. And with this advance in effective control and calculability, the inhuman distinction between violence and violence, sacrifice and sacrifice becomes increasingly rational. For throughout history, the happiness and freedom, and even the life of individuals, have been sacrificed. If we consider human life *per se* sacred under all conditions, the distinction is meaningless, and we have to admit that history is *per se* amoral and immoral, because it has never respected the sanctity of human life as such. But in fact we do distinguish between sacrifices which are legitimate and sacrifices which are not legitimate. This distinction is an historical one, and with this qualification, ethical standards are also applicable to violence.

Let me now recapitulate and reformulate. In absolute ethical terms, that is to say, in terms of suprahistorical validity, there is no justification for any suppression and sacrifice for the sake of future freedom and happiness, revolutionary or otherwise. But in historical terms we are confronted with a distinction and a decision. For suppression and sacrifice are daily exacted by all societies, and one cannot start—indeed I would like to say this with all possible emphasis—one cannot start becoming moral and ethical at an arbitrary but expedient point of cut off: the point of revolution. Who can quantify and who can compare the sacrifices exacted by an established society and those exacted by its subversion? Are ten thousand victims more ethical than twenty thousand? Such is in fact the inhuman arithmetic of history, and in this inhuman historical context operates the historical calculus. Calculable are the material and intellectual resources available, calculable are the productive and distributive facilities in a society, and the extent of unsatisfied vital needs and of satisfied non-vital needs. Quantifiable and calculable are the quantity and size of the labor force and of the population as a whole. That is the empirical material at the disposal of the historical calculus. And on the basis of this quantifiable material the question can be asked whether the available resources and capabilities are utilized most rationally, that is to say, with a view to the best possible satisfaction of needs under the priority of vital needs and with a minimum of toil, misery and injustice. If the analysis of a specific historical situation suggests a negative answer, if conditions exist in which technological rationality is impeded or even superseded by repressive political and social interests which define the general welfare, then the reversal of such conditions in favor of a more rational and human use of the available resources would also be a maximalization of the chance of progress in freedom. Consequently, a social and political movement in this direction would, in terms of the calculus, allow the presumption of historical justification. It can be no more than a presumption, subject to correction as the movement actually develops, reveals its potential and establishes new facts, or in other words, as it sustains or as it cuts the links between the means which the revolution employs and the end which it professes to attain.

And this leads to the last question which I want to raise here, namely, can the revolutionary end justify *all* means? Can we distinguish between rational and irrational, necessary and arbitrary, suppression? When can such suppression be called rational in terms of the objective of a respective revolution? I shall briefly illustrate the scope of this question by the Bolshevik Revolution. The professed objective of the Bolshevik Revolution was socialism. It implied the socialization of the means of production, the dictatorship of the proletariat as preparatory to a classless society. In the specific historical situation in which the Bolshevik Revolution occurred, socialism called for industrialization in competition with the advanced capitalist countries of the West, for the building up of the armed forces, and for propaganda on a global scale. Now can we apply a distinction between rational and irrational to these objectives and to the degree of suppression involved in them? In terms of the revolution, rational would be accelerated industrialization, the elimination of non-cooperative layers of management from the economy, the enforcement of work discipline, sacrifices in the satisfaction of needs imposed by the priority of heavy industry in the first stages of industrialization, and suspension of civil liberties if they were used for sabotaging these objectives. And we can reject, without long discussion, as not justifiable, even in terms of the revolution, the Moscow trials, the permanent terror, the concentration camps, and the dictatorship of the Party over the working classes. Futher examination would require introducing into the discussion the situation of global coexistence; but time forbids us to do so. We have also made abstraction from the human element in the leadership of the revolution, that is to say, from the so-called historical individuals.

And here I want to add one remark. It seems to me characteristic that, the more calculable and the more controllable the technical apparatus of modern industrial society becomes, the more does the chance of human progress depend on the intellectual and moral qualities of the leaders, and on their willingness and ability to educate the controlled population and to make it recognize the possibility, nay, the necessity of pacification and humanization. For today, the technical apparatus of advanced industrial society is in itself authoritarian, requiring service, submission, subordination to the objective mechanism of the machine system, that is to say, submission to those who control the apparatus. Technology has been made into a powerful instrument of streamlined domination—the more powerful the more it proves its efficiency and delivers the goods. And as such, it serves the politics of domination.

I come to the conclusion. The means-end relation is the ethical problem of revolution. In one sense, the end justifies the means, namely, if they demonstrably serve human progress in freedom. This legitimate end, the only legitimate end, demands the creation of conditions which would facilitate and expedite its realization. And the creation of these conditions may justify sacrifices, as it has justified sacrifices throughout history. But this relation between means and ends is a dialectical one. The end must be operative in the repressive means for attaining the end. But no matter how rational, how necessary, how liberating—revolution involves violence. The non-violent history is the promise and possibility of a society which is still to be fought for. At present, the triumphant violence seems to be on the other side.

Section II
Popular
Concerns

V. I. Lenin

V. I. Lenin (1870–1924) was the most important and influential
leader in the Russian revolution of October-November 1917. In
addition to pamphlets aimed at revolutionary and governmental
policy he wrote theoretical works on Marxism which form the
basis for the interpretation and expansion of Marx often referred
to as Marxism-Leninism. In the selection from *State and Revolution* which appears below, Lenin argues for his conception of
anarchism, which he said was the aim of political action. He
presents his argument as an explanation of Marx's writings.

State and Revolution

V. THE ECONOMIC BASIS FOR THE WITHERING AWAY OF THE STATE

A most detailed elucidation of this question is given by Marx in his *Critique
of the Gotha Programme* (letter to Bracke, May 15, 1875, printed only in 1891
in the *Neue Zeit*, IX—1, and in a special Russian edition). The polemical part of
this remarkable work, consisting of a criticism of Lassalleanism, has, so to speak,
overshadowed its positive part, namely, the analysis of the connection between
the development of Communism and the withering away of the state.

1. Formulation of the Question by Marx

From a superficial comparison of the letter of Marx to Bracke (May 15,
1875) with Engels' letter to Bebel (March 28, 1875), analysed above, it might
appear that Marx was much more "prostate" than Engels, and that the difference of opinion between the two writers on the question of the state is very
considerable.

Engels suggests to Bebel that all the chatter about the state should be thrown
overboard; that the word "state" should be eliminated from the programme and
replaced by "community". Engels even declares that the Commune was really no
longer a state in the proper sense of the word. And Marx even speaks of the
"future state in Communist society," *i.e.*, he is apparently recognising the
necessity of a state even under Communism.

But such a view would be fundamentally incorrect. A closer examination
shows that Marx's and Engels' views on the state and its withering away were

completely identical, and that Marx's expression quoted above refers merely to this withering away of the state.

It is clear that there can be no question of defining the exact moment of the *future* withering away—the more so as it must obviously be a rather lengthy process. The apparent difference between Marx and Engels is due to the different subjects they dealt with, the different aims they were pursuing. Engels set out to show to Bebel, in a plain, bold and broad outline, all the absurdity of the current superstitions concerning the state, shared to no small degree by Lassalle himself. Marx, on the other hand, only touches upon *this* question in passing, being interested mainly in another subject—the *evolution* of Communist society.

The whole theory of Marx is an application of the theory of evolution—in its most consistent, complete, well considered and fruitful form—to modern capitalism. It was natural for Marx to raise the question of applying this theory both to the *coming* collapse of capitalism and to the *future* evolution of *future* Communism.

On the basis of what *data* can the future evolution of future Communism be considered?

On the basis of the fact that *it has its origin* in capitalism, that it develops historically from capitalism, that it is the result of the action of a social force to which capitalism *has given birth.* There is no shadow of an attempt on Marx's part to conjure up a Utopia, to make idle guesses about that which cannot be known. Marx treats the question of Communism in the same way as a naturalist would treat the question of the evolution of, say, a new biological species, if he knew that such and such was its origin, and such and such the direction in which it changed.

Marx, first of all brushes aside the confusion the Gotha Programme brings into the question of the interrelation between state and society.

> "Contemporary society" is the capitalist society—he writes-which exists in all civilized countries, more or less free of mediaeval admixture, more or less modified by each country's particular historical development, more or less developed. In contrast with this, the "contemporary state" varies with every state boundary. It is different in the Prusso-German Empire from what it is in Switzerland, and different in England from what it is in the United States. The "contemporary state" is therefore a fiction. Nevertheless, in spite of the motley variety of their forms, the different states of the various civilised countries all have this in common: they are all based on modern bourgeois society, only a little more or less capitalistically developed. Consequently, they also have certain essential characteristics in common. In this sense, it is possible to speak of the "contemporary state" in contrast to the future, when its present root, bourgeois society, will have perished.
>
> Then the question arises: what transformation will the state undergo in a Communist society? In other words, what social functions analogous to the present functions of the state will then still survive? This question can only be answered scientifically, and however many thousand times the word people is combined with the word state, we get not a flea-jump closer to the problem. . . .

Having thus ridiculed all talk about a "people's state," Marx formulates the question and warns us, as it were, that to arrive at a scientific answer one must rely only on firmly established scientific data.

The first fact that has been established with complete exactness by the whole theory of evolution, by science as a whole—a fact which the Utopians forgot, and which is forgotten by the present-day opportunists who are afraid of the Socialist revolution—is that, historically, there must undoubtedly be a special stage or epoch of *transition* from capitalism to Communism.

2. Transition from Capitalism to Communism

> Between capitalist and Communist society—Marx continues—lies the period of the revolutionary transformation of the former into the latter. To this also corresponds a political transition period, in which the state can be no other than *the revolutionary dictatorship of the proletariat.*

This conclusion Marx bases on an analysis of the rôle played by the proletariat in modern capitalist society, on the data concerning the evolution of this society, and on the irreconcilability of the opposing interests of the proletariat and the bourgeoisie.

Earlier the question was put thus: to attain its emancipation, the proletariat must overthrow the bourgeoisie, conquer political power and establish its own revolutionary dictatorship.

Now the question is put somewhat differently: the transition from capitalist society, developing towards Communism, towards a Communist society, is impossible without a "political transition period," and the state in this period can only be the revolutionary dictatorship of the proletariat.

What, then, is the relation of this dictatorship to democracy?

We have seen that the *Communist Manifesto* simply places side by side the two ideas: the "transformation of the proletariat into the ruling class" and the "establishment of democracy." On the basis of all that has been said above, one can define more exactly how democracy changes in the transition from capitalism to Communism.

In capitalist society, under the conditions most favourable to its development, we have more or less complete democracy in the democratic republic. But this democracy is always bound by the narrow framework of capitalist exploitation, and consequently always remains, in reality, a democracy for the minority, only for the possessing classes, only for the rich. Freedom in capitalist society always remains just about the same as it was in the ancient Greek republics: freedom for the slave-owners. The modern wage-slaves, owing to the conditions of capitalist exploitation, are so much crushed by want and poverty that "democracy is nothing to them," "politics is nothing to them"; that, in the ordinary peaceful course of events, the majority of the population is debarred from participating in social and political life.

The correctness of this statement is perhaps most clearly proved by Germany, just because in this state constitutional legality lasted and remained stable for a remarkably long time—for nearly half a century (1871–1914)—and because Social-Democracy in Germany during that time was able to achieve far more than in other countries in "utilising legality," and was able to organise into a political party a larger proportion of the working class than anywhere else in the world.

What, then, is this largest proportion of politically conscious and active wage-slaves that has so far been observed in capitalist society? One million members of the Social-Democratic Party—out of fifteen million wage-workers! Three million organised in trade unions—out of fifteen million!

Democracy for an insignificant minority, democracy for the rich—that is the democracy of capitalist society. If we look more closely into the mechanism of capitalist democracy, everywhere, both in the "petty"—so-called petty—details of the suffrage (residential qualification, exclusion of women, etc.), and in the technique of the representative institutions, in the actual obstacles to the right of assembly (public buildings are not for "begars"!), in the purely capitalist organisation of the daily press, etc., etc.—on all sides we see restriction after restriction upon democracy. These restrictions, exceptions, exclusions, obstacles for the poor, seem slight, especially in the eyes of one who has himself never known want and has never been in close contact with the oppressed classes in their mass life (and nine-tenths, if not ninety-nine hundredths, of the bourgeois publicists and politicians are of this class), but in their sum total these restrictions exclude and squeeze out the poor from politics and from an active share in democracy.

Marx splendidly grasped this *essence* of capitalist democracy, when, in analysing the experience of the Commune, he said that the oppressed were allowed, once every few years, to decide which particular representatives of the oppressing class should be in parliament to represent and repress them!

But from this capitalist democracy—inevitably narrow, subtly rejecting the poor, and therefore hypocritical and false to the core—progress does not march onward, simply, smoothly and directly, to "greater and greater democracy," as the liberal professors and petty-bourgeois opportunists would have us believe. No, progress marches onward, *i.e.*, towards Communism, through the dictatorship of the proletariat; it cannot do otherwise, for there is no one else and no other way to *break the resistance* of the capitalist exploiters.

But the dictatorship of the proletariat—*i.e.*, the organisation of the vanguard of the oppressed as the ruling class for the purpose of crushing the oppressors—cannot produce merely an expansion of democracy. *Together* with an immense expansion of democracy which *for the first time* becomes democracy for the poor, democracy for the people and not democracy for the rich folk, the dictatorship of the proletariat produces a series of restrictions of liberty in the case of the oppressors, the exploiters, the capitalists. We must crush them in order to free humanity from wage-slavery; their resistance must be broken by force; it is clear that where there is suppression there is also violence, there is no liberty, no democracy.

Engles expressed this splendidly in his letter to Bebel when he said, as the reader will remember, that "as long as the proletariat still *needs* the state, it needs it not in the interests of freedom, but for the purpose of crushing its antagonists; and as soon as it becomes possible to speak of freedom, then the state, as such, ceases to exist."

Democracy for the vast majority of the people, and suppression by force, *i.e.*, exclusion from democracy, of the exploiters and oppressors of the people—this is the modification of democracy during the *transition* from capitalism to Communism.

Only in Communist society, when the resistance of the capitalists has been completely broken, when the capitalists have disappeared, when there are no classes (*i.e.*, there is no difference between the members of society in their relation to the social means of production), *only then* "the state ceases to exist," and "*it becomes possible to speak of freedom.*" Only then a really full democracy, a democracy without any exceptions, will be possible and will be realised. And only then will democracy itself begin to *wither away* due to the simple fact that, freed from capitalist slavery, from the untold horrors, savagery, absurdities and infamies of capitalist exploitation, people will gradually *become accustomed* to the observance of the elementary rules of social life that have been known for centuries and repeated for thousands of years in all school books; they will become accustomed to observing them without force, without compulsion, without subordination, without the *special apparatus* for compulsion which is called the state.

The expression "the state *withers away*," is very well chosen, for it indicates both the gradual and the elemental nature of the process. Only habit can, and undoubtedly will, have such an effect; for we see around us millions of times how readily people get accustomed to observe the necessary rules of life in common, if there is no exploitattion, if there is nothing that causes indignation, that calls forth protest and revolt and has to be *suppressed.*

Thus, in capitalist society, we have a democracy that is curtailed, poor, false; a democracy only for the rich, for the minority. The dictatorship of the proletariat, the period of transition to Communism, will, for the first time, produce democracy for the people, for the majority, side by side with the necessary suppression of the minority—the exploiters. Communism alone is capable of giving a really complete democracy, and the more complete it is the more quickly will it become unnecessary and wither away of itself.

In other words: under capitalism we have a state in the proper sense of the word, that is, special machinery for the suppression of one class by another, and of the majority by the minority at that. Naturally, for the successful discharge of such a task as the systematic suppression by the exploiting minority of the exploited majority, the greatest ferocity and savagery of suppression are required, seas of blood are required, through which mankind is marching in slavery, serfdom, and wage-labour.

Again, during the *transition* from capitalism to Communism, suppression is *still* necessary; but it is the suppression of the minority of exploiters by the majority of exploited. A special apparatus, special machinery for suppression, the "state," is *still* necessary, but this is now a transitional state, no longer a state in the usual sense, for the suppression of the minority of exploiters, by the majority of the wage slaves *of yesterday*, is a matter comparatively so easy, simple and natural that it will cost far less bloodshed that the suppression of the risings of slaves, serfs or wage labourers, and will cost mankind far less. This is compatible with the diffusion of democracy among such an overwhelming majority of the population, that the need for *special machinery* of suppression will begin to disappear. The exploiters are, naturally, unable to suppress the people without a most complex machinery for performing this task; but *the people* can suppress the exploiters even with very simple "machinery," almost without any "machinery," without any special apparatus, by the simple *organisation of the armed masses* (such as the Soviets of Workers' and Soldiers' Deputies, we may remark, anticipating a little).

Finally, only Communism renders the state absolutely unnecessary, for there is *no one* to be suppressed—"no one" in the sense of a *class*, in the sense of a systematic struggle with a definite section of the population. We are not Utopians, and we do not in the least deny the possibility and inevitability of excesses on the part of *individual persons*, nor the need to suppress *such* excesses. But, in the first place, no special machinery, no special apparatus of repression is needed for this; this will be done by the armed people itself, as simply and as readily as any crowd of civilised people, even in modern society, parts a pair of combatants or does not allow a woman to be outraged. And, secondly, we know that the fundamental social cause of excesses which consist in violating the rules of social life is the exploitation of the masses, their want and their poverty. With the removal of this chief cause, excesses will inevitably begin to *"wither away."* We do not know how quickly and in what succession, but we know that they will wither away. With their withering away, the state will also *wither away.*

Without going into Utopias, Marx defined more fully what can *now* be defined regarding this future, namely, the difference between the lower and higher phases (degrees, stages) of Communist society.

3. First Phase of Communist Society

In the *Critique of the Gotha Programme*, Marx goes into some detail to disprove the Lassallean idea of the workers' receiving under Socialism the "undiminished" or "full product of their labour." Marx shows that out of the whole of the social labour of society, it is necessary to deduct a reserve fund, a fund for the expansion of production, for the replacement of worn-out machinery, and so on; then, also, out of the means of consumption must be deducted a fund for the expenses of management, for schools, hospitals, homes for the aged, and so on.

Instead of the hazy, obscure, general phrase of Lassalle's—"the full product of his labour for the worker"—Marx gives a sober estimate of exactly how a Socialist society will have to manage its affairs. Marx undertakes a *concrete* analysis of the conditions of life of a society in which there is no capitalism and says:

> What we are dealing with here [analysing the programme of the party] is not a Communist society which has *developed* on its own foundations, but, on the contrary, one which is just *emerging* from capitalist society, and which therefore in all respects—economic, moral and intellectual—still bears the birthmarks of the old society from whose womb it sprung.

And it is this Communist society—a society which has just come into the world out of the womb of capitalism, and which, in all respects, bears the stamp of the old society—that Marx terms the "first," or lower, phase of Communist society.

The means of production are no longer the private property of individuals. The means of production belong to the whole of society. Every member of society, performing a certain part of socially-necessary work, receives a certificate from society to the effect that he has done such and such a quantity of work. According to this certificate, he receives from the public warehouses, where articles of consumption are stored, a corresponding quantity of products. Deducting that portion of labour which goes to the public fund, every worker, therefore, receives from society as much as he has given it.

"Equality" seems to reign supreme.

But when Lassalle, having in view such a social order (generally called Socialism, but termed by Marx the first phase of Communism), speaks of this as "just distribution," and says that this is "the equal right of each to an equal product of labour," Lassalle is mistaken, and Marx exposes his error.

"Equal right," says Marx, we indeed have here; but it is *still* a "bourgeois right," which, like every right, *presupposes inequality*. Every right is an application of the *same* measure to *different* people who, in fact, are not the same and are not equal to one another; this is why "equal right" is really a violation of equality, and an injustice. In effect, every man having done as much social labour as every other, receives an equal share of the social products (with the above-mentioned deductions).

But different people are not alike: one is strong, another is weak, one is married, the other is not; one has more children, another has less, and so on.

> ... With equal labour—Marx concludes—and therefore an equal share in the social consumption fund, one man in fact receives more than the other, one is richer than the other, and so forth. In order to avoid all these defects, rights, instead of being equal, must be unequal.

The first phase of Communism, therefore, still cannot produce justice and equality; differences, and unjust differences, in wealth will still exist, but the *exploitation* of man by man will have become impossible, because it will be impossible to seize as private property the *means of production*, the factories, machines, land, and so on. In tearing down Lassalle's petty-bourgeois, confused phrase about "equality" and "justice" *in general*, Marx shows the *course of development* of Communist society, which is forced at first to destroy *only* the "injustice" that consists in the means of production having been seized by private individuals, and which *is not capable* of destroying at once the further injustice consisting in the distribution of the articles of consumption "according to work performed" (and not according to need).

The vulgar economists, including the bourgeois professors and also "our" Tugan-Baranovsky, constantly reproach the Socialists with forgetting the inequality of people and with "dreaming" of destroying this inequality. Such a reproach, as we see, only proves the extreme ignorance of the gentlemen propounding bourgeois ideology.

Marx not only takes into account with the greatest accuracy the inevitable inequality of men; he also takes into account the fact that the mere conversion of the means of production into the common property of the whole of society ("Socialism" in the generally accepted sense of the word) *does not remove* the defects of distribution and the inequality of "bourgeois right" which *continue to rule* as long as the products are divided "according to work performed."

> But these defects—Marx continues—are unavoidable in the first phase of Communist society, when, after long travail, it first emerges from capitalist society. Justice can never rise superior to the economic conditions of society and the cultural development conditioned by them.

And so, in the first phase of Communist society (generally called Socialism) "bourgeois right" is *not* abolished in its entirety, but only in part, only in proportion to the economic transformation so far attained, *i.e.*, only in respect of the means of production. "Bourgeois right" recognises them as the private property of separate individuals. Socialism converts them into common property. *To that extent*, and to that extent alone, does "bourgeois right" disappear.

However, it continues to exist as far as its other part is concerned; it remains in the capacity of regulator (determining factor) distributing the products and allotting labour among the members of society. "He who does not work, shall not eat"—this Socialist principle is *already* realised; "for an equal quantity of labour, an equal quantity of products"—this Socialist principle is also *already* realised. However, this is not yet Communism, and this does not abolish "bourgeois right," which gives to unequal individuals, in return for an unequal (in reality unequal) amount of work, an equal quantity of products.

This is a "defect," says Marx, but it is unavoidable during the first phase of Communism; for, if we are not to fall into Utopianism, we cannot imagine that, having overthrown capitalism, people will at once learn to work for society *without any standards of right*; indeed, the abolition of capitalism *does not immediately lay* the economic foundations for *such* a change.

And there is no other standard yet than that of "bourgeois right." To this extent, therefore, a form of state is still necessary, which, while maintaining public ownership of the means of production, would preserve the equality of labour and equality in the distribution of products.

The state is withering away in so far as there are no longer any capitalists, any classes, and, consequently, no *class* can be suppressed.

But the state has not yet altogether withered away, since there still remains the protection of "bourgeois right" which sanctifies actual inequality. For the complete extinction of the state, complete Communism is necessary.

Higher Phase of Communist Society

Marx continues:

> In a higher phase of Communist society, when the enslaving subordination of individuals in the division of labour has disappeared, and with it also the antagonism between mental and physical labour; when labour has become not only a means of living, but itself the first necessity of life; when, along with the all-round development of individuals, the productive forces too have grown, and all the springs of social wealth are flowing more freely—it is only at that stage that it will be possible to pass completely beyond the narrow horizon of bourgeois rights, and for society to inscribe on its banners: from each according to his ability; to each according to his needs!

Only now can we appreciate the full correctness of Engels' remarks in which he mercilessly ridiculed all the absurdity of combining the words "freedom" and "state." While the state exists there is no freedom. When there is freedom, there will be no state.

The economic basis for the complete withering away of the state is that high stage of development of Communism when the antagonism between mental and physical labour disappears, that is to say, when one of the principal sources of modern *social* inequality disappears—a source, moreover, which it is impossible to remove immediately by the mere conversion of the means of production into public property, by the mere expropriation of the capitalists.

This expropriation will make a gigantic development of the productive forces *possible*. And seeing how incredibly, even now, capitalism *retards* this development, how much progress could be made even on the basis of modern technique at the level it has reached, we have a right to say, with the fullest confidence, that the expropriation of the capitalists will inevitably result in a gigantic development of the productive forces of human society. But how rapidly this development will go forward, how soon it will reach the point of breaking away from the division of labour, of removing the antagonism between mental and physical labour, of transforming work into the "first necessity of life"—this we do not and *cannot* know.

Consequently, we have a right to speak solely of the inevitable withering away of the state, emphasising the protracted nature of this process and its dependence upon the rapidity of development of the *higher phase* of Communism; leaving quite open the question of lengths of time, or the concrete forms of withering away, since material for the solution of such questions is *not available*.

The state will be able to wither away completely when society has realised the rule: "From each according to his ability; to each according to his needs," *i.e.*, when people have become accustomed to observe the fundamental rules of social life, and their labour is so productive, that they voluntarily work *according to their ability*. "The narrow horizon of bourgeois rights," which compels one to calculate, with the hard-heartedness of a Shylock, whether he has not worked half an hour more than another, whether he is not getting less pay than another—this narrow horizon will then be left behind. There will then be no need for any exact calculation by society of the quantity of products to be distributed to each of its members; each will take freely "according to his needs."

From the bourgeois point of view, it is easy to declare such a social order "a pure Utopia," and to sneer at the Socialists for promising each the right to receive from society without any control of the labour of the individual citizen, any quantity of truffles, automobiles, pianos, etc. Even now, most bourgeois "savants" deliver themselves of such sneers, thereby displaying at once their ignorance and their self-seeking defence of capitalism.

Ignorance—for it has never entered the head of any Socialist to "promise" that the highest phase of Communism will arrive; while the great Socialists, in *foreseeing* its arrival, presupposed both a productivity of labour unlike the present and a person not like the present man in the street, capable of spoiling, without reflection, like the seminary students in Pomyalovsky's book, the stores of social wealth, and of demanding the impossible.

Until the "higher" phase of Communism arrives, the Socialists demand the *strictest* control, *by society and by the state*, of the quantity of labour and the quantity of consumption; only this control must *start* with the expropriation of the capitalists, with the control of the workers over the capitalists, and must be carried out, not by a state of bureaucrats, but by a state of *armed workers*.

Self-seeking defence of capitalism by the bourgeois ideologists (and their hangers-on like Tsereteli, Chernov and Co.) consists in that they *substitute* disputes and discussions about the distant future for the essential imperative questions of present-day policy: the expropriation of the capitalists, the conversion of *all* citizens into workers and employees of *one* huge "syndicate"—the whole state—and the complete subordination of the whole of the work of this syndicate to the really democratic state of the *Soviets of Workers' and Soldiers' Deputies.*

In reality, when a learned professor, and following him some philistine, and following the latter Messrs. Tsereteli and Chernov, talk of the unreasonable Utopians, of the demagogic promises of the Bolsheviks, of the impossibility of "introducing" Socialism, it is the higher stage or phase of Communism which they have in mind, and which no one has ever promised, or even thought of "introducing," for the reason that, generally speaking, it cannot be "introduced."

And here we come to that question of the scientific difference between Socialism and Communism, upon which Engels touched in his above-quoted discussion on the incorrectness of the name "Social-Democrat." The political difference between the first, or lower, and the higher phase of Communism will in time, no doubt, be tremendous; but it would be ridiculous to emphasise it now, under capitalism, and only, perhaps, some isolated Anarchist could invest it with primary importance (if there are still some people among the Anarchists who have learned nothing from the Plekhanov-like conversion of the Kropotkins, the Graveses, the Cornelissens, and other "leading lights" if Anarchism to social-chauvinism or Anarcho-*Jusquaubout*-ism as Ge, one of the few Anarchists still preserving honour and conscience, has expressed it).

But the scientific difference between Socialism and Communism is clear. What is generally called Socialism was termed by Marx the "first" or lower phase of Communist society. In so far as the means of production become *public* property, the word "Communism" is also applicable here, providing we do not forget that it is *not* full Communism. The great significance of Marx's elucidations consists in this: that here, too, he consistently applies materialist dialectics, the doctrine of evolution, looking upon Communism as something which evolves *out of* capitalism. Instead of artificial, "elaborate," scholastic definitions and profitless disquisitions on the meaning of words (what Socialism is, what Communism is), Marx gives an analysis of what may be called stages in the economic ripeness of Communism.

In its first phase or first stage Communism *cannot* as yet be economically ripe and entirely free of all tradition and of all taint of capitalism. Hence the interesting phenomenon of Communism retaining, in its first phase, "the narrow horizon of bourgeois rights." Bourgeois rights, with respect to distribution of articles of *consumption*, inevitably presupposes, of course, the existence of the *bourgeois state,* for rights are nothing without an apparatus capable of *enforcing* for a certain time not only bourgeois rights, but even the bourgeois state remains under Communism, without the bourgeoisie!

This may look like a paradox, or simple a dialectical puzzle for which Marxism is often blamed by people who would not make the least effort to study its extraordinarily profound content.

But, as a matter of fact, the old surviving in the new confronts us in life at every step, in nature as well as in society. Marx did not smuggle a scrap of "bourgeois" rights into Communism of his own accord, he indicated what is economically and politically inevitable in a society issuing *from the womb* of capitalism.

Democracy is of great importance for the working class in its struggle for freedom against the capitalists. But democracy is by no means a limit one may not overstep; it is only one of the stages in the course of development from feudalism to capitalism, and from capitalism to Communism.

Democracy means equality. The great significance of the struggle of the proletariat for equality, and the significance of equality as a slogan, are apparent, if we correctly interpret it as meaning the abolition of *classes*. But democracy means only *formal* equality. Immediately after the attainment of equality for all members of society *in respect of* the ownership of the means of production, that is, of equality of labour and equality of wages, there will inevitably arise before humanity the question of going further from formal equality to real equality, *i.e.*, to realising the rule, "From each according to his ability; to each according to his needs." By what stages, by means of what practical measures humanity will proceed to this higher aim—this we do not and cannot know. But it is important to realise how infinitely mendacious is the usual bourgeois presentation of Socialism as something lifeless, petrified, fixed once for all, whereas in reality, it is *only* with Socialism that there will commence a rapid, genuine, real mass advance, in which first the *majority* and then the whole of the population will take part—an advance in all domains of social and individual life.

Democracy is a form of the state—one of its varieties. Consequently, like every state, it consists in organised, systematic application of force against human beings. This on the one hand. On the other hand, however, it signifies the formal recognition of the equality of all citizens, the equal right of all to determine the structure and administration of the state. This, in turn, is connected with the fact that, at a certain stage in the development of democracy, it first rallies the proletariat as a revolutionary class against capitalism, and gives it an opportunity to crush, to smash to bits, to wipe off the face of the earth the bourgeois state machinery—even its republican variety: the standing army, the police, and bureaucracy; then it substitutes for all this a *more* democratic, but still a state machinery in the shape of armed masses of workers, which becomes transformed into universal participation of the people in the militia.

Here "quantity turns into quality": *such* a degree of democracy is bound up with the abandonment of the framework of bourgeois society, and the beginning of its Socialist reconstruction. If *every* one really takes part in the administration of the state, capitalism cannot retain its hold. In its turn, capitalism, as it develops, itself creates *prerequisites* for "every one" *to be able* really to take part in the administration of the state. Among such prerequisites are: universal literacy, already realised in most of the advanced capitalist countries, then the "training and disciplining" of millions of workers by the huge, complex, and socialised apparatus of the post-office, the railways, the big factories, large-scale commerce, banking, etc., etc.

With such *economic* prerequisites it is perfectly possible, immediately, within twenty-four hours after the overthrow of the capitalists and bureaucrats, to replace them, in the control of production and distribution, in the business of *control* of labour and products, by the armed workers, by the whole people in arms. (The question of control and accounting must not be confused with the question of the scientifically educated staff of engineers, agronomists and so on. These gentlemen work today, obeying the capitalists; they will work even better tomorrow, obeying the armed workers.)

Accounting and control—these are the *chief* things necessary for the organising and correct functioning of the *first phase* of Communist society. *All* citizens are here transformed into hired employees of the state, which is made up of the armed workers. *All* citizens become employees and workers of *one* national state "syndicate." All that is required is that they should work equally, should regularly do their share of work, and should receive equal pay. The accounting and control necessary for this have been *simplified* by capitalism to the utmost, till they have become the extraordinarily simple operations of watching, recording and issuing receipts, within the reach of anybody who can read and write and knows the first four rules of arithmetic.

When the *majority* of the people begin everywhere to keep such accounts and maintain such control over the capitalists (now converted into employees) and over the intellectual gentry, who still retain capitalist habits, this control will really become universal, general, national; and there will be no way of getting away from it, there will be "nowhere to go."

The whole of society will have become one office and one factory, with equal work and equal pay.

But this "factory" discipline, which the proletariat will extend to the whole of society after the defeat of the capitalists and the overthrow of the exploiters, is by no means our ideal, or our final aim. It is but a *foothold* necessary for the radical cleansing of society of all the hideousness and foulness of capitalist exploitation, *in order to advance further.*

From the moment when all members of society, or even only the overwhelming majority, have learned how to govern the state *themselves*, have taken this business into their own hands, have "established" control over the insignificant minority of capitalists, over the gentry with capitalist leanings, and the workers thoroughly demoralised by capitalism—from this moment the need for any government begins to disappear. The more complete the democracy, the nearer the moment when it begins to be unnecessary. The more democratic the "state" consisting of armed workers, which is "no longer a state in the proper sense of the word," the more rapidly does *every* state begin to wither away.

For when *all* have learned to manage, and independently are actually managing by themselves social production, keeping accounts, controlling the idlers, the gentlefolk, the swindlers and similar "guardians of capitalist traditions," then the escape from this national accounting and control will inevitably become so increasingly difficult, such a rare exception, and will probably be accompanied by such swift and severe punishment (for the armed workers are men of practical life, not sentimental intellectuals, and they will scarcely allow any one to trifle with them), that very soon the *necessity* of observing the simple, fundamental rules of every-day social life in common will have become a *habit.*

The door will then be wide open for the transition from the first phase of Communist society to its higher phase, and along with it to the complete withering away of the state.

Mao Tse-tung

Mao Tse-tung (b. 1893) was the leader in the Chinese Communists' long battle to assume control of China. He has been and perhaps still is the top Chinese leader. Like Lenin, he both theorized and acted; and also like Lenin, he adapted Marxs' theories and recommendations for an industrialized nineteenth-century country to situations in an essentially nonindustrialized country. The last three selections from Mao's work are self-explanatory. The first is Mao's own interpretation of "dialectical materialism"; in particular, he speaks to the question of how one is to deal with the conflicts which will arise in a nation under Communist rule.

Political Thought

ON THE CORRECT HANDLING OF CONTRADICTIONS AMONG THE PEOPLE[1]

Never has our country been so united as it is today. The victories of the bourgeois-democratic revolution and the socialist revolution, coupled with our achievements in socialist construction, have rapidly changed the face of old China. Now we see before us an even brighter future. The days of national disunity and turmoil, which the people detested, have gone forever. Led by the working class and the Communist Party, and united as one, our 600 million people are engaged in the great work of building socialism. . . . However, this does not mean that there are no longer any contradictions in our society. It would be naïve to imagine that there are no more contradictions. To do so would be to fly in the face of objective reality. We are confronted by two types of social contradictions—contradictions between ourselves and the enemy and contradictions among the people. These two types of contradictions are totally different in nature. . . .

The term "the people" has different meanings in different countries and in different historical periods in each country. . . . At this stage of building socialism, all classes, strata, and social groups that approve, support, and work for the

[1] Extracted from a speech of February 27, 1957, published (in revised form) on June 10, 1957, under the same title. My source was *Kuan-yü Cheng-ch'üeh Ch'u-li Jen-min Nei-pu Mao-tun ti Wen-t'i* (Peking: Jen Min Ch'u Pan She, 1960), pp. 1-6, 10, 25-28, 30-33.

Available translations: Mao Tse-tung. *On the Correct Handling of Contradictions Among the People.* Peking: Foreign Languages Press, 1957.

From *The Political Thought of Mao Tse-tung,* ed. and trans. by Stuart R. Schram. By permission of Frederick A. Praeger Co., New York. The footnotes citing sources of the material are those of the translator.

cause of socialist construction belong to the category of the people, while those social forces and groups that resist the socialist revolution and are hostile to and try to wreck socialist construction are enemies of the people.

The contradictions between ourselves and our enemies are antagonistic ones. Within the ranks of the people, contradictions among the working people are nonantagonistic, whereas those between the exploiters and exploited classes have a nonantagonistic aspect as well as an antagonistic one.... In the conditions existing in China today what we call contradictions among the people include the following: contradictions within the working class, contradictions within the peasantry, contradictions within the intelligentsia, contradictions between the working class and the peasantry, contradictions between the working class and other sections of the working people on the one hand and the national bourgeoisie on the other, contradictions within the national bourgeoisie, and so forth. Our people's government is a government that truly represents the interests of the people and serves the people, yet certain contradictions do exist between the government and the masses. These include contradictions between the interests of the state, collective interests, and individual interests; between democracy and centralism; between those in positions of leadership and the led; and contradictions arising from the bureaucratic practices of certain state functionaries in their relations with the masses. All these are contradictions among the people. Generally speaking, underlying the contradictions among the people is the basic identity of the interests of the people.

In our country, the contradiction between the working class and the national bourgeoisie is a contradiction among the people.... This is because of the dual character of the national bourgeoisie in our country.... Exploitation of the working class for profit is one aspect, while support of the Constitution and willingness to accept socialist transformation is the other.... The contradiction between exploiter and exploited that exists between the national bourgeoisie and the working class is in itself an antagonistic one. But, in the concrete conditions existing in China, such an antagonistic contradiction, if properly handled, can be transformed into a nonantagonistic one and resolved in a peaceful way. But if it is not properly handled, if, say, we do not follow a policy of uniting with, criticizing, and educating the national bourgeoisie, or if the national bourgeoisie does not accept this policy, then the contradiction between the working class and the national bourgeoisie can turn into an antagonistic contradiction as between ourselve and the enemy....

Our state is a state of the people's democratic dictatorship, led by the working class and based on the worker-peasant alliance. What is this dictatorship for? Its first function is to suppress the reactionary classes and elements and those exploiters in the country who range themselves against the socialist revolution, to suppress all those who try to wreck our socialist construction, that is to say, to solve the contradictions between ourselves and the enemy within the country....

The second function of this dictatorship is to protect our country from subversive activities and possible aggression by the external enemy....

Our constitution states that citizens of the People's Republic of China enjoy freedom of speech, of the press, of assembly, of association, of procession, of religious practices, and so on.... Our socialist democracy is democracy in the widest sense, such as is not to be found in any capitalist country...

But this freedom is freedom with leadership and this democracy is democracy under centralized guidance, not anarchy. Anarchy does not conform to the interests or wishes of the people.

Certain people in our country were delighted when the Hungarian events took place. They hoped that something similar would happen in China, that thousands upon thousands of people would demonstrate in the streets against the People's Government. Such hopes ran counter to the interests of the masses and therefore could not possibly get their support. In Hungary, a section of the people, deceived by domestic and foreign counterrevolutionaries, made the mistake of resorting to acts of violence against the people's government, with the result that both the state and the people suffered for it. . . .

Democracy sometimes seems to be an end, but it is in fact only a means. Marxism teaches us that democracy is part of the superstructure and belongs to the realm of politics. That is to say, in the last analysis, it serves the economic base. The same is true of freedom. Both democracy and freedom are relative, not absolute, and they come into being and develop under specific historical circumstances. Within the ranks of our people, democracy stands in relation to centralism, and freedom to discipline. They are two conflicting aspects of a single entity, contradictory as well as united, and we should not one-sidedly emphasize one to the detriment of the other. Within the ranks of the people, we cannot do without freedom, nor can we do without discipline; we cannot do without democracy, nor can we do without centralism. . . . Under democratic centralism, the people enjoy a wide measure of democracy and freedom, but at the same time they have to keep themselves within the bounds of socialist discipline. All this is well understood by the masses of the people.

While we stand for freedom with leadership and democracy under centralized guidance, in no sense do we mean that coercive measures should be taken to settle ideological matters and questions involving the distinction between right and wrong among the people. Any attempt to deal with ideological matters or questions involving right and wrong by administrative orders or coercive measures will not only be ineffective but harmful. . . . Administrative orders issued for the maintenance of social order must be accompanied by persuasion and education, for in many cases administrative orders alone will not work. . . .

Contradictions in a socialist society are fundamentally different from contradictions in old societies, such as capitalist society. Contradictions in capitalist society find expression in acute antagonisms and conflicts, in sharp class struggle, which cannot be resolved by the capitalist system itself, but only by socialist revolution. But contradictions in socialist society are not antagonistic and can be resolved one after the other by the socialist system itself.

The basic contradictions in socialist society are still those between the relations of production and the productive forces, and between the superstructure and the economic base. . . .

"Let a hundred flowers bloom," and "let a hundred schools contend," "long-term coexistence and mutual supervision"—how did these slogans come to be?

They were put forward in the light of the specific conditions in China, on the basis of the recognition that various kinds of contradictions still exist in a socialist society, and in response to the country's urgent need to speed up its economic and cultural development.

The policy of letting a hundred flowers bloom and a hundred schools contend is designed to promote the flourishing of the arts and the progress of science; it is designed to enable socialist culture to thrive in our land. . . .

Questions of right and wrong in the arts and sciences should be settled through free discussion in artistic and scientific circles and in the course of practical work in the arts and sciences. They should not be settled in summary fashion. A trial period is often needed to determine whether something is right or wrong. In the past, new and correct things often failed at the outset to win recognition from the majority of people and had to develop by twists and turns in struggle. . . . Copernicus' theory of the solar system and Darwin's theory of evolution were once dismissed as erroneous and had to win over bitter opposition. Chinese history offers many similar examples. In a socialist society, conditions for the growth of new things are radically different from and far superior to those in the old society. Nevertheless, it still often happens that new, rising forces are held back and reasonable suggestions smothered. . . .

Marxism has also developed through struggle. At the beginning, Marxism was subjected to all kinds of attack and regarded as a poisonous weed. It is still being attacked and regarded as a poisonous weed in many parts of the world. But in the socialist countries it enjoys a different position. Yet even in these countries there are non-Marxist as well as anti-Marxist ideologies. . . . In China . . . remnants of the overthrown landlord and comprador classes still exist, the bourgeoisie still exists, and the petty bourgeoisie has only just begun to remold itself. The class struggle is not yet finished. The class struggle between the proletariat and the bourgeoisie, the class struggle between various political forces, and the class struggle in the ideological field between the proletariat and the bourgeoisie will still be long and arduous and at times may even become very acute. The proletariat seeks to transform the world according to its own world outlook. So does the bourgeoisie. In this respect, the question whether socialism or capitalism will win is still not really settled. Marxists are still a minority of the entire population as well as of the intellectuals. Marxism therefore must still develop through struggle. . . . That which is correct always develops in the course of struggling against that which is wrong. . . . As mankind in general rejects an untruth and accepts a truth, a new truth will begin struggling with new erroneous ideas. Such struggles will never end. This is the law of the development of truth and it is certainly also the law of the development of Marxism. . . .

Ideological struggle is not like other forms of struggle, Crude, coercive methods should not be used in this struggle, only the method of painstaking reasoning. Today, socialism enjoys favorable conditions in the ideological struggle. The main power of the state is in the hands of the working people led by the proletariat. The Communist Party is strong and its prestige stands high. Although there are defects and mistakes in our work, every fair-minded person can see that we are loyal to the people, that we are both determined and able to build up our country together with the people, and that we have achieved great successes and will achieve still greater ones. The vast majority of the bourgeoisie and intellectuals who come from the old society are patriotic; they are willing to serve their flourishing socialist motherland, and they know that if they turn away from the socialist cause and the working people led by the Communist Party, they will have no one to rely on and no bright future to look forward to.

People may ask: Since Marxism is accepted by the majority of the people in our country as the guiding ideology, can it be criticized? Certainly it can. Marxism, being a scientific truth, fears no criticism.... Quite the contrary. Marxists need to steel and improve themselves and win new positions in the teeth of criticism and the storm and stress of struggle. Fighting against wrong ideas is like being vaccinated—a man develops greater immunity from disease after the vaccine takes effect. Plants raised in hothouses are not likely to be robust. Carrying out the policy of letting a hundred flowers bloom and a hundred schools contend will strengthen, not weaken the leading position of Marxism in the ideological field.

What should our policy be toward non-Marxist ideas? As far as unregenerate counterrevolutionaries and wreckers of the socialist cause are concerned, the matter is easy: We simply deprive them of their freedom of speech. But it is quite a different matter when we are faced with incorrect ideas among the people.... It is not only futile but very harmful to use crude and summary methods to deal with ideological questions among the people, with questions relating to the spiritual life of man. You may ban the expression of wrong ideas, but the ideas will still be there. On the other hand, correct ideas, if pampered in hothouses without exposure to the elements or immunization against disease, will not win out against wrong ones. ...

What, from the point of view of the broad masses of the people, should be the criteria today for distinguishing between fragrant flowers and poisonous weeds? ...

Basing ourselves on the principles of our Constitution, the will of the overwhelming majority of our people and the political programs jointly proclaimed on various occasions by our political parties and groups, we believe that, broadly speaking, words and actions can be judged right if they:

1. Help to unite the people of our various nationalities rather than divide them:
2. Are beneficial, not harmful, to socialist transformation and socialist construction;
3. Help to consolidate, not undermine or weaken, the people's democratic dictatorship;
4. Help to consolidate, not undermine or weaken, democratic centralism;
5. Tend to strengthen, not to cast off or weaken, the leadership of the Communist Party;
6. Are beneficial, not harmful, to international socialist solidarity and the solidarity of the peace-loving peoples of the world.

Of these six criteria, the most important are the socialist path and the leadership of the Party.... These are political criteria. Naturally, in judging the truthfulness of scientific theories or assessing the aesthetic value of works of art, other pertinent criteria are needed, but these six political criteria are also applicable to all activities in the arts or sciences. In a socialist country like ours, can there possibly be any useful scientific or artistic activity that runs counter to these political criteria? ...

In 1956, small numbers of workers and students in certain places went on strike. The immediate cause of these disturbances was the faillure to satisfy certain of their demands for material benefits, of which some should and could be met, while others were out of place or excessive, and therefore could not be met for the time being. But a more important cause was the bureaucratism of those in positions of leadership. In some cases, responsibility for such bureaucratic mistakes should be placed on the higher authorities, and those at lower levels should not be made to bear all the blame. Another cause for these disturbances was the inadequacy of the ideological and political educational work done among the workers and students. In the same year, members of a small number of agricultural cooperatives also created disturbances, and the main causes were also bureaucratism on the part of the leadership and lack of educational work among the masses. . . .

We do not approve of disturbances, because contradictions among the people can be resolved in accordance with the formula "unity—criticism—unity," while disturbances inevitably cause losses and are detrimental to the advance of socialism. . . . With regard to this question, we should pay attention to the following:

1. In order to get rid of the root cause of disturbances, we must stamp out bureaucratism, greatly improve ideological and political education, and deal with all contradictions in a proper way. If this is done, there usually will not be any disturbances.

2. If disturbances should occur as a result of bad work on our part, then we should guide those involved in such disturbances toward the correct path, make use of these disturbances as a special means of improving our work and educating the cadres and the masses, and work out solutions to questions neglected in the past. . . . The guiding spirits of disturbances should not be removed from their jobs or expelled without good reason, except for those who have committed criminal offenses or active counterrevolutionaries who should be dealt with according to law. In a big country like ours, it is nothing to get alarmed about if small numbers of people create disturbances; rather we should turn such things to advantage to help us get rid of bureaucratism.

In our society, there is . . . a small number of people who, unmindful of public interests, refuse to listen to reason, commit crimes, and break the law. They may take advantage of our policies and distort them, deliberately put forward unreasonable demands in order to stir up the masses, or deliberately spread rumors to create trouble and disrupt social order. We do not propose to let these people have their way. On the contrary, proper legal action must be taken against them. The masses demand that these persons be punished. Not to do so would run counter to popular will. . . .

GUERRILLA WARFARE IS THE INEVITABLE PATH[2]

. . . .What is guerrilla warfare? It is, in a backward country, in a big semi-colonial country, and for a long period of time, the inevitable and therefore the best form of struggle for the people's armed forces to overcome the armed enemy and create their own strongholds. For eighteen years the political line and the building of our Party have been closely linked with this form of struggle. Apart from armed struggle, apart from guerrilla warfare, it is impossible to understand our political line, and consequently, to understand our Party-build-

[2] Extracted from an editorial for the first issue of *The Communist*, an intraparty journal, October 1939. (*Hsüan Chi* [1947], Supplement, pp. 47-48.)

ing. . . . We know that in China there would be no place for the proletariat, no place for the people, no place for the Communist Party, and no victory for the revolution without armed struggle. For eighteen years the development, consolidation, and Bolshevization of our Party have been undertaken in the midst of revolutionary wars *and have been inseparable from guerrilla warfare.* Without armed struggle, *without guerrilla warfare,* there would not have been such a Communist Party as exists today. Comrades throughout the Party must never forget this experience gained at the cost of blood.

REACTIONARIES AND ATOM BOMBS ARE PAPER TIGERS[3]

. . . I do not mean to say that the U.S. reactionaries have no intention of attacking the Soviet Union. The Soviet Union is a defender of world peace and a powerful factor in preventing the domination of the world by U.S. reactionaries. . . . That is why the U.S. reactionaries rabidly hate the Soviet Union and actually dream of destroying this socialist state. . . . I think the American people and the peoples of all countries menaced by U.S. aggression should unite and struggle against the attacks of the U.S. reactionaries and their running dogs in these countries. Only by victory in this struggle can a third world war be avoided; otherwise it is unavoidable.

Strong: That is well put. But suppose the United States uses the atom bomb? Suppose the United States bombs the Soviet Union from its bases in Iceland, Okinawa, and China?

Mao: The atom bomb is a paper tiger used by the U.S. reactionaries to scare people. It looks terrible, but in fact it isn't. Of course, the atomb bomb is a weapon of mass slaughter, but the outcome of a war is decided by the people, not by one or two new types of weapon.

All reactionaries are paper tigers. In appearance, the reactionaries are terrifying, but in reality they are not so powerful. From a long-range point of view, it is not the reactionaries but the people who are really powerful. In Russia, before the February Revolution of 1917, which side was really strong? On the surface the Czar seemed strong, but he was swept away by a single gust of wind in the February Revolution. In the final analysis, the strength in Russia was on the side of the Soviets of Workers, Peasants, and Soldiers. The Czar was merely a paper tiger. Wasn't Hitler once considered very strong? But history proved that he was a paper tiger. So was Mussolini, so was Japanese imperialism. But the strength of the Soviet Union and of the people in all countries who loved democracy and freedom proved much greater than had been foreseen.

Chiang Kai-shek and his supporters, the U.S. reactionaries, are all paper tigers, too. Speaking of U.S. imperialism, people seem to feel that it is terrifically strong. . . . But it will be proved that the U.S. reactionaries, like all the reactionaries in history, do not have much strength. In the United States there are others who are really strong—the American people.

Take the case of China. We have only millet plus rifles to rely on, but ultimately history will prove that our millet plus rifles is more powerful than

[3] Extracts from Mao's interview with Anna Louise Strong, August 1946. (*Hsüan Chi,* IV, pp. 1192-93.)

Available translations: Mao Tse-tung. *Selected Works.* Vol IV. Peking: Foreign Languages Press, 1961, pp. 100-101.

Chiang Kai-shek's aeroplanes plus tanks. Although the Chinese people still face many difficulties and will long suffer hardships from the joint attacks of U.S. imperialism and the Chinese reactionaries, the day will come when these reactionaries are defeated and we are victorious. The reason is simply this: The reactionaries represent reaction, we represent progress.

AMERICAN IMPERIALISM IS SITTING ON A VOLCANO[4]

... America's strength is superficial and transient. The crisis is like a volcano that menaces American imperialism every day. American imperialism is sitting on this volcano. This situation has driven the American imperialists to draw up a plan for enslaving the world; to run amuck like wild beasts in Europe, Asia, and other parts of the world; to muster the reactionary forces in all countries, the human dregs cast off by their peoples; to form an imperialist, antidemocratic camp against all the democratic forces headed by the Soviet Union; and to prepare for war in the hope that in the future, at a distant time, some day, they can start a third world war to defeat the democratic forces. This is a preposterous plan. The democratic forces of the world must and certainly can defeat this plan. The strength of the world anti-imperialist camp has surpassed that of the imperialist camp. It is we, not the enemy, who are in the superior position. The anti-imperialist camp headed by the Soviet Union has already been formed. The socialist Soviet Union is free from crises, on the ascendancy, and cherished by the world's broad masses; its strength has already surpassed that of the imperialist United States, which is seriously menaced by crises, on the decline, and opposed by the world's broad masses. The people's democracies in Europe are consolidating themselves internally and are uniting with each other. In the European capitalist countries the people's anti-imperialist forces are developing, with those in France and Italy taking the lead. Within the United States, there are people's democratic forces that are getting stronger every day. The peoples of Latin America are not slaves obedient to U.S. imperialism. In the whole of Asia a great national liberation movement has arisen. All the forces of the anti-imperialist camp are uniting and forging ahead. The Communist and workers' parties of nine European countries have established their Information Bureau and issued a call to the people of the world to rise against the imperialist plan of enslavement. This call to battle has inspired the oppressed people of the world, charted the course of their struggle, and strengthened their confidence in victory. It has thrown world reaction into panic and confusion. All the anti-imperialist forces in the countries of the East, too, should unite, oppose oppression by imperialism and by their domestic reactionaries, and make the emancipation of the more than one billion oppressed people of the East the goal of their struggle. We must grasp our own destiny in our own hands. We should rid our ranks of all impotent thinking. All views that overestimate the strength of the enemy and underestimate the strength of the people are wrong. If everyone makes strenuous efforts, we, together with all the democratic forces of the world, can surely defeat the imperialist plan of enslavement, prevent the

[4] Extracted from a report of December 25, 1947 (see note to Text VI). Available translations. Mao Tse-tung. *Selected Works.* Vol IV. Peking: Foreign Languages Press, 1961, pp. 172-73.

outbreak of a third world war, overthrow all reactionary regimes, and win lasting peace for mankind.... This is the historic epoch in which world capitalism and imperialism are going down to their doom and world socialism and democracy[5] are marching to victory. The dawn is in sight, we must exert ourselves.

Benito Mussolini

Benito Mussolini (1883–1945) was the Fascist leader of Italy from 1919 to 1945 (actually in power from 1921-1945). The following is an explanation of fascist ideals.

Fundamental Ideas

Like all sound political conceptions, fascism is action and it is thought; action in which doctrine is immanent, and doctrine arising from a given system of historical forces in which it is inserted, and working on them from within. It has therefore a form correlated to contingencies of time and space; but it has also an ideal content which makes it an expression of truth in the higher region of the history of thought. There is no way of exercising a spiritual influence in the world as a human will dominating the will of others unless one has a conception both of the transient and the specific reality on which that action is to be exercised, and of the permanent and universal reality in which the transient dwells and has its being. To know men one must know man; and to know man one must be acquainted with reality and its laws. There can be no conception of the State which is not fundamentally a conception of life: philosophy or intuition, system of ideas evolving within the framework of logic or concentrated in a vision or a faith, but always, at least potentially, an organic conception of the world.

Thus many of the practical expressions of fascism—such as party organization, system of education, discipline—can only be understood when considered in relation to its general attitude toward life, a spiritual attitude. Fascism sees in the world not only those superficial, material aspects in which man appears as an individual, standing by himself, self-centered, subject to natural law which instinctively urges him toward a life of selfish momentary pleasure; it sees not only the individual but the nation and the country; individuals and generations

[5] In the current edition, this reads "people's democracy."

bound together by a moral law, with common traditions and a mission which, suppressing the instinct for life closed in a brief circle of pleasure, builds up a higher life, founded on duty, a life free from the limitations of time and space, in which the individual by self-sacrifice, the renunciation of self-interest, by death itself can achieve that purely spiritual existence in which his value as a man consists.

The conception is therefore a spiritual one, arising from the general reaction of the century against the flaccid materialistic positivism of the nineteenth century. Anti-positivistic but positive; neither skeptical nor agnostic; neither pessimistic nor supinely optimistic as are, generally speaking, the doctrines (all negative) which place the center of life outside man; whereas, by the exercise of his free will, man can and must create his own world.

Fascism wants man to be active and to engage in action with all his energies; it wants him to be manfully aware of the difficulties besetting him and ready to face them. It conceives of life as a struggle in which it behooves a man to win for himself a really worthy place, first of all by fitting himself (physically, morally, intellectually) to become the implement required for winning it. As for the individual, so for the nation and so for mankind. Hence the high value of culture in all its forms (artistic, religious, scientific), and the outstanding importance of education. Hence also the essential value of work, by which man subjugates nature and creates the human world (economic, political, ethical, intellectual).

This positive conception of life is obviously an ethical one. It invests the whole field of reality as well as the human activities which master it. No action is exempt from moral judgment; no activity can be despoiled of the value which a moral purpose confers on all things. Therefore life, as conceived of by the fascist, is serious, austere, religious; all its manifestations are poised in a world sustained by moral forces and subject to spiritual responsibilities. The fascist disdains an "easy" life.

The fascist conception of life is a religious one, in which man is viewed in his immanent relation to a higher law, endowed with an objective will transcending the individual and raising him to conscious membership in a spiritual society. Those who perceive nothing beyond opportunistic considerations in the religious policy of the fascist regime fail to realize that fascism is not only a system of government but also and above all a system of thought.

In the fascist conception of history, man is man only by virtue of the spiritual process to which he contributes as a member of the family, the social group, the nation, and in the function of history to which all nations bring their contribution. Hence the great value of tradition in records, in language, in customs, in the rules of social life. Outside history man is a nonentity. Fascism is therefore opposed to all individualistic abstractions based on eighteenth-century materialism; and it is opposed to all Jacobinistic utopias and innovations. It does not believe in the possibility of "happiness" on earth as conceived by the economistic literature of the eighteenth century, and it therefore rejects the teleological notion that at some future time the human family will secure a final settlement of all its difficulties. This notion runs counter to experience which teaches that life is in continual flux and in process of evolution. In politics fascism aims at realism; in practice it desires to deal only with those problems which are the spontaneous product of historic conditions and which find or suggest their own solutions. Only by entering into the process of reality and taking possession of the forces at work within it can man act on man and on nature.

Anti-individualistic, the fascist conception of life stresses the importance of the State and accepts the individual only in so far as his interests coincide with those of the State, which stands for the conscience and the universal will of man as a historic entity. It is opposed to classical liberalism, which arose as a reaction to absolutism and exhausted its historical function when the State became the expression of the conscience and will of the people. Liberalism denied the State in the name of the individual; fascism reasserts the right of the State as expressing the real essence of the individual. And if liberty is to be the attribute of living men and not of abstract dummies invented by individualistic liberalism, then fascism stands for liberty, and for the only liberty worth having, the liberty of the State and of the individual within the State. The fascist conception of the State is all-embracing; outside of it no human or spiritual values can exist, much less have value. Thus understood, fascism is totalitarian, and the fascist State—a synthesis and a unit inclusive of all values—interprets, develops, and potentiates the whole life of a people.

No individuals or groups (political parties, cultural associations, economic unions, social classes) are outside the State. Fascism is therefore opposed to socialism to which unity within the State (which amalgamates classes into a single economic and ethical reality) is unknown, and which sees in history nothing but the class struggle. Fascism is likewise opposed to trade-unionism as a class weapon. But when brought within the orbit of the State, fascism recognizes the real needs which gave rise to socialism and trade unionism, giving them due weight in the guild or corporative system in which divergent interests are coordinated and harmonized in the unity of the State.

Grouped according to their several interests, individuals form classes; they form trade-unions when organized according to their several economic activities; but first and foremost they form the State, which is no mere matter of numbers, the sum of the individuals forming the majority. Fascism is therefore opposed to that form of democracy which equates a nation to the majority, lowering it to the level of the largest number; but it is the purest form of democracy if the nation be considered—as it should be—from the point of view of quality rather than quantity, as an idea, the mightiest because the most ethical, the most coherent, the truest, expressing itself in a people as the conscience and will of the few, if not, indeed, of one, and tending to express itself in the conscience and the will of the mass, of the whole group ethnically molded by natural and historical conditions into a nation, advancing, as one conscience and one will, along the self-same line of development and spiritual formation. Not a race, or a geographically defined region, but a people, historically perpetuating itself; a multitude unified by an idea and imbued with the will to live, the will to power, self-consciousness, personality.

In so far as it is embodied in a State, this higher personality becomes a nation. It is not the nation that generates the State; that is an antiquated naturalistic concept which afforded a basis for nineteenth-century publicity in favor of national governments. Rather is it the State that creates the nation, conferring volition and therefore real life on a people made aware of their moral unity.

The right to national independence does not arise from any merely literary and idealistic form of self-consciousness; still less from a more or less passive and unconscious *de facto* situation, but from an active, self-conscious, political will expressing itself in action and ready to prove its rights. It arises, in short, from the existence, at least *in fieri*, of a State. Indeed, it is the State which, as the expressions of a universal ethical will, creates the right to national independence.

A nation, as expressed in the State, is a living, ethical entity only in so far as it is progressive. Inactivity is death. Therefore the State is not only Authority which governs and confers legal form and spiritual value on individual wills, but it is also Power which makes its will felt and respected beyond its own frontiers, thus affording practical proof of the universal character of the decisions necessary to insure its development. This implies organization and expansion, potential if not actual. Thus the State equates itself to the will of man, whose development cannot be checked by obstacles and which, by achieving self-expression, demonstrates its own infinity.

The fascist State, as a higher and more powerful expression of personality, is a force, but a spiritual one. It sums up all the manifestations of the moral and intellectual life of man. Its functions canot therefore be limited to those of enforcing order and keeping the peace, as the liberal doctrine had it. It is no mere mechanical device for defining the sphere within which the individual may duly exercise his supposed rights. The fascist State is an inwardly accepted standard and rule of conduct, a discipline of the whole person; it permeates the will no less than the intellect. It stands for a principle which becomes the central motive of man as a member of civilized society, sinking deep down into his personality; it dwells in the heart of the man of action and of the thinker, of the artist and of the man of science: soul of the soul.

Fascism, in short, is not only a lawgiver and a founder of institutions, but an educator and promoter of spiritual life. It aims at refashioning not only the forms of life but their content—man, his character, and his faith. To achieve this purpose it enforces discipline and uses authority, entering into the soul and ruling with undisputed sway. Therefore it has chosen as its emblem the lictor's rods, the symbol of unity, strength, and justice.

M. K. Gandhi

M. K. Gandhi (1869–1948) was spiritual leader of the Indian liberation movement, and was highly effective in bringing about the independence of India. He was assassinated in 1948. The technique Gandhi proposed for convincing Great Britain to grant India her independence was a variety of nonviolent civil disobedience. Gandhi defended this technique in the following selections.

Nonviolent Resistance

SATYAGRAHA

For the past thirty years I have been preaching and practising Satyagraha. The principles of Satyagraha, as I know today, constitute a gradual evolution.

Satyagraha differs from Passive Resistance as the North Pole from the South. The latter has been conceived as a weapon of the weak and does not exclude the use of physical force or violence for the purpose of gaining one's end, whereas the former has been conceived as a weapon of the strongest and excludes the use of violence in any shape or form.

The term *Satyagraha* was coined by me in South Africa to express the force that the Indians there used for full eight years and it was coined in order to distinguish it from the movement then going on in the United Kingdom and South Africa under the name of Passive Resistance.

Its root meaning is holding on to truth, hence truth-force. I have also called it Love-force or Soul-force. In the application of Satyagraha I discovered in the earliest stages that pursuit of truth did not admit of violence being inflicted on one's opponent but that he must be weaned from error by patience and sympathy. For what appears to be truth to the one may appear to be error to the other. And patience means self-suffering. So the doctrine came to mean vindication of truth not by infliction of suffering on the opponent but on one's self.

But on the political field the struggle on behalf of the people mostly consists in opposing error in the shape of unjust laws. When you have failed to bring the error home to the lawgiver by way of petitions and the like, the only remedy open to you, if you do not wish to submit to error, is to compel him by physical force to yield to you or by suffering in your own person by inviting the penalty for the breach of the law. Hence Satyagraha largely appears to the public as Civil Disobedience or Civil Resistance. It is civil in the sense that it is not criminal.

The lawbreaker breaks the law surreptitiously and tries to avoid the penalty, not so the civil resister. He ever obeys the laws of the State to which he belongs, not out of fear of the sanctions but because he considers them to be good for the welfare of society. But there come occasions, generally rare, when he considers certain laws to be so unjust as to render obedience to them a dishonour. He then openly and civilly breaks them and quietly suffers the penalty for their breach. And in order to register his protest against the action of the law givers, it is open to him to withdraw his cooperation from the State by disobeying such other laws whose breach does not involve moral turpitude.

In my opinion, the beauty and efficacy of Satyagraha are so great and the doctrine so simple that it can be preached even to children. It was preached by me to thousands of men, women and children commonly called indentured Indians with excellent results.

From *Nonviolent Resistance*, Schocken Books, 1961. By permission of Navajivan Trust.

EVIDENCE BEFORE THE HUNTER COMMITTEE
(EXTRACTS)

1. Examination by Lord Hunter

Q.: I take it, Mr Gandhi, that you are the author of the Satyagraha movement.

A.: Yes, Sir.

Q.: Will you explain it briefly?

A.: It is a movement intended to replace methods of violence and a movement based entirely upon truth. It is, as I have conceived it, an extension of the domestic law on the political field, and my experience has led me to the conclusion that that movement, and that alone, can rid India of the possibility of violence spreading throughout the length and breadth of the land, for the redress of grievances.

Q.: It was adopted by you in connection with the opposition to the Rowlatt Act. And in that connection you asked the people to sign the Satyagraha pledge.

A.: Yes, Sir.

Q.: Was it your intention to enlist as many men as possible in the movement?

A.: Yes, consistently with the principle of truth and nonviolence. If I got a million men ready to act according to those principles, I would not mind enlisting them all.

Q.: It is not a movement essentially antagonistic to Government because you substitute the determination of the Satyagraha Committee for the will of the Government?

A.: That is not the spirit in which the movement has been understood by the people.

Q.: I ask you to look at it from the point of view of the Government. If you were a Governor yourself, what would you say to a movement that was started with the object of breaking those laws which your Committee determined?

A.: That would not be stating the whole case of the Satyagraha doctrine. If I were in charge of the Government and brought face to face with a body who, entirely in search of truth, were determined to seek redress from unjust laws without inflicting violence, I would welcome it and would consider that they were the best constitutionalists, and, as a Governor I would take them by my side as advisers who would keep me on the right path.

Q.: People differ as to the justice or injustice of particular laws?

A.: That is the main reason why violence is eliminated and a Satyagrahi gives his opponent the same right of independence and feelings of liberty that he reserves to himself, and he will fight by inflicting injuries on his own person.

Lord Hunter: I was looking at it from the point of view of the continuance of Government. Would it be possible to continue the Government if you had set up against the Government a body of men who would not accept the Government view but the view of an independent Committee?

A.: I have found from my experience that it was possible to do so during the eight years of continuous struggle in South Africa. I found General Smuts, who went through the whole of that campaign, at the end of it saying that if all conducted themselves as the Satyagrahis had done, they should have nothing to fear.

Q.: But there was no such pledge in that campaign as is prescribed here?

A.: Certainly there was. Every Satyagrahi was bound to resist all those laws which he considered to be unjust and which were not of a criminal character, in order to bend the Government to the will of the people.

Q.: I understand your vow contemplates breaking of laws which a Committee may decide.

A.: Yes, my Lord. I want to make it clear to the Committee that that part of the vow was meant to be a restraint on individual liberty. As I intended to make it a mass movement, I thought the constitution of some such Committee as we had appointed was necessary, so that no man should become a law unto himself, and, therefore, we conceived the plan that the Committee would be able to show what laws might be broken.

Q.: We hear that doctors differ, and, even Satyagrahis might differ?

A.: Yes, I found it so to my cost.

Q.: Supposing a Satyagrahi was satisfied that a particular law was a just law and that the Committee did not obey this law, what is a Satyagrahi to do?

A.: He is not bound to disobey that law. We had such Satyagrahis in abundance.

Q.: Is it not rather a dangerous campaign?

A.: If you will conceive the campaign as designed in order to rid the country of violence, then you will share with me the same concern for it; I think that at any cost a movement of this character should live in the country in a purified state.

Q.: By your pledge are you not binding a man's conscience?

A.: Not according to my interpretation of it. If my interpretation of the pledge is found to be incorrect, I shall mend my error if I have to start the movement again. (*Lord Hunter*—No, no, Mr Gandhi, I do not pretend to advise you.)

I wish I could disabuse the Committee of the idea that it is a dangerous doctrine. It is conceived entirely with the object of ridding the country of the idea of violence.

Lord Hunter here briefly detailed the circumstances preceding the passage of the Rowlatt Act, the widespread general Indian opposition to the Act etc., and asked Mr Gandhi to describe the essence of his objection to the legislation.

A.: I have read the Rowlatt Committee's report to the end and the legislation foreshadowed in it, and I came to the conclusion that the legislation was not warranted by the facts produced by the Committee. I thought it was very restrictive of human liberty and that no self-respecting person or nation could allow such legislation. When I saw the debates in the Legislative Council, I felt that the opposition to it was universal. When I found the agitation against it, I felt that for me as a self-respecting individual and a member of a vast Empire, there was no course left open, but to resist that law to the utmost.

Q.: So far as the objects of that legislation are concerned, have you any doubt that they are to put down revolutionary and anarchical crimes?

A.: They are quite laudable objects.

Q.: Your complaint, then, must be as regards the methods adopted?

A.: Entirely.

Q.: The method is, I understand, that greater power has been given to the executive than they enjoyed before.

A.: That is so.

Q.: But is it not the same power that the executive enjoyed under the Defence of India Act?

A.: That is true, but that was essentially an emergency measure designed to secure the co-operation of everybody in order to put down any violence that may be offered by any section of the community in connection with the successful carrying on of the war. It was assented to with the greatest reluctance. The Rowlatt legislation is of a different character altogether, and now the experience of the working of the former Act has strengthened my objections to the Rowlatt Act.

Q.: Mr Gandhi, the Rowlatt legislation is only to operate if the local Government is satisfied that there is anarchy.

A.: I would not, as a legislator, leave that power in the hands of an executive whom I have known to run mad in India at times.

Q.: Then really, your objection comes to this, that the Government of India, in the prosecution of a laudable object, adopted a wrong method. Therefore, is not the proper method of dealing with that, from a constitutional point of view, to endeavour to get the legislation remedied by satisfying Government of the inexpediency of it?

A.: I approached on bended knees Lord Chelmsford. and pleaded with him and with every English officer I had the pleasure of meeting, and placed my views before them, but they said they were helpless, and that the Rowlatt Committee's recommendations had to be given effect to. We had exhausted all the methods open to us.

Q.: If an opponent differs from you, you cannot satisfy him all of a sudden. You must do it by degrees. It is not rather a drastic way of attempting it by refusing to obey the law?

A.: I respectfully beg to differ from Your Lordship. If I find that even my father has imposed upon me a law which is repugnant to my conscience, I think it is the least drastic course that I could adopt, to respectfully tell him that I cannot obey it. By that course I do nothing but justice to my father, and, if I may say so without any disrespect to the Committee, I have myself followed that course with the greatest advantage and I have preached that ever since. If it is not disrespectful to say so to my father, it is not so to a friend and for that matter to my Government.

Lord Hunter: In the prosecution of your Satyagraha movement against the Rowlatt legislation you resolved upon a general *hartal* throughout India, That *hartal* was to be a day when no business was to be done and people were generally to indicate by their attitude that they disapproved of the Government's action. A *hartal* means a general cessation throughout the whole country. Would it not create a very difficult situation?

A.: Cessation for a great length of time would create a difficult situation.

Mr Gandhi here explained how the observance of the *hartal* in some part of the country on the 30th March, and all over the country on the 6th April came about not on account of any miscalculation, but on account of the people in one part coming to know of the Viceregal assent to the Act earlier than the people in other parts.

Q.: You agree that the abstention from work should be entirely voluntary?

A.: Yes, entirely voluntary, in the sense that persuasion on the day of the *hartal* would not be allowed, whereas persuasion by means of leaflets and other propaganda work on the other days would be perfectly legitimate, so long as no physical force was employed.

Q.: You disapprove of people interfering with *tongas* on the day of the *hartal?*

A.: Certainly.

Q.: You would not object to the police interfering in the case of such a disapprovable interference on the people's part?

A.: I would not if they acted with proper restraint and forbearance.

Q.: But you agree that on the day of the *hartal* it was highly improper to jostle with other people and stop *tongas?*

A.: From a Satyagrahi standpoint I would hold it to be criminal.

Lord Hunter: Your leading lieutenant in Delhi, Swami Shraddhananda—Mr *Gandhi* interrupting: I would not call him my lieutenant, but an esteemed coworker.—Did he write you a letter on the subject, and indicate to you that after what had occurred in Delhi and the Punjab, it was manifest that you could not prosecute a general *hartal* without violence inevitably ensuing?

A.: I cannot recall the contents of that letter. I think he went much further and said that it was not possible that the law-breaking campaign could be carried on with impunity among the masses. He did not refer to *hartal* proceeding. There was a difference of opinion between me and Swami Shraddhananda when I suspended civil disobedience. I found it necessary to suspend it because I had not obtained sufficient control, to my satisfaction, over the people. What Swami Shraddhananda said was that Satyagraha could not be taken as a mass movement. But I did not agree with his view and I do not know that he is not converted to my view today. The suspension of civil disobedience was as much necessary as prosecution for offences against law. I would like the Committee to draw a sharp distinction between *hartal* and civil disobedience. *Hartal* was designed to strike the imagination of the people and the Government. Civil disobedience was a discipline for those who were to offer disobedience. I had no means of understanding the mind of India except by some such striking movement. *Hartal* was a proper indication to me how far I would be able to carry civil disobedience.

Q.: If there is a *hartal* side by side with the preaching of Satyagraha would it not be calculated to promote violence?

A.: My experience is entirely to the contrary. It was an amazing scene for me to see people collected in their thousands—men, women and even little children and babies marching peacefully in procession. The peaceful *hartals* would not have been at all possible if Satyagraha was not preached in the right way.

But as I have said a *hartal* is a different thing from civil disobedience in practice.

Lord Hunter: Now, the only matters that we have got to deal with here are as regards Ahmedabad itself. In Ahmedabad, as we have been told, you enjoy great popularity among the mill workers?

Mr Gandhi: Yes.

Lord Hunter: And your arrest seems to have caused great resentment on their part and led to the very unfortunate actions of the mob on April 10, 11 and 12 in Ahmedabad and Viramgam?

Mr Gandhi: Yes.

Lord Hunter: So far as those incidents are concerned you have no personal knowledge of them?

Mr Gandhi: No.

Lord Hunter: I don't know whether there is anything that you can communi-cate to us in connection with those events to help us to form an opinion.

Mr Gandhi: I venture to present the opinion that I considered that the action of the mob, whether at Ahmedabad or at Viramgam, was totally unjustified, and I think that it was a sad thing that they lost self-control. But, at the same time, I would like to say that the people among whom, rightly or wrongly, I was popular, were put to a severe test by Government. They should have known better. I do not say that the Government committed an unpardonable error of judgment and the mob committed no error. On the contrary, I hold that it was more unpardonable on the part of the mob than on the part of Government.

Proceeding, Mr Gandhi narrated how he endeavoured to do what he could to repair the error. He placed himself entirely at the disposal of the authorities. He had a long interview with Mr Pratt and other officials. He was to have held a meeting of the people on the 13th but he was told that it would not be possible to hold it that day, not on account of Colonel Fraser's order, because he was promised every assistance in connection with the meeting, but that the notice of the meeting would not reach all the people that day. The meeting took place on the 14th. There he adumbrated what had happened. There he had to use the terms *organized* and *educated* both of which terms had been so much quoted against him and against the people. The speech was in Gujarati. Mr Gandhi explained and hoped Sir Chimanlal Setalwad would bear him out on a reference to the Gujarati speech that the word only means those who can read and write, and that he used the word and expressed the opinion as he sensed the thing at that time.

He emphasized it was not a previous organization that he meant; he only meant to say, and there could be no mistaking the actual words in his speech, that the acts were done in an *organized manner.* He further emphasized that he was speaking of Ahmedabad only, that he had then no knowledge of what had happened even at Viramgam, and that he would not retract a single statement from that speech. In his opinion, said Mr Gandhi, violence was done in an organized manner. It cannot be interpreted to mean a deep-laid conspiracy. He laid special emphasis on the fact that while he used these expressions he was addressing the people, and not the police authorities.

If Mr Guider stated that a single name of the offenders was not forthcoming from him, he was entirely mistaken about his mission and had put an improper valuation upon the term *organization.* The crimes committed by the mob were the result of their being deluded by the wicked rumour of the arrest of Miss Anasuya. There was a class of half-educated people who possessed false ideas obtained from sources such as cinematographs and from silly novels and from political leaders. He knew that school. He had mixed with them and endeavoured to wean them. He had so far succeeded in his endeavours that there were today hundreds of people who had ceased to belong to the school of revolution.

Proceeding, Mr Gandhi said he had now given the whole meaning of what he had said. He had never meant that there were University men behind the disturbances. He did not say they were incapable of those acts, but he was not aware of any highly educated man directing the mob.

Lord Hunter: Do you imply that there was a common purpose on the part of the rioters?

Mr Gandhi: I don't say that. It would be exaggerating to say that, but I think the common purpose was restricted to two or three men or parties who instigated the crimes.

Q.: Did the agitation take an anti-European character?

A.: It was certainly an anti-Government movement. I would fain believe it was not anti-European, but I have not yet made up my mind as to that.

Lord Hunter: I do not know whether you want to answer this or not. According to the Satyagraha doctrine, is it right that people who have committed crimes should be punished by the civil authorities?

Mr Gandhi: It is a difficult question to answer, because (through punishment) you anticipate pressure from outside. I am not prepared to say that it is wrong, but there is a better method. But I think, on the whole, it would be proper to say that Satyagrahi cannot possibly quarrel with any punishment that might be meted out to an offender, and therefore he cannot be anti-Government in that sense.

Lord Hunter: But apparently it is against the doctrine of Satyagraha to give assistance to Government by way of placing the information that a Satyagrahi has that would lead to the convictions of offenders?

Mr Gandhi: According to the principle of Satyagraha it is inconsistent, for the simple reason that a Satyagrahi's business is not to assist the police in the method which is open to the police, but he helps the authorities and the police to make the people more law-abiding and more respectable to authority.

Lord Hunter: Supposing a Satyagrahi has seen one of the more serious crimes committed in these riots in his own presence. Would there be no obligation on him to inform the police?

Mr Gandhi: Of course I answered that question to Mr Guider before and I think I must answer it to Your Lordship. I don't want to misguide the youth of the country, but even then he cannot go against his own brother. When I say brother, I do not, of course, make any distinction of country or nationality. A Satyagrahi is wholly independent of such a distinction. The Satyagrahi's position is somewhat similar to that of a counsel defending an accused. I have known criminals of the deadliest type and I may humbly claim to have been instrumental in weaning them from crimes. I should be forfeiting their confidence if I disclosed the name of a single man. But supposing I found myself wanting in weaning them I would surely not take the next step to go and inform the police about them; I do not hesitate to say that for a Satyagrahi it is the straightest thing not to give evidence of a crime done even under his nose. But there can be only the rarest uses of this doctrine and even today I am not able to say whether I would not give evidence against a criminal whom I saw caught in the act.

(*Young India*, 21-1-'20)

2. Examination by Sir Chimanlal Setalwad

Sir Chimanlal: With regard to your Satyagraha doctrine, so far as I understand it, it involves the pursuit of truth and in that pursuit you invite suffering on yourself and do not cause violence to anybody else.

Mr Gandhi: Yes Sir.

Q.: However honestly a man may strive in his search for truth his notions of truth may be different from the notions of others. Who then is to determine the truth?

A.: The individual himself would determine that.

Q.: Different individuals would have different views as to truth. Would that not lead to confusion?

A.: I do not think so.

Q.: Honestly striving after truth is different in every case.

A.: That is why the non-violence part was a necessary corollary. Without that there would be confusion and worse.

Q.: Must not the person wanting to pursue truth be of high moral and intellectual equipment?

A.: No. It would be impossible to expect that from every one. If A has evolved a truth by his own efforts which B, C and others are to accept I should not require them to have the equipment of A.

Q.: Then it comes to this that a man comes to a decision and others of lower intellectual and moral equipment would have to blindly follow him.

A.: Not blindly. All I wish to urge is that each individual, unless he wants to carry on his pursuit of truth independently, needs to follow someone who has determined truth.

Q.: Your scheme involves the determination of truth by people of high moral and intellectual equipment and a large number of people may follow them blindly being themselves unable to arrive at similar conclusions by reason of their lower intellectual equipment.

A.: I would exact from them nothing more than I would expect from an ordinary being.

Q.: I take it that the strength of the propaganda must depend on the number of its followers.

A.: No. In Satyagrahi success is possible even if there is only one Satyagrahi of the proper stamp.

Q.: Mr Gandhi, you said you do not consider yourself a perfect Satyagrahi yet. The large mass of people are then even less so.

A.: No. I do not consider myself an extraordinary man. There may be people more capable of determining truth than myself. Forty thousand Indians in South Africa, totally uncultured, came to the conclusion that they could be Satyagrahis and if I could take you through those thrilling scenes in the Transvaal you will surprized to hear what restraint your countrymen in South Africa exhibited.

Q.: But there you were all unanimous.

A.: I have more solidity of opinion here than in South Africa.

Q.: But there you had a clear-cut issue, not here.

A.: Here too we have a clear-cut issue, viz. the Rowlatt Act.

Mr Gandhi then explained how he presented Satyagraha as an instrument of infinitely greater power than violence.

Q.: Does not suffering and going on suffering require extraordinary self-control?

A.: No; no extraordinary self-control is required. Every mother suffers. Your countrymen, I submit, have got such control and they have exhibited that in a very large measure.

Q.: Take Ahmedabad. Did they exhibit control here?

A.: All I say is, throughout India where you find these isolated instances of violence you will find a very large number of people who exercised self-restraint. Ahmedabad and other places show that we had not attained proper mastery over self. The Kaira people in the midst of grave provocation last year acted with the greatest self-restraint.

Q.: Do you mean to say these acts of violence were mere accidents?

A.: Not accidents. But they were rare and would be rarer for a clear conception of Satyagraha. The country, I think, has sufficiently well realized the doctrine to warrant a second trial. I do feel sure that the country is all the purer and better for having gone through the fire of Satyagraha.

Q.: Ordinarily your doctrine contemplates co-operation with the Government and elimination of race-hatred and inviting self-suffering. Does not suffering create ill-will?

A.: It is contrary to my thirty years' experience that people have by suffering been filled with any ill-will against the Government. In South Africa after a bitter struggle the Indians have lived on the best of terms with the Government, and Gen. Smuts was the recipient of an address which was voluntarily voted by the Indians.

Q.: Is it possible to take part in the movement without taking the Satyagraha vow?

A.: I would ask them to take part in the non-civil-resistance part of the movement. The masses unless they took the pledge were not to do the civil-disobedience part of the pledge. For those who were not civil resisters, therefore, another vow was devised asking people to follow truth at all costs and to refrain from violence. I had suspended civil resistance then, and as it is open to a leader to emphasize one part of the vow, I eliminated the civil-resistance part which was not for that season suited to the people, and placed the truth part before them.

Q.: Is not the underlying idea embarrassment of Government?

A.: Certainly not. A Satyagrahi relies not upon embarrassment but upon self-suffering for securing relief.

Q.: Would not ordered Government be impossible?

A.: Ordered Government cannot be impossible if totally inoffensive people break the laws. But I would certainly make Government impossible if I found it had taken leave of its senses.

Q.: In your message you ask people to refrain from violence and still violence occurred. Does it not show that the ordinary mind finds it very difficult to practise the theory of non-violence?

A.: After having used methods of violence for years it is difficult for them to practice abstention.

(*Young India*, 21-1-'20)

3. Examination by Pandit Jagatnarain

Q.: It is alleged that the Satyagraha movement would embarrass the Government. Are you not afraid of any such result of your movement?

A.: The Satyagraha movement is not started with the intention of embarrassing the Government while ordinary political agitation is often started with that object. If a Satyagrahi finds his activities resulting in embarrassing the Government, he will not hesitate to face it.

Q.: But you will agree with me that every political agitation depends for its success on the numbers of followers?

A.: I do not regard the force of numbers as necessary in a just cause, and in such a cause every man, be he high or low, can have his remedy.

Q.: But you would certainly try to have as many men in your movement as possible?

A.: Not exactly so. A Satyagrahi depends only on truth and his capacity to suffer for truth.

Q.: But in politics, Mahatmaji, how can a single man's voice be heard?

A.: That is exactly what I have been attempting to disprove.

Q.: Do you believe that an English officer will take any notice of isolated attempts?

A.: Why, that is my experience. Lord Bentinck became an ordinary Mr at the instance of Keshavachandra Sen.

Q.: Oh, you cite an example of an extraordinary man.

A.: Men of ordinary abilities also can develop morality. No doubt I regard illiteracy among my people as deplorable and I consider it necessary to educate them, but it is not at all impossible for an absolutely illiterate man to imbibe the Satyagraha principle. This is my long-standing experience.

Here Mr Gandhi briefly cleared the distinction between *hartal* and Satyagraha. *Hartal* was no integral part of Satyagraha. It should be resorted to only when necessary. He tried and tried it successfully in connection with the deportation of Mr Horniman and the Khilafat movement.

Q.: You can resort to no other remedy to oppose the irresponsible, foreign officials and that is why you have started this movement. Is it not?

A.: I cannot say that with certainty. I can conceive the necessity of Satyagraha in opposition to the would-be full responsible self-government. Our ministers can never claim to defend themselves on the score of their ignorance, whereas such a defence is available today for the English officers.

Q.: But with all the rights of self-government we shall be able to dismiss the ministers.

A.: I cannot feel on that point so assured for ever. In England it often happens that ministers can continue in the executive even though they lose all the confidence of the public. The same thing may happen here too and therefore I can imagine a state of things in this country which would need Satyagraha even under Home Rule.

Q.: Would you think that there should be no unrest coming after the Satyagraha movement?

A.: Not only I do not think so, I would be disappointed if there were no unrest in case Anasuyabehn and I were arrested. But that unrest will not take the shape of violence. It pains a Satyagrahi to see others suffering; Satyagrahis will follow each other to jail. I do wish for such unrest.

(*Young India*, 4-2-'20)

Martin Luther King, Jr.

The Rev. Dr. Martin Luther King, Jr. (1929-1968), head of the Southern Christian Leadership Conference until his death by assassination in 1968, used nonviolent civil disobedience to gain for American Negroes some of the political and social rights denied them. The "Letter from Birmingham City Jail" explains Rev. Dr. King's justifications for breaking certain kinds of law. It was written in response to a statement critical of his activities issued by a group of prominent clergymen.

Letter from Birmingham City Jail

My dear Fellow Clergymen,

While confined here in the Birmingham City Jail, I came across your recent statement calling our present activities "unwise and untimely." Seldom, if ever, do I pause to answer criticism of my work and ideas. If I sought to answer all of the criticisms that cross my desk, my secretaries would be engaged in little else in the course of the day, and I would have no time for constructive work. But since I feel that you are men of genuine goodwill and your criticisms are sincerely set forth, I would like to answer your statement in what I hope will be patient and reasonable terms.

I think I should give the reason for my being in Birmingham, since you have been influenced by the argument of "outsiders coming in." I have the honor of serving as president of the Southern Christian Leadership Conference, an organization operating in every southern state, with headquarters in Atlanta, Georgia. We have some eighty-five affiliate organizations all across the South—one being the Alabama Christian Movement for Human Rights. Whenever necessary and possible we share staff, educational and financial resources with our affiliates. Several months ago our local affiliate here in Birmingham invited us to be on call to engage in a nonviolent direct action program if such were deemed necessary. We readily consented and when the hour came we lived up to our promises. So I am here, along with several members of my staff, because we were invited here. I am here because I have basic organizational ties here.

Beyond this, I am in Birmingham because injustice is here. Just as the eighth century prophets left their little villages and carried their "thus saith the Lord" far beyond the boundaries of their home towns; and just as the Apostle Paul left

"Letter from Birmingham City Jail—April 16, 1963" from *Why We Can't Wait* by Martin Luther King, Jr. Copyright 1963 by Martin Luther King, Jr. By permission of Harper & Row, Publishers, Inc.

his little village of Tarsus and carried the gospel of Jesus Christ to practically every hamlet and city of the Graeco-Roman world; I too am compelled to carry the gospel of freedom beyond my particular home town. Like Paul, I must constantly respond to the Macedonian call for aid.

Moreover, I am cognizant of the interrelatedness of all communities and states. I cannot sit idly by in Atlanta and not be concerned about what happens in Birmingham. Injustice anywhere is a threat to justice everywhere. We are caught in an inescapable network of mutuality, tied in a single garment of destiny. Whatever affects one directly affects all indirectly. Never again can we afford to live with the narrow, provincial "outside agitator" idea. Anyone who lives inside the United States can never be considered an outsider anywhere in this country.

You deplore the demonstrations that are presently taking place in Birmingham. But I am sorry that your statement did not express a similar concern for the conditions that brought the demonstrations into being. I am sure that each of you would want to go beyond the superficial social analyst who looks merely at effects, and does not grapple with underlying causes. I would not hesitate to say that it is unfortunate that so-called demonstrations are taking place in Birmingham at this time, but I would say in more emphatic terms that it is even more unfortunate that the white power structure of this city left the Negro community with no other alternative.

In any nonviolent campaign there are four basic steps: 1) Collection of the facts to determine whether injustices are alive. 2) Negotiation. 3) Self-purification and 4) Direct Action. We have gone through all of these steps in Birmingham. There can be no gainsaying of the fact that racial injustice engulfs this community.

Birmingham is probably the most thoroughly segregated city in the United States. Its ugly record of police brutality is known in every section of this country. Its injust treatment of Negroes in the courts is a notorious reality. There have been more unsolved bombings of Negro homes and churches in Birmingham than any city in this nation. These are the hard, brutal and unbelievable facts. On the basis of these conditions Negro leaders sought to negotiate with the city fathers. But the political leaders consistently refused to engage in good faith negotiation.

Then came the opportunity last September to talk with some of the leaders of the economic community. In these negotiating sessions certain promises were made by the merchants—such as the promise to remove the humiliating racial signs from the stores. On the basis of these promises Rev. Shuttlesworth and the leaders of the Alabama Christian Movement for Human Rights agreed to call a moratorium on any type of demonstrations. As the weeks and months unfolded we realized that we were the victims of a broken promise. The signs remained. Like so many experiences of the past we were confronted with blasted hopes, and the dark shadow of a deep disappointment settled upon us. So we had no alternative except that of preparing for direct action, whereby we would present our very bodies as a means of laying our case before the conscience of the local and national community. We were not unmindful of the difficulties involved. So we decided to go through a process of self-purification. We started having workshops on nonviolence and repeatedly asked ourselves the questions, "Are you able to accept blows without retaliating?" "Are you able to endure the ordeals of jail?" We decided to set our direct action program around the Easter season, realizing that with the exception of Christmas, this was the largest shopping period of the year. Knowing that a strong economic withdrawal program would be the byproduct of direct action, we felt that this was the best time to bring pressure on the merchants for the needed changes. Then it occurred to us that the March election was ahead and so we speedily decided to postpone action until after election day. When we discovered that Mr. Connor was in the run-off, we decided again to postpone action so that the demonstrations could not be used to cloud the issues. At this time we agreed to begin our nonviolent witness the day after the run-off.

This reveals that we did not move irresponsibly into direct action. We too wanted to see Mr. Connor defeated; so we went through postponement after postponement to aid in this community need. After this we felt that direct action could be delayed no longer.

You may well ask, "Why direct action? Why sit-ins, marches, etc.? Isn't negotiation a better path?" You are exactly right in your call for negotiation. Indeed, this is the purpose of direct action. Nonviolent direct action seeks to create such a crisis and establish such creative tension that a community that has constantly refused to negotiate is forced to confront the issue. It seeks so to dramatize the issue that it can no longer be ignored. I just referred to the creation of tension as a part of the work of the nonviolent resister. This may sound rather shocking. But I must confess that I am not afraid of the word tension. I have earnestly worked and preached against violent tension, but there is a type of constructive nonviolent tension that is necessary for growth. Just as Socrates felt that it was necessary to create a tension in the mind so that individuals could rise from the bondage of myths and half-truths to the unfettered realm of creative analysis and objective appraisal, we must see the need of having nonviolent gadflies to create the kind of tension in society that will help men to rise from the dark depths of prejudice and racism to the majestic heights of understanding and brotherhood. So the purpose of the direct action is to create a situation so crisis-packed that it will inevitably open the door to negotiation. We, therefore, concur with you in your call for negotiation. Too long has our beloved Southland been bogged down in the tragic attempt to live in monologue rather than dialogue.

One of the basic points in your statement is that our acts are untimely. Some have asked, "Why didn't you give the new administration time to act?" The only answer that I can give to this inquiry is that the new administration must be prodded about as much as the outgoing one before it acts. We will be sadly mistaken if we feel that the election of Mr. Boutwell will bring the millennium to Birmingham. While Mr. Boutwell is much more articulate and gentle than Mr. Connor, they are both segregationists, dedicated to the task of maintaining the status quo. The hope I see in Mr. Boutwell is that he will be reasonable enough to see the futility of massive resistance to desegregation. But he will not see this without pressure from the devotees of civil rights. My friends, I must say to you that we have not made a single gain in civil rights without determined legal and nonviolent pressure. History is the long and tragic story of the fact that privileged groups seldom give up their privileges voluntarily. Individuals may see the moral light and voluntarily give up their unjust posture; but as Reinhold Niebuhr has reminded us, groups are more immoral than individuals.

We know through painful experience that freedom is never voluntarily given by the oppressor; it must be demanded by the oppressed. Frankly, I have never yet engaged in a direct action movement that was "well timed," according to the timetable of those who have not suffered unduly from the disease of segregation. For years now I have heard the words "Wait!" It rings in the ear of every Negro with a piercing familiarity. This "Wait" has almost always meant "Never." It has been a tranquilizing thalidomide, relieving the emotional stress for a moment, only to give birth to an ill-formed infant of frustration. We must come to see with the distinguished jurist of yesterday that "justice too long delayed is justice denied." We have waited for more than three hundred and forty years for our constitutional and God-given rights. The nations of Asia and Africa are moving with jet-like speed toward the goal of political independence, and we still creep at horse and buggy pace toward the gaining of a cup of coffee at a lunch counter. I guess it is easy for those who have never felt the stinging darts of segregation to say, "Wait." But when you have seen vicious mobs lynch your mothers and fathers at will and drown your sisters and brothers at whim; when you have seen hate-filled policemen curse, kick, brutalize and even kill your black brothers and sisters with impunity; when you see the vast majority of your twenty million Negro brothers smothering in an air-tight cage of poverty in the midst of an affluent society; when you suddenly find your tongue twisted and your speech stammering as you seek to explain to your six-year-old daughter why she can't go to the public amusement park that has just been advertised on television, and see tears welling up in her little eyes when she is told that Funtown is closed to colored children, and see the depressing clouds of inferiority begin to form in her little mental sky, and see her begin to distort her little personality by unconsciously developing a bitterness toward white people; when you have to concoct an answer for a five-year-old son asking in agonizing pathos: "Daddy, why do white people treat colored people so mean?"; when you take a cross country drive and find it necessary to sleep night after night in the uncomforable corners of your automobile because no motel will accept you; when you are humiliated day in and day out by nagging signs reading "white" and "colored"; when your first name becomes "nigger" and your middle name becomes "boy" (however old you are) and your last name becomes "John," and when your wife and mother are never given the respected title "Mrs."; when you are harried by day and haunted at night by the fact that you are a Negro, living constantly at tip-toe stance never quite knowing what to expect next, and plagued with inner fears and outer resentments; when you are forever fighting a degenerating sense of "nobodiness"; then you will understand why we find it difficult to wait. There comes a time when the cup of endurance runs over, and men are no longer willing to be plunged into an abyss of injustice where they experience the blackness of corroding despair. I hope, sirs, you can understand our legitimate and unavoidable impatience.

You express a great deal of anxiety over our willingness to break laws. This is certainly a legitimate concern. Since we so diligently urge people to obey the Supreme Court's decision of 1954 outlawing segregation in the public schools, it is rather strange and paradoxical to find us consciously breaking laws. One may well ask, "How can you advocate breaking some laws and obeying others?" The answer is found in the fact that there are two types of laws: There are *just* and there are *unjust* laws. I would agree with Saint Augustine that "An unjust law is no law at all."

Now what is the difference between the two? How does one determine when a law is just or unjust? A just law is a man-made code that squares with the moral law or the law of God. An unjust law is a code that is out of harmony with the moral law. To put it in the terms of Saint Thomas Aquinas, an unjust law is a human law that is not rooted in eternal and and natural law. Any law that uplifts human personality is just. Any law that degrades human personality is unjust. All segregation statutes are unjust because segregation distorts the soul and damages the personality. It gives the segregator a false sense of superiority, and the segregated a false sense of inferiority. To use the words of Martin Buber, the great Jewish philosopher, segregation substitutes an "I—it" relationship for the "I-thou" relationship, and ends up relegating persons to the status of things. So segregation is not only politically, economically and sociologically unsound, but it is morally wrong and sinful. Paul Tilich has said that sin is separation. Isn't segregation an existential expression of man's tragic separation, an expression of his awful estrangement, his terrible sinfulness? So I can urge men to disobey segregation ordinances because they are morally wrong.

Let us turn to a more concrete example of just and unjust laws. An unjust law is a code that a majority inflicts on a minority that is not binding on itself. This is difference made legal. On the other hand a just law is a code that a majority compels a minority to follow that it is willing to follow itself. This is sameness made legal.

Let me give another explanation. An unjust law is a code inflicted upon a minority which that minority had no part in enacting or creating because they did not have the unhampered right to vote. Who can say that the legislature of Alabama which set up the segregation laws was democratically elected? Throughout the state of Alabama all types of conniving methods are used to prevent Negroes from becoming registered voters and there are some counties without a single Negro registered to vote despite the fact that the Negro constitutes a majority of the population. Can any law set up in such a state be considered democratically structured?

These are just a few examples of unjust and just laws. There are some instances when a law is just on its face and unjust in its application. For instance, I was arrested Friday on a charge of parading without a permit. Now there is nothing wrong with an ordinance which requires a permit for a parade, but when the ordinance is used to preserve segregation and to deny citizens the First Amendment privilege of peaceful assembly and peaceful protest, then it becomes unjust.

I hope you can see the distinction I am trying to point out. In no sense do I advocate evading or defying the law as the rabid segregationist would do. This would lead to anarchy. One who breaks an unjust law must do it *openly*, *lovingly* (not hatefully as the white mothers did in New Orleans when they were seen on television screaming "nigger, nigger, nigger"), and with a willingness to accept the penalty. I submit that an individual who breaks a law that conscience tells him is unjust, and willingly accepts the penalty by staying in jail to arouse the conscience of the community over its injustice, is in reality expressing the very highest respect for law.

Of course, there is nothing new about this kind of civil disobedience. It was seen sublimely in the refusal of Shadrach, Meshach and Abednego to obey the laws of Nebuchadnezzar because a higher moral law was involved. It was practiced superbly by the early Christians who were willing to face hungry lions and the excruciating pain of chopping blocks, before submitting to certain unjust laws of the Roman empire. To a degree academic freedom is a reality today because Socrates practiced civil disobedience.

We can never forget that everything Hitler did in Germany was "legal" and everything the Hungarian freedom fighters did in Hungary was "illegal." It was "illegal" to aid and confort a Jew in Hitler's Germany. But I am sure that if I had lived in Germany during that time I would have aided and comforted my Jewish brothers even though it was illegal. If I lived in a Communist country today where certain principles dear to the Christian faith are suppressed, I believe I would openly advocate disobeying these anti-religious laws. I must make two honest confessions to you, my Christian and Jewish brothers. First, I must confess that over the last few years I have been gravely disappointed with the white moderate. I have almost reached the regrettable conclusion that the Negro's great stumbling block in the stride toward freedom is not the White Citizen's Council-er or the Ku Klux Klanner, but the white moderate who is more devoted to "order" than to justice; who prefers a negative peace which is the absence of tension to a positive peace which is the presence of justice; who constantly says, "I agree with you in the goal you seek, but I can't agree with your methods of direct action"; who paternalistically feels that he can set the timetable for another man's freedom; who lives by the myth of time and who constantly advises the Negro to wait until a "more convenient season." Shallow understanding from people of goodwill is more frustrating than absolute misunderstanding from people of ill will. Lukewarm acceptance is much more bewildering than outright rejection.

I had hoped that the white moderate would understand that law and order exist for the purpose of establishing justice, and that when they fail to do this they become dangerously structured dams that block the flow of social progress. I had hoped that the white moderate would understand that the present tension of the South is merely a necessary phase of the transition from an obnoxious negative peace, where the Negro passively accepted his unjust plight, to a substance-filled positive peace, where all men will respect the dignity and worth of human personality. Actually, we who engage in nonviolent direct action are not the creators of tension. We merely bring to the surface the hidden tension that is already alive. We bring it out in the open where it can be seen and dealt with. Like a boil that can never be cured as long as it is covered up but must be opened with all its pus flowing ugliness to the natural medicines of air and light, injustice must likewise be exposed, with all of the tension its exposing creates, to the light of human conscience and the air of national opinion before it can be cured.

In your statement you asserted that our actions, even though peaceful, must be condemned because they precipitate violence. But can this assertion be logically made? Isn't this like condemning the robbed man because his possession of money precipitated the evil act of robbery? Isn't this like condemning Socrates because his unswerving commitment to truth and his philosophical delvings precipitated the misguided popular mind to make him drink the hemlock? Isn't this like condemning Jesus because His unique God-Consciousness and never-ceasing devotion to His will precipitated the evil act of crucifixion? We must come to see, as federal courts have consistently affirmed, that it is immoral to urge an individual to withdraw his efforts to gain his basic constitutional rights because the quest precipitates violence. Society must protect the robbed and punish the robber.

I had also hoped that the white moderate would reject the myth of time. I received a letter this morning from a white brother in Texas which said: "All Christians know that the colored people will receive equal rights eventually, but it is possible that you are in too great of a religious hurry. It has taken Christianity almost 2000 years to accomplish what it has. The teachings of Christ take time to come to earth." All that is said here grows out of a tragic misconception of time. It is the strangely irrational notion that there is some-thing in the very flow of time that will inevitably cure all ills. Actually time is neutral. It can be used either destructively or constructively. I am coming to feel than the people of ill will have used time much more effectively that the people of goodwill. We will have to repent in this generation not merely for the vitriolic words and actions of the bad people, but for the appalling silence of the good people. We must come to see that human progress never rolls in on wheels of inevitability. It comes through the tireless efforts and persistent work of men willing to be co-workers with God, and without this hard work time itself becomes an ally of the forces of social stagnation. We must use time creatively, and forever realize that the time is always ripe to do right. Now is the time to make real the promise of democracy, and transform our pending national elegy into a creative psalm of brotherhood. Now is the time to lift our national policy from the quicksand of racial injustice to the solid rock of human dignity.

You spoke of our activity in Birmingham as extreme. At first I was rather disappointed that fellow clergymen would see my nonviolent efforts as those of the extremist. I started thinking about the fact that I stand in the middle of two opposing forces in the Negro community. One is a force of complacency made up of Negroes who, as a result of long years of oppression, have been so completely drained of self-respect and a sense of "somebodiness" that they have adjusted to segregation, and, of a few Negroes in the middle class who, because of a degree of academic and economic security, and because at points they profit by segregation, have unconsciously become insensitive to the problems of the masses. The other force is one of bitterness and hatred, and comes perilously close to advocating violence. It is expressed in the various black nationalist groups that are springing up over the nation, the largest and best known being Elijah Muhammad's Muslim movement. This movement is nourished by the contemporary frustration over the continued existence of racial discrimination. It is made up of people who have lost faith in America, who have absolutely repudiated Christianity, and who have concluded that the white man is an incurable "devil." I have tried to stand between these two forces, saying that we need not follow the "do-nothingism" of the complacent or the hatred and despair of the black nationalist. There is the more excellent way of love and nonviolent protest. I'm grateful to God that through the Negro church, the dimension of nonviolence entered our struggle. If this philosophy had not emerged, I am convinced by now many streets of the South would be flowing with floods of blood. And I am further convinced that if our white brothers dismiss as "rabble rousers" and "outside agitators" those of us who are working through the channels of nonviolent direct action and refuse to support our nonviolent efforts, millions of Negroes, out of frustration and despair, will seek solace and security in black nationalist ideologies, a development that will lead inevitably to a frightening racial nightmare.

Oppressed people cannot remain oppressed forever. The urge for freedom will eventually come. This is what happened to the American Negro. Something within has reminded him of his birthright of freedom; something without has reminded him that he can gain it. Consciously and unconsciously, he has been swept in by what the Germans call the *Zeitgeist*, and with his black brothers of Africa, and his brown and yellow brothers of Asia, South America and the Caribbean, he is moving with a sense of cosmic urgency toward the promised land of racial justice. Recognizing this vital urge that has engulfed the Negro community, one should readily understand public demonstrations. The Negro has many pent-up resentments and latent frustrations. He has to get them out. So let him march sometime; let him have his prayer pilgrimages to the city hall; understand why he must have sit-ins and freedom rides. If his repressed emotions do not come out in these nonviolent ways, they will come out in ominous expressions of violence. This is not a threat; it is a fact of history. So I have not said to my people "get rid of your discontent." But I have tried to say that this normal and healthy discontent can be channelized through the creative outlet of nonviolent direct action. Now this approach is being dismissed as extremist. I must admit that I was initially disappointed in being so categorized.

But as I continued to think about the matter I gradually gained a bit of satisfaction from being considered an extremist. Was not Jesus an extremist in love—"Love your enemies, bless them that curse you, pray for them that despitefully use you." Was not Amos an extremist for justice—"Let justice roll down like waters and righteousness like a mighty stream." Was not Paul an extremist for the gospel of Jesus Christ—"I bear in my body the marks of the Lord Jesus." Was not Martin Luther an extremist—"Here I stand; I can do none other so help me God." Was not John Bunyan an extremist—"I will stay in jail to the end of my days before I make a butchery of my conscience." Was not Abraham Lincoln an extremist—"This nation cannot survive half slave and half free." Was not Thomas Jefferson an extremist—"We hold these truths to be self-evident, that all men are created equal." So the question is not whether we will be extremist but what kind of extremist will we be. Will we be extremists for hate or will we be extremists for love? Will we be extremists for the preservation of injustice—or will we be extremists for the cause of justice? In that dramatic scene on Calvary's hill, three men were crucified. We must not forget that all three were crucified for the same crime—the crime of extremism. Two were extremists for immorality, and thusly fell below their environment. The other, Jesus Christ, was an extremist for love, truth and goodness, and thereby rose above his environment. So, after all, maybe the South, the nation and the world are in dire need of creative extremists.

I had hoped that the white moderate would see this. Maybe I was too optimistic. Maybe I expected too much. I guess I should have realized that few members of a race that has oppressed another race can understand or appreciate the deep groans and passionate yearnings of those that have been oppressed and still fewer have the vision to see that injustice must be rooted out by strong, persistent and determined action. I am thankful, however, that some of our white brothers have grasped the meaning of this social revolution and committed themselves to it. They are still all too small in quantity, but they are big in quality. Some like Ralph McGill, Lillian Smith, Harry Golden and James Dabbs have written about our struggle in eloquent, prophetic and understanding terms. Others have marched with us down nameless streets of the South. They have languished in filthy roach-infested jails, suffering the abuse and brutality of angry policemen who see them as "dirty nigger lovers." They, unlike so many of their moderate brothers and sisters, have recognized the urgency of the moment and sensed the need for powerful "action" antidotes to combat the disease of segregation.

Let me rush on to mention my other disappointment. I have been so greatly disappointed with the white church and its leadership. Of course, there are some notable exceptions. I am not unmindful of the fact that each of you has taken some significant stands on this issue. I commend you, Rev. Stallings, for your Christian stand on this past Sunday, in welcoming Negroes to your worship service on a non-segregated basis. I commend the Catholic leaders of this state for integrating Springhill College several years ago.

But despite these notable exceptions I must honestly reiterate that I have been disappointed with the church. I do not say that as one of the negative critics who can always find something wrong with the church. I say it as a minister of the gospel, who loves the church; who was nurtured in its bosom; who has been sustained by its spiritual blessings and who will remain true to it as long as the cord of life shall lengthen.

I had the strange feeling when I was suddenly catapulted into the leadership of the bus protest in Montgomery several years ago that we would have the support of the white church. I felt that the white ministers, priests and rabbis of the South would be some of our strongest allies. Instead, some have been outright opponents, refusing to understand the freedom movement and misrepresenting its leaders; all too many others have been more cautious than courageous and have remained silent behind the anesthetizing security of the stained-glass window.

In spite of my shattered dreams of the past, I came to Birmingham with the hope that the white religious leadership of this community would see the justice of our cause, and with deep moral concern, serve as the channel through which our just grievances would go to the power structure. I had hoped that each of you would understand. But again I have been disappointed. I have heard numerous religious leaders of the South call upon their worshippers to comply with a desegregation decision because it is the *law*, but I have longed to hear white ministers say. "Follow this decree because integration is morally *right* and the Negro is your brother." In the midst of blatant injustices inflicted upon the Negro, I have watched white churches stand on the sideline and merely mouth pious irrelevancies and sanctimonious trivialities. In the midst of a mighty struggle to rid our nation of racial and economic injustice, I have heard so many ministers say, "Those are social issues with which the gospel has no real concern," and I have watched so many churches commit themselves to a completely other-wordly religion which made a strange distinction between body and soul, the sacred and the secular.

So here we are moving toward the exit of the twentieth century with a religious community largely adjusted to the status quo, standing as a tail-light behind other community agencies rather than a headlight leading men to higher levels of justice.

I have traveled the length and breadth of Alabama, Mississippi and all the other southern states. On sweltering summer days and crisp autumn mornings I have looked at her beautiful churches with their lofty spires pointing heavenward. I have beheld the impressive outlay of her massive religious education buildings. Over and over again I have found myself asking: "What kind of people worship here? Who is their God? Where were their voices when the lips of Governor Barnett dripped with words of interposition and nullification? Where were they when Governor Wallace gave the clarion call for defiance and hatred? Where were their voices of support when tired, bruised and weary Negro men and women decided to rise from the dark dungeons of complacency to the bright hills of creative protest?"

Yes, these questions are still in my mind. In deep disappointment, I have wept over the laxity of the church. But be assured that my tears have been tears of love. There can be no deep disappointment where there is not deep love. Yes, I love the church; I love her sacred walls. How could I do otherwise? I am in the rather unique position of being the son, the grandson and the great-grandson of preachers. Yes, I see the church as the body of Christ. But, oh! How we have blemished and scarred that body through social neglect and fear of being nonconformists.

There was a time when the church was very powerful. It was during that period when the early Christians rejoiced when they were deemed worthy to suffer for what they believed. In those days the church was not merely a thermometer that recorded the ideas and principles of popular opinion; it was a thermostat that transformed the mores of society. Wherever the early Christians entered a town the power structure got disturbed and immediately sought to convict them for being "disturbers of the peace" and "outside agitators." But they went on with the conviction that they were "a colony of heaven," and had to obey God rather than man. They were small in number but big in commitment. They were too God-intoxicated to be "astronomically intimidated." They brought an end to such ancient evils as infanticide and gladiatorial contest.

Things are different now. The contemporary church is often a weak, ineffectual voice with an uncertain sound. It is so often the arch supporter of the status quo. Far from being disturbed by the presence of the church, the power structure of the average community is consoled by the church's silent and often vocal sanction of things as they are.

But the judgment of God is upon the church as never before. If the church of today does not recapture the sacrificial spirit of the early church, it will lose its authentic ring, forfeit the loyalty of millions, and be dismissed as an irrelevant social club with no meaning for the twentieth century. I am meeting young people every day whose disappointment with the church has risen to outright disgust.

Maybe again, I have been too optimistic. Is organized religion too inextricably bound to the status quo to save our nation and the world? Maybe I must turn my faith to the inner spiritual church, the church within the church, as the true *ecclesia* and the hope of the world. But again I am thankful to God that some noble souls from the ranks of organized religion have broken loose from the paralyzing chains of conformity and joined us as active partners in the struggle for freedom. They have left their secure congregations and walked the streets if Albany, Georgia, with us. They have gone through the highways of the South on tortuous rides for freedom. Yes, they have gone to jail with us. Some have been kicked out of their churches, and lost support of their bishops and fellow ministers. But they have gone with the faith that right defeated is stronger than evil triumphant. These men have been the leaven in the lump of the race. Their witness has been the spiritual salt that has preserved the true meaning of the Gospel in these troubled times. They have carved a tunnel of hope through the dark mountain of disappointment.

I hope the church as a whole will meet the challenge of this decisive hour. But even if the church does not come to the aid of justice, I have no despair about the future. I have no fear about the outcome of our struggle in Birmingham, even if our motives are presently misunderstood. We will reach the goal of freedom in Birmingham and all over the nation, because the goal of America is freedom. Abused and scorned though we may be, our destiny is tied up with the destiny of America. Before the pilgrims landed at Plymouth we were here. Before the pen of Jefferson etched across the pages of history the majestic words of the Declaration of Independence, we were here. For more than two centuries our foreparents labored in this country without wages; they made cotton king; and they built the homes of their masters in the midst of brutal injustice and shameful humiliation—and yet out of a bottomless vitality they continued to thrive and develop. If the inexpressible cruelties of slavery could not stop us, the opposition we now face will surely fail. We will win our freedom because the sacred heritage of our nation and the eternal will of God are embodied in our echoing demands.

I must close now. But before closing I am impelled to mention one other point in your statement that troubled me profoundly. You warmly commended the Birmingham police force for keeping "order" and "preventing violence." I don't believe you would have so warmly commended the police force if you had seen its angry violent dogs literally biting six unarmed, nonviolent Negroes. I don't believe you would so quickly commend the policemen if you would observe their ugly and inhuman treatment of Negroes here in the city jail; if you would watch them push and curse old Negro women and young Negro girls; if you would see them slap and kick old Negro men and young boys; if you will observe them, as they did on two occasions, refuse to give us food because we wanted to sing our grace together. I'm sorry that I can't join you in your praise for the police department.

It is true that they have been rather disciplined in their public handling of the demonstrators. In this sense they have been rather publicly "nonviolent." But for what purpose? To preserve the evil system of segregation. Over the last few years I have consistently preached that nonviolence demands that the means we use must be as pure as the ends we seek. So I have tried to make it clear that it is wrong to use immoral means to attain moral ends. But now I must affirm that it is just as wrong, or even more so, to use moral means to preserve immoral ends. Maybe Mr. Connor and his policemen have been rather publicly nonviolent, as Chief Pritchett was in Albany, Georgia, but they have used the moral means of nonviolence to maintain the immoral end of flagrant racial injustice. T. S. Eliot has said that there is no greater treason than to do the right deed for the wrong reason.

I wish you had commended the Negro sit-inners and demonstrators of Birmingham for their sublime courage, their willingness to suffer and their amazing discipline in the midst of the most inhuman provocation. One day the South will recognize its real heroes. They will be the James Merediths, courageously and with a majestic sense of purpose facing jeering and hostile mobs and the agonizing loneliness that characterizes the life of the pioneer. They will be old, oppressed, battered Negro women, symbolized in a seventy-two year old woman of Montgomery, Alabama, who rose up with a sense of dignity and with her people decided not to ride the segregated buses, and responded to one who inquired about her tiredness with ungrammatical profundity: "My feet is tired, but my soul is rested." They will be the young high school and college students, young ministers of the Gospel and a host of their elders courageously and nonviolently sitting-in at lunch counters and willingly going to jail for conscience's sake. One day the South will know that when these disinherited children of God sat down at lunch counters they were in reality standing up for the best in the American dream and the most sacred values in our Judeo-Christian heritage, and thusly, carrying our whole nation back to those great wells of democracy which were dug deep by the founding fathers in the formulation of the Constitution and the Declaration of Independence.

Never before have I written a letter this long (or should I say a book?). (I'm afraid that it is much too long to take your precious time. I can assure you that it would have been much shorter if I had been writing from a comfortable desk, but what else is there to do when you are alone for days in the dull monotony of a narrow jail cell other than write long letters, think strange thoughts, and pray long prayers?

If I have said anything in this letter that is an overstatement of the truth and is indicative of an unreasonable impatience, I beg you to forgive me. If I have said anything in this letter that is an understatement of the truth and is indicative of my having a patience that makes me patient with anything less than brotherhood, I beg God to forgive me.

I hope this letter finds you strong in the faith. I also hope that circumstances will soon make it possible for me to meet each of you, not as an integrationist or a civil-rights leader, but as a fellow clergyman and a Christian brother. Let us all hope that the dark clouds of racial prejudice will soon pass away and the deep fog of misunderstanding will be lifted from our fear-drenched communities and in some not too distant tomorrow the radiant stars of love and brotherhood will shine over our great nation with all of their scintillating beauty.

Yours for the cause of Peace and Brotherhood,
Martin Luther King, Jr.

Sidney Hook

Sidney Hook (b. 1902) is Professor of Philosophy at New York University. In addition to numerous scholarly books and articles, Professor Hook has written on many topics of popular interest. In the following article "Social Protest and Civil Disobedience," he explains and defends his views concerning the role of civil disobedience in seeking social and political change.

Social Protest and Civil Disobedience

In times of moral crisis what has been accepted as commonplace truth sometimes appears questionable and problematic. We have all been nurtured in the humanistic belief that in a democracy, citizens are free to disagree with a law but that so long as it remains in force, they have a *prima facie* obligation to obey it. The belief is justified on the ground that this procedure enables us to escape the twin evils of tyranny and anarchy. Tyranny is avoided by virtue of the freedom and power of dissent to win the uncoerced consent of the community. Anarchy is avoided by reliance on due process, the recognition that there is a right way to correct a wrong, and a wrong way to secure a right. To the extent that anything is demonstrable in human affairs, we have held that democracy as a political system is not viable if members systematically refused to obey laws whose wisdom or morality they dispute.

Nonetheless, during the past decade of tension and turmoil in American life there has developed a mass phenomenon of civil disobedience even among those who profess devotion to democratic ideals and institutions. This phenomenon has assumed a character similar to a tidal wave which has not yet reached its crest. It has swept from the field of race relations to the campuses of some universities, subtly altering the connotation of the term "academic." It is being systematically developed as an instrument of influencing foreign policy. It is leaving its mark on popular culture. I am told it is not only a theme of comic books but that children in our more sophisticated families no longer resort to tantrums in defying parental discipline—they go limp!

More seriously, in the wake of civil disobedience there has occasionally developed *uncivil* disobedience, sometimes as a natural psychological development, and often because of the failure of law enforcement agencies especially in the South to respect and defend legitimate expressions of social protest. The line

This article first appeared in *The Humanist*, Fall, 1967, and is reprinted by permission.

between civil and uncivil disobedience is not only an uncertain and wavering one in practice, it has become so in theory. A recent prophet of the philosophy of the absurd in recommending civil disobedience as a form of creative disorder in a democracy cited Shay's Rebellion as an illustration. This Rebellion was uncivil to the point of bloodshed. Indeed, some of the techniques of protesting American involvement in Vietnam have departed so far from traditional ways of civil disobedience as to make it likely that they are inspired by the same confusion between civil and uncivil disobedience.

All this has made focal the perennial problems of the nature and limits of the citizen's obligation to obey the law, of the relation between the authority of conscience and the authority of the state, of the rights and duties of a democratic moral man in an immoral democratic society. The classical writings on these questions have acquired a burning relevance to the political condition of man today. I propose briefly to clarify some of these problems.

To begin with I wish to stress the point that there is no problem concerning "social protest" as such in a democracy. Our Bill of Rights was adopted not only to make protest possible but to encourage it. The political logic, the very ethos of any democracy that professes to rest, no matter how indirectly, upon freely given consent *requires* that social protest be permitted—and not only permitted but *protected* from interference by those opposed to the protest, which means protected by agencies of law enforcement.

Not social protest but *illegal* social protest constitutes our problem. It raises the question: "When, if ever, is illegal protest justified in a democratic society?" It is of the first importance to bear in mind that we are raising the question as principled democrats and humanists in a democratic society. To urge that illegal social protests, motivated by exalted ideals are sanctified in a democratic society by precedents like the Boston Tea Party, is a lapse into political illiteracy. Such actions occurred in societies in which those affected by unjust laws had no power peacefully to change them.

Further, many actions dubbed civilly disobedient by local authorities, strictly speaking, are not such at all. An action launched in violation of a local law or ordinance, and undertaken to test it, on the ground that the law itself violates state or federal law, or launched in violation of a state law in the sincerely held belief that the state law outrages the Constitution, the supreme law of the land, is not civilly disobedient. In large measure the original sympathy with which the original sit-ins were received, especially the Freedom Rides, marches, and demonstrations that flouted local Southern laws, was due to the conviction that they were constitutionally justified, in accordance with the heritage of freedom, enshrined in the Amendments, and enjoyed in other regions of the country. Practically everything the marchers did was sanctioned by the phrase of the First Amendment which upholds "the right of the people peaceably to assemble and to petition the Government for a redress of grievances." Actions of this kind may be wise or unwise, timely or untimely, but they are not civilly disobedient.

They become civilly disobedient when they are in deliberate violation of laws that have been sustained by the highest legislative and judicial bodies of the nation, e.g., income tax laws, conscription laws, laws forbidding segregation in education, and discrimination in public accommodations and employment. Another class of examples consists of illegal social protest against local and state laws that clearly do not conflict with Federal Law.

Once we grasp the proper issue, the question is asked with deceptive clarity: "Are we under an obligation in a democratic community always to obey an unjust law?" To this question Abraham Lincoln is supposed to have made the classic answer in an eloquent address on "The Perpetuation of Our Political Institution," calling for absolute and religious obedience until the unjust law is repealed.

I said that this question is asked with deceptive clarity because Lincoln, judging by his other writings and the pragmatic cast of his basic philosophy, could never have subscribed to this absolutism or meant what he seemed literally to have said. Not only are we under no moral obligation *always* to obey unjust laws, we are under no moral obligation *always* to obey a just law. One can put it more strongly: sometimes it may be necessary in the interests of the greater good to violate a just or sensible law. A man who refused to violate a sensible traffic law if it were necessary to do so to avoid a probably fatal accident would be a moral idiot. There are other values in the world besides legality or even justice, and sometimes they may be of overriding concern and weight. Everyone can imagine some situation in which the violation of some existing law is the lesser moral evil, but this does not invalidate recognition of our obligation to obey just laws.

There is a difference between disobeying a law which one approves of in general but whose application in a specific case seems wrong, and disobeying a law in protest against the injustice of the law itself. In the latter case the disobedience is open and public; in the former, not. But if the grounds of disobedience in both cases are moral considerations, there is only a difference in degree between them. The rejection, therefore, of legal absolutism or the fetishism of legality—that one is never justified in violating any law in any circumstances—is a matter of common sense.

The implications drawn from this moral commonplace by some ritualistic liberals are clearly absurd. For they have substituted for the absolutism of law something very close to the absolutism of individual conscience. Properly rejecting the view that the law, no matter how unjust, must be obeyed in all circumstances, they have taken the view that the law is to be obeyed only when the individual deems it just or when it does not outrage his conscience. Fantastic comparisons are made between those who do not act on the dictates of their conscience and those who accepted and obeyed Hitler's laws. These comparisons completely disregard the systems of law involved, the presence of alternatives of action, the differences in the behavior commanded, in degrees of complicity of guilt, in the moral costs and personal consequences of compliance and other relevant matters.

It is commendable to recognize the primacy of morality to law but unless we recognize the centrality of intelligence to morality, we stumble with blind self-righteousness into moral disaster. Because, Kant to the contrary notwithstanding, it is not wrong sometimes to lie to save a human life; because it is not wrong sometimes to kill in defense to save many from being killed, it does not follow that the moral principles: "Do not lie!" "Do not kill!" are invalid. When more than one valid principle bears on a problem of moral experience the very fact of their conflict means that not all of them can hold unqualifiedly. One of them must be denied. The point is that such negation or violation entails upon us the obligation of justifying it, and moral justification is a matter of reasons not of conscience. The burden of proof rests on the person violating the rules. Normally, we don't have to justify telling the truth. We do have to justify *not* telling the truth. Similarly, with respect to the moral obligation of a democrat who breaches his political obligation to obey the laws of a democratic community, the resort to conscience is not enough. There must always be reasonable justification.

This is all the more true because just as we can, if challenged, give powerful reasons for the moral principle of truth-telling, so we can offer logically coercive grounds for the obligation of a democrat to obey the laws of a democracy. The grounds are many and they can be amplified beyond the passing mention we give here. It is a matter of fairness, of social utility, of peace, of ordered progress, of redeeming an implicit commitment.

There is one point, however, which has a particular relevance to the claims of those who counterpose to legal absolutism the absolutism of conscience. There is the empirically observable tendency for public disobedience to law to spread from those who occupy high moral ground to those who dwell on low ground, with consequent growth of disorder and insecurity.

Conscience by itself is not the measure of high or low moral ground. This is the work of reason. Where it functions properly the democratic process permits this resort to reason. If the man of conscience loses in the court of reason, why should he assume that the decision or the law is mistaken rather than the deliverances of his conscience?

The voice of conscience may sound loud and clear. But it may conflict at times not only with the law but with another man's conscience. Every conscientious objector to a law knows that at least one man's conscience is wrong, *viz.,* the conscience of the man who asserts that *his* conscience tells him that he must not tolerate conscientious objectors. From this if he is reasonable he should conclude that when he hears the voice of conscience, he is hearing not the voice of God, but the voice of a finite, limited man in this time and in this place, and that conscience is neither a special nor an infallible organ of apprehending moral truth, that conscience without conscientiousness, conscience which does not cap the process of critical reflective morality, is likely to be prejudice masquerading as a First Principle or a Mandate from Heaven.

The mark of an enlightened democracy is, as far as is possible with its security, to respect the religious commitment of a citizen who believes, on grounds of conscience or any other ground, that his relation to God involves duties superior to those arising from any human relation. It, therefore, exempts him from his duty as a citizen to protect his country. However, the mark of the genuine conscientious objector in a democracy is to respect the democratic process. He does not use his exemption as a political weapon to coerce where he has failed to convince or persuade. Having failed to influence national policy by rational means within the law, in the political processes open to him in a free society, he cannot justifiably try to defeat that policy by resorting to obstructive techniques outside the law and still remain a democrat.

It is one thing on grounds of conscience or religion to plead exemption from the duty of serving one's country when drafted. It is quite another to adopt harassing techniques to prevent others from volunteering or responding to the call of duty. It is one thing to oppose American involvement in Vietnam by teach-ins, petitions, electoral activity. It is quite another to attempt to stop troop trains: to take possession of the premises of draft boards where policies are not made; to urge recruits to sabotage their assignments and feign illness to win discharge. The first class of actions fall within the sphere of legitimate social protest; the second class are implicitly insurrectionary since it is directed against the authority of a democratic government which it seeks to overthrow not by argument and discussion but by resistance—albeit passive resistance.

Nonetheless, since we have rejected legal absolutism we must face the possibility that in protest on ethical grounds individuals may refuse to obey some law which they regard as uncommonly immoral or uncommonly foolish. If they profess to be democrats, their behavior must scrupulously respect the following conditions:

First, it must be nonviolent—peaceful not only in form but in actuality. After all, the protesters are seeking to dramatize a great evil that the community allegedly has been unable to overcome because of complacency or moral weakness. Therefore, they must avoid the guilt of imposing hardship or harm on others who in the nature of the case can hardly be responsible for the situation under protest. Passive resistance should not be utilized merely as a safer or more effective strategy than active resistance of imposing their wills on others.

Secondly, resort to civil disobedience is never morally legitimate where other methods of remedying the evil complained of are available. Existing grievance procedures should be used. No grievance procedures were available to the southern Negroes. The Courts often shared the prejudices of the community and offered no relief, not even minimal protection. But such procedures *are* available in the areas of industry and education. For example, where charges against students are being heard such procedures may result in the dismissal of the charges not the students. Or the faculty on appeal may decide to suspend the rules rather than the students. To jump the gun to civil disobedience in bypassing these procedures is telltale evidence that those who are calling the shots are after other game than preserving the rights of students.

Thirdly, those who resort to civil disobedience are duty bound to accept the legal sanctions and punishments imposed by the laws. Attempts to evade and escape them not only involve a betrayal of the community, but erode the moral foundations of civil disobedience itself. Socrates' argument in the *Crito* is valid only on democratic premises. The rationale of the protesters is the hope that the pain and hurt and indignity they voluntarily accept will stir their fellow citizens to compassion, open their minds to second thoughts, and move them to undertake the necessary healing action. When, however, we observe the heroics of defiance being followed by the dialectics of legal evasion, we question the sincerity of the action.

Fourth, civil disobedience is unjustified if a major moral issue is not clearly at stake. Differences about negotiable details that can easily be settled with a little patience should not be fanned into a blaze of illegal opposition.

Fifth, where intelligent men of good will and character differ on large and complex moral issues, discussion and agitation are more appropriate than civilly disobedient action. Those who feel strongly about animal rights and regard the consumption of animal flesh as foods as morally evil would have a just cause for civil disobedience if *their* freedom to obtain other food was threatened. They would have no moral right to resort to similar action to prevent their fellow citizens from consuming meat. Similarly with fluoridation.

Sixth, where civil disobedience is undertaken, there must be some rhyme and reason in the time, place, and targets selected. If one is convinced, as I am not, that the Board of Education of New York City is remiss in its policy of desegregation, what is the point of dumping garbage on bridges to produce traffic jams that seriously discomfort commuters who have not the remotest connection with educational policies in New York. Such action can only obstruct the progress of desegregation in the communities of Long Island. Gandhi, who inspired the civil disobedience movement in the twentieth century, was a better tactician than many who invoke his name but ignore his teachings. When he organized his campaign of civil disobedience against the Salt Tax, he marched with his followers to the sea to make salt. He did not hold up food trains or tie up traffic.

Finally, there is such a thing as historical timing. Democrats who resort to civil disobedience must ask themselves whether the cumulative consequences of their action may in the existing climate of opinion undermine the peace and order on which the effective exercise of other human rights depend. This is a cost which one may be willing to pay but which must be taken into the reckoning.

These observations in the eyes of some defenders of the philosophy of civil disobedience are far from persuasive. They regard them as evading the political realities. The political realities, it is asserted, do not provide meaningful channels for the legitimate expression of dissent. The "Establishment" is too powerful or indifferent to be moved. Administrations are voted into office that are not bound by their election pledges. The right to form minority parties is hampered by unconstitutional voting laws. What does even "the right of the people to present petitions for the redress of grievances" amount to if it does not carry with it the right to have those petitions paid attention to, at least to have them read, if not acted upon?

No, the opposing argument runs on. Genuine progress does not come by enactment of laws, by appeals to the good will or conscience of one's fellow citizens, but only by obstructions which interfere with the functioning of the system itself, by actions whose nuisance value is so high that the Establishment finds it easier to be decent and yield to demands than to be obdurate and oppose them. The time comes, as one student leader of the civilly disobedient Berkeley students advised, "when it is necessary for you to throw your bodies upon the wheels and gears and levers and bring the machine to a grinding halt." When one objects that such obstruction, as a principle of political action, is almost sure to produce chaos, and that it is unnecessary and undesirable in a democracy, the retort is made: "Amen, if only this were a democracy, how glad we would be to stop!"

It is characteristic of those who argue this way to define the presence or absence of the democratic process by whether or not *they* get their political way, and not by the presence or absence of democratic institutional processes. The rules of the game exist to enable them to win and if they lose that's sufficient proof the game is rigged and dishonest. The sincerity with which the position is held is no evidence whatsoever of its coherence. The right to petition does not carry with it the right to be heard, if that means influence on those to whom it is addressed. What would they do if they received incompatible petitions from two different and hostile groups of petitioning citizens? The right of petition gives one a chance to persuade, and the persuasion must rest on the power of words, on the effective appeal to emotion, sympathy, reason, and logic. Petitions are weapons of criticism, and their failure does not justify appeal to other kinds of weapons.

It is quite true that some local election laws do hamper minority groups in the organization of political parties; but there is always the right of appeal to the Courts. Even if this fails there is a possibility of influencing other political parties. It is difficult but so long as one is free to publish and speak, it can be done. If a group is unsuccessful in moving a majority by the weapons of criticism, in a democracy it may resort to peaceful measures of obstruction, provided it is willing to accept punishment for its obstructionist behavior. But these objections are usually a preface to some form of elitism or moral snobbery which is incompatible with the very grounds given in defending the right of civil disobedience on the part of democrats in a democracy.

All of the seven considerations listed above are cautionary, not categorical. We have ruled out only two positions—blind obedience to any and all laws in a democracy, and unreflective violation of laws at the behest of individual consciences. Between these two obviously unacceptable extremes, there is a spectrum of views which shade into each other. Intelligent persons can differ on their application to specific situations. These differences will reflect different assessments of the historical mood of a culture, of the proper timing of protest and acquiescence, and of what the most desirable emphasis and direction of our teaching should be in order to extend "the blessing of liberty" as we preserve "domestic tranquility."

Without essaying the role of a prophet, here is my reading of the needs of the present. It seems to me that the Civil Rights Acts of 1964 and the Voting Acts of 1965 mark a watershed in the history of social and civil protest in the U.S. Upon their enforcement a great many things we hold dear depend, especially those causes in behalf of which in the last decade so many movements of social protest were launched. We must recall that it was the emasculation of the 15th Amendment in the South which kept the Southern Negro in a state of virtual peonage. The prospect of enforcement of the new civil rights legislation is a function of many factors—most notably the law-abiding behavior of the hitherto recalcitrant elements in the southern white communities. Their *uncivil*, violent disobedience has proved unavailing. We need not fear this so much as that they will adopt the strategies and techniques of the civil disobedience itself in their opposition to long-delayed and decent legislation to make the ideals of American democracy a greater reality.

On the other hand, I think the movement of civil disobedience, as distinct from legal protest, in regions of the country in which Negroes have made slow but substantial advances are not likely to make new gains commensurate with the risks. Those risks are that what is begun as civil disobedience will be perverted by extremists into uncivil disobedience, and alienate large numbers who have firmly supported the cause of freedom.

One of the unintended consequences of the two World Wars is that in many ways they strengthened the position of the Negroes and all other minorities in American political life. We do not need another, a third World War, to continue the process of liberation. We can do it in peace—without war and without civil war. The Civil Rights and Voting Acts of 1964 and 1965 are far in advance of the actual situation in the country where discrimination is so rife. Our present task is to bring home and reinforce popular consciousness of the fact that those who violate their provisions are violating the highest law of the land, and that their actions are outside the law. Therefore, our goal must *now* be to build up and strengthen a mood of respect for the law, for civil obedience to laws, even by those who deem them unwise or who opposed them in the past. Our hope is that those who abide by the law may learn not only to tolerate them but, in time, as their fruits develop, to accept them. To have the positive law on the side of right and justice is to have a powerful weapon that makes for voluntary compliance—but only if the *reasonableness* of the *prima facie* obligation to obey the law is recognized.

To one observer at least, that reasonableness is being more and more disregarded in this country. The current mood is one of growing indifference to and disregard of even the reasonable legalities. The headlines from New York to California tell the story. I am not referring to the crime rate which has made frightening strides, nor to the fact that some of our metropolitan centers have become dangerous jungles. I refer to a growing mood toward law generally, something comparable to the attitude toward the Volstead Act during the Prohibition era. The mood is more diffuse today. To be lawabiding in some circles is to be "a square."

In part, the community itself has been responsible for the emergence of this mood. This is especially true in those states which have failed to abolish the *unreasonable* legalities, particularly in the fields of marriage, divorce, birth control, sex behavior, therapeutic abortion, voluntary euthanasia, and other intrusions on the right of privacy. The failure to repeal foolish laws, which makes morally upright individuals legal offenders, tends to generate skepticism and indifference toward observing the reasonable legalities.

This mood must change if the promise of recent civil rights legislation is to be realized. Respect for law today can give momentum to the liberal upswing of the political and social pendulum in American life. In a democracy we cannot make an absolute of obedience to law or to anything else except "the moral obligation to be intelligent," but more than ever we must stress that dissent and opposition—the oxygen of free society—be combined with civic obedience, and that on moral grounds it express itself as legal dissent and legal opposition.

Frantz Fanon

Frantz Fanon (1925–1961), a French-educated psychoanalyst, became sympathetic to the Algerian cause while working in Algeria during its war for independence. He has become famous recently because of his work on the psychology of colonized peoples. His writings have been adopted and adapted by radical black groups in the United States. Of particular interest in the following selection from *The Wretched of the Earth* is Fanon's defense of violence as playing a role in the growth and maturation of individuals—particularly colonized individuals. His thesis on violence is not new; Hegel too defended something close to it. But its application to the colonized man has brought the argument to life. In its broad outlines, Fanon's work is Marxist in character.

The Wretched of the Earth

CONCERNING VIOLENCE

National liberation, national renaissance, the restoration of nationhood to the people, commonwealth: whatever may be the headings used or the new formulas introduced, decolonization is always a violent phenomenon. At whatever level we study it—relationships between individuals, new names for sports clubs, the human admixture at cocktail parties, in the police, on the directing boards of national or private banks—decolonization is quite simply the replacing of a certain "species" of men by another "species" of men. Without any period of transition, there is a total, complete, and absolute substitution. It is true that we could equally well stress the rise of a new nation, the setting up of a new state, its diplomatic relations, and its economic and political trends. But we have precisely chosen to speak of that kind of *tabula rasa* which characterizes at the outset all decolonization. Its unusual importance is that it constitutes, from the very first day, the minimum demands of the colonized. To tell the truth, the proof of success lies in a whole social structure being changed from the bottom up. The extraordinary importance of this change is that it is willed, called for, demanded. The need for this change exists in its crude state, impetuous and compelling, in the consciousness and in the lives of the men and women who are colonized. But the possibility of this change is equally experienced in the form of a terrifying future in the consciousness of another "species" of men and women: the colonizers.

Decolonization, which sets out to change the order of the world, is, obviously, a program of complete disorder. But it cannot come as a result of magical practices, nor of a natural shock, nor of a friendly understanding. Decolonization, as we know, is a historical process: that is to say that it cannot be understood, it cannot become intelligible nor clear to itself except in the exact measure that we can discern the movements which give it historical form and content. Decolonization is the meeting of two forces, opposed to each other by their very nature, which in fact owe their originality to that sort of substantification which results from and is nourished by the situation in the colonies. Their first encounter was marked by violence and their existence together—that is to say the exploitation of the native by the settler—was carried on by dint of a great array of bayonets and cannons. The settler and the native are old acquaintances. In fact, the settler is right when he speaks of knowing "them" well. For it is the settler who has brought the native into existence and who perpetuates his existence. The settler owes the fact of his very existence, that is to say, his property, to the colonial system.

Decolonization never takes place unnoticed, for it influences individuals and modifies them fundamentally. It transforms spectators crushed with their inessentiality into privileged actors, with the grandiose glare of history's floodlights upon them. It brings a natural rhythm into existence, introduced by new men, and with it a new language and a new humanity. Decolonization is the veritable creation of new men. But this creation owes nothing of its legitimacy to any supernatural power; the "thing" which has been colonized becomes man during the same process by which it frees itself.

In decolonization, there is therefore the need of a complete calling in question of the colonial situation. If we wish to describe it precisely, we might find it in the well-known words: "The last shall be first and the first last." Decolonization is the putting into practice of this sentence. That is why, if we try to describe it, all decolonization is successful.

The naked truth of decolonization evokes for us the searing bullets and bloodstained knives which emanate from it. For if the last shall be first, this will only come to pass after a murderous and decisive struggle between the two protagonists. That affirmed intention to place the last at the head of things, and to make them climb at a pace (too quickly, some say) the well-known steps which characterize an organized society, can only triumph if we use all means to turn the scale, including, of course, that of violence.

You do not turn any society, however primitive it may be, upside down with such a program if you have not decided from the very beginning, that is to say from the actual formulation of that program, to overcome all the obstacles that you will come across in so doing. The native who decides to put the program into practice, and to become its moving force, is ready for violence at all times. From birth it is clear to him that this narrow world, strewn with prohibitions, can only be called in question by absolute violence.

The colonial world is a world divided into compartments. It is probably unnecessary to recall the existence of native quarters and European quarters, of schools for natives and schools for Europeans; in the same way we need not recall apartheid in South Africa. Yet, if we examine closely this system of compartments, we will at least be able to reveal the lines of force it implies. This approach to the colonial world, its ordering and its geographical layout will allow us to mark out the lines on which a decolonized society will be reorganized.

The colonial world is a world cut in two. The dividing line, the frontiers are shown by barracks and police stations. In the colonies it is the policeman and the soldier who are the official, instituted go-betweens, the spokesmen of the settler and his rule of oppression. In capitalist societies the educational system, whether lay or clerical, the structure of moral reflexes handed down from father to son, the exemplary honesty of workers who are given a medal after fifty years of good and loyal service, and the affection which springs from harmonious relations and good behavior—all these aesthetic expressions of respect for the established order serve to create around the exploited person an atmosphere of submission and of inhibition which lightens the task of policing considerably. In the capitalist countries a multitude of moral teachers, counselors and "bewilderers" separate the exploited from those in power. In the colonial countries, on the contrary, the policeman and the soldier, by their immediate presence and their frequent and direct action maintain contact with the native and advise him by means of rifle butts and napalm not to budge. It is obvious here that the agents of government speak the language of pure force. The intermediary does not lighten the oppression, nor seek to hide the domination; he shows them up and puts them into practice with the clear conscience of an upholder of the peace; yet he is the bringer of violence into the home and into the mind of the native.

The zone where the natives live is not complementary to the zone inhabited by the settlers. The two zones are opposed, but not in the service of a higher unity. Obedient to the rules of pure Aristotelian logic, they both follow the principle of reciprocal exclusivity. No conciliation is possible, for of the two terms, one is superfluous. The settlers' town is a strongly built town, all made of stone and steel. It is a brightly lit town; the streets are covered with asphalt, and the garbage cans swallow all the leavings, unseen, unknown and hardly thought about. The settler's feet are never visible, except perhaps in the sea; but there you're never close enough to see them. His feet are protected by strong shoes although the streets of his town are clean and even, with no holes or stones. The settler's town is a well-fed town, an easygoing town; its belly is always full of good things. The settler's town is a town of white people, of foreigners.

The town belonging to the colonized people, or at least the native town, the Negro village, the medina, the reservation, is a place of ill fame, peopled by men of evil repute. They are born there, it matters little where or how; they die there, it matters not where, nor how. It is a world without spaciousness; men live there on top of each other, and their huts are built one on top of the other. The native town is a hungry town, starved of bread, of meat, of shoes, of coal, of light. The native town is a crouching village, a town on its knees, a town wallowing in the mire. It is a town of niggers and dirty Arabs. The look that the native turns on the settler's town is a look of lust, a look of envy; it expresses his dreams of possession—all manner of possession: to sit at the settler's table, to sleep in the settler's bed, with his wife if possible. The colonized man is an envious man. And this the settler knows very well; when their glances meet he ascertains bitterly, always on the defensive, "They want to take our place." It is true, for there is no native who does not dream at least once a day of setting himself up in the settler's place.

This world divided into compartments, this world cut in two is inhabited by two different species. The orginality of the colonial context is that economic reality, inequality, and the immense difference of ways of life never come to mask the human realities. When you examine at close quarters the colonial context, it is evident that what parcels out the world is to begin with the fact of belonging to or not belonging to a given race, a given species. In the colonies the economic substructure is also a superstructure. The cause is the consequence; you are rich because you are white, you are white because you are rich. This is why Marxist analysis should always be slightly stretched every time we have to do with the colonial problem.

Everything up to and including the very nature of precapitalist society, so well explained by Marx, must here be thought out again. The serf is in essence different from the knight, but a reference to divine right is necessary to legitimize this statutory difference. In the colonies, the foreigner coming from another country imposed his rule by means of guns and machines. In defiance of his successful transplantation, in spite of his appropriation, the settler still remains a foreigner. It is neither the act of owning factories, nor estates, nor a bank balance which distinguishes the governing classes. The governing race is first and foremost those who come from elsewhere, those who are unlike the original inhabitants, "the others."

The violence which has ruled over the ordering of the colonial world, which has ceaselessly drummed the rhythm for the destruction of native social forms and broken up without reserve the systems of reference of the economy, the customs of dress and external life, that same violence will be claimed and taken over by the native at the moment when, deciding to embody history in his own person, he surges into the forbidden quarters. To wreck the colonial world is henceforward a mental picture of action which is very clear, very easy to understand and which may be assumed by each one of the individuals which constitute the colonized people. To break up the colonial world does not mean that after the frontiers have been abolished lines of communication will be set up between the two zones. The destruction of the colonial world is no more and no less that the abolition of one zone, its burial in the depths of the earth or its expulsion from the country.

The natives' challenge to the colonial world is not a rational confrontation of points of view. It is not a treatise on the universal, but the untidy affirmation of an original idea propounded as an absolute. The colonial world is a Manichean world. It is not enough for the settler to delimit physically, that is to say with the help of the army and the police force, the place of the native. As if to show the totalitarian character of colonial exploitation the settler paints the native as a sort of quintessence of evil. Native society is not simply described as a society lacking in values. It is not enough for the colonist to affirm that those values have disappeared from, or still better never existed in, the colonial world. The native is declared insensible to ethics; he represents not only the absence of values, but also the negation of values. He is, let us dare to admit, the enemy of values, and in this sense he is the absolute evil. He is the corrosive element, destroying all that comes near him; he is the deforming element, disfiguring all that has to do with beauty or morality; he is the depository of maleficent powers, the unconscious and irretrievable instrument of blind forces. Monsieur Meyer could thus state seriously in the French National Assembly that the Republic must not be prostituted by allowing the Algerian people to become part of it. All values, in fact, are irrevocably poisoned and diseased as soon as they are allowed in contact with the colonized race. The customs of the colonized people, their traditions, their myths—above all, their myths—are the very sign of that poverty of spirit and of their constitutional depravity. That is why we must put the DDT which destroys parasites, the bearers of disease, on the same level as the Christian religion which wages war on embryonic heresies and instincts, and on evil as yet unborn. The recession of yellow fever and the advance of evangelization form part of the same balance sheet. But the triumphant *communiqués* from the missions are in fact a source of information concerning the implantation of foreign influences in the core of the colonized people. I speak of the Christian religion, and no one need be astonished. The Church in the colonies is the white people's Church, the foreigner's Church. She does not call the native to God's ways but to the ways of the white man, of the master, of the oppressor. And as we know, in this matter many are called but few chosen.

At times this Manicheism goes to its logical conclusion and dehumanizes the native, or to speak plainly, it turns him into an animal. In fact, the terms the settler uses when he mentions the native are zoological terms. He speaks of the yellow man's reptilian motions, of the stink of the native quarter, of breeding swarms, of foulness, of spawn, of gesticulations. When the settler seeks to describe the native fully in exact terms he constantly refers to the bestiary. The European rarely hits on a picturesque style; but the native, who knows what is in the mind of the settler, guesses at once what he is thinking of. Those hordes of vital statistics, those hysterical masses, those faces bereft of all humanity, those distended bodies which are like nothing on earth, that mob without beginning or end, those children who seem to belong to nobody, that laziness stretched out in the sun, that vegetative rhythm of life—all this forms part of the colonial vocabulary. General de Gaulle speaks of "the yellow multitudes" and François Mauriac of the black, brown, and yellow masses which soon will be unleashed. The native knows all this, and laughs to himself every time he spots an allusion to the animal world in the other's words. For he knows that he is not an animal; and it is precisely at the moment he realizes his humanity that he begins to sharpen the weapons with which he will secure its victory.

As soon as the native begins to pull on his moorings, and to cause anxiety to the settler, he is handed over to well-meaning souls who in cultural congresses point out to him the specificity and wealth of Western values. But every time Western values are mentioned they produce in the native a sort of stiffening or muscular lockjaw. During the period of decolonization the native's reason is appealed to. He is offered definite values, he is told frequently that decolonization need not mean regression, and that he must put his trust in qualities which are well-tried, solid, and highly esteemed. But it so happens that when the native hears a speech about Western culture he pulls o 't his knife—or at least he makes sure it is within reach. The violence with which the supremacy of white values is affirmed and the aggressiveness which has permeated the victory of these values over the ways of life and of thought of the native mean that, in revenge, the native laughs in mockery when Western values are mentioned in front of him. In the colonial context the settler only ends his work of breaking in the native when the latter admits loudly and intelligibly the supremacy of the white man's values. In the period of decolonization, the colonized masses mock at these very values, insult them, and vomit them up.

This phenomenon is ordinarily masked because, during the period of decolonization, certain colonized intellectuals have begun a dialogue with the bourgeoisie of the colonialist country. During this phase, the indigenous population is discerned only as an indistinct mass. The few native personalities whom the colonialist bourgeois have come to know here and there have not sufficient influence on that immediate discernment to give rise to nuances. On the other hand, during the period of liberation, the colonialist bourgeoisie looks feverishly for contacts with the elite and it is with these elite that the familiar dialogue concerning values is carried on. The colonialist bourgeoisie, when it realizes that it is impossible for it to maintain its domination over the colonial countries, decides to carry out a rearguard action with regard to culture, values, techniques, and so on. Now what we must never forget is that the immense majority of colonized peoples is oblivious to these problems. For a colonized people the most essential value, because the most concrete, is first and foremost the land: the land which will bring them bread and, above all, dignity. But this dignity has nothing to do with the dignity of the human individual: for that human individual has never heard tell of it. All that the native has seen in his country is that they can freely arrest him, beat him, strave him: and no professor of ethics, no priest has ever come to be beaten in his place, nor to share their bread with him. As far as the native is concerned, morality is very concrete; it is to silence the settler's defiance, to break his flaunting violence—in a word, to put him out of the picture. The well-known principle that all men are equal will be illustrated in the colonies from the moment that the native claims that he is the equal of the settler. One step more, and he is ready to fight to be more than the settler. In fact he has already decided to eject him and to take his place; as we see it, it is a whole material and moral universe which is breaking up. The intellectual who for his part has followed the colonialist with regard to the universal abstract will fight in order that the settler and the native may live together in peace in a new world. But the thing he does not see, precisely because he is permeated by colonialism and all its ways of thinking, is that the settler, from the moment that the colonial context disappears, has no longer any interest in remaining or in co-existing. . . .

Thus the native discovers that his life, his breath, his beating heart are the same as those of the settler. He finds out that the settler's skin is not of any more value than a native's skin; and it must be said that this discovery shakes the world in a very necessary manner. All the new, revolutionary assurance of the native stems from it. For if, in fact, my life is worth as much as the settler's, his glance no longer shrivels me up nor freezes me, and his voice no longer turns me into stone. I am no longer on tenterhooks in his presence; in fact, I don't give a damn for him. Not only does his presence no longer trouble me, but I am already preparing such efficient ambushes for him that soon there will be no way out but that of flight.

We have said that the colonial context is characterized by the dichotomy which it imposes upon the whole people. Decolonization unifies that people by the radical decision to remove from it its heterogeneity, and by unifying it on a national, sometimes a racial, basis. We know the fierce words of the Senegalese patriots, referring to the maneuvers of their president, Senghor: "We have demanded that the higher posts should be given to Africans; and now Senghor is Africanizing the Europeans." That is to say that the native can see clearly and immediately if decolonization has come to pass or not, for his minimum demands are simply that the last shall be first.

But the native intellectual brings variants to this petition, and, in fact, he seems to have good reasons: higher civil servants, technicians, specialists—all seem to be needed. Now, the ordinary native interprets these unfair promotions as so many acts of sabotage, and he is often heard to declare: "It wasn't worthwhile, then, our becoming independent . . ."

In the colonial countries where a real struggle for freedom has taken place, where the blood of the people has flowed and where the length of the period of armed warfare has favored the backward surge of intellectuals toward bases grounded in the people, we can observe a genuine eradication of the superstructure built by these intellectuals from the bourgeois, colonialist environment. The colonialist bourgeoisie, in its narcissistic dialogue, expounded by the members of its universities, had in fact deeply implanted in the minds of the colonized intellectual that the essential qualities remain eternal in spite of all the blunders men may make: the essential qualities of the West, of course. The native intellectual accepted the cogency of these ideas, and deep down in his brain you could always find a vigilant sentinel ready to defend the Greco-Latin pedestal. Now it so happens that during the struggle for liberation, at the moment that the native intellectual comes into touch again with his people, this artificial sentinel is turned into dust. All the Mediterranean values—the triumph of the human individual, of clarity, and of beauty—become lifeless, colorless knickknacks. All those speeches seem like collections of dead words; those values which seemed to uplift the soul are revealed as worthless, simply because they have nothing to do with the concrete conflict in which the people is engaged.

Individualism is the first to disappear. The native intellectual had learnt from his masters that the individual ought to express himself fully. The colonialist bourgeoisie had hammered into the native's mind the idea of a society of individuals where each person shuts himself up in his own subjectivity, and whose only wealth is individual thought. Now the native who has the opportunity to return to the people during the struggle for freedom will discover the falseness of this theory. The very forms of organization of the struggle will suggest to him a different vocabulary. Brother, sister, friend—these are words outlawed by the colonialist bourgeoisie, because for them my brother is my purse, my friend is part of my scheme for getting on. The native intellectual takes part, in a sort of auto-da-fé, in the destruction of all his idols: egoism, recrimination that springs from pride, and the childish stupidity of those who always want to have the last word. Such a colonized intellectual, dusted over by colonial culture, will in the same way discover the substance of village assemblies, the cohesion of people's committees, and the extraordinary fruitfulness of local meetings and groupments. Henceforward, the interests of one will be the interests of all, for in concrete fact everyone will be discovered by the troops, everyone will be massacred—or everyone will be saved. The motto "look out for yourself," the atheist's method of salvation, is in this context forbidden.

Self-criticism has been much talked about of late, but few people realize that it is an African institution. Whether in the *djemaas*[1] of northern Africa or in the meetings of western Africa, tradition demands that the quarrels which occur in a village should be settled in public. It is communal self-criticism, of course, and with a note of humor, because everybody is relaxed, and because in the last resort we all want the same things. But the more the intellectual imbibes the atmosphere of the people, the more completely he abandons the habits of calculation, of unwonted silence, of mental reservations, and shakes off the spirit of concealment. And it is true that already at that level we can say that the community triumphs, and that it spreads its own light and its own reason.

But it so happens sometimes that decolonization occurs in areas which have not been sufficiently shaken by the struggle for liberation, and there may be found those same know-all, smart, wily intellectuals. We find intact in them the manners and forms of thought picked up during their association with the colonialist bourgeoisie. Spoilt children of yesterday's colonialism and of today's national governments, they organize the loot of whatever national resources exist. Without pity, they use today's national distress as a means of getting on through scheming and legal robbery, by import-export combines, limited liability companies, gambling on the stock exchange, or unfair promotion. They are insistent in their demands for the nationalization of commerce, that is to say the reservation of markets and advantageous bargains for nationals only. As far as doctrine is concerned, they proclaim the pressing necessity of nationalizing the robbery of the nation. In this arid phase of national life, the so-called period of austerity, the success of their depredations is swift to call forth the violence and anger of the people. For this same people, poverty-stricken yet independent, comes very quickly to possess a social conscience in the African and international context of today; and this the petty individualists will quickly learn.

In order to assimilate and to experience the oppressor's culture, the native has had to leave certain of his intellectual possessions in pawn. These pledges include his adoption of the forms of thought of the colonialist bourgeoisie. This is very noticeable in the inaptitude of the native intellectual to carry on a two-sided discussion; for he cannot eliminate himself when confronted with an object or an idea. On the other hand, when on .e he begins to militate among the people he is struck with wonder and amazement; he is literally disarmed by their good faith and honesty. The danger that will haunt him continually is that of becoming the uncritical mouthpiece of the masses; he becomes a kind of yes-man who nods assent at every word coming from the people, which he interprets as considered judgments. Now, the *fellah*, the unemployed man, the starving native do not lay a claim to the truth; they do not *say* that they ₌epresent the truth, for they *are* the truth.

Objectively, the intellectual behaves in this phase like a common opportunist. In fact he has not stopped maneuvering. There is never any question of his being either rejected or welcomed by the people. What they ask is simply that all resources should be pooled. The inclusion of the native intellectual in the upward surge of the masses will in this case be differentiated by a curious cult of detail. That is not to say that the people are hostile to analysis; on the contrary, they like having things explained to them, they are glad to understand a line of

[1] Village assemblies.—*Trans.*

argument and they like to see where they are going. But at the beginning of his association with the people the native intellectual over-stresses details and thereby comes to forget that the defeat of colonialism is the real object of the struggle. Carried away by the multitudinous aspects of the fight, he tends to concentrate on local tasks, performed with enthusiasm but almost always too solemnly. He fails to see the whole of the movement all the time. He introduces the idea of special disciplines, of specialized functions, of departments within the terrible stone crusher, the fierce mixing machine which a popular revolution is. He is occupied in action on a particular front, and it so happens that he loses sight of the unity of the movement. Thus, if a local defeat is inflicted, he may well be drawn into doubt, and from thence to despair. The people, on the other hand, take their stand from the start on the broad and inclusive positions of *bread and the land:* how can we obtain the land, and bread to eat? And this obstinate point of view of the masses, which may seem shrunken and limited, is in the end the most worthwhile and the most efficient mode of procedure.

The problem of truth ought also to be considered. In every age, among the people, truth is the property of the national cause. No absolute verity, no discourse on the purity of the soul, can shake this position. The native replies to the living lie of the colonial situation by an equal falsehood. His dealings with his fellow-nationals are open; they are strained and incomprehensible with regard to the settlers. Truth is that which hurries on the break-up of the colonialist regime; it is that which promotes the emergence of the nation; it is all that protects the natives, and ruins the foreigners. In this colonialist context there is no truthful behavior: and the good is quite simply that which is evil for "them."

Thus we see that the primary Manicheism which governed colonial society is preserved intact during the period of decolonization; that is to say that the settler never ceases to be the enemy, the opponent, the foe that must be overthrown. The oppressor, in his own sphere, starts the process, a process of domination, of exploitation and of pillage, and in the other sphere the coiled, plundered creature which is the native provides fodder for the process as best he can, the process which moves uninterruptedly from the banks of the colonial territory to the palaces and the docks of the mother country. In this becalmed zone the sea has a smooth surface, the palm tree stirs gently in the breeze, the waves lap against the pebbles, and raw materials are ceaselessly transported, justifying the presence of the settler: and all the while the native, bent double, more dead than alive, exists interminably in an unchanging dream. The settler makes history; his life is an epoch, an Odyssey. He is the absolute beginning: "This land was created by us"; he is the unceasing cause: "If we leave, all is lost, and the country will go back to the Middle Ages." Over against him torpid creatures, wasted by fevers, obsessed by ancestral customs, form an almost inorganic background for the innovating dynamism of colonial mercantilism.

The settler makes history and is conscious of making it. And because he constantly refers to the history of his mother country, he clearly indicates that he himself is the extension of that mother country. Thus the history which he writes is not the history of the country which he plunders but the history of his own nation in regard to all that she skims off, all that she violates and starves.

The immobility to which the native is condemned can only be called in question if the native decides to put an end to this history of colonization—the history of pillage—and to bring into existence the history of the nation—the history of decolonization. . .

Conclusion

Come, then, comrades; it would be as well to decide at once to change our ways. We must shake off the heavy darkness in which we were plunged, and leave it behind. The new day which is already at hand must find us firm, prudent, and resolute.

We must leave our dreams and abandon our old beliefs and friendships from the time before life began. Let us waste no time in sterile litanies and nauseating mimicry. Leave this Europe where they are never done talking of Man, yet murder men everywhere they find them, at the corner of every one of their own streets, in all the corners of the globe. For centuries they have stifled almost the whole of humanity in the name of a so-called spiritual experience. Look at them today swaying between atomic and spiritual disintegration.

And yet it may be said that Europe has been successful in as much as everything that she has attempted has succeeded.

Europe undertook the leadership of the world with ardor, cynicism, and violence. Look at how the shadow of her palaces stretches out ever further. Every one of her movements has burst the bounds of space and thought. Europe has declined all humility and all modesty; but she has also set her face against all solicitude and all tenderness.

She has only shown herself parsimonious and niggardly where men are concerned; it is only men that she has killed and devoured.

So, my brothers, how is it that we do not understand that we have better things to do than to follow that same Europe?

That same Europe where they were never done talking of Man, and where they never stopped proclaiming that they were only anxious for the welfare of Man: today we know with what sufferings humanity has paid for every one of their triumphs of the mind.

Come, then, comrades, the European game has finally ended; we must find something different. We today can do everything, so long as we do not imitate Europe, so long as we are not obsessed by the desire to catch up with Europe.

Europe now lives at such a mad, reckless pace that she has shaken off all guidance and all reason, and she is running headlong into the abyss; we would do well to avoid it with all possible speed.

Yet it is very true that we need a model, and that we want blueprints and examples. For many among us the European model is the most inspiring. We have therefore seen in the preceding pages to what mortifying setbacks such an imitation has led us. European achievements, European techniques, and the European style ought no longer to tempt us and to throw us off our balance.

When I search for Man in the technique and the style of Europe, I see only a succession of negations of man, and an avalanche of murders.

The human condition, plans for mankind, and collaboration between men in those tasks which increase the sum total of humanity are new problems, which demand true inventions.

Let us decide not to imitate Europe; let us combine our muscles and our brains in a new direction. Let us try to create the whole man, whom Europe has been incapable of bringing to triumphant birth.

Two centuries ago, a former European colony decided to catch up with Europe. It succeeded so well that the United States of America became a monster, in which the taints, the sickness, and the inhumanity of Europe have grown to appalling dimensions.

Comrades, have we not other work to do than to create a third Europe? The West saw itself as a spiritual adventure. It is in the name of the spirit, in the name of the spirit of Europe, that Europe has made her encroachments, that she has justified her crimes and legitimized the slavery in which she holds the four-fifths of humanity.

Yes, the European spirit has strange roots. All European thought has unfolded in places which were increasingly more deserted and more encircled by precipices; and thus it was that the custom grew up in those places of very seldom meeting man.

A permanent dialogue with oneself and an increasingly obscene narcissism never ceased to prepare the way for a half delirious state, where intellectual work became suffering and the reality was not at all that of a living man, working and creating himself, but rather words, different combinations of words, and the tensions springing from the meanings contained in words. Yet some Europeans were found to urge the European workers to shatter this narcissism and to break with this unreality.

But in general, the workers of Europe have not replied to these calls; for the workers believe, too, that they are part of the prodigious adventure of the European spirit.

All the elements of a solution to the great problems of humanity have, at different times, existed in European thought. But the action of European men has not carried out the mission which fell to them, and which consisted of bringing their whole weight violently to bear upon these elements, of modifying their arrangement and their nature, of changing them and finally of bringing the problem of mankind to an infinitely higher plane.

Today we are present at the stasis of Europe. Comrades, let us flee from this motionless movement where gradually dialectic is changing into the logic of equilibrium. Let us reconsider the question of mankind. Let us reconsider the question of cerebral reality and of the cerebral mass of all humanity, whose connections must be increased, whose channels must be diversified and whose messages must be re-humanized.

Come, brothers, we have far too much work to do for us to play the game of rearguard. Europe has done what she set out to do and on the whole she has done it well; let us stop blaming her, but let us say to her firmly that she should not make such a song and dance about it. We have no more to fear; so let us stop envying her.

The Third World today faces Europe like a colossal mass whose aim should be to try to resolve the problems to which Europe has not been able to find the answers.

But let us be clear: what matters is to stop talking about output, and intensification, and the rhythm of work.

No, there is no question of a return to Nature. It is simply a very concrete question of not dragging men toward mutilation, of not imposing upon the brain rhythms which very quickly obliterate it and wreck it. The pretext of catching up must not be used to push man around, to tear him away from himself or from his privacy, to break and kill him.

No, we do not want to catch up with anyone. What we want to do is to go forward all the time, night and day, in the company of Man, in the company of all men. The caravan should not be stretched out, for in that case each line will hardly see those who precede it; and men who no longer recognize each other meet less and less together, and talk to each other less and less.

It is a question of the Third World starting a new history of Man, a history which will have regard to the sometimes prodigious theses which Europe has put forward, but which will also not forget Europe's crimes, of which the most horrible was committed in the heart of man, and consisted of the pathological tearing apart of his functions and the crumbling away of his unity. And in the framework of the collectivity there were the differentiations, the stratification, and the bloodthirsty tensions fed by classes; and finally, on the immense scale of humanity, there were racial hatreds, slavery, exploitation, and above all the bloodless genocide which consisted in the setting aside of fifteen thousand millions of men.

So, comrades, let us not pay tribute to Europe by creating states, institutions, and societies which draw their inspiration from her.

Humanity is waiting, for something from us other than such an imitation, which would be almost an obscene caricature.

If we want to turn Africa into a new Europe, and America into a new Europe, then let us leave the destiny of our countries to Europeans. They will know how to do it better than the most gifted among us.

But if we want humanity to advance a step further, if we want to bring it up to a different level than that which Europe has shown it, then we must invent and we must make discoveries.

If we wish to live up to our peoples' expectations, we must seek the response elsewhere than in Europe.

Moreover, if we wish to reply to the expectations of the people of Europe, it is no good sending them back a reflection, even an ideal reflection, of their society and their thought with which from time to time they feel immeasurably sickened.

For Europe, for ourselves, and for humanity, comrades, we must turn over a new leaf, we must work out new concepts, and try to set afoot a new man.

Eldridge Cleaver

Eldrige Cleaver (b. 1935) has been minister of information of the Black Panther Party and was the 1968 Presidential candidate of the Peace and Freedom Party. Because of legal problems with the State of California he has left the United States and is living in Algeria. His friends and supporters consider him a political exile, his detractors call him a fugitive from justice.

Soul on Ice, written while he was in Folsom State Prison, established Cleaver as one of the most articulate spokesmen for
militant American blacks. The following chapter, "Domestic Law
and International Order", explains his view of the enforcement
agencies of existing governments.

Soul on Ice

DOMESTIC LAW AND INTERNATIONAL ORDER

The police department and the armed forces are the two arms of the power
structure, the muscles of control and enforcement. They have deadly weapons
with which to inflict pain on the human body. They know how to bring about
horrible deaths. They have clubs with which to beat the body and the head.
They have bullets and guns with which to tear holes in the flesh, to smash bones,
to disable and kill. They use force, to make you do what the deciders have
decided you must do.

Every country on earth has these agencies of force. The people everywhere
fear this terror and force. To them it is like a snarling wild beast which can put
an end to one's dreams. They punish. They have cells and prisons to lock you up
in. They pass out sentences. They won't let you go when you want to. You have
to stay put until they give the word. If your mother is dying, you can't go to her
bedside to say goodbye or to her graveside to see her lowered into the earth, to
see her, for the last time, swallowed up by that black hole.

The techniques of the enforcers are many: firing squads, gas chambers,
electric chairs, torture chambers, the garrote, the guillotine, the tightening rope
around your throat. It has been found that the death penalty is necessary to
back up the law, to make it easier to enforce, to deter transgressions against the
penal code. That everybody doesn't believe in the same laws is beside the point.

Which laws get enforced depends on who is in power. If the capitalists are in
power, they enforce laws designed to protect their system, their way of life.
They have a particular abhorrence for crimes against property, but are prepared
to be liberal and show a modicum of compassion for crimes against the
person—unless, of course, an instance of the latter is combined with an instance
of the former. In such cases, nothing can stop them from throwing the whole
book at the offender. For instance, armed robbery with violence, to a capitalist,
is the very epitome of evil. Ask any banker what he thinks of it.

If Communists are in power, they enforce laws designed to protect their
system, their way of life. To them, the horror of horrors is the speculator, that
man of magic who has mastered the art of getting something with nothing and

who in America would be a member in good standing of his local Chamber of Commerce.

"The people," however, are nowhere consulted, although everywhere everything is done always in their name and ostensibly for their betterment, while their real-life problems go unsolved. "The people" are a rubber stamp for the crafty and sly. And no problem can be solved without taking the police department and the armed forces into account. Both kings and bookies understand this, as do first ladies and common prostitutes.

The police do on the domestic level what the armed forces do on the international level: protect the way of life of those in power. The police patrol the city, cordon off communities, blockade neighborhoods, invade homes, search for that which is hidden. The armed forces patrol the world, invade countries and continents, cordon off nations, blockade islands and whole peoples; they will also overrun villages, neighborhoods, enter homes, huts, caves, searching for that which is hidden. The policeman and the soldier will violate your person, smoke you out with various gases. Each will shoot you, beat your head and body with sticks and clubs, with rifle butts, run you through with bayonets, shoot holes in your flesh, kill you. They each have unlimited firepower. They will use all that is necessary to bring you to your knees. They won't take no for an answer. If you resist their sticks, they draw their guns. If you resist their guns, they call for reinforcements with bigger guns. Eventually they will come in tanks, in jets, in ships. They will not rest until you surrender or are killed. The policeman and the soldier will have the last word.

Both police and the armed forces follow orders. Orders. Orders flow from the top down. Up there, behind closed doors, in antechambers, in conference rooms, gavels bang on the tables, the tinkling of silver decanters can be heard as icewater is poured by well-fed, conservatively dressed men in hornrimmed glasses, fashionably dressed American widows with rejuvenated faces and tinted hair, the air permeated with the square humor of Bob Hope jokes. Here all the talking is done, all the thinking, all the deciding. Gray rabbits of men scurry forth from the conference room to spread the decisions throughout the city, as News. Carrying out orders is a job, a way of meeting the payments on the house, a way of providing for one's kiddies. In the armed forces it is also a duty, patriotism. Not to do so is treason.

Every city has its police department. No city would be complete without one. It would be sheer madness to try operating an American city without the heat, the fuzz, the man. Americans are too far gone, or else they haven't arrived yet; the center does not exist, only the extremes. Take away the cops and Americans would have a coast-to-coast free-for-all. There are, of course, a few citizens who carry their own private cops around with them, built into their souls. But there is robbery in the land, and larceny, murder, rape, burglary, theft, swindles, all brands of crime, profit, rent, interest—and these blasé descendants of Pilgrims are at each other's throats. To complicate matters, there are also rich people and poor peole in America. There are Negroes and whites, Indians, Puerto Ricans, Mexicans, Jews, Chinese, Arabs, Japanese—all with equal rights but unequal possessions. Some are haves and some are have-nots. All have been taught to worship at the shrine of General Motors. The whites are on top in America and they want to stay there, up there. They are also on top in the world, on the international level, and they want to stay up there, too. Everywhere there are those who want to smash this precious toy clock of a system, they want ever so much to change it, to rearrange things, to pull the whites down off their high horse and make them equal. Everywhere the whites are fighting to prolong their status, to retard the erosion of their position. In America, when everything else fails, they call out the police. On the international level, when everything else fails, they call out the armed forces.

A strange thing happened in Watts, in 1965, August. The blacks, who in this land of private property have all private and no property, got excited into an uproar because they noticed a cop before he had a chance to wash the blood off his hands. Usually the police department can handle such flare-ups. But this time it was different. Things got out of hand. The blacks were running amok, burning, shooting, breaking. The police department was powerless to control them; the chief called for reinforcements. Out came the National Guard, that ambiguous hybrid from the twilight zone where the domestic army merges with the international; that hypocritical force poised within America and capable of action on either level, capable of backing up either the police or the armed forces. Unleashing their formidable firepower, they crushed the blacks. But things will never be the same again. Too many people saw that those who turned the other cheek in Watts got their whole head blown off. At the same time, heads were being blown off in Vietnam. America was embarrassed, not by the quality of her deeds but by the surplus of publicity focused upon her negative selling points, and a little frightened because of what all those dead bodies, on two fronts, implied. Those corpses spoke eloquently of potential allies and alliances. A community of interest began to emerge, dripping with blood, out of the ashes of Watts. The blacks in Watts and all over America could now see the Viet Cong's point: both were on the receiving end of what the armed forces were dishing out.

So now the blacks, stung by the new knowledge they have unearthed, cry out: *"POLICE BRUTALITY!"* From one end of the country to the other, the new war cry is raised. The youth, those nodes of compulsive energy who are all fuel and muscle, race their motors, itch to do something. The Uncle Toms, no longer willing to get down on their knees to lick boots, do so from a squatting position. The black bourgeoisie call for Citizens' Review Boards, to assert civilian control over the activity of the police. In back rooms, in dark stinking corners of the ghettos, self-conscious black men curse their own cowardice and stare at their rifles and pistols and shotguns laid out on tables before them, trembling as they wish for a manly impulse to course through their bodies and send them screaming mad into the streets shooting from the hip. Black women look at their men as if they are bugs, curious growths of flesh playing an inscrutable waiting game. Violence becomes a homing pigeon floating through the ghettos seeking a black brain in which to roost for a season.

In their rage against the police, against police brutality, the blacks lose sight of the fundamental reality: that the police are only an instrument for the implementation of the policies of those who make the decisions. Police brutality is only one facet of the crystal of terror and oppression. Behind police brutality there is social brutality, economic brutality, and political brutality. From the perspective of the ghetto, this is not easy to discern: the TV newscaster and the radio announcer and the editorialists of the newspapers are wizards of the smoke screen and the snow job.

What is true on the international level is true also at home; except that the ace up the sleeve is easier to detect in the international arena. Who would maintain that American soldiers are in Vietnam on their own motion? They were conscripted into the armed forces and taught the wisdom of obeying orders. They were sent to Vietnam by orders of the generals in the Pentagon, who receive them from the Secretary of Defense, who receives them from the President, who is shrouded in mystery. The soldier in the field in Vietnam, the man who lies in the grass and squeezes the trigger when a little half-starved, trembling Vietnamese peasant crosses his sights, is only following orders, carrying out a policy and a plan. He hardly knows what it is all about. They have him wired-up tight with the slogans of TV and the World Series. All he knows is that he has been assigned to carry out a certain ritual of duties. He is well trained and does the best he can. He does a good job. He may want to please those above him with the quality of his performance. He may want to make sergeant, or better. This man is from some hicky farm in Shit Creek, Georgia. He only knew whom to kill after passing through boot camp. He could just as well come out ready to kill Swedes. He will kill a Swede dead, if he is ordered to do so.

Same for the policeman in Watts. He is not there on his own. They have all been assigned. They have been told what to do and what not to do. They have also been told what they better not do. So when they continually do something, in every filthy ghetto in this shitty land, it means only that they are following orders.

It's no secret that in America the blacks are in total rebellion against the System. They want to get their nuts out of the sand. They don't like the way America is run, from top to bottom. In America, everything is owned. Everything is held as private property. Someone has a brand on everything. There is nothing left over. Until recently, the blacks themselves were counted as part of somebody's private property, along with the chickens and goats. The blacks have not forgotten this, principally because they are still treated as if they are part of someone's inventory of assets—or perhaps, in this day of rage against the costs of welfare, blacks are listed among the nation's liabilities. On any account, however, blacks are in no position to respect or help maintain the institution of private property. What they want is to figure out a way to get some of that property for themselves, to divert it to their own needs. This is what it is all about, and this is the real brutality involved. This is the source of all brutality.

The police are the armed guardians of the social order. The blacks are the chief domestic victims of the American social order. A conflict of interest exists, therefore, between the blacks and the police. It is not solely a matter of trigger-happy cops, of brutal cops who love to crack black heads. Mostly it's a job to them. It pays good. And there are numerous fringe benefits. The real problem is a trigger-happy social order.

The Utopians speak of a day when there will be no police. There will be nothing for them to do. Every man will do his duty, will respect the rights of his neighbor, will not disturb the peace. The needs of all will be taken care of. Everyone will have sympathy for his fellow man. There will be no such thing as crime. There will be, of course, no prisons. No electric chairs, no gas chambers. The hangman's rope will be the thing of the past. The entire earth will be a land of plenty. There will be no crimes against property, no speculation.

It is easy to see that we are not on the verge of entering Utopia: there are cops everywhere. North and South, the Negroes are the have-nots. They see property all around them, property that is owned by whites. In this regard, the black bourgeoisie has become nothing but a ridiculous nuisance. Having waged a battle for entrance into the American mainstream continually for fifty years, all of the black bourgeoisie's defenses are directed outward, against the whites. They have no defenses against the blacks and no time to erect any. The black masses can handle them any time they choose, with one mighty blow. But the white bourgeoisie presents a bigger problem, those whites who own everything. With many shackled by unemployment, hatred in black hearts for this system of private property increases daily. The sanctity surrounding property is being called into question. The mystique of the deed of ownership is melting away. In other parts of the world, peasants rise up and expropriate the land from the former owners. Blacks in America see that the deed is not eternal, that it is not signed by God, and that new deeds, making blacks the owners, can be drawn up.

The Black Muslims raised the cry, "*WE MUST HAVE SOME LAND!*" "*SOME LAND OF OUR OWN OR ELSE!*" Blacks in America shrink from the colossus of General Motors. They can't see how to wade through that thicket of common stocks, preferred stocks, bonds and debentures. They only know that General Motors is huge, that it has billions of dollars under its control, that it owns land, that its subsidiaries are legion, that it is a repository of vast powers. The blacks want to crack the nut of General Motors. They are meditating on it. Meanwhile, they must learn that the police take orders from General Motors. And that the Bank of America has something to do with them even though they don't have a righteous penny in the bank. They have no bank accounts, only bills to pay. The only way they know of making withdrawals from the bank is at the point of a gun. The shiny fronts of skyscrapers intimidate them. They do not own them. They feel alienated from the very sidewalks on which they walk. This white man's country, this white man's world. Overflowing with men of color. An economy consecrated to the succor of the whites. Blacks are incidental. The war on poverty, that monstrous insult to the rippling muscles in a black man's arms, is an index of how men actually sit down and plot each other's deaths, actually sit down with slide rules and calculate how to hide bread from the hungry. And the black bourgeoisie greedily sopping up what crumbs are tossed into their dark corner.

There are 20,000,000 of these blacks in America, probably more. Today they repeat, in awe, this magic number to themselves: there are 20,000,000 of us! They shout this to each other in humiliated astonishment. No one need tell them that there is vast power latent in their mass. They know that 20,000,000 of anything is enough to get some recognition and consideration. They know also that they must harness their number and hone it into a sword with a sharp cutting edge. White General Motors also knows that the unity of these 20,000,000 ragamuffins will spell the death of the system of its being. At all costs, then, they will seek to keep these blacks from uniting, from becoming bold and revolutionary. These white property owners know that they must keep the blacks cowardly and intimidated. By a complex communications system of hints and signals, certain orders are given to the chief of police and the sheriff, who pass them on to their men, the footsoldiers in the trenches of the ghetto.

We experience this system of control as madness. So that Leonard Deadwyler, one of these 20,000,000 blacks, is rushing his pregnant wife to the hospital and is shot dead by a policeman. An accident. That the sun rises in the east and sets in the west is also an accident, by design. The blacks are up in arms. From one end of America to the other, blacks are outraged at this accident, this latest evidence of what an accident-prone people they are, of the cruelty and pain of their lives, these blacks at the mercy of trigger-happy Yankees and Rebs in coalition against their skin. They want the policeman's blood as a sign that the Viet Cong is not the only answer. A sign to save them from the deaths they must die, and inflict. The power structure, without so much as blinking an eye, wouldn't mind tossing Bova to the mob, to restore law and order, but it knows in the vaults of its strength that at all cost the blacks must be kept at bay, that it must uphold the police department, its Guardian. Nothing must be allowed to threaten the set-up. Justice is secondary. Security is the byword.

Meanwhile, blacks are looking on and asking tactical questions. They are asked to die for the System in Vietnam. In Watts they are killed by it. Now—*NOW!*—they are asking each other, in dead earnest: Why not die right here in Babylon fighting for a better life, like the Viet Cong? If those little cats can do it, what's wrong with big studs like us?

A mood sets in, spreads across America, across the face of Babylon, jells in black hearts everywhere.

William F. Buckley, Jr.

William F. Buckley, Jr. (b. 1925) has established himself as one of the foremost spokesmen for American conservatism. He is the editor of *The National Review* and the author of numerous articles and books.

The selection printed here contains a thoughtful statement of principles which conservatives (or at least some conservatives, since conservatives do not like to be categorized) would consider in approaching the problems which beset society.

From *Up from Liberalism*, Hillman Books 1961. Copyright © 1959 William F. Buckley, Jr. Used by permission of the author.

Up from Liberalism

THE CONSERVATIVE FRAMEWORK AND MODERN REALITIES

Up where from Liberalism? There is no conservative political manifesto which, as we make our faltering way, we can consult, confident that it will point a sure finger in the direction of the good society. Indeed, sometimes the conservative needle appears to be jumping about as on a disoriented compass. My professional life is lived in an office battered by every pressure of contemporary conservatism. Some of the importunities upon a decent American conservatism are outrageous, or appear so to me, at any rate. (*"We should have high tariffs because the farmers have high subsidies, and they shouldn't, by the way."*) Some are pathological (*"Alaska is being prepared as a mammoth concentration camp for pro-McCarthyites"*). Some are deeply mystical (*"The state can do no good."* My answer: it can arrest Communists, can't it?); some ambitiously spiritual (*"Conservatism has no extrinsic significance except in relation to religion"*). Some urge the schematization of conservatism. (*"What passes for conservatism these days is nothing more than sentimentality and nostalgia. Let us give it structure . . ."*); or the opposite (*"Beware the ideologization of conservatism."*).

Still, for all the confusion and contradiction, I venture to say it is possible to talk about "the conservative position" and mean something by it. At the political level, conservatives are bound together for the most part by negative response to Liberalism; but altogether too much is made of that fact. Negative action is not necessarily of negative value. Political freedom's principal value is negative in character. The people are politically stirred principally by the necessity for negative affirmations. Cincinnatus was a farmer before he took up his sword, and went back to farming after wielding some highly negative strokes upon the pates of those who sought to make positive changes in his way of life.

The weakness of American conservatives does not reduce neatly to the fact that some want tariffs, others not. Dr. Robert Oppenheimer is much taken these days by what goes by the name of "complementarity," a notion having to do with revised relationships in the far reaches of philosophical thought, where "opposites" come under a single compass, and fuse into workable philosophical and physical unities. No doubt Physicist Oppenheimer is sticking an irreverent finger in the higher chemistry of metaphysics: but his theory, like the Hegelian synthesis, serves to remind us that there is almost always conceivable the vantage point from which the seemingly incongruous, the apparently contradictory, can be viewed in harmony. A navigator for whom two lighthouses can mark extreme points of danger relative to his present position, knows that by going back and making a wholly different approach, the two lighthouses will fuse together to form a single object to the vision, confirming the safety of his position. They are then said to be "in range."

There is a point from which opposition to the social security laws and a devout belief in social stability are in range; as also a determined resistance to the spread of world Communism—and a belief in political non-interventionism; a disgust with the results of modern education—and sympathy for the indvidual educational requirements of the individual child; a sympathetic understanding of the spiritual essence of human existence—and a desire to delimit religious influence in political affairs; a patriotic concern for the nation and its culture—and a genuine respect for the integrity and differences of other peoples' culture; a millitant concern for the Negro—and a belief in decentralized political power even though, on account of it, the Negro is sometimes victimized; a respect for the omni-competence of the free marketplace—and the knowledge of the neccessity for occasional interposition. There is a position from which these views are "in range"; and that is the position, generally speaking, where conservatives now find themselves on the political chart. Our most serious challenge is to restore principles—the right principles; the principles Liberalism has abused, forsaken, and replaced with "principles" that have merely a methodological content—our challenge is to restore principles to public affairs.

I mentioned in the opening pages of this book that what was once a healthy American pragmatism has deteriorated into a wayward relativism. It is one thing to make the allowances to reality that reality imposes, to take advantage of the current when the current moves in your direction, while riding at anchor at ebb tide. But it is something else to run before political or historical impulses merely because fractious winds begin to blow, and to dismiss resistance as foolish, or perverse idealism. And it is supremely wrong, intellectually and morally, to abandon the norms by which it becomes possible, viewing a trend, to pass judgment upon it; without which judgment we cannot know whether to yield, or to fight.

Are we to fight the machine? Can conservatism assimilate it? Whittaker Chambers once wrote me that "the rock-core of the Conservative Position can be held realistically only if Conservation will accommodate itself to the needs and hopes of the masses—needs and hopes which like the masses themselves, are the product of machines."

It is true that the masses have asserted themselves, all over the world; have revolted, Ortega said, perceiving the revolutionary quality of the cultural convulsion. The question: how can conservatism accommodate revolution? Can the revolutionary essence be extravasated and be made to diffuse harmlessly in the network of capillaries that rushes forward to accommodate its explosive force? Will the revolt of the masses moderate when the lower class is rising, when science has extirpated misery, and the machine has abolished poverty? Not if the machines themselves are irreconcilable, as Mr. Chambers seems to suggest when he writes that ". . . of course, our fight is with machines," adding: "A Conservatism that cannot face the facts of the machine and mass production, and its consequences in government and politics, is foredoomed to futility and petulance. A Conservatism that allows for them has an eleventh-hour chance of rallying what is sound in the West."

What forms must this accommodation take? *The welfare state!* is the non-Communist answer one mostly hears. It is necessary, we are told, to comprehend the interdependence of life in an industrial society, and the social consequences of any action by a single part of it, on other parts. Let the steel workers go on strike, and spark-plug salesmen will in due course be out of work. There must be laws to mitigate the helplessness of the individual link in the industrial chain that the machine has built.

What can conservatism do? Must it come to terms with these realities? "To live is to maneuver [Mr. Chambers continues]. The choices of maneuver are now visibly narrow. In the matter of social security, for example, the masses of Americans, like the Russian peasants in 1918, are signing the peace with their feet. I worked the hay load last night against the coming rain—by headlights, long after dark. I know the farmer's case for the machine and for the factory. And I know, like the cut of hay-bale cords in my hands, that a Conservatism that cannot find room in its folds for these actualities is a Conservatism that is not a political force, or even a twitch: it has become a literary whimsy."

Indeed. The machine must be accepted, and conservatives must not live by programs that were written as though the machine did not exist, or could be made to go away: that is the proper kind of realism. The big question is whether the essential planks of conservatism were anachronized by the machine; the big answer is that they were not. "Those who remain in the world, if they will not surrender on its terms, must manuever within its terms [says Mr. Chambers]. That is what Conservatives must decide: how much to give in order to survive at all; how much to give in order not to give up the basic principles. And, of course, that results in a dance along a precipice. Many will drop over, and, always, the cliff-dancers will hear the screaming curses of those who fall, or be numbed by the sullen silence of those, nobler souls perhaps, who will not join in the dance." We cliff-dancers, resolved not to withdraw into a petulant solitude, or let ourselves fall over the cliff into Liberalism, must do what maneuvering we can, and come up with a conservative program that speaks to our time.

It is the chronic failure of Liberalism that it obliges circumstance—because it has an inadequate discriminatory apparatus which might cause it to take any other course. There are unemployed in Harlan Country? *Rush them aid.* New Yorkers do not want to pay the cost of subways? *Get someone else to pay it.* Farmers do not want to leave the land? *Let them till it, buy and destroy the produce.* Labor unions demand the closed shop? *It is theirs.* Inflation goes forward in all industrial societies? *We will have continued inflation.* Communism is in control behind the Iron Curtain? *Coexist with it.* The tidal wave of industrialism will sweep in the welfare state? *Pull down the sea walls.*

Conservatism must insist that while the will of man is limited in what it can do, it can do enough to make over the face of the world; and that the question that must always be before us is, What shape should the world take, given modern realities? How can technology hope to invalidate conservatism? Freedom, individuality, the sense of community, the sanctity of the family, the supremacy of the conscience, the spiritual view of life—can these verities be transmuted by the advent of tractors and adding machines? These have had a smashing social effect upon us, to be sure. They have created a vortex into which we are being drawn as though irresistibly; but that, surely, is because the principles by which we might have made anchor have not been used, not because of their insufficiency or proven inadaptability. "Technology has succeeded in extracting just about the last bit of taste from a loaf of bread," Columnist Murray Kempton once told me spiritedly. "And when we get peacetime use of atomic energy, we'll succeed in getting *all* the taste out!"

How can one put the problem more plainly? I assume by now Mrs. Kempton has gone to the archives, dusted off an ancient volume, and learned how to bake homemade bread. And Lo! the bread turns out to be as easy to make as before, tastes as good as before, and the machine age did not need to be roasted at an *auto-da-fe* to make it all possible. A conservative solution to *that* problem. But when the atom does to politics what it threatens to bread, what *then* is the solution? Can one make homemade freedom, under the eyes of an omnipotent state that has no notion of, or tolerance for, the flavor of freedom?

Freedom and order and community and justice in an age of technology: that is the contemporary challenge of political conservatism. How to do it, how to live with mechanical harvesters and without socialized agriculture. The direction we must travel requires a broadmindedness that, in the modulated age, strikes us as antiquarian, and callous. As I write there is mass suffering in Harlan County, Kentucky, where coal mining has become unprofitable, and a whole community is desolate. The Liberal solution is: immediate and sustained federal subsidies. The conservative, breasting the emotional surf, will begin by saying that it was many years ago foreseeable that coal mining in Harlan County was becoming unprofitable, that the humane course would have been to face up to that realism by permitting the marketplace, through the exertion of economic pressures of mounting intensity, to require resettlement. That was not done for the coal miners (they were shielded from reality by a combination of state and union aid)—any more than it is now being done for marginal farmers; so that we are face-to-face with an acute emergency for which there is admittedly no thinkable alternative to immediate relief—if necessary (though it is not) by the federal government; otherwise, by the surrounding communities, or the state of Kentucky. But having made arrangements for relief, what then? Will the grandsons of the Harlan coal miners be mining coal, to be sold to the government at a pegged price, all this to spare today's coal miners the ordeal of looking for other occupations?

The Hoover Commission on government reorganization unearthed several years ago a little rope factory in Boston, Massachusetts, which had been established by the federal government during the Civil War to manufacture the textile specialties the Southern blockade had caused to be temporarily scarce. There it was, ninety years after Appomattox, grinding out the same specialties, which are bought by the government, and then sold at considerable loss. "Liquidate the plant," the Hoover Commission was getting ready to recommend. Whereupon a most influential Massachusetts Senator interceded. "You cannot," he informed a member of the Commission, "do so heinous a thing. The plant employs 136 persons, whose only skill is in making this specialty." "Very well then," said the spokesman for the Commission, anxious to cooperate. "Suppose we recommend to the Government that the factory retain in employment every single present employee until he quits, retires, or dies—but on the understanding that none of them is to be replaced. That way we can at least look forward to the eventual liquidation of the plant. Otherwise, there will be 136 people making useless specialties generations hence; an unreasonable legacy of the Civil War."

The Senator was unappeased. What a commotion the proposal would cause in the textile-specialty enclave in Boston! The solution, he warned the Commission, was intolerable, and he would resist it with all his prodigious political might.

The relationship of force being what it is, the factory continues to operate at full force.

To be sure, a great nation can indulge its little extravagances, as I have repeatedly stressed; but a long enough series of little extravagances, as I have also said, can add up to a stagnating if not a crippling economic overhead. What is disturbing about the Civil War factory incident is first the sheer stupidity of the thing, second the easy victory of Liberal sentimentalism over reason. Subsidies are the form that modern circuses tend to take, and, as ever, the people are unaware that it is they who pay for their circuses.

But closing down the useless factories—a general war on featherbedding—is the correct thing to do, if it is correct to cherish the flavor of freedom and economic sanity. There is a sophisticated argument that has to do with the conceivable economic beneficences of pyramid building, and of hiring men to throw rocks out into the sea. But even these proposals, when advanced rhetorically by Lord Keynes, were meliorative and temporary in concept: the idea was to put the men to work *until* the regenerative juices of the economy had done their work. Now we wake to the fact that along the line we abandoned our agreement to abide, as a general rule, by the determinations of the marketplace. We once believed that useless textile workers and useless coal miners and useless farmers—and useless carriagemakers and pony expressmen—should search out other means of employment.

It is the dawning realization that, under the economics of illusion, pyramid building is becoming a major economic enterprise in America, that has set advanced Liberals to finding more persuasive ways to dispose of the time of the textile specialty workers. And their solution—vide Galbraith—is great social enterprises, roads, schools, slum clearance, national parks. The thesis of the Affluent Society is that simple. We have 1) an earned surplus, 2) unemployment, 3) "social imbalance." (I.e., too many cars, not enough roads; too much carbon monoxide, not enough air purification; too many children, not enough class-rooms.) So let the government 1) take over the extra money, 2) use it to hire the unemployed, and 3) set them to restoring the social balance, i.e., to building parks, schools, roads.

The program prescribed by Mr. Galbraith is unacceptable, conservatives would agree. Deal high-handedly as he would have us do with the mechanisms of the marketplace, and the mechanisms will bind. Preempt the surplus of the people, and surpluses will dwindle. Direct politically the economic activity of a nation, and the economy will lose its capacity for that infinite responsiveness to individual tastes that gives concrete expression to the individual will in material matters. Centralize the political function, and you will lose touch with reality, for the reality is an intimate and individualized relationship between individuals and those among whom they live; and the abstractions of wide-screen social draftsmen will not substitute for it. Stifle the economic sovereignty of the individual by spending his dollars for him, and you stifle his freedom. Socialize the individual's surplus and you socialize his spirit and creativeness; you cannot paint the *Mona Lisa* by assigning one dab each to a thousand painters.

Conservatives do not deny that technology poses enormous problems; they insist only that the answers of Liberalism create worse problems than those they set out to solve. Conservatism cannot be blind, or give the appearance of being blind, to the dismaying spectacle of unemployment, or any other kind of suffering. But conservatives can insist that the statist solution to the problem is inadmissible. It is not the single conservative's responsibility or right to draft a concrete program—merely to suggest the principles that should frame it.

What then *is* the indicated course of action? It is to maintain and wherever possible enhance the freedom of the individual to acquire property and dispose of that property in ways that he decides on. To deal with unemployment by eliminating monopoly unionism, featherbedding, and inflexibilities in the labor market, and be prepared, where residual unemployment persists, to cope with it locally, placing the political and humanitarian responsibility on the lowest feasible political unit. Boston can surely find a way to employ gainfully its 136 textile specialists—and its way would be very different, predictably, from Kentucky's with the coal miners; and let them be different. Let the two localities experiment with different solutions, and let the natural desire of the individual for more goods, and better education, and more leisure, find satisfaction in individual encounters with the marketplace, in the growth of private schools, in the myriad economic and charitable activities which, because they took root in the individual imagination and impulse, take organic form. And then let us see whether we are better off than we would be living by decisions made between nine and five in Washington office rooms, where the oligarchs of the Affluent Society sit, allocating complaints and solutions to communities represented by pins on the map.

Is that a program? Call it a No-Program, if you will, but adopt it for your own. I will not cede more power to the state. I will not willingly cede more power to anyone, not to the state, not to General Motors, not to the CIO. I will hoard my power like a miser, resisting every effort to drain it away from me. I will then use *my* power, as *I* see fit. I mean to live my life an obedient man, but obedient to God, subservient to the wisdom of my ancestors; never to the authority of political truths arrived at yesterday at the voting booth. That is a program of sorts, is it not?

It is certainly program enough to keep conservatives busy, and Liberals at bay. And the nation free.

Students for a Democratic Society

Tom Hayden drafted the Port Huron Statement for the convention of the Students for a Democratic Society in 1962. Students for a Democratic Society no longer exists in anything like its form of the early and mid-1960s; but the Statement remains an important position paper which is probably the best-known statement of the beliefs of the New Left.

The Port Huron Statement

Introduction: Agenda for a Generation

We are people of this generation, bred in at least modest comfort, housed now in universities, looking uncomfortably to the world we inherit.

When we were kids the United States was the wealthiest and strongest country in the world; the only one with the atom bomb, the least scarred by modern war, an initiator of the United Nations that we thought would distribute Western influence throughout the world. Freedom and equality for each individual, government of, by, and for the people—these American values we found good, principles by which we could live as men. Many of us began maturing in complacency.

As we grew, however, our comfort was penetrated by events too troubling to dismiss. First, the permeating and victimizing fact of human degradation, symbolized by the Southern struggle against racial bigotry, compelled most of us from silence to activism. Second, the enclosing fact of the Cold War, symbolized by the presence of the Bomb, brought awareness that we ourselves, and our friends, and millions of abstract "others" we knew more directly because of our common peril, might die at any time. We might deliberately ignore, or avoid, or fail to feel all other human problems, but not these two, for these were too immediate and crushing in their impact, too challenging in the demand that we as individuals take the responsibility for encounter and resolution.

While these other problems either directly oppressed us or rankled our consciences and became our own subjective concerns, we began to see complicated and disturbing paradoxes in our surrounding America. The declaration "all men are created equal. . ." rang hollow before the facts of Negro life in the South and the big cities of the North. The proclaimed peaceful intentions of the United States contradicted its economic and military investments in the Cold War status quo.

We witnessed, and continue to witness, other paradoxes. With nuclear energy whole cities can easily be powered, yet the dominant nation-states seem more likely to unleash destruction greater than that incurred in all wars of human history. Although our own technology is destroying old and creating new forms of social organization, men still tolerate meaningless work and idleness. While two-thirds of mankind suffers undernourishment, our own upper classes revel amidst superfluous abundance. Although world population is expected to double in forty years, the nations still tolerate anarchy as a major principle of international conduct and uncontrolled exploitation governs the sapping of the earth's physical resources. Although mankind desperately needs revolutionary leadership, America rests in national stalemate, its goals ambiguous and tradition-bound instead of informed and clear, its democratic system apathetic and manipulated rather than "of, by, and for the people."

Not only did tarnish appear on our image of American virtue, not only did disillusion occur when the hypocrisy of American ideals was discovered, but we began to sense that what we had originally seen as the American Golden Age was actually the decline of an era. The worldwide outbreak of revolution against colonialism and imperialism, the entrenchment of totalitarian states, the menace of war, overpopulation, international disorder, supertechnology—these trends were testing the tenacity of our own commitment to democracy and freedom and our abilities to visualize their application to a world in upheaval.

Our work is guided by the sense that we may be the last generation in the experiment with living. But we are a minority—the vast majority of our people regard the temporary equilibrium of our society and world as eternally-functional parts. In this is perhaps the outstanding paradox: we ourseles are imbued with urgency, yet the message of our society is that there is no viable alternative to the present. Beneath the reassuring tones of the politicians, beneath the common opinion that America will "muddle through," beneath the stagnation of those who have closed their minds to the future, is the pervading feeling that there simply are no alternatives, that our times have witnessed the exhaustion not only of Utopias, but of any new departures as well. Feeling the press of complexity upon the emptiness of life, people are fearful of the thought that at any moment things might be thrust out of control. They fear change itself, since change might smash whatever invisible framework seems to hold back chaos for them now. For most Americans, all crusades are suspect, threatening. The fact that each individual sees apathy in his fellows perpetuates the common reluctance to organize for change. The dominant institutions are complex enough to blunt the minds of their potential critics, and entrenched enough to swiftly dissipate or entirely repel the energies of protest and reform, thus limiting human expectancies. Then, too, we are a materially improved society, and by our own improvements we seem to have weakened the case for further change.

Some would have us believe that Americans feel contentment amidst prosperity—but might it not be better be called a glaze above deeply-felt anxieties about their role in the new world? And if these anxieties produce a developed indifference to human affairs, do they not as well produce a yearning to believe there *is* an alternative to the present, that something *can* be done to change circumstances in the school, the workplaces, the bureaucracies, the government? It is to this latter yearning, at once the spark and engine of change, that we direct our present appeal. The search for truly democratic alternatives to the present, and a commitment to social experimentation with them, is a worthy and fulfilling human enterprise, one which moves us and, we hope, others today. On such a basis do we offer this document of our convictions and analysis: as an effort in understanding and changing the conditions of humanity in the late twentieth century, an effort rooted in the ancient, still unfulfilled conception of man attaining determining influence over his circumstances of life.

Values

Making values explicit—an initial task in establishing alternatives—is an activity that has been devalued and corrupted. The conventional moral terms of the age, the politician moralities—"free world," "people's democracies"—reflect realities poorly, if at all, and seem to function more as ruling myths than as descriptive principles. But neither has our experience in the universities brought us moral enlightenment. Our professors and administrators sacrifice controversy to public relations; their curriculums change more slowly than the living events of the world; their skills and silence are purchased by investors in the arms race; passion is called unscholastic. The questions we might want raised—what is really important? can we live in a different and better way? If we wanted to change society, how would we do it?—are not thought to be questions of a "fruitful, empirical nature," and thus are brushed aside.

Unlike youth in other countries we are used to moral leadership being exercised and moral dimensions being clarified by our elders. But today, for us, not even the liberal and socialist preachments of the past seem adequate to the forms of the present. Consider the old slogans: Capitalism Cannot Reform Itself, United Front Against Fascism, General Strike, All Out on May Day. Or, more recently, No Cooperation with Commies and Fellow Travellers, Ideologies are Exhausted, Bipartisanship, No Utopias. These are incomplete, and there are few new prophets. It has been said that our liberal and socialist predecessors were plagued by vision without program, while our own generation is plagued by program without vision. All around us there is astute grasp of method, technique—the committee, the ad hoc group, the lobbyist, the hard and soft sell, the make, the projected image—but, if pressed critically, such expertise is incompetent to explain its implicit ideals. It is highly fashionable to identify oneself by old categories, or by naming a respected political figure, or by explaining "how we would vote" on various issues.

Theoretic chaos has replaced the idealistic thinking of old—and, unable to reconstitute theoretic order, men have condemned idealism itself. Doubt has replaced hopefulness—and men act out a defeatism that is labelled realistic. The decline of utopia and hope is in fact one of the defining features of social life today. The reasons are various: the dreams of the older left were perverted by Stalinism and never recreated; the congressional stalemate makes men narrow their view of the possible; the specialization of human activity leaves little room for sweeping thought; the horrors of the twentieth century, symbolized in the gas-ovens and concentration camps and atom bombs, have blasted hopefulness. To be idealistic is to be considered apocalyptic, deluded. To have no serious aspirations, on the contrary, is to be "toughminded."

In suggesting social goals and values, therefore, we are aware of entering a sphere of some disrepute. Perhaps matured by the past, we have no sure formulas, no closed theories—but that does not mean values are beyond discussion and tentative determination. A first task of any social movement is to convince people that the search for orienting theories and the creation of human values is complex but worthwhile. We are aware that to avoid platitudes we must analyze the concrete conditions of social order. But to direct such an analysis we must use the guideposts of basic principles. Our own social values involve conceptions of human beings, human relationships, and social systems.

We regard *men* as infinitely precious and possessed of unfulfilled capacities for reason, freedom, and love. In affirming these principles we are aware of countering perhaps the dominant conceptions of man in the twentieth century: that he is a thing to be manipulated, and that he is inherently incapable of directing his own affairs. We oppose the depersonalization that reduces human beings to the status of things—if anything, the brutalities of the twentieth century teach that means and ends are intimately related, that vague appeals to "posterity" cannot justify the mutilations of the present. We oppose, too, the doctrine of human incompetence because it rests essentially on the modern fact that men have been "competently" manipulated into incompetence—we see little reason why men cannot meet with increasing skill the complexities and responsibilities of their situation, if society is organized not for minority, but for majority, participation in decision-making.

Men have unrealized potential for self-cultivation, self-direction, self-understanding, and creativity. It is this potential that we regard as crucial and to which we appeal, not to the human potentiality for violence, unreason, and submission to authority. The goal of man and society should be human independence: a concern not with image of popularity but with finding a meaning in life that is personally authentic; a quality of mind not compulsively driven by a sense of powerlessness, nor one which unthinkingly adopts status values, nor one which represses all threats to its habits, but one which has full, spontaneous access to present and past experiences, one which easily unites the fragmented parts of personal history, one which openly faces problems which are troubling and unresolved; one with an intuitive awareness of possibilities, an active sense of curiosity, an ability and willingness to learn.

This kind of independence does not mean egotistic individualism—the object is not to have one's way so much as it is to have a way that is one's own. Nor do we deify man—we merely have faith in his potential.

Human relationships should involve fraternity and honesty. Human interdependence is contemporary fact; human brotherhood must be willed, however, as a condition of future survival and as the most appropriate form of social relations. Personal links between man and man are needed, especially to go beyond the partial and fragmentary bonds of function that bind men only as worker to worker, employer to employee, teacher to student, American to Russian.

Loneliness, estrangement, isolation describe the vast distance between man and man today. These dominant tendencies cannot be overcome by better personnel management, nor by improved gadgets, but only when a love of man overcomes the idolatrous worship of things by man. As the individualism we affirm is not egoism, the selflessness we affirm is not self-elimination. On the contrary, we believe in generosity of a kind that imprints one's unique individual qualities in the relation to other men, and to all human activity. Further, to dislike isolation is not to favor the abolition of privacy; the latter differs from isolation in that it occurs or is abolished according to individual will.

We would replace power rooted in possession, privileged, or circumstance by power and uniqueness rooted in love, reflectiveness, reason, and creativity. As a *social system* we seek the establishment of a democracy of individual participation, governed by two central aims: that the individual share in those social decisions determining the quality and direction of his life; that society be organized to encourage independence in men and provide the media for their common participation.

In a participatory democracy, the political life would be based in several root principles.

that decision-making of basic social consequence be carried on by public groupings;

that politics be seen positively, as the art of collectively creating an acceptable pattern of social relations;

that politics has the function of bringing people out of isolation and into community, thus being a necessary, though not sufficient, means of finding meaning in personal life;

that the political order should serve to clarify problems in a way instrumental to their solution; it should provide outlets for the expression of personal grievance and aspiration; opposing views should be organized so as to illuminate choices and facilitate the attainment of goals; channels should be commonly available to relate men to knowledge and to power so that private problems—from bad recreation facilities to personal alienation—are formulated as general issues.

The economic sphere would have as its basis the principles:

that work should involve incentives worthier than money or survival. It should be educative, not stultifying; creative, not mechanical; self-directed, not manipulated, encouraging independence, a respect for others, a sense of dignity and a willingness to accept social responsibility, since it is this experience that has crucial influence on habits, perceptions and individual ethics;

that the economic experience is so personally decisive that the individual must share in its full determination;

that the economy itself is of such social importance that its major resources and means of production should be open to democratic participation and subject to democratic social regulation.

Like the political and economic ones, major social institutions—cultural, educational, rehabilitative, and others—should be generally organized with the well-being and dignity of man as the essential measure of success.

In social change or interchange, we find violence to be abhorrent because it requires generally the transformation of the target, be it a human being or a community of people, into a depersonalized object of hate. It is imperative that the means of violence be abolished and the institutions—local, national, international—that encourage non-violence as a condition of conflict be developed.

There are our central values, in skeletal form. It remains vital to understand their denial or attainment in the context of the modern world.

The Students

In the last few years, thousands of American students demonstrated that they at least felt the urgency of the times. They moved actively and directly against racial injustices, the threat of war, violations of individual rights of conscience and, less frequently, against economic manipulation. They succeeded in restoring a small measure of controversy to the campuses after the stillness of the McCarthy period. They succeeded, too, in gaining some concessions from the people and institutions they opposed, especially in the fight against racial bigotry.

The significance of these scattered movements lies not in their success or failure in gaining objectives—at least not yet. Nor does the significance lie in the intellectual "competence" or "maturity" of the students involved—as some pedantic elders allege. The significance is in the fact the students are breaking the crust of apathy and overcoming the inner alienation that remain the defining characteristics of American college life.

If student movements for change are still rarities on the campus scene, what is commonplace there? The real campus, the familiar campus, is a place of private people, engaged in their notorious "inner emigration." It is a place of commitment to business-as-usual, getting ahead, playing it cool. It is a place of mass affirmation of the Twist, but mass reluctance toward the controversial public stance. Rules are accepted as "inevitable," bureaucracy as "just circumstances," irrelevance as "scholarship," selflessness as "martyrdom," politics as "just another way to make people, and an unprofitable one, too."

Almost no students value activity as citizens. Passive in public, they are hardly more idealistic in arranging their private lives: Gallup concludes they will settle for "low success, and won't risk high failure." There is not much willingness to take risks (not even in business), no settling of dangerous goals, no real conception of personal identity except one manufactured in the image of others, no real urge for personal fulfillment except to be almost as successful as the very succesful people. Attention is being paid to social status (the quality of shirt collars, meeting people, getting wives or husbands, making solid contacts for later on); much, too, is paid to academic status (grades, honors, the med school rat race). But neglected generally is real intellectual status, the personal cultivation of the mind.

"Students don't even give a damn about the apathy," one has said. Apathy toward apathy begets a privately-constructed universe, a place of systematic study schedules, two nights each week for beer, a girl or two, and early marriage; a framework infused with personality, warmth, and under control, no matter how unsatisfying otherwise.

Under these conditions university life loses all relevance to some. Four hundred thousand of our classmates leave college every year.

But apathy is not simply an attitude; it is a product of social institutions, and of the structure and organization of higher education itself. The extracurricular life is ordered according to *in loco parentis* theory, which ratifies the Administration as the moral guardian of the young.

The accompanying "let's pretend" theory of student extracurricular affairs validates student government as a training center for those who want to spend their lives in political pretense, and discourages intitiative from the more articulate, honest and sensitive students. The bounds and style of controversy are delimited before controversy begins. The university "prepares" the student for "citizenship" through perpetual rehearsals and, usually, through emasculation of what creative spirit there is in the individual.

The academic life contains reinforcing counterparts to the way in which extracurricular life is organized. The academic world is founded on a teacher-student relation analogous to the parent-child relation which characterizes *in loco parentis*. Further, academia includes a radical separation of the student from the material of study. That which is studied, the social reality, is "objectified" to sterility, dividing the student from life—just as he is restrained in active involvement by the deans controlling student government. The specialization of function and knowledge, admittedly necessary to our complex technological and social structure, has produced an exaggerated compartmentalization of study and understanding. This has contributed to an overly parochial view, by faculty, of the role of its research and scholarship, to a discontinuous and truncated understanding, by students, of the surrounding social order; and to a loss of personal attachment, by nearly all, to the worth of study as a humanistic enterprise.

There is, finally, the cumbersome academic bureaucracy extending throughout the academic as well as the extracurricular structures, contributing to the sense of outer complexity and inner powerlessness that transforms the honest searching of many students to a ratification of convention and, worse, to a numbness to present and future catastrophes. The size and financing systems of the university enhance the permanent trusteeship of the administrative bureaucracy, their power leading to a shift within the university toward the value standards of business and the administrative mentality. Huge foundations and other private financial interests shape the underfinanced colleges and universities, not only making them more commercial, but less disposed to diagnose society critically, less open to dissent. Many social and physical scientists, neglecting the liberating heritage of higher learning, develop "human relations" or "morale-producing" techniques for the corporate economy, while others exercise their intellectual skills to accelerate the arms race.

Tragically, the university could serve as a significant source of social criticism and an initiator of new modes and molders of attitudes. But the actual intellectual effect or the college experience is hardly distinguishable from that of any other communications channel—say, a television set—passing on the stock truths of the day. Students leave college somewhat more "tolerant" than when they arrived but basically unchallenged in their values and political orientations. With administrators ordering the institution, and faculty the curriculum, the student learns by his isolation to accept elite rule within the university, which prepares him to accept later forms of minority control. The real function of the educational system—as opposed to its more rhetorical function of "searching for truth"—is to impart the key information and styles that will help the student get by, modestly but comfortably, in the big society beyond.

The Society Beyond

Look beyond the campus, to America itself. That student life is more intellectual, and perhaps more comfortable, does not obscure the fact that the fundamental qualities of life on the campus reflect the habits of society at large. The fraternity president is seen at the junior manager levels; the sorority queen has gone to Grosse Pointe; the serious poet burns for a place, any place, to work; the once-serious and never-serious poets work at the advertising agencies. The desperation of people threatened by forces about which they know little and of which they can say less; the cheerful emptiness of people "giving up" all hope of changing things; the faceless ones polled by Gallup who listed "international affairs" fourteenth on their list of "problems" but who also expected thermonuclear war in the next few years; in these and other forms, Americans are in withdrawal from public life, from any collective effort at directing their own affairs.

Some regard these national doldrums as a sign of healthy approval of the established order—but is it approval by consent or manipulated acquiescence? Others declare that the people are withdrawn because compelling issues are fast disappearing—perhaps there are fewer breadlines in America, but is Jim Crow gone, is there enough work and work more fulfilling, is world war a diminishing threat, and what of the revolutionary new peoples? Still others think the national quietude is a necessary consequence of the need for elites to resolve complex and specialized problems of modern industrial society—but, then, why should *business* elites help decide foreign policy, and who controls the elites anyway, and are they solving mankind's problems? Others, finally, shrug knowingly and announce that full democracy never worked anywhere in the past—but why lump qualitatively different civilizations together, and how can a social order work well if its best thinkers are skeptics, and is man really doomed forever to the domination of today?

There are no convincing apologies for the contemporary malaise. While the world tumbles toward the final war, while men in other nations are trying desperately to alter events, while the very future is uncertain—America is without community, impulse, without the inner momentum necessary for an age when societies cannot successfully perpetuate themselves by their military weapons, when democracy must be viable because of the quality of life, not its quantity of rockets.

The apathy here is first, *subjective*—the felt powerlessness of ordinary people, the resignation before the enormity of events. But subjective apathy is encouraged by the *objective* American situation—the actual structural separation of people from power, from relevant knowledge, from pinnacles of decision-making. Just as the university influences the student way of life, so do major social institutions create the circumstances in which the isolated citizen will try hopelessly to understand his world and himself.

The very isolation of the individual—from power and community and ability to aspire—means the rise of a democracy without publics. With the great mass of people structurally remote and psychologically hesitant with respect to democratic institutions, those institutions themselves attenuate and become, in the fashion of the vicious circle, progressively less accessible to those few who aspire to serious participation in social affairs. The vital democratic connection between community and leadership, between the mass and the several elites, has been so wrenched and perverted that disastrous policies go unchallenged time and again.

Politics Without Publics

The American political system is not the democratic model of which its glorifiers speak. In actuality it frustrates democracy by confusing the individual citizen, paralyzing policy discussion, and consolidating the irresponsible power of military and business interests.

A crucial feature of the political apparatus in America is that greater differences are harbored within each major party than the differences existing between them. Instead of two parties presenting distinctive and significant differences of approach, what dominates the system is a natural interlocking of Democrats from Southern states with the more conservative elements of the Republican Party. This arrangement of forces is blessed by the seniority system of Congress which guarantees Congressional committee domination by conservatives—ten of seventeen committees in the Senate and thirteen of twenty-one in the House of Representatives are chaired currently by Dixiecrats.

The party overlap, however, is not the only structural antagonist of democracy in politics. First, the localized nature of the party system does not encourage discussion of national and international issues: thus problems are not raised by and for people, and political representatives usually are unfettered from any responsibilities to the general public except those regarding parochial matters. Second, whole constituencies are divested of the full political power they might have: many Negroes in the South are prevented from voting, migrant workers are disenfranchised by various residence requirements, some urban and suburban dwellers are victimized by gerrymandering, and poor people are too often without the power to obtain political representation. Third, the focus of political attention is significantly distorted by the enormous lobby force, composed predominantly of business interests, spending hundreds of millions each year in an attempt to conform facts about productivity, agriculture, defense, and social services, to the wants of private economic groupings.

What emerges from the party contradiction and insulation of privately held power is the organized political stalemate: calcification dominates flexibility as the principle of parliamentary organization, frustration is the expectancy of legislators intending liberal reform, and Congress becomes less and less central to national decision-making, especially in the area of foreign policy. In this context, confusion and blurring is built into the formulation of issues, long-range priorities are not discussed in the rational manner needed for policy-making, the politics of personality and "image" become a more important mechanism than the construction of issues in a way that affords each voter a challenging and real option. The American voter is buffeted from all directions by pseudo-problems, by the structurally initiated sense that nothing political is subject to human mastery. Worried by his mundane problems which never get solved, but constrained by the common belief that politics is an agonizingly slow accommodation of views, he quits all pretense of bothering.

A most alarming fact is that few, if any, politicians are calling for changes in these conditions. Only a handful even are calling on the President to "live up to" platform pledges; no one is demanding structural changes, such as the shuttling of Southern Democrats out of the Democratic Party. Rather than protesting the state of poltics, most politicians are reinforcing and aggravating that state. While in practice they rig public opinion to suit their own interests, in word and ritual they enshrine "the sovereign public" and call for more and more letters. Their speeches and campaign actions are banal, based on a degrading conception of what people want to hear. They respond not to dialogue, but to pressure: and knowing this, the ordinary citizen sees even greater inclination to shun the political sphere. The politician is usually a trumpeter to "citizenship" and "service to the nation," but since he is unwilling to seriously rearrange power relationships, his trumpetings only increase apathy by creating no outlets. Much of the time the call to "service" is justified not in idealistic terms, but in the crasser terms of "defending the free world from Communism"—thus making future idealistic impulses harder to justify in anything but Cold War terms.

In such a setting of status quo politics, where most if not all government activity is rationalized in Cold War anti-Communist terms, it is somewhat natural that discontented, super-patriotic groups would emerge through political channels and explain their ultra-conservatism as the best means of Victory over Communism. They have become a politically influential force within the Republican Party, at a national level through Senator Goldwater, and at a local level through their important social and economic roles. Their political views are defined generally as the opposite of the supposed views of Communists: complete individual freedom in the economic sphere, non-participation by the government in the machinery of production. But actually "anti-Communism" becomes an umbrella by which to protest liberalism, internationalism, welfare-ism, the active civil rights and labor movements. It is to the disgrace of the United States that such a movement should become a prominent kind of public participation in the modern world—but, ironically, it is somewhat to the interests of the United States that such a movement should be a public constituency pointed toward realignment of the political parties, demanding a conservative Republican Party in the South and an exclusion of the "leftist" elements of the national GOP.

The University and Social Change

There is, perhaps little reason to be optimistic about the above analysis. True, the Dixiecrat-GOP coalition is the weakest point in the dominating complex of corporate, military and political power. But the civil rights, peace, and student movements are too poor and socially slighted, and the labor movement too quiescent, to be counted with enthusiasm. From where else can power and vision be summoned? We believe that the universities are an overlooked seat of influence.

First, the university is located in a permanent position of social influence. Its educational function makes it indispensable and automatically makes it a crucial institution in the formation of social attitudes. Second, in an unbelievably complicated world, it is the central institution for organizing, evaluating, and transmitting knowledge. Third, the extent to which academic resources presently are used to buttress immoral social practice is revealed first, by the extent to which defense contracts make the universities engineers of the arms race. Too, the use of modern social science as a manipulative tool reveals itself in the "human relations" consultants to the modern corporations, who introduce trivial sops to give laborers feelings of "participation" or "belonging," while actually deluding them in order to further exploit their labor. And, of course, the use of motivational research is already infamous as a manipulative aspect of American politics. But these social uses of the universities' resources also demonstrate the unchangeable reliance by men of power on the men and storehouses of knowledge: this makes the university functionally tied to society in new ways, revealing new potentialities, new levers for change. Fourth, the university is the only mainstream institution that is open to participation by individuals of nearly any viewpoint.

These, at least, are facts, no matter how dull the teaching, how paternalistic the rules, how irrelevant the research that goes on. Social relevance, the accessibility to knowledge, and internal openness—these together make the university a potential base and agency in a movement of social change.

1. Any new left in America must be, in large measure, a left with real intellectual skills, committed to deliberativeness, honesty, reflection as working tools. The university permits the political life to be an adjunct to the academic one, and action to be informed by reason.
2. A new left must be distributed in significant social roles throughout the country. The universities are distributed in such a manner.
3. A new left must consist of younger people who matured in the post-war

world, and partially be directed to the recruitment of younger people. The university is an obvious beginning point.

4. A new left must include liberals and socialists, the former for their relevance, the latter for their sense of thoroughgoing reforms in the system. The university is a more sensible place than a political party for these two traditions to begin to discuss their differences and look for political synthesis.

5. A new left must start controversy across the land, if national policies and national apathy are to be reversed. The ideal university is a community of controversy, within itself and in its effects on communities beyond.

6. A new left must transform modern complexity into issues that can be understood and felt close-up by every human being. It must give form to the feelings of helplessness and indifference, so that people may see the political, social, and economic sources of their private troubles and organize to change society. In a time of supposed prosperity, moral complacency, and political manipulation, a new left cannot rely on only aching stomachs to be the engine force of social reform. The case for change, for alternatives that will involve uncomfortable personal efforts, must be argued as never before. The university is a relevant place for all of these activities.

But we need not indulge in illusions: the university system cannot complete a movement of ordinary people making demands for a better life. From its schools and colleges across the nation, a militant left might awaken its allies, and by beginning the process towards peace, civil rights, and labor struggles, reinsert theory and idealism where too often reign confusion and political barter. The power of students and faculty united is not only potential; it has shown its actuality in the South, and in the reform movements of the North.

The bridge to political power, though, will be built through genuine cooperation, locally, nationally, and internationally, between a new left of young people, and an awakening community of allies. In each community we must look within the university and act with confidence that we can be powerful, but we must look outwards to the less exotic but more lasting struggles for justice.

To turn these possibilities into realities will involve national efforts at university reform by an alliance of students and faculty. They must wrest control of the educational process from the administrative bureaucracy. They must make fraternal and functional contact with allies in labor, civil rights, and other liberal forces outside the campus. They must import major public issues into the curriculum—research and teaching on problems of war and peace is an outstanding example. They must make debate and controversy, not dull pedantic cant, the common style for educational life. They must consciously build a base for their assault upon the loci of power.

As students for a democratic society, we are committed to stimulating this kind of social movement, this kind of vision and program in campus and community across the country. If we appear to seek the unattainable, as it has been said, then let it be known that we do so to avoid the unimaginable.

Michael Harrington

Michael Harrington (b. 1928) is a prominent Leftist critic of American society. His book *The Other America,* in which he clearly presented the extent of poverty in the United States, played an important role in arousing the interest of the Kennedy and Johnson administrations in the problems of poverty in the midst of abundance. The selection included here is "Utopian Pragmatism" from his book *Toward a Democratic Left.* In this selection he criticizes certain assumptions which he believes have unwittingly guided much recent public policy.

Toward a Democratic Left

UTOPIAN PRAGMATISM

The American system doesn't seem to work any more.

The nation's statesmen proclaim that they seek only to abolish war, hunger and ignorance in the world and then follow policies which make the rich richer, the poor poorer and incite the globe to violence. The Government says that it will conduct an unconditional war on poverty and three years later announces that life in the slums has become worse. And supposedly practical people propose that the country make a social revolution but without the inconvenience of changing any basic institutions.

Before the escalation of the tragic war in Vietnam signaled the retreat from all his domestic social promises, Lyndon Johnson's rhetoric soared. Ending poverty and abolishing racism were, he said, "just the beginning." He looked forward to nothing less that a Great Society, "a place where men are more concerned with the quality of their goals than the quantity of their goods," where leisure would mean "a welcome chance to build and reflect, not a feared cause of boredom and restlessness," where the city would serve "the desire for beauty and the hunger for community."

An excellent case can be made for dismissing this talk as windy futurism.

America has not yet even bothered to fulfill the hopes of the last generation of reform. In 1944, for instance, Franklin Roosevelt advocated a genuine, legally guaranteed right to work (if the private sector failed to provide a man with a job, the public sector would be obliged to create a useful employment for him). By the time a conservative Congress got through with this fine affirmation in the Employment Act of 1946, the President's binding pledge had been degraded to a pious wish. There followed two decades in which intolerable rates of unemployment were chronic. In November 1966, the Department of Labor showed that, if one defined joblessness realistically, the black and white poor of the urban slums were living under Depression conditions during the greatest boom in the economy's history and twenty years after the society had committed itself to full employment.

This Department of Labor report is typical of the Sixties. For the Government of the United States has carefully counted, classified and computer-taped all of the outrages which it does so little about.

The statistics would frighten a Jeremiah, but the laws must be written to satisfy stolid businessmen. Housing is a case in point. In 1949 Senator Robert Taft concluded that the private sector would not provide decent dwellings for the poor and urged the construction of better than 200,000 low-cost units a year. That was not done. Then, in 1966, the White House Conference on Civil Rights totted up the deficit that had accrued from ignoring Taft's advice, surveyed the new needs and concluded that America must construct 2,000,000 housing units annually, 500,000 of them for the impoverished. The next year Mr. Johnson advocated 165,000 low-cost units, or about a third of what his own conference had told him was desperately needed. However, there was not the slightest possibility that Congress would honor this utterly inadequate request, since it is in the habit of appropriating funds for about 35,000 units a year. Mr. Johnson then persuaded the insurance industry to put up $1 billion, but even if that Federally guaranteed investment were to be spent exclusively on housing for the poor (it will not be), it would yield only 80,000 new units.

So the Administration's own figures convict it of perpetuating — and even worsening — conditions the Administration says lead to social explosions. After the next riot the Federal statistics thus predict, another commission will presumably be empaneled to explain why it took place.

This contradiction between bold words and sordid deeds does not, however, stop at the water's edge. The United Nations officially designated the Sixties as the "Development Decade." After five years of this effort, the Secretary General bluntly admitted the failure of this hope and pointed out that the gap between the fat and the starving lands was increasing. Fully informed of this trend, the affluent economies proceeded to reduce the percentage of their national products devoted to foreign aid, shifted disbursements from grants to loans and, in the Kennedy Round, rejected all the urgent pleas for the reform of world trade addressed to them by the developing countries.

Given these intolerable contrasts of American pretense and practice both at home and abroad, we have good reason to suspect the new utopias urged by men who will not even carry out the old reforms. This is particularly true when President Johnson suggests that fundamental transitions in the nation's life and values are to be achieved almost effortlessly. The corporations and the unions, the racial majority and the minorities, the religous believers and the atheists, the political machines and the reformers are all supposed to unite in making a gentle upheaval. And in a society where making money has traditionally been the most respected activity, spiritual considerations are suddenly going to come first.

Yet it would be wrong to dismiss all these unfulfilled promises as mere dishonesty. These pathetic utopias of the practical men are an admission—and a reflection—of the fact that the United States must take some first steps toward utopia in the best sense of that word. It is of some moment that tough minded manipulators have been driven to visions even if they do little about them. Then there are now the rudiments of a public awareness of the national plight, and the case for radical change can therefore be made with the help of official figures. Finally, our documented inadequacies make a precise statement of what needs to be done, and the program for reform can thus be more specific than ever before.

But this analysis should not be taken to argue that all that is required is to draw the humane conclusions implicit in the public premises. Nor should it be thought, as some of those struggling to end the war in Vietnam have said, that the nation's problems are simply a function of the pride and perversity of Lyndon B. Johnson. Our social irrationality is not a product of the Presidential psyche nor of faulty logic but a coherent, consistent feature of our social structure. There are powerful, organized and, I am sure, sincere forces committed to the maintenance of the injustices chronicled by the Government. They are not the bloated Wall Street plutocracy of Leftist myth, and that is why it is all the more difficult, and all the more imperative, to recognize them. They most certainly do not enjoy seeing people suffer at home or in the Third World of Africa, Asia and Latin America, and they just as certainly refuse, out of a sophisticated self-interest, to do what is necessary to end their agony.

To take America's urgent goals seriously and to make the system work again will demand vigorous democratic conflict and a vivid social imagination. Such an undertaking, which is the work of the democratic Left, challenges an orthodoxy which prevails both in the groves of Academe and in the smoke-filled rooms.

ONE

America believes in utopian pragmatism.

The pragmatism of this formula is familiar enough. All of the politicians and most of the professors hold that this country is a blessedly unideological land where elections are naturally won at the Center rather than on the Right or Left. The utopianism of this no-nonsense creed is not so obvious, since it is either shamefaced or unconscious. It is found in the assumption that the world has been so benevolently created that the solutions to problems of revolutionary technological, economic and social change are invariably to be discovered in the middle of the road. Not since Adam Smith's invisible hand was thought to vector a myriad of private greeds into a common good has there been such a touching faith in secular providence.

Utopian pragmatism became fashionable after World War II, in part as a reaction to the rigid intellectual categories popular during the Depression. In that era Marxism was regularly vulgarized so as to project a United States which was the mere reflex of oversimplified class antagonisms. This attitude produced more than its share of crudities and, as befits a dialectical method, therefore provoked its own negation. In the postwar years semi-affluence intensified the revulsion from this theory, and many thinkers proceeded to ignore the crises of the Fifties, Sixties and Seventies on the grounds that the bread-lines of the Thirties had not returned. So it was said on all sides that America is a pluralist nation in which power is shared, statesmen are quite properly the brokers of interest groups and endless progress is possible as long as no one gets too principled.

The notion that America is a unique place exempt from the polarizations of the class struggle is hardly new. At the beginning of the century Werner Sombart was already claiming that the abundance of roast beef and apple pie explained the absence of a mass socialist movement in this country. But the current belief in utopian pragmatism goes far beyond this simple sociology. Everything in American life—its geography, its constitutional institutions and even its latest technology—are seen as conspiring to deliver this society from the European curse of ideology. And these happy accidents are, often enough, supposed to have converged in the best of all possible worlds.

Here, for instance, is how Samuel Lubell pictures American politics: "To win the Presidency each party must appeal to a cross section of voters, to Midwest-erners as well as Easterners, to employers as well as to factory workers. Extreme differences must be conciliated, thus putting a premium upon the arts of compromise which have helped hold this country together." In this vast land, Lubell says, the basic drama is not the battle of Left and Right but "the constant struggle for national unification." So the sectional deal becomes one of our most typical arrangements.

Others, like James MacGregor Burns, trace the diffuseness of American politics back to a conscious decision. The Madisonians are said to have been so intent on thwarting the triumph of factionalism that they fragmented power through an intricate system of checks and balances. Since practically every group had a veto over every other group, even a clear and democratic majority was forced to the arts of wheedling. At its worst, Burns says, this structure could produce a "deadlock of democracy." Yet, in a bow to the prevailing optimism, he still believes that the "overlapping, jostling, crisscrossing, mutually inter-dependent networks of leaders and followers" are a prime, and praiseworthy, source of stability in the society. In the end, however, Burns is an academic who does understand the need for changing ancient habits.

More recently the futuristic potential of economic and social accounting has been seen as reinforcing the hallowed anti-ideological ideology. Government intervention, according to Daniel Patrick Moynihan, is more and more a matter for experts drawing on the latest academic research. Therefore the days of the "mile-long petitions and mass rallies" are over; there is a decline "in the moral exhilaration of public affairs at the domestic level." Where the social classes once fought, the specialists now discuss. Max Ways of *Fortune* magazine has taken up this theme on behalf of private enterprise. Now that there is going to be neutral problem-solving rather than passionate political contention, he proposes that the corporations contract to redesign the society.

There is clearly a great deal of truth in these various explanations of the American reality. Yet even as history they tend to be overly neat. America has the most violent and bloody trade-union history of any advanced nation, and the workers, as Seymour Martin Lipsett has documented in *Political Man*, support the Democratic Party more cohesively than their counterparts in class-conscious Britain back the Labor Party. But most important of all, the utopian pragmatists underestimate the significance of the realigning elections in the nation's past. There were great issues at stake in the Republican victory of 1860, the triumph of the East and the Midwest over the Populist South and West in 1896, the New Deal victories of 1934 and 1936. At such moments an entirely new political context was created. Then the deals, the compromises and the coalition took place within a transformed framework.

In the turmoil of the Thirties there were thinkers who saw only the dilalectical leaps of society; in the semi-affluence of the Fifties and Sixties the fashion was and is to notice only the evolutionary increments. Both perspectives distort. But what is at issue is not a scholarly quarrel over the past but a political debate over the future. For even if it were true that this country has stumbled through its history without any particular idea of where it is going, it can no longer afford to do so.

In *To Move a Nation*, Roger Hilsman gives a summary description of the utopian pragmatist way of doing things: "Rather than through grand decisions or grand alternatives, policy changes seem to come through a series of modifications of existing policy, with the new policy emerging slowly and haltingly by small and usually tentative steps, a process of trial and error in which policy zigs and zags, reverses itself and then moves forward in a series of incremental steps." My thesis, simply put, is that this method cannot possibly cope with the profound social crises which have been officially defined—and then catalogued— by the United States Government

It has been recognized (ironically, on the initiative of defense planners) that the evils of the society are not random but systematic. In the megalopolitan complexes, for instance, inadequate transportation, central-city decay, racial segregation and high rates of unemployment all reinforce one another. Reality itself is, in short, demanding "grand decisions or grand alternatives" whether American history likes it or not. The decision to rebuild Europe under the Marshall Plan was not an "incremental step," and neither is a commitment to rebuild America.

In a sense, the emerging situation is so radical that it changes at least some of the evidence on which Lubell and Burns base their analyses. The interdependence of the United States is becoming so marked that one could even say that the country is finally nationalizing itself and thus is moving toward a Left-Right, rather than a regional, opposition. For a few years after the murder of John F. Kennedy the Dixiecrat-Republican Congressional coalition which symbolized the deadlock of democracy was defeated, and there were those who thought that merica had escaped from the paralysis of its Madisonian institutions. But in 1967 that famed alliance for reaction returned more vigorous than ever. So even Burns's and Lubell's own terms, the need for truly decisive change is becoming more and more insistent.

A personal anecdote might make this point clearer. In 1964, immediately after President Johnson appointed Sargent Shriver to head the War on Poverty, I spent two weeks as a consultant to the task force which eventually drew up the Economic Opportunity Act of 1964. At my first meeting with Shriver I told him that the billion dollars the White House then planned to invest in the project was nickels and dimes" ("Oh really, Mr. Harrington," Shriver said. "I don't know about you, but this is the first time I've spent a billion dollars"). But as the days went on I became conscious that the intellectual deficit was even greater than the financial. The task-force members were dedicated, often brilliant. Yet all of us suffered from the fact that, during the Eisenhower years, few people had thought of what to do about poverty. When the moment for action finally came, practical men were hamstrung because not enough visionaries had preceded them.

But the limitations of utopian pragmatism did not just bedevil the War on Poverty. They led Lyndon Johnson to miss one of the greatest opportunities in recent American history. For his incredible personal triumph in the landslide of 1964 was also a failure of leadership.

In the aftermath of that election there were many who believed that the victory had been so total that the country had turned a political corner. Now, said Samuel Lubell, there was a decisive majority which "opened a new political epoch." And in 1965 Congress seemed to confirm this optimistic analysis. There were Federal aid to education, Medicare, a civil-rights, anti-poverty action, a Cabinet seat for the cities, and so on. It seemed that, were it not for the escalation of the war in Vietnam, Mr Johnson would have achieved his youthful ambition of becoming a second Franklin Roosevelt. Yet, for all the very real achievements of the Johnson Administration in those days, 1964 and 1965 marked the end of an old era, not the beginning of a new one.

John F. Kennedy had been stymied by the Dixiecrat-Republican coalition that had ruled Congress since 1938. He was forced to adopt a strategy of prudence in order to win a few Southern Democratic congressmen to his side. So he regularly proposed bills that were judged inadequate by his own planners. If these managed to pass, they were further compromised in the process. By the year of Kennedy's death there was hardly a political analyst in the land who did not agree with Burns that democracy had become deadlocked.

The emotional shock of the President's assassination made it possible for Mr Johnson to move even before November 1964. But it was Barry Goldwater who truly prepared the way for the liberal legislative triumphs of 1965. Goldwater's campaign strategy was precisely an attempt to force a realigning election. He proposed to win the South away from the Democratic Party and, by uniting it with Republican strength in the Midwest, create a completely new political context. In fact, Goldwater drove the moderates and independents into the Johnson camp, and a fantastic coalition was assembled, stretching from Martin Luther King Jr, to Russell Long and from Walter Reuther to Henry Ford.

In The Making of the President 1964, Theodore H. White describes a debate that took place within the Johnson staff during the election: "Among the speech-writers the dialogue was different from the dialogue among the strategists. What was the object of the Johnson campaign, asked some of the speech writers—to "broaden the base" or "to shape the mandate." It was a luxurious internal argument open only to men certain of victory. Should they state a campaign whose purpose was to harvest the greatest majority in American history? . . . Or should they press the campaign in another way? To spend in advance some of the certain margin of victory by putting before the people such hard, cleaving issues as must lose a few million votes but would shape an explicit mandate to give the President clear authority for the new programs of his next administration."

White believes that Johnson both expanded the safe middle ground and shaped his mandate. In fact, he sought new votes but not new ideas. This was one reason why his Congressional troubles started even before the Democratic defeats of 1966. The program Johnson put forth in 1964 and legislated in 1965 was essentially the culmination of the New Deal. Most of the measures in it — such as Medicare — had been debated for a generation and had been postponed because of the strength of the Dixiecrat-Republican coalition. There was a clear popular majority in favor of these bills and, once Barry Goldwater performed the invaluable service of getting the reactionary coalition out of the cloakroom and onto the ballot, it was inevitable that this social legislation would be passed. So the 1964 election finally vindicated the New Deal of Franklin Roosevelt. It did not, however, inaugurate the Great Society of Lyndon Johnson, for, among other things, no one really knew what that Great Society was supposed to be.

Even before the 1966 election the very same Congress which had been so enthusastic about completing the New Deal became recalcitrant about rent subsidies, the Teacher Corps and Model Cities. These were, for all their inadequacy, new ideas and principles, and the President had neglected the opportunity to win the American people to them under the euphoric conditions of the 1964 election. More broadly, his obsession with consensus had kept Mr Johnson from informing the electorate about the conflict-ridden practicalities of the future. He helped Henry Ford and other captains of industry to make their belated peace with Franklin Roosevelt, and he even persuaded them to join in a united front with Walter Reuther. But he secured this agreement on the conquests of the Thirties by avoiding the divisive challenges of the Sixties and Seventies.

So it is necessary to speak of major social changes as the Sixties come to an end, even though the forces of reform and renewal are everywhere on the defensive. For the history I have just sketched makes it clear that the democratic Left cannot wait for political victory and only then begin to work out a program. When Franklin Roosevelt began to improvise the New Deal after his electoral triumph in 1932, his audacious pragmatism accomplished many things —but it did not end the Depression. Now the problems before the nation are infinitely more complex that the gross catastrophe which confronted the Thirties, and the Johnson Administration proves that they are not susceptible to jerry-built solutions. Therefore it is precisely in the dark days when the horrible war in Vietnam has put an end to innovation that we must prepare for an advance that cannot even be foreseen. For the next time the nation decides to start moving again, there must be a democratic Left with some idea of where it is going.

Last generation's reforms will not solve this generation's crises. For all the official figures prove that it is now necessary to go far beyond Franklin Roosevelt. And this, as Washington has so magnificently documented, cannot be done by trusting in the incremental zigs and zags of utopian pragmatism somehow to come out right. The country has no choice but to have some larger ideas and to take them seriously.

TWO

Liberalism, as it has been known for three decades, cannot respond to this challenge unless it moves sharply to the democratic Left.

One consequence of that extraordinary consensus which Barry Goldwater organized among his enemies was to make the traditional liberal domestic program the official, national ideology of the United States. Everyone except the Neanderthals agreed on Federal management of the economy, the goal of full employment, Medicare, formal legal equality for Negroes and, above all, economic growth. There was even a vague unanimity about a misty future called the Great Society. So liberalism was no longer a subversive, prophetic force. It had arrived at the very center of the society.

To be sure, the liberal demands were adopted more on principle than in practice. Harry Truman's call for universal national medical insurance was turned into a Medicare program which covered some of the needs of people over sixty-five and some of the poor. In this area, and in many others, a struggle is still demanded to get the nation to honor its own commitments. But that is a matter, however important, of quantitive change. And liberalism, which is as far Left as this country has ever gone, must propose qualitatively new innovations if it is to be true to its own traditions.

The most intelligent and radical of the American youth sensed this impasse before any scholar defined it. They began to scandalize their liberal elders, charging them with having become agents of the corporations and the Establishment. The theories in which the young expressed their anger were intemperate, unhistorical, much too sweeping and contained a substantial truth. In *The New Industrial State*, John Kenneth Galbraith, the chairman of Americans for Democratic Action, provided a brilliant, reasoned analysis which substantiated many of the most bitter attacks on the liberal movement which he led.

"Except as he may stress more equitable distribution of income," Galbraith wrote, "the reformer's goals are identical with those of the industrial system. Except as he concerns himself with the poor he has become the political voice of the industrial system. It is an effortless role; no loud controversy is involved, there are no unseemly quarrels, no one need be persuaded. It is merely necessary to stand modestly at attention and take a bow as the Gross National Product goes up again, perhaps by a record amount. Reformers who so spend their time are, in effect, unemployed."

In other words, what used to be the Left is now the Center. Yet the problems that remain are even greater than the ones that have been solved. So liberalism must recover from its own intemperate victory, and it can do this only by a move toward the democratic Left. In saying this I do not propose a socialist reorganization of society even though I most emphatically favor it. The horizon of this book is set roughly twenty years in the distance and it is not, alas, realistic to expect that the American people will decide to transform capitalism during that period. So I use the term 'Left' here to describe a program and movement which socialists and radicals can—and must—support but which appeals to the more traditional American aspirations for reform as well.

I make no secret of the fact that I believe that extending democracy into significant areas of economic and social life, as I urge here, is a first step toward a completely new society. For myself, I make these proposals in precisely this transitional sense. Yet it is not at all necessary to agree with the socialist philosophy which I outlined in *The Accidental Century* in order to favor these ideas. They are grounded in liberal, religious and humanist, as well as socialist, values, and their urgency is attested to by the statistical authority of the United States Government itself.

Moreover, recent, and very hopeful, events make it particularly important thus to locate a radical program midway between immediate feasibility and ultimate utopia. For if the radical youth of the Sixties have rightly understood that liberalism must transcend its now established truths, they have been quite vague about what that means. They are precise about the bureacratic, technocratic and hypocritical society they reject, but, despite some anarchist yearnings, they have not really addressed themselves to the problem of how one can actually infuse a complex technological order with a democratic and humane spirit.

A hazy apocalypse is no substitute for an inadequate liberalism. This can be seen most dramatically in the confusions of the Left with regard to the revolutionary movements of the world. In analyzing the failures of a purely negative radicalism in this area, it becomes clear why the Left must state what it is for as well as what it is against.

The tendencies toward totalitarianism in the Third World of Asia, Africa and Latin America are not the invention of agents from Moscow, Peking, Havana or anywhere else. The bureaucratic and terrorist accumulation of capital in a developing nation is a rational, intolerable response to a real problem and it appeals to elites in the ex-colonies whether they are 'pro-Communist' or not. As Senator J. William Fulbright put it: "The reconstitution of a traditional society requires great discipline and enormous human sacrifice: not only must the rich be persuaded to give up privileges which they regard as their birthright, *but the poor who have practically nothing must be persuaded to do with even less in order to provide investment capital.*" (Italics added.)

In this setting, the terms "socialism" and "Left" are often used to express meanings diametrically opposed to the definitions made by the people of Europe and America in the course of their struggles. These words were originally intended to express the possibilities of a rich society producing for popular need under popular control, but they are now regularly employed to rationalize a coercive system in which the masses work harder for less and any independent organization, be it a union or a political party, is treated as a dangerous claimant for a scarce surplus. So on the basis of economics as much as, if not more than, ideology, the states of the Third World tend toward dictatorship when they seek to develop themselves.

The terrible necessities of this process are not necessary at all. They are the invention of Western power; they are imposed from without, and they can be substantially changed. But what is particularly relevant here is the simple-minded reaction of some Leftists to the complexities involved. France and the United States are cases in point.

French youth played a heroic, vanguard role in leading the opposition to the Algerian war. The socialists were divided on the issue, the Communists were afraid of acting because they were not at all sure the workers would follow them, and the students, professors and intellectuals courageously fought their own Government and the terrorists of the Right. But in the course of denouncing the colonialist horrors which France was perpetrating, many in the youthful resistance assumed that, if only the imperial power were withdrawn, then it would be a simple matter to create a regime of socialism and liberty in North Africa. When De Gaulle finally made his historic settlement with the National Liberation Front, the first half of the process described by Senator Fulbright was successfully concluded: the privileges of the rich had been successfully challenged. But then came the second part of the current development equation, the struggles against poverty—and, more often than not, against the poor.

At this point the loss of French expertise imposed a terrible social cost on the new republic. Unemployment became chronic, production declined, and there was an internal crisis which led to Boumedienne's coup against Ben Bella. For a considerable period the country was dependent on the largess of the United States in order to feed its own people. And at the beginning of 1968 those Algerians who proclaimed themselves "revolutionary" were mainly in an underground opposition. Thus did reality take its revenge on the libertarian fantasies of the French Left. The ideas of the youth were as shallow as their deeds were courageous.

There were analogous tendencies in the American movement to end the war in Vietnam. Here again students played a major role. Very few of them belonged to the various Communist organizations, and most were sincere democrats who were horrified at what their own Government was doing. Yet more than a few saw only the fight against American policy. They were romantic about what would come after the peace, supporting the Vietcong, or indifferent, not thinking about the problem at all. In their justified rage against Washington they did not concern themselves with the agonizing choices before the Vietnamese when the killing stopped. They saw Ho Chi Minh only as the hero of nationalist resistance and not as the man who had forcibly collectivized the peasants of the North. He was both.

These Vietnamese and Algerian examples are instances of a larger truth: it is not enough simply to be against the *status quo*. In the Third World the economic necessities as they have been artificially defined by the West provide a strong argument for anti-democratic rule. In such circumstances to think that the world of human liberation is accomplished simply by dismantling the old order is often to make way for a new tyranny. In the advanced nations the application of science to production collectivizes intelligence and creates huge, impersonal organizations. Thus there are tendencies toward an inhuman, manipulative society in the poverty of the ex-colonies and the affluence of the big powers. So in addition to excoriating the past and present, one must propose the future.

The old liberalism does not offer an adequate response to these massive historic trends and can even be used as a screen for corporate collectivism. And so long as the new Leftism is only an opposition it may help people to change their masters but not to free themselves. To deal with the crises it has officially certified at home and abroad, the United States will have to be quite concrete. It must, among other things, redefine economics, recover its passion for equality and, in the doing, reduce the profit motive to fourth-rate importance and raise the non-profit motive to the first rank.

THREE

According to the prevailing, but not universal, notion of economics in the Western world, it is uneconomical:

for advanced countries to trade with impoverished nations so as to improve the relative position of the latter and help close the global gap between the rich and the poor;

for private capital to be invested in balanced economic development in the Third World;

for the corporations to abolish the slums of America; for urban space to be "wasted" on beauty, history or civility; to subsidize the humanities and not just the physical and social sciences.

These are only a few examples. They express the fact that there is much more to be made by investing in the misshapen development of the world economy and in the distortion of affluence than in human decency. Decisions to act in this way are not necessarily made by malevolent men and are, often enough, the work of sincere people. It is just that these choices are economical and justice is not.

Here is how Charles J. Hitch and Roland McKean, the authors of one of the most influential books of political economy in recent times, *The Economics of Defense in the Nuclear Age*, put the prevailing orthodoxy: "But always economics or economizing means trying to make *the most efficient use* of the resources available in all activities and in any circumstances." (Italics added). The crucial phrase is, of course, 'the most efficient use.' With some important exceptions, economists have understood this term in a quantitative, commercial sense. That which produces the most units in the shortest time at the cheapest cost and therefore yields the highest profit is "economic."

There are economists who have made a much broader and humane reading of the textbook doctrine. Theodore Shultz had demonstrated that education made a relatively greater contribution to increased production in the United States than the combined inputs of capital and labor. Fritz Machlup of Princeton pleaded with his colleagues, "We must not put economic values to one side and other values—say ethical, social, political or human—to the other side." And in a speech to the Urban American Conference, John Kenneth Galbraith argued that market determination of land value, though once justified, made it impossible for society to take social or aesthetic considerations into account. He therefore proposed to take a great deal of property out of the speculative realm altogether by making it public.

But on the whole, professionals have understood the 'most efficient use' of resources in the crass, obvious sense of the phrase. Moreover, it has been this definition that has guided Government policy. And yet the most urgent needs of the times—economic progress in the less developed countries, an end to poverty and racism in America, the design of a humane environment for human beings— are not economical within this definition. Suburban sprawl is a more "efficient" use of resources than the abolition of slums; rigging the world market to tax the poor for the benefit of the rich is more "efficient" than the other way around.

These facts of life have been recognized in one relatively small area of American life: television. The Ford and Carnegie foundations, the White House, and even Congress, have come to realize that commercial television slights some rather important values. As Robert Sarnoff of RCA stated an excellently uneconomical philosophy in a 1967 speech, "Although non-commercial television may attract only a small fraction of the audience, *its value cannot be measured in these terms alone*. It should be measured by the vitality of its service to minority interest. The results of such efforts often find their way to

the majority of the people, helping to enrich and elevate the quality of life."
(Italics added.)

Sarnoff's rejection of the commercial measure of television time which his company—and all the others—have so religiously used is a gain. Yet the conclusions he drew from this insight illustrate another important theme of this book; that executives usually propose to serve the public interest in a way that maximizes their own corporate interest as well. Sarnoff rejected two suggested methods of financing public television: the Carnegie notion of a tax on sets and Ford's idea of a non-profit domestic satellite company which would use its surplus to underwrite a quality network. Both of those reforms might cost the industry something, so Sarnoff held that the funds be paid from the general -- taxpayers'—revenues. (This was not an isolated instance but a typical case of the moneymaker's perspective on social service.)

In any case, foundations, businessmen and politicians all recognize that television cannot be made to serve truly social ends as long as it is operated on commercial principles. Such a shocking admission can be made in this area of the economy because public television will not cost very much and will not require any structural innovation in the society. And the chief beneficiaries of such an undertaking (and I still support it even though this is the case) would be the educated middle class. As will be seen, such a discriminatory expenditure of Federal funds in favor of the well-off is the one form of uneconomics the Congress usually approves.

Decent housing for the poor is as uneconomical as good television for the cultured, but General Sarnoff's philosophy is not normally applied in this case. It would be too dangerous. To end the slums will take the expenditure of billions of dollars, the creation of new institutions of democratic planning and a system of fiscal priorities which would actually subsidize the poor to the same degree as the middle class and the rich. That comes to a little more than a contribution for good video theatre. Yet the democratic Left cannot permit the redefinition of economics to be confined to the genteel, middle-class side of American life — public television, highway beautification and the like. Therefore one of the most basic strategies of the Left will be to commit the state to make massive public investments which are not "economical" in the traditional sense of the word.

In short, there must be a social determination of what is economic. Building homes for the impoverished is not profitable from the point of view of a corporate investor because it does not provide a high enough rate of return on capital. But the social investor — which is to say the democratic society — has a different point of view. Poverty is, of course, enormously costly in terms of increasing the risks of crime, fire, disease and every other ill, and America already pays a high price for being unjust. But much more basically, human beings are being squandered, and this is a tragic waste from the point of view of both the individual and the society.

As the Harvard psychiatrist Robert Coles told a Senate sub-committee in 1966, "I have found in the most apathetic or lawless people enough unused energy and sidetracked morality to make of them different people, given different circumstances in their actual, everyday life." But in order to reach these people — and the millions of the Third World — the democratic Left must carry out a concerted attack on the old notion of the "efficient" uses of resources.

John Maynard Keynes anticipated this point even though he was a radical conservative rather than a revolutionist. In his *General Theory of Employment, Interest and Money*, he wrote that "strict business principles" led people to prefer wholly wasteful expenditures to the partly wasteful. It was, he said, more acceptable to finance unemployment relief by a loan than to put people to work recreating the society and financing the improvements with a subsidized interest rate. So it is today. America would rather administer a humiliating, utterly inadequate, annual dole than to make a massive multi-billion-dollar investment in people for an abolition of poverty which will yield enormous human and social profit.

In saying these things I am not advocating charity. For, as later chapters will show, the power of the American state has been used to reinforce the maldistribution of wealth in the society, and the rich and the middle class have received more handouts than the poor. In these circumstances it would be justice, not *noblesse oblige*, to channel public funds to those who most desperately need them. In the process, the nation might even resurrect one of its most hallowed, and forgotten, ideals: equality.

The current rediscovery of the problems of the American underclass is not, by far and large, a response to an egalitarian movement. It came as a result of mass pressure only in the sense that the country would never have noticed its own poverty were it not for the Negro movement. In their struggle for equality before the law, black Americans also laid bare the inequalities of the economy and probably did more for their white fellow citizens than for themselves. Beyond that, the War on Poverty derived from reformist conscience at the top of the society rather than from revolutionary consciousness at the bottom. The Cold War slackened and social criticism became less suspect, the intelligentsia less complacent; John Kennedy awakened the idealism of the youth and middle class; and in the wake of the ghetto riots of the mid-Sixties there was a fearful advocacy of amelioration. When, for instance, Henry Ford came out in support of the anti-poverty effort in 1966, he did so out of the explicit worry that, if these miseries were not attended to, they might menace the *status quo*. The Detroit riots of 1967 proved him prescient.

So there is now considerable talk of raising minimum standards up to a semi-humane level, but no one speaks of increasing the justice of the society. For despite many journalistic, and even scholarly, proclamations of recent social "revolutions" the American system of inequality has shown a depressing vitality in the last two decades. In 1947 the poorest 20 percent of the population received 5 percent of the income, and it held this same 5 percent share in 1964 (all figures are taken from the Current Population Report of the Department of Commerce, the Federal agency assigned to record this Federal scandal). The second lowest fifth got 12 percent in 1947 and 12 percent in 1964. In short, 40 percent of the American people were held to a 17 percent share of the income throughout the entire postwar period. The 5 percent at the top got about the same portion as that 40 percent. These figures, it must be realized, underestimate the evil, since they are taken from tax returns; and the highest income recipients hire expensive lawyers and accountants in order to conceal as much of their wealth as possible, while the rest of the nation pays as it goes.

Such a stagnant, unfair distribution of wealth mocks the American egalitarian spirit. But more than that, the regressive division of wealth within America and throughout the globe has been encouraged by Washington. For one of the most important economic mechanisms to be described in this book shows that in a world, or in a society, dominated by the economic power of larger corporations (or, for that matter, by fat Communist bureaucracies), policies to foster the economic common good will, in the absence of determined political counter-measures, strengthen the existing order of injustice. When foreign aid is given, trade pacts are negotiated or the domestic pump is primed, it is "natural" that the rich individuals and institutions will be the brokers of the public investment and the greatest gainers from the publicly induced prosperity.

So the democratic Left must not only commit itself to "uneconomic" investments in human beings but must do so in such a way as to increase the equality of the society. It is important that people have "enough" — and morally impera-tive that they should have what is rightfully theirs. Henry Ford seeks ameliora-tions to keep the natives happy at home and abroad; and every summer the mayors of the Big American cities throw a few crumbs into the ghetto in the hope that a riot can be bought off. That is social engineering. And, by way of sharp contrast, the democratic Left is concerned with justice.

Finally, these broad changes in social philosophy will challenge the primacy of the profit motive as the principle of social and individual life.

Businessmen, as I pointed out in *The Accidental Century*, have been the main subverters of the classic capitalist ethic. The gigantic corporation is a private collective that engages in planning, administers prices and dispenses with the test of the market by generating its own future capital rather than by borrowing it. There is still a diminishing function for the money market and the law of supply and demand, but it really does not have much to do with the dominant industrial sector of the society. As a result, the Horatio Alger myth, whatever validity it had in the past, is now a nostalgic lie.

A growing number of young people have been recognizing the new facts of life. In 1964 the *Wall Street Journal* reported that 14 percent of Harvard's senior class entered business, as opposed to 39 percent in 1960. In 1966 a Harris poll found that the trend was deepening. Only 12 percent of a sample of college seniors were looking forward to business careers — and twice as many wanted to be teachers. In that year the *Wall Street Journal* "Labor Letter" also noted that corporate personnel officers were stressing the social contribution of the private sector, with a company like General Electric recruiting trained youth to the struggle against air pollution rather than to the making of money. And in 1967 *Newsweek* reported that business executives were worried because the Peace Corps was attracting a disproportionate number of the brightest students from the finest colleges.

Late in 1967 Albert R. Hunt of the *Wall Street Journal* summarized the trend: "It looks as if selling refrigerators to Eskimos may be only a little harder than selling the virtues of a corporate career to today's collegians." Hunt reported that in a poll at wealthy Stanford University only 8 percent of the freshman class were intending to have business careers.

But then perhaps the most authoritative testimonial to the possibility of dispensing with the profit motive comes from a millionaire businessman and stock speculator. I speak once again of John Maynard Keynes.

In 1925 Keynes wrote, ". . . the moral problem of our age is concerned with the love of money, with the habitual appeal to the money motive in nine tenths of the activities of life, with the unversal striving after individual security as the prime object of endeavor, with the social approbation of money as the measure of constructive success, and with the social appeal to the hoarding instinct as the foundation of the necessary provision for the family and for the future." Yet, as I noted earlier, Keynes was not a revolutionary, and his *General Theory* explicitly defended "the environment of private wealth ownership." How is the contradiction resolved?

Two years after his attack on the love of money Keynes published a sophisticated and paradoxical distinction. There were two separate issues, he said, and one concerned the efficiency of capitalism, the other the desirability of the system. "For my part," Keynes wrote, "I think that capitalism, wisely managed, can probably be made more efficient for obtaining economic ends than any alternative system yet in sight; but that in itself is in many ways objectionable." Eventually, Keynes believed, the economy would become so productive (he even imagined a zero interest rate for capital) that society would no longer need to be immoral in order to be efficient. At that point, "The love of money — as distinguished from the love of money as a means to the enjoyments and realities of life — will be recognized for what it is, a somewhat disgusting morbidity; one of those semi-criminal, semi-pathological propensities which one hands over with a shudder to the specialists in mental disease."

This distinction between money as means and money as an end is crucial if the issues are not to be muddled. For the immediate future, and even into the visionary middle distance, almost everyone is going to be raising his standard of life and even pursuing luxuries. One accepts, then, a modicum of self-interest and anti-neighborliness at this point in history. Moreover, it is absolutely imperative that an economy produce a surplus (a "profit," if you will) in excess of what is consumed in order to provide for future investment and, above all from the point of view of the democratic Left, future social investment.

Yet these relatively functional concepts of money-making are a far cry from the profit mythology which is still taught to innocent school children in this society. For Americans are told that buying cheap and selling dear, gaining an advantage over one's neighbor, making a killing out of a rise in the value of stock or land which the individual did nothing to promote are the basic principles which should guide the citizen and the society. It is indeed a "somewhat disgusting morbidity" that the country thus reverences.

Many college students have, as noted earlier, turned their backs on this dog-eat-dog ethic. More generally, educators have a major contribution to make on this count. They can begin to teach the young about economic reality and assign personal greed a relatively modest role in the society. And they can discuss the humane, cooperative motives which can induce people to action. Indeed, there are many signs that the youth have understood the necessity for such a pedagogy before it occurred to their teachers.

But homilies will not change the motivational structure of an entire society. What is needed in addition is action to create an evironment in which it is more "natural" to help one's fellow man than to profit from him. And this is precisely what follows from the main argument of this book. An analysis of international and domestic social issues shows over and over that there is an objective need for some public, as opposed to private, investment; for social, as opposed to individual, consumption; and for giving aesthetic and other non-commercial values a claim on material resources. These reforms, it should be emphasized, are required in order to redeem the existing, official pledges of the Untited States of America. If they are carried out, however, they will have a profound byproduct. For as the social, non-profit and aesthetic sectors of the society expand, more and more people will be able to live their lives and express themselves in the actual practice of a cooperative, rather than a competitive, ethic. And that fact will be the most powerful sermon of all.

FOUR

Finally, the ideas in this book are not presented as blueprints for legislative draftsmen but as practical intimations of a new civilization.

I am not proposing another exercise in futurism, an attempt to guess the inventions that will take place in the next twenty or so years. There are already distinguished study commissions engaged in that undertaking. Throughout this book I simply assume that unprecedented change will be a commonplace, as in the recent past. If the pace of the next twenty years is only as headlong as that of the last twenty, that will provide imperative enough for the kinds of political, social and economic reform urged here. If, as is quite possible, there is some unforseen scientific breakthrough, then a transformation of our minds and institutions becomes even more urgent. In either case, America desperately needs a democratic Left.

I do not here pretend to have made an exhaustive description of that Left. I have identified some of the most important evils in the society and tried to see them not as isolated outrages but as part of a social system in motion. They are typical instances of what is grievously wrong with America rather than a comprehensive inventory. And the solutions are put forth to illustrate new ways of thinking to initiate, rather than to close, the discussion.

And yet in saying that there must be first steps toward a new civilization I do not mean to effect a vague rhetoric. Along with the social tragedies, the Government has also catalogued the awesome possibilities that are already present among us. It is quite clear that this nation, and the world, are in for profound, qualitative change; that we are heading, willy-nilly, for a new epoch in man's history.

The National Commission on Technology, Automation and Economic Progress reported that, if America were to take all of its productivity gains from 1965 to 1985 in the form of increased leisure, it would be able to choose between a twenty-two-hour week, a twenty-seven-week year and retirement at thirty-eight.

There are now around sixty million housing units in the United States. By the year 2000 it will be necessary to build an *additional* seventy million, or more than now exist. This means, in the Johnson Administration's phrase, the construction of a "second America." On what principles and according to what design?

By 1975, according to the special Counsel to the Senate Sub-committee on Anti-Trust, three hundred corporations will own 75 percent of the industrial assets of the world.

George Ball, formerly of the State Department and now chairman of the foreign-operations branch of Lehman Brothers, predicted in 1967, "Before many years we may see supernational corporations incorporated under treaty arrangements without a domicile in any particular nation state." Such entities, one might add, could well turn out to be more powerful than the United Nations.

There are thus fundamental choices to be made, choices which will affect the relation of man to himself, his fellow citizen and the entire world. And yet all that America has really done is to take note of this tremendous fact and then file it in the Library of Congress. As a result, the system no longer seems to work, for it cannot keep its own promises.

That is why there must be a democratic Left.

Donald A. Wells

Donald A. Wells (b. 1917) is Professor of Philosophy at the University of Illinois, Chicago Circle. In the article which follows, "How Much Can 'The Just War' Justify?", he subjects to critical analysis the leading traditional theory of the justification of war. The question of what conditions must be met if a nation is to be justified in going to war is, of course, important in its own right. This question has additional significance in that it also bears directly on other questions of importance, such as those concerning the duties of men called to serve in a war. Both these questions have, of course, been of much more than theoretical interest in the recent experience of citizens of the United States.

How Much Can
"The Just War" Justify?

Justification, as is well known, is not an unambiguous term. Even in the context of logical justification the criteria are debatable, but at least in this milieu justification is assumed to be a function of a set of given rules in an agreed-upon system. Within a context of a set of truth claims consistency is a

From *The Journal of Philosophy*, Vol. LXVI No. 23, December 4, 1969. By permission of the Editor and the Author.

necessary and almost sufficient criterion. In normative discourse, however, justification takes on an honorific and emotion-laden aura. Adequacy here entails notions of "rightness" or "goodness" in addition to putative truth claims. The problem of "The Just War" is, in this latter sense, more than a matter of the occurrence of matters of fact, more than a matter of consistency within a system of given axioms, more than a matter of demonstrating what is permissible legally, and more than an exercise in casuistry.

In a very ordinary sense of the term 'justify' we may merely seek an explanation of why war is waged in the sense of showing the premises that prompted us to the conclusion to wage war. When asked, "Why did you wage this war?" we could reply, "I did it because x, y, and z had occurred," and we now conclude that the war in question had now been justified. If, on the other hand, we justify war the way an appellant defends himself before the judge, we would then need to show that what we did was consistent with the laws under which we have agreed to operate. But suppose that the justification of war is like the famous "justification of induction" and that its resolution involves us in a metalinguistic search. In fact, the attempts to justify war, or to identify what a just war would be like, share common properties with all these interpretations. In addition, however, there is an implicit contradiction which discussants of war and justice ordinarily recognize. Since the havoc of war is normally classed with immoral actions and evil consequences, what the notion of "the just war" attempts to do is to show that under some circumstances it would be "just" to perform immoral acts and to contribute to evil consequences. Some justifications of war aim to show that actions deemed normally forbidden by moral mandates are now permissible when performed under the aegis of war.

Since the history of ethical speculation has virtually no other instance of the defense of immoral acts under the extenuating circumstance of prudential risk, the "just war" concept needs special attention. It constitutes an anomalous instance in moral discourse, namely, a glaring exception to an otherwise accepted prohibition of acts of human brutality.

Traditionally the doctrine of "the just war" intended to curb excessively inhumane war practices, reduce the likelihood of war, identify who may properly declare war, ensure that the means of war bore a relation of proportion to the ends of war, and generally to promote a conscience on the practice. Incidentally, the concept functioned as a defense of national sovereignty and of the "right" of nations to defend themselves in a basically lawless world. It made national survival feasible, while making international organization unlikely.

Since the notion of "the just war" has been revived after nearly two centuries of silence on the issue, it seems appropriate to look again at the medieval claims to see whether, if they had a defense then, they have any rationale now. The entire discussion for the medievalist rested, of course, on a concession which itself needs reassessment; namely, that war has a place in the moral scheme. The traditional questions about war were prudential, and the discussion centered around such questions as the time, place, and cause for war. Wars were presumed to be neutral means which could be given moral properties under the appropriate conditions. Wars were criticized, if at all, in practice rather than in principle. In this, medieval war discussion shared a common starting point with medieval speculation on capital punishment. It wasn't the fact of killing that was the determinant; rather the reasons given for the acts of killing were decisive.

THE CRITERIA OF SAINT THOMAS

In order for a war to be just, three conditions had to be met: (1) an authoritative sovereign must declare the war; (2) there must be a just cause; and (3) the men who wage the war must have just intentions, so that good actually results from the war. In application of these criteria, the criticisms that did emerge of particular wars were so few as to suggest that princes were basically moral men or that the criteria were too vague to be useful. In addition, the critics were commonly persons not officially in government, so that their protests were a kind of baying at the moon. George Fox, for example, challenged the wars of Cromwell, but then Fox rejected the war method utterly. Franciscus de Victoria, a theological professor at the University of Salamanca in the sixteenth century, chastised his Spanish superiors for the wars against the Indians[1]—but the remarks of university professors, then as now, were rarely influential in the determination of foreign policy, particularly when such remarks were critical of decisions of state already made.

More recently, Joseph McKenna[2] has revived the "just war" doctrine with an expanded list of seven conditions. They are: (a) the war must be declared by the duly constituted authority; (2) the seriousness of the injury inflicted on the enemy must be proportional to the damage suffered by the virtuous; (3) the injury to the aggressor must be real and immediate; (4) there must be a reasonable chance of winning the war; (5) the use of war must be a last resort; (6) the participants must have right intentions; and (7) the means used must be moral. Our question is: "Can such criteria be made applicable to modern war?" Let us consider this in terms of some general "just war" claims.

A JUST WAR IS ONE DECLARED BY THE DULY CONSTITUTED AUTHORITY

For a theologian like Saint Augustine or Saint Thomas, who presumed some prevading and ameliorating power from Christian prelates, such a criterion could be considered to be a limitation on careless scoundrels, as well as a limitation on the number of wars that would actually be waged. By the sixteenth century, however, with the proliferation of princes and the fading away of the influence of Christian prelates, a radically new situation had emerged. By this time, the "reasons of state," as Machiavelli elaborated them, permitted every prince to wage war whenever he saw fit. Since by the eighteenth century war had become the sport of kings, it was clear that authorities were not very reliable nor sensitive.

The rise of nationalism made this first criterion undifferentiating. It became increasingly obvious that to grant to any prince the privilege of judging his neighboring prelates was an odd situation. It was this anomaly that led Grotius and Victoria to insist that, although only one side of a war could properly be considered just, in fact persons on both sides could, in good conscience, presume

[1] Franciscus de Victoria, *On the Law of War* (Washington, D.C.: The Carnegie Institute, 1917), sec. 22.

[2] "Ethics and War: A Catholic View," *American Political Science Review* (September 1960): 647-658.

that they had justice on their side. In the absence of any international judge, who could determine the justice of the various national claims? What this criterion did do was to make clear that revolution was not to be allowed. What it could not do was to persuade or compel some prince to forego a war.

If rulers were saints and scholars there might be some reason to suppose that their judgements on war were adequate. Actually, there are no plausible reasons to suppose that secular leaders have intentions that will meet even minimal standards of humaneness. It is not necessary to have in mind Hitler, Tojo, DeGaulle, or Thieu to see that this is so. There is nothing in the nature of the process by which leaders are selected to give assurance that Johnson, Trudeau, or Wilson have moral insights that are even as good as the average, let alone sufficiently discerning to be used as the criterion for a just war. These leaders are not presumed by their loyal opposition to be especially gifted in domestic policy. Why imagine that they are so for foreign policy?

Even clerics have a rather poor reputation for moral insight or sound judgment. Witness, for example, the stand of Archbishop Groeber of Freiburg-im-Breisgau, who rejected Christian pacifism for German Catholics on the grounds that Hitler was the duly constituted authority. Pope Pius XII showed no better insight when he rejected the right of conscientious objection for German Catholics at the time of the formation of NATO. This first criterion, therefore, seems to serve no helpful purpose at all. In Vietnam, for example, it would rule out Thieu, since he is warring against his own people, while granting that L.B.J. might be right, and Ho Chi Minh just in killing American troops but not so for killing Vietnamese from the South.

A JUST WAR USES MEANS PROPORTIONAL TO THE ENDS

Franciscus de Victoria had observed (*op cit.*, secs. 33, 37) that if to retake a piece of territory would expose a people to "intolerable ills and heavy woes" then it would not be just to retake it. We must be sure, he continued, that the evils we commit in war do not exceed the evils we claim to be averting. But how do we measure the relative ills? This is the problem of a hedonic calculus on which Mill's system foundered. Since Victoria granted princes the right to despoil innocent children if military necessity required it, it ceased to be clear what proportionality meant or whether any limit at all was being proposed.

In a recent paper on this issue Father John A. Connery[3] stated that the morality of the violence depends on the proportionality to the aggression. What is required is some calculus to make this measurement. The latitude with which conscientious persons have interpreted this suggests (what was clear enough to Mill) that we possess neither the quantitative nor the qualitative yardstick for this decision. Pope Pius XII thought the annihilation of vast numbers of persons would be impermissible. John Courtney Murray[4] thought this prohibition was too restrictive. Herbert Hoover thought in 1939 that the aerial bombing of cities should be banned, although he did urge the U.S. to build bombing planes to

[3] "Morality and Nuclear Armament," in William J. Nagle, ed., *Morality and Modern Warfare* (Baltimore: Helicon, 1960), p. 92.

[4] "War and the Bombardment of Cities," *Commonweal* (Sept. 2, 1938).

perform this banned action. Jacques Maritain put bombing from the air in the category of as absolutely proscribed act.[5] In the early period of World War II "Saturation bombing" was considered to be too inhumane for American citizens to accept. We then practiced what was euphemistically called "Precision bombing." That the terms were empty became obvious when the Air Force announced at the time of the first test shot of the Atlas missile, that a bomb that lands within fifty miles of its target is considered accurate.

Does the notion of proportionality have any discriminatory meaning? During World War II the English writer, Vera Brittain, attacked both Britain and America in her book *Massacre by Bombing. The Christian Century* urged in editorials that its subscribers should read the book, while taking the position that the bombing of civilians is a necessary part of a just war. The American Bar Association defeated a resolution calling for a condemnation of the bombing of civilians.[6] The *Saturday Evening Post* maintained that anyone who questioned the bombing of civilians was "unstable."[7] McKinlay Kantor said the book was "soft-hearted." The Reverend Carl McIntyre called the position of the sensitive Mrs. Brittain "un-American and pro-Fascist," and the conservative Boston clergyman, H. J. Ockenga, called the view "un-American" and said it gave aid and comfort to the enemy. Not only do Christian prelates seem a fairly callous lot, but the notion of proportionality has lost sense.

Where should we draw the line? Pope Pius XII decided that Communism was such a cosmic threat that atomic, chemical, and biological bombs could all be justifiably used. But where then is the proportion? The dilemma is not aided by the clerical dictum that "there are greater evils than the physical death and destruction wrought in war" (Nagle, 80). What civilian would be impressed by this amid the rain of bombs? Like "better dead than Red," this is a fiction, enthusiasm for which is directly proportional to the square of the distance from the potential havoc. In any case, there is simply too much horror to be subsumed under the medieval notion of proportionality. Indeed, our State Department's White Paper, which was intended to explain the ends that justified our means in Vietnam, is a monstrously casuistic document. It seems to make no proportional sense to do what we are doing against the Vietnamese if the only reward is American-style elections or freedom from the threat of creeping Communism.

The medieval thinkers rejected religion as a proper cause of a just war, and it is not egregious to point out that politics is in the same general class as religion. After all, is there really any doubt that men can live well under a variety of systems: capitalistic, communistic, monarchic, or democratic? It is equally obvious, I assume, that men may live poorly under any of these systems. Witness the blacks in Georgia, Mississippi, or Washington, D.C. Would any theologian wish to make a case for the bomb on Selma or Chicago? Surely the crimes against men are great there, and if there is any proportion in Hanoi, it would seem to follow that similar acts could be justified in Little Rock.

If there is any reasonable doubt left that the criterion calling for "just means" is simply a verbal genuflection, a brief look at what is currently called "rational

[5] Nagle, *op cit.*, p. 107.

[6] *New York Times* (July 15, 1939), p. 3.

[7] *Saturday Evening Post* (Nov. 21, 1942): 128.

nuclear armament" will banish it. A contemporary recommendation by proponents of "rationality" here is to limit bombs to the ½-megaton class. This is fifty times greater than the bomb dropped on Hiroshima. Limitation, proportion, or rationality do not seem to apply to the language of mega-kill. Once a bomb is big enough to kill every person in an area, it is not an expansion of war to use a bomb big enough to kill everyone twice, any more than it can be considered a reduction to reduce from a bomb twice as large as is needed to one the precise size that is needed to decimate the population. And, in addition, to call such a consideration "rational" may be proper to military tacticians, but alien to a concept that aimed at a moral distinction.

WAR MAY BE JUSTLY TAKEN ONLY AS A LAST RESORT

In conventional language the notion of "last resort" presupposes a notion of "first resorts." Thus, unless a nation could show that it indeed exhausted first resorts, it would make no sense to claim the right of last resort. Presumably, first resorts would be such alternatives as economic, social, or political boycott, negotiations either through unilateral or multilateral means, or through such an agency as the United Nations, or even the contemplation of some kind of compromise. After these had been exhausted and there appeared to be no further nonviolent alternatives, we would still need to show that the last resort ought, in this case, to be taken. It is always possible that the final resort that can be defended morally is the first resort taken. Too much of the discussion about the "justice" of war as a last resort presumes war to be proper in any case, so that the only genuine questions have to do with timing. With this kind of concession, in the first place, imagine what would happen to discussion of the War Crimes Trials after World War II. The problem facing the German Nazis was simply: "After having exhausted every resort, may we now as a last resort exterminate the Jews?"

The problem facing contemporary theorists of the "just war" is whether modern war is a means that may "justly" be granted as any resort at all. When we begin to speak of "massive retaliation" then perhaps it is time to question war itself. Is there any end at all of sufficient value that the sacrifice of persons on such a scale as is now possible could become "justified?" Something has happened to the medieval notion of last resort when our leaders destroy a city to save it. But the horror of war has never functioned as much of an intellectual deterrent to the justice of war. Thus it is antecedently unlikely that the ability to "overkill" or "megakill" makes any rational difference to the medieval concept. If war is a just resort at all, it makes no sense to deny nations its use as a last resort. Once the killing has been sanctioned in the first place, moral discussion, such as the medieval man carried out, takes on the aura of Pentagon calculations.

We find, in this vein, Paul Ramsey, a Protestant advocate of the "just war," endorsing the use of thermonuclear weapons, provided that an important *military target* could not otherwise be eliminated. While Ramsey deplored the death of so many civilians, he assured the survivors that this is not too great a price to pay for civilization. The possibility that surrender would be more moral than war is not even conceded a probability, making it clear that the discussants are speaking only for nations that win wars. The demand for "unconditional surrender" which American statesmen have regularly made, makes it clear that last resorts are the only ones they have in mind. For example, in August, 1958, the U.S. Senate voted 82 to 2 to deny government funds to any person or institution that proposes or actually conducts any study regarding the possible results of the surrender of the U.S. as an alternative to war. The sheer presence of the doctrine of "last resort" makes the compromise contingent on negotiations inadmissable.

What does our "just war" theory say to the American Indians back in the seventeenth century when they were confronted with the white man's power? Was war justified for the Indian as a last resort? It was surely a case of defense, and even white historians grant that the Indians tried many resorts short of war. Since nations with arms are loath to succumb to similar national neighbors, and more especially to do so over concern with whether war is a last resort or whether first resorts still remain, about all the theory tells us is that the "last resort" is bound to be a resort that we actually take.

A JUST WAR MUST BE WAGED BY MEN WITH RIGHT INTENTIONS

The medieval hub of this argument was the doctrine of the "double effect." A just belligerent intended only as much death as would be proportional to the threat or the offense, and he would intend to kill only combatants. It was presumed that we ought not to kill noncombatants. In the middle ages the weapons made such concern practical. Although the archer might shoot his arrow into the air and not be too clear about where it landed, he was not in doubt about whether he was shooting it at combatant enemies. He might miss a small barn, but he hit the right city. Modern weapons make such sensitivity about the recipients of our missiles inoperable and unfeasible. Not only this, but the number of noncombatants killed in modern war usually far exceeds that of soldiers. Whereas medieval man might pardonably weep for the accidentally slain civilians, modern man intends the death of every civilian slain when he drops his bombs from the air.

In every age, however, the problem of unintended death proved a harrassing one, and the pattern of resolution seems to have been to deplete the scope of the class of the noncombatant, until in the present this is a null class. Modern war is total at least in the sense that there are no innocents. We could never have dropped the bombs on Dresden, Nagasaki. Hiroshima, or Tokyo if the class of innocents had had members. But quite apart from whether one could or did intend the death of noncombatants, there would still remain the question whether the end justified the means at all. It was this sheer inapplicability of the doctrine of the "double effect" that prompted John Bennett to reject the notion completely.[8] There is, also, another procedural problem here. The doctrine of the "double effect" is one that does not trouble military or political strategists. Their interest is to win the war, and not to make theological calculations. Indeed, the only concern the military appears to have had over such niceties as intentionality is whether there would be a moral response from the public. We

[8] Cf. Paul Ramsey, *War and the Christian Conscience* (Durham, N.C..: Duke University Press, 1961), p. 148.

did not, initially, practice saturation bombing in Europe, and we were told later that the military feared a public outcry against it. Once we had practiced it on the Japanese and once military necessity demanded it, Americans lost most of their sensitivity on the problem.

No defense of the intentions of a belligerent could be satisfactorily made unless it could also be shown that the means used were also moral, and this would be so even for the combatants considered to be fair game. Nowhere has the ability of man to tolerate increasing doses of violence and brutality been more evident than in his history of attempts to humanize the weapons. Richard J. Krickus[9] believed that chemical bombs were moral, whereas biological bombs were not, and this because of the difficulty of control in the case of the latter. On the other hand, napalm, anti-personnel shrapnel, and thermonuclear bombs were all "just" in their intended uses. To speak of the just use of the bayonet is difficult enough for mere mortals to grasp, but to use the same approbation for mega-weapons makes the terms 'just' and 'moral' lose their conventional distinguishing function. Modern man has had long practice in handling these theoretically difficult problems. Since we use gas chambers in the United States for our domestic offenders, it must not have been their method that led to the War Crimes Trials against the Nazis, but simply that they gassed and cremated the wrong persons. Although there may be no way to calculate the relative horror of gas chambers in the two countries or the hedonic ratios of the death of twenty Japanese as compared with the death of twenty Americans, it is precisely this kind of question that the "just war" theorists must answer.

The discussion of "intention" in the thirteenth century, when the weapons were relatively limited in scope so that a king could implement his wish not to harm noncombatants and could practice some kind of proportionality, is something that modern men can no longer carry out. All we can consider is whether to set the projectiles in motion. From that moment on, it makes no sense to speak of proportionality, intentionality, or limitation. But here, men have attempted to think the "unthinkable." What seemed too brutal in one age becomes militarily necessary and, hence, just in the next age. As recently as twenty years ago the arms agencies deleted mention of their chemical-biological research from the public agendas for fear of a public outcry. Now there is no need for secrecy, and everyone can witness on television the operations of our nerve gas plant in Newport, Indiana, our disease-bomb research at Fort Detrick, Maryland, and the bubonic plague research of the Hartford Travellers Research Corporation to discover the most efficient means to spread the disease by airplane or on foot. The history of prudential calculation reveals that every weapon sooner or later is added to the list of morally approved ones.

There may be credible case for claiming that the medieval discussions of the war added to man's moral insights and implemented his humane concerns. Perhaps without such discussions, the history of war would be even worse than it now is. Such counter-factual conditionals are, however, technically incapable of being assigned weights of probability as to truth or falsity. But what can be determined is that the use of the terms "just", "limited", "humane", "proportional", or "intention" in the context of modern war robs these terms of most of their traditional moral flavor. If it was poor military strategy to assert "thou shalt

[9] "On the Morality of Chemical/Biological War," *Journal of Conflict Resolution* (June 1965): 200-210.

not kill," it was even worse ethics to claim, "thou mayest napalm thine enemy if thy country is threatened."

One could have hoped that as the scope of weapons increased there would have been an escalation of sensitivity as to their use. But all that happened was that there was an escalation of insensitivity, until today it is hard to imagine what an unjustly fought war would look like that is not already exhibited in the just variety. Conceivably some medieval sword thrusts might have been made justly, and some fortified cities justly sacked. The entire distinction vanishes, however, once we admit weapons that shoot farther than the eye can see. And clearly this distinction has been lost once we use mega-weapons, and even what are called "conventional" weapons like fragmentation bombs and napalm. Since we no longer admit the combatant-noncombatant distinction, what have we left to adjudicate? If the just war ever had moral significance in the past, it is clear today that it justifies too much. In the middle ages the just war was less tragic than the alternatives. Today the just war justifies Armageddon if our hearts be pure, and this is to justify too much.

Let me close with an analogy. Suppose that, instead of national war, we were discussing the battles of Aryans against Jews. Suppose we approach this subject with medieval language and modern skill. We would, of course, consistent with the position taken on war, grant to Aryans the right to wage the war of extermination of the Jews, provided of course that the pogrom be declared by the duly constituted authority, be carried out with due decorum proportional to the threat, and with a just end in view. With this much granted, citizens would then see that they must kill Jews if their prince commanded it in the name of national defense (not unlike the Aryan concern with racial defense.) Citizens would then implement the State department plan of containment of Judaism (not unlike containment of Communism) and seek by every means to rid the world of the threat of creeping Judaism. With no more effort than our war leaders now exert, we would carry out essentially what the Nazis did carry out, and do it according to the laws of pogroms (not unlike the much advertised "laws of wars"). Our means would naturally be humane gas chambers and sanitary ovens. If we put it this way, then the doctrine of the "just war"—like that of the "just pogrom"—would justify too much.

Selected General Bibliography

In order to aid students beginning research in political philosophy we cite below selected general works on political philosophy and political theory. Particularly good bibliographies on the historical figures can be found in the McDonald book, while useful references to recent work by political philosophers can be found in the Quinton book.

I. General Histories of Philosophy Covering Political Philosophy

Copleston, Frederick. *A History of Philosphy.* 8 vols. London: Burns Oates and Washbourne, 1946-1966.
Jones, W. T. A History of Western Philosophy. 2d ed. revised. 4 vols. New York: Harcourt, Brace, and World, 1969.

II. Histories of Political Philosophy and Political Theory

McDonald, Lee Cameron. *Western Political Theory: From Its Origins to the Present.* New York: Harcourt, Brace, and World, 1968.
Sabine, George H. *A History of Political Theory.* New York: Henry Holt, 1937.

III. General Systematic Treatments of Political Philosophy

Benn, S.I. and Peters, R.S. *The Principles of Political Thought.* New York: The Free Press, 1965.
Mabbott, J.D. *The State and The Citizen.* London: Hutchinson, 1948.

IV. Collections of Essays

Brandt, Richard B. (ed.) *Social Justice.* Englewood Cliffs, New Jersey: Prentice-Hall, 1962.
Friedrich, C.J. *Nomos.* Vols. 1-8. New York: Atherton Press. These are the yearbooks of the American Society for Political and Legal Philosophy and include volumes on *Authority, Community, Responsibility, Liberty, The Public Interest, Justice, Rational Decision,* and *Revolution.*
Laslett, Peter. *Philosophy, Politics, and Society.* Oxford: Basil Blackwell, 1956.
Laslett, Peter and Runciman, W.G. *Philosophy, Politics, and Society* (Second Series and Third Series). Oxford: Basil Blackwell, 1962 and 1967.
Olafson, Frederick A. *Justice and Social Policy.* Englewood Cliffs, New Jersey: Prentice-Hall, 1961.
Quinton, Anthony. *Political Philosophy.* London: Oxford University Press, 1967.

Syllabi

These four syllabi are offered as *examples* of the ways in which courses using different approaches can be constructed using this book. They certainly are neither definitive nor complete. We hope that these syllabi will not only illustrate the differing uses of this volume, but will also, together with the Index and Selected Bibliography, provide an aid to students carrying out individual projects.

In constructing the syllabi we have listed the names of the authors to be read under the various topics mentioned. If more than one work from an author is included in this book and not all are relevant to a particular topic, then we have listed the title of the relevant work as well.

Syllabus I   History of Political Philosophy

The Contents for Part I provides a basic syllabus for the history of political philosophy. To it can be added as much or as little of the contemporary material as the instructor finds of sufficient importance to yield a history of political philosophy from classical times to the present.

Syllabus II   Types of Political Philosophy

Critics as well as advocates of the approaches concerned are included at times.

I. Natural Law and Natural Right Theories
   Plato—*Republic*
   Aristotle—*Politics*
   Aquinas
   Hobbes
   Locke
   Rousseau
   Hart—"Are There Any Natural Rights?"

II. Social Contract Theories
   Plato—*Crito* and *Statesman*
   Hobbes
   Locke
   Rousseau
   Hume—"Of The Original Contract"
   Rawls

III. Utilitarianism
 Hume—"Of Justice"
 Bentham
 Mill
 Dostoyevsky
 Barry
 Rawls
 Mabbott

IV. Organic Theories of the State
 Plato
 Aristotle—*Politics*
 Rousseau
 Hegel
 Nietzsche—*Thus Spake Zarathustra*
 Mussolini
 Buckley

V. Anarchism
 Hobbes
 Kropotkin
 Nietzsche—*Thus Spake Zarathustra*
 Lenin

VI. Marxism
 Marx
 Petrovic
 Marcuse
 Lenin
 Mao Tse-tung
 Fanon

VII. Varieties of Democratic Theory
 Plato—*Statesman*
 Aristotle—*Politics*
 Locke
 Rousseau
 Mill
 Marx—*Communist Manifesto* and *Economic and Philosophical Manuscripts*
 Niebuhr
 Students for a Democratic Society
 Harrington

Syllabus III   Problems of Political Philosophy

This syllabus is constructed so as to reflect the outline of the problems of political philosophy presented in the Introduction.

I. Political Obligation and the Nature and Authority of the State

(A large proportion of the selections are relevant to this general problem area. The following list is constructed to show the balance which can be achieved. Alternative lists can easily be arranged.)

Plato
Aristotle—*Politics*
Aquinas
Machiavelli
Hobbes
Locke
Rousseau
Jefferson—"On Republican Government"
Hegel
Marx
Kropotkin
Lenin
Mussolini

II. The Evaluation of Social and Political Institutions
  A. Justice
     Plato—*Republic*
     Aristotle—*Nicomachean Ethics*
     Aquinas
     Locke
     Rousseau
     Hume—"Of Justice"
     Hart—"The Principles of Justice"
     Vlastos
     Rawls

  B. Liberty
     Locke
     Rousseau
     Mill
     Hegel
     Dostoyevsky
     Kropotkin
     Rawls
     Berlin
     Dworkin
     Petrovic

  C. Rights
     See V, Human Rights and Civil Rights

  D. The Common Good and the Public Interest
     Aristotle—*Politics*
     Aquinas

Rousseau
Hume—"Of Justice"
Dostoyevsky
Barry
Harrington

E. Alienation
   Marx
   Petrovic

III. Ideals of Society
   (Again many selections are relevant, but we have made a list balancing different views.)
   Plato—*Republic*
   Aristotle—*Politics*
   Hegel
   Kropotkin
   Niebuhr
   Lenin
   Buckley
   Students for a Democratic Society
   Harrington

IV. Social and Political Change
   A. Legal Reform
      Jefferson—"On Progress in the Laws"
      Buckley
      Harrington

   B. Civil Disobedience and Nonviolence
      Thoreau
      Gandhi
      King
      Hook

   C. Resistance and Revolution
      Locke
      Rousseau
      Marx—*The Communist Manifesto*
      Marcuse
      Lenin
      Mao Tse-tung
      Fanon
      Cleaver
      Students for a Democratic Society

V. Human Rights and Civil Rights
   Aristotle—*Politics*
   Locke
   Rousseau
   Mill
   Marx—*Economic and Philosophical Manuscripts*

Hart—"Are There Any Natural Rights?"
Vlastos
Rawls
Dworkin
Petrovic
Gandhi
King
Cleaver
Buckley

VI. War and Violence
Machiavelli
Hobbes
Locke
Rousseau
Mao Tse-tung
Students for a Democratic Society
Wells

VII. Punishment
Bentham
Kant
Nietzsche—*On the Genealogy of Morals*
Kropotkin
Dworkin
Louch
Mabbott
Pincoffs

Syllabus IV Contemporary Political Issues

I. Law, Morality, and Punishment
Bentham
Kant
Mill
Nietzsche—*On the Genealogy of Morals*
Kropotkin
Dworkin
Louch
Mabbott
Pincoffs
Cleaver

II Civil Rights, Civil Liberty, and Racism
Aristotle—*Politics*
Mill
Rawls
Gandhi

King
Hook
Fanon
Cleaver
Buckley
Students for a Democratic Society
Harrington

III. Social Control
Mill
Hegel
Marx
Dostoyevsky
Kropotkin
Dworkin
Louch
Petrovic
Mussolini
Cleaver
Students for a Democratic Society

IV. Violence and Nonviolence
Machiavelli
Thoreau
Mao Tse-tung
Gandhi
King
Hook
Fanon
Cleaver

V. War and Violence
Hobbes
Locke
Mao Tse-tung
Fanon
Cleaver
Wells

VI. Civil Disobedience
Plato—*Crito*
Jefferson—"On Obedience to Law"
Thoreau
Gandhi
King
Hook

VII Resistance and Revolution
Locke

Marx—*The Communist Manifesto*
Marcuse
Lenin
Mao Tse-tung
Fanon
Cleaver
Students for a Democratic Society

VIII. Freedom
Hobbes
Rousseau
Mill
Hegel
Marx—*The Communist Manifesto*
Dostoyevsky
Kropotkin
Berlin
Petrovic
Buckley
Students for a Democratic Society

Index

Family, 116, 126 f., 139, 208, 219, 296, 353
Fanon, Frantz, 481-492
  bourgeoisie, 486 f.
  capitalist society, 483
  colonialism, 481 ff.
  decolonization, 486 ff.
  individualism, 487
  Marxism, 484
  nationalism, 481 ff.
  role of the intellectual in revolution, 488 ff.
  social change, 481 ff.
  Third World and ends of government, 491 ff.
  truth, 489
  violence, 481 ff.
Fascism, 447 ff.
Feuerbach, 222, 223
Fomes, 70
Force, 127, 403 ff., 493 ff.
Forgiveness, 377
Frankena, W. K., 6, 311, 314n.
Freedom:
  and bondage, 126
  bourgeois, 218
  and contract, 131
  and democracy, 341 ff.
  economic, 336 f.
  and general will, 137
  and governmental ideals, 416 ff.
  and human worth, 312 ff.
  and individual liberty, 340
  interference with, 297 f.
  and law, 78 f., 116, 206, 207 ff.
  libertarian, 188, 199, 337 f.
  marxist, 222, 289n.
  and moral right, 290 ff., 298
  and nature of man, 127 f., 261, 262 f.
  and natural right, 289 ff.
  negative sense, 336, 339 f., 412
  and New Left, 505 ff., 508
  and oppression, 464 f., 468
  political, 499
  positive sense, 341 ff., 412 ff.
  and religion, 191, 235 ff.
  and revolution, 419 ff.
  and right, 117 f., 120

Freedom:
  and self-determination, 412 ff.
  as self-mastery, 342 f.
  and society, 413 ff.
  of speech, 10, 188 ff.
  and state, 204, 207 ff., 212 ff., 431
  and state of nature, 105, 109 f.
  of thought, 188 f., 443
Fulbright, J. Wm., 524

Galbraith, J. K., 503, 523, 526
Galsworthy, John, 400n.
Game theory, 322n., 322 ff., 324n
Gandhi, M. K., 450-460
  civil disobedience, 451 ff.
  conscience, 457 ff.
  justice and social change, 452 ff.
  law and morals, 451 ff.
  nonviolent resistance, 451 ff.
  satyagraha, 451 ff.
  social change, justification of, 451 ff.
  violence, 452, 457 f., 459
General interest, 144
General rights, 296 f., 298
General will, 132 f., 134, 135, 137, 283 f., 404
Gods, 264
Goffman, Erving, 370n.
Goldwater, Barry, 513, 521, 522
Government, 123 ff., 136, 491 ff., 502 ff., 508 ff., 525, 531 ff., ends of, 107, 120 ff., 124, 132 f., 138, 165 f., 168, 198, 205, 206, 244, 416 ff., 447
Green, T. H., 343n.
Guerilla warfare, 444
Guilt, 259 f., 263 ff., 265 ff.

Happiness, 416 ff., 448
Hare, R. M., 285, 321n.
Harrington, Michael, 516-532
  capitalism, 529 f.
  class struggle, 519
  democracy, 516 ff.
  democratic left, 522, 523 ff., 527 ff.

Hobbes, Thomas:
  equality, 93
  equity, 93
  freedom, 337*n.*, 338 f., 414
  human nature, 86 ff.
  justice, 87, 90 ff., 322*n.*
  law, 100
  liberty, 95, 101, 103
  monarchy, 99
  natural law, 88 f., 90 ff.
  peace, 88 f., 95 ff.
  punishment, 92
  reason, 89
  right, 87 f., 89 f.
  security, 99
  sovereign, 98
  sovereignty, 101 ff.
  state of nature, 86 ff.
  war, 88 f., 96 f.
  will, 87, 97
Hook, Sidney, 473-480
  civil disobedience, 473 ff.
  conscience, 475 ff.
  conscientious objection, 476 f.
  democracy, 473 ff., 477 ff.
  democratic progress, 478 f.
  duty, 477
  law, respect for, 480
  nonviolence, 477
  political obligation, 474 ff.
  reason, 476 f.
  social protest, 474 ff.
  uncivil disobedience, 473 ff., 479
Homosexuality, 348 ff., 353 ff.
Human law, 67 f., 76 ff.
Human nature, 86 ff., 206, 395, 402 f.,
    407
Human rights, 10
Human worth, 306 ff., 309 ff., 311 ff.
Humanity, 390 ff., 398 ff., 507 ff.
Hume, David, 137-150
  divine right, 146
  duty, 148 ff.
  equality, 143 f.
  family, 139
  general interest, 144
  government, ends of, 138
  justice, 138 ff., 149, 318, 322*n.*
  labor, 144

Hume, David:
  laws of nature, 144
  monarchy, 146
  political obligation, 149 f.
  property, 138 ff., 143 ff., *145*
  punishment, 140
  social contract, 146 ff.
  state, 147 ff.
  state of nature, 141 f.
  utility, 138 ff., 144 ff. 318*n.*
  war, 140

Ideals of government, 132 f., 209
Ideals of society, 7 ff., 22 ff., 443
Imperialism, 446 f.
Imprisonment, 400 f.
Indebtedness, 263 ff.
Individualism, 330, 448 f., 487
Individuality, 197 f., 198 ff., 204 ff.,
    211, 217 f.
Individual worth, 309 ff.
Inhibition, 261 f., 265
Initial position, 317 ff.
Injustice, 34, 55 f., 90 ff., 249 f., 299,
    407 ff.
Insurrection, 9
Interest, 280 ff., *281*
Interference, 297 f.
Internalization, 261 f.
Interpretation, 257
Isidore, 64, 65, 74, 76

James, William, 343 f.
Jefferson, Thomas, 154-160
  equality, 468
  individual liberty, 339 f.
  law, 157 ff.
  majority rule, 160
  national debt, 154, 156, 158
  political obligation, 157 f.
  republic, *155*
  republican government, 154 ff.
  representation, 155 f.
  state, 155 f.
  state of war, 159
Johnson, Lyndon, 516, 521 f., 535
Justice, 34, 60, 316, 323

Justice:
   and administering law, 301 f.
   applied to actions, 316
   applied to persons, 316
   applied to practices, 316 ff.
   as basis of criticism of social insti-
      tutions, 324
   and civil disobedience, 475 ff.
   commutative, 91
   compensatory, 303 f.
   concept of, 334 f.
   contractarian view, 6
   distributive, 91
   and economic resources, 307n., 309
      402, 433
   and economics, 526, 528
   as efficiency, 329 ff.
   equalitarian, 6
   and equality, 300 f., 303 f., 306 ff.,
      316 ff.
   and fairness, 299 f.
   and individual, 32 ff.
   of institutions, 5
   and law, 135, 299 ff.
   as limiting principles, 390 ff., 390n.
   as mean, 55 f.
   and morality, 299 f., 302, 338
   nature of, 26 f. 54 ff., 90 ff.,
      138 ff., 149, 245, 247
   political, 60 ff.
   and power, 403 ff.
   principles of, 299 ff.
   and procedural regularity, 5 f.
   proportional, 58
   and punishment, 151 ff., 379f.,
      387 ff., 392n.
   and rationality, 319 ff.
   and reason, 87
   rectificatory, 59
   and relevant differences, 302,
      317 ff.
   and self-interest, 319 ff.
   and social change, 452 ff., 462 ff.
   and social contract, 315, 322, 323,
      324
   and social role, 318 ff.
   as standard, 5
   utilitarian, 6, 138 ff., 318, 328 ff.
   and war, 533 ff.

Justification, 294 ff., 297 ff., 388 ff.,
   532 ff.

Kant, Immanuel, 150-153
   death sentence, justification of,
      152 f.
   equality, 151, 316n.
   freedom, 415
   human worth, 311 f., 311n.
   justice, 151 ff.
   morality, 475
   moral right, 291
   punishment, 151 ff.
   reason, 153
   retaliation, 151
   revolution, 418
   utilitarianism, 151 ff.
   wickedness, 152
Kelsen, Hans, 6
Kennedy, John F., 521, 528
Keynes, John Maynard, 503, 527, 529
King, Martin Luther, 461-472
   civil disobedience, 461 ff.
   freedom, 464 ff., 468
   justice, 462 ff., 464 f.
   law, 464 ff.
   non-violent resistance, 462 f.
      471 f.
   segregation, 468
   social change, 462 ff.
   state and religion, 470 ff.
Kropotkin, Peter, 268-275
   anarchism, defense of, 269 ff.
   authority, 269 ff.
   equality, 271
   labor, 272 f.
   law, 269 ff.
   middle class, 271
   property, 272 f.
   punishment, 274 f.

Labor, 110 ff., 144, 217 f., 224 ff.,
      228 ff., 272 f., 432 ff.
Laslett, Peter, 12
Law:
   anarchist critique of, 269 ff.
   authority, 115 ff., 122
   concept of, 299 ff.

Punishment:
   and guilt, 259 f.
   and humanity, 398 ff.
   and imprisonment, 400
   justification of, 385 ff.
   and justice, 140, 151 ff., 304,
      387 ff., 398 f.
   and law, 274 f., 376 f., 380 f.
   and mental illness, 367 ff.
   and morals, 375
   and oppression, 493 ff.
   origin of, 256 ff.
   as persuasion, 393 ff.
   philosophical questions about, 11
   and popular will, 444
   and property, 117 ff.
   and psychiatry, 364 ff., 396 f.
   purpose of, 256 ff.
   reformatory, 374
   as retaliation, 151 ff.
   retributive, 373 ff.
   as revenge, 256 ff.
   and science, 363 ff.
   as social game, 371 f.
   and social suasion, 393 ff.
   types, 258 f.
   and utilitarianism, 168 ff., 174 ff.,
      187, 374, 376 f., 389 ff.
   and vengeance, 372
   and wickedness, 152

Racial discrimination, 10, 461 ff.,
   481 ff., 492 ff.
Rationality, 319 f., 537
Rawls, John, 6, 315-335
   acceptance, 327 f.
   common good, 316
   community, 325
   duty, 322, 325
   equality, 316 ff., 321 f., 333 ff.
   fairness, 315 ff., 324n., 325 ff.,
      328 ff.
   fair play, 326
   game theory, 322 ff., 322n., 324n.
   individualism, 330
   initial position, 317 ff.
   justice, 315 ff., 316, 323, 319 ff.,
      324, 328 ff., 333 ff., 390n.
   liberty, 316 ff., 320, 333 ff.

Rawls, John:
   morality, 321 ff., 324n., 327 f.,
      332 ff.
   practice, 316 ff., 316n., 326, 328,
      333 ff.
   political obligation, 325 f.
   rights, 322, 325
   rules, 317, 323 f., 325
   self-interest, 319 ff.
   slavery, 331 f.
   social contract, 315, 322 f., 334
   social institutions, 316
   utilitarianism, 315, 318, 318n.,
      328 ff.
   utility, 329 ff., 333 ff.
   welfare economics, 328 ff., 330n.
Reactionaries, 445 f.
Reason, 64 ff., 89, 117, 153, 204 ff.,
   475 f.
Reasons and causes, 368
Rebellion, 123, 125, 495 ff.
Reform, 9
Religion, 212 ff., 223, 536
Representative government, 211, 288
Republic, 136, 155, 210
Republican government, 136, 154 ff.
Resistance, 9
Responsibility, 364 ff.
Ressentiment, 262
Restraint, 289n.
Retaliation, 151
Revolution, 9, 125, 222, 246 f.,
   416 ff., 420 ff., 488 ff., 500 ff.
Reward, 394 f.
Right, 3, 87 f., 89 f., 101 ff., 106,
   117 ff., 126 f., 245, 289 ff.,
   296 f., 312 ff., 322, 350 ff.,
   353 ff.
Robespierre, 418
Roosevelt, F. D. R., 282, 516, 522
Ross, Alf, 5, 386n.
Rousseau, Jean Jacques, 126-137
   agreement, 126, 128, 134
   alienation, 128, 131
   association, 130, 133, 136
   autonomy, 128
   body politic, 130, 132, 134
   bondage, 126 f.
   common good, 132 f.
   convention, 126 f.

State of nature, 86 ff., 105 ff., 107 ff.,
   120 f., 141 f., 207
State of war, 108 ff., 129, 159, 410 ff.
Statesmanship, 35 ff., 43, 255, 518
Students for a Democratic Society,
   504-515
   alienation, 508
   apathy, 510 ff.
   cold war, 505
   community, 508
   conservatism, 513 f.
   democracy, 505 ff.
   economics and values, 509
   equality, 505
   freedom, 505 f., 508
   humanity, 507 ff.
   majority rule, 507 f.
   New Left, 505 ff.
   New Left, goals of, 514 f.
   political parties, 512 ff.
   social change, 506 ff.
   university, role of in social change,
      509 ff., 514 f.
   utopia, 507
   values, 506 ff.
Szasz, Thomas, 369n.

Taxation, 250
Technology, 500 f.
Third World, 491 f., 524 ff.
Thoreau, Henry David, 244-255
   citizen, 248 ff.
   civil disobedience, 244 ff., 250 ff.
   conscience, 245
   conscientious objection, 244 ff.,
      250 ff.
   democracy, 255
   government, ends of, 244
   injustice, 249 f.
   justice, 245, 247
   majority rule, 245
   money, 251
   revolution, 246 f.
   right, 245
   slavery, 246 f.
   social contract, 252
   state, relation to citizens, 245 ff.

Thoreau, Henry David:
   statesman, 255
   taxation, 250
   voting, 247 f.
Tolstoy, 385, 386, 392, 397
Totalitarianism, 449, 524
Toulmin, S. E., 318n.
Truman, Harry, 523
Truth, 489
Tyranny, 45

Uncivil disobedience, 473 ff.
Utilitarianism, 151 ff., 168 ff, 174 ff.,
   186 ff., 295, 315, 318, 318n.,
   328 ff., 331 f., 337 ff., 374,
   376 f., 389 ff.
Utility, 138, 144 ff., 161 ff., *162*, 187,
   329 ff., 333 ff., 380 f.
Utopia, 402, 428, 435 ff., 507, 516 ff.

Value, 311 ff., 344 ff., 347, 506 ff.,
   526 f.
Vietnam War, 496, 536
Violence, 417 ff., 430, 452, 457,
   459 ff., 481 ff.
Virtue, 73, 80 ff.
Virtues in individual, 32 ff., *35*, 51,
   54 ff., 74
Virtues of states, 21 ff., 27 ff., 52 f.,
   57 ff., 316
Vlastos, Gregory, 6, 305-314
   distributive justice, 306 ff.
   equality, 306 ff.
   equality and human worth, 308,
      312 f.
   freedom, 312 ff.
   human rights, 312 ff.
   human worth, 306 ff.
   individual worth, 309 ff.
   intrinsic value, 311 ff.
   justice, 306 ff.
   Marx, 307
   merit, 308 ff.
   moral obligation, 310 f.
   natural law, 306
   punishment, 311

Vlastos, Gregory:
 value, 311 ff.
 well-being, 312 ff.
Voting, 136 f., 247 f., 288

War, 11, 88 f., 96 f., 128 ff., 140,
 408 f., 532 ff.
Welfare economics, 328 ff., 330n.
Welfare state, 500 f.
Well-being, 312 ff.
Wells, Donald A., 532-540
 citizens, 540
 double effect, 538 ff.
 justice and war, 533 ff.

Wells, Donald A.:
 justification, in moral discourse,
  535 ff.
 justification of war, 532 ff.
 last resort, 537 ff.
 morality, 539 f.
 nationalism, 533 ff.
 war, justification of, 533 ff.
White, Theodore H., 521
Will, 87, 97, 123 f., 132 f., 134,
 204 ff., 210, 211, 206,
 450
Will of all, 133, 283 f.
Will to power, 257 f., 263
Wittgenstein, Ludwig, 327n.